D0509438

Dynamic Web Publishing

Second Edition

72816

TK 5105.888 .D96 1998

Dynamic web publishing
unleashed

Shelley Powers, et al.

DATE DUE		
MAY 0 5 2007		
GAYLORD		PRINTED IN U.S.A.

RED ROCKS
COMMUNITY COLLEGE LIBRARY

sams
.net

201 West 103rd Street
Indianapolis, IN 46290

UNLEASHED

Copyright © 1998 by Sams.net Publishing

SECOND EDITION

All rights reserved. No part of this book shall be reproduced, stored in a retrieval system, or transmitted by any means, electronic, mechanical, photocopying, recording, or otherwise, without written permission from the publisher. No patent liability is assumed with respect to the use of the information contained herein. Although every precaution has been taken in the preparation of this book, the publisher and author assume no responsibility for errors or omissions. Neither is any liability assumed for damages resulting from the use of the information contained herein. For information, address Sams.net Publishing, 201 W. 103rd St., Indianapolis, IN 46290.

International Standard Book Number: 0-57521-363-x

Library of Congress Catalog Card Number: 97-68546

2001   2000   99   98   4   3   2   1

Interpretation of the printing code: The rightmost double-digit number is the year of the book's printing; the rightmost single-digit, the number of the book's printing. For example, a printing code of 98-1 shows that the first printing of the book occurred in 1998.

Composed in AGaramond and MCPdigital by Macmillan Computer Publishing

Printed in the United States of America

Trademarks

All terms mentioned in this book that are known to be trademarks or service marks have been appropriately capitalized. Sams.net Publishing cannot attest to the accuracy of this information. Use of a term in this book should not be regarded as affecting the validity of any trademark or service mark.

A 38451743

72816

TK

5105.888

·D96

1998

Senior Vice-President of Publishing	Richard K. Swadley
Publisher	Jordan Gold
Executive Editor	Beverly M. Eppink
Managing Editor	Patrick Kanouse
Indexing Manager	Johnna L. VanHoose
Director of Brand Management	Alan Bower
Brand Associate	Kim Spilker
Director of Software and User Services	Cheryl Willoughby

Acquisitions Editor
David B. Mayhew

Development Editor
Scott D. Meyers

Software Development Specialist
Adam Swetnam

Production Editor
Andrew Cupp

Copy Editors
Tonya Maddox, Julie McNamee, Patricia Kinyon, Margaret Berson, Nancy Allbright

Indexer
Erika Millen

Technical Reviewers
Lee Anne Phillips, Rob Falla

Editorial Coordinators
Mandie Rowell, Katie Wise

Resource Coordinators
Deborah Frisby
Charlotte Clapp

Team Coordinator
Lorraine E. Schaffer

Editorial Assistants
Andi Richter
Rhonda Tinch-Mize

Brand Coordinator
Linda B. Beckwith

Cover Designer
Jason Grisham

Book Designer
Gary Adair

Copy Writer
Eric Borgert

Production Manager
Juli Cook

Production Team Supervisor
Andrew Stone

Production Team
Elizabeth Deeter, Terri Edwards, Donna Martin, Becky Stutzman

Overview

RED ROCKS
COMMUNITY COLLEGE LIBRARY

RED ROCKS
COMMUNITY COLLEGE

Contents

Acknowledgments

Shelley Powers would like to acknowledge the Microsoft Internet Explorer 4.0 beta support team for their outstanding support during the writing of this book. In particular, we would like to specifically mention the newsgroup support people, including a special thanks to Summet Shrivastava, as well as the members of the Microsoft Internet Explorer 4.0 development and "bug" teams that tracked down and responded to even the most obscure problem report.

Additionally, she would like to acknowledge all the vendors mentioned in this book that provided easy, downloadable access to their software in order for people like her to work with and write about.

Dedication

To all our friends for their love and support.
-David and Rhonda Crowder

I would like to thank Anna Armendariz de Klaasmeyer for her vim and vigor.
-Corey Klaasmeyer

About the Authors

Lead Author

Shelley Powers is an independent developer, consultant, and author within her own company, YASD, which is located in the New England area. She has worked with Web, client-server, database, and distributed applications for years for some of the nation's leading companies. In addition, Shelley has authored or co-authored seven books on subjects such as PowerBuilder 5.0, Web programming with Perl, JavaScript, Java, cross-browser-compatible Dynamic HTML, and other Web technologies, in addition to providing articles for several online magazines. She can be reached at shelleyp@yasd.com, and her Web site can be seen at http://www.yasd.com.

Contributing Authors

David and Rhonda Crowder were hypertext pioneers and have been involved in the online community for over a decade. Their company, Far Horizons Software, a Web site design firm, created the award-winning LinkFinder and NetWelcome sites. They and their cats live in Miami, Florida.

Rob Falla (roberto@brant.com) has spent most of the past year in cyberspace. His fingers have developed permanent indents from filling in all those online questionnaire forms, and his wife claims to be an Internet widow. During that time, Rob still managed to work on a few books and write a couple of magazine articles. His complete list of published works, both computer-related and sci-fi, is located at http://www.cwebdev.com/. You should use IE 4.0 on that site. Well, maybe not. Rob is considering developing a multi-browser version of the site. There are also some neat CSS style sheet and JavaScript tips at that URL. Thanks for reading this bio.

Nana Gilbert-Baffoe is a Web designer at JBG Web, a Web design company located in Chicago, Illinois. When he's not working on a Web site, he's busy studying more about every new aspect of the Web. He has been in love with computers ever since he got his first one at about age 12, and quickly started to program in QuickBasic and C (in an attempt to write his own games). Now he's interested only in the Web. You can reach Nana via e-mail at nekpomhi@geocities.com.

David Gulbransen is currently a partner with Vervet Logic, an Internet technologies development company specializing in cutting-edge Internet/intranet technology development. He is also the author of *Creating Web Applets with Java* (Sams.net), the *Netscape Server Survival Guide* (Sams.net), and *Inside Dynamic HTML* (Que). In addition to JavaScript, David works with cross-platform Java development, CGI/Perl, the Channel Definition Format, and Dynamic HTML. When he is not coding or learning new technologies, he can often be found watching, editing, and creating short films. David holds a Bachelor of Arts in Computer Science and Theatre from Indiana University.

Blake Benet Hall is a freelance consultant for his own firm, Benet Systems. His broad background began with a Bachelors of Science in Computer Science from the University of Mississippi. He currently designs and implements custom multi-user applications, designs and creates conference videos, stays abreast of evolving technologies, and expands his interest in 3D animation/video techniques.

Corey Klaasmeyer teaches Java at the University of Denver and works as a Java mentor and consultant. He hopes to someday telecommute from someplace with no roads or cars.

Rita Lewis uses her Master of Arts degree in Cultural Anthropology to study the habits of the online world. She has been a technical writer and proposal manager for over ten years before chucking it all to become a freelance writer. Rita has written over 11 books on various subjects dealing with networks and personal computers, including *PageMill 2 Handbook* (Hayden Books), *Maclopedia* (Hayden Books), *WordPerfect 3.5 Visual Quickstart Guide* (Peachpit Press), and the as-yet-unpublished *Special Edition Using Mac OS 8, Special Edition* (Hayden Books).

Robert McDaniel is an Internet technology enthusiast who has been active with the Web since its early days. Some of his other works include the *CGI Manual of Style, PC Magazine Webmaster's Ultimate Resource Guide, Late Night Microsoft Visual J++,* and *How to Program Microsoft Visual Basic Scripting Edition.* He is currently working on an intranet project at Walt Disney Imagineering Research and Development.

Kelly Murdock (kelleym@waterford.org) works as a full-time programmer and spends much of his spare time exploring the graphics frontier. He especially enjoys dabbling in 3D. He is the lead author of *Laura Lemay's Web Workshop: 3D Graphics and VRML 2* and has contributed to several other titles. He also writes a regular column, "Kel's Eye Inside Reviews" for www.3dreview.com.

Simon North's background includes working as a helicopter repair technician, as a software quality assurance engineer, and as a technical translator. He is an experienced technical writer, specializing in online, multimedia, and interactive delivery methods. He is one of the authors of the Dutch national standard for consumer documentation, and is co-author of *Presenting XML.* Simon has been involved with SGML since 1989, and was an active participant in Dutch CALS/SGML standardization activities. Simon is an avid Internet surfer, having built his first intranet in 1993. His latest hobby (since giving up free-fall parachuting) is collecting e-mail accounts, but Simon can be contacted via sintac@xs4all.nl.

Leena Prasad worked as a software engineer for nine years before founding Montage Productions (http://montageproductions.com) in December 1996 in order to transition to working independently as a contractor/consultant. She has expertise in developing sophisticated database software and interactive/dynamic Web pages using state-of-the-art Internet technologies. Her background includes working as a software engineering consultant for a high-tech company, developing artificial-intelligence software, participating in the development of a transaction-processing language, developing a test suite for a graphics package, and teaching computer science. She has a B.S. in Computer Science from Tulane University and an M.A. in Journalism from Stanford University.

Tell Us What You Think!

As a reader, you are the most important critic and commentator of our books. We value your opinion and want to know what we're doing right, what we could do better, what areas you'd like to see us publish in, and any other words of wisdom you're willing to pass our way. You can help us make strong books that meet your needs and give you the computer guidance you require.

Do you have access to the World Wide Web? Then check out our site at http://www.mcp.com.

NOTE

If you have a technical question about this book, call the technical support line at (317) 581-3833 or send e-mail to support@mcp.com.

As the team leader of the group that created this book, I welcome your comments. You can fax, e-mail, or write me directly to let me know what you did or didn't like about this book—as well as what we can do to make our books stronger. Here's the information:

FAX: 317-581-4669
E-mail: HTML@mcp.com
Mail: Beverly M. Eppink
         Comments Department
         Sams Publishing
         201 W. 103rd Street
         Indianapolis, IN 46290

Introduction

In the chapters to come, you are going to have a chance to review and work with virtually every aspect of Web development and authoring technology that exists. Following the tradition established by the *Unleashed* books, the chapters provide working examples of the technology, as well as discussions on each technology or product's use, how it fits into the overall Web development framework, and tips and "gotchas" about which you should be aware.

How This Book Is Organized

Part I. Web Publishing: A Quick Look: These chapters explore the basics of a Web document by working with HTML, including a look at some of the new draft HTML 4.0 elements and attributes. Additionally, controlling the presentation of one or more Web pages through the use of Cascading Style Sheets (CSS1) is demonstrated, as well as an in-depth examination of HTML tables and forms. The section also includes a look at the new CSS1 positioning capability that both Netscape Navigator and Internet Explorer 4.0 support, as well as looking at how each browser works with multimedia.

Part II. HTML 4.0: The Web Publishing Foundation: This section continues the review of Web development technologies by focusing on scripting. Scripting basics, client-side imagemaps, and the use of the most popular scripting language, JavaScript, are discussed and examples that you can work with are provided. The section also provides a discussion and demonstration of VBScript, Microsoft's Visual Basic for Application version of VB for the Web. Netscape's JavaScript style sheets also are demonstrated.

Part III. Client-Side Scripting: You can't have a book on Web development technologies without including a section on Java, and this section does just that. The section provides an overview of the language and how it can be used to create applets. The section also provides a look at JavaBeans, the new Java-based component technology that is becoming increasingly popular. Finally, the section ends with a discussion about integrating JavaScript and Java within one Web page.

Part IV. Web Publishing with Java: Another popular embedded object technology is the use of ActiveX controls. These controls are designed mainly to work with Internet Explorer but can be used in other applications, and can be created relatively easily using a variety of tools. This section discusses ActiveX technology, how to create and distribute ActiveX controls, and how to integrate ActiveX and VBScript within a Web page.

Part V. CGI and Controlling the Web from the Server: Server-side applications are becoming more popular, and are being used for anything from a simple online e-mail form, to complex banking transaction Web sites. This section discusses several server-side techniques, beginning with the traditional Common Gateway Interface (CGI) techniques and ending with a look at Microsoft's and Netscape's server technologies. Actual examples of the technologies are provided, giving you a chance to see how each of the approaches works even if you don't have access to all the servers discussed.

Part VI. Putting It All Together: Engineering a Web Site: These chapters discuss the new Dynamic HTML technology that both Internet Explorer 4.0 and Netscape Navigator 4.0 have implemented. The section provides several examples of using Dynamic HTML, including examples of each browser's capability, and examples that work with both browsers. One problem with Dynamic HTML is that reloading the browser, or accessing a Web page at a later time, erases the dynamic HTML effect you might want to keep. The section also addresses this with a discussion about using Netscape-style cookies to persistently store Dynamic HTML state information and to re-create an effect at a later time.

Part VII. Emerging and Alternate Web Technologies: Finally, the book rounds out this Web development technology review by looking at the new technologies, such as the Extended Markup Language (XML) standard.

Enjoy!

Web Publishing: A Quick Look

PART

I

A Melding of Technologies

by Rita Lewis

IN THIS CHAPTER

The world of the 21st Century will be one where the line between your computer and the rest of the world dissolves. People will share data, programs, and information across computer platforms and space. People will not care about the origin of information because their computers will be able to view or use data whether it comes from a mainframe, a workstation, or even a PC; or whether it comes from a hard disk, a CD-ROM, or China. They will use video, sounds, graphics, motion pictures, animations, and text fluidly within any program without worrying about its origin. All of this magic takes place using a nearly universal network called the Internet. The Internet provides interactive communications in the form of electronic mail, telephony, published documents, and avenues to gain direct access to software and information. This is the Information Superhighway.

Seems like a dream.

About the Internet

You hear the terms internet and intranet bandied about a lot these days. An *internet* is a conglomeration of computers linked by a myriad of networks into a baffling, decentralized global network. The *Internet* with a capital "I" is one manifestation of internet technology—the one typically spoken of when one mentions the Information Superhighway. An *intranet* is a corporation's version of an internet—an internal internet for that firm. In this chapter, Internet and internet are used to mean the same thing: the vast system of networks governed by the World Wide Web Consortium and the Internet Society.

The Internet and intranets provide several types of services to their members, all based on the ability to pass information along wires and other telecommunications equipment between disparate computers and have the contents of these information packets understood and usable on the other side. Internet services are functional, meaning they are the means of using the internet technology. You can use the network of networks to perform the following types of tasks:

- **Electronic mail.** The reason most people connect to the Internet is to pass messages among computers. The ability to send and receive short bursts of text, pictures, sounds, and moving images almost instantaneously between two points no matter where they are in the world, makes e-mail one of the most compelling uses of the Internet.

- **Research.** The second reason most people connect to internets is to perform research. Originally, you could search for titles of papers or their abstracts, which had been laboriously entered onto computer files. The technology that performs searches is called Gopher. The articles themselves were not available on the network. Later, the articles were converted to computer files and made available on the network. You can download files from servers over the Internet using special software that uses the File Transfer Protocol (FTP) to gain access to special servers called FTP servers.

RESEARCH EXPANDS ON THE WORLD WIDE WEB

Most recently, the use of hypertext and interactive images makes retrieval of information almost instantaneous, opening the Internet for use as a medium for broadcasting news and entertainment, corporate information, research data and images, advertising, consumer goods, and on and on. The World Wide Web gives people the ability to view pictures and text and hear sounds over the Internet—the most popular format for Internet use. You gain access to this Internet format through the use of a piece of software called a browser, which is used to translate and display the information sent over the Internet. Click a picture and hear a sound snippet in real-time if you have the proper plug-in installed; or view an animation right on the screen. The WWW is a seductive medium.

■ **Discussion**. One of the oldest uses of the Internet is a form of e-mail that is broadcast to many people at once called Usenet. Think of an interest and you can probably find a group of people who are receiving and responding to lists of messages about their pet subjects via a List Server. These interest groups are called *newsgroups*. Once you subscribe, you receive all of the messages submitted by members of the group in a certain time period determined by the group's system operator (sysop). You can read threads of queries and responses of newsgroups using a News browser, which is usually included in your browser software as an adjunct of your e-mail browser.

The *mailing list* is an adjunct of Usenet. Mailing lists enable you to receive batches of messages from members of a newsgroup via e-mail when you subscribe to the specific List Server. Whereas Usenet requires software to type interactively, mailing lists only require an e-mail address to participate, although the resulting conversation is slower and considerably less interactive, given that you have to wait for your mail in order to read a response.

One of the newest forms of Internet use is the ability to send and receive messages in real-time, called *chatting*. E-mail allows you to send and receive messages as packets of information that you must open, reply to, and send back to an address. Chatting lets a group of people get together anywhere in the world and type messages to each other over the Internet. There are chat rooms for just about every interest. You need special software—Global Chat and IRCLE for the Macintosh or mIRC and MS-Chat for Windows—to use the Internet to chat.

■ **Interactive Games**. One of the Internet's fastest-growing features is the capability of playing computer games in real-time. Online gaming is an adjunct of chat rooms and newsgroups melding with the WWW and a dose of virtual reality thrown in for good measure. Games are played throughout the Internet, such as Quake, Gunship 2000, Wipeout, even chess; not to mention the America Online games like Air Warrior and the Multi-User Dungeons (M.U.D. or MUD), where one can wander for days getting points by buying and selling body parts or other weirdness. Such games are played using client software and a modem connection to the Internet. Responses to your moves are reflected in your game as they happen and vice versa. Heady stuff!

WHAT IS THIS INTERNET THING?

The Internet is the invention of the Defense Department and its affiliated labs and universities. It is old and complicated; the network is based on 1960s software technology, namely UNIX. The military and its affiliated university departments, such as Lawrence Livermore Labs, needed a fail-safe way to keep computers running in case of a nuclear attack. Because there was no such thing as dial-up connections, scientists first made their computer networks fail-safe by inventing a common code that all computers would recognize and that told them to accept a transmission. This was called *Internet Protocol* (IP). Information was sent between computers in bunches, called *packets*, but the route the information took from computer A to computer B might be circuitous. The computers decided the optimal transmission route. Thus, if one computer went down, the packets were simply sent in another direction and ended up at the intended destination. By 1969, this system was in place and called the Advanced Research Agency Project Network or ARPAnet.

Because the IP protocol caught on like wildfire, the Department of Defense turned over the upkeep of the Internet structure in the 1980s to the National Science Foundation. Soon, early commercial online services began to appear, such as FidoNet and DECnet. These online services were still based on command-line, text-based dumb terminals supported by IP.

In 1991, The National Science Foundation lifted its restrictions on commercial use of the Net, and "Net surfing" tools proliferated. During the early 1990s, scientists developed uniform rules that allowed the uploading and downloading of files (FTP), a graphical way to see what was on other computers (Gopher—a search engine for UseNets published by Paul Lindner and Mark McCahill of the University of Minnesota), ways to send electronic mail reliably between computers (SMTP), and word-based ways to identify each computer and server, called a *domain*, whose address is a *Uniform Resource Locator* (URL).

Remember that until the 1990s, mainframes and medium-sized minicomputers stored the information shared by dumb terminals on networks. These *servers* controlled access to the information. In the meantime, a need arose to provide support for personal computers— smart terminals. These computers were self-booting and multitudinous and wanted to share information at any time by dialing into the Internet using a modem. A new dial-up method called *Serial Line Internet Protocol* (SLIP) was invented; another, faster method was later developed and called *Point-to-Point Protocol* (PPP).

Enter the World Wide Web, Stage Left

Meanwhile, due to the popularity of graphical-user interfaces and hypertext (such as the Mac and HyperCard), in 1989 Tim Berners-Lee at the University of Illinois' National Center for Supercomputing Applications developed the graphical entryway to the Internet, called *Hypertext Transfer Protocol* (HTTP)—and by 1991 was appearing on the Internet and called the *World Wide Web* (WWW).

The World Wide Web is a front end, a human interface design, not a place or network. Berners-Lee's invention provided a way to intuitively navigate through gallons of data via pictures and hypertext. The invention of the Web (the HTTP you see in URLs when you surf the Web indicates that you are using this method to communicate on the Internet) is a way to move around the Internet by exchanging documents via hyperlinks (internal and external computer addresses included with the documents). It was revolutionary.

By 1992, there were one million host computers connected to the Internet. The public's interest in using these networks to communicate was astounding. There are more than 10 million Web users today.

A Short History of Hypertext Markup Language

The secret of the Internet (and later the World Wide Web) is the separation of the act of transmission of data from the display of data. By separating the processes, transmission could be greatly speeded because the server did not have to worry about how the data looked at the other end, since display was left to the local receiving computer. The problem to be solved was how to tell disparate computer platforms that there is understandable data and how to get them to translate it into something that could be displayed on a monitor. The solution was to send information alongside the data (called *tags*) telling the receiving computer how to display different types of information. This form of tagged typesetting information is very familiar to UNIX users as roff, nroff, and troff (all "runoff" languages), as well as Tex; all are widely used in the character-only world of early UNIX systems.

Several methods of tagging over networks were developed based on this experience with UNIX systems to assist in data display (ways to tell your computer that a stream of data is a paragraph, a list, or a citation, for example). These coding methods, called *markup languages,* travel with the data and are interpreted by the retrieving software. Hypertext (such as Apple's Hypercard) supplies ways to connect disparate pieces of data. Codes to tell the computer how to interpret hypertext documents are called Hypertext Markup Language (HTML). HTML became the standard way to tag pages of information traveling over the Internet.

Figure 1.1 shows you the raw HTML for a Web page. Each paragraph is identified as such, as are tabular data, graphics, hypertext links, and titles. It is like drawing a picture without being able to see the paper.

The browser interprets these tags and properly displays the page (see Figure 1.2).

FIGURE 1.1.

HTML tells the browser how to display information received over the Internet on any computer.

FIGURE 1.2.

This is the same Web page interpreted by the Netscape Navigator browser.

The Birth of the WWW

So, there are two parts to using the Internet: managing the data (the data creators and later the server's job) and retrieving and displaying it on your computer (the computer user's job). Early users had to be UNIX gurus to understand UNIX communications protocols because they were still dealing with the server software to query and receive information. Data coming across the Internet was in textual form because nothing stood between the user and the server except UNIX.

Then a revolution quietly occurred. Computer science students began to write programs, called Web browsers, that served as intermediaries, interpreting the HTML tags and speaking the multitudinous server languages. Browsers assisted users in finding information on the Web and properly displaying it on computer screens. At first, only text was supported. As browsers became more sophisticated at interpreting HTML codes, graphics, sounds, movies, real-time animations, and so forth started to appear as ways to present information.

Browsers and the Web

Let's review.

The Web is simply a way of looking at the Internet. This vast network consists of computers that manage data and the communications links via software and hardware called *servers*. Web servers receive requests for information, go out and find it in their databases, and return the proper pages of data to the requesting computer. The operating system running the servers' computer is a set of routines that allow the user (and other system processes) to interact with and control the machine's hardware resources while preventing conflicts that might arise when two users want to access the same resource at the same time. OSs are written in various languages, which may be C, C++, assembly language, or even firmware or machine language. The OS communicates by means of standard protocols and system routines, which are different for each OS, although the various flavors of UNIX, for example, share many of the same process names and system calls. The operating system is the brains of the computer, and it speaks to itself in many different ways, called *languages*—mostly variations on UNIX, such as SCO, Xenix, SunOS, AIX, A/UX, and so forth; but also Windows variations and, of course, Macintosh. The challenge of early efforts to share information was cutting through this Tower of Babel to share information among dissimilar computer environments. Hypertext Transfer Protocol (HTTP) was developed as a way to find information and retrieve it over telephone lines in a coherent fashion. HTTP is a common set of communications protocols that allow any client to query a server, no matter what OS it's running, and request files or other information from the server.

The revolutionary portion of HTTP is the separation of collecting data from displaying the data. A primary advantage of HTTP was that the server didn't need to know anything about the client, but could serve up the information blindly and could depend on the client to figure out how to display it on local hardware. For example, an audio browser might speak the words on the page rather than displaying them on a video screen, or a robot could extract pertinent information and discard the rest. Graphics, for example, could be "left behind" if the user didn't need them.

You hear the term *bandwidth* a lot when talking about the Internet. This is the capacity of telephone lines and direct connections among computers to handle the electronic pulses required to transmit different types of information. The more bytes it takes to store information, the more bandwidth needed. Graphics need bytes to describe the lines of which they are composed, the colors of the lines, and how to draw the lines. Sound and animation need even more storage area—too much to be sent over a telephone line and be coherent on the other side. By lowering the amount of data crossing the telecommunications links, HTTP found a way to communicate using pictures and sounds without needing to actually transmit all of the information.

On your computer, a Web browser translates what is sent over the wires into the pictures and words you see onscreen as a Web page. Figure 1.3 shows Earthlink's home page as an example of such a display.

FIGURE 1.3.

The browser controls how a page appears on your computer screen.

How did browsers come to be? Early users of the Internet, prior to the advent of HTTP, had to be UNIX gurus because they had to deal with the server software to query and receive information. Data coming across the Internet was in textual form because nothing stood between the users and the server except UNIX. Of course, the question of how to increase the amount of data that crossed a limited amount of bandwidth could not go unanswered. Computer science students began to write programs that resided on local computers (*clients*) that could understand the HTTP protocol. These browsers served as intermediaries between the server and the user.

Now that there was a way to send virtually unlimited amounts of data over limited resources, a way to communicate *how* the data should be displayed on the other side was needed. Print shops were already accepting print jobs on tape from their clients. The digital version of a print job used tags that told the printers how to output data, (ways to tell your computer that a stream of data is a paragraph, or a list, or a citation, for example). One tagging method is called *Standard Generalized Markup Language* (SGML). Computer scientists looked at SGML and simplified it considerably. The simplified version of the markup tags was to travel with the data and be interpreted by the retrieving software—the browser.

Hypertext (such as Apple's HyperCard) supplied ways to connect disparate pieces of data that resided on separate computers using more tags. Together, the hypertext and display tags that tell the computer how to interpret Internet documents came to be called HTML. It became the standard way to tag pages of information that traveled over the Internet via the WWW.

Internet Access Matures

By 1994, commercial online services also made the WWW available to their subscribers by building gateways and browsers from their proprietary sites. Currently, America Online, CompuServe, and Prodigy all have gateways to the Web. With commercial access providers becoming more ubiquitous and prices for access becoming cheaper, millions of regular folks are exploring what used to be the sole province of scientists and students. Meanwhile, the growth in users and resulting marketing possibilities of the Internet made commercial tools for browsing the Web a possibility.

Today, 90 percent of all Internet users use commercial browsers rather than public domain browsers such as Mosaic or Lynx. Commercial browsers are growing in the capabilities of what they can interpret and display. So, the problem of displaying retrieved information has been and is being solved.

A QUICK LESSON ON NETWORKS

A *network* is a system of computers and other devices connected to share data. Networks consist of both hardware (the physical devices such as file server computers, computers, print server computers, printers, and routers) and software (the operating systems containing network client systems and the server operating systems). The connected physical devices are called *nodes*. Nodes are interconnected but may not be on the same physical line. *Bridges* and *routers* connect networks. Bridges are non-intelligent connections and routers contain addressing and routing information that let the machine determine from a message's address the most efficient route the message should take to its destination.

Nodes exchange data using a common set of rules that define the data's format and how it should be transmitted. These rules are called *protocols*. Protocols are implemented using software that carries out the functions specified by the rule.

Are you keeping up?

When networks do not use the same rules to communicate, a *gateway* is needed to convert addresses and protocols to fit the dissimilar network. A set of networks connected by routers or gateways is called an *internet*. The Internet is the internet being discussed—a worldwide conglomeration of networks, routers, gateways, and systems. Just as there are layers of complexity in networks, protocols build their rules by using other, more elementary protocols. That is why there is such alphabet soup in networking talk. For example, on the Macintosh, The AppleTalk Data Stream Protocol (ADSP) uses the Datagram Delivery

continues

continued

Protocol (DDP) to encapsulate the data and deliver it over an AppleTalk network. Thus, rules can be stacked up based on dependencies. This hierarchy is called a *protocol stack*.

You should now understand nodes, routers, gateways, internets and the rules that govern their operation, called protocols, as well as the software written that implements the rules, such as ADSP and DDP.

Then wizards began to fiddle with HTML's boundaries so that more and more things could be transmitted to people's desktops. And so a whole new programming language called Java was begot, which included ways to create small programs that do specific things, ways to personalize information called *push technology*, and other proprietary methods of adding interactivity and animation to Web pages, such as ActiveX controls and OpenStep. HTML standards generation got way behind the types of information that was being transmitted over the Internet. For example, HTML 3.2 does not discuss how to insert applets, how to display different fonts, or how to create frames. Yet, Microsoft Internet Explorer 3.0 (and now 4.0) and Netscape Navigator 3.0 (and now 4.0) can do these things and more. Other, older browsers could not interpret all the multimedia jazz being transmitted because they did not support the new tags being incorporated into newer browsers. In addition, because HTML is not good at graphical layout (for example, you cannot overlap images or create layers of images deeper than a background and foreground, nor place an object in an exact spot and know that it will be viewed in that spot on all types of computers), Web designers needed a more powerful tool to create Web content.

Today, the W3 Consortium has developed an update to the HTML standard that encompasses all of these new multimedia inclusions. HTML 4.0 changes the way you use tags to let Web content grow while keeping it accessible to all types of users. The key to HTML 4.0 is twofold: style sheets separate formatting from information and let designers use more tags defined in a style guide to be read by the browser separate from HTML; and a new OBJECT tag that replaces the applet and IMG tags to allow many more types of data to be transmitted and used. HTML is now a framework for the inclusion of components based on many technologies.

Component Software and the Web

The newest trend in programming, called *component-based programming*, is extending its reaches to the World Wide Web. Currently, a battle is raging for the right to be the ultimate standard for how components work on the Web. *Components* are small programs that can be fit together to form a modular, customized application in real-time (as you need them). The beauty of components is that they can be written in cross-platform languages and rapidly compiled to work on many platforms. For example, if you want a spell checker for your spreadsheet, use a component and you don't have to purchase a large program such as Microsoft Excel to gain that functionality.

Component-based programming has come to the Web in the form of a fight for acceptance as standards between Sun's Java programming language, Apple/IBM's OpenDoc technology, and Microsoft's ActiveX technology (formerly called OLE). Netscape Navigator has chosen to use Java applets and its own JavaScript to provide extensions to basic browser functions.

Today, everything about component software is in flux. A few months ago, Netscape announced it is including OpenDoc support for Navigator on the Macintosh, but then Apple retired OpenDoc to support Java and OPENSTEP. Microsoft has built Internet Explorer from ActiveX technologies but plans to support JavaScript as well as Java virtual machines. This is confusing, isn't it? Wait, it gets better.

Basically, the battle is over two models of how Web browsers will grow, and hence, how Web pages are going to enhance using component software. Microsoft depends on the Distributed Component Object Model (DCOM) whereas Netscape, Apple, IBM, and Sun have agreed upon the Object Management Group's Common Object Request Broker Architecture (CORBA). These competing models make you decide which browser to use, but you must publish your Web pages for both Internet Explorer and Netscape Navigator (as well as other browsers, such as UNIX's Lynx and NCSA's Mosaic). Luckily, the technologies do the same thing, enabling you to view objects such as GIF animations, Virtual Reality, and Shockwave objects placed into HTML. The difference is in how they do it.

ALL ABOUT PLUG-INS

Netscape Navigator began enhancing the capabilities of its browser in 1994 through inline plug-ins and browser- and file-specific software (called *helpers*), which display or play foreign files referenced in HTML. Plug-ins are platform-specific; you have to know which computer operating system the plug-in operates with, because not all of them work on every operating system. The benefit of using plug-ins is that Web designers can control where their data appears on the page and how it relates to other HTML text and graphics on the page (because the foreign file object is embedded in the HTML). The plug-in recognizes the data by its file extension.

The problem is that you must have either the plug-in or access to a player that works on your computer in order to enjoy the enhanced visuals and sound produced by the embedded object. Plug-ins are on the wane, and are being replaced by Java applets, JavaScript, and ActiveX. These are programming technologies, not just single-function applications. They extend the functionality of the Web server as well as the client's browser because they are written directly onto the Web page and call on external programs to operate as needed. Their goal is to integrate the computer operating system with the browser more completely so you can use Internet-based data with more local applications.

Java and JavaScript

The hottest thing to hit the Web is the programming language Java, which Sun Microsystems introduced to make programs portable. This is important because the nature of the Web is that you don't know anything about what your reader is using to access your site. Netscape created a lighter version of Java, which lets users customize their browsers and create a more interactive environment on the Web. This capability is called *Web-delivered scripting*, which enables you to execute programs within a browser. The scripting language based on Java is called JavaScript.

Having the ability to create dynamic interactive features that play on anyone's computer, are relatively easy to create, and are virus-free and relatively tamper-proof is very powerful. Java is used to write fully compiled programs that perform processes such as a visitor counter or an analog clock that you can add to your Web pages. JavaScript is useful for writing small instruction sets used for processing simple user actions, such as how HTML-based documents are displayed (scrolling title bars, flashing buttons, scrolling scroll bar messages, and so forth).

Java applets are small, independent, pre-compiled programs. These programs can be used to create a word processing program that operates over the Web or bounces pretty balls across your screen. Java applets require browsers to understand the language, because the beauty of the language is that it is interpreted in real-time. There are two browsers that understand Java— Sun's HotJava browser and Netscape Navigator 2.0 or higher. Microsoft has invented a competitor called ActiveX and their own "Java" called J++ that is supported by its browser, Internet Explorer. To find more on Java applets, visit the Gamelan Web site at `http://www.gamelan.com`.

Java and JavaScript provide Web pages with the capability to interact with the user. The fact that you can perform all kinds of calculations and display the results on a reader's computer enables you to suddenly personalize your Web pages. You can add, for example, a JavaScript to calculate how many days until your reader's birthday and give him or her the result. Now all you have to do is learn how to write JavaScript-based macros (*scripts*) and add them to your HTML source code.

Cool.

ActiveX

ActiveX is a set of technologies that lets you create more interactive Web pages. ActiveX is a redesign of Microsoft's OLE technology that lets you open external programs and create active documents within another document.

ActiveX technologies provide support for programs on both the client- and server sides. There are several ActiveX components used to perform different functions:

- **ActiveX Controls**. These are applets that function as objects you can embed in your HTML that provide interactive and user-controllable functions.
- **ActiveX Documents**. Let you view non-HTML documents through a Web browser.
- **Active Scripting**. Lets you integrate the functions of several ActiveX controls or Java applets from the browser or server.
- **ActiveX Server Framework**. Provides Web server functions such as security, database access, and others to Web pages.

ActiveX controls (formerly called OLE custom controls) are small applications that run inside a container, such as a Web browser. Because ActiveX controls must be recompiled for each computer system, they are generally incompatible with any operating systems except Windows.

ActiveX requires Microsoft's software to fully function. This is because the beauty of ActiveX is that after ActiveX controls are downloaded into Internet Explorer 3.0 or Netscape Navigator with ScriptActive, the controls can be shared among any OLE-aware application, such as Microsoft Excel or Word, just like any other OLE object. ActiveX documents contain code that launches applications identified as the originating programs for Web page objects, such as Shockwave Director files or Adobe Portable Document Files (PDFs), so that more types of files can be viewed and manipulated within Internet Explorer.

ActiveX documents, built into future versions of Internet Explorer, enable users to interact with local and networked data almost transparently. Although ActiveX controls are more flexible than plug-ins because they use the Windows Registry system for identification of file extensions, this limits ActiveX to Windows environments. Netscape Navigator plug-ins and Java applets use the MIME (Multipurpose Internet Mail Extension) system, which is less flexible than Windows Registry but is available on all platforms. Remember, ActiveX is machine dependent. Java applets are machine independent and download as needed via software interpreters.

ActiveX controls can also function as servers. The DCOM standard allows client and server controls to communicate with each other and distribute the workload across multiple networks. In addition, VBScript (Visual Basic Script) enables you to write ActiveX scripts to provide controls on your Web pages automated from within the browser.

Many vendors have developed ActiveX controls; for example, Macromedia Shockwave is both a plug-in for Netscape Navigator and an ActiveX control. If you use the Microsoft Internet Explorer as your browser to visit a Web site where the ActiveX Shockwave is used, the control is downloaded and installed automatically. Netcompass offers a plug-in called ScriptActive to provide ActiveX control for Netscape Navigator for Windows users.

FOR MORE INFORMATION...

For more information about component-based software, surf the following Web sites:

- **ActiveX** `http://www.microsoft.com/activex/` or `http://www.activex.org/`

You can learn more about JavaScript at the following sites:

- **Netscape's Official JavaScript Reference Guide** `http//home.netscape.com/eng/mozilla/2.0/handbook/javascript/index.html`

- **Tecfa's JavaScript Manual** A JavaScript tutorial. (`http://tecfa.unige.ch/guides/java/tecfaman/java-1.html`)

continues

continued

- **JavaScript 411** A JavaScript FAQ, tutorial, and more. (`http://www.freqgrafx.com/411`)
- **JavaScript 411's Snippet Page** Provides advanced JavaScript code. (`http://freqgrafx.com/411/library.html`)
- **Example Site** Provides examples of JavaScript macros, including a temperature converter, a metric converter, a calendar greeting program, and a loan interest calculator. (`http://www.cis.syr.edu/~bhu/javascript.d/`)

Multimedia Tools

The buzz in the news is about multimedia on the Web. We are standing on the edge of the ability to broadcast on-demand video and audio over the Web, such as a live event (the Presidential debates?) while they are in progress. In addition, working in three dimensions in real-time motion (called *virtual reality*) opens up new vistas.

You are not quite there yet. The problem is bandwidth and browser compatibility. These are huge programs. Even on the speediest of telecommunications lines, these communications get bogged down when transmitting over today's fastest connections (a 128Kbps ISDN Internet connection).

The question of whether you want to spend the very large amount on hardware to broadcast what most users cannot afford to see is dubious today, but who knows about tomorrow…

Databases for Multimedia

More and more Web sites serve as front ends for very large relational databases. Databases keep tabs on content of sites, track copyright information during the production of a site, create templates for Web pages, and manage transmission traffic. Multimedia databases such as Illustra Information Technologies automatically open information sent via e-mail and store images, captions, and text in separate fields. Because of the growing size and number of HTML pages, Java code snippets, and audio/video files that make up a site, you need databases to manage the storage and use of multimedia items.

There are four types of databases available for managing Web sites: traditional relational databases such as Oracle and FileMaker Pro; object-oriented databases such as ObjectDesign's ObjectStore; relational-object hybrid databases such as Illustra; and specialty databases such as Cinebase.

The biggest players are the traditional SQL-based relational database companies: Oracle, Informix, Sybase, Computer Associates, and IBM. Webmasters use these monster databases to manage huge transaction loads such as customer orders and inventory management. You can't store images, sounds, or video on SQL databases because the software handles text, images, and video as one large object (called a BLOB—binary large object), which is difficult to search and retrieve.

Oracle now supports multimedia storage via its new Universal Server Enterprise Edition, which includes Oracle Spatial Data option for storage and retrieval of images, the ConText Option for full text retrieval through SQL, and Oracle Video Option, which serves video files to multiple clients via switched Ethernet and fiber optic cable systems. IBM also has multimedia extensions for its DB/2 relational database that support text, audio, video, image, and fingerprint data.

Object-oriented databases are useful for storing images, video, and audio because they use an object model rather than a tabular model in the database design. An object, as in PageMill, can be anything, whereas in relational databases it can't be easily managed if it cannot fit in a field. There are many small companies producing these more graphic-oriented databases, such as Objectivity, ObjectDesign, and Versant Object Technology. Computer Associates is set to release Jasmine, a joint-development venture with Fujitsu using Fujitsu's ODB-II technology that defines images in terms of their parts. Because component-relationship information is stored with the data, you can easily call up images by selecting a single part of the file name.

Hybrid mixtures of object-oriented and relational databases use the benefits of tabular data and object-based data. The hybrid system is scalable for large amounts of data and uses SQL, yet it can handle complex relationships and new media types and formats. You can extend the database's capabilities by adding plug-ins (called DataBlades in Illustra) that handle complex tasks, such as searching using a visual keyword or Web page authoring. You can create HTML page templates with embedded SQL statements that do not require a CGI script to perform a search and build a resulting Web page on-the-fly. Informix recently bought Illustra and plans to speed its performance and add streaming audio and video capabilities. Its new Universal Server will incorporate Illustra's hybrid systems with Informix' Dynamic Scalable Architecture.

Specialty databases are built for single purposes, such as Media-On-Demand, which is an asset and work flow management program built by Bulldog Group. Media-On-Demand uses Illustra but tailored it for use by commercial art production departments to provide database storage alongside Web authoring capabilities using video, audio, and text objects. A companion database that manages Web transactions is being designed. Cinebase is used for archiving large amounts of video materials.

A new development are Web servers that function as relational databases. The DynaWeb server from Electronic Book Technologies (EBT) manages large libraries of multi-page manuals for storage and retrieval. EBT is also developing DynaBase, a combination Web development and content-management system that would run on Windows NT, Solaris, and Silicon Graphic's IRIX systems. DynaBase produces Web pages on-the-fly based on the results of database searches by browsers.

Audio Broadcasting

One of the exciting new technologies coming out of multimedia developers' workshops is the browser capability to play sound data as it is received. This technology is based on a data type called MIME (Multipurpose Internet Mail Extensions), where the computer sends the data packet first so that the browser can interpret information as it comes screaming down the wire. The benefits of this system are that users do not have to store large chunks of data to enjoy the music, and servers do not have to take up large chunks of storage space processing the sounds. Live audio data is highly compressed (typically 44:1), meaning that an hour's worth of music can be saved in a 3.6MB file.

The problem today is that telecommunications lines are not screaming, but sputtering—there is no such thing as a continuous, error-free flow of data. So you have to install a plug-in that *buffers* (saves in memory) some of the information so that lost or delayed data can be accommodated. You hear this as a long pause before the music starts. In addition, data does not usually flow at a continuous rate, but slows down if the host or client computer is occupied with other matters while surfing (such as printing or traffic surges on the server side of things).

Live music requires two pieces of software: server software and player software. Typically, the server software you buy and the player software is offered free for downloading. PageMill supports files (plays their contents) that you place on a page if you put a copy of the plug-in in the PageMill Plug-ins folder and restart your computer prior to placing the file. Today, Netscape's Web page (`http://home.netscape.com/comprod/products/navigator/`) offers the following plug-in players for Macs and/or Windows 3.1/NT/95.

> **NOTE**
>
> Your player plug-in only supports the data type for which it was written. There are two types of music systems on the computer: MIDI (*Musical Instrument Digital Interface*) and digital audio. Digital audio files are recorded audio waveforms stored as data (bits and bytes). The most common general audio format of the Macintosh is AIFF (*Audio Interchange File Format*) and on the PC, the most common digital audio format is Microsoft's Wave (.wav). The Internet also supports Sun Microsystems' uLaw format. In addition, the Web supports MPEG (*Motion Picture Expert's Group*) compression format for video and audio. You can only hear audio that your browser and computer support. Be careful when embedding digital audio files in PageMill; check that they are in a format your listeners can accept. MIDI is just the opposite of digital audio in that what is stored is information about the music that the player software uses to produce the sounds. The player is usually a sound synthesizer or sound card in the user's computer.

- ■ **Crescendo Plus** by LiveUpdate. Crescendo is a MIDI player that uses QuickTime's built-in MIDI synthesizer to play the music. Crescendo downloads the MIDI sound file and plays it as a continuous sound loop (you cannot stop it from playing until you leave the page). You place a MIDI object in your HTML document, and Macs and Windows 3.1/NT/95 systems with Crescendo automatically play the file.

- **InterVU** MPEG Player by Intervu, Inc. InterVU provides streaming MPEG audio/ video downloads for Netscape Navigator 2.0 or better browsers. You can play any MPEG file without requiring decoders. The InterVU plug-in is available for Macs and Windows NT/95 systems.

- **Koan** by Sseyo. Koan plays MIDI music formatted in Koan Music on all types of Windows systems. The music is generated locally in real-time by the PC's sound card.

- **Maczilla** by Knowledge Engineering. Maczilla supports just about any audio format from QuickTime, MIDI background sound, WAV, AU, and AIFF audio, MPEG and AVI video on a Macintosh.

- **MidPlug** by Yamaha. MidPlug plays MIDI background music on PowerMacs and Windows 3.1/95 systems. You may require external MIDI playback equipment to hear the MidPlug-downloaded music on your computer.

- **RealAudio** by Progressive Networks. RealAudio is the grandmaster plug-in (the first and probably the best) for playing live, on-demand, real-time audio over 14.4Kbps or faster connections to the Internet. RealAudio players and creation software (server-side) are available for Macs and all Windows 3.1/95/NT systems.

- **StreamWorks** by Xing Technology. A high-end counterpart to RealAudio. StreamWorks plug-in supports high-speed digital Internet connections not supported by RealAudio, including 44.1kHz CD-quality stereo sound transmitted over 128Kbps ISDN line. There is no server software available for the Mac to create StreamWorks files, but you can play these files or place them in PageMill on the Mac or any Windows system.

Digital Video

There are two video compression formats vying for power on the Web: QuickTime and MPEG. Digital video does not have the picture quality of broadcast video because personal computers (both Macs and Intels) cannot support the bandwidth required to transmit all the data involved. Digital video is also called *animation* because the images that comprise a moving picture are sent one-by-one in a single pass without interlacing and at half the number of frames per second as broadcast video (digital video is typically transmitted at 15 frames per second).

The pictures on the screen are small (typically 160×120 pixels) to also save bandwidth. There are three ways to compress digital video for the Web: Cinepak, TrueMotion-S, and Indeo. Digital video files are saved as `.mov`, `.moov`, `.qt`, `.avi`, `.mpeg`, and `.mpg` files. QuickTime (`.qt`, `.moov`, and `.mov`) is the most common file format for combined audio/video files. AVI is Microsoft's file format for Windows. You can convert your QuickTime files to AVI files using shareware on both Mac and Windows platforms. MPEG is a new medium that is just beginning to provide combined audio and video in a single file. With the advent of cable modems, you will see more live broadcasts using MPEG compression technology.

Netscape supports the following plug-ins for viewing and creating digital video animations:

- ■ **Action** by Open2U. This Windows 95/NT plug-in lets you embed MPEG movies with synchronized sound into your pages and play them back offline.
- ■ **CineWeb** by Digigami. Plays standard movie and audio files (AVI, MOV, MPG, WAV, MID, and MP2) on Windows systems. You can create standard movies using Weblisher and MegaPEG, also by Digigami.
- ■ **CoolFusion** by Iterated Data Systems. CoolFusion plug-in plays streaming video for Windows (AVI) files. Using CoolFusion, you can preview AVI video in real-time as it downloads on Windows 95 systems.
- ■ **InterVU** by InterVu, Inc. InterVu is an MPEG player that lets you play audio and video MPEG files without decoders or video servers. Videos are transmitted in streams so that they can be previewed as they download on Macs and Windows NT/95 systems.
- ■ **MovieStar** by Intelligence at Large. This plug-in plays QuickTime movies. If the QuickTime files have been optimized with MovieStar Maker, users of the plug-in can preview the films as they are downloading on Macs and Windows 95 systems.
- ■ **QuickTime for Netscape** by Apple Computer. The Netscape Navigator comes with a QuickTime viewer plug-in that previews streaming downloads of QuickTime files. You have to prepare standard Macintosh QuickTime movies before they are useable on the Web by moving the meta data located at the end of the file to the beginning. The QuickTime Web page at `http://quicktime.apple.com/` tells you how to do this. PageMill treats QuickTime movies as objects and will play them back if the QuickTime plug-in is placed in its Plug-ins folder.
- ■ **ViewMovie** by Ivan Cavero Belaunde. This shareware plug-in lets Macs view QuickTime movies, whether linked with anchors or embedded as active images directly on the Page, as they download.

Animation

There are three popular ways to provide animation on Web pages: server-push animated GIFs (GIF files composed of multiple frames), a Java animation applet, and Macromedia Shockwave.

Server-push uses commands embedded in the HTML that create an open connection between the server and the browser. A CGI script is used to push images to the Web page until the script stops the pushing or the user pushes a Stop button. You cannot control image speed, but you can produce montages of photographs or cool moving pictures. For more information about server-push animation, check out Meng Weng Wong's Web site at `http://www.seas.upenn.edu/~menwong/perlhtml.html`.

The GIF89 format and programs, such as GIF Construction Set on Windows machines or GIFBuilder for Macintosh, assist you in implementing the building of GIF frames. The GIF89 format lets you take all of the separate drawings you pushed on the Web page using a server-push CGI script and consolidate them in one file that downloads as a single unit. These files are more compact than server-push animations and take the load off of the server.

As described in the paragraphs on Java, you can use Java applets to provide sound- and motion-interactive animations on your Web page. You can get pre-built applets from shareware or you can write your own Java applets. Check out Sun Microsystems's Web site at `http://java.sun.com/` for examples of applets and a discussion of writing Java programs.

Macromedia, Incorporated has led the way in the production of animated presentations. The Director program is unique in the way it stores animated sequences: It tracks the paths that objects take along with transformations in an object's appearance rather than simply recording frames-per-second transmissions. This makes Director files smaller and more compressed than typical animated film files. You can insert Director files in your Web page using PageMill if you have the Shockwave plug-in installed. ShockWave plays both audio and video and is used to animate logos and banners, because the animations should be kept short to save bandwidth. You use Macromedia's AfterBurner program to convert and compress Director files before inserting them into your Page. ShockWave is available for Macs and all Windows systems. Contact the Macromedia Web site at `http://www.macromedia.com` for information about the various ShockWave products for viewing other Macromedia graphic package outputs over the Web.

Narrative Communications (`http://www.narrative.com`) has developed a product that supports streaming animation and audio called Enliven. Enliven is a server-based technology for streaming 2D animation sequences for Windows 95 and Windows NT servers. Enliven competes against RealAudio and Shockwave to provide fast downloading and real-time playing of animations with sounds. The technology is comprised of a viewer, a server, and a post-production authoring package called Producer that converts Macromedia Director applications into Enliven-compatible files. The viewer is a Netscape plug-in.

3D Images and Virtual Reality

There is currently competition as to whose 3D animation standard will become Virtual Reality Markup Language (VRML) 2.0. Two proposals have been submitted to the VRML Architecture Group: Moving Worlds from Silicon Graphics, Sony, WorldMaker, and Apple, among others, and Active VRML from Microsoft. Both proposals build on existing `.wrl` (World) format files, adding innovations such as timed events, 2D and 3D animation, user interaction with objects (*avatars*), sound effects, collision detection, and automatic frame generation.

You can create the illusion of three dimensions on the two-dimensional computer screen using a new markup language called Virtual Reality Markup Language (VRML), derived from HTML. You need a VRML browser, such as Netscape's Live3D, to view the results. QuickTime VR lets you create panoramic shots, turn them into a QuickTime movie, and view them as QuickTime videos without VRML on Macs. You place QuickTime VR files in PageMill the same way you would QuickTime files. You need to have the QuickTime VR plug-in installed in the PageMill Plug-in folder to view the results in PageMill's Preview window.

For more information about VRML, surf the following sites: `http://www.sdsc.edu/vrml` or `http://www.w3.org/hypertext/WWW/MarkUp/VRML`.

Helper Applications

A helper application is basically a program that cooperates with Netscape and other browsers to perform functions such as displaying the contents of files, which the browser cannot do.

If you surf the Web, you know that you don't really use just one application. The browser software (such as Netscape or Internet Explorer) is your chief tool for clicking through the Web and reading pages, but the Web is a multimedia environment complete with sounds, images, and movies. In general, there are more types of data on the Web than Web browser software can display. JPEG images are one example.

Currently, only Netscape Navigator can display JPEG images inside its main window. Other browsers use what is called a helper application to display JPEG images. On the Macintosh, the helper application to view JPEG images is called JPEG View. If your page's reader is using a browser that does not support direct JPEG image viewing, and comes across a JPEG image, that image is handed off to the helper application, which displays it in a separate window. Other helper applications are listed in Table 1.1.

Table 1.1. Helper applications for Macs and Windows.

Purpose	*Macintosh*	*Windows*
VRML viewing	Whurlwind (requires 3D plug-in), WebSpace for PowerQuickDraw Macs (`www.sgi.com/Products/WebFORCE/WebSpace/`), Web FX for viewing 3D spaces in Internet Chat Rooms (`www.paperinc.com`), Virtus browser (`www.webmaster.com:80/`)	Cosmo Player is the current VRML standard in Windows and UNIX. Live3D by Netscape (formerly Paper Software's WebFX); Microsoft Explorer
Movie viewing	Shockwave Director Internet Player, Apple MoviePlayer	AVI video player for Windows; MPEGPLAY Ver 1.61 for UNIX and win3; VT motion-scalable MPEG player; MPEG players for windows
MPEG animation viewing	Sparkle	Ghostscript; lview 3.1
QuickTime VR movie viewing	Apple QuickTime VR Player	—

Purpose	*Macintosh*	*Windows*
MPEG audio playback	MPEG/CD Player	—
AIFF or AU audio playback	SoundMachine	WHAM 1.33 audio player

WANTED: MORE AND MORE BANDWIDTH

Multimedia transmissions over networks take a lot of bandwidth. Even with compression, multimedia downloads are slow. On the other hand, MIDI and VRML do not have great bandwidth requirements but require extensive preparatory work. There are limited applications available to perform this work and so are of limited usefulness today. Useful media types such as audio, video, and animation, need broader bandwidth, called *fat pipes* in Internet jargon, to be efficient.

ISDN has slightly sped up performance by providing speeds five times greater than that of the fastest modems. That is only half the necessary performance jump necessary to truly provide real-time multimedia on the Web. The next bandwidth jump will use a new technology called Asymmetrical Digital Subscriber Loop (ADSL), video cable modems, and spread-spectrum radio signals. This is just on the end-user side. The backbone of the Internet also needs to speed up. Currently, the backbone can handle transmissions at 45Mbps. Work is starting to extend that performance to 155Mbps. It is already assumed that this increase in bandwidth is not enough to support all of the data being transmitted.

Electronic Publishing

It is one thing to use HTML to send pictures and text over telephone wires to remote computers where a browser interprets arcane codes to display a replica of what was broadcast. It is quite another to be able to reproduce published documents with their complex layouts, colors, and art on a remote computer. The remote computer may not have the fonts installed that were used to produce the document nor the software used to lay out the document. What is needed is a way to make documents electronically portable.

The Web would be a great way to share work among organizations, if this problem of fonts and layout were solved. Adobe Systems has one solution called the portable digital file (*PDF*). Adobe invented PostScript, the printing description language. Encapsulated PostScript (*EPS*) was developed as a way to print vector-based objects using PostScript. PDFs use PostScript to print documents to a file with their fonts and images embedded. PDFs need a reader that is able to translate the Postscript and display the file. Adobe Acrobat, among several competing software applications, is able to create and display PDFs.

The newest version of Adobe Acrobat, code-named Amber and in public beta testing as Acrobat 3.0, is able to transmit PDFs over the Internet containing hypertext links, animation, movies, and so forth, that are readable by a PDF plug-in to Netscape Navigator or Internet Explorer directly on the Web. Now you can use the Web to electronically distribute documents with all of their layout, plus multimedia features, intact.

For more information about PDFs and Adobe Acrobat, surf the Adobe Acrobat site at `http://www.adobe.com/acrobat`.

Summary

When Tim Berners-Lee developed Hypertext Markup Language, he probably never imagined using it to present live information, movies, information on demand, multimedia, and other commercialized presentations. HTML standards as represented by HTML 4.0 build a framework through which you can use the various technologies of Java, ActiveX, DirectX, JBScript, JavaScript, and so forth, to construct your Web pages.

Setting Up an Extensible Web Publishing Framework

by Rita Lewis

CHAPTER 2

Introduction

What does *extensible* mean? This word encompasses the entire history of HTML specification development in a single thought—that the specification has to hold and support all of the new technologies driving the Web. HTML specifications as they stand today do not readily support the inclusion of HTML extensions, such as FONT, or new technologies such as TrueDoc fonts, ActiveX controls, and Java applets. HTML 4.0 promises to be extensible because it includes broader tags for embedding objects, style sheets to separate page layout from paragraph formatting, more flexible table elements, and additional form elements to support the burgeoning use of backend databases.

This chapter provides an overview of how the World Wide Web Consortium and its HTML version 4.0 Specification is designed to both extend the reach of HTML specifications and yet retain the interoperability of Web contents.

What Is the World Wide Web Consortium (W3C)?

It is hard to believe that the World Wide Web as an entity is actually only five years old (as of late 1997). So much has happened since the W3C was founded in October, 1994, to manage the evolution of the World Wide Web and its design components. Already, there are four generations of specifications dictating how *user agents* (as the W3C calls browsers and other devices used to view Web pages) display information from the Internet.

The first HTML specification, 2.0, was a document defining which tags would be accepted as legitimate by browsers. W3C saw its role as that of arbitrator, defining how the Web would behave. This would have been well and good, but the World Wide Web design and content took off ahead of where W3C members could all agree on how pages should be displayed. Netscape introduced its own series of enhancements to the HTML specification, including tables, frames, JavaScript, animated graphics, and client-side image maps, which only users of its browser could see. Microsoft also jumped in with its proprietary enhancements, including font faces, style sheets, ActiveX controls, which only users of its browser could see. Both companies made agreements outside the Consortium to support each others's versions of these HTML tags, but this left the HTML specification in the dust. All of a sudden people were asking what the W3C's role was and how HTML specifications could be extended to support new technologies while remaining interoperable with older user agents.

Part of the answer was for W3C to give up trying to be the definer of true HTML. With the recommendation of HTML 3.2 (3.0 was withdrawn), W3C played catch-up with HTML supported by the popular browsers, incorporating those rendering attributes that were truly interoperable, such as tables and applets. The latest iteration of the Hypertext Markup Language Specification, version 4.0, consolidates popular extensions and attempts to build a framework for the incorporation of future extensions that are supported by all manner of Web browsers (even those yet unimagined).

W3C was founded by a coalition of hardware, software, and content providers to ensure that the Internet remains open, meaning that the Web continues to be interoperable and has not become the province of one major provider. It cannot be stressed enough, how important this concept of interoperability is to the future evolution of the Internet and World Wide Web. Here is a quote from the HTML 4.0 Specification (W3C Working Draft 8, July 1997), page 8:

HTML 4.0 SPECIFICATION ON INTEROPERABILITY

Each version of HTML attempts to reach greater consensus among industry players so that the investment made by content providers will not be wasted and that their documents will not become unreadable in a short period of time.

HTML has been developed with the vision that all manner of devices should be able to use information on the Web: PCs with graphics displays of varying resolution and color depths, cellular telephones, hand-held devices, devices for speech for output and input, computers with high or low bandwidth, and so on.

The World Wide Web Consortium (W3C) was founded by CERN (Centre Européen pour la Recherche Nucléaire) in Switzerland and the Massachusetts Institute of Technology (MIT) Laboratory for Computer Science to "...develop common protocols that enhance the interoperability and promote the evolution of the World Wide Web." When CERN could no longer afford to host the Consortium in April 1995, responsibility for the group's European component passed to France's National Institute for Research in Computer Science and Control (INRIA). In August 1996, Keio University of Japan was invited to be the third host and represent Asian interests.

The W3C is both a library of sample code to promote standards, information about the World Wide Web, prototype applications demonstrating new technologies, and a series of meetings where Web-related issues can be discussed in a vendor-neutral environment.

There are currently 180 commercial and academic members worldwide. W3C members include representatives from hardware and software vendors, telecommunications providers, content developers, corporations, and government and academic users of the Internet. The W3C is governed by an Advisory Committee comprised of one representative from each member organization. The W3C's output is a set of specifications defining the operations of the World Wide Web, including HTML, security issues, Internet issues, and so forth.

How Is the W3C Organized?

The World Wide Web Consortium is organized around three domains: User Interface, Technology and Society, and Architecture. The User Interface group works on issues dealing with Web content and design. The Technology and Society group works on issues dealing with security, privacy, copyrights, intellectual property rights, and self-censorship. The Architecture group works on issues dealing with infrastructure, such as addressing, object technology, new forms of hypertext, and new ways to transmit and receive pages.

As shown in Figure 2.1, the HTML Activity area lies under the User Interface Domain.

FIGURE 2.1.

*Here is the organiza-
tion chart for the World
Wide Web Consortium.*

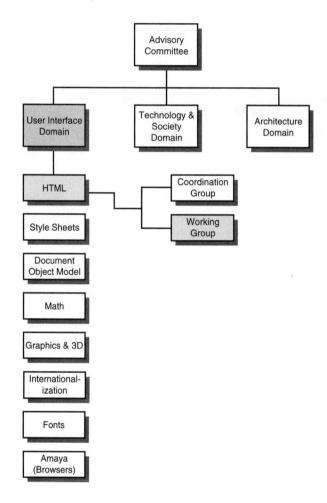

What Is the HTML Working Group?

The HTML Working Group is the current organization within W3C responsible for developing HTML specifications and standards. This year the Working Group replaced an older
organization called the Editorial Review Board (ERB), which was formed in 1995, to incorporate vendor developments and gain agreement among Web vendors on the HTML feature set.

A Quick Review of Markup Concepts

The goal of markup languages is to create a universal way to identify the structure and content
of a document. Standardized Markup Language (SGML) is the earliest specification for markup

(and HTML's father). The origin of SGML and its baby, HTML, was the recognition that information is a commodity that can be used repeatedly, in the same way a computer can be repeatedly accessed. The problem was that different output devices could not figure out where a document began or ended. SGML took the concept of generic markup and developed a hierarchical model in which every element of a document fits into a logical, predictable structure.

SO WHAT IS MARKUP, ANYWAY?

The earliest use of markup was when an editor took a red pen and added editorial comments to typewritten text to instruct the typesetter or compositor how the document should be constructed (what typefaces to use, where chapters began and ended, which lines were subheadings, and so forth). This *manual markup* process evolved with desktop publishing into what is called procedural markup.

Procedural markup is what your word processor does when it adds codes to your document, telling the printer how to format different portions (styles, fonts, and so forth). WordPerfect is a very obvious user of procedural markup—you can even see the tokens (tiny codes telling the word processor how to present your information) right on your screen. The problem with procedural markup is that it is dedicated to a single user—whether a typesetting machine, word processing program, or desktop processing program; it cannot be transferred to another computer that does not have the requisite software installed.

Software developers went on and figured out what is called generic or descriptive markup. *Generic markup* tells any output device how to format the contents of a document. Generic markup is not concerned with the physical appearance of a page, but rather its structure—headings, chapters, footnotes, figures, and so forth. Generic markup identifies entire *elements* within a document's structure (chapters, sections, and so forth) by describing those element's start and finish (not how the element should look). SGML takes generic markup one step further by organizing its element codes into a hierarchical structure that describes an entire document by its sections and their relationship to the whole.

SGML is based upon the use of a special file called a Document Type Description (DTD) document. The *DTD* describes the structure of a document, much like a Data Description Document describes the structure of a database. The document's basic framework is defined, including types of elements used and how these elements are related to each other. For example, a chapter heading element would be defined so that it is understood by the document's interpreter software that the text following a chapter heading tag would contain the title of the chapter. DTDs always travel with a document. Remember DTDs? HTML 4.0 returns to them with a vengeance (only now they are called style sheets).

The contents of a document are labeled with tags that identify the document's structure. Each tag has a beginning and ending. Tags can be nested within tags.

Notice that layout has not yet been addressed.

For the past ten years or so, a series of standards have been developed for describing the layout or presentation portion of a document so that the information can be used by any computer to correctly output a document. The oldest initiative was called Output Specification (OS), which used a special DTD for creating a Formatting Output Specification (FOSI). FOSI is a special file expressed in SGML tags. FOSI is a large style sheet specifying the formatting characteristics of every tag in the DTD. Later, the OS and its FOSI developed into an international standard called Document Style Semantics and Specifications Language (DSSSL).

So what does this have to do with HTML?

HTML was developed as a subset of SGML for handling hypertext links in a fashion that allowed the collection of links and their compilation and display by a user agent (called a *browser*). HTML uses a type of DTD based on the specifications designated by the W3C because every browser is supposed to interpret HTML elements in the same fashion based on these specifications.

What is interesting about HTML 4.0 compared to earlier specifications is that the specification is returning to the idea of separating presentation from content and structure. Style sheets are a type of DTD in the same way FOSIs are to SGML. The document becomes interoperable to the degree that layout information can be separated from a document's structure. An added bonus is that a tagged document is more usable as a database component, because its tags can also be set up as index elements for a search engine. Multiple style sheets enable you to create one site, but indicate a series of ways it can be displayed depending upon its audience (people with disabilities, non-graphic browsers, and WebTV, for example). In addition, separate style sheets for printing eliminate the need for hard-wiring layout to a page via table tags and invisible GIFs, making pages more universal.

So what is the meaning of all of this? You need to understand how SGML works in order to comprehend how HTML 4.0 changes your Web page development.

What Is HTML 4.0?

The HTML Specification 4.0 is a working draft. That is the first stage in a three-step process to reach consensus among members. The next stage is called a Proposed Recommendation, and when a majority of the membership approves the specification it becomes a recommendation. HTML Specification 3.2 is the current recommended specification. Upon acceptance as a recommendation, the specification becomes an RFC (Request for Comment). RFCs are slightly less than standards but more than recommendations. The current HTML RFC is version 2.0 (called RFC 1866 just to make things confusing). Everything is in limbo depending upon how many large-scale Web producers (such as Microsoft and Netscape) intend to accept the RFC or recommendation. You'll hear a lot about HTML 4.0, even as HTML 3.2 and HTML 2.0 are being phased out and later HTML drafts are developed.

EXPLAINING HTML SPECIFICATION VERSIONS

HTML has an interesting development history. When HTML (termed simply HTML 1) was first written by Tim Berners-Lee, it was very basic. During the time HTML was unfolding, Marc Andresson wrote the Mosaic browser that used extensions to HTML that were not in Berners-Lee's original specification. The Internet Engineering Task Force (IETF) (a precursor to the W3C and an existing standards-setting organization) worked up the HTML 2.0 specification in mid-1994 to try to make sense of this outgrowth of HTML extensions and commonly used tags that weren't specified in HTML 2.0. (See a pattern here?)

HTML 2.0 was outdated by the time the W3C was founded. W3C formed the Editorial Review Board expressly to rein in Microsoft and Netscape's divergent adoption of HTML features and extensions. The resulting specification was published in 1996 and called HTML 3.2. Because it did not address Java, ActiveX, streaming audio, and other multimedia and Web programming developments, HTML 3.2 was also already obsolete when it became a recommendation. The HTML Working Group has a broader vendor base and should receive wider acceptance for its specification, code-named "Cougar" and now called HTML 4.0, because the group's goal is to map out future directions for HTML, rather than simply ratifying existing HTML.

HTML 4.0 corrects design deficiencies produced by HTML 3.2, especially in the support of forms and tables. Table 2.1 presents differences between HTML 4.0 and HTML 3.2.

Table 2.1. Changes between HTML 3.2 and HTML 4.0.

Changes	Resulting Tags and Attributes
New elements and attributes (added to address formatting and localization enhancements)	Q, INS, DEL, ACRONYM, LEGEND, COLORGROUP, BUTTON, LABEL, FIELDSET, and FIELDSET. TABLE style attribute; FORM accesskey, disabled, readonly, and accept charset attributes; INPUT accept attribute; new FORM script-support attributes, including onchange INPUT
Modified elements and attributes (changed to avoid SGML name clashes—especially with align and valign attributes)	TABLE frame and rules attributes
Deprecated Elements (tags and attributes that are being phased out)	ISINDEX, APPLET, CENTER, FONT, BASEFONT, STRIKE, S, U, DIR, and MENU
Obsolete Elements (The PRE tag replaces these dead tags)	XMP, PLAINTEXT, and LISTING

Design Concepts Underlying HTML 4.0

HTML 4.0 can be viewed as a battle plan to keep the Web truly worldwide by making sure that all people (no matter their nationality or ability) and all computers (no matter their power, size, or range) can access the Web. The Working Group used the following concepts to ensure that their specifications met that goal:

- Interoperability
- Internationalization
- Accessibility
- Enhanced tables
- Compound documents-enabled
- Style sheets
- Scripting-enabled
- Enhance printing of entire Web sites
- Maintain HTML's ease of use

HTML 4.0 is an extensible Web framework because it incorporates these listed things, which allow the specification to grow with the times. By being more general in its application, HTML 4.0 enables you to create more efficient and effective pages by separating the page's structure from its information. HTML elements are no longer concerned with the type of link they call (be it an image, a block of text, a file, an applet, a CGI, or a script), but with broadening the ability of the specification to accept new media. The more you can split the layout from the structure, the broader the range of platforms, media, and audiences you can reach without having to constantly redesign your pages. HTML 4.0 builds on this concept of interoperability by providing various new tools (active buttons, text-to-speech script hooks, and the new accesskey and alt attributes) to let nontraditional browsers access the Web. HTML 4.0 supports the Unicode document character set, as well as various new elements and attributes that make it easier to internationalize your pages. HTML 4.0 also increases the efficiency with which browsers render pages by redesigning how tables and frames work (incremental rendering of tables, new table and frame elements that increase your control of tabular materials).

There is a downside to this change in direction: You have to go back to school.

Because HTML 4.0 represents a departure from earlier efforts to standardize the features of HTML, Web developers will find that broadening the scope of HTML comes at the price of learning new Web page design techniques, namely the separation of information presentation to style sheets, the reduction of your dependence on tables for layout assistance, the addition of alternative versions of images for physically disabled users, and the use of new HTML 4.0 features to increase the download efficiency of their pages.

Summary

HTML did not spring up fully grown from the head of Tim Berners-Lee. The markup language is a subset of a non-proprietary language standard used to write markup schemes that can be interpreted by any computer. HTML enables you to receive proper layouts over a network by using hypertext to pull together parts of a page. SGML is based on the concept of separating a document's content from its structure and then applying formatting. HTML 4.0 returns to this idea by introducing the concept of multiple style sheets used to lay out a single document for a multitude of user types with differing needs (physical needs as well as technological capabilities to view your page).

The end result? Throw out those tables and one-pixel GIFs and use style sheets for layout. Use HTML 4.0's standardized set of tags to ensure that your page is readable by any browser, anywhere in the world.

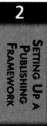

II

PART

HTML 4.0: The Web Publishing Foundation

With all the excitement about style sheets and dynamic scripting, it is easy to lose sight of the fact that all this new functionality is built around the old, solid core of the Hypertext Markup Language. None of it has any meaning apart from its relationship to HTML. Whether it is the ability to define HTML elements in a new way or the ability to dynamically alter HTML elements, the central part of all these new approaches to handling and manipulating Web documents is still HTML.

HTML is a subset of SGML, Standard Generalized Markup Language. SGML is itself a rigorous format meant for designing other markup languages. The basic concept behind HTML or any other markup languages is to embed commands that describe how different elements within a document should be interpreted in that document. Thus, unlike a word-processing file, which operates with a proprietary formatting scheme useable only within that program unless converted to another format, an HTML document can be read and displayed by different user agents (such as Web browsers).

The particular display may be interpreted in different ways. For example, the embedded command represented by the <STRONG> tag is usually rendered as bold text, but the exact method is optional. Instead of bold text, it is perfectly permissible to render it as italics or as all caps. A voice-oriented client agent may speak the affected terms at a higher volume. None of these approaches is a violation of the HTML code's intent, which is that this text should stand out from the text preceding and following it.

HTML is changing these days, though, and the major thrust of that change is to give greater control to the HTML author. Most people have always preferred to have more say in the final appearance of their work; for instance, rather than using <EM> or <STRONG> and hoping that it shows up respectively as italic or bold text, you would instead use the more specific <I> and <B> tags. Now, the advent of style sheets, with their control over such things as font-family specifications and absolute positioning, means that the era of full control over Web development is finally here—but the one thing that remains constant is the foundation upon which these new capabilities are built—the venerable Hypertext Markup Language itself.

The Web's Defining Framework

HTML provides Web designers with both a matrix and a mechanism. As a matrix, its purpose is to be the basic framework in which content is embedded. As a mechanism, it provides ways to specify the manner in which that content is presented and, to a limited extent, allows various options for its functioning. Paired with the newer developments of scripting languages and style sheets, the true potential of HTML seems about to be fully realized, and the World Wide Web to really come into flower.

It was the melding of hardware and software that first brought the World Wide Web to life. Without the interconnectivity of the worldwide network called the Internet, hypertext would be limited to local presentations at best. Indeed, hypertext was around for a very long time before the Web was even conceived. The first written record referring to it was an article titled

"As We May Think," in the July, 1945 issue of *Atlantic Monthly* magazine. Written by Vannevar Bush, who was in charge of the War Department's scientific division during World War II, it referred to a hypothetical device he called a *memex*, which would contain vast amounts of data, all of which cross-linked with one another.

Over the years, there were sporadic attempts to implement the hypertext concept, though nothing much came of it until Apple's Hypercard and the Windows help file system brought it into the daily life of the average computer user. It was not until 1990, though, that Tim Berners-Lee, working at CERN in Geneva, Switzerland, proposed a globe-girdling system of hypertext. The Hypertext Markup Language was off and running from that point. Very few people in the world would have had the forward vision to even begin to imagine what impact it would have.

Combined with the vast internetwork of computers that exists today, HTML and the World Wide Web finally brought to life the memex of Dr. Bush's imagination. At first, it was a simple system—even primitive by today's standards, a mere seven years later. Text-oriented and lacking even such elementary capabilities as centering a paragraph, it nevertheless contained the critical element, the hyperlink.

As the name of the language implies, the heart of HTML is the hypertext link. With it, HTML documents combine disparate elements into a single, coherent whole. In a single document, HTML today allows text, images, sound, and video to become a unitary environment. In the World Wide Web as a whole, it allows all the documentation on the entire planet to be melded together as the single largest book ever written, with the largest group of authors ever gathered. It is truly a landmark in the history of humankind.

Tags and Elements in HTML

Tags are the main resources for HTML authors. They define the existence of all the elements a Web page contains. Indeed, they define the existence of the page itself. Each element is said to be "contained" by tags. In many cases, elements can also contain other elements, although the containment is still defined by the element's tags.

When a Web browser or other client agent parses the HTML code in a Web page, it looks for these defining indicators to tell it how to process and display the elements.

The code structure of elements is a start tag (which contains not only the name of the element, but also any attributes assigned to that element), followed by the content, if any, and the end tag. Content varies from element to element; some have no content portion at all.

Most elements have required start and end tags, the function of which is to delimit the beginning and ending of the element. For instance, the FORM element begins with <FORM> and ends with </FORM>. Leaving out either tag means the form will not work (and will probably generate other errors in adjacent elements).

Other elements have required start tags, but optional end tags. In these cases, there is some other event besides reaching the end tag that tells the parser that the element is complete and another is about to begin. The paragraph element, for example, only requires a start tag (<P>). Although you can add an end tag (</P>), it is not required because anything following a paragraph is likely to be a block-level element, and all HTML parsers know this. There are, of course, cases in which an inline element (such as an image) follows a paragraph, but this is sufficiently unusual that the HTML specification does not require an end tag for paragraphs.

> **NOTE**
>
> Elements are either block-level or inline. *Block-level elements* are things like paragraphs, forms, lists, and headings, which form separate, coherent blocks from the surrounding elements. *Inline elements*, by contrast, are character-level and do not cause a new block to be created. Examples of inline elements include superscripts, images, and italic text.

Still other elements have only a start tag and no end tag—the IMG element, for instance. Everything required to insert an image is contained within the start tag and its attributes.

There are no elements with optional start tags; every element must have a start tag.

Each element has its own attributes that are peculiar to it. The A (anchor) element, for instance, has the href (hypertext reference) attribute, which is necessary in order for the element to identify to which URL it needs to link. The TABLE element, on the other hand, has no use whatsoever for the href attribute.

Every element, though, has certain generic attributes. These include the core attributes (see Chapter 6, "Style Sheets: Formatting for the Future"), the i18n (international language) attributes, and the intrinsic events (for use with scripting languages, see Chapter 13, "Scripting Basics."). They are outlined in Tables 3.1, 3.2, and 3.3, along with their official definitions from the World Wide Web Consortium's transitional document type definition (DTD).

Table 3.1. Core attributes.

Attribute	DTD Definition
id	Document-wide unique ID
class	Space-separated list of classes
style	Associated-style information
title	Advisory title/amplification

Table 3.2. i18n (international language) attributes.

Attribute	DTD Definition
lang	RFC1766 language value
dir	Direction for weak/neutral text

Table 3.3. Intrinsic events.

Event	DTD Definition
onclick	A pointer button was clicked.
ondblclick	A pointer button was double-clicked.
onmousedown	A pointer button was pressed down.
onmouseup	A pointer button was released.
onmouseover	A pointer was moved onto.
onmousemove	A pointer was moved within.
onmouseout	A pointer was moved away.
onkeypress	A key was pressed and released.
onkeydown	A key was pressed down.
onkeyup	A key was released.

The page is HTML's fundamental element. Despite the existence of billions of other Web pages in the world, and despite the interconnected nature of the World Wide Web, there is no container element in the Hypertext Markup Language that has scope beyond one single HTML page.

The main structural elements of the Web page itself are covered in Chapter 4, "Basic Structural Elements and Their Usage." Briefly, the start of an HTML page is defined by the <HTML> start tag and the end is defined by the </HTML> end tag. The HEAD and BODY elements are within that HTML element. The material between the <HEAD></HEAD> tags is largely informational, although this is also where JavaScript and style-connection information are placed. The BODY element (found, of course, between the <BODY></BODY> tags) contains the majority of the other elements—at least, everything your site's visitor will be able to see. It is also more and more common today to see the BODY element replaced by frames, which are defined by the FRAMESET element. Like the BODY element, it has start and end tags (<FRAMESET> and </FRAMESET>). Framesets are covered in Chapter 10, "Frames and Framesets."

The elements contained within a Web page's body tags are many and various. They include elements for controlling the insertion of images and sounds, tying in Java applets and other objects, setting the appearance and size of text, adding tables and forms, and just about anything else that seven years of frantic, explosive development have been able to see to fruition.

Although they can still be used to fully define a Web page's appearance and structure, their use with current technology is becoming less a matter of defining the specific look of every detail, and more a matter of page layout. The fine details of the page—element sizing, alignment, and color, the choice of font faces, and the like—are being left more to the arena of cascading style sheets.

Still, the basic design phase of Web site development is mostly involved with HTML itself. Even the use of scripting languages to bring true programmatic control to the Web must rely on the solid foundation of HTML; style sheets ultimately do little that HTML was not already capable of doing, though they admittedly do it in a more elegant and organized manner.

Summary

The Hypertext Markup Language (HTML) is a subset of the Standard Generalized Markup Language (SGML). HTML describes the layout and content of a Web page so that it can be understood by a wide variety of user agents; these various user agents are permitted to interpret the HTML markup in different ways. Today, HTML is moving in the direction of giving total power to the Web designer over a page's appearance and interpretation. HTML provides the basic framework within which content is included; it also gives control over the appearance and functionality of the various elements that comprise a Web page. The hypertext link is the heart of the Hypertext Markup Language, the one element without which it would simply be another standalone page-layout system. Tags are the factors that define the elements in a Web page. Some elements require start and end tags, some have optional end tags, and others have no end tags at all. Every element has attributes, some of which are particular to it, and others that are common to all elements. The Web page is the fundamental element of HTML, and it encapsulates all the other elements.

Basic Structural Elements and Their Usage

by David and Rhonda Crowder

IN THIS CHAPTER

CHAPTER 4

There are four basic structural elements in HTML. The <!DOCTYPE> tag represents the Document Type Declaration (DTD), which defines the version of HTML used on the page. The next is the <HTML> tag itself, which simply states that the page is an HTML document. The third is the HEAD element, which contains the document's title and, sometimes, other information. Then there is the BODY element, where the actual Web page itself is contained.

A basic HTML page looks like this:

```
<!DOCTYPE HTML PUBLIC "-//W3C//DTD HTML 4.0 //EN">

<HTML>

<HEAD>
<TITLE>Page Title Goes Here</TITLE>
Optional metadata goes here.
</HEAD>

<BODY>
Web page goes here.
</BODY>

</HTML>
```

Note how the start and end tags for each of the last three elements denote the container relationships in the Web page. The <HTML></HTML> tags surround the HEAD and BODY elements, which, in turn, surround their own content and are denoted by their own start and end tags. Thus, HEAD and BODY are contained within the HTML element, but not within each other.

The DOCTYPE Element

Although <!DOCTYPE> is technically required at the start of any HTML document, it is almost never used, and its absence does not cause any of the usual Web browsers to balk. Its purpose is to declare to browsers exactly what version of HTML was used to create the document. There are different DOCTYPE declarations, depending upon the elements you have included in your HTML document. The general DOCTYPE declaration for HTML 4.0 is

```
<!DOCTYPE HTML PUBLIC "-//W3C//DTD HTML 4.0 //EN">
```

The reason for the EN is that the HTML specification has not yet been developed in any language but English.

The previous document declaration is for the strictest possible implementation of the HTML 4.0 specification. If you intend to include elements that are currently deprecated, such as the <CENTER> tag, you should use the following declaration:

```
<!DOCTYPE HTML PUBLIC "-//W3C//DTD HTML 4.0 Transitional//EN">
```

Finally, if you are replacing the BODY element with FRAMESET, you should use the following DTD:

```
<!DOCTYPE HTML PUBLIC "-//W3C//DTD HTML 4.0 Frameset//EN">
```

Note that DOCTYPE has no end tag; there is no such thing as </!DOCTYPE>.

It seems likely at this stage that HTML 4.0's final specification will be issued at some point in the near future, but this is not a foregone conclusion. The HTML 3.0 specification never got beyond the draft stage, left behind as a footnote when it was superseded by the HTML 3.2 specification.

> **CAUTION**
>
> You should not use the DOCTYPE declaration if there is a single element in your Web pages that deviates from the official standard. If, for instance, you use Microsoft's MARQUEE tag or Netscape's LAYERS tag, the DOCTYPE could cause problems.

There is another technique for supplying the DOCTYPE declaration. This is called the *System Identifier* DTD. A System Identifier DTD is declared as follows:

```
<!DOCTYPE
HTML
SYSTEM
"http://www.w3.org/DTD/HTML4-strict.dtd">
```

The difference in this approach is that the DTD is referenced not by name, but by specifying the URL where it is found. The Web browser can then download the DTD and any special characters (or *entity sets*) needed to properly display the Web page. Obviously, this can require a longer connect time before everything is ready to go.

Table 4.1 shows the URLs the World Wide Web Consortium supplies for use with this method.

Table 4.1. URLs for use with System Identifier DTDs.

URL	*DTD*
http://www.w3.org/DTD/HTML4-strict.dtd	Default strict DTD
http://www.w3.org/DTD/HTML4-loose.dtd	Loose DTD
http://www.w3.org/DTD/HTML4-frameset.dtd	DTD for frameset documents
http://www.w3.org/DTD/ISOlat1.ent	Latin-1 entities
http://www.w3.org/DTD/HTMLsymbol.ent	Symbol entities
http://www.w3.org/DTD/HTML4special.ent	Special entities

4

BASIC STRUCTURAL ELEMENTS AND THEIR USAGE

The standard document type declaration and the system-identifier document type declaration can be used together. Such a declaration would be as follows:

```
<!DOCTYPE
HTML
PUBLIC
"-//W3C//DTD
HTML
4.0//EN"
"http://www.w3.org/DTD/HTML4-frameset.dtd">
```

The HTML Element

The HTML tag, on the other hand, is an absolute necessity. It is the first and the last thing in a Web page, and its absence means that no Web browser recognizes your work as an HTML page. Unlike DOCTYPE, the HTML element must have both start and end tags in order to function properly. Thus, the document begins with <HTML> and ends with </HTML>.

Generally speaking, the HTML start tag contains no other content. Technically, however, it does have three attributes. The first is version, and it takes a URL value. The URL points to a location that has the Document Type Definition (DTD) for the version of HTML in use on that page. However, because that information is already included in the DOCTYPE, or is included at peril (see previous Caution), it has little use and is almost never seen in practice.

The HTML start tag can also contain the lang and dir attributes, which, respectively, establish the human language in which the Web page is written (for example, en for English and fr for French) and the direction of the printing (right to left or left to right, with RTL being the default). These attributes, which have little or no use in current practice, are common to other elements as well.

An HTML element's start tag, which fully utilizes every possible attribute, instead of simply consisting of the usual <HTML>, might look like:

```
<HTML version="http://www.w3.org/DTD/HTML4-strict.dtd" lang=en dir=rtl>
```

The HEAD Element

The HEAD element is a container for an HTML document's header information. It contains one required element—TITLE—and several other optional attributes, most of which are rare in actual usage. The HEAD element has both start and end tags, beginning with <HEAD> and ending with </HEAD>. A typical HEAD element looks like this:

```
<HEAD>
<TITLE>Olga's Home Page</TITLE>
</HEAD>
```

> **NOTE**
>
> Believe it or not, neither the start tag nor the end tag for the HEAD element is required at the top of an HTML document. However, it is good form to use them, as they help to clearly and unequivocally distinguish the header information from the body of the document.

The sole content permitted in a TITLE element is the text used to identify the Web page. The text between the TITLE tags is displayed in the title bar of a visitor's Web browser. This is also the text that is used to identify the page when a bookmark is added in a browser, or when the page is indexed by a Web search service such as Webcrawler or Excite. Thus, you should take care to make the text descriptive and coherent.

Most Web designers choose to repeat the same text as is used in the title as an <H1> element to begin their page, as in the following example:

```
<HTML>
<HEAD>
<TITLE>Information Acquisition, Inc.</TITLE>
</HEAD>
<BODY>
<H1>Information Acquisition, Inc.</H1>
...
</BODY>
</HTML>
```

This means that, when viewed in a Web browser, the displayed page starts with the same text as is displayed in the browser's title bar (see Figure 4.1).

FIGURE 4.1.

The title and the first line match.

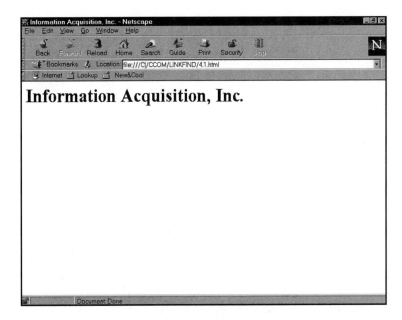

Still, some others prefer to utilize the differences between the two, and place different text in the title and first page element, as in the following example:

```
<HTML>
<HEAD>
<TITLE>Begonias, Orchids, Ferns, Gesneriads, Sellizinella</TITLE>
</HEAD>
<BODY>
<H1>Palm Hammock Orchid Estate</H1>
...
</BODY>
</HTML>
```

In this technique, the displayed page does not start with the same text as is displayed in the browser's title bar (see Figure 4.2). However, by taking advantage of the different techniques, the title shows up in a search engine as a very descriptive line detailing the contents of the Web site, while not detracting from the pleasing appearance of the page in a Web browser.

Figure 4.2.

The title and the first line do not match.

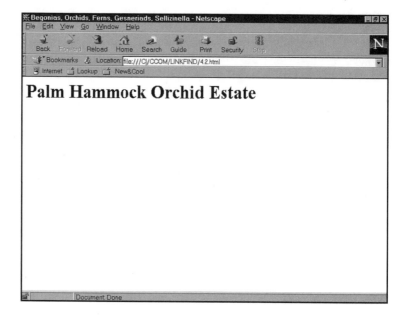

CAUTION

There has been a regrettable choice of terminology that is bound to cause a great deal of confusion to HTML authors. The TITLE element, which has existed as long as HTML itself, is not the same thing as the new title attribute, which is found in most elements. While the title attribute is used to create ToolTips such as (depending on the user agent) status bar messages or floating help balloons that present the user with more information about the element, the TITLE element is used to give an overall title to the entire HTML document and exists only within the HEAD element.

Metadata

In addition to the title, a HEAD element can contain other elements known as *metadata*. Metadata is information other than that contained in the body of the HTML page. It is data that is not shown to the person viewing the page in a Web browser, but is still available and, if constructed properly, useful to user agents and search engines.

Metadata includes a broad and ever-expanding group of data, ranging from copyright information to ratings systems. The HEAD element currently has two separate methods for using metadata. One is an attribute of the HEAD element itself, and the other is to use separate elements that are required to be contained within the HEAD element.

The profile attribute of the HEAD element is largely unimplemented at this time. In fact, no format for profiles has been developed for the HTML 4.0 specification. There seems to be no coherent concept of exactly what a profile might be useful for (the official documentation states that user agents could "perform some activity"). The one example given is to name keywords that are later defined by the META element. Because defining keywords via the META element is already a well-established approach requiring no other assistance, it is difficult to say what good a profile might be to an HTML author.

Be that as it may, the profile is specified as a URL. An example of this might be:

```
<HEAD profile="http://www.whatever.com/profile/data.html">
```

There are several elements that can be contained within HEAD for the provision of various types of metadata. Two of these, ISINDEX and NEXTID, are no longer used. The currently used elements in this class are:

- BASE
- LINK
- META
- SCRIPT
- STYLE

The BASE Element

The BASE element establishes a base URL from which relative URLs referenced in the HTML document can be calculated. If BASE is not present in the HEAD element, the URL of the document itself (minus the document name) is used by default. BASE, of course, takes a URL as its argument, as in the following example:

```
<BASE href="http://www.test.org/">
```

The result of this declaration is that any relative URL in the HTML document is appended to this base URL to achieve the full URL. Thus, a relative URL of tubes.HTML would be interpreted as http://www.test.org/tubes.html, and an image referenced at images/beaker.gif would be searched for at http://www.test.org/images/beaker.gif.

It is generally unnecessary to specify the base URL, because the Web browser or other client agent is fully capable of determining it. However, there are special cases where this is desirable. For example, if you have an advertiser-sponsored Web site where you are paid for the number of hits, you might want to make your Web pages non-portable, so that any links followed from a downloaded copy of your pages will cause hits on your site, not on the copy.

The BASE element has one other attribute besides href. Although it is rarely used, you can specify the frame in which the document referred to by a relative URL will appear. Of course, this is only useful if you are using frames to begin with. This is done with the target attribute. The following HTML code shows how this is done:

```
<BASE target="framename">
```

For a complete exploration of frames, their naming conventions, and the various options available to the HTML author when using them, refer to Chapter 10, "Frames and Framesets."

Both attributes can be used simultaneously, as in the following example:

```
<BASE href="http://www.test.org/" target="framename">
```

The LINK Element

The LINK element has been around for a while, though it has never seen much use. Its purpose is to establish relationships among different HTML documents. Usually, these are the various documents in a Web site, but there is actually no requirement that all the associated documents be at the same base URL.

Theoretically, LINK metadata can be used to set up navigation bars and to control the order of printing when hard copies are made of Web sites, but these uses have never materialized in the real world of the Web.

Used only in the HEAD element and not to be confused with hyperlink anchors (<A>), which are found only in the body of an HTML document, the LINK element first specifies the relationship a referenced document has with the current document, then gives its URL. For example:

```
<LINK rel="Next" href="chapter3.html">
```

LINK elements can be stacked to identify numerous relationships. For example, Chapter 2 of a book on the Web might reference the following documents:

```
<LINK rel="Previous" href="chapter1.html">
<LINK rel="Next" href="chapter3.html">
```

This would establish to a LINK-sensitive Web browser that Chapter 2 comes between Chapter 1 and Chapter 3. It is possible to use this information to build a tree-based layout of the Web site, or to print the entire site in correct order, rather than one document at a time.

LINK takes three main attributes in addition to href: rel, rev, and title. The first two specify the relationship as far as which end of the link is the source and which the destination; rel defines a forward relationship and rev defines a reverse one. Other than that difference, they work in the same manner. Thus, the previous example could also (and more properly) be written:

```
<LINK rev="Previous" href="chapter1.html">
<LINK rel="Next" href="chapter3.html">
```

The `title` attribute simply gives a title to the document referenced by the URL. This title need not be the same as the one given in that document's TITLE element, and can be anything the HTML author desires.

You can use one LINK element to state multiple relationships. For example, the earlier listing could just as well be rendered in this manner:

```
<LINK rev="Previous" href="chapter1.html" rel="Next" href="chapter3.html">
```

Other attributes that can be used are `charset` (which specifies what character encoding the linked resource uses), `type` (MIME type), `media` (screen, print, Braille, and the like), and `target` (which functions in the same manner as the same attribute in `base`).

The `Previous` and `Next` from the previous listings are examples of *link types*. Link types are not case sensitive; `Next` is interpreted as the same thing as `next` or `NexT`. One of the problems that has kept the LINK element from being put into use is the fact that anyone can make up any link type, and there is no functional mechanism for defining the meaning and handling of new link types. If you like, you could say `rel="hamburger"` or `rev="myuncle"` and it would be perfectly proper HTML. It would, of course, also be meaningless to any Web browser.

The only method accepted for providing definitions for homemade link types is the `profile` method. As noted earlier, profiles have not had any format developed, nor has their usage been determined.

The W3C-approved link types that can be specified are listed in Table 4.2. Each of these link types describes an individual document (except for Bookmark, which points to a named anchor within a document).

Table 4.2. Officially recognized link types.

Link Type	Meaning
Alternate	Points to an optional replacement for the current document, such as a translation
Appendix	Points to an appendix
Bookmark	Points to a named anchor within an HTML document
Chapter	Points to a chapter
Contents (or ToC)	Points to a table of contents
Copyright	Points to a copyright statement
Glossary	Points to a glossary of terms
Help	Points to a help document
Index	Points to an index
Next	Points to the document that comes after the current one

4

BASIC STRUCTURAL ELEMENTS AND THEIR USAGE

continues

Table 4.2. continued

Link Type	Meaning
Previous (or Prev)	Points to the document that comes before the current one
Section	Points to a section
Start (or Begin)	Points to the beginning document
Stylesheet	In concert with Alternate, points to one of several optional style sheets
Subsection	Points to a subsection

There are several obvious problems with these definitions. What, for instance, is the difference between a chapter and a section? Other than possibly describing the manner in which parts of books versus parts of other documents such as technical specifications are described, there is no real difference in how the HTML author applies them. Also, the act of specifying an Index document, which is not called `index.html`, and specifying a Start document, which is called `index.html`, is begging for confusion.

It seems likely that much of this chaos will be cleared up in the future. Some of the ideas will doubtless find practical application on the Web, such as in navigation bars, though it appears improbable that many Web designers will supply multiple style sheets for a single document.

The META Element

The META element element has been around for a while, though it has many facets. When used with the `name` and `content` attributes, its main function is to establish metadata variable information for use by Web search agents. Perhaps the most common use of these name/value pairs is to establish descriptions and keywords for Web pages.

A typical description might be coded like this:

```
<META name="description" content="The finest baked goods in the southeastern
U.S."
```

The keywords for this same Web site could look like this:

```
<META name="keywords" content="cakes, cookies, pies, rolls, cinnamon buns,
garlic bread">
```

Multiple META elements can be contained within one HEAD element.

The META element's other major use is to simulate HTTP (Hypertext Transfer Protocol) header information. An element beginning with META `http-equiv` affects the Web browser just as though it had received that information from the HTTP server as part of its header information. This can create a variety of potentially unpleasant situations, and therefore should not be used by anyone who does not understand the HTTP protocol. In particular, the HTML author must take care not to attempt to override valid HTTP header information without a thorough comprehension of the possible consequences.

There are, however, several safe and ready uses. The most common—and probably the safest—use of http-equiv is redirecting a visitor from an old Web site address to a new one via the refresh attribute. This is accomplished as follows:

```
<META http-equiv="Refresh" content="5;URL=http://www.baseball.com/index.html">
```

This code tells the browser that after waiting five seconds, it should replace the existing Web page with the one specified in the URL. Of course, you can vary the time delay and address to suit your particular situation. A time delay of 0 means to take the redirection action immediately.

Of course, the resource at the URL does not have to be a Web page. It could just as easily be an image or a sound.

Another use of http-equiv is to set an expiration date for an HTML document. This is useful in preventing an old cached version from being used, rather than the Web browser loading an updated version. The code for performing this is as follows:

```
<META http-equiv="expires" content="Fri 29 Aug 1997 09:00:00 GMT">
```

The content attribute should be in valid HTTP DATE header dateformat, as shown. Setting content to 0 forces a reload with every access.

The previous example uses the original HTTP 1.0 method. The same outcome can be achieved with any browser that supports HTTP 1.1 by using the following code:

```
<META http-equiv="Cache-Control" content="must-revalidate">
```

One of the newer http-equiv uses is declaring a PICS Rating. *PICS* stands for *Platform for Internet Content Selection* and is a method of including information in the HEAD element about a Web site's adult content (whether it contains sexual material, profanity, violence, and so on). This metadata is utilized by filtering software to, for instance, lock children (and office workers) out of adults-only, sex-oriented sites. There are a number of variations on the exact scheme, and you need to contact a self-rating service (see the PICS information at http://www.w3.org/PICS/ for the latest updates), which generates the appropriate code for inclusion, based upon your statements about the content of your site.

The SCRIPT and STYLE Elements

For details on the SCRIPT element, see Part III, "Client-Side Scripting." For information on the STYLE element, see Chapter 6, "Style Sheets: Formatting for the Future."

The BODY Element

The BODY element is where the displayable Web page is found. Along with the </HTML> end tag, it is one of the last things found in a Web page. The BODY element also starts by defining various key factors (all of which are now deprecated in favor of using style sheets, but still work just fine on their own).

NOTE

Technically, neither the start nor the end tags for the BODY element are required in an HTML document. However, it is good form to use them, as they help to clearly and unequivocally distinguish the body information from the rest of the document.

A typical BODY in an HTML document looks something like this:

```
<BODY background="bg.gif" text="000000" link="0000FF" vlink="FF8C00"
alink="000000">
Text, images, etc. are found here.
</BODY>
```

The code sets the background image to read in the file bg.gif, and sets the text and link colors (link is an unvisited hyperlink, vlink is a visited hyperlink, and alink is a hyperlink at the moment of activation). The colors can be specified, as in this example, as hexadecimal numbers for RGB values, or you can use one of 16 colors, for which words can be assigned. The hexadecimal notation, of course, gives you a larger number of colors to choose from, but many people feel uncomfortable with them. If you want to use words for the colors, you can use those in this listing: Aqua, Black, Blue, Fuchsia, Gray, Green, Lime, Maroon, Navy, Olive, Purple, Red, Silver, Teal, White, Yellow.

NOTE

These attributes can also be set by using Cascading Style Sheets, which is the currently preferred method. See Chapter 6.

Make sure you have a very good reason before changing the links' colors either by this method— deprecated or not—or by using style sheets. These are already set by default to certain colors Web surfers have come to expect (link, for instance, is blue—or 0000FF—by default).

NOTE

It is possible to develop an HTML page that , through the use of frames, has no BODY element. See Chapter 10 for full details on how to work with frames.

The DIV and SPAN Elements

The DIV and SPAN elements form a sort of "BODY within the BODY." Each serves the similar function of dividing a portion of the page into separate sections without affecting any of the elements inside them. The difference between the elements is that while DIV can be used to mark off block-level elements such as paragraphs, horizontal rules, and list items, SPAN can be used only inside them. Indeed, DIV is a block-level element itself, and most browsers insert a line feed before a <DIV> tag and after a </DIV> tag.

> **NOTE**
>
> It is clear that SPAN is technically not a structural element like DIV, but an inline element. However, its close association with DIV means that it is best handled in the same section.

These elements are intended to be used with the class and id attributes to mark areas of text and other elements for handling by style sheets (see Chapter 6).

While SPAN contains only the usual core attributes, DIV also has the align attribute which, in this case, can be left, right, or center. The following code shows how to center text using DIV.

```
<DIV align="center">
This text is centered.
</DIV>
```

Summary

The basic structural elements in HTML are DOCTYPE, HTML, HEAD, and BODY. The latter three have end tags and act as containers for other elements. The DOCTYPE element is rarely used and not recommended if you are using anything other than the actual HTML standard; vendor-specific elements can cause problems if you use the DOCTYPE element. The HTML element, however, is absolutely required; it is what defines your work as an HTML document. The HEAD element is a container for HTML header information. The only thing required within a HEAD element is the TITLE element, which establishes a title for the entire document. HEAD elements can also contain metadata, or data other than the document itself. BASE, which defines the base URL upon which relative URLs referenced in the HTML document are calculated, is an example of metadata. Other examples of metadata are implemented within the META element, which can contain both data and instructions. The former use includes such information as the document author and copyright information, as well as keywords and a document description. The latter use includes such things as loading a new document to replace the original and controlling how often a cached document is updated. The LINK element, despite not being of much current use, can establish relationships among Web pages that can be used in navigation bars and printing. The BODY element, in which the displayable Web page is held, is HTML's main container. BODY elements have certain properties, such as background color, which can duplicate the efforts of style sheets. Finally, the DIV element can be used to further divide the BODY into smaller segments.

4

BASIC STRUCTURAL ELEMENTS AND THEIR USAGE

Traditional Text and Formatting

*by David and
Rhonda Crowder*

Because the bulk of material on the World Wide Web is text, an understanding of the ways in which text is organized, structured, placed, and altered is critical to an HTML author. Although the current trend is to take Web design more in the direction of traditional programming, using predefined variables in style sheets instead of detailed in-place markup (see Chapter 6, "Style Sheets: Formatting for the Future"), the basic tools for accomplishing the task are the same, no matter the approach you take. Whether in an attached style sheet or in straight HTML, a paragraph is still a paragraph and you still use a <P> tag to denote it.

Deprecated and Obsolete Elements

As HTML evolves, the function of some elements is replaced or superseded by newer and, presumably, better approaches. Some are still fully functional and useful, but can be done more economically or efficiently. Some just don't seem to fit the World Wide Web Consortium's vision for the future of HTML. Others are just plain lousy ideas to begin with and never work out. For example, both the <IMG> and <APPLET> tags still work, but both perform similar tasks—embedding a particular object in the HTML page. With the prospect of confusing the language as more kinds of objects came under development and implementation, it was decided that a single <OBJECT> element would be designed that would encompass all possible embeddable objects, both present and future, instead of developing separate tags for each new type of object. Thus, both <IMG> and <APPLET> are now deprecated in favor of the all-inclusive <OBJECT> tag.

Another example of this kind is shown by the <DIR> and <MENU> elements, which were both interpreted by most browsers exactly as if they were an unordered list. Thus, though the <UL> element is not new, both <DIR> and <MENU> are now deprecated in favor of <UL>.

What exactly do deprecated and obsolete mean, and what is the difference between them? When an element is *deprecated*, that means that the World Wide Web Consortium recommends that you no longer use it, but use, instead, the newer solution in place of the deprecated element. However, deprecated elements are still a part of the official HTML specification, and should still be supported by Web browsers and other client agents. Elements that are currently deprecated, however, may well end up on the list of obsolete elements in future specifications.

Obsolete elements, on the other hand, are no longer defined in the official HTML specification, and W3C does not require that client agents support them. This does not necessarily mean that you cannot still use them; neither Netscape nor Microsoft follows every recommendation of the W3C slavishly, but may freely choose to support whatever elements they want to, whether they are in the official specification or not. However, deciding to use an element for which there is no longer any official definition or support is a risky choice to make.

Text Layout

There are two basic types of text-affecting elements in HTML. The first kind performs text layout tasks, such as setting up paragraphs and line breaks or ordering text into lists. The second kind, which is dealt with in the section titled "Text Styles," affects mainly the text's appearance.

TIP

Whitespace, with rare exception, is generally ignored by client agents and, although it can be inserted into HTML source code to improve readability, does not affect the resultant display of the Web page.

The P Element

The `<P>` tag is used to denote the beginning of a new paragraph. Although the end tag `</P>` exists, its use is optional. However, most HTML authors feel it is good form to include all existing end tags, whether they are required or not. If the end tag is not used, the beginning of the next block level element is interpreted as the end of the paragraph. This is illustrated in the following code and in Figure 5.1.

```
<P>
This is an example of a paragraph without an end tag.
<P>
The next P element (or any other block level element) causes the preceding
paragraph to be terminated just as though it had an end tag like this
paragraph does.
</P>
```

FIGURE 5.1.

P *elements and end tags.*

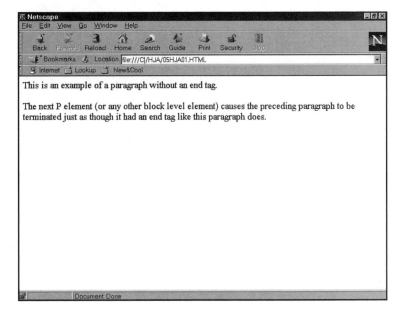

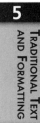

5

TRADITIONAL TEXT
AND FORMATTING

NOTE

Although the terms are commonly used interchangeably, there is, technically, a difference between a tag and an element. For example, in the code `<H2>This is a second level heading</H2>`, the `<H2>` and `</H2>` parts are the tags, but the element itself includes both the tags and the matter between them.

If the paragraph is contained within another block level element, the end tag of that element is interpreted as ending the paragraph as well. This is illustrated in the following code and in Figure 5.2.

```
<DIV>
<P>
This paragraph is terminated just as though it had an end tag since it is
contained within a block level element which does have an end tag.
</DIV>
This paragraph needs no tag to be recognized as a separate element since
the preceding paragraph has already been terminated. It will not be
terminated until some other block level element is encountered.
```

CAUTION

The previous example uses an HTML trick to illustrate the point about block level elements. The final paragraph in the example code is not proper HTML because it lacks the required start tag `<P>`. This, by the way, is why it rides directly under the preceding paragraph in Figure 5.2—because there is no instruction to properly space it.

The P elements must have content or they are treated as though they do not exist. Using `<P><P><P><P><P>This is a paragraph</P>` is effectively the same code as `<P>This is a paragraph</P>`. You could, of course, simply put a blank space after each opening tag to create content, but if you need to add vertical whitespace between paragraphs, it is better to use the `<BR>` tag, which is designed for that task (see the next section).

Paragraphs can be aligned flush left, flush right, justified, or centered, depending on the settings in the `align` attribute of the P element. The following code and Figure 5.3 illustrate this.

```
<P align=left>
This paragraph is left-aligned.
</P>
<P align=center>
This paragraph is centered.
</P>
<P align=right>
This paragraph is right-aligned.
</P>
<P align=justify>
```

This paragraph is justified. Of course, for any paragraph to actually
show justification, it has to be pretty long, so this one has some extra
verbiage just to make it longer. Really, you wouldn't believe how long a
paragraph has to be to properly show justification. If you only have a few
lines, you shouldn't even bother with justifying it, since it just won't
show up.
</P>

FIGURE 5.2.

*The P elements within
block level elements.*

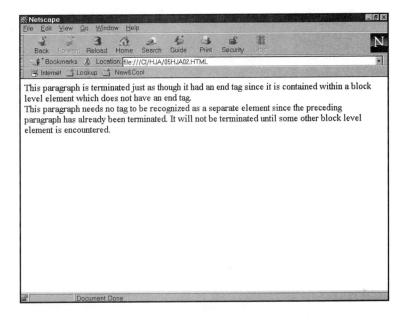

FIGURE 5.3.

Aligning P elements.

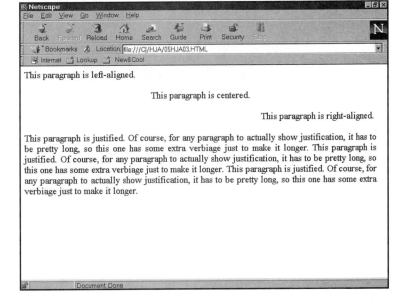

It should be noted that the ALIGN attribute has been deprecated in favor of CSS (which will not work in older browsers), but is still functional.

The BR Element

The BR element forces a line break. A line break is the same as a CR/LF (carriage return/line feed) combination (in DOS and Windows; UNIX uses <LF> alone while Mac uses <CR> alone). As mentioned in "The P Element," you can use it to add vertical whitespace between paragraphs (or other elements). Stacking several BR elements in a row (

) causes several blank lines to be generated. There is no end tag.

Other than its simple use, the BR element has a special function. When placed after a floating image (or images), the clear attribute controls how text is handled when wrapping around those images (for more information on images, see Chapter 11, "Using Images with HTML"). The clear attribute has four possible values: none, left, right, and all. Examples of this usage are shown in the following code samples and in Figures 5.4, 5.5, and 5.6.

This code sample shows how the results in Figure 5.4 were achieved:

```
<IMG align="left" src="133162.gif">
<BR>
This text will show up next to the image.
```

FIGURE 5.4.

Plain <BR> with image.

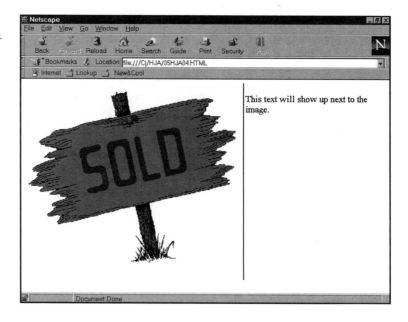

Using <BR> without specifying the clear attribute is the same thing as using <BR clear="none">.

This code sample shows how the results in Figure 5.5 were achieved:

```
<IMG align="left" src="133162.gif">
<BR clear="left">
This text will show up below the image.
```

FIGURE 5.5.

`<BR clear="left">`
with image.

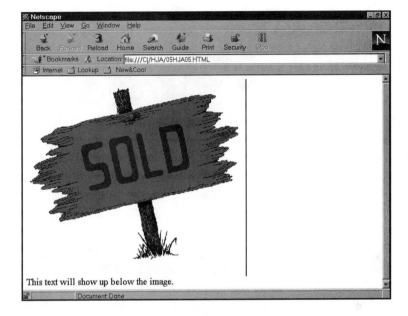

This time, the text was pushed to the bottom of the image. Note that both the image and the line break are left-aligned. This is necessary for this effect to occur. If the image had been right-aligned, the line break would have to be right-aligned, as well; otherwise, the clear attribute does not affect the flow of the text. Using clear="all" means that the text starts at the bottom of any image, either left-aligned or right-aligned.

There is one further consideration when placing the line break: it does not have to come between the image and the text. If it is placed in the middle of the text that follows the image instead of at the beginning, then the text before the line break shows up next to the image, and the text after it follows whatever behavior is appropriate to the value of the clear attribute used. This is illustrated in the following code and in Figure 5.6.

```
<IMG align="left" src="133162.gif">
This text will show up beside the image
<BR clear="left">
and this text will show up below the image.
```

FIGURE 5.6.

Line break within the text with image.

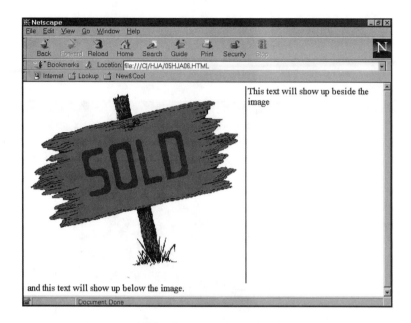

CAUTION

`<BR clear="none">` does not work properly in Netscape Navigator; it acts the same as `<BR clear="all">`. It works fine in Internet Explorer. This is not a major problem, however, because this value is rarely used. If you want to achieve the same effect, use `<BR>`; it defaults to a value of `clear="none"`, and this approach works fine in both browsers.

The CENTER Element

The CENTER element causes all text between its start and end tags to be centered between the margins (whether those be page margins, table margins, or whatever). The proper usage is this:

```
<CENTER>Text goes here.</CENTER>
```

This element is now deprecated. W3C recommends using either style sheets or the following approach instead:

```
<DIV align="center">
Text goes here.
</DIV>
```

Because the CENTER element is an easier and more intuitive solution for centering text, it seems likely that, deprecated or not, HTML authors will continue to use it.

The HN Element

In the early versions of HTML heading elements, default font styles and indentation were specified for each different level of heading. In practice, however, it developed into simply changing the size of the text, so that each successively lower heading led to successively smaller text.

The highest level of heading is represented by the <H1> tag, the lowest by the <H6> tag (see Figure 5.7). Heading elements are required to have end tags as well as start tags.

FIGURE 5.7.

Various heading levels.

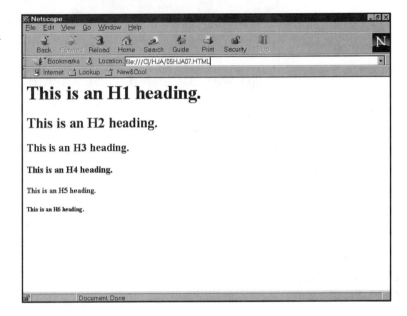

FIGURE 5.7.

Various heading levels.

This is the proper way to code a heading element:

```
<H1>This is the highest heading level.</H1>
```

If you forget to put in an end tag for a heading element, subsequent text in your HTML document might be different from what you intended. Any text following an <H1> tag, for instance, is in large text until an </H1> tag is found, or, because any heading start tag begins a new heading element, until another heading size is specified.

This can be illustrated by the following code. The effect is shown in Figure 5.8:

```
<H1>This is an H1 heading without an end tag.
<P>
This was supposed to be normal body text.
</P>
<H6>This is an H6 heading without an end tag.
<P>
This was also supposed to be normal body text.
```

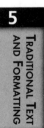

5

TRADITIONAL TEXT
AND FORMATTING

```
</P>
<H1>This is an H1 heading with a proper end tag.</H1>
<P>
This is normal body text.
</P>
```

FIGURE 5.8.

Heading levels and end tags.

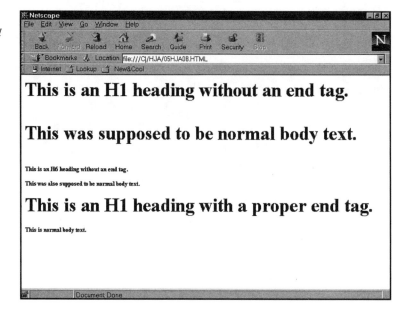

The HR Element

Horizontal rules are used to visually divide different segments of Web pages from one another. Although many HTML authors prefer to use a variety of clever images for horizontal rules, HTML has a built-in method for creating these dividing lines—the HR element.

A simple horizontal rule is coded as follows:

```
<HR>
```

The HR element has no end tag. By default, it is a shaded line, two pixels thick, which stretches from one side of the page to the other. However, it has various attributes that can be used to change its width, thickness, and appearance.

A horizontal rule can be aligned as follows:

```
<HR align="left">
```

Although it can be aligned to the left, center, or right, these settings only have meaning if the horizontal rule to which they are applied is less than the full width of the browser window. The width attribute can be set to either an absolute width in pixels or a percentage of the page width.

An example of the percentage method is as follows:

```
<HR width="33%">
```

The absolute pixel method looks like this:

```
<HR width="300">
```

The thickness of the horizontal rule can also be set by using the `size` attribute:

```
<HR size="10">
```

Note that the `size` (thickness) attribute takes only an absolute pixel setting as its value; there is no possibility of setting a percentage of page height, because there is no way of knowing the size of that dimension.

The horizontal rule can also be rendered as a solid line rather than its shadowed default. This option uses the `noshade` attribute:

```
<HR noshade>
```

Of course, all these attributes can be used together, as in the following code:

```
<HR align="center" width="300" size="5" noshade>
```

Examples of how various options among these values appear are shown in Figure 5.9.

FIGURE 5.9.

Horizontal rule variations.

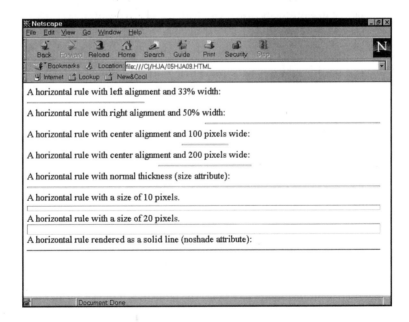

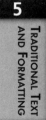

FIGURE 5.11.

Different bullets.

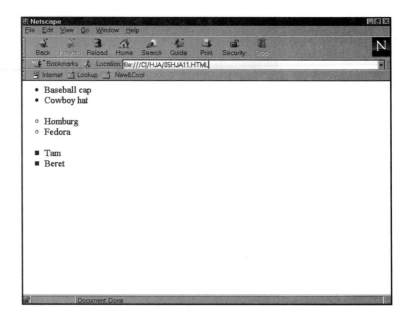

A typical ordered list may be presented with the following code:

```
<OL>
<LI>Shut off electrical power at the circuit breaker.
<LI>Use circuit tester to double check that power is off.
<LI>Remove screws holding cover plate in place.
<LI>Remove cover plate.
<LI>Remove screws holding outlet in place.
<LI>Remove outlet from wall.
<LI>Loosen screws which hold wires in place, noting position of colored wires.
<LI>Place wires in same position on new outlet, then tighten screws.
<LI>Replace outlet in wall, then tighten screws holding it in place.
<LI>Replace cover plate, then tighten screw holding it in place.
</OL>
```

This example would display as shown in Figure 5.12.

Like the UL element, OL elements have the type and compact attributes. In addition, there is the start attribute. The type attribute works a bit differently with an ordered list; instead of the type of bullet, it selects the kind of numbering system utilized to order the list. The following code and Figure 5.13 illustrate the use of the type attribute in an ordered list:

```
<OL type="a">
<LI>Pull on left pants leg.
<LI>Put on right pants leg.
</OL>
<OL type="A">
<LI>Put on left sock.
<LI>Put on right sock.
</OL>
<OL type="i">
```

```
<LI>Put on left shoe.
<LI>Put on right shoe.
</OL>
<OL type="I">
<LI>Put on shirt.
<LI>Put on necktie.
</OL>
<OL type="1">
<LI>Put on vest.
<LI>Put on coat.
</OL>
```

FIGURE 5.12.

An ordered list.

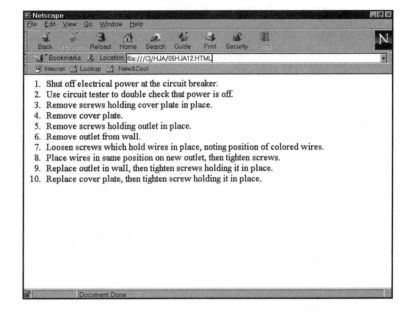

The starting value can also be specified through the start attribute. This is illustrated in the following code and in Figure 5.14:

```
<OL type="a" start="10">
<LI>Pull on left pants leg.
<LI>Put on right pants leg.
</OL>
<OL type="A" start="10">
<LI>Put on left sock.
<LI>Put on right sock.
</OL>
<OL type="i" start="10">
<LI>Put on left shoe.
<LI>Put on right shoe.
</OL>
<OL type="I" start="10">
<LI>Put on shirt.
<LI>Put on necktie.
</OL>
```

```
<OL type="1" start="10">
<LI>Put on vest.
<LI>Put on coat.
</OL>
```

FIGURE 5.13.

Ordered list with specified types.

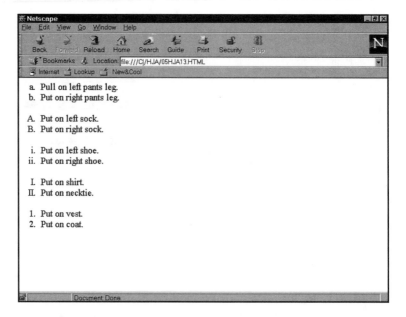

FIGURE 5.14.

Ordered list with start values.

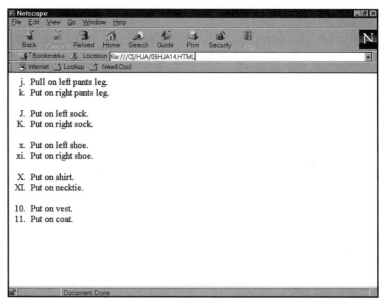

> **TIP**
>
> Interestingly, the type attribute is also present in the LI element and with it, the type attribute works the same way as either an ordered or unordered list. However, you must use the type associated with the kind of list the LI element is contained within. Thus, you cannot use type="I" with an unordered list, nor can you use type="disc" with an ordered list.
>
> You can also use the value attribute with any list item in an ordered list to change the numbering sequence. Thus, if the normal numbering sequence causes the next number to equal 8, then setting <LI value="12"> causes the next number to be 12 instead of 9.

Definition Lists

Definition lists are specified with the <DL> tag. As mentioned earlier, definition lists consist of pairs of values, the first being the term to be defined, and the second being the definition of the term. In place of list items, however, are definition terms and definitions.

A typical definition list may be presented with the following code:

```
<DL>
<DT><B>Satellite Dish</B>
<DD><I>A concave antenna-like device which functions to receive and
concentrate television signals which have been relayed through Earth
orbiting communications satellites.</I>
<DT><B>Video Cassette Recorder (VCR)</B>
<DD><I>A video tape recorder (VTR) which, instead of using a reel-to-reel
arrangement for spooling variable amounts of videotape, utilizes a plastic
cassette which holds a fixed amount of videotape.</I>
</DL>
```

Both the <DT> and <DD> tags work much like the <LI> tag in the other types of lists, except that dd elements are indented slightly. Like the <LI> tag, they, too, have optional end tags (</DT> </DD>) that are not generally used. It is a good idea to use either text styles (as you did in the previous example) or style sheets to create distinct differences between the definition terms and the definitions themselves, rather than to simply rely on indentation. This example displays as shown in Figure 5.15.

Nested Lists

Any kind of list—ordered, unordered, or definition—can be nested within another list. For instance, you might want to have items inserted in the midst of an ordered list, and the order of those inserted items might not itself be important. By way of example, take a look at the following code and Figure 5.16:

```
<OL>
<LI>Shut off electrical power at the circuit breaker.
<LI>Make sure you have the following tools available:
<UL>
<LI>Circuit tester
```

```
<LI>Screwdriver
<LI>Wire cutters
<LI>Wire stripper
</UL>
<LI>Use circuit tester to double check that power is off.
etc....
</OL>
```

FIGURE 5.15.

A definition list.

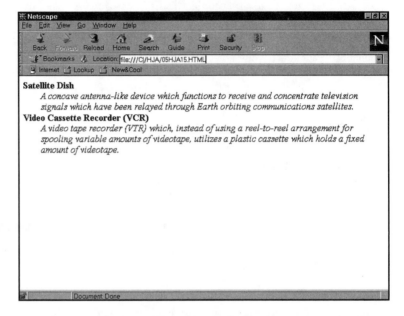

FIGURE 5.16.

Nested lists.

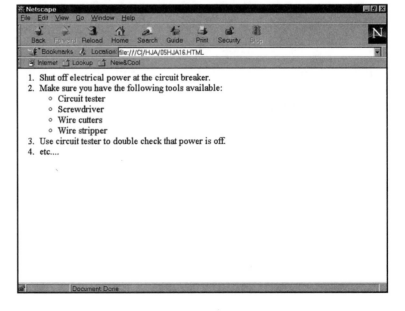

Text Styles

Text styles are inline elements that change the appearance of text. The two most commonly used are the I element, which makes text italic, and the B element, which makes it bold. Others perform such tasks as creating a typewriter-style monospaced font, increasing or decreasing text size, or raising and lowering characters for superscripting and subscripting.

The B and STRONG Elements

In most browsers or other user agents, using the <B> and <STRONG> tags has the effect of rendering text in bold print. The tags can be inserted anywhere in text. Both have required end tags (</B> and </STRONG>, respectively). Because the STRONG element essentially duplicates the b element, it is not generally used anymore, though it is not officially deprecated. The use of these two tags and the resultant browser display is illustrated in the following code and in Figure 5.17:

```
<P>
The use of either the b or strong element results in bold text:
<B>bold text</B> or <STRONG>bold text</STRONG>.
</P>
```

FIGURE 5.17.

B *and* STRONG *elements.*

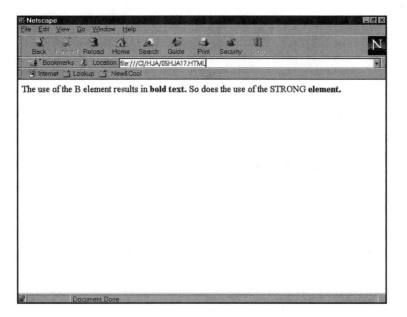

The use of the B element results in **bold text**. So does the use of the STRONG **element.**

The I and EM Elements

In most browsers or other user agents, using the <I> and <EM> (emphasis) tags has the effect of rendering text in italicized print. The tags can be inserted anywhere in text. Both have required end tags (</I> and </EM>, respectively). Because the EM element essentially duplicates the I element, it is not generally used anymore, though it is not officially deprecated.

Three other elements, ADDRESS, CITE, and VAR, also place text in italics. The ADDRESS element is usually used at the bottom of a home page for the purpose of stating contact addresses and copyright notices. Unlike the other three italicizing elements, it is not normally used within text to emphasize a word or phrase, but is applied to entire paragraphs at a time. The CITE element italicizes the title of a book or other citation. The VAR element indicates a program variable.

Although there is no official statement to this effect, it is commonly believed that CITE, ADDRESS, and other elements that seem to be unnecessarily specialized and duplicate other, more straightforward approaches, are part of a long-term plan to develop an entire series of tags geared toward text indexing.

The use of these tags and the resultant browser display are illustrated in the following code and in Figure 5.18:

```
<P>
```

The use of either the I or EM element results in italicized text. As a matter of fact, it is difficult to distinguish the effect of either the CITE or VAR elements from them.

```
</P>
<P>
<ADDRESS>The ADDRESS element does pretty much the same thing.</ADDRESS>
<P>
```

TT and Similar Elements

Several different elements have the same effect—setting the affected text into a monospaced font. Each has some differing trait, however. The TT (teletype) element, for instance, simply causes the text to be monospaced in a typewriter-style face. The PRE element, on the other hand, also causes carriage return/line feed (CR/LF) combinations, which are normally treated as whitespace to be recognized.

The elements CODE, SAMP, and KBD do the same thing as the TT element. The only difference is in the intent. CODE is for displaying snippets of program code; SAMP is for sample program output; KBD is for text to be entered by the user.

Because there is no functional difference between these tags, it seems probable that this is another example of different tags for the purpose of indexing.

Three other elements that had this same effect—PLAINTEXT, LISTING, and XMP—are now obsolete and are no longer part of HTML specification.

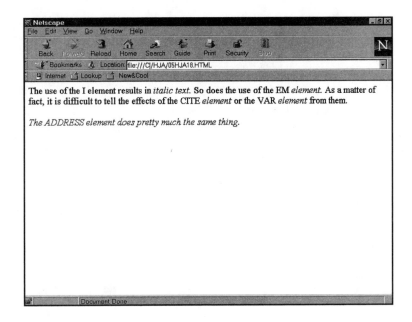

FIGURE 5.18.

I, EM, CITE, *and*
ADDRESS *elements.*

The use of these tags and the resultant browser display is illustrated in the following code and in Figure 5.19:

```
<P>
The use of the TT element results in <TT>monospaced, typewriter style
text.</TT>
So does the use of the CODE <CODE>element.</CODE>
As a matter of fact, it is difficult to tell the effects of the SAMP
<SAMP>element</SAMP> or the CITE <CITE>element</CITE> from them.
</P>
<P>
<PRE>The PRE element has one major difference.
The carriage return/line feed in this paragraph will show up in the display,
but the ones in the paragraph above will not.</PRE>
</P>
```

The STRIKE and U Elements

The STRIKE element (also called the S element) causes text to be struck through. The U element underlines the affected text. Both of these elements are now deprecated. In the case of the U element, it is easy to see why: Users are accustomed to seeing hyperlinks represented as underlined text. The only drawback to the STRIKE element, however, is that its output looks just like that proposed for the new DEL element. Because there are several elements that produce indistinguishable output, it is difficult to understand why this would be considered a problem in this case.

The use of these tags and the resultant browser display are illustrated in the following code and in Figure 5.20.

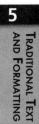

Figure 5.19.

The TT and similar elements.

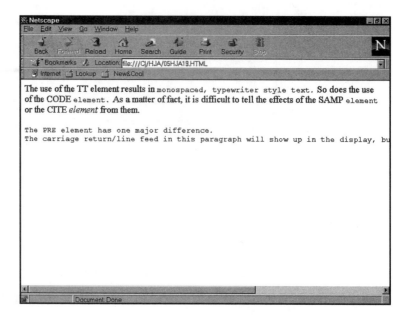

```
<P>
The use of the STRIKE element results in <STRIKE>text which has a line drawn
through it.</STRIKE> The S element results in <S>the exact same thing.</S>
The U element results in <U>underlined text</U> which is difficult to
distinguish from a hyperlink.
<P>
```

Figure 5.20.

The STRIKE and U elements.

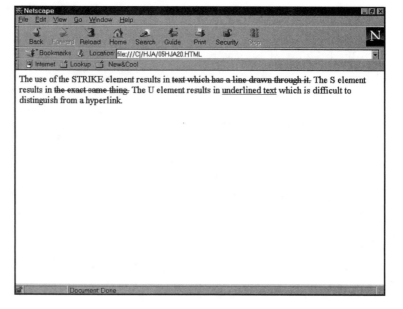

The BIG, SMALL, SUP, and SUB Elements

These four elements actually change the size or position of the affected text. The BIG element increases the size of the affected text, and the SMALL element decreases it. Stacking multiples of these elements in a row has an incremental effect.

The SUP and SUB elements are used, respectively, to create superscripts and subscripts. Depending on the client agent, the display may simply raise or lower the affected text, or it may also present it in a smaller font size.

The use of these tags and the resultant browser display are illustrated in the following code and in Figure 5.21:

```
<P>
The use of the BIG element results in <BIG>text which is larger than the
rest of the line.</BIG> Stacking multiple BIGs <BIG><BIG>causes incremental
increases in text size.</BIG></BIG> The SMALL element results in <SMALL>the
reverse effect.</SMALL> Stacking multiple SMALLs <SMALL><SMALL>causes
incremental decreases in text size.</SMALL></SMALL>
</P>
<P>
The SUB element comes in handy with chemical formulae like HCNO<SUB>3 </SUB>,
while the SUP element is a common need in mathematical equations such as
E=mc<SUP>2</SUP>.
</P>
```

FIGURE 5.21.

The SMALL, BIG, SUB, *and* SUP *elements.*

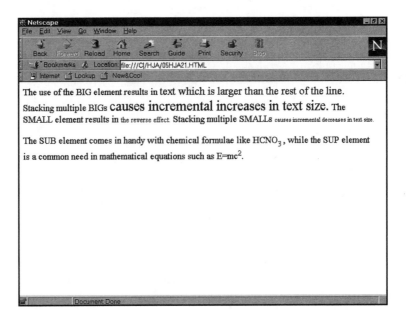

The Q and BLOCKQUOTE Elements

The Q and BLOCKQUOTE elements serve very similar functions; they are both used to denote quoted material. Although BLOCKQUOTE has been around for a while, Q is new with HTML 4.0. The difference between the two is that Q is for short sections of inline quotation, whereas BLOCKQUOTE is for larger selections, and is, as the name implies, a block level element that cannot be used inline. The Q element does not affect the appearance of the quoted text, but the BLOCKQUOTE element causes the text to be indented from both left and right margins.

> **NOTE**
>
> Many HTML authors have traditionally used BLOCKQUOTE because it can be used for a quick-and-dirty indentation even when its use has nothing to do with quoting a source. The World Wide Web Consortium, in a baffling attempt to control how Web developers use elements, has officially stated that this usage of the BLOCKQUOTE element is deprecated. W3C, of course, has no power to enforce this dictum; if you want to use BLOCKQUOTE for purposes of indentation, you can still do so.

Both Q and BLOCKQUOTE use the cite attribute to provide a URL that points to the online source (if any) for the quotation. For example, you could have something like the following:

```
<BLOCKQUOTE cite="http:\\www.microsoft.com\">
Quoted material goes here.
</BLOCKQUOTE>
```

As things presently stand, this URL information is only available if the user looks at the page source and reads through the code to find the cited URL. Perhaps W3C plans to make such information available as a hyperlink in the future, though it is hard to see how, because the hyperlink would either have to be invisible, or the quoted material would have to be colored and underlined.

The INS and DEL Elements

The INS and DEL elements are both new to HTML 4.0. They are intended to deal with situations in which several drafts of a document must be sorted through and the history of the changes is significant. These might be used, for instance, with government legislation, where lawyers need to see what earlier versions said and when those versions were in effect.

Although neither Netscape Navigator nor Internet Explorer support these elements, W3C hopes that the eventual appearance of the text affected by these elements may be something like a strikethrough for the deleted sections and a different color font for the inserted sections.

As with the Q and BLOCKQUOTE elements, INS and DEL use the cite attribute to specify a URL where the earlier version of the document (or perhaps some other document explaining the changes) may be found, if it is available online. Additionally, they use the datetime attribute to specify the date and time when the document has been amended (`datetime` must be formatted as specified by the ISO8601 standard). This is illustrated in the following code:

```
<P>
This is an unchanged part of the text.
<DEL cite="http:\\www.legislation.gov\oldtext.html"
datetime="1997-09-11T09:00:00-05:00">This is the old text, which has been
superseded.</DEL> <INS cite="http:\\www.legislation.gov\newtext.html"
datetime="1997-09-14T10:00:00-05:00">This is the new text, which has been
added.</INS>
</P>
```

The FONT and BASEFONT Elements

The FONT and BASEFONT elements perform the same task and use the same methods for doing so. The difference between them is the scope of their effect. Both set the size, color, and font face for the text in an HTML document, but the BASEFONT element is global for all body text in the document, whereas the FONT element is strictly local and affects only the text between its start and end tags. The BASEFONT element, if used, must be the first thing on the HTML page after the BODY element. Although they are both deprecated by the W3C, they are still functional. The FONT element has both start and end tags; BASEFONT has no end tag.

The size attribute works a little differently for the two elements. With BASEFONT, the value of size is an absolute value that ranges from 1 to 7, with 1 being the smallest and 7 being the largest. The default value for size, if no BASEFONT element is used, is 3. For the FONT element, size is a relative value, which is expressed as greater or less than the base font size. For instance, if the base font size were 4, then size=+2 would mean the value for size was 6.

The color attribute works the same for both elements. It uses a hexadecimal number to describe the RGB value of the desired color. The face attribute also works the same for both of them. It is simply the name of the desired font face.

The use of these tags and the resultant browser display are illustrated in the following code and in Figure 5.22:

```
<BASEFONT size=4 color="#000000" face="ARIAL">
<P>
This is the normal body text using the base font size.
<P>
<P>
<FONT size=+3>This is a locally increased font.</FONT> The size reverts to
the base font size outside the scope of the FONT element.
</P>
```

The ACRONYM and DFN Elements

Neither ACRONYM (which is new to HTML with the 4.0 specification) nor DFN actually affect the output of text in any way. The ACRONYM element is used, of course, to delineate acronyms such as WWW, SGML, and so forth. HTML authors are supposed to use the title attribute to expand the acronym. For example, `<ACRONYM title="World Wide Web">WWW</ACRONYM>`. The rationale behind this is that it aids in the functioning of speech synthesizers and spell checkers.

The DFN element, on the other hand, is a bit obscure, to put it mildly. It is not new, and has never seen much popular usage. It is used, according to the official specification, to denote "the defining instance of the enclosed term." Despite the similarity in terminology, this "instance definition" has nothing to do with definition lists.

FIGURE 5.22.

The BASEFONT *and* FONT *elements.*

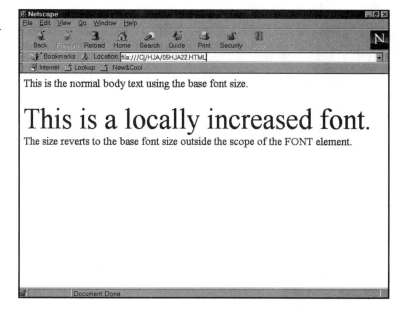

Summary

Most of the World Wide Web is composed of text. A thorough understanding of how text is structured and styled in traditional HTML is critical, even if you are planning to use cascading style sheets to control text, because the tags and elements are the same for both approaches. In HTML 4.0, many of the commonly used elements and attributes are deprecated (meaning their use is discouraged), and some others are declared obsolete (meaning that they may not be supported at all). However, most of these elements and attributes are still fully functional.

Conversely, some of the newer elements exist only on paper, and cannot be used in the real world yet. The P (paragraph) element is the most common text structuring tool available, and can be aligned left, center, right, or with the text justified to both left and right margins. The BR (line break) element is also broadly used, serving the function of a carriage return/line feed; it also has a specialized function through the use of the clear attribute when it comes to wrapping text around an image. The CENTER element, although officially deprecated, is still the easiest way to center text. HN (heading) elements, with sizes ranging from H1 through H6, offer another way to structure a Web page by allowing the HTML author to establish marked breaks in the flow of text. The HR (horizontal rule) elements provide a similar function in a nontextual manner; their size, color, and shading characteristics can be varied at the HTML author's whim.

Lists are another method of text organization. There are three kinds: ordered, unordered, and definition. Ordered lists use numbers, letters, and Roman numerals to lay out a specific chain of events. Unordered lists use bullets of various shapes to denote list items when the sequence of them is unimportant. Definition lists are used to set up a glossary of terms. Any of these types may be nested within one another. There are also a variety of elements whose purpose is to alter affected text by changing it to bold or italic print; a monospaced, typewriter-like font; and altering text size and position. Font size, color, and face can also be directly and specifically controlled on both global and local levels by use of the BASEFONT and FONT elements.

HTML provides the syntax for defining the structure of a Web page, such as including a header, inserting a line break between two paragraphs, or listing items. HTML does not, however, provide for Web page presentation.

In January, 1997, the W3C issued a recommendation for Cascading Style Sheets in order to control Web page presentation. This chapter provides an overview of this standard and several examples of its use.

The CSS1 Standard

Style sheets are embedded directly into a page, or linked in from an external file, and provide Web page developers and authors the ability to redefine the appearance of all elements of a certain type, a group of possibly different elements, or one specific element. As an example, the following code is a simple style sheet, embedded into the head section of the Web page. It sets the style for H1 headers to a red font, to have a font family of Arial, and to have a margin, relative to containing element, of one inch on all sides:

```
<STYLE type="text/css">
    H1 { color: red; font-family: Arial; margin: 1.0in }
</STYLE>
```

With this style sheet setting, all H1 elements within the document are set to use the new style.

Both Netscape Navigator and Microsoft Internet Explorer have adopted the CSS1 standard, though neither company implements the full standard as defined within the Level 1 specification. To be a compliant application, the browser only needs to implement what is defined to be the core specification. For the most part, IE has incorporated more of CSS1 into IE 4.0 then Netscape did with Navigator 4.0, and most of the examples in this chapter are demonstrated in IE 4.0, and most only work with IE 4.0.

There are also many implementation details that are not defined within the standard, implementations that are up to the browser to determine how to handle. Because of both of these issues, you can get different results for the same page when viewed with IE compared to viewing with Navigator.

Including Style Sheets

There are four different techniques you can use to include style sheet definitions in a Web page. They are:

- Including a style sheet in the document's head section
- Linking in a style sheet stored externally
- Importing in a style sheet stored externally
- Including an inline style sheet definition directly in an HTML element

Each of these techniques and how style sheet rules are defined and used are covered in this section.

To demonstrate the CSS1 features in this chapter, an HTML document that uses several elements is used for all the examples. Listing 6.1 contains the HTML for the Web page.

Listing 6.1. Stock HTML Web page used for all examples in this chapter.

```
<HTML>
<HEAD><TITLE>CSS1 Test Content</TITLE>
</HEAD>
<BODY>
<H1>This is the CSS1 Test Content</H1>
<P>
In order to demonstrate <strong>CSS1 Style Sheets</strong> I created this
test content document, which contains samples of most types of web page
content.
</P>
<P>
CSS1 can impact on a document generally, as well as individual elements
such as:
</p>
<UL>
<LI> Lists
<LI> Headers
<LI> Images
<LI> Paragraphs
<LI> Inline elements
<LI> Tables
<LI> Forms and Form elements
</UL>
<P>
<img src="button.jpg"> CSS1 can also alter the presentation of certain
psuedo-elements such as <a href="#next">hypertext links</a> or the first
line or character within a line.
There actually isn't <a name="next">anything</a> that can't in some way
be controlled by CSS1. You can do some fun things with images, and add
effects to most elements with borders.
</p>
</BODY>
</HTML>
```

As you can see from the listing, the Web page contains a couple of paragraphs, a header, an image, a hypertext link and a named link, and an unordered list. Figure 6.1 shows this page without any formatting.

COMPANION **Web site** There is more than one technique you can use to include style sheets within your Web page. Probably the most common approach is to embed style sheets directly into the HEAD of the Web page and provide settings for all of the elements within the Web page. The sample file include1.htm contains an example of a simple style sheet, shown in the following code, that uses the embedded style sheet format:

Now, regardless of what other style settings occur earlier in the document, these paragraphs have a lime-colored font and a yellow italic font, respectively. The style sheet attributes color, font-style, and background-color are discussed in more detail later in the chapter.

The complete HTML and CSS1 for creating the page is shown in Listing 6.2.

Listing 6.2. Using CSS1 to alter the font colors and style for several paragraph elements.

```
<HTML>
<HEAD><TITLE>CSS1 Test Content</TITLE>
<LINK REL=STYLESHEET TYPE="text/css"
    HREF="style1.css" TITLE="stylesheet1">
</HEAD>
<BODY>
<H1>This is the CSS1 Test Content</H1>
<P style="color: lime">
In order to demonstrate <strong>CSS1 Style Sheets</strong> I created this
test content document, which contains samples of most types of web page
content.
</P>
<P style="color: yellow; font-style: italic">
CSS1 can impact on a document generally, as well as individual elements
such as:
</p>
<UL>
<LI> Lists
<LI> Headers
<LI> Images
<LI> Paragraphs
<LI> Inline elements
<LI> Tables
<LI> Forms and Form elements
</UL>
<P>
<img src="button.jpg"> CSS1 can also alter the presentation of certain
psuedo-elements such as <a href="#next">hypertext links</a>
or the first line or character within a line.
There actually isn't <a name="next">anything</a> that can't in some way
be controlled by CSS1. You can do some fun things with images, and add
effects to most elements with borders.
</p>
</BODY>
</HTML>
```

Applying Styles to Specific Groups of Elements

The previous examples in this chapter demonstrated altering the style settings based on the type of element, such as for the entire body of the Web page. You can also provide style settings for groups of items or even one specific item.

A *selector*, which is an element tag, class name, or ID, identifies the style sheet settings and is used to determine the elements that are altered within the Web page.

Using the Class Name Style Sheet Selector

A class name is a way to apply style sheet settings to a group of named elements, using the following style syntax:

```
<STYLE type="text/css">
<!--
    P.someclass { color: red; margin-left: 1.5in }
    .otherclass { color: blue; font-size: 18pt }
-->
</STYLE>
...
<P class=someclass>
...
</P>
<H1 class=otherclass>…</H1>
<P class=otherclass>
```

In this code, two classes are created, one specifically for paragraphs and named `someclass`, the other for any element and named `otherclass`. The syntax is an optional tag name, followed by a period, followed by the class name. If the tag name is not given, the class can be applied to several elements.

To demonstrate the class selector, three classes have been added to this chapter's sample Web page: one specifically for paragraphs and two generic classes. The paragraph class was applied to one of the paragraphs and to one of the list items, and the unordered list's first generic class and last paragraph, and the header's second generic class and a couple of the list items, as shown in Listing 6.3.

Listing 6.3. Using classes to apply style sheet settings to groups of elements.

```
<HTML>
<HEAD><TITLE>CSS1 Test Content</TITLE>
<STYLE type="text/css">
<!--
    P.first { font-variant: small-caps }
    .second { color: blue; background-color: yellow }
    .third { color: yellow; background-color: blue }
-->
</STYLE>
</HEAD>
<BODY>
<H1 class=third>This is the CSS1 Test Content</H1>
<P class=first>
In order to demonstrate <strong>CSS1 Style Sheets</strong> I created this
test content document, which contains samples of most types of web page
content.
</P>
<P>
CSS1 can impact on a document generally, as well as individual elements
such as:
</p>
<UL class=second>
```

continues

Listing 6.3. continued

```
<LI> Lists
<LI class=first> Headers
<LI> Images
<LI class=third> Paragraphs
<LI> Inline elements
<LI> Tables
<LI class=third> Forms and Form elements
</UL>
<P class=second>
<img src="button.jpg"> CSS1 can also alter the presentation of certain
psuedo-elements such as<a href="#next">hypertext links</a> or the first line
or character within a line.
There actually isn't <a name="next">anything</a> that can't in some way
be controlled by CSS1. You can do some fun things with images, and add
effects to most elements with borders.
</p>
</BODY>
</HTML>
```

COMPANION Website Figure 6.2 shows the impact of these style sheet settings, which you can view for yourself by opening the file class.htm. Note that the first paragraph is transformed to small caps, per the use of the class first, but this same class had no impact on the first of the list items because it did not fit the HTML element type defined for the style sheet class. The list and the last paragraph reflect the use of the second generic class, which sets the background to yellow and the font color to blue. Two of the list items and the header, though, are set to a blue background and yellow font color because they have been assigned the third class style sheet setting.

FIGURE 6.2.

Page showing impact on Web page using class-specified style sheets.

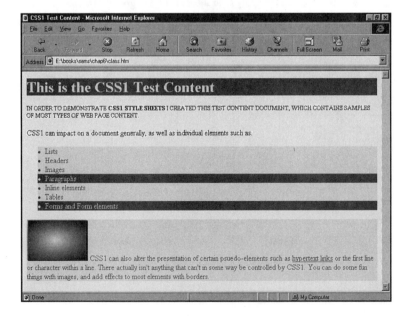

The style sheet for the individual list items takes precedence over the style sheet for the containing or parent element, the list. You can try out this example yourself by opening the file class.htm.

DYNAMICALLY ASSIGNING A STYLE SHEET CLASS

COMPANION Web site Dynamic HTML is covered later in this book, beginning with Chapter 30, "Using the HTML Object Model and Creating Dynamic HTML Pages." However, one aspect of IE-specific Dynamic HTML worth mentioning is that you can assign a style sheet class to an element dynamically. In the example file class2.htm, the example is extended with one simple script block:

```
<SCRIPT language="jscript" FOR=document EVENT=onclick>
<!--
    var elem = window.event.srcElement;
    elem.className = "third";
//-->
</SCRIPT>
```

This script assigns the style sheet third to whatever element received the clicked event. This is an effective approach to take to dynamically alter several element properties based on one event.

Using the ID Style Sheet Specifier

The W3C does not recommend the use of the ID style sheet specifier, primarily because it is used for creating style sheets for specific elements, rather than for classes of elements. The purpose of style sheets is to apply global changes that can then be altered within the sheet, rather than having to access individual elements. Using the ID specifier does imply adding styles to individual elements. However, the ID style sheet specifier is supported in both Navigator and IE.

The ID style selector uses a pound sign (#) instead of the period that the class selector used, as demonstrated in the following abbreviated code:

```
<STYLE type="text/css">
    P#someid { color: red; margin-left: 1.5in }
    #otherid { color: blue; font-size: 18pt }
</STYLE>
...
<P id=someid>
...
</P>
<H1 id=otherid>…</H1>
<P id=otherid>
```

This example is the same as the first in the section on using the class specifier. It also sets the paragraph that uses the otherid style sheet to red font with a margin of 1 1/2 inches, and the header and second paragraph to using a larger blue font.

COMPANION Web site A file called id.htm was created to demonstrate the use of the ID selector. This example redefines the font and color of font used for one generic ID selector, increases the size and alters the font for the header using another selector, and adds a border to elements using the third selector, as shown in Listing 6.4.

Listing 6.4. Using the ID selector to apply a style sheet to a specific element.

```
<HTML>
<HEAD><TITLE>CSS1 Test Content</TITLE>
<STYLE type="text/css">
<!--
    #one { font-family: Cursive; font-weight: 800; color: red }
    H1#two { font-family: Fantasy; font-size: 48pt }
    #three { border-width: 8px; border-style: inset; border-color: yellow}
-->
</STYLE>
</HEAD>
<BODY>
<H1 id=two>This is the CSS1 Test Content</H1>
<P id=two>
In order to demonstrate <strong>CSS1 Style Sheets</strong> I created this
test content document, which contains samples of most types of web page
content.
</P>
<P id=one>
CSS1 can impact on a document generally, as well as individual elements
such as:
</p>
<UL id=three>
<LI> Lists
<LI> Headers
<LI id=two> Images
<LI> Paragraphs
<LI id=one> Inline elements
<LI> Tables
<LI> Forms and Form elements
</UL>
<P>
<img src="button.jpg" id=three style="float:left">
CSS1 can also alter the presentation of certain psuedo-elements such as
<a href="#next">hypertext links</a>
or the first line or character within a line.
There actually isn't <a name="next">anything</a> that can't in some way
be controlled by CSS1. You can do some fun things with images, and add
effects to most elements with borders.
</p>
</BODY>
</HTML>
```

Figure 6.3 shows the results of style sheet settings on the sample Web page created for this chapter. Note, as with the class selector, applying a style sheet defined for a specific element does not work with elements of a different type.

FIGURE 6.3.

The impact on a Web page using style sheets attached to an element by ID *specifier.*

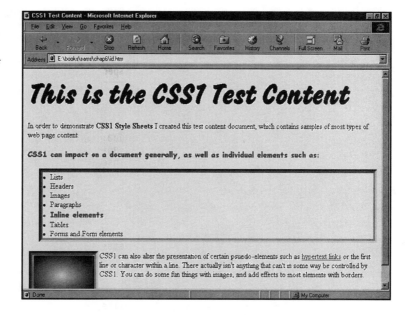

Creating an Overall Look for the Web Page

The previous examples in this chapter demonstrated several of the CSS1 attributes that can be altered for a Web page. This section describes applying attribute changes to impact the entire document.

The BODY tag is the tag specifier to use when applying style sheets to an entire document page. background-color and image and setting the page margins are among the more common attributes used with the BODY tag. The following style sheet changes the document to a background image, except if image loading is turned off, in which case the background is set to white. Also, the font color for the document is set to a dark green. The margins for the Web page are also set to 0.3 inches all around the document:

```
<STYLE type="text/css">
    BODY { margin: 0.3in; color: darkgreen;
        background-color: white; background-image: url(back1.jpg)}
</STYLE>
```

COMPANION
Web site   It's amazing what a few lines can do to a document. You can see this for yourself by opening the file body1.htm. Figure 6.4 shows the sample Web page with the style sheet setting just shown.

FIGURE 6.4.

Presentation as a result of altering Web page by adding background image, font color, and adjusting margins.

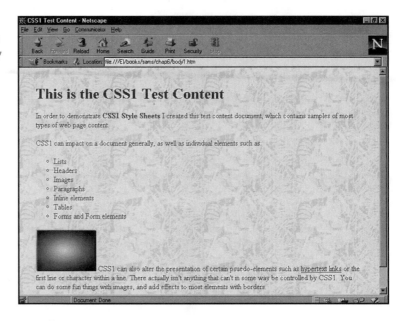

To fully appreciate how much of an impact you can create with a Web page by adjusting these attributes, Figure 6.5 shows an entirely different Web page with slight alterations in the style sheet:

```
<STYLE type="text/css">
    BODY { margin: 0.5in 1.0in; color: white;
        background-color: black; background-image: url(vertbar2.jpg);
        background-repeat: repeat-x; background-attachment: fixed}
</STYLE>
```

 You can try out this style sheet yourself by checking out `body2.htm` at the Companion Web Site.

The CSS1 attributes just demonstrated are the `background`, `margin`, and `color` attributes. Table 6.1 shows these attributes and sample values.

Table 6.1. The background, margin, and color CSS1 attributes.

Attribute	Sample Value
background	black url (`vertbar2.jpg`) repeat-x fixed
background-color	#FFFFFF // white
background-image	url (`somefile.gif`)
background-repeat	repeat-x // repeat horizontally
background-attachment	scroll // scroll with page
background-position	top center

Attribute	Sample Value
color	white
margin	20px 10px // top/bottom set to 20 pixels, left/right margins set to 10 pixels
margin-left	0.1in
margin-top	20px
margin-right	10
margin-bottom	auto

FIGURE 6.5.

Page appearance after changing the CSS1 style attributes for the background image, font color, and margins.

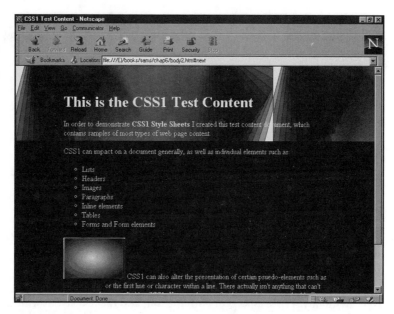

The CSS1 attributes also contain *shortcut* references, which are keywords that designate all the properties within the family of properties. In Table 6.1, background and margin are shortcuts, and the value in the table demonstrates how these types of attributes are set. For a shortcut reference, and for all of the attributes, if a value is specified, it is used; otherwise, whatever the default determined by the browser or the W3C is used. For the margin, when you specify the top and left values (which are the first two properties to be set for the margin shortcut), the bottom property is set the same as the top property, and the right property is set the same as the left.

Notice also that colors can be specified in two formats. The first is to use a named color, such as "white" or "magenta," and the second uses the hexadecimal RGB syntax, such as #FFFF00.

The hexadecimal value begins with the pound sign and is followed by the hexadecimal value for the colors red, green, and, finally, blue. Each of the RGB settings can have a value from 0-255 in decimal, which is 00 to FF in hexadecimal value.

The color CSS1 attribute is the font color. The background color is set using the background shortcut, or using background-color directly. The color names that each browser supports are unique to the browser, though many of the names overlap, such as green, magenta, or white. Use the hexadecimal notation to ensure the most accurate color match.

When using a background image, it can be positioned within the Web page and can be fixed so that it doesn't scroll with the page. You can also control how the image repeats, vertically only, horizontally only, no repetition, or in both directions, which is the default. A common approach to creating the sidebars you see in many Web pages is to use very thin, long images, and hope that the page isn't so wide that the image repeats. Now you can create the sidebar image the size you want and specify that the image repeats along the Y-axis—vertically—only.

CREATING A WATERMARK FOR THE WEB PAGE

COMPANION Web site A *watermark* is an image that remains in a fixed position on the page, regardless of how much the reader scrolls vertically or horizontally. It should be a larger image, set to be unobtrusively transparent, and positioned in the middle of the page. The file bodywtrmrk.htm contains an example of using a watermark. The style sheet for the example is:

```
<STYLE type="text/css">
<!--
    BODY { margin: 0.5in 0.5in; color: darkorchid;
        background-color: white; background-image: url(watermrk.jpg);
        background-repeat: no-repeat; background-attachment: fixed;
        background-position: 50% 50%}
-->
</STYLE>
```

Modifying Font and Text Appearance

You can modify several aspects of both the font and the text layout within a Web page. As you have seen, you can adjust the font color, the font family, style, and size. You can also convert the text to display as small caps, or control whether each word within a block is capitalized. You can also remove or add text decoration such as an underline or strikethrough, and control the spacing of text.

The CSS1 attributes that can control these properties are listed in Table 6.2, along with example values for each.

Table 6.2. Font and text CSS1 properties.

CSS1 Attribute	Sample Value
font	italic bold 18pt Arial
font-family	"times new roman" Arial

CSS1 Attribute	Sample Value
font-style	oblique
font-variant	small caps
font-size	larger
font-weight	800
letter-spacing	0.1em
word-spacing	0.5em
text-decoration	underline
vertical-align	super
text-transform	capitalize
text-align	center
text-indent	10%
line-height	110%

Sometimes some of the CSS1 attribute values are enclosed in quotes, such as "times new ro-man," because it is a multi-word value.

The shortcut font provides a method to designate one or more CSS1 properties, including the font weight, style, and family. Again, as with other shortcut methods, if a property is not set, the default value is applied. The defaults for each of these can be found in the specification, or within the browser documentation, as defaults may differ between browsers.

Notice that the attributes that can control spacing can take values of inches or *ex* units (the average size of the letter x for the font), *em* units (average height of font letter), or pixels. Font sizes can also be specified in font points, or *pt*. Many CSS1 attributes can also take a percent-age, which becomes a value derived from the sibling elements, the parent element, or itself. For instance, the line-height attribute is set to 110%, which is the default height of the line times 1.1. The text-indent value is derived from the parent element.

The example Web page has been modified to use most of these properties. The new style sheet is in Listing 6.5.

Listing 6.5. Using the font and text properties to modify the page presentation.

```
<HTML>
<HEAD><TITLE>CSS1 Test Content</TITLE>
</HEAD>
<STYLE type="text/css">
<!--
    BODY { margin-left: 2.0in; color: magenta;
        background-color: black; background-image: url(sidebar.jpg);
```

continues

Listing 6.5. continued

```
         background-repeat: repeat-y; background-attachment: scroll}
    H1 { color: yellow; font-family: Fantasy; font-size: 28pt;
         margin-left: -1.5in }
    P { text-indent: 0.25in }
    P.small { font-variant: small-caps; letter-spacing: 0.1em;
              line-height: 80% }
    P.upper { text-transform: uppercase; font-weight:bold }
    IMG {float: left}
    A { text-decoration: none; color: yellow }
    STRONG { vertical-align: super; color: orange }
-->
</STYLE>
<BODY>
<H1>This is the CSS1 Test Content</H1>
<P class=small>
In order to demonstrate <strong>CSS1 Style Sheets</strong> I created this
test content document, which contains samples of most types of web page
content.
</P>
<P>
CSS1 can impact on a document generally, as well as individual elements
such as:
</p>
<UL>
<LI> Lists
<LI> Headers
<LI> Images
<LI> Paragraphs
<LI> Inline elements
<LI> Tables
<LI> Forms and Form elements
</UL>
<P>
<img src="button.jpg"> CSS1 can also alter the presentation of certain
psuedo-elements such as<a href="#next">hypertext links</a> or the first line
or character within a line.
There actually isn't <a name="next">anything</a> that can't in some way
be controlled by CSS1. You can do some fun things with images, and add
effects to most elements with borders.
</p>
</BODY>
</HTML>
```

The header for the page has a different font family and size. All the paragraphs are indented 1/4 inch. The paragraphs with the small class are scrunched in by shrinking the line height and letter spacing, and setting all the letters to small caps. The paragraphs with the upper class are set to be uppercase only, and bold. Additionally, the anchor tags are set to yellow, and any text decoration, such as the underline, is removed. This setting impacts all the anchor tags, whether they are name tags or contain links. The strong tag is set to be superscript, which means it is placed slightly above the other text. Figure 6.6 shows what the page looks like with the style sheet.

FIGURE 6.6.
Results of adding text and font style sheet settings, with some background and color changes, to the basic Web page.

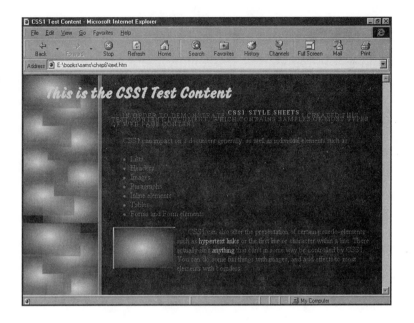

COMPANION **Web site** You can access this example by opening the file text.htm. Try changing any of the text or font attributes and see what the impact is.

Creating Borders Around Elements

There are certain CSS1 attributes that impact the "box" that surrounds a block-level HTML element. This box is the rectangular area large enough to enclose the element. A `block-level` element is any that is prefaced and followed by some form of line break, such as a paragraph or header.

Table 6.3 contains the `padding` and `border` attributes. The `border` attributes control the border drawn around the box, which is normally invisible. The `padding` attributes control the amount of whitespace between the border (visual or not) and the element contents. Margins are the other CSS1 attributes the W3C considers box attributes.

Table 6.3. Padding and border CSS1 attributes.

CSS1 Attribute	Value
border	thick groove yellow
border-color	yellow red blue
border-width	thin thick
border-style	inset

continues

Table 6.3. continued

CSS1 Attribute	Value
border-top	3px solid red
border-right	yellow
border-bottom	5px solid
border-left	solid
border-top-style	ridge
border-bottom-style	double
border-left-style	none
border-right-style	groove
border-top-color	#FFFF00
border-bottom-color	black
border-right-color	#0000CC
border-left-color	blue
border-top-width	thin
border-left-width	thick
border-right-width	medium
border-bottom-width	8px
padding	12% 18px
padding-left	18px
padding-top	4%
padding-right	0.25in
padding-bottom	5px

The padding shortcut is a technique that sets the padding of all four sides of an element at once. The border shortcut is a shortcut for eight other shortcut attributes: border-color, border-width, border-style, border-top, border-left, border-right, and border-bottom. With these shortcuts, you can apply one color or style to all sides at one time, or you can apply all the attributes to one side at a time.

Setting these attributes can cause an HTML element to stand out from a page dramatically, or the attributes can be used to align elements or to provide an attractive 3D effect to the page. Listing 6.6 contains the sample Web page with the box CSS1 attributes applied to several different HTML elements.

Listing 6.6. Using borders and padding to enhance page alignment and appearance.

```
<HTML>
<HEAD><TITLE>CSS1 Test Content</TITLE>
</HEAD>
<STYLE type="text/css">
<!--
    BODY { margin-left: 2.0in; margin-right: 05.in; color: magenta;
        background-color: black; background-image: url(sidebar.jpg);
        background-repeat: repeat-y; background-attachment: scroll}
    P { padding: 5px }
    .border1 { color: yellow; margin-left: -1.5in;
        border-width: thin; border-style: groove;
        border-color: orange; padding-top: 0.1in;
        padding-left: 0.2in }
    IMG { float: left; margin: -2.0in }
    .border2 { border: ridge 5px lime }
    UL { padding-left: 1.5in }
-->
</STYLE>
<BODY>
<H1 class=border1>This is the CSS1 Test Content</H1>
<P>
In order to demonstrate <strong>CSS1 Style Sheets</strong> I created this
test content document, which contains samples of most types of web page
content.
</P>
<P>
CSS1 can impact on a document generally, as well as individual elements
such as:
</p>
<UL>
<LI> Lists
<LI> Headers
<LI> Images
<LI> Paragraphs
<LI> Inline elements
<LI> Tables
<LI> Forms and Form elements
</UL>
<P>
<img src="button.jpg" class=border2>
 CSS1 can also alter the presentation of certain psuedo-elements such as
<a href="#next">hypertext links</a>
or the first line or character within a line.
There actually isn't <a name="next">anything</a> that can't in some way
be controlled by CSS1. You can do some fun things with images, and add
effects to most elements with borders.
</p>
</BODY>
</HTML>
```

COMPANION
Web site A border is used around the title, and its margin is set to a negative value, meaning that it will move to the left, beyond the normal margin set for the page. This will

cause it to overlap the sidebar, providing a more cohesive look to the Web page. Another border is also applied to the image, framing it. It, too, is moved to the left into the sidebar area. Padding is added to the tops of paragraphs to add more whitespace between paragraph elements, and padding is added to the left of the unordered list to help center the list within the page. Figure 6.7 contains the sample Web page, and the example can be found in the file box.htm.

FIGURE 6.7.

border *and* padding *properties applied to the sample Web page.*

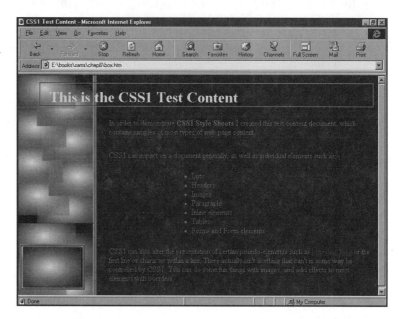

The border, padding, and margin properties are terrific techniques for adding whitespace to elements, without having to use HTML tables, or using one-pixel transparent GIF file gimmicks. Chapter 8, "Advanced Layout and Positioning with Style Sheets," extends this by discussing the CSS1 positioning attributes, and how they can be used to position elements directly.

Controlling the Appearance of Lists and Other HTML Elements

The last CSS1 attributes discussed in this chapter are the classifying attributes, such as those that control the appearance of lists, how HTML elements display, and pseudo-attributes.

The Classifying and Display Attributes

Table 6.4 contains the final CSS1 attributes discussed in this chapter.

6

Table 6.4. The classifying and display CSS1 attributes.

CSS1 *Attribute*	*Value*
display	none
white-space	pre
list-style	square outside
list-style-type	disc
list-style-image	url (someimage.jpg)
list-style-position	inside
float	right
clear	left
width	150px
height	25%

The `display` attribute is very useful. It can define that an element display as a list item or not display at all. The following example turns off the display of any element using the `nodisplay` class:

```
<STYLE type="text/css">
    .nodisplay { display: none }
</STYLE>
```

The `white-space` property controls whether whitespace contained within an element is displayed as it is typed, similar to using the PRE tags, or whether the whitespace is compressed. The following code specifies that all paragraphs are displayed with whitespace as it is typed:

```
P { white-space: pre }
```

The `list-style` attributes control how an ordered or unordered list is displayed. With these attributes you can alter the list bullet, whether the bullet is an image, and how additional list text displays in relation to the bullet. The following example code alters the bullet of the ordered list to be uppercase Roman characters, and that all text for the list item align to the right of the bullet:

```
OL { list-style-type: upper-roman }
```

The `list-style-position` attribute is set to a value of `outside` by default, which means that the list text is aligned to the right of the bullet symbol.

The `float`, `clear`, `width`, and `height` attributes can be used with most HTML elements, but they are mainly defined for use with images. You have seen the use of `float` in earlier examples, and it controls how other elements align with the target element, in these cases the image within the Web page. As an example, the following code aligns text surrounding the image to the left of the image:

```
IMG { float: left}
```

With this style sheet setting, all images within the Web page are aligned to the left of all the surrounding text. The `clear` attribute clears any elements to the right or left of the target element.

The `width` and `height` CSS1 attributes define the width and height of what the W3C terms *replaced* elements, such as images. These attributes can also be used with `other` `block-level` elements, but are mainly defined for the replaced elements.

COMPANION Website To demonstrate some of these attributes, the file `float.htm` contains a style sheet that hides the list within the page, floats the image to the right, and applies the clear attribute to any anchors. It also alters the header border, the body background, the paragraphs, and the use of the strong HTML element. Listing 6.7 contains the source for this page.

Listing 6.7. Using `float` and `clear` to align text and an image, and using `display` to hide the list.

```
<HTML>
<HEAD><TITLE>CSS1 Test Content</TITLE>
</HEAD>
<STYLE type="text/css">
<!--
    BODY { margin-left: 2.0in; margin-right: 0.5in;
        background-color: silver; background-image: url(vertbar.jpg);
        background-repeat: repeat-x; background-attachment: scroll}
    #header { color: firebrick; font-family: FANTASY; font-size: 28pt;
        background-color: silver;
        margin-top: 0.5in; margin-left: -1.5in;
        border-top: 15px outset red;
        border-left: 15px outset red;
        border-right: 15px inset yellow;
        border-bottom: 15px inset yellow }
    IMG { float: right; width: 50; height: 50  }
    LI { display: none }
    A { color: red; clear: right }
    P { margin-left: -1.5in; color: firebrick;
        font-family: Cursive; font-weight: 700}
    STRONG { color: yellow; font-family: fantasy; font-size: 14pt }
-->
</STYLE>
<BODY>
<DIV id=header><CENTER>This is the CSS1 Test Content</CENTER></div>
<P style="margin-top: 1in; white-space: pre">
In order to demonstrate <strong>CSS1 Style Sheets</strong> I created this
test content document, which contains samples of most types of web page
content.
</P>
<P>
```

```
CSS1 can impact on a document generally, as well as individual elements
such as:
</p>
<UL>
<LI> Lists
<LI> Headers
<LI> Images
<LI> Paragraphs
<LI> Inline elements
<LI> Tables
<LI> Forms and Form elements
</UL>
<P>
<img src="button.jpg"> CSS1 can also alter the presentation of certain
psuedo-elements such as <a href="#next">hypertext links</a>
or the first line or character within a line.
There actually isn't <a name="next">anything</a> that can't in some way
be controlled by CSS1. You can do some fun things with images, and add
effects to most elements with borders.
</p>
</BODY>
</HTML>
```

Notice from the listing that the first paragraph is given an inline style sheet, which sets the white-space attribute to a value of pre, which means that the whitespace within the paragraph should not be compressed. IE does not, at this time, process the white-space attribute, which means, for this browser, that using the attribute makes no impact on the whitespace. The whitespace is not maintained as typed and is compressed following standard HTML whitespace compression, as shown in Figure 6.8.

FIGURE 6.8.

Applying the classifying and display attributes to the example Web page.

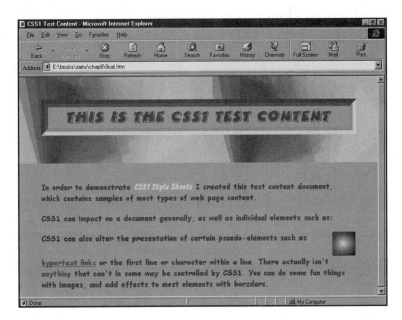

Navigator, however, does honor this attribute, as you can see in Figure 6.9. It does not, unfortunately, honor many other attributes such as the header border, the display property for the list, or the width and height properties for the image. Future releases of the browser should provide more support for these other attributes.

FIGURE 6.9.

The same Web page loaded into Navigator.

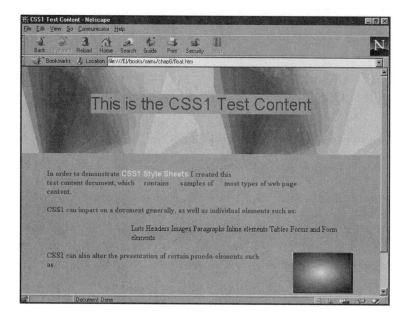

The Pseudo-Elements and Classes

The last CSS1 attributes discussed here are what the W3C defines as pseudo-elements and classes. A *pseudo-element* is an HTML element in which some external factor influences the presentation of the element. Style settings can be applied based on this external factor.

As an example, IE and Navigator have displayed different font colors for a visited link versus an unvisited link. If an anchor style sheet setting sets the font to red and this color is applied to both visited and unvisited links, this information is then lost. The anchor pseudo-class works with this link state information and allows you to define different colors, styles, and so on to each state of the link. The following code demonstrates the use of this pseudo-class:

```
a.classname:visited { color: red }
a:unvisited { color: yellow }
a:active { color: lime}
```

The active color is the one displayed when you actually press the mouse button down while over the link, and before you release the button. Also, you can use class names with the pseudo-class as long as the class name precedes the pseudo-class, as shown with the visited link in the example.

Other pseudo-elements are those associated with typographical conventions, such as the first letter in an element or the first line. The following code demonstrates the use of these attributes:

```
p:first-line { font-variant: small-caps }
p:first-letter { font-size: 18pt; color: red }
```

Listing 6.8 contains an example that uses these psuedo-classes and HTML elements, in addition to some others already discussed in this chapter.

Listing 6.8. Applying the pseudo-classes and elements to provide style-sheet settings for elements.

```
<HTML>
<HEAD><TITLE>CSS1 Test Content</TITLE>
</HEAD>
<STYLE type="text/css">
    BODY { margin: 0.5in; background-color: white}
    UL { list-style-image: url(box1.gif);
        list-style-position: outside; padding-left: 20}
    PRE { font-family: Arial; color: red; background-color: yellow }
    A {color: red; clear: left }
    A:link { color: lime }
    A:visited { color: firebrick }
    A:active { color: yellow}
    P.firsttype:first-letter { color: red }
    P.firsttype:first-line { font-variant: small-caps}
</STYLE>
<BODY>
<H1><CENTER>This is the CSS1 Test Content</CENTER></H1>
<P style="white-space: pre">
In order to demonstrate <strong>CSS1 Style Sheets</strong> I created this
test content document, which contains samples of most
types of web page
content.
</P>
<P class=firsttype>
CSS1 can impact on a document generally, as well as individual elements
such as:
</p>
<UL>
<PRE>
<LI>    Lists
<LI>    Headers
<LI>    Images
<LI>    Paragraphs
<LI>    Inline elements
<LI>    Tables
<LI>    Forms and Form elements
</PRE>
</UL>
<P>
<img src="button.jpg" style="float:right"> CSS1 can also alter the presentation
of certain psuedo-elements such as
<a href="#next">hypertext links</a>
or the first line or character within a line.
There actually isn't <a name="next">anything</a> that can't in some way
```

continues

Listing 6.8. continued

```
be controlled by CSS1. You can do some fun things with images, and add
effects to most elements with borders.
</p>
</BODY>
</HTML>
```

The Web page source redefines the color for the links, and applies the paragraph-based pseudo-elements. At this time neither IE nor Navigator supports the latter, but both support the former. You can also use an image as the bullet for the list, and use the PRE tag to maintain the whitespace within the list. Without adding in the additional whitespace, the list item text abuts directly against the bullet image. The image is set to float toward the right, and the text color is redefined within the PRE tags. Figure 6.10 shows the Web page loaded in IE.

FIGURE 6.10.

Using the pseudo-elements and classes to alter Web page presentation.

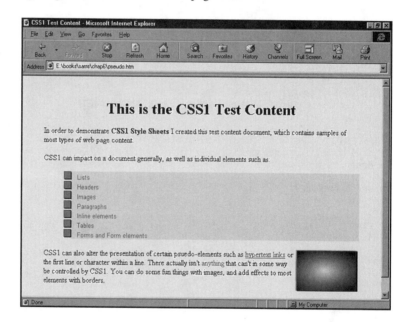

COMPANION Web site You can also try the page yourself by opening the file pseudo.htm. Try clicking the unvisited link and notice the color changes. Also note that the anchor tags are set to be red unless they are redefined. This means that the named anchor tag is red, and remains red. The actual link anchors pick up their colors from the pseudo-elements. A second example file, pseudo2.htm, switches the color of the visited and unvisited pseudo-elements, in addition to making other page alterations. This file's contents aren't covered, but you can try it out yourself, or modify the example given in Listing 6.7, to see the impact to the page when the presentation settings are altered.

Summary

This chapter provides an overview and demonstrations of the Cascading Style Sheets, Level 1 specification (CSS1).

The chapter also covers the four techniques to include style-sheet settings, which are to link in a CSS1 style-sheet file, to import a file, to embed the style-sheet setting directly into the Web page, or to embed the setting inline within a specific element.

The chapter also covers the CSS1 attributes, such as `font-variant`, `font-style`, and `text-transform`, that control the appearance of text and font. Also covered are border CSS1 attributes such as `border-color` and `border-style`.

In addition to these properties, the chapter also demonstrates how to apply style-sheet settings to all elements of a specific type, to a group of elements, or to individual elements. How to modify and align images, lists, and using the pseudo-elements and classes are also discussed and demonstrated.

Chapter 7, "Using Tables for Organization and Layout," begins to take a look at how to group page contents and control the layout of elements using HTML tables.

Using Tables for Organization and Layout

by Shelley Powers

IN THIS CHAPTER

CHAPTER 7

Prior to the release of the W3C recommendation for Cascading Style Sheets (CSS), HTML tables were the main technique used to control the placement of elements within a Web page.

Using tables, you can create two side-by-side columns of text, control the placement of images to create a menu bar, and align links, text, and graphics to create an attractive and easily read resource list. You can also use tables to control the layout of form elements in order to present a more professional appearance for your Web page forms.

Though CSS has redefined some of the necessity for using HTML tables, it hasn't replaced it. Tables are still an effective and simple-to-use solution for many Web page layout needs. Additionally, as demonstrated in this chapter and in the next, you can use tables in conjunction with CSS within a single page, to control not only layout but presentation.

A final and compelling reason to maintain the use of HTML tables is that older browsers, such as Navigator 3.x and to some extent IE 3.x, either don't support CSS1 fully, or only support a subset of the capability. Also, only Navigator 4.x and IE 4.x support CSS1 positioning, discussed in more detail in Chapter 8, "Advanced Layout and Positioning with Style Sheets."

HTML tables have also been used with most data accessing server-side scripting techniques, such as Microsoft's Active Server Pages (ASP) and Netscape's LiveWire, discussed in Chapter 27, "Server-Specific Technologies: Netscape ONE Versus Microsoft WindowsDNA." These techniques use tables as a method of presenting database data returned as the result of the Web page reader's request or action. CGI data applications also generate HTML tables in order to present data from databases or other sources. Microsoft also supports a new technique, called *data binding*, in which data sources are accessed from the server and the data is cached on the client. The data is bound to tables and other HTML elements for presentation.

Whatever the reason, the use of HTML tables for control of page layout and organization will continue.

> **NOTE**
>
> Note that several elements and attributes discussed in this chapter are based on the HTML 4.0 specification, which was a draft document when this book was written. Additionally, only IE 4.x supported HTML 4.0. Netscape has committed support for HTML 4.0 in Navigator when the W3C HTML 4.0 specification has moved from being a draft to a recommendation. New or changed elements and attributes with HTML 4.0 are identified.

What Are the HTML Table Elements?

HTML tables begin and end with the tables tags, `<TABLE>` and `</TABLE>`. They contain rows, defined with the row tags `<TR>` and `</TR>`, and cells, defined with cell tags, `<TD>` and `</TD>`. Captions for tables are created with the begin and end caption tags, `<CAPTION>` and `</CAPTION>`.

Some cells can be designated as table row headers with the use of the `<TH>` and `</TH>` tags. These cells then display using a bolder script than the other table cells.

The Basic Table Elements

Each of the tables begins and ends with the table tags (`<TABLE>` and `</TABLE>`). Table, row, cell, and caption specific elements have several attributes that control spacing and overall table appearance. The table element attributes control the background color, alignment, padding, spacing, height, and width of the table. Several of the attributes are *deprecated*, which means that they are included with the HTML 4.0 specification for backward compatibility and may not be supported in the future. Table 7.1 contains the table attributes, including whether the attribute is deprecated.

Table 7.1. Table element attributes.

Attribute	Description
align	How table aligns with other document elements—deprecated
bgcolor	Background color for table—deprecated
width	Width of table
cols	Number of columns within table
border	Width in pixels of frame around table
frame	Which sides of the frame surrounding table are visible
rules	Which rules appear between table columns and rows
cellspacing	The space between cell border and table frame
cellpadding	The space between cell border and cell contents
style	Used to set CSS1 style sheet
title	May display as ToolTip, or used with audio browsers
id	Element identifier, also specific style sheet setting identifier
class	Style sheet class name
lang	Primary language, such as en for English
dir	Direction text flows, used for new international formatting

The `frame` attribute has several acceptable values, given in the following list:

- ■ void—No frame
- ■ above—Top side only
- ■ below—Bottom side only

- `hsides`—Horizontal sides (top and bottom) only
- `vsides`—Vertical sides (left and right) only
- `lhs`—Left side only
- `rhs`—Right side only
- `box`—All four sides
- `border`—All four sides

The acceptable values for the `rules` attribute are given in the next list:

- `none`—No rules
- `groups`—Rules appear only between groups
- `rows`—Rules appear between rows
- `cols`—Rules appear between columns
- `all`—Rules appear between all elements

The `CAPTION` element has one specific attribute, `align`, which determines how the caption displays with the table, such as above or below the table. The table row element, `TR`, has the `bgcolor` attribute, though this is deprecated. The table column header and cell elements, `TH` and `TD`, have several attributes, given in Table 7.2.

Table 7.2. TH and TD element attributes.

Attribute	Description
axes	Used with speech synthesis and data binding—label of column for cell contents
axis	Used with speech synthesis and data binding—label of specific cell location
nowrap	Disable automatic text wrapping—deprecated
bgcolor	Background color of cell—deprecated
rowspan	Number of rows spanned by cell
colspan	Number of columns spanned by cell

Note that for all elements contained with tables, such as the table rows, cells, groups (discussed next), or captions, values can be specified to control alignment through the `align` attribute, though this attribute is deprecated. The W3C recommends the use of style sheets to control element alignment.

As an example of these attributes, the HTML file shown in Listing 7.1 creates a table set to a width of 60 percent of page width, with a border around the table set to 8 pixels. The table uses rules between rows only, and there are three columns. The caption is placed below the table, and four cells are created. The first cell spans two rows and the next two occupy just one cell each. The last cell, created in the second row, spans two columns. Each of the table cells is set to a center, left, or right alignment.

Listing 7.1. HTML to create a table with two rows and four cells.

```
<HTML>
<HEAD>
<TITLE>Table Examples</TITLE>
</HEAD>
<BODY>
<table width=60% frame=border border=8 rules=rows
    cols=3 cellspacing=5 cellpadding=5>
<CAPTION align=bottom>This is an example Table</CAPTION>
<TR><TH>First Value</TH>
<TH>Second Value</TH>
<TH>Third Value</TH></TR>
<TR>
<TD rowspan=2>1.88899</TD>
<TD align=center>1.444</TD>
<TD align=left>.0005</TD>
</TR>
<TR>
<TD align=center colspan=2>1.444</TD>
</TR>

</TABLE>
</BODY>
```

COMPANION **Web site** Figure 7.1 shows the table created with the source code. Again, note that no rules are drawn between the cells, and that one cell spans two rows, another two columns. You can try this example by opening the `tables1.htm` file.

FIGURE 7.1.

Web page containing HTML table with column headers, two rows of data, and three columns.

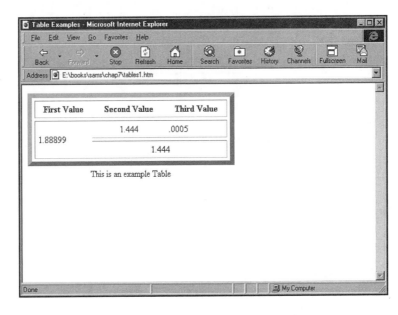

7

USING TABLES FOR
ORGANIZATION
AND LAYOUT

Column Grouping with COLGROUP and COL

Beginning with the HTML 4.0 draft, new elements add grouping capability within tables. You can group columns using the new colgroup element. This element, which begins with <COLGROUP> and may or may not have an ending </COLGROUP> tag, groups one or more columns. Once grouped, you can apply a width to all of the columns included within the group. A second element, COL, can also supply specific width and alignment information for one or more columns within the group. Also, style information and events can be accessed for the specific group. In the absence of a defined COLGROUP, the columns for the entire table are grouped.

Additional attributes that you can use with these elements are the char attribute, which sets the alignment of the column to a specific character, and charoff, which provides an offset to the first occurrence of the alignment character, if any. This attribute provides the ability to align a column's data to a decimal point if the column data is numeric or shows currency, or you can align on any other character. When using the char attribute, the align attribute is set to a value of char. The values for the align attribute are given in the following list:

- left—Left-justify contents
- right—Right-justify contents
- center—Center-justify contents
- justify—Double-justify contents
- char—Align around specified character

COMPANION **Web site** To demonstrate column grouping, the tables2.htm file uses the COLGROUP and COL elements, sets the first column to overlap the rows for the table, and sets the last two columns to align on the period. Listing 7.2 shows that the width of the columns is set to 30 pixels wide for the first column, and to distribute the horizontal space for the last two columns within the remaining space for the table, but as close to 10 pixels wide as possible.

Listing 7.2. Table using COL and COLGROUP elements.

```
<HTML>
<HEAD>
<TITLE>Table Examples</TITLE>
</HEAD>
<BODY>
<table width=60% frame=border border=8 rules=rows
    cols=3 cellspacing=5 cellpadding=5 align=center>
<CAPTION align=bottom>This is an example Table</CAPTION>
<COLGROUP span=3>
<COL align=center width="40">
<COL align="char" char="." width="10*">
<COL align="char" char="." width="10*"
<TR><TH>First Value</TH>
<TH>Second Value</TH>
<TH>Third Value</TH></TR>
<TR>
<TD rowspan=2>subtotals:</TD>
```

```
<TD>1.444</TD>
<TD>.0005</TD>
</TR>
<TR>
<TD>1444.444</TD>
<TD>18889.003</TD>
</TR>

</TABLE>
</BODY>
```

Figure 7.2 contains the Web page showing the HTML table just defined. Note that, at this time, neither Internet Explorer 4.0 nor Navigator 4.x correctly parse the char attributes, and the last two columns are not aligned on the period.

FIGURE 7.2.

Page with HTML table using COLGROUP *and* COL *elements to group the columns and add formatting.*

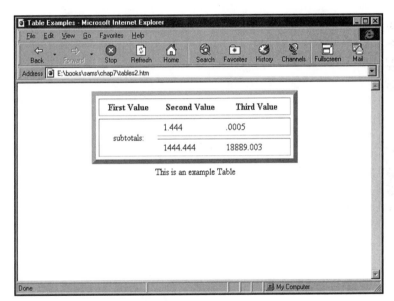

Row Grouping with THEAD, TFOOT, and TBODY Elements

Grouping the table rows is another table grouping technique. Each table has at least one row, and this becomes the default table body. However, the rows that make up the body can also be delimited with one or more TBODY elements. Additionally, the rows that make up the table head for a specific row grouping can be delimited with the THEAD element, and the foot of the table row grouping can be delimited with the TFOOT element. Each of these elements is defined by begin and end tags, though the end tags may be omitted if the begin tag for another of the elements is used. For the table body, the TBODY tags may be omitted if neither the THEAD nor TFOOT elements is used.

The only attributes for these elements are the general ones available to most elements: id, class, lang, char, charoff, valign, align, style, and several events. The values for the align attribute are given earlier in the section on column grouping. The values for the valign attribute are given in the following list:

- top—Align contents flush with cell top
- bottom—Align contents flush with cell bottom
- middle—Align contents vertically in middle of cell
- baseline—Align cell contents for first line with text in other cells

To demonstrate the row level grouping, Listing 7.3 contains the definition for another HTML table, this one using the THEAD, TBODY, and TFOOT elements, and with rules drawn around the groups.

Listing 7.3. Table created with TBODY, THEAD, and TFOOT row grouping elements.

```
<HTML>
<HEAD>
<TITLE>Table Examples</TITLE>
</HEAD>
<BODY>
<table width=60% frame=border border=8 rules=groups
    cols=3 cellspacing=5 cellpadding=5 align=center>
<CAPTION>This is an example Table</CAPTION>
<THEAD valign="top" align="left">
<TR><TH> </TH>
<TH>Second Value</TH>
<TH>Third Value</TH></TR>
<TFOOT valign="bottom">
<TR>
<TD>Month Two Subtotals (rounded): </TD>
<TD> 1446</TD>
<TD> 18889</TD>
</TR>
</TFOOT>
<TBODY valign="middle">
<TR>
<TD rowspan=2>Month One values:</TD>
<TD>0.5</TD>
<TD>.5</TD>
</TR>
<TR>
<TD>4.4</TD>
<TD>89.3</TD>
</TR>
<TFOOT valign="bottom">
<TR>
<TD>Month One Subtotals (rounded): </TD>
<TD> 1 </TD>
<TD> 1 94</TD>
</TR>
<TBODY valign="middle">
<TR>
```

```
<TD rowspan=2>Month Two values:</TD>
<TD>1.444</TD>
<TD>.0005</TD>
</TR>
<TR>
<TD>1444.444</TD>
<TD>18889.003</TD>
</TR>
</TBODY>
</TABLE>
</BODY>
```

COMPANION Web site The THEAD element is defined before the TBODY rows in order to draw the THEAD element contents before displaying the associated value rows. Figure 7.3 shows the table created with this HTML page definition, and `tables3.htm` contains the source code for the example.

FIGURE 7.3.

Web page showing HTML table with one THEAD *element, and two* TBODY *and associated* TFOOT *elements.*

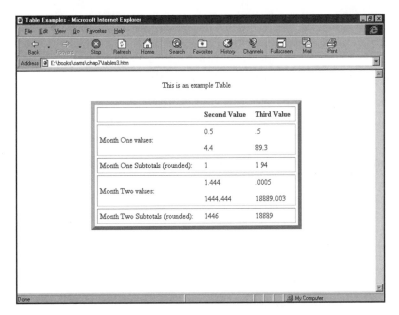

This section demonstrates the table elements and their associated attributes. The next section demonstrates how to use HTML tables with CSS1 style sheets, and the sections after that demonstrate how to use tables for certain Web page presentations.

Combining the Use of HTML Tables and CSS1 Style Sheets

In the previous section, you learned that some of the table attributes have been deprecated, meaning that they are included for backward compatibility only and that Web page developers and authors should use other techniques for the same results. The most common of these deprecated attributes is the bgcolor attribute. The bgcolor attribute sets the background color of the element's contents. This attribute has been deprecated because the W3C recommends the use of CSS1 style sheets to provide presentation definitions for HTML elements.

As an example, the file tables4.htm is a re-creation of tables3.htm, except for the style sheet settings being defined for several of the table elements. First, the table's border style is changed to the groove style, the border color is set to blue, the overall table font is set to green, serif, and with a size of 14 point. A margin of 0.5 inches is applied to the left and right sides of the table, and one of 0.2 inches is applied to the top and bottom sides of the table. Listing 7.4 contains the Web page contents.

Listing 7.4. Mixing CSS1 style sheets and tables for presentation and control of layout.

```
<TITLE>Table Examples</TITLE>
<STYLE type="text/css">
    THEAD { background-color: red; color: yellow }
    TBODY { background-color: black; color: yellow }
    TFOOT { background-color: lime; color: red }
    TABLE { border-style: groove; border-color: blue;
            font-family: serif; font-size: 14pt;
            color: darkgreen; margin: 0.2in 0.5in }
    TH { font-family: Fantasy }
</STYLE>
</HEAD>
<BODY>
<table width=60% frame=border border=8 rules=groups
    cols=3 cellspacing=5 cellpadding=5 >
<CAPTION>This is an example Table</CAPTION>
<THEAD valign="top" align="left">
<TR><TH> </TH>
<TH>Second Value</TH>
<TH>Third Value</TH></TR>
<TFOOT valign="bottom">
<TR>
<TD style="font-family: cursive">Month Two Subtotals (rounded): </TD>
<TD> 1446</TD>
<TD> 18889</TD>
</TR>
</TFOOT>
<TBODY valign="middle">
<TR>
<TD rowspan=2 style="text-decoration:underline">Month One values:</TD>
<TD>0.5</TD>
<TD>.5</TD>
</TR>
<TR>
<TD>4.4</TD>
<TD>89.3</TD>
</TR>
<TFOOT valign="bottom">
<TR>
<TD style="font-family: cursive">Month One Subtotals (rounded): </TD>
<TD> 1 </TD>
```

```
<TD> 1 94</TD>
</TR>
<TBODY valign="middle">
<TR>
<TD rowspan=2 style="text-decoration:underline">Month Two values:</TD>
<TD>1.444</TD>
<TD>.0005</TD>
</TR>
<TR>
<TD>1444.444</TD>
<TD>18889.003</TD>
</TR>
</TBODY>
</TABLE>
</BODY>
```

In addition to the style settings for the table, the TBODY elements are set to a black background and yellow font. These redefine the settings of the parent element, the table. Each of the table elements inherit style settings from the TABLE element, unless there are styles defined for either the element, or a specific instance of one or more of the elements.

The THEAD elements are set to red with a yellow font, and the TFOOT elements are set to lime with a red font. Additionally, the TH elements (the column headers) are set to the Fantasy font family.

Within the Web page itself, inline style sheets are provided for the table cells that contain the Subtotal and values writing. The cells containing the numeric data are left alone.

Figure 7.4 shows the Web page defined from Listing 7.4. As you can see, the results are dramatically different from the Web page in Figure 7.3. Yet the Web page is identical, except the align attribute has been removed from the table and the style sheets have been added.

Using an HTML Table to Create a Layout for Links

A popular use of HTML tables is to maintain the layout of a links page or a section of a page that contains resource links. You want Web page content such as this to have a cohesive appearance, and you also want to control spacing between a graphic and a link, or between a link and its associated descriptive text.

To create a links layout table, you need to decide how many columns you want. You might want one column for one or more graphics (such as a "new" graphic to show that the link is new), one column for the link, and one column for the description. However, if you have a simple link list, you can create a one-column table to hold a small, evenly sized graphic and a link. You would use this table mainly for Web page placement and spacing.

Listing 7.5 contains the source for a Web page that contains several different links, positioned and organized using a one-column table.

FIGURE 7.4.

Page with HTML table using CSS1 style sheets defined for the table elements.

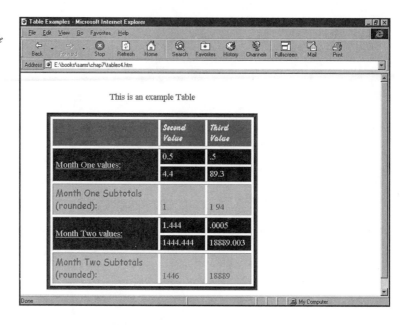

Listing 7.5. One-column table used to control layout of a links list.

```
<HTML>
<HEAD>
<TITLE>My Dynamic HTML Resources</TITLE>
</HEAD>
<BODY>
<TABLE width=80% CELLPADDING=10 cellspacing=15 border=5
frame=border rules=none align=center>
<CAPTION align=bottom>Internet Explorer Dynamic HTML links</CAPTION>
<TR><TD>
<H1>My IE Dynamic HTML Resources</H1>
</td></tr>
<tr><td>
<IMG SRC="box3.gif" width=17 height=17 hspace=5>
<a href=
    "http://www.w3.org/pub/WWW/TR/WD-positioning">
W3C Positioning Draft</a>
Positioning HTML Elements with Cascade Style Sheets
</TD></TR>

<TR><TD>
<IMG SRC="box3.gif" width=17 height=17 hspace=5>
<a href=
   "http://www.microsoft.com/ie/ie40/">
Internet Explorer 4.0 Platform Preview</a>
</TD></TR>

<TR><TD>
<IMG SRC="box3.gif" width=17 height=17 hspace=5>
<a href=
  "http://www.microsoft.com/ie/ie40/authors/">
```

```
IE 4.0 Authors/Developers page</a>
</TD></TR>

<TR><TD>
<IMG SRC="box3.gif" width=17 height=17 hspace=5">
</a>
<a href=
    "http://www.microsoft.com/sitebuilder/workshop/prog/ie4/">
Internet Explorer 4.0 Technologies</a></TD>
</TD></TR>

<TR><TD>
<IMG SRC="box3.gif" width=17 height=17 hspace=5">
<a href="http://www.microsoft.com/workshop/prog/inetsdk/docs/">
IE 4.0 Internet Client SDK Docs</a>
</TD></TR>
</TABLE>
</BODY>
```

COMPANION **Web site**   Figure 7.5 shows the Web page with this HTML table. Each link is next to an identical image, a small box, and the space between the link and the image is controlled with the use of the hspace attribute for the image. The first row in the table is a header element naming the table. The table also has a caption located at the bottom of the table. Then both the cellpadding and cellspacing attributes are used to stretch the table out and create whitespace around and between the links. A border is drawn around the whole, and the table is aligned in the middle of the page and set to 80 percent of the page width. You can find the example in tbllnks.htm.

FIGURE 7.5.

Web page with a one-column table used to organize resource list for inclusion within the page.

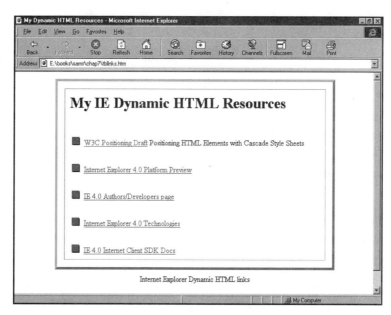

This approach is actually very workable and one you can use for resource lists. However, for a full page, you can use a multi-column table and CSS1 to create an attractive and organized resource page.

COMPANION Web site Figure 7.6 shows a page from a Web site that contains links to resources geared to assist independent computer consultants. You can view this page by opening the file center.htm. The page uses a table to organize the links, but it doesn't use CSS1 and is not as organized as it could be. Time for a makeover.

Figure 7.6.

A resource page with several links and their associated descriptions.

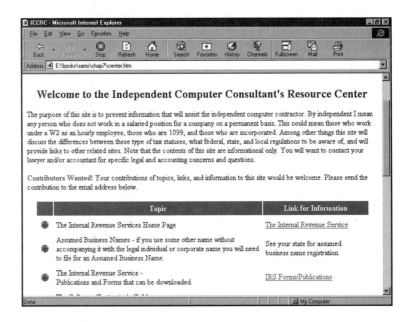

First, change the table to reverse the link and description, putting the link first and the description second, as shown in the following code:

```
<TR>
<TD><IMG SRC="ball.gif" height=16 width=16 alt="o"  align=left hspace=5></TD>
<TD><A href="http://www.scguild.com/">The Software Contractor's Guild </A></TD>
<TD>The Software Contractor's Guild <BR>
Post your resume for a nominal yearly fee.  </TD>
</TR>
```

Next, move the text to explain the purpose of the Web page to the THEAD element of the table, and the text asking for contributions to the TFOOT section of the page, as shown in the following code block:

```
<!-- table header -->
<THEAD>
The purpose of this site is to present information that will assist the
independent computer contractor. By independent I mean any person who does
not work in a salaried position for a company on a permanent basis. This
could mean those who work under a W2 as an hourly employee, those who are
```

```
1099, and those who are incorporated. Among other things this site will
discuss the differences between these type of tax statuses, what federal,
state, and local regulations to be aware of, and will provide links to
other related sites. Note that the contents of
this site are informational only. You will want to contact your lawyer
and/or accountant for specific legal and accounting concerns and questions.
<TR>
<TH> Link for Information </TH>
<TH colspan=2> Topic </TH>
</TR>

<!-- table footer -->
<TFOOT>
<TR><TD colspan=3>
<strong>Contributors Wanted!</strong> Your contributions of topics, links,
and information to this site would be welcome. Please send the contribution
to the email address below.
</TD></TR>
</TFOOT>
```

Notice that the colspan attribute of both the THEAD and TFOOT elements spans across all the columns within the table. The text supporting the resource listing is moved to be a part of the table so it is impacted by style sheet settings for the table, providing a consistent presentation.

Next, all of the old presentation formatting, such as the use of the FONT element and the bgcolor attribute in the column headers are removed. These are replaced with style sheets. The table width is set to 100 percent as margins for the document are controlled with style sheets and the table can size to fit the document space within the margins. The first column header is set to span two columns, which contain the graphic and link, as shown in the following code:

```
<TH colspan=2> Link </TH>
```

The new COLGROUP and COL elements provide widths for the columns. The width of each column is set to 0*, which specifies that the column is expanded to a width—within the given table width—to contain the contents. The column grouping is set to below the TABLE tag, but before any columns are created, including the table header columns.

NOTE

Note that using a relative sizing technique such as 0* with a table column usually picks up the size by the contents of the first row.

The column grouping code and the table tag code are shown next:

```
<TABLE Border=0 cellpadding=5 cellspacing=5 cols=3>

<!-- group columns and set width -->
<COLGROUP span=3>
<COL width="0*">
<COL width="0*">
<COL width="0*">
```

After adding the table element definitions, the page is ready for style sheet settings. The sheet sets the page margins and creates a background color and border for the column headers. Then the sheet sets the STRONG font for the page to a red color, with a font family of Fantasy, and redefines the font size, family, and color for the H2 header within the page. This style sheet is shown next:

```
<STYLE type="text/css">
    BODY { margin: 0.25in 0.35in; background-color:white }
    TH { background-color: navy; color: white;
        border-style:inset; border-color: blue; border-width: 5 }
    STRONG { color: red; font-family: Fantasy }
    H2 { color: maroon; font-family: sans-serif; font-size: 16pt }
</STYLE>
```

Figure 7.7 shows the resource page with these changes. You can also view this interim effort by opening the file center2.htm.

FIGURE 7.7.

Resource page using new table elements and some style sheet settings.

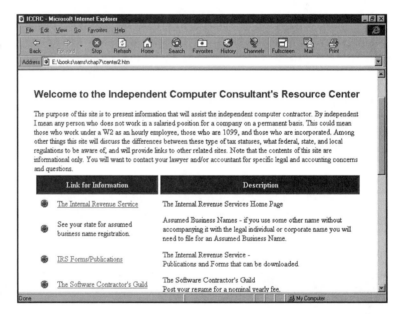

To finish the page, the style sheet sets the font size for the table head and foot to a smaller font, adding padding to inset the text. Because the TH tag-defined column headers are included within the head, they are redefined to not have the same padding, and to be a larger font (to override the changes made to their parent element, THEAD). The altered font variant attribute is set for the column headers, as shown next:

```
THEAD { font-size: 10pt; padding: 0.2in }
TFOOT { font-size: 10pt; padding: 0.2in }
TH { background-color: navy; color: white;
    border-style:inset; border-color: blue; border-width: 5;
    padding: 5px; font-size: 12pt; font-variant: small-caps }
```

The color of the links is altered to make them stand out a bit more. The font for the column with the link is changed to be different from the font for the column with the description. In order to avoid having to repeat style information for each table cell, the COL elements for each of these columns are used, and a style sheet for each column is defined, assigning the style sheet a class name and assigning a class to each of the elements, as shown next:

```
A:link { color: red }
A:visited { color: maroon}
A:active { color: yellow }
COL.link { font-family: Arial; font-size: 10pt }
COL.desc { font-family: serif; font-size: 10pt }
...
<!-- group columns and set width -->
<COLGROUP span=3>
<COL width="0*">
<COL width="0*" class=link>
<COL width="0*" class=desc>
```

This demonstrates how useful the new grouping columns are, especially when used with CSS1. Lastly, a couple of the listings are actually multiple links, with one description, but this is very hard to see. To compensate, look at a new style sheet class for these types of table cells:

```
TD.multi { border-width: 3px; border-style: groove;
         border-color: blue }
```

This could also be an effective approach to making a specific link stand out but defining it for a row element, TR, instead of a table cell.

COMPANION Web site The modified resource page is contained within center3.htm, and you can open it and try different style settings to see their impact with the table elements. Listing 7.6 contains the complete page.

Listing 7.6. Web page defining two page columns and sidebar.

```
<HTML>
<HEAD><TITLE>ICCRC</TITLE>
<STYLE type="text/css">
<!--
    BODY { margin: 0.25in 0.35in; background-color:white }
    THEAD { font-size: 10pt; padding: 0.2in }
    TFOOT { font-size: 10pt; padding: 0.2in }
    TH { background-color: navy; color: white;
        border-style:inset; border-color: blue; border-width: 5;
        padding: 5px; font-size: 12pt; font-variant: small-caps }
    STRONG { color: red; font-family: Fantasy }
    H2 { color: maroon; font-family: sans-serif; font-size: 16pt }
    A:link { color: red }
    A:visited { color: maroon}
    A:active { color: yellow }
    COL.link { font-family: Arial; font-size: 10pt }
    COL.desc { font-family: serif; font-size: 10pt }
    TD.multi { border-width: 3px; border-style: groove;
            border-color: blue }
```

continues

Listing 7.6. continued

```
-->
</STYLE>
<HEAD>
<BODY>
<IMG SRC="logo.gif"  width=98 height=69 alt="logo" hspace=20>
<IMG SRC="banner.gif" width=495 height=53 hspace=20
    alt="Independent Computer Consultant's Resource Center">
<p>
<IMG SRC="bar.jpg" width=100% height=8 alt="horizontal rule">
<H2>Welcome to the Independent Computer Consultant's Resource Center</H2>

<TABLE Border=0 cellpadding=5 cellspacing=5 cols=3>

<!-- group columns and set width -->
<COLGROUP span=3>
<COL width="0*">
<COL width="0*" class=link>
<COL width="0*" class=desc>

<!-- table header -->
<THEAD>
The purpose of this site is to present information that will assist
the independent computer contractor. By independent I mean any person
who does not work in a salaried position for a company on a permanent
basis. This could mean those who work under a W2 as an hourly employee,
those who are 1099, and those who are incorporated. Among other
things this site will discuss the differences between these type of tax
statuses, what federal, state, and local regulations to be aware of,
and will provide links to other related sites. Note that the contents
of this site are informational only. You will want to contact your lawyer
and/or accountant for specific legal and accounting concerns and questions.
<TR>
<TH colspan=2> Link for Information </TH>
<TH> Description </TH>
</TR>

<!-- table footer -->
<TFOOT>
<TR><TD colspan=3>
<strong>Contributors Wanted!</strong> Your contributions
of topics, links, and information to this site would be welcome.
Please send the
contribution to the email address below.
</TD></TR>
</TFOOT>

<!-- table body -->
<TBODY>
<tr>
<TD> <IMG SRC="ball.gif" height=16 width=16 alt="o"  align=left hspace=5> </td>
<TD> <a href="http://www.irs.ustreas.gov/prod/">
The Internal Revenue Service</A>
</TD>
<td>The Internal Revenue Services Home Page
</TD>
</TR>
```

```
<TR>
<TD><IMG SRC="ball.gif" height=16 width=16 alt="o"  align=center hspace=5>
</td>
<TD> See your state for assumed business name registration.</TD>
<td> Assumed Business Names - if you
use some other name without accompanying it with the legal
individual or corporate name you will
need to file for an Assumed Business Name.</TD>
</TR>


<TR>
<TD><IMG SRC="ball.gif" height=16 width=16 alt="o"  align=left hspace=5></td>
<TD><a href="http://www.irs.ustreas.gov/prod/forms_pubs/pubs.html">
IRS Forms/Publications</A></TD>
<td> The Internal Revenue Service - <br>
Publications and Forms that can be downloaded. </TD>
</TR>


<TR>
<TD><IMG SRC="ball.gif" height=16 width=16 alt="o"  align=left hspace=5></td>
<TD><a href="http://www.scguild.com/">The Software Contractor's Guild </a>
</td>
<td>The Software Contractor's Guild <br>
Post your resume for a nominal yearly fee.  </TD>
</tr>


<TR>
<TD> <IMG SRC="ball.gif" height=16 width=16 alt="o"  align=left hspace=5></td>
<TD class=multi>
<a href="http://www.nolo.com/nn273.html">Hiring Independent Contractors:
What your business needs to know</A><p>
<a href="http://www.nolo.com/item/hici.html">Hiring Independent Contractors:
The Employer's Legal Guide</A>
</td>
<td>Stephan Fishman has both an
on-line article and a book that cover the legal issues of hiring an
independent.
Both are absolute must-reads. </TD>
</TR>


<TR>
<TD> <IMG SRC="ball.gif" height=16 width=16 alt="o"  align=left hspace=5></td>
<TD> <a href="http://www.sbaonline.sba.gov/">The SBA </A></TD>
<td> The Small Business Administration </TD>
</TR>


<TR>
<TD> <IMG SRC="ball.gif" height=16 width=16 alt="o"  align=left hspace=5></td>
<TD> <a href="devcent.html">A listing of Small Business Development Center
Web Sites</A>
<td> The Small Business Development Centers <br>
These centers provide help, training, and referrals for the small business.
An exceptionally helpful resource. </TD>
</TD></TR>


<TR>
<TD> <IMG SRC="ball.gif" height=16 width=16 alt="o"  align=left hspace=5></td>
```

continues

Listing 7.6. continued

```
<TD> <a href="http://www.Cued.org/cued/index.html"> CUED</A></TD>
<td> The National Council for Urban Economic Development</TD>
</tr>

<tr>
<TD> <IMG SRC="ball.gif" height=16 width=16 alt="o"  align=left hspace=5></td>
<TD> <a href="http://www.icca.org/"> ICCA </A></TD>
<td> The Independent Computer
Consultants Association <br>
A non-profit organization dedicated to the independent computer consultant.
</TD>
</TR>
<TR>
<TD> <IMG SRC="ball.gif" height=16 width=16 alt="o"  align=left hspace=5></td>
<TD> <a href="http://www.aimnet.com/~software/csia/csia.htm">CSIA</A></TD>
<td> The Computer Software Industry Association <br>
This organization monitors legislative actions that can impact of the
computer software industry. Emphasis is on California and Federal.</TD>
</TR><TR>

<TD> <IMG SRC="ball.gif" height=16 width=16 alt="o"  align=left hspace=5></td>
<TD> <a href="http://www.aimnet.com/~software/industry_issues/">
Software Industry Issues </A></TD>
<td> The Software Industry Issues <br>
Issues affecting the Software Industry </TD>
</TR>
<TR>
<TR>
<TD> <IMG SRC="ball.gif" height=16 width=16 alt="o"  align=left hspace=5></td>
<TD class=multi> <a href=
"http://www.yahoo.com/Business_and_Economy/Companies/Consulting/
        Independent_Consultants/">Independent Consultants</A><p>
<a href=
    "http://www.yahoo.com/Business_and_Economy/Companies/Computers/Services/">
Computer Services</A><p>
<a href=
"http://www.yahoo.com/Business_and_Economy/Companies/
    Internet_Services/Internet_Consulting/">
Internet Consulting</A><p>
<a href="http://www.yahoo.com/Business_and_Economy/Companies/
    Internet_Services/Web_Presence_Providers/">
Web Presence Providers</A>
</TD>
<td> Yahoo! Sub-Directories for the Independent
<br> Submit your site for inclusion at one of these </TD>
</TR><TR>
<TD><IMG SRC="ball.gif" height=16 width=16 alt="o"  align=left hspace=5> </td>
<TD> <a href="http://www.yahoo.com/Business_and_Economy/
Small_Business_Information/"> Small Business Information</A></TD>
<td>Yahoo! Small Business Information</TD>
</TR>
</TABLE>
</BODY>
```

Notice the use of spacing between each table row, and the use of HTML comments to differentiate the table header, footer, and column grouping. Figure 7.8 shows a section of the resource page after all the modifications.

FIGURE 7.8.

Finished resource listing page using an HTML table for layout and CSS1 for presentation.

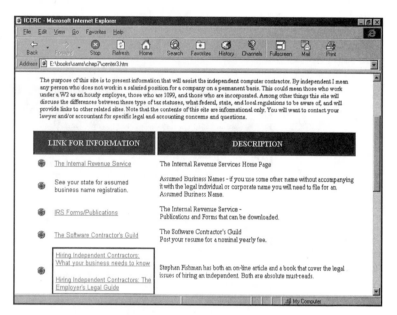

Creating Page Columns with a Table

Another popular use of HTML tables is to create columns within a page. The normal display of text within a Web page is to display the text from left to right, until the text meets the right margin and then wrap the text around to the left. This presentation approach is acceptable if you want a book-like look, but there are times when you want to lay text out in a manner similar to magazines or newspapers—as columnar text.

You can grab some content from the same page used to create the listing resource page, in the last section. This time access text-based content only. Figure 7.9 shows the content as it is normally displayed without any table layout, or style sheet setting.

COMPANION Web site The page is acceptable and the content is readable, but it's not very attractive and there is nothing that makes any part of the text stand out. You can access this Web page by opening the file `columns.htm`.

The first change is to split the data into three columns. The first column acts as a sidebar and contains text that appears highlighted. The other two columns contain the remainder of the text. In order to make the sidebar work, two rows are created in addition to the three columns, and the text is split between the "regular" columns to achieve approximately the same height with both columns. A COLGROUP element and three COL elements size the columns, as shown in the following HTML:

```
<table width=100% cols=3 cellspacing=10>
<COLGROUP span=3>
<COL width="30%">
<COL width="0*">
<COL width="0*">
```

FIGURE 7.9.

Web page containing several paragraphs and a header.

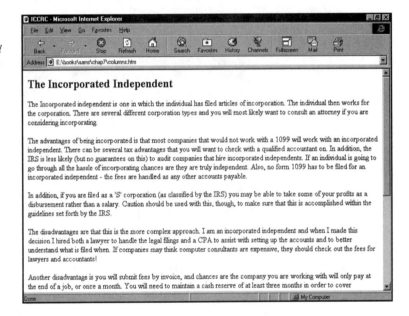

This HTML contains the table definition and the column group. Note that the table sets the cellspacing to 10 pixels and the width of the table to 100 percent. Also, the first of the columns is set to a width of 30 percent, and the others are set to use relative sizing, to adapt the width to a best fit for column contents.

Figure 7.10 shows the page with the three columns. Note the page layout improvement—three distinct columns appear. Also note that one column has less content than the other two do as it is the *sidebar* column. Because the columns are actually split into two rows, the first regular column flows around the sidebar by filling the area beneath the sidebar at the bottom of the page. You can see this page by opening the file columns2.htm.

As in Figure 7.10, you now have three columns, but the sidebar looks like a mis-sized column, rather than important text, which is normally what sidebars contain. This is where style sheets come in.

FIGURE 7.10.

Web page showing contents split into three columns.

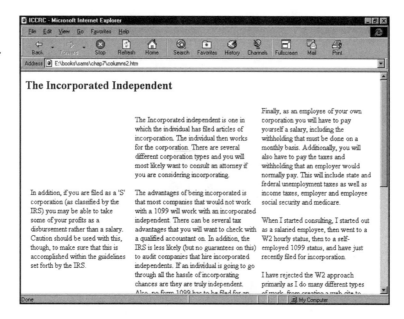

First, a margin is added to the page so the text doesn't abut directly up to the browser edges. The font size of the table text is altered to a smaller size in order to match more closely to the smaller type used in magazines and newspapers. The page header's color is changed and centered.

The most important changes are adding padding to the columns to create more visual separation between the columns, and aligning all text within the columns to the top. However, for the sidebar table cell, a border is added, the background color is set to maroon and the font color to white, the font is changed to a more distinctive font, and the sidebar text is aligned in the middle of the sidebar, as shown in the following style sheet setting:

```
<STYLE type="text/css">
    BODY { margin: 0.2in }
    TABLE { font-size: 10pt }
    H2 { color: maroon; text-align: center }
    TD { vertical-align: top; padding-left: 0.3in; padding-right: 0.2in;
        text-indent: 0.2in }
    TD.first {  border-width: 3px; border-style: inset; border-color: silver;
            background-color: maroon; color:white; font-family: Arial;
            vertical-align: middle; font-size: 10pt }
</STYLE>
```

With the style setting, the page has a much more professional look, and the sidebar stands out in a more dramatic manner. Figure 7.11 shows the finished results of converting the standard HTML text Web page into columns, using an HTML table and style sheets.

FIGURE 7.11.

Finished Web page with contents split into two columns and sidebar.

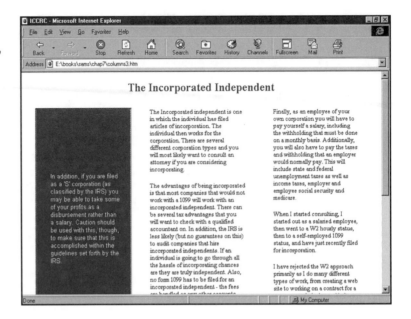

COMPANION
Web site

The file `columns3.htm` on the companion Web site contains the source for the finished Web page.

Controlling a Form Layout with a Table

There is no layout capability built into forms or form elements. Without an HTML table, you would have a difficult time aligning form labels with each other and with their associated input elements.

Forms and form elements are discussed in more detail in the following chapter, "Advanced Layout and Positioning with Style Sheets." However, a small example of using an HTML table to control the display of form elements is a useful way of ending this chapter.

A form was created with four text fields, two listboxes, two radio buttons, and two push buttons. A table with four columns is used to control the layout of the elements, each column set to 25 percent of the table width. Lines are drawn around the form input elements and the Reset and Submit buttons. When an element has a label, such as with the text fields, the label is set into the first column, followed by the `input` element, with the label right justified and the text field left justified. This aligns the label next to the element. For the other elements, the `colspan` attribute is used to overlap the column boundaries with the elements. Listing 7.7 contains the Web page source.

Listing 7.7. Form with spacing controlled by an HTML table.

```
<HTML>
<HEAD>
<TITLE>Table Examples</TITLE>
</HEAD>
<BODY>
<FORM>
<table width=70% frame=border border=4 rules=groups align=center
    cols=4 cellspacing=5 cellpadding=10>
<CAPTION align=top>Please enter the following information:</CAPTION>
<COLGROUP span=4 width="25%">

<!-- the submit and reset buttons -->
<TFOOT>
<TR>
<TD> </TD>
<TD>
<input type=submit>
</TD>
<TD>
<input type=reset>
</TD>
<TD></TD>
</TR>

<TBODY>
<!-- first form row -->
<TR><TH align=right>First Name:</TH>
<TD><input type=text name=firstname></td>
<TH align=right>Last Name:</TH>
<TD><input type=text name=lastname>//td>
</tr>

<!-- second form row -->
<TR><TH align=right>Address:</TH>
<TD><input type=text name=address></td>
<TH align=right>City and State:</TH>
<TD><input type=text name=citystate></td>
</tr>

<!-- third form row -->
<TR>
<TH align=right>Primary Colors:</TH>
<TD>
<SELECT name="colors">
<OPTION VALUE="ig">ivory/dark green
<OPTION SELECTED VALUE="ir">ivory/rust
<OPTION VALUE="wl">white/black
<OPTION VALUE="wb">white/blue
<OPTION VALUE="ar">aqua/rust
</SELECT>
</td>
<TH align=right>Secondary Colors:</TH>
<TD>
<SELECT name="colors2">
```

continues

Listing 7.7. continued

```
<OPTION VALUE="ig">ivory/dark green
<OPTION SELECTED VALUE="ir">ivory/rust
<OPTION VALUE="wl">white/black
<OPTION VALUE="wb">white/blue
<OPTION VALUE="ar">aqua/rust
</SELECT>
</td>
</TR>


<!-- last form row -->
<TR>
<TD colspan=2 align=right>
Low Resolution Images: <INPUT TYPE="radio" NAME="imageon" VALUE="Low Res"
CHECKED>
</TD>
<TD colspan=2 align=left>
High Resolution Images: <INPUT TYPE="radio" NAME="imageon" VALUE="Hi Res">
</td>
</tr>

</TABLE>
</FORM>
</BODY>
```

COMPANION **Web site**   As you can see, the Submit and Reset buttons are set into the page within the TFOOT element, and the other elements follow. Also note that the radio buttons are set to span two columns, providing enough space to contain the entire element, including the element label. The labels added to input elements that don't have their own built-in labels are set using the TH, or column header format, which means the text is bolder than regular page text. You see the form in Figure 7.12, and open it directly from the file forms.htm.

Summary

This chapter looks at the various uses of HTML tables to control layout of various HTML elements and to organize HTML contents.

The table elements and their attributes are discussed, and examples of their use are given. Following this, a demonstration of working with HTML tables and CSS1 style sheets to control page layout and presentation are provided.

Two examples of using an HTML table to organize hypertext links are provided. The first is a simple one-column table used to demonstrate how to organize resource links at the bottom of a Web page. The second example is more complex and demonstrates a full-page resource page. The latter example also uses CSS1 in conjunction with the HTML table to control the page presentation.

FIGURE 7.12.

Page showing how an HTML table is used to organize form elements.

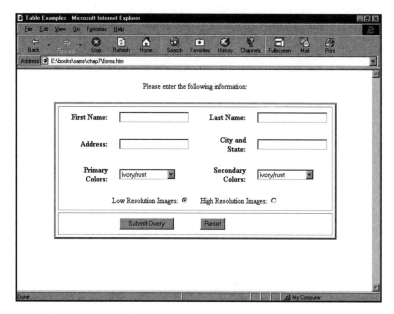

Following the resource page demonstration, a demonstration of creating a Web page with co-lumnar content is given, including how to create a sidebar that stands out from the page but is integrated with the overall page layout.

Finally, an HTML table used to control the layout of form elements is provided.

A discussion of forms and form elements continues with Chapter 9, "Creating Forms with HTML." Using CSS1 positioning to control Web page layout is covered in the next chapter.

Advanced Layout and Positioning with Style Sheets

by Shelley Powers

IN THIS CHAPTER

CSS Positioning, sometimes abbreviated as CSSP or CSS-P, is based on a draft recommendation co-created by Netscape and Microsoft and covers the static positioning of elements within a Web page. In addition to being able to position elements two dimensionally, you can also layer elements, hide or display them, or even alter the element's clipping area.

Both companies have also extended their scripting object models to dynamically incorporate positioning, hiding, and clipping elements. This is covered in detail in Chapter 30, "Using the HTML Object Model and Creating Dynamic HTML Pages," and Chapter 31, "Manipulating Objects and Responding to User Interaction."

At the time this book was written, Navigator 4.03 had just been released and had some problems with CSS positioning. Most specifically, Navigator 4.03 had difficulty determining the width of the Web page, and percentage-based values did not always work correctly. Most of the examples in this chapter are demonstrated with IE 4.0.

CSS Positioning Attributes

You can see all standards, proposed standards, recommendations, and drafts undergoing review by the W3C at `http://www.w3.org/TR/`. This includes the draft recommendation paper titled, "Positioning HTML Elements with Cascading Style Sheets," co-authored by Scott Isaacs of Microsoft and Scott Furman of Netscape, and edited by Robert Stevahn of Hewlett-Packard.

In their paper, Isaacs and Furman propose a specification that provides for explicit 2D positioning of HTML elements, including stacking order if the elements are stacked and whether an element is visible. Table 36.1 contains the proposed CSS positioning attributes.

Table 36.1. CSS positioning attributes.

Attribute	Description
position	Determines whether element is positioned explicitly or relative to the natural flow of the Web page document
left	Position of the left side of the rectangular area enclosing the element
top	Position of the top side of the rectangular area enclosing the element
width	Width of the rectangular area enclosing the element
height	Height of the rectangular area enclosing the element
clip	The clipping shape and dimensions used to control what portion of the element displays
overflow	The portion of the element contents that exceeds the bounds of the rectangular area enclosing the element
z-index	The stacking order of the element if two or more elements are stacked on top of each other
visibility	Whether element is visible

As you can see from the table, there aren't many CSS positioning attributes, but they can have a powerful influence on your Web page presentation.

Positioning Images and Other Elements

Images have had some positioning capability, with the hspace and vspace IMG attributes, and can be aligned with the align attribute. In fact, a one-pixel transparent GIF image has been used to create more esoteric Web page layouts. Images and other HTML elements have also been positioned within a Web page using HTML tables.

One technique Web developers did not have before Internet Explorer 4.0 and Netscape Navigator 4.0 is the ability to layer text and other HTML elements on images, or to layer images themselves. Also, developers could not exactly position images or any other element. The most the developer could do was use HTML tables or transparent GIFs to approximate the positioning effect being attempted. CSS positioning changes all of this.

As an example, look at Figure 8.1, which is a Web page containing three images beginning 100 pixels from the left, with exactly 10 pixels between each of the images. The images are each 90 pixels square. Figure 8.1 shows the images as they display without any CSS positioning or style sheets applied.

FIGURE 8.1.

Example of three images in a page using regular HTML positioning.

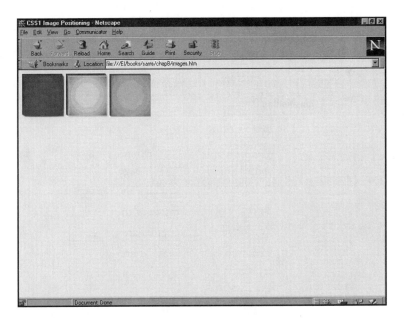

Notice that the first image is positioned at the left side of the browser, and the other images are located directly after the first one with a small space between, which is set by default. Figure 8.2 shows the same images, each with an hspace attribute set to 30, and a vspace attribute set to 20.

FIGURE 8.2.

Example of three images in a page using hspace *and* vspace IMG *attributes.*

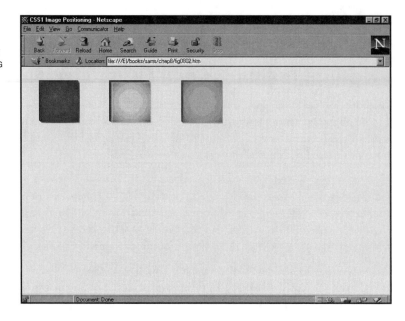

Unfortunately, using the hspace attribute applies the same horizontal space evenly around the image. If you want the first image to start 100 pixels from the left, you provide an hspace value of 100 pixels and then set the image alignment to the left. However, all other elements following the image are pushed over 100 pixels to the left.

With CSS, the position attribute is set to a value of absolute, which means that the element is positioned exactly, regardless of how any other element is positioned. The top, width, and height attributes are the same for all images, so the IMG selector sets the same values for all images within the page. The left attribute is defined for each image, using an ID selector. Listing 8.1 contains the complete source for the Web page.

Listing 8.1. Using CSS positioning to position three images.

```
<HTML>
<HEAD><TITLE>CSS Image Positioning</TITLE>
<STYLE type="text/css">
    IMG { position: absolute; width: 90; height: 90;
       top: 100 }
    #one { left: 100 }
    #two { left: 200 }
    #three { left: 300 }
</STYLE>
</HEAD>
<BODY>
<IMG src="red.jpg" id=one>
<IMG src="yellow.jpg" id=two>
<IMG src="green.jpg" id=three>
</BODY>
</HTML>
```

COMPANION
Web site Note that the IMG selector contains the style-sheet settings that apply to all the images, and the individual images then have their own settings for the left position. This style-sheet setting could also have been embedded directly into each image using an inline style sheet. You can see this Web page by opening the file `images.htm`.

If you try this file with Navigator, you find that the style sheet did not work for this browser. Netscape does not apply positioning to replaced elements such as images—at least not at this time. However, there is a way to work around this and have the same effect for both IE and Navigator: Enclose each image within a DIV block, and then position these elements, rather than the image, directly. Based on this, Listing 8.2 contains the altered source file.

Listing 8.2. Using DIV blocks to position images.

```
<HTML>
<HEAD><TITLE>CSS Image Positioning</TITLE>
<STYLE type="text/css">
    DIV { position: absolute; top: 100 }
    #one { left: 100; }
    #two { left: 200; }
    #three { left: 300; }
</STYLE>
</HEAD>
<BODY>
<DIV id=one>
<IMG src="red.jpg" width=90 height=90>
</DIV>
<DIV id=two>
<IMG src="yellow.jpg" width=90 height=90>
</DIV>
<DIV id=three>
<IMG src="green.jpg" width=90 height=90>
</DIV>
</BODY>
</HTML>
```

COMPANION
Web site As with the images and IE, you can move the repeated information into one style sheet and then use individual style sheets to create the unique definitions. You can try the altered file by opening `images2.htm`. Figure 8.3 contains the altered Web page with the three images, displayed in Navigator.

You can layer HTML elements, including placing text above images. One key to successfully using layers is to set the z-index CSS positioning attribute to a higher integer for the element you want to display at the top of the stack.

COMPANION
Web site IE assigns, as default, a z-index value of 1 to all elements. Navigator does not. Using a copy of `images2.htm`, the z-index value of 1 was added to the images so that both browsers are set to the same value. Three new DIV blocks are created, this time containing text that displays on the images. The z-index values of these DIV blocks are set to 2 so that they are placed on top.

FIGURE 8.3.

Web page showing use of DIV *blocks to apply absolute positioning that works with both Navigator and IE.*

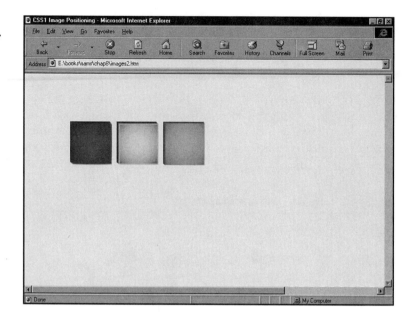

FIGURE 8.3.

Web page showing use of DIV *blocks to apply absolute positioning that works with both Navigator and IE.*

COMPANION
Web site Listing 8.3 contains the source code for the new file, which is named images3.htm and can be found on the Companion Web Site.

Listing 8.3. Layering text and images with z-index ordering.

```
<HTML>
<HEAD><TITLE>CSS Image Positioning</TITLE>
<STYLE type="text/css">
    BODY { font-family: Arial; color: white;
        font-weight: bold }
    DIV { position: absolute}
    #one { top: 25; left: 20; z-index:1}
    #two { top: 125; left: 20; z-index:1}
    #three { top: 225; left: 20; z-index: 1}
</STYLE>
</HEAD>
<BODY>

<!-- text -->
<DIV style="top:50; left: 40; z-index:2">
Item <br> One
</DIV>
<DIV style="top: 150; left: 40; z-index:2">
Item <br>Two
</DIV>
<DIV style="top: 250; left: 40; z-index:2">
Item <br>Three
</DIV>


<!-- images -->
```

```
<DIV id=one>
<IMG src="red.jpg" width=90 height=90>
</DIV>
<DIV id=two>
<IMG src="yellow.jpg" width=90 height=90>
</DIV>
<DIV id=three>
<IMG src="green.jpg" width=90 height=90>
</DIV>

</BODY>
</HTML>
```

A DIV block is used for the text because IE, at this time, does not support positioning for regular text block-level elements such as paragraphs. Figure 8.4 contains the page with the images aligned vertically and the text layered on top. Notice that the text for the body is also redefined to a white font, with font family of Arial, and with a weight of bold. This applies to all text in the page, including the text layered with the images.

FIGURE 8.4.

Web page showing vertical images with text layered on top.

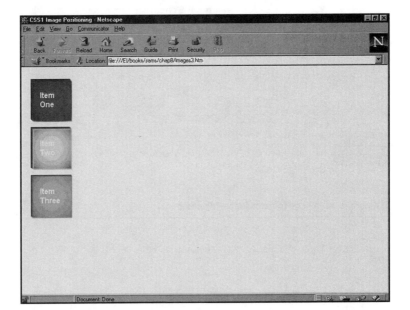

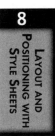

Creating Page Columns and Using HTML Tables and CSS Positioning Together

Web developers and authors use HTML tables to create columnar contents. This section goes into detail about how you can use CSS positioning to create multi-column Web page content. In addition, you can use HTML tables and CSS positioning for one Web page, as demonstrated here.

The Basic Page

At my Web site is an example page that demonstrates creating a client-side imagemap. To create the original page layout, I used tables to control the placement of the image menus at the top, and tables to control the positioning of the content. Figure 8.5 shows this page.

FIGURE 8.5.

Basic Web page that will be converted into CSS positioning columns.

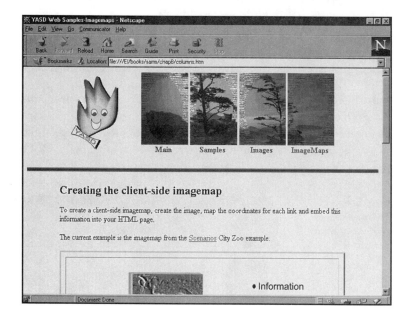

COMPANION
Web site You can see the Web page by opening the file columns.htm. Listing 8.4 contains the page's text.

Listing 8.4. Web page contents for Imagemap page.

```html
<html>
<head>
    <title> YASD Web Samples-Imagemaps </title>
</head>
<body>
<center>

<table border=0>

<tr><td width=150>
<img align=top src="yasd.gif" border=0 width=104 height=152 align=top>
</td>

<td align=center width=101>
<a href="http://www.yasd.com"><img src="menuaa.jpg" width=101 height=150
    hspace=0 align=top border=0 alt="main"></a>
<strong><font color="#660000">Main</font></strong>
</td>
```

```
<td align=center width=101>
<a href="http://www.yasd.com/samples/">
<img src="menuab.jpg" width=101 height=150 hspace=0 border=0 align=top
    alt="samples"></a>
<strong><font color="#990000">Samples</font></strong>
</td>

<td align=center valign=top width=101>
<a href="http://www.yasd.com/samples/images/">
<img src="menuac.jpg" width=101 height=150 hspace=0 border=0 align=top
    alt="images"></a>
<strong><font color="#333399">Images</font></strong>
</td>

<td align=center valign=top width=101>
<a href="http://www.yasd.com/samples/images/imagemap/">
<img src="menuad.jpg" width=101 height=150 hspace=0 border=0 align=top
alt="imagemap"></a>
<strong><font color="#3333cc">ImageMaps</font></strong>
</td></tr></table>
</center>

<p>
<img src="barblue.jpg" width=100% height=8 alt="hr">
<p>

<center>
<table border=0 width=80%>
<tr><td>
<a name="test"><h2> Creating the client-side imagemap</h2></a>
<p>

To create a client-side imagemap, create the image,
map the coordinates for each link and embed this information into your HTML page.
<p>

The current example is the imagemap from the
<a href="http://www.yasd.com/samples/scenarios/"> Scenarios</a>
City Zoo example.
<p>

<table border=3 cellspacing=10 cellpadding=10>
<tr><td>
<!-- create menu mapping for navigation -->
<map name=menu>
<area shape=rect coords="343,26,440,51" href="#test"
    onMouseOver="alert('over')" alt="some alt">
<area shape=rect coords="343,51,402,76" href= "#test">
<area shape=rect coords= "343,76,486,120" href="#test">
<area shape=rect coords="343,120,445,150" href="#test">
<area shape=rect coords= "343,150,466,180" href="#test">
<area shape=rect coords="343,180,424,210" href="#test">
<area shape=default href="#test">
</map>

<center>
```

continues

Listing 8.4. continued

```
<img src="menu.gif" width=530 height=226 border=0
    hspace=20 vspace=20 usemap="#menu"
    alt="menu map, or use text menu below">
<p></center>

<center>
<!-- create text based menu as an alternative -->
<small>¦ <a href="#test">Information</a>
        ¦ <a href="#test" onMouseOver="alert('clicked here')">Events</a>
        ¦ <a href="#test"> Announcements</a>
        ¦ <a href="#test"> Photos </a>
        ¦ <a href="#test"> Animal House </a>
        ¦ <a href="#test"> Gift Shop Catalog </a>
        ¦
</small></center>
</td></tr>
</table>
<p>
As can be seen above, the image contains text to describe the sites.
As the image was created a rectangle was created and placed over each of the text
fields in turn. The location(beginning
x,y positions) of the rectangle was recorded,
as well as its height and width.
<p>

After the image is embedded into the HTML page, the Image(IMG)
reference also includes a
"usemap" attribute. This attribute links the image with the
imagemap specification. This specification
uses the HTML "map" and associated "area" tags to define
the link for the specific area of the
image. If you check the source of this page you will be
able to see this definition. You will also see
that the page uses the "rect" shape attribute. This will
define an area of a given size and that forms
a rectangle.
<p>

A "default" entry is also listed, which links a default
location for any part of the image that
is not defined by previous in the specification.
<p>

<font color="#ff0000">Design Note</font>: Note two important
components to this imagemap.
<p>

First, the image has alternative text. This informs people
what the image is while it is being downloaded, and also
lets people who are using audio browsers (browsers that
translate an HTML page into
an audio alternative) know what is going on. Always, always
use alternative text particularly with
an imagemap.
<p>
```

```
Second, an alternative text based menu is given directly under
the menu map. Again, for those who are
using an audio browser, this is essential. It is also helpful
for those who do not want to download the image, or wait for
the image to finish downloading. Always, always include an
alternative text based menu.
<p>

One advantage to an imagemap is that the graphic is accessed
once resulting in less hits to the
web server. For a popular site (such as one that gets 10,000 hits per day),
there is a big difference between one graphic access and four or five or more.
<p>

The YASD site does not use imagemaps, primarily because we
want generic images that can be used
regardless of the location of the page. In this case, each
image has an associated hypertext link rather than one
image with many hypertext links.
</td></tr>
</table>
</center>

<p>
<img src="barblue.jpg" width=100% height=8 alt="HR">
<p>
<small><p>&copy; Shelley Powers, YASD, 1996, 1997</small>
<p>
<address>
Send any comments or inquiries to the
<a href="mailto:shelleyp@yasd.com">YASD Webmaster</a>.
</body>
</html>
```

> **NOTE**
>
> If you have not worked with client-side imagemaps, Listing 8.3 also includes an example of how these are defined. For more details on client-side imagemaps, see Chapter 14, "Client-Side Imagemaps: A Quick Demonstration of Client-Side Scripting."

Only the text contents are converted into columns, leaving the table to control the menu images and the table surrounding the imagemap alone. The last section of this chapter details how an entire page can be converted using CSS positioning.

The new page needs to be designed first. The menu bar from the top is removed, and the imagemap is placed into the text as a sidebar at the bottom of the page. The text is broken into two side-by-side columns, surrounding the imagemap. Additionally, the text margins are moved over to the left and right, adding some CSS style attributes in to redefine the font and some other page characteristics.

The CSS style sheet is added first. Working with positioning, you need to know what size the font will be and how much space the text will take. You also need to work within what will be the final margins. The following code contains the contents for the style sheet redefining the Web page document, header, and anchors, as well as the SMALL, ADDRESS, and STRONG elements.

```
<STYLE type="text/css">
    BODY { font-family: Times; font-size: 10pt;
        margin-left: 0.2in; margin-right: 0.2in;
        background-color: white  }
    H1 { color: blue }
    A { text-decoration: none }
    A:visited { color: darkblue }
    A:link { color: blue}
    A:active { color:red }
    SMALL { color: red}
    ADDRESS { color: red}
    STRONG { color: red}
</STYLE>
```

The next step is removing the table that controls the Web page contents, and creating the columns.

Creating the Columns

To convert the Web page contents into using CSS positioning, except around the imagemap, remove the HTML table references from the body of the document. Move the imagemap to the bottom of the document to get it out of the way while working on the columns. Remove the menu bar images from the top.

The Web page content is split in a logical place, creating two DIV blocks: one for the first half of the content and one for the second. The style settings for each block are embedded directly into the blocks rather than into the style sheet in the HEAD section. The DIV block definitions look, at this point, as follows:

```
<DIV style="position:absolute; left: 0.2in; top: 0.2in; width:45%">
<DIV style="position:absolute; left: 47%; top: 0.2in; width:45%">
```

The page is loaded so the results can be checked; it looks similar to Figure 8.6.

As you can see, the work for this page is not over. When the two DIV blocks were created using absolute positioning, they were removed from the normal flow of the HTML elements. Based on this, the imagemap located after the DIV blocks moved to the top of the Web page, with the contents overlaying each other. To test this page without any other elements, the imagemap and address information from the bottom of the document were temporarily removed, and the page was loaded again. The text is still not aligned properly, so the contents of the blocks were changed and the style settings redefined to the following:

```
<DIV style="position:absolute; left: 2%; top: 0.2in; width:45%">
<DIV style="position:absolute; left: 50%; top: 0.2in; width:48%">
```

Notice the percentages are used for all the widths; the right column moves over to create more whitespace. Figure 8.7 shows the Web page after the column width adjustments.

FIGURE 8.6.

Page showing two side-by-side, absolute positioned DIV *blocks, overlayed by Web page contents positioned using the natural page flow.*

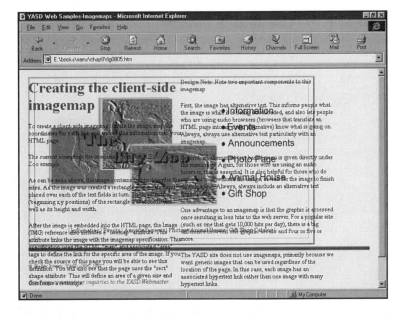

FIGURE 8.7.

Web page with columns and adjusted to more evenly distribute content.

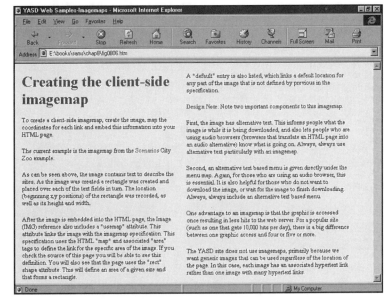

Now that the columns have been created, it's time to add the imagemap sidebar and the content for the bottom of the page.

Creating the Imagemap Sidebar

In the example, the columns are created with width but not height. With this approach, the height of the DIV blocks increases automatically to fit the height necessary for the content. However, a problem is that you have no idea where to position the block containing the imagemap and the block for the content at the end of the page.

You could dynamically access the positions and heights of the blocks, using script, and move the imagemap block to the correct position. This Dynamic HTML use is covered in detail in Chapter 31, "Manipulating Objects and Responding to User Interaction." However, in this chapter, static positioning is used.

There is not a trick for positioning elements within a page, except to try different positions and see if they fit. If you are using Netscape layers, you can use inline scripting to access the element's height, but this won't work with CSS positioning.

The imagemap is at the bottom of the page and needs to be moved toward the center. To do this, the text columns are split into four and the map is positioned toward the center of the document.

The columns are split first, and the imagemap is positioned just after the first half of the columns. Physically, in the document, the text is kept together to make content adjustments easier. The style sheet settings are pulled from the blocks into the HEAD style sheet, in order to find the settings more easily. The new settings for the blocks are:

```
DIV { position: absolute }
#first { left: 2%; top: 5%; width:45% }
#second { left: 2%; top: 625; width:45% }
#third { left: 50%; top: 5%; width:48% }
#fourth { left: 50%; top: 625; width:48%  }
#themap { left: 2%; top: 250 }
```

The final change is adding the bottom text. Again, this is located within a DIV block and positioned absolutely. The setting for this block is as follows:

```
#theend { left: 2%; top: 900; height: 100 }
```

This block has a height to create some whitespace below the contents.

COMPANION Web site That's the last of the page's modifications. Figure 8.8 shows the top portion of the Web page, and Figure 8.9 shows the bottom portion. You can also view the results by opening the file columns2.htm on the Companion Web Site.

Listing 8.5 contains the source code for the new file. Notice that HTML tables are still used for the imagemap itself, demonstrating that you can combine the two layout techniques.

FIGURE 8.8.

Top half of Web page after conversion to using CSS positioning.

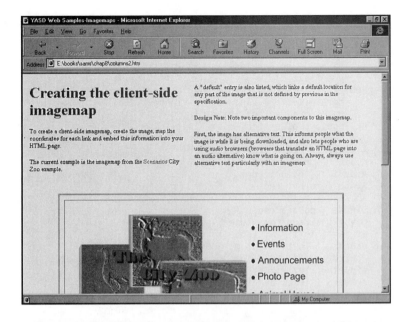

FIGURE 8.9.

Bottom half of Web page after conversion to using CSS positioning.

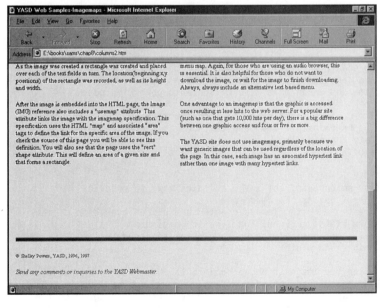

Listing 8.5. Web page source file after conversion to text columns using CSS Positioning.

```html
<html>
<head>
    <title> YASD Web Samples-Imagemaps </title>
<STYLE type="text/css">
    BODY { font-family: Times; font-size: 10pt;
        margin-left: 0.2in; margin-right: 0.2in;
        background-color: white  }
    H1 { color: blue; font-size: 24pt }
    A { text-decoration: none }
    A:visited { color: darkblue }
    A:link { color: blue}
    A:active { color:red }
    SMALL { color: red}
    ADDRESS { color: red}
    STRONG { color: red}
    DIV { position: absolute }
    #first { left: 2%; top: 5%; width:45% }
    #second { left: 2%; top: 150%; width:45% }
    #third { left: 50%; top: 5%; width:48% }
    #fourth { left: 50%; top: 150%; width:48% }
    #themap { left: 2%; top: 60% }
    #theend { left: 2%; top: 220%; height: 100 }
</STYLE>
</head>
<body>

<DIV id=first>
<h1> Creating the client-side imagemap</h1>

To create a client-side imagemap, create the image, map
the coordinates for each
link and embed this information into your HTML page.
<p>
The current example is the imagemap from the
 <a href="http://www.yasd.com/samples/scenarios/"> Scenarios</a>
City Zoo example.
</DIV>

<DIV id=second>
As can be seen, the image contains text to describe
the sites. As the image was
created a rectangle was created and placed over each of the
text fields in turn. The location(beginning
x,y positions) of the rectangle was recorded, as well as its
height and width.
<p>
After the image is embedded into the HTML page, the Image(IMG)
reference also includes a
"usemap" attribute. This attribute links the image with the
imagemap specification. This specification
uses the HTML "map" and associated "area" tags to define the
link for the specific area of the
image. If you check the source of this page you will be able
to see this definition. You will also see
that the page uses the "rect" shape attribute. This will define
an area of a given size and that forms
```

```
a rectangle.
</DIV>

<DIV id=third>
A "default" entry is also listed, which links a default location
for any part of the image that
is not defined by previous in the specification.
<p>
<strong>Design Note</strong>: Note two important components to this imagemap.
<p>
First, the image has alternative text. This informs people what
the image is while it is being
downloaded, and also lets people who are using audio browsers
(browsers that translate an HTML page into
an audio alternative) know what is going on. Always, always use
alternative text particularly with
an imagemap.
</DIV>

<DIV id=fourth>
Second, an alternative text based menu is given directly under the
menu map. Again, for those who are
using an audio browser, this is essential. It is also helpful for
those who do not want to download the image, or wait for the image
to finish downloading. Always, always include an alternative text based menu.
<p>
One advantage to an imagemap is that the graphic is accessed once
resulting in less hits to the
web server. For a popular site (such as one that gets 10,000
hits per day), there is a big difference between one
graphic access and four or five or more.
<p>
The YASD site does not use imagemaps, primarily because we want
generic images that can be used
regardless of the location of the page. In this case, each image
has an associated hypertext link rather than one image with many hypertext links.
</DIV>

<DIV id=themap>
<CENTER>
<table border=3 cellspacing=10 cellpadding=10>
<tr><td>
<!-- create menu mapping for navigation -->
<map name=menu>
<area shape=rect coords="343,26,440,51" href="#test"
    onMouseOver="alert('over')" alt="some alt">
<area shape=rect coords="343,51,402,76" href= "#test">
<area shape=rect coords= "343,76,486,120" href="#test">
<area shape=rect coords="343,120,445,150" href="#test">
<area shape=rect coords= "343,150,466,180" href="#test">
<area shape=rect coords="343,180,424,210" href="#test">
<area shape=default href="#test">
</map>

<center>
<img src="menu.gif" width=530 height=226 border=0
    hspace=20 vspace=20 usemap="#menu"
```

continues

Listing 8.5. continued

```
     alt="menu map, or use text menu below">
<p></center>

<center>
<!-- create text based menu as an alternative -->
<small>¦  <a href="#test">Information</a>
           ¦  <a href="#test" onMouseOver="alert('clicked here')">Events</a>
           ¦  <a href="#test"> Announcements</a>
           ¦  <a href="#test"> Photos </a>
           ¦  <a href="#test"> Animal House </a>
           ¦  <a href="#test"> Gift Shop Catalog </a>
           ¦
</small></center>
</td></tr>
</table>
</CENTER>
</DIV>

<DIV id=theend>
<p>
<img src="barblue.jpg" width=100% height=8 alt="HR">
<p>
<small><p>&copy; Shelley Powers, YASD, 1996, 1997</small>
<p>
<address>
Send any comments or inquiries to the
<a href="mailto:shelleyp@yasd.com">YASD Webmaster</a>.
</DIV>

</body>
</html>
```

Using the columns is a better approach to display this article. Due to the scrolling of the Web page, you can reverse the positions of the second half of the first column and the first half of the second column. Then, the Web page reader can follow the text across the page before scrolling down. However, because CSS positioning is used, all it takes to accomplish this is changing the names of the IDs used with the blocks. When the second block is identified by the style sheet ID selector of third, it has all the style sheet settings associated with this selector; the same applies to the third text block. There is a real advantage to using CSS positioning.

Converting an Existing Table-Based Web Page

Before CSS positioning was implemented within either Navigator or IE, tables were used to format a Web page, as shown in Figure 8.10. Notice the two columns, with text and photos alternating between them. A one-cell table is used around each of the photos to create a raised border effect.

COMPANION **Web site** Also note that the display of the menu bar and logo at the top of the page are controlled with another table. This table specification is given in Listing 8.6, and you can view the page by opening the file menu.htm.

FIGURE 8.10.

Sample Web page containing a mix of text and images.

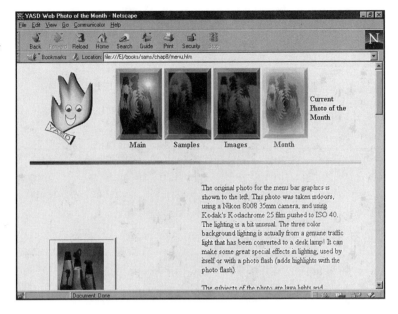

Listing 8.6. Web page document with menu bar controlled by HTML table.

```
<center>
<table height=170 border=0>
<tr><td width=150>
<img align=top src="http://www.yasd.com/mm/yasd.gif"
alt="logo" border=0 width=104 height=152 align=top>
</td>

<td align=center width=101>
<a href="http://www.yasd.com"><img src="menua.jpg" width=101
height=150 hspace=0 align=top alt="main" border=0></a>
<strong><font color=##660000>Main</font></strong>
</td>

<td align=center width=101>
<a href="http://www.yasd.com/samples/"><img src="menub.jpg"
width=101 height=150 hspace=0 border=0 align=top alt="samples"></a>
<strong><font color=#990000>Samples</font></strong>
</td>

<td align=center valign=top width=101>
<a href="http://www.yasd.com/samples/images/"><img src="menuc.jpg"
width=101 height=150 hspace=0 border=0 align=top alt="images"></a>
<strong><font color=#333399>Images</font></strong>
</td>

<td align=center valign=top width=101>
<a href="http://www.yasd.com/samples/images/photomo/">
<img src="menud.jpg" width=101 height=150 hspace=0 border=0
align=top alt="photo of the month"></a>
```

continues

8

LAYOUT AND
POSITIONING WITH
STYLE SHEETS

Listing 8.6. continued

```
<strong><font color=#3333cc>Month</font></strong>
</td>

<td>
<strong>Current<br>
Photo of the<br>
Month</strong></td>
</tr></table>
</center>
```

For the menu bar, the width of the table columns is set to the same size as the menu bar images. Also, the menu bar table is centered so the menu bar and logo are always in the middle of the page.

Using a table to control page layout isn't a bad approach, and is covered in detail in Chapter 7, "Using Tables for Organization and Layout," but there are limitations. First, with the menu bar, you should layer the menu bar text on the image itself, rather than having to set each text block below the image. You don't want to have to create a new set of images for each Web page just to change the associated text. Not only would this take a long time, it also means that the Web page reader has to load a new set of images for each page accessed from the site, rather than using one set of images and taking advantage of image caching. A second limitation is that because the text and images alternate, the images tend to have a large space surrounding them, when you would rather embed the images within the text and have the text flow around them. This was attempted by placing the images directly in the text but it was hard to control the alignment of the images.

Finally, another reason tables are not used with this page is it needed a little layout variety. Unlike print media, a Web page is not restricted to rigidly defined columns and carefully delimited margins. Additionally, and also unlike print media, you might have to scroll in order to view all the contents with a Web page. It's also fun to try something new, as long as the content is clearly readable and the reader has no trouble following the flow of the document.

COMPANION **Web site**   To convert the page just described to using CSS positioning, the first step is to recreate the menu bar at the top of the page. A new document is started. DIV blocks were used as Netscape does not, at least with 4.01, support positioning directly with images. Listing 8.7 contains the style sheet and elements for the menu bar, including the logo image and the bar separating the menu section from the rest of the document. You can access the new Web page by opening the file menunew.htm and following along.

Listing 8.7. New Photo of the Month Web page menu bar section.

```
<STYLE type="text/css">
    BODY { background-color: white; font-size: 10pt}
    H1 { font-family: Fantasy; color: red; font-size: 20pt }
    .diva {text-decoration: none; color: yellow}
```

```
       DIV { position: absolute; font-size: 10pt; font-family:Arial }
       #logo { position: absolute; top: 50px; left: 50px;
              z-index: 5; width: 105}
       #image1 { position: absolute; top: 10px; left: 185}
       #image2 { position: absolute; top: 10px; left: 290 }
       #image3 { position: absolute; top: 10px; left: 395}
       #image4 { position: absolute; top: 10px; left: 500 }
       #title1 { position: absolute; top: 20px; left: 200px;
              z-index: 5; height: 20px; width: 80px }
       #title2 { position: absolute; top: 20px; left: 300px;
              z-index: 5; height: 20px; width: 80px }
       #title3 { position: absolute; top: 20px; left: 410px;
              z-index: 5; height: 20px; width: 80px }
       #title4 { position: absolute; top: 20px; left: 510px;
              z-index: 5; height: 20px; width: 80px }
</STYLE>
</head>
<body>
<!-- Set menu images-->
<DIV id=logo>
<img src="yasd.gif" width=104 height=152>
</DIV>
<DIV id=image1>
<a href="http://www.yasd.com">
<img src="menua.jpg" border=0 width=101 height=153></a>
</DIV>
<DIV id=image2>
<a href="http://www.yasd.com/samples">
<img src="menub.jpg" border=0 width=101 height=153></a>
</DIV>
<DIV id=image3>
<a href="http://www.yasd.com/samples/images">
<img src="menuc.jpg" border=0 width=101 height=153></a>
</DIV>
<DIV id=image4>
<a href="http://www.yasd.com/samples/images/photomo">
<img src="menud.jpg" border=0 width=101 height=153></a>
</DIV>

<!-- Set menu titles -->
<DIV id=title1>
<h3><a class=diva href="http://www.yasd.com">Main</a></h3>
</DIV>
<DIV id=title2>
<h3><a class=diva href="http://www.yasd.com/samples">
    Samples</a></h3>
</DIV>
<DIV id=title3>
<h3><a class=diva href="http://www.yasd.com/samples/images">
    Images</a></h3>
</DIV>
<DIV id=title4>
<h3><a class=diva href="http://www.yasd.com/samples/images/photomo">
    Photo of the Month</a></h3>
</DIV>
<DIV style="position:absolute; left:10; top:180; z-index:0">
<img src="bar.jpg" width=620 height=8>
</DIV>
```

Notice that DIV blocks are used for the menu text, because IE did not support positioning for header elements at the time this was written. Notice also that the menu text blocks have a higher z-order value. The z-order attribute controls the ordering of layered or stacked elements, and setting this value to a higher number for the text ensures that the text displays on the images.

Both the menu bar images and text are surrounded by hypertext links. To prevent the underline from showing with the menu bar text, a new class, diva, was created; it sets the CSS1 text-decoration attribute to none and the font to yellow so the menu text shows against the darker images. Figure 8.11 shows the Web page contents after creating the menu bar.

FIGURE 8.11.

Page showing re-created menu bar using CSS positioning rather than HTML table.

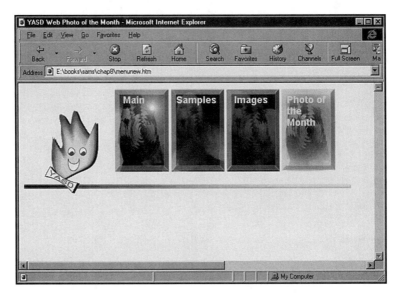

Once the menu bar is set, each section of the original document is converted over to using CSS positioning only. The entire document is not converted at once, so each element's position can be tested as it is moved over to the new document.

DIV blocks are used for all the content, as this is one of the few HTML elements that both Navigator and IE position in a manner consistent between both browsers. New classes are defined for each image, not only positioning them, but surrounding them with a colorful border to give the image a more polished look, and to add a little three-dimensional effect to the page. The CSS positioning information is embedded directly into the DIV blocks for the text.

The text blocks are sized to work with the placement of the images. The header is not placed directly in the middle of the page, but offset to the right, overlapping a little into the space reserved for the first text block. The first image is placed to the left, in from the page margins and positioned to balance both the header and the text. Listing 8.8 contains the HTML and CSS1 and CSS-P style settings for these elements.

Listing 8.8. HTML and CSS settings for the first three document elements, the first image, the header, and the first block of text.

```
    .image1 { border-width: 6; border-style: groove; border-color:lime;
          position:absolute; left: 100; top: 250; width: 101; height: 150}
...
<DIV class=image1 >
<img src="photo1.jpg" width=101 height=150 align=center>
</DIV>
<DIV style="position:absolute; left: 260; top: 210">
<H1>
January Photos of the Month
</H1></DIV>
<DIV style="position:absolute; left:260; top: 275; width: 350">
The original photo for the menu bar graphics is shown to the left. This photo was
taken indoors, using a Nikon 8008 35mm camera, and using Kodak's Kodachrome 25 film
pushed to ISO 40. The lighting is a bit unusual. The three color background
lighting is actually from a genuine traffic light that has been converted to a desk
lamp! It can make some great special effects in lighting, used by itself or with a
photo flash (adds highlights with the photo flash).
<p>
The subjects of the photo are lava lights and crystals from two different
collections.
</DIV>
```

The image style setting is the listing's first two lines and is contained within the style sheet located in the head of the document. The rest of the code is the definition for the header and text. Figure 8.12 shows the contents of the Web page at this time.

FIGURE 8.12.

Web page after adding the first three page elements: the header, the first image, and the first text block.

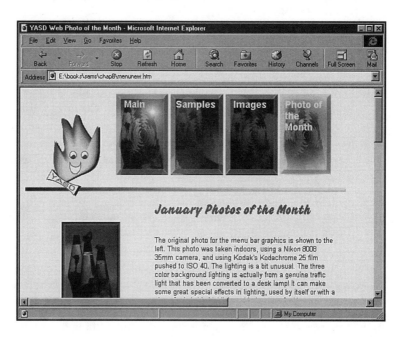

In the next section of the document, the image is placed in the middle of the text. This is accomplished by breaking the text into two separate parts of about equal size. Three DIV blocks are used, two for the text and one for the image itself, as shown in Listing 8.9.

Listing 8.9. Second section of the Web page document, containing two more text blocks and another image.

```
.image2 { position:absolute; left:275; top: 480; width: 101; height: 151;
         border-width: 6; border-color: lime; border-style: groove }
...
<DIV style="position:absolute; left:20; top:455; width: 250">
The slides were taken with the camera mounted on a tripod
(with that slow of a film speed and the equivalent long exposure
 time a tripod was a must). Exposure settings and time were
 unfortunately not recorded. The lens used was the Nikon
 70-210mm f/4- .6D AF Zoom lens which does very well for
indoor still lifes. The image was digitalized using
 the Nikon Coolscan II slide scanner.
</DIV>
<DIV class=image2>
<img src="photo2.jpg" width=101 height=150 align=center>
</DIV>
<DIV style="position:absolute; left: 415; top: 460; width:240">
I used Adobe PhotoShop as the software tool to scan in the
image, and work with it once digitalized. Once the image was
 scanned into the computer, the fun could really begin. By
itself the image is rough and a bit flat, though colorful.
To add a little dimension to the picture I experimented with
several of the Photoshop filters. I decided to use the ZigZag
 distortion filter with the Pond ripple effect on the picture,
as shown to the right.
</DIV>
```

Again, the first two lines of the listing are the style sheet setting for the image, located in the page style sheet. Notice from the code that the text blocks' widths—not their heights—are set. This controls the placement of the width and lets the text block's height extend in order to fit the contents. If a block is created too small in both width and height for the text, each individual browser then determines what to do with the overlap, and you lose control of the contents positioning. By default, both IE and Netscape allow the contents to overflow the container, but there is nothing to prevent them from changing this, or determining how to display the overflow.

If the contents do overflow, you can override the default behavior for overflow by explicitly using the overflow attribute, and setting the attribute to some other value. A value of none means that the text overflows the boundaries and isn't clipped. With Navigator, a value of clip clips the contents at the overflow point. With IE, you can use scroll to add scrollbars specific to that element only. Which attribute values are available is browser-dependent. To try this, open the example file and deliberately set the container for one of the text blocks to a size too small for the contents; then add the overflow attribute to the inline style setting for the element.

In the next section of the document, you can see something different: a long text block and four images grouped tightly together. When the results were tested, the text overlapped the images in length, so the images were moved to a point that vertically aligned them with the text block, as shown in Listing 8.10.

Listing 8.10. Source code grouping four images together and aligning with large text block.

```
.image3a { position:absolute; left:375;top:710; height: 150; width: 100;
        border-width: 6; border-color: yellow; border-style: groove }
.image3b { position:absolute; left:495;top:710; width: 100;
        border-width: 6; border-color: lime; border-style:groove }
.image3c { position:absolute; left:375;top:880; width: 100;
        border-width: 6; border-color: blue; border-style: groove }
.image3d { position:absolute; left:495;top:880; width: 100;
        border-width: 6; border-color: red; border-style:groove }
...
<DIV class=image3a>
<img src="photo3.jpg" width=101 width=150 align=center>
</DIV>

<DIV class=image3b>
<img src="photo4.jpg" width=101 height=150 align=center>
</DIV>

<DIV class=image3c>
<img src="photo5.jpg" width=101 height=150 align=center>
</DIV>

<DIV class=image3d>
<img src="photo6.jpg" width=101 height=150 align=center>
</DIV>

<DIV style="position:absolute;left:20; top:680; width: 330">
After the base object was created, each of the menu graphics was
generated. The YASD site goes to a depth of 4 levels (directories)
for most of the site, which means that I needed to create 4
images. The first image, as shown in the top row at the near
right was the base image with a Rendering filter of Lens Flare added.
<p>

The next image shown in the top row far right, was the base
image altered using the Rendering Filter and then using Lighting
effects. In this case the effect was the RGBLIGHT and using
the Spotlight option.
<p>

On the lower near right, the image was altered by selecting
the Adjust option of the Image main menu,and then selecting
Color Balance. The colors of the image were adjusted to be
100% red in the Midtones and Shadows, and -100 in Magenta-Green
and Yellow-Blue ranges. The Highlights balance was left as is.
As a final touch, the Lighting Effects Rendering Filter with
the spotlight option was used.
<p>

The final image, as shown in the far right, bottom row, was not
adjusted in Photoshop. Instead I used Corel Xara product. I applied
the transparency tool to the image, using the Circular style and
setting the transparency value to 65%.
</DIV>
```

8

LAYOUT AND
POSITIONING WITH
STYLE SHEETS

Notice that the text block actually contains several paragraphs. One real advantage to using the DIV block is that it is a container element, meaning it can enclose more than one HTML element. You can read more about the difference between container and noncontainer elements in Chapter 4, "Basic Structural Elements and Their Usage." The DIV element is also a block-level element, meaning that by default there is a line break separating the element from other HTML elements when using relative positioning. This is compared with an inline element such as the STRONG element or the SPAN element, which do not have this line break. Again, this is also discussed in detail in Chapter 4. Also notice that the images used within the Web page body all use the align attribute. Navigator, and to some extent IE, add space between the DIV block, and the contents and centering ensures that the image is surrounded evenly by whitespace.

The next section breaks up any hope of columnar alignment in the document by alternating two images and two text blocks. Again, because the images and the space surrounding the images take up considerable space, the text blocks are kept slim, as shown in Listing 8.11.

Listing 8.11. Final section of the document.

```
    .image4a { position:absolute; left:10;top:1110; height: 150; width: 100;
            border-width: 6; border-color: blue; border-style: groove }
    .image4b { position:absolute; left:335 ;top:1110; height: 150; width: 100;
            border-width: 6; border-color: yellow; border-style: groove }
...
<DIV class=image4a>
<img src="photo7.jpg" width=101 height=150 align=center>
</DIV>

<DIV style="left: 140; top: 1110; width: 180">
Finally, the images were modified using Corel Xara to add a 'frame'.
This was accomplished by creating a long slim darker gray rectangle
the exact height of the images and creating another rectangle,
perpendicular to the first, that was the exact width of the menu images.
</DIV>

<DIV class=image4b>
<img src="photo8.jpg" width=101 height=150 align=center>
</DIV>

<DIV style="left: 470; height: 200; top: 1100; width: 150">
Both the rectangles were made transparent (at a value of about
75% using the flat option). The images were also moulded using
the Mould tool. This allowed us to mitre the edges of the rectangles.
</DIV>
```

The document's last section groups the remaining two images to the left. The end-of-document content, another bar, any copyright information, and contact information follows this section, as shown in Listing 8.12.

Listing 8.12. The Web page footer, containing copyright and contact information.

```
    .image4c { position:absolute; left:375 ;top:1310; height: 150; width: 100;
            border-width: 6; border-color: red; border-style: groove }
```

```
    .image4d { position:absolute; left:495 ;top:1310; height: 150; width: 100;
         border-width: 6; border-color: lime; border-style: groove }
</STYLE>
...
<DIV style="left: 20; top: 1310; width: 340">
The rectangles were duplicated and the color was set to a light gray in the
new images. The new rectangles were
also flipped to face in the opposite direction. All of the
rectangles were placed in such a way as to form a frame, with the darker
rectangles forming the
right and bottom parts of the frame; the lighter forming the top and left
side of the frame.
<p>
The frames were then placed on each of the menu images (sizing to best
possible fit) and then the new
combined image was grouped and exported using the JPEG format.
</DIV>

<DIV class=image4c>
<img src="photo9.jpg" width=101 height=150 align=center>
</DIV>

<DIV class=image4d>
<img src="photo10.jpg" width=101 height=150 align=center>
</DIV>

<DIV style="top: 1500; left: 2.5%; width: 95%">
<img src="bar.jpg" width=620 height=8>
<p>
<small>
CorelXara is a trademark of the Corel Corporation<br>
Photoshop is a trademark of Adobe Systems, Inc.<br>
Nikon is a trademark of Nikon Inc.
<p>
&copy; Shelley Powers, YASD, 1996, 1997</small>
</p>
<p>
<address>
Send any comments or inquiries to the
<a href="mailto:shelleyp@yasd.com">YASD Webmaster</a>.
</address>
</p>
</DIV>
```

The document's last two images are the last elements that have styles defined in the style sheet, so they are followed by the STYLE closing tag. It is important to remember the DIV block and STYLE closing tags because the page does not display correctly without them. However, you won't get an error and it can be very difficult to find the problem.

COMPANION Website That's it for the new document, and Figure 8.13 shows the last of the document. Again, you can try this by opening the older version of the page using HTML tables, located in menu.htm, or the newer version of the page using CSS Positioning, located in menunew.htm.

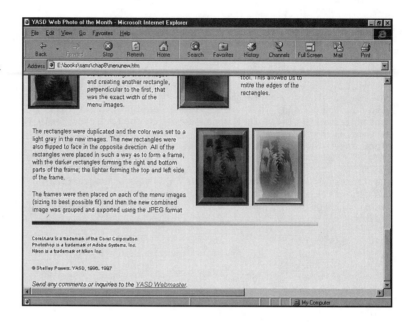

This section covers statically positioning HTML elements. Later in this book, you see several examples of dynamically positioning elements after the Web page loads and based on the Web page reader's actions.

Summary

This chapter provides demonstrations of CSS positioning, including a listing of the CSS positioning attributes currently undergoing review by the W3C.

The CSS positioning techniques are applied to several examples, such as positioning several images within a Web page and then overlaying the images with text. Additionally, an existing Web page is converted into columns using CSS positioning. This example also uses HTML tables, demonstrating that both techniques can be used together.

The last demonstration converts another Web page, which contains several text blocks and images. This example uses CSS1 positioning only and also demonstrates that you can use different layout approaches with Web pages, when not constrained by normal typesetting machines.

The next chapter discusses HTML forms. Though they are some of the older components in use with Web pages, HTML forms are still the most widely used techniques.

Creating Forms with HTML

by Shelley Powers

IN THIS CHAPTER

CHAPTER 9

The HTML form element was the first extension to HTML and the one most needed. Interactivity and doing business on the Web required some method of obtaining information from the Web page reader, and a method of providing information to the same reader.

HTML forms have also been one of the most stable components of Web-based developments. Though browsers now support dynamic HTML and channels, and XML extends the very objects that define a Web page, a form remains a method of getting and providing information.

What Are HTML Forms

An HTML form is not a visual element. It is a container, and can contain one or more buttons, text boxes, or other form elements. The form elements can be used to access information from the reader and then process that information within the Web page. The information can also be sent to a CGI or Web server application for further processing.

The FORM Object and Its Attributes

A form is created by using the begin and end form tags <FORM> and </FORM>. Though not required, there are form attributes that can control what happens to the form information, the method used to deliver this form information, and where feedback derived from the form contents should be sent.

> **NOTE**
>
> Internet Explorer does not require the ending FORM tag, but Navigator does. Because you want to create to the most common denominator, include the ending as well as beginning form tags when you create a form.

The following code shows a named form as an example of creating a form and setting the values of some attributes. When the Web page reader presses the Submit button, the browser sends the form information to the URL of the CGI application in the ACTION attribute, using the post method:

```
<FORM name="mailform"
ACTION="http://www.somecompany.com/cgi-bin/somescript.cgi" METHOD="post">
...
</FORM>
```

The FORM attributes are shown in the following list:

- name—Form name.
- target—Location of window where form responses are sent.
- action—URL of Web server application that processes form information.

- enctype—By default this attribute has a value of `application/x-www-form-urlencoded`, but can be set to `multipart/form-data` if the file upload element is used. Not all browsers support the latter encoding type.
- method—A value of `get` or `post`, which determines how form information is sent.

The `action` attribute contains the location of the application that processes the form information. Traditionally this is a CGI application, covered in more detail in Chapter 25, "Traditional CGI Programming." However, the application can also be a Web server-based application such as LiveWire for Netscape's server, or Active Server Pages for Microsoft's server.

By default the results of the form processing are returned to the window where the form was contained, but the `target` attribute allows you to specify a different window. This can be another frame window if you are using frames, or a parent window if your form is in a separate child window. You could also create a new window for holding form results, and open this window before the form is submitted.

The `enctype` attribute is set to `application/x-www-form-urlencoded` by default, or when the POST method is used. However, if you include a `fileupload` element, discussed later in the section titled "Uploading Files with `fileupload`," then set this value to `multipart/form-data`.

Finally, the two methods of sending the form information to the server are the POST and GET methods. The POST method encapsulates the information into a data structure accessible from the environment variable `stdin`. The GET method attaches the form information to the end of the URL. This is usually accessed by the environment variable `QUERY_STRING`.

How each of these attributes works with a Web server application is discussed in more detail in Chapters 24, "Putting Your Server to Work," through 28, "Serious Applications for Serious Web Publishing," and Chapters 30, "Using the HTML Object Model and Creating Dynamic HTML Pages," through 34, "XML."

The forms Array

Each form has a separate entry in a built-in array called `forms`. This array can be accessed in script through the `document` object, which contains this array as a property.

Chapter 17, "Using JavaScript for Forms," goes into more detail about accessing forms and form elements from script, but a small introduction to the forms array is in order here.

To find the length of a form, each `forms` array has a `length` property that contains the number of forms in the array. Also each form element, in turn, has a built-in `elements` array that contains all of the form elements. This array also has a `length` property that contains the number of elements within that specific form.

As a quick demonstration of these two arrays, the code in Listing 9.1 contains two forms. The first form contains a text box and a push button. The second form contains a selection list and a push button. Figure 9.1 contains the Web page with the two forms.

FIGURE 9.1.

A Web page with two forms, each form containing two form elements.

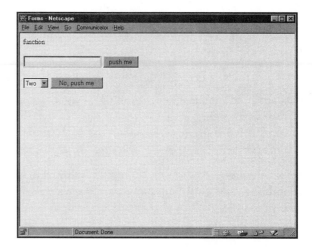

Pressing the second button triggers the button's `onclick` event, which has an event handler that calls the JavaScript function `list_values`. This function accesses each form, prints out the form name, and then accesses the `element` array for each form; it then prints out the element names and the current value.

Listing 9.1. Web page with two forms and four form elements.

```
<HTML>
<HEAD>
<TITLE> Forms </TITLE>
<SCRIPT language="javascript">
<!--

// list out element values, and all names
function list_values() {
   var strng = "";
   for (i = 0; i < document.forms.length; i++) {
    strng+= "form name: " + document.forms[i].name + "<br>";
      for (j = 0; j < document.forms[i].elements.length; j++)
        strng+= document.forms[i].elements[j].name + " " +
         document.forms[i].elements[j].value + "<br>";
    strng+="<p>";
    }
   document.writeln(strng);
}
//-->
</SCRIPT>
function
</HEAD>
<BODY>

<!-- form 1 -->
<FORM name="form1">
<input type=text name="textname">
<input type=button name="button1" value="push me">
</FORM>
```

```
<!-- form 2 -->
<FORM name="form2">
<SELECT name="randomvalues">
<OPTION VALUE="1">One
<OPTION SELECTED VALUE="2">Two
</SELECT>
<input type=button name="button2" value="No, push me"
    onclick="list_values()">
</FORM>
</BODY>
```

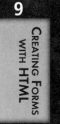 As each of the form and `form element` attributes is accessed, the values are concatenated. After the code has accessed all the forms within the page and all the elements in each form, the resulting string containing the attribute values is printed out to the current Web page. This erases the page contents and replaces it with the string contents. Figure 9.2 shows the Web page after the reader has pressed the second button. You can try this example by opening the file `form1.htm`.

The example from Listing 9.1 also demonstrates a couple of the form element types. The following section covers each of these types in detail.

FIGURE 9.2.

Forms Web page after second button has been pressed.

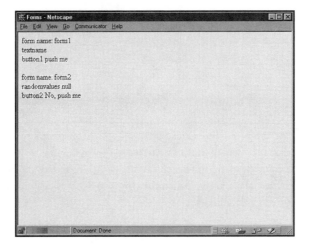

The Form Elements

At this time there are eleven different form elements: `button`, `check box`, `fileupload`, `hidden`, `password`, `radio`, `reset`, `select`, `submit`, `text`, and `textarea`. Each element has a different look and performs a different function.

The INPUT tag creates most of these elements. As an example of creating an element, the following code creates a text field:

```
<INPUT type="text" name=somefield>
```

The only elements that are not created using the INPUT element tag are the `textarea` and `select` elements. Creating and using each of these elements is detailed in the following sections.

The button Element

Probably the most common of the form elements is the button element. Using this type of input element, a button is created on the page with the traditional Windows-based 3D appearance including a gray background with shaded sides. You can create a button using the following code:

```
<button TYPE="button" NAME="somebutton" VALUE="Push Me">
```

This code creates a button, named somebutton and with the words Push Me appearing on it. Figure 9.3 shows a page with this type of form element.

FIGURE 9.3.

A simple form button with the words Push Me.

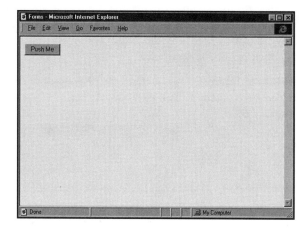

The only attributes for the button element are the name attribute, which becomes the element name, and value, which contains the words for the button. If the button is named, you can access this element using the button name rather than having to access the element by its position in the elements array. The following code shows how to access a named element that is also contained in a named array:

```
document.theform.theelement.value = "changed title";
```

As you can see from this code, this button's value can be changed in script.

COMPANION Web site Internet Explorer 4.0 also allows you to change the button's appearance using CSS1 attributes. As an example, the file button.htm contains a sampling of the same type of button, but with different style settings. Listing 9.2 contains the source for this example.

Listing 9.2. Applying CSS1 style sheets to several buttons.

```
<HTML>
<HEAD>
<TITLE> Buttons </TITLE>
<STYLE type="text/css">
    #one { color: red; font-weight: bold }
```

```
    #two { color: darkgreen; font-weight: bold;
        background-image: url(snow.jpg);
        width: 200; height: 150 }
    #three { color: firebrick; background-color: ivory;
        border-color: firebrick; font-family: Cursive }
    #four { color: white; background-color: blue;
        border-color: yellow; border-style: groove;
        border-width: 10; width: 200 }
    #five { text-decoration: underline; background-color: green;
        color: lime }
</STYLE>
</HEAD>
<BODY>

<!-- form 1 -->
<FORM name="form1">
<!-- button 1 -->
<input id="one" type=button name="button1" value="Push Me">

<!-- button 2 -->
<input id="two" type=button name="button1" value="Push Me">

<!-- button 3 -->
<input id="three" type=button name="button1" value="Push Me">
<p>

<!-- button 4 -->
<input id="four" type=button name="button1" value="Push Me">

<!-- button 5 -->
<input id="five" type=button name="button1" value="Push Me">

<!-- button 6 -->
<input type=button name="button1" value="Push Me">
</FORM>

</BODY>
```

Figure 9.4 shows what this page looks like. As you can see, different style settings can create very different looks. Though the CSS1 style settings only work with IE at this time, it is likely that Netscape Navigator will support these settings in the future.

THE HTML 4.0 BUTTON ELEMENT

BUTTON is a new element released with the 4.0 HTML draft. This element does not require that the button be embedded within a form. It is a container element and can be used to enclose several different HTML elements such as images, text, or other elements. It creates a button-like effect on anything the element encloses. For an example, see the following BUTTON element definition:

```
<BUTTON
style="background-color: yellow; color: red; font-weight: bold">
```

continues

```
continued

<table border=5>
<tr><td>
<img src="photo6.jpg" align=top>
</td></tr></table>
<p>
Push Me
</p>
</BUTTON>
```

COMPANION Website Figure 9.5 shows the results of this element, and `btnelem.htm` contains the page source code. At this time only IE 4.0 supports the BUTTON element.

Figure 9.4.

The resultant Web page after applying CSS1 style settings to several different button elements.

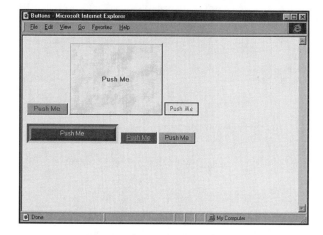

Figure 9.5.

Using the button *element to enclose HTML elements.*

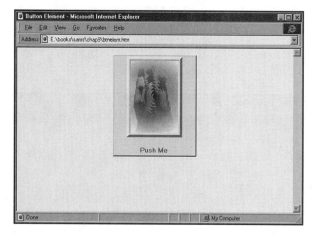

The BUTTON element generates several events such as the onclick event. Trapping for these by providing an event handler for the event and providing code to process the event is covered in Chapter 17, "Using JavaScript for Forms."

Creating a Selection List

A selection list, or drop-down listbox, is really a couple of different elements. The first is the select element, which is the box, and the second is one or more option elements, which contain the box entries. Creating a selection list generates a text-field-sized element with an arrow. Clicking the down arrow in the box next to the list exposes the list elements in a drop-down box big enough to hold all the elements.

As an example of using these elements, you can create a selection list using the following code, which creates the list with four options:

```
<SELECT NAME="selection">
   <OPTION> One
   <OPTION> Two
   <OPTION SELECTED> Three
   <OPTION> Four
</SELECT>
```

The selection list is named selection and the third option, with the text Three, is selected and appears in the box when the page opens. Clicking the arrow associated with the box drops the box down and displays all the items in the list, as shown in Figure 9.6.

FIGURE 9.6.

Web page showing selection list with four options.

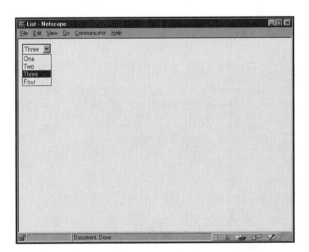

There are three attributes for the SELECT object:

- name—element name
- size—number of options visible when page opens, set to one by default
- multiple—specifies that more than one option can be selected

Options within the list are delimited by the OPTION tag, which has a beginning tag but no ending tag. This element has two attributes, the value attribute, which contains the value submitted with the form if the option is selected, and selected, which selects a specific option when the Web page is opened. The selected item is listed in the top of the box if only one option is displayed when the page opens, or is highlighted within the list. The text that is displayed to the Web page reader for the option follows the OPTION tag.

The selection is accessible in code from the elements array, and the options are accessible from the selection element as the options array, as shown in the following code:

```
document.forms[0].elements[0].options[0].selected;
```

Additionally, options can be added or removed from the selection using the following code:

```
// create option and add to array
newoption = new Option("Displayed Text", value, false, false);
document.forms[0].elements[0].options[num]=newoption;
...
// delete option
document.forms[0].elements[0].options[num]=null;
```

As with the button element in the earlier section, you can also apply CSS1 style attributes to a selection list, though the attributes you can change are more limited. Again, these modifications only work with Internet Explorer 4.x and up. Listing 9.3 contains the source for a Web page with a selection and four options. Style sheets have been applied to the select element and the options. A style sheet class was created and applied to two of the options.

Listing 9.3. Applying CSS1 attributes to a select and option elements.

```
<HTML>
<HEAD>
<TITLE> List </TITLE>
<STYLE type="text/css">
    OPTION{ background-color: lime; color: red}
    OPTION.TWO { background-color: blue; color: yellow }
    SELECT { background-color: red; margin: 1.0in;
            font-family: Fantasy; font-weight: bold;
            font-size: 18pt }
</STYLE>
</HEAD>
<BODY>

<!-- form 1 -->
<FORM name="form1">
<SELECT NAME="selection">
    <OPTION VALUE=1> First Selection
    <OPTION class=TWO VALUE=2> Second Selection
    <OPTION VALUE=3 SELECTED> Third Selection
    <OPTION class=TWO VALUE=4> Fourth Selection
</SELECT>
</FORM>
</BODY>
```

Unlike the button element, many of the style sheet attributes are ignored. If I tried to alter the border for the selection, nothing would happen. The result of this page, shown in Figure 9.7, shows that the font and background colors for the options are changed, as well as the background color for the select element and the margins.

FIGURE 9.7.

A select *element and options, modified using CSS1 attributes.*

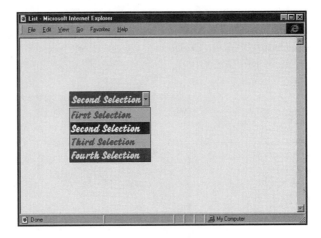

To match the look in the figure, the font for the options was modified. In order to accomplish this, the font style sheet specifications needed to be added to the selection element rather than to the option. If the font information is added to the options, it would be ignored, providing visual proof that some of the presentation information for the options is derived from the parent element, and the rest from the element itself. You can try the example by opening the file select.htm in IE 4.0.

Adding Radio Buttons and Check Boxes to a Web Page

The radio button is a way to provide a set of mutually exclusive choices. Only one button can be checked with the radio button, and clicking one of the buttons deselects any previous selection. Check boxes, on the other hand, provide a method of selecting several mutually inclusive choices. You can select one box or more of the options represented by the boxes.

The radio button usually consists of a small, checked "dot" or triangle and text located next to the dot. Clicking one of the buttons fills in the dot. Check boxes have a box, and clicking it creates a check within the box.

As an example, the following code creates three grouped radio buttons and three check boxes:

```
<!-- radio buttons -->
<INPUT TYPE="radio" NAME="thegroup" VALUE="one" CHECKED> One
<INPUT TYPE="radio" NAME="thegroup" VALUE="two"> Two
```

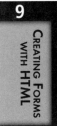

```
<INPUT TYPE="radio" NAME="thegroup" VALUE="three"> Three
<p>
<!-- checkboxes -->
<INPUT TYPE="checkbox" NAME="ckbox1" VALUE="checkone" CHECKED>Check One
<INPUT TYPE="checkbox" NAME="ckbox2" VALUE="checktwo">Check Two
<INPUT TYPE="checkbox" NAME="ckbox3" VALUE="checkthree" CHECKED>Check Three
```

Notice that a major difference between radio button and the check box use is that the radio buttons' names are all the same. This groups the buttons so that selecting one deselects the previous selection. This isn't necessary for the check boxes. Figure 9.8 shows the Web page with these form elements.

Figure 9.8.

A Web page with three related radio buttons and three check boxes.

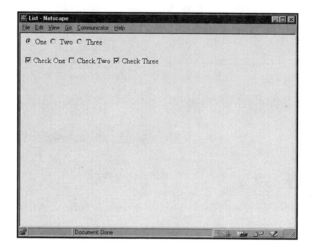

The attributes for both elements are the same. Both are created using the INPUT element, and the type attribute creates each different type of control. The name attribute for the radio button has the group name, but for the check box, name is the name of the individual control. Both attributes have a CHECKED attribute, which selects the control. Only one applies to the radio button group, but all the check boxes can be checked. Conversely, one of the radio buttons must be checked, but none of the check boxes needs to be selected.

As just noted, each of the radio buttons has the same name, which forms them into a group. What would happen if each of the check boxes was also given the same name? When one or more input elements is given the same name, they become their own array. Each individual control is then accessed as an array element. To demonstrate this, Listing 9.4 has the source for a Web page with one form that contains three check boxes and one push button. Each of the three check box controls is given the same name, and when you select the button, a function that prints out the value of each check box and whether it is checked or not is called.

Listing 9.4. Form with three identically named check boxes forming a named array.

```
<HTML>
<HEAD>
<TITLE> List </TITLE>
<SCRIPT language="javascript">
<!--

// iterate through checkboxes and print
// out status
function iterate() {
   var strng = "";
   var control = document.forms[0].ckbox1;
   for (i = 0; i < control.length; i++) {
    strng = "Control " + control[i].value;
    if (control[i].checked)
       alert(strng + " is checked");
    else
       alert(strng + " is not checked");
   }
}
//-->
</SCRIPT>
</HEAD>
<BODY>

<!-- form 1 -->
<center>
<FORM name="form1">
<p>
<!-- checkboxes -->
<INPUT TYPE="checkbox" NAME="ckbox1" VALUE="checkone" CHECKED>Check One
<INPUT TYPE="checkbox" NAME="ckbox1" VALUE="checktwo">Check Two
<INPUT TYPE="checkbox" NAME="ckbox1" VALUE="checkthree" CHECKED>Check Three
<p>
<INPUT TYPE="button" VALUE="Checkbox Status" onclick="iterate()">
</FORM>
</center>
</BODY>
```

COMPANION
Web site As you can see from the code, the check boxes' names are the same, and the function accesses these controls by their array index. You can try this code yourself by accessing the file ckbox.htm. This is a useful technique when you have a larger form that can have several different check boxes, and which you may add to and drop over time. As an example of using this automatic array creation, you could use the text within the VALUE attribute to act as an array index into another array and then use code to only access those array entries that are checked, as the following code demonstrates:

```
var tmp = document.forms[0].ckbox1;
if (tmp[0].checked)
    new_array[tmp[0].value] = ...
```

9

CREATING FORMS
WITH HTML

With this technique the form elements can change over time with a minimum of code change necessary to compensate for the changing number of elements.

Uploading Files with `fileupload`

The `fileupload` element provides a means for the Web page reader to specify a file for loading to the Web server. When you create one of these controls, a text box for the filename and a button labeled Browse… are created within the Web page. The Web page reader can type a filename and path into the box or click the Browse button to select a file. When the form is submitted, the file is also appended to the form data being sent to the server.

Listing 9.5 contains an example of using the `fileupload` control. Notice that the form attributes have changed to accommodate this type of control.

Listing 9.5. `fileupload` example, with form attributes set to support this type of element.

```
<HTML>
<HEAD>
<TITLE> File Upload </TITLE>

</HEAD>
<BODY>

<!-- form 1 -->
<FORM name="form1" ACTION="results.htm" METHOD="GET"
 ENCTYPE="multipart/form-data">

<INPUT TYPE="file" NAME="FileUpload">
<p>
<INPUT TYPE="submit">
</FORM>

</BODY>
```

COMPANION Web site   To support file uploading, `enctype` is set to `multipart/form-data`, which is the appropriate MIME type for a form containing a `fileupload` control. Submitting the form from this Web page using a local Web server, you get a `501 Not Supported` error because the URL listed with the `action` attribute is not a CGI application and does not support this type of control. You can try this yourself by opening the file `fileup.htm`. However, if you remove the `enctype` attribute and resubmit the page, you get a result similar to that shown in Figure 9.9. Note the data appended to the URL in the Location window.

You want to use the `multipart/form-data enctype` when using `fileupload`. Chapters 24, "Putting your Server to Work," through 26, "The Anatomy of a CGI Application," cover the CGI applications that would process form data such as this.

Figure 9.9.

Web page displayed after submitting form with fileupload *control.*

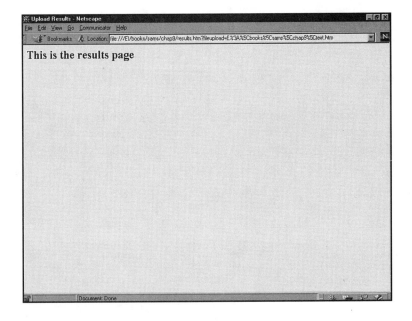

Accessing Text with the Text Controls: text, textarea, and password

The text, textarea, and password input elements are all methods of accessing text from the Web page reader. The text element provides for single-line text values such as a name, and textarea provides a control that can accept a block of text several words wide and several lines long. The password element hides the value being entered with the usual display of asterisks.

To demonstrate the similarities and differences, between these three controls, the following code sample shows a form with one of each:

```
<INPUT TYPE="text" VALUE="Enter Information Here" NAME="text1" size=80>
<p>
<TEXTAREA ROWS=20 COLS=50> </TEXTAREA>
<p>
<INPUT TYPE="password" SIZE=20>
```

Each of these controls has a name attribute, which becomes the specific element's name. The password and text controls have a size attribute that controls the width of the control. The value specified is how many characters can be displayed, using current font, without the element scrolling. The textarea control has two values to control its size: rows for the number of lines (it defines the control's height), and cols for the number of characters (it defines the control's width). Figure 9.10 shows these three controls with content entered into the textarea and password controls, and the default text showing in the text control.

9

CREATING FORMS WITH HTML

FIGURE 9.10.

Three HTML INPUT *elements, a* text *control, a* textarea *control, and a* password *control.*

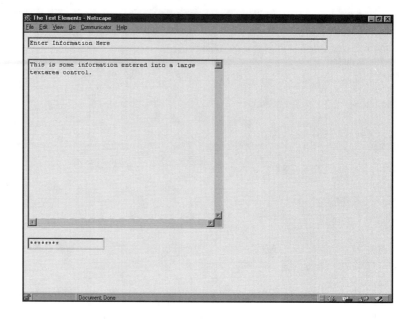

These controls can be modified with the use of CSS positioning and style attributes, though most uses of these attributes currently only work with IE 4.x. Listing 9.6 contains a form with a Text, TextArea, and Password control. Each of these elements has an associated label, and the positioning of the elements in relation to each other and their label is controlled through the use of an HTML table. The table is enclosed within a DIV block and CSS positioning is used to position the form within the Web page. Up to this point, the source code for the page works with both Navigator and IE. However, CSS1 attributes are used to alter the appearance of the labels and the text associated with the controls, and surround the elements with an aqua box, which is surrounded with a red border.

Listing 9.6. Form with text fields, with presentation and position controlled through CSS-P attributes.

```
<HTML>
<HEAD>
<TITLE> The Text Controls </TITLE>
<STYLE type="text/css">
    #formlayout { background-color: aqua;
            border-color: red; border-style: groove; border-width: 6;
            padding: 10;
            position:absolute; left: 50; top: 50; width: 600 }
    TD.label { width: 150; text-align: right;
            color: red; font-family: Univers; font-size: 18pt }
    TD.control { text-align: left }
    INPUT { color: red;  font-family: Cursive; font-style: italic;
            font-size: 18pt }
</STYLE>
</HEAD>
<BODY>

<!-- form 1 -->
```

```
<DIV id="formlayout">
<FORM name="form1" ACTION="results.htm" METHOD="GET">
<TABLE cols=2 border=0 cellspacing=10>

<!-- first row -->
<tr><td class=label>Enter your name:</td>
<td class=control>
<INPUT NAME="personname" id="first" type="text" size=50></td></tr>

<!-- second row -->
<tr><td class=label>Enter your address:</td>
<td class=control>
<TEXTAREA NAME="address" id="second" rows=10 cols=50
style="color:maroon; font-family: sans-serif; font-variant: small-caps">
</TEXTAREA>
</td></tr>

<!-- third row -->
<tr><td class=label>Enter your password:</td>
<td class=control><INPUT TYPE="password" NAME="psswrd" ID="third" size=20></td>
</tr>
</table>
</FORM>
</DIV>

</BODY>
```

The Web page appears similar to that shown in Figure 9.11. Text is entered in all three fields to demonstrate the impact of the CSS1 style-sheet settings. Note that the name element has a script-like effect (at least in Windows 95), and the address remains in small caps regardless of how the reader enters the information.

COMPANION **Web**site The colors have also been altered to complement the background's and border's colors. This form is much more attractive and has much more visual appeal than the one created without using CSS1. Using these attributes does not prevent the form from showing correctly with Navigator, as shown in Figure 9.12. The result is that the form does not show in the same manner as that shown with IE. You can try this for yourself by opening the file text.htm.

GETTING THE CSS1 ATTRIBUTES TO WORK

Note that whatever element is embedded in what other element can impact on what does or does not show. If you exchange the embedding positions of the FORM and DIV elements, embedding the DIV block within the FORM block, the form elements do not show correctly with Navigator 4.x.

Also note that sometimes CSS1 attributes must be applied directly into the element, using the inline style technique, in order for them to work. As an example, in Listing 9.6 the style sheet for the TEXTAREA element is placed directly into the element. Placing this information into the STYLE block at the top of the page did not work correctly, at least with the version of IE 4.0 used at the time this was written.

9

CREATING FORMS
WITH HTML

FIGURE 9.11.

A form with text elements, using CSS positioning and attributes and shown in IE.

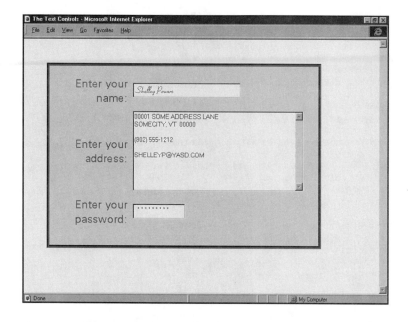

FIGURE 9.12.

A form with the same elements and CSS attributes as the Web page shown in Figure 9.11, but presented in Navigator.

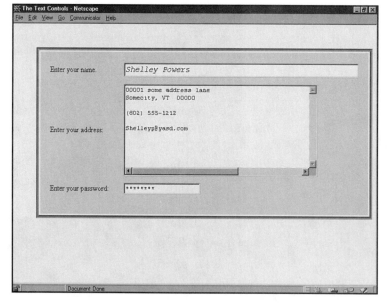

Creating Interpage Persistence with the `hidden` Element

There is a great trick to use when maintaining information persistently between the Web server application and the Web pages showing on the client. This technique is accomplished using the `hidden` form element.

The `hidden` form element is an element that contains information stored within the Web page but not displayed to the Web page reader. It is created using the following syntax:

```
<INPUT type="hidden" name="somevalue" value="the hidden text">
```

CGI and Web server applications can use the hidden field as a way of storing persistent information from page to Web page, by generating the hidden field within a form on each Web page the application generates. If the Web site has a shopping cart application, as an example, as the reader moves from page to page, each Web page is generated as they access the page, and each one includes the hidden field as part of the page. This can maintain information such as the customer ID or order information.

Another technique is to use Netscape cookies, covered in more detail in Chapter 32, "Saving User Preferences: Cookies and OPS."

Submitting and Resetting the Form with `submit` and `reset`

The final two traditional HTML form elements discussed are `submit` and `reset`. These two `INPUT` elements submit the form to the form processing application, or reset the form values, respectively.

To create either of these elements, the following code is used:

```
<INPUT TYPE="submit" VALUE="Send Form">
<INPUT TYPE="reset" VALUE="Reset Form Values">
```

Using the `submit` element submits the form. An alternative approach could be to create some other element, and based on trapping an element event, issue the form `submit` method, as shown here:

```
document.forms[0].submit();
```

The reset button clears the form elements from all values that the Web page reader has entered within a page session. This is an important button to use, particularly if the form is large and the reader may want to start over. An alternative approach to using the `reset` control is to trap some other event and issue the form `reset` method, as shown here:

```
document.forms[0].reset();
```

Either using the element or invoking the form methods works equally well.

Working with the New HTML 4.0 Form Elements and Extensions

The HTML 4.0 draft specification was issued in July of 1997 and has several new form elements and form element attributes. This section details each of these.

> **NOTE**
>
> Note that the information covered in this section is based on a W3C draft recommendation, which may go through changes before the recommended specification is released. These changes could impact the accuracy of the content of this section.

label, image, and fieldset are the three new HTML 4.0 form elements. The label element is used to provide a label for a control, such as the text or textarea controls discussed earlier in this chapter. The image control creates an image-based control that can be clicked in a manner similar to a button. The fieldset control is an element that provides a visual grouping of other form elements, such as a group of radio buttons.

accesskey, tabindex, disabled, and readonly are the new HTML 4.0 element attributes. The accesskey attribute can be used to associate an accelerator key with a specific form element. *Accelerator keys* are single keys, such as the letter A for address, that when used in conjunction with the Alt key, move the focus to the element that is associated with the specific accelerator key.

The disabled attribute disables the focus from an element and prevents that same element's value from being submitted with the form. You also cannot enter a value, or select a value from that element. The readonly attribute prevents any changes to an element. It is there to be read but not changed.

The tabindex attribute associates a specific tab order with an element. With this, you have a greater degree of control in the flow the Web page reader takes through a form.

To demonstrate all of these new elements and attributes, the sample source page shown in Listing 9.6 has been altered to include three radio buttons. The source for this new page is shown in Listing 9.7.

Listing 9.7. HTML 4.0 attribute page.

```
<HTML>
<HEAD>
<TITLE> The Text Controls </TITLE>
<STYLE type="text/css">
    #formlayout { background-color: aqua;
            border-color: red; border-style: groove; border-width: 6;
```

```
              padding: 10;
              position:absolute; left: 10; top: 10; width: 600 }
     TD.label { width: 150; text-align: right;
            color: red; font-family: Univers; font-size: 18pt }
     TD.control { text-align: left }
     INPUT { color: red;  font-family: Cursive; font-style: italic;
            font-size: 14pt }
</STYLE>
</HEAD>
<BODY>

<!-- form 1 -->
<DIV id="formlayout">
<FORM name="form1" ACTION="results.htm" METHOD="GET">
<TABLE cols=2 border=0 cellspacing=10>

<!-- first row -->
<tr><td width=150 class=label><LABEL for="first" accesskey="N">
Enter your <SPAN style="text-decoration: underline">N</SPAN>ame:
</LABEL></td>

<td class=control>
<INPUT tabindex=2 NAME="personname" id="first" type="text" size=50></td></tr>

<!-- second row -->
<tr><td class=label><LABEL disabled for="second" accesskey="A">
Enter your <SPAN style="text-decoration: underline">A</SPAN>ddress:
</LABEL></a></td>

<td class=control>
<TEXTAREA disabled tabindex=3 NAME="address" id="second" rows=10 cols=50
style="color:maroon; font-family: sans-serif; font-variant: small-caps">
</TEXTAREA>
</td></tr>

<!-- third row -->
<tr><td class=label><LABEL for="third" accesskey="P">
Enter your <SPAN style="text-decoration: underline">P</span>assword:</LABEL>
</td>
<td class=control>
<INPUT tabindex=1 TYPE="password" NAME="psswrd" ID="third" size=20></td></tr>

<!-- fourth row -->
<tr><td colspan=2 class=label>
<FIELDSET>
<LEGEND align=left>Color Preferences:</LEGEND>
<INPUT type="radio" name="colors" value="Blue" CHECKED>Blue
<INPUT type="radio" name="colors" value="Red">Red
<INPUT type="radio" name="colors" value="Green">Green
</FIELDSET>
</td></tr>
<tr><td class=label colspan=2>This image is actually a button
<INPUT type="IMAGE" SRC="box4.gif" ALT="button"></td></tr></table>
</FORM>
</DIV>
</BODY>
```

COMPANION **Web site** A `label` element is added to `name`, `address`, and `password`, and set to the accelerator key, via the `accesskey` attribute, to N, A, and P, respectively. A `tabindex` is also added to these three fields, setting the first tab to the password, then name, and finally address fields. Three radio buttons are added and enclosed within a `fieldset` element. A legend is added to `fieldset` to identify the groupings for the elements. At the bottom of the form an `image input` element with its own label is added. Lastly, the password field is disabled, meaning that it can no longer receive mouse or keyboard events. Figure 9.13 shows the page with these new elements, and you can access the source from the file `html40.htm`. As stated earlier in this chapter, these new HTML 4.0 elements do not, at this time, work with Navigator 4.x.

FIGURE 9.13.

Web page showing some of the new HTML 4.0 elements.

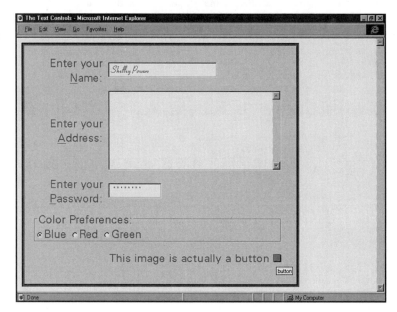

Summary

This chapter reviews the use of HTML forms and examines each of the HTML forms elements.

The push button and selection elements are detailed and demonstrated as are the check boxes and radio buttons. Additionally, the similarities and differences among the `text`, `textarea`, and `password` elements are demonstrated. How hidden fields can be used for persistence is briefly discussed, as is using the `submit` and `reset` elements to submit the form contents and reset the form contents, respectively. Several of the elements are demonstrated using CSS attributes to alter their appearance, position them within the Web page, or both.

Finally, the new HTML 4.0 elements such as `fieldset`, `label`, `legend`, and `image` are discussed in addition to the `accesskey`, `tabindex`, `disabled`, and `readonly` attributes.

Chapter 17, "Using JavaScript for Forms," covers using JavaScript with forms and form elements.

Frames and Framesets

by Shelley Powers

IN THIS CHAPTER

Frames have been and still are one of the most controversial HTML elements, inspiring either great interest or great loathing.

HTML frames slip the Web page window into separate window views, each capable of holding a different HTML document. Used correctly, frames are a terrific technique for displaying a site map or other supporting Web pages, accessible from all Web pages. Used incorrectly, they waste valuable space by holding useless graphics or other content.

This chapter discusses how to wisely create and use HTML frames and what some of the issues are with using frames. This chapter also discusses how to load pages from external sites so that these pages don't load within the frame. Finally, the new HTML 4.0 IFRAME element is demonstrated, which creates a frame within a Web page.

Creating and Working with Frames

Frame windows are made from more than one HMTL file. One file contains the FRAMESET definition, including which source files make up the frames and how much space each will occupy. This file also contains the NOFRAME element, if the FRAMESET element is used.

The FRAMESET Element

COMPANION
Web site
As an example of a FRAMESET, the code in Listing 10.1 creates a frame window with two frames, each created as a row. The first frame takes up 80 pixels of the window's height, and the second takes up the remainder. The listing also contains the code for the main.htm and menu.htm files.

Listing 10.1. Frameset with two frames.

```
// parent1.htm
<HTML>
<FRAMESET rows="80, *">
    <FRAME SRC="menu1.htm">
    <FRAME SRC="main1.htm">
</FRAMESET>
</HTML>

// main1.htm
<HTML>
<HEAD>
<STYLE type="text/css">
    body { background-color: black;
           color: yellow;
         margin: 0.1in 0.4in }
</STYLE>
</HEAD>
<BODY>
<H1> Main Body </H1>
The top part of this window is the menu frame, and the rest of the window
is taken up with the main window text, such as this.
</BODY>
```

```
// menu1.htm
<HTML>
<HEAD>
<STYLE type="text/css">
    body { background-color: white }
    #heading1 { color: yellow; position:absolute;
            left: 15; top: 10; font-size: 24pt }
    #heading2 { color: black; position:absolute;
            left: 17; top: 12; font-size: 24pt }

</STYLE>
</HEAD>
<BODY>
<SPAN id="heading1">Welcome</SPAN>
<SPAN id="heading2">Welcome</SPAN>
<img align=right src="menu.jpg" width=504 height=57>

</BODY>
```

The only element this frame parent file has is the FRAMESET, which is creating the two frames. Figure 10.1 shows the page split into the two frames.

FIGURE 10.1.

Web page with frame window consisting of two frames: a menu frame and a main body frame.

The FRAMESET element's attributes are rows, which sets the number of rows each frame within the frameset will occupy, and cols, which sets the width of each frame. In the example just shown, the frameset creates two frames that occupy the width of the page. The first is set to a specific value, which is 80 pixels. The second is set to a value of *, which instructs the browser to assign to the second frame the remaining height of the Web page. If the page were 200 pixels, the second frame would occupy 120 pixels. If the page were 400 pixels, the second frame would occupy 320 pixels, and so on.

You can specify that each frame occupy the same amount of space, using the following code:

```
<FRAMESET rows="*, *">
    <FRAME SRC="menu.htm">
    <FRAME SRC="main.htm">
</FRAMESET>
```

Figure 10.2 shows the result of this action. Notice that both frames occupy an equal amount of space.

FIGURE 10.2.

Web page using `Frameset` *to Create two equal-sized frames.*

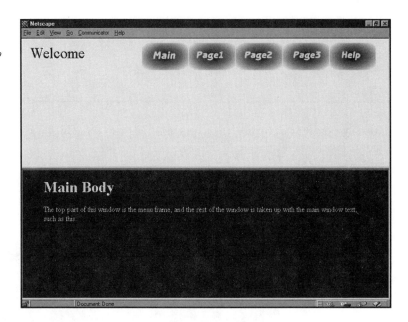

Instead of creating two rows, you can also create two columns and load the Web page contents into each. The following code shows how to create two frames as side-by-side columns:

```
<FRAMESET cols="80, *">
    <FRAME SRC="menu.htm">
    <FRAME SRC="main.htm">
</FRAMESET>
```

Nested Framesets

Sometimes you might want to create nested framesets, which are framesets that contain other framesets in addition to frames. You might use this technique to show a split menu frame window at the top or side of a page, and the body of the Web page occupying the rest of the space.

COMPANION **Web site** To create nested framesets, instead of specifying a FRAME element as one of the frameset elements, you specify another FRAMESET. Listing 10.2 shows one frameset nested within another. The outer frameset creates two rows, and the inner creates three columns from the last row. The listing also demonstrates that HTML files are not the only source

that can be loaded into a frameset window. The source code for this listing can be found in
`crystals.htm`.

Listing 10.2. A frameset nested within another frameset.

```
<HTML>
<FRAMESET rows="*, 250">
    <FRAME SRC="main.htm">
    <FRAMESET cols="225,225,*">
        <FRAME SRC="cinnabar1.JPG">
        <FRAME SRC="barite1.JPG">
        <FRAME SRC="cerussite1.JPG">
    </FRAMESET>
</FRAMESET>
</HTML>
```

The result of this nested frameset is shown in Figure 10.3. Note that when an image is loaded
directly into a browser *window,* or frame, the background around the image is set to whatever
the default browser background color is.

FIGURE 10.3.

Web page showing the results of a nested frameset and loading images directly into frames.

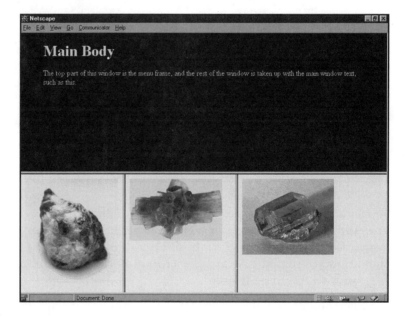

The FRAME Element

In the previous examples, you have used the FRAME element and supplied a value for the src
attribute, but have not used any other frame attributes. There are several frame attributes, given
in Table 10.1.

Table 10.1. Frame element attributes.

Attribute	Short Description	Long Description
name	Frame name	This can be used with script to direct content or actions to one specific frame.
src	Frame source	This forms the contents of the frame window, and may be an HTML file or other content, such as an image.
frameborder	Frame border	Setting this value to 1, which is the default, draws a border around the frame; setting the value to 0 removes the border.
noresize	Frame resizing	Using this attribute turns off frame resizing.
marginwidth	Frame horizontal margin	Setting this value provides whitespace for the frame's left and right margins.
marginheight	Frame vertical margin	Setting this value provides whitespace for the frame's top and bottom margins.
scrolling	Frame scroll bars	Setting this value to auto provides scrolling only when frame content does not fit within frame space. Setting this value to yes always provides a scroll bar. Setting this value to no always turns off the scroll bar.

If you want to direct code or content to any specific frame, you can access the frame using the frames array, or you can access the frame by its name. To provide a "frameless" look, set the frameborder attribute to 0, and set the scrolling attribute to no, to make sure no scrollbars show. However, you also have to make sure that the contents of the frame are displayed, totally, when the frame page is loaded.

To demonstrate some of these attributes, the original frame example shown in Listing 10.1 is modified. The menu image is turned into a client-side imagemap using the MAP and AREA elements, and code is added to call a function when the mouse is over any one of the image's "buttons." Two scripting blocks are included, one using the Javascript1.2 language, and one using JScript, IE's scripting language. The JScript block is placed after the JavaScript 1.2 block so that IE picks up the JScript block. Navigator ignores the JScript block.

> **NOTE**
>
> A default behavior for both Navigator and IE is to access the function in the bottommost scripting block that the browser is capable of parsing. This is a handy fact to remember when providing different code for the same function for two different browsers.

The function that is called from the mouseover event modifies an element in the main frame page, using the Navigator layer write technique for Navigator, and the innerHTML attribute for IE. Both of these are discussed in more detail in Chapters 30, "Using the HTML Object Model and Creating Dynamic HTML Pages," through 32, "Saving User Preferences: Cookies and OPS." But for now, these techniques replace existing content with new HTML content. The replacement HTML provides a message that states which image map button the mouse is over. Listing 10.3 contains the source for the parent HTML file, which creates the frameset, and the two frame windows.

Listing 10.3. FRAMESET page creating two frames, both without borders and without scroll bars.

```
<!-- Main Frameset HTML page parent2.htm -->
<HTML>
<FRAMESET rows="*,80">
    <FRAME SRC=main2.htm NAME="workFrame"
        frameborder=0 scrolling=no>
    <FRAME SRC=menu2.htm NAME="menuFrame"
        frameborder=0 scrolling=no>
</FRAMESET>
</HTML>

<!-- Main Frame Page main2.htm-->
<HTML>
<HEAD>
<STYLE type="text/css">
    body { background-color: black;
            color: yellow;
        margin: 0.1in 0.4in }
    H2 { color: lime; font-size: 48pt;
        font-family: Cursive; font-style: italic     }
</STYLE>
</HEAD>
<BODY>
<H1> Main Body </H1>
<DIV id="content" style="position:absolute; left:50; top:100; color: lime">
<h1> Starting Contents</h1>
</DIV>
</BODY>

<!-- Main menu page menu2.htm -->
<HTML>
<HEAD>
<STYLE type="text/css">
```

continues

10

FRAMES AND FRAMESETS

Listing 10.3. continued

```
    body { background-color: white }
    #heading { color: yellow; position:absolute;
          left: 15; top: 10; font-size: 24pt }
    #heading2 { color: black; position:absolute;
          left: 17; top: 12; font-size: 24pt }

</STYLE>
<SCRIPT language="javascript1.2">
<!--
// change layer to reflect image map mouse position
function change_content(item) {
    strng = "<H2> Over " + item + "</h2>";
    parent.workFrame.document.content.
        document.write(strng);
    parent.workFrame.document.content.document.
        close();
}
//-->
</SCRIPT>

<SCRIPT language="jscript">
<!--
// change layer to reflect image map mouse position
function change_content(item) {
    strng = "<H2> Over " + item + "</h2>";
    parent.workFrame.content.innerHTML = strng;
}
//-->
</SCRIPT>
</HEAD>
<BODY>
<map name=menu>
<area shape=rect coords="0,0,100,57" href="#test" onMouseOver=
➥"change_content('main')">
<area shape=rect coords="101,0,201,57" href= "#test" onMouseOver=
➥"change_content('page1')">
<area shape=rect coords= "202,0,302,57" href= "#test" onMouseOver=
➥"change_content('page2')">
<area shape=rect coords="303,0,403,57" href="#test" onMouseOver=
➥"change_content('page3')">
<area shape=rect coords= "404,0,504,57" href="#test" onMouseOver=
➥"change_content('help')">
<area shape=default href="#test" onMouseOver="change_content('menu page')">
</map>

<img align=right src="menu.jpg" width=504 height=57
    onclick="change_content()" usemap="#menu" border=0>
<SPAN id="heading">Welcome</SPAN>
<SPAN id="heading2">Welcome</SPAN>

</BODY>
```

COMPANION **Web site** Each of the frames was named when created. The scripting function `change_content` uses the frame name to access the frame contents in order to change the displayed text for the document DIV block. Additionally, the frames are created without borders and scroll bars, giving the page a frameless look. In actuality, the Web page reader will not know that the page had a frame unless they view the page source. Figure 10.4 shows the Web page frames when the mouse is over one of the menu items. You can also access this example by opening the file parent2.htm.

FIGURE 10.4.

Page with two frame windows without a frame border or scrollbars.

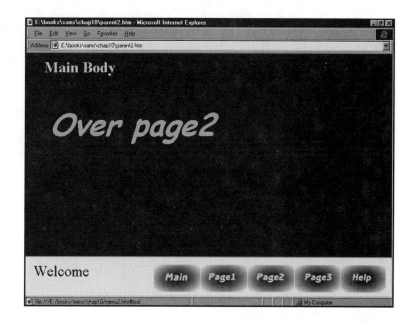

With IE 4.0, you can also add a style sheet to the parent window and create a colorful border for the frames. Figure 10.5 shows the same frames from Listing 10.3, but with the following parent page source:

```
<HTML>
<HEAD>
<STYLE type="text/css">
    FRAME { border-width: 5; border-style: groove;
            border-color: red }
</STYLE>
</HEAD>
<FRAMESET rows="*,80">
    <FRAME SRC=main2.htm NAME="workFrame"
        frameborder=0 scrolling=no>
    <FRAME SRC=menu2.htm NAME="menuFrame"
        frameborder=0 scrolling=no>
</FRAMESET>
</HTML>
```

COMPANION
Web site   Note, though, that adding this style sheet to the FRAMESET page prevents the page from loading correctly with Navigator 4.x. You can try this variation of the FRAMESET page by opening the file parent2ie.htm.

10

FRAMES AND
FRAMESETS

FIGURE 10.5.

Adding a style sheet to frame parent to alter the type of border shown for the frame windows.

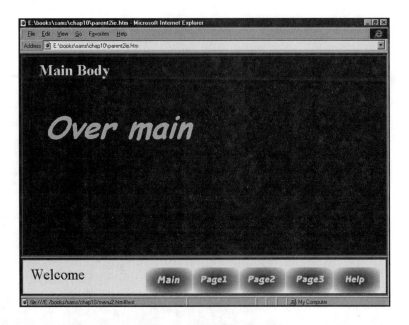

THE NOFRAMES ELEMENT

You can use the NOFRAMES element to provide content for those browsers that do not support frames, or browsers that do support frames and the frames have been turned off. An effective approach to using this element is to include a reference to a non-frames page that the reader can click to see the site contents. The following demonstrates this:

```
<NOFRAMES>
This site uses frames. Click <a href="content.htm">here</a>
to see a non-frames version of this site.
</NOFRAMES>
```

Browsers that support frames should ignore NOFRAMES, except, as stated earlier, when the reader has turned off frames (if that is a browser option).

Accessing External References from Frames

One disadvantage with using frames is that the Back or Forward buttons have seldom worked correctly with frame-based content. The open question is, when the reader presses the Back button, did he or she want to go to the page before the FRAMESET window, or did he or she want to go to the page previous to the page in the frame that currently has focus? Both Navigator 4.0 and IE 4.0 provide better frame navigation, but you still might want to code navigation directly into the frame page.

Another disadvantage to using frames is that including a hypertext link within a frame page to a Web page at an external Web site loads that page into the frame, rather than directly into the browser window. If that page, in turn, had frames, it got confusing as to which frame was for what page. Also, most people think it is discourteous to load others' Web pages into another Web site's frame-based setup. To work around this problem, there are techniques to redirecting links in such a way that you can control whether a page loads into the parent window, the frame, or even into a brand new browser window.

To demonstrate both frames-based navigation and re-directing links, the two-frame example presented previously in this chapter is modified to incorporate several different URL-loading techniques. Several new HTML pages map to the `Main`, `Page1`, `Page2`, `Page3`, and `Help` menu items on the menu bar. In each of these pages, there are links to take the reader through the frame pages, and links to external sites (note that these external site links are real and contain references to several Dynamic HTML pages). Several different techniques are used to redirect page loading.

The link elements (`A`, `LINK`), imagemap (`AREA`), and form elements all share an attribute called `target`. This attribute contains the location of the browser window that holds the loaded Web page or contents. There are several different reserved keywords that can serve as the `target` attribute value:

- `blank`—loads page to new unnamed window
- `self`—loads page to current frame or window
- `parent`—loads page to parent window if frame, or to current window
- `top`—loads page to original window, or if current window is original window, to current window

In addition, pages can be loaded to another frame by specifying the frame's name, or they can be loaded to a new named window by specifying the window's name.

First, I created the new `FRAMESET` page, named parent3.htm, which creates two frame windows, one for the main Web page and one for the menu. This is really no different than previous `FRAMESET` pages described in this chapter, except that I allow scrolling in the main Web page frame, as shown in the following code:

```
<HTML>
<FRAMESET rows="*,80">
    <FRAME SRC=main3.htm NAME="workFrame"
        frameborder=0>
    <FRAME SRC=menu3.htm NAME="menuFrame"
        frameborder=0 scrolling=no>
</FRAMESET>
</HTML>
```

Next, the menu Web page is modified to load the appropriate Web page when the Web page reader moves his or her mouse over the associated menu button, as shown in Listing 10.4.

10

FRAMES AND FRAMESETS

Listing 10.4. Menu page that loads the page associated with menu items into work frame.

```
<HTML>
<HEAD>
<STYLE type="text/css">
    body { background-color: white }
    #heading { color: yellow; position:absolute;
            left: 15; top: 10; font-size: 24pt }
    #heading2 { color: black; position:absolute;
            left: 17; top: 12; font-size: 24pt }

</STYLE>
<SCRIPT language="javascript">
<!--
// change layer to reflect image map mouse position
function change_content(item) {
    parent.workFrame.location = item + ".htm";
}
//-->
</SCRIPT>

</HEAD>
<BODY>
<map name=menu>
<area shape=rect coords="0,0,100,57" href="#test"
    onMouseOver="change_content('main3')">
<area shape=rect coords="101,0,201,57" href= "#test"
    onMouseOver="change_content('page1')">
<area shape=rect coords= "202,0,302,57" href="#test"
    onMouseOver="change_content('page2')">
<area shape=rect coords="303,0,403,57" href="#test"
    onMouseOver="change_content('page3')">
<area shape=rect coords= "404,0,504,57" href="#test"
    onMouseOver="change_content('help')">
<area shape=default href="#test" onMouseOver="change_content('menu page')">
</map>

<img align=right src="menu.jpg" width=504 height=57
    onclick="change_content()" usemap="#menu" border=0>
<SPAN id="heading">Welcome</SPAN>
<SPAN id="heading2">Welcome</SPAN>

</BODY>
```

COMPANION **Web site** As the code shows, moving the mouse over the menu item calls a function with an associated page name. This name is concatenated to the extension .htm and is set to the work frame's location attribute, automatically loading the associated page. You can view this source code directly in menu3.htm.

COMPANION **Web site** Next, the first page, the main Web page, is created for the work frame window. The file is titled main3.htm, and the source for this page is shown in Listing 10.5.

Listing 10.5. Main Web page in file `main3.htm`.

```
<HTML>
<HEAD>
<STYLE type="text/css">
    body { background-color: black;
           color: yellow;
        margin: 0.1in 0.4in }
    A { color: magenta }
    CAPTION { color: red ; font-size: 18pt; font-weight: bold }
</STYLE>
<BASE TARGET="_top">
</HEAD>
<BODY>
<TABLE align=center width=90% CELLPADDING=5 cellspacing=5
frame=none rules=none align=center>
<CAPTION align=top>Internet Explorer and Navigator Dynamic HTML links</CAPTION>
<tr><td>
<a href="page1.htm" TARGET=_self>This Site - Page 1</a>
</TD></TR>

<tr><td>
<a href="http://www.w3.org/pub/WWW/TR/WD-positioning">
W3C Positioning Draft</a>
Positioning HTML Elements with Cascade Style Sheets
</TD></TR>

<TR><TD>
<a href="http://www.microsoft.com/ie/ie40/">
Internet Explorer 4.0 Platform Preview</a>
</TD></TR>

<TR><TD>
<a href="http://www.microsoft.com/ie/ie40/authors/">
IE 4.0 Authors/Developers page</a>
</TD></TR>
</TABLE>

</BODY>
```

Notice that the page contains one navigational link to the next page in the Web site series, and several links to external sources. The BASE element redirects the external references to the topmost window. When using the BASE element and the target attribute, any element with an associate target attribute redirects the page loading to the value specified for the BASE element (unless this is overridden by using the target attribute directly in the element itself). With the main page, the "navigational" link uses the target attribute to set the page to self, meaning that the page loads into the current frame. Because they have not specified the target attribute, all the other links load directly into the topmost original window. Figure 10.6 shows the browser window after clicking the navigational link to go to the page labeled Page 1.

FIGURE 10.6.

*Frames example after
clicking navigational
link from main page.*

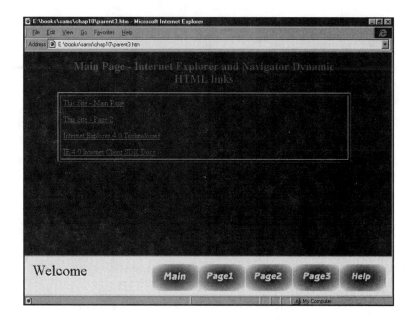

The Page 1 contents page is shown in Listing 10.6.

Listing 10.6. Page 1 source for frames example.

```
<HTML>
<HEAD>
<STYLE type="text/css">
    body { background-color: black;
           color: yellow;
         margin: 0.1in 0.4in }
    A { color: magenta }
    CAPTION { color: red ; font-size: 18pt; font-weight: bold }
</STYLE>
</HEAD>
<BODY>
<TABLE align=center width=90% CELLPADDING=5 cellspacing=5
frame=none rules=none align=center>
<CAPTION align=top>Main Page - Internet Explorer and
➡Navigator Dynamic HTML links</CAPTION>
<tr><td>
<a href="main3.htm">This Site - Main Page</a>
</TD></TR>

<tr><td>
<a href="page2.htm">This Site - Page 2</a>
</TD></TR>

<TR><TD>
</a><a href="http://www.microsoft.com/sitebuilder/workshop/prog/ie4/"
target="_top">
Internet Explorer 4.0 Technologies</a></TD>
</TD></TR>
```

```
<TR><TD>
<a href="http://www.microsoft.com/workshop/prog/inetsdk/docs/"
target="_top">IE 4.0 Internet Client SDK Docs</a>
</TD></TR>

</TABLE>

</BODY>
```

A different technique redirects page loading with this page. The `target` attribute is coded for the two external links, and the default targeting is used for the two navigational links. As the `target` attribute is set to `self` by default, the two navigational links load directly into the frame. The two external links load into the topmost browser window. `page1.htm` is shown in Listing 10.6.

`page2.htm` is next, and the source for this is shown in Listing 10.7.

Listing 10.7. Page 2 source from file `page2.htm`.

```
<HTML>
<HEAD>
<STYLE type="text/css">
    body { background-color: black;
             color: yellow;
        margin: 0.1in 0.4in }
    A { color: magenta }
    CAPTION { color: red ; font-size: 18pt; font-weight: bold }
</STYLE>
<BASE TARGET="newwindow">
</HEAD>
<BODY>
<TABLE align=center width=90% CELLPADDING=5 cellspacing=5
frame=none rules=none align=center>
<CAPTION align=top>Main Page - Internet Explorer and
Navigator Dynamic HTML links</CAPTION>
<tr><td>
<a href="page1.htm" target="_self">This Site - Page 1</a>
</TD></TR>

<tr><td>
<a href="page3.htm" target="_self">This Site - Page 3</a>
</TD></TR>

<TR><TD>
<a href=
"http://developer.netscape.com/library/documentation/
communicator/dynhtml/index.htm">
The Guide to Dynamic HTML in Netscape Communicator</a> <br>
Document has been updated
</TD></TR>

<TR><TD>
<a href="http://developer.netscape.com/library/documentation/
```

continues

Listing 10.7. continued

```
communicator/index.html">
Netscape Communicator Documentation</a>
</TD></TR>
</TABLE>

</BODY>
```

The BASE element is used with this page, except this time the output is set to a window named newwindow. The first time the browser attempts to load a page into newwindow, it discovers that this window has not been created, and creates it. From that point on, all output directed to newwindow goes to this newly created window. Figure 10.7 shows what happens when one of the external links is clicked with this page.

FIGURE 10.7.

New browser window opened when one of the external links from Page 2 was clicked.

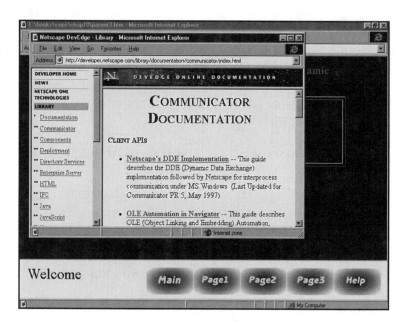

Page 3 and its source are shown in Listing 10.8.

Listing 10.8. Page 3 source from the file page3.htm.

```
<HTML>
<HEAD>
<STYLE type="text/css">
    body { background-color: black;
             color: yellow;
          margin: 0.1in 0.4in }
    A { color: magenta }
```

```
        CAPTION { color: red ; font-size: 18pt; font-weight: bold }
</STYLE>
</HEAD>
<BODY>
<TABLE align=center width=90% CELLPADDING=5 cellspacing=5
frame=none rules=none align=center>
<CAPTION align=top>Main Page - Internet Explorer and
Navigator Dynamic HTML links</CAPTION>
<tr><td>
<a href="page2.htm" target="_self" >This Site - Page 2</a>
</TD></TR>

<tr><td>
<a href="help.htm" target="menuFrame">This Site - Help</a>
</TD></TR>

<TR><TD>
<a href="http://developer.netscape.com/library/
documentation/communicator/layers/index.htm"
    target="newwindow">
Navigator Positioning HTML elements Documentation</a></TD>
</TD></TR>

<TR><TD>
<a href="http://developer.netscape.com/library/documentation/
communicator/jsguide/js1_2.htm"
    target="_parent">
What's new in JavaScript for Navigator 4.0</a>
</TD></TR>

<TR><TD>
<a href="http://developer.netscape.com/library/documentation/
htmlguid/dynamic_resources.html"
    target="_blank">
Navigator Dynamic HTML Resources</a>
</TD></TR>
</TABLE>

</BODY>
```

This page uses several redirection techniques. The first navigation link, to Page 2, is directed to self, which means the page loads into the current frame. The second navigational page, to Help, is directed to the menuFrame window. Figure 10.8 shows this page where the Help link is selected.

COMPANION
Web site   The first of the external links loads into a new browser window named newwindow. The second external link loads the page into the parent window, which is equivalent to the use of top when the frames are only one level deep (the frame pages themselves do not contain frames). The last external link loads to a new, unnamed window. Figure 10.9 shows the results of clicking the first external link, then the last external link, and finally the middle external link, which replaces the frame page. The source for Page 3 can be found in page3.htm.

FIGURE 10.8.

Clicking the Help link in Page 3 redirects the Help page to the menu bar frame.

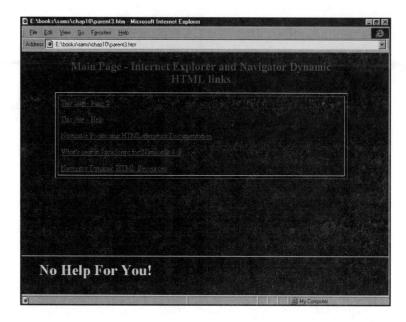

FIGURE 10.8.

Clicking the Help link in Page 3 redirects the Help page to the menu bar frame.

The final page is the Help page, and it has the following source, which displays a header saying No Help For You! and can be found in `help.htm`:

```
<HTML>
<HEAD>
<STYLE type="text/css">
    body { background-color: black;
           color: yellow;
        margin: 0.1in 0.4in }
</STYLE>
</HEAD>
<BODY>
<H1> No Help For You!</H1>

</BODY>
```

This example demonstrates all the techniques you can use to redirect output from a frame page. As Internet copyright issues become clarified, one issue that may become law is that you cannot include a link to an external page from within a frame and have that page loaded to your frame, as it would violate the original page's copyright law Issues of law aside, Web authors and developers consider it a courtesy to redirect an external link to outside a frame, either by opening a new window or loading the page directly into the main browser window.

AVOIDING FRAMES FOR YOUR PAGES

There are several techniques you can use if you want to avoid your pages being opened within a frame. One approach is to use the following script within the page you want to protect from frames:

```
<SCRIPT language="javascript">
    if (self != top)
        top.location = self.location;
</SCRIPT>
```

This code checks to see if the current page is the top page. If it isn't, the page is set to be the topmost page.

Inline Frames with IFRAME

HTML 4.0 created a new frame element called the *inline frame*, which uses the tags <IFRAME> and </IFRAME>. At this time only Microsoft's Internet Explorer supports inline frames.

Inline frames have the same attributes regular frames have, except that each inline frame window is embedded within a Web page and attributes are specified directly for the frame window. Instead of specifying the rows and cols of a frameset, each inline frame has a width and a height, which can be specified in inches or pixels. However, the frame does support the marginHeight, marginWidth, frameborder, and scrolling attributes. The IFRAME element also supports the target and align attributes. Best of all, the source can load directly into the frame dynamically using script.

COMPANION **Web site** A page using two IFRAME elements—one for holding the contents of menu3.htm, and one for holding the contents of main3.htm—demonstrates the INFRAME element. The page also has a header at the top. Listing 10.9 contains the source for this page.

Listing 10.9. Using the IFRAME element to create inline frames.

```
<HTML>
<HEAD>
<STYLE type="text/css">
    body { background-color: black;
           color: yellow;
        margin: 0.1in 0.4in }
    H2 { color: lime; font-size: 16pt }
</STYLE>
</HEAD>
<BODY>
<H2>This demonstrates INLINE FRAMES </H2>
<IFRAME src="menu3.htm" frameborder=0 scrolling=no height=120 width=95%
    align=center name="menuFrame">
    Your browser does not support inline frames
</IFRAME>
<IFRAME src="main3.htm" frameborder=0 width=95% height=300 align=center
    name="workFrame">

</IFRAME>

</BODY>
```

The first frame is created directly below the header, and is large enough to hold the menu page. The second frame is just below the menu inline frame, and should be large enough to hold any frame pages created for the example in the last section. The first inline frame has the words Your browser does not support inline frames contained within the <IFRAME> and </IFRAME> tags. This is equivalent to the NORFRAME element when using FRAMESET.

> COMPANION Website You can try this page yourself in Internet Explorer 4.0 by opening the Companion Web Site and opening inframe.htm source file. Figure 10.9 shows the page just after it is opened.

FIGURE 10.9.

Example demonstrating two inline frames using IFRAME.

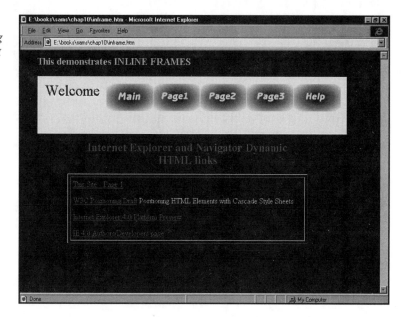

Clicking any of the external links results in the same behavior as that demonstrated in the last section using a FRAMESET and FRAME. However, loading the page into Navigator results in a page similar to that shown in Figure 10.10, as Navigator has not yet implemented IFRAME.

Summary

This chapter provides an overview and examples of using the FRAMESET and FRAME elements. In addition, the chapter covers using the new inline frame element IFRAME.

You also had a chance to review and try several different techniques for redirecting page loading when using frames, and how to provide for intraframe navigation.

Using the NOFRAMES element is demonstrated for the FRAMESET element, and the equivalent technique is demonstrated for use with the IFRAME element.

FIGURE 10.10.

*Results of opening a
page using inline frames
with Navigator.*

Some of the examples in this chapter also use dynamic HTML, and you can read more about
this technology in Chapters 30, "Using the HTML Object Model and Creating Dynamic
HTML Pages," through 32, "Saving User Preferences: Cookies and OPS."

Using Images with HTML

by Shelley Powers

IN THIS CHAPTER

Web pages would be pretty dull without images. If pages consisted only of text on a plain background, the Web would not have achieved the enormous popularity it has today. Images are also, unfortunately, probably the number one reason the Internet has to handle an increasingly heavy traffic burden, as more Web sites are posting pages with increasing numbers of images and other multimedia content.

This chapter discusses how to embed an image within a Web page, and the attributes available to modify the image. The chapter also discusses how to create a client-side image map, and the pros and cons of using this type of technology.

This chapter also reveals some tricks you can use with images, such as how to cache images on the client's machine to decrease the burden to the server and the Web page reader. You also have a chance to work with images from scripting blocks, including creating the popular rollover effect. This effect is used to alter the image displayed when the Web page reader moves his or her mouse over the image or clicks the image.

> **NOTE**
>
> Note that the examples in this chapter have been tested with IE 4.0 and Navigator 4.0 unless otherwise specified. Also, not all effects work with all browsers, but most will work with IE 3.x and up and Navigator 3.x and up unless specified otherwise. If you must provide support for browsers outside of those, be careful in using some of the technologies mentioned in this chapter, as many will not work with older browsers.

Embedding Images Within an HTML Document

Images are embedded within a Web document page with the use of the IMG tag. This tag contains the source of the image file and other information, and does not have an end tag. The images used are commonly GIF or JPEG files, though a new image formatting specification—the PNG format—is now supported.

The Image Formats

The Graphics Interface Format was created by CompuServe and is probably the most popular image format in use within HTML files at this time. The GIF89a specific version of this format, supported by most graphics programs, allows for the specification of the number of colors to include within the image file; it also allows the image creator to designate which color becomes transparent when the image is displayed.

The Joint Photographic Experts Group format retains all the image's colors—which makes it especially useful with photos dependent on higher color densities—but also supports a compression technique that discards data from the image nonessential to the display. The downside to the compression technique is that once an image has been compressed, and then decompressed, it is no longer the same as the original image. Higher levels of compression lead to smaller file sizes, but also decrease the quality of the image. Additionally, the JPEG format does not support the GIF89a ability to mark a color as transparent.

The Portable Network Graphics format is considered a replacement for the GIF format. It supports alpha channels, which can contain masks to alter or protect parts of the image and can be used to create transparency variations. Additionally, PNG supports a more efficient compression routine and two-dimensional interlacing, which controls how an image is displayed while it downloads.

The PNG format is very new, and most image formats use GIF and JPEG. However, more uses of the PNG format are expected for images in the near future as more browsers provide support for it. Internet Explorer 4.0 currently supports the PNG format, and there is a Navigator plug-in for support , the PNG Live plug-in, available for download at the Netscape plug-in Web site. To access the Netscape plug-in site, access the About Plug-Ins option from the Help menu and click the hypertext link at the top labeled `For more information on Netscape plug-ins, click here.`

The IMG Attributes

As stated earlier, images are embedded within a Web page using the IMG tag, as shown in the following code:

```
<IMG src="some.gif" width=100 height=100 alt="Sunrise
over Lake Champlaign" hspace=20>
```

This image is 100 pixels wide and 100 pixels tall, has alternative text of "Sunrise over Lake Champlaign" associated with it, and has a horizontal space of 20 pixels on either side. The image source is the file `some.gif`.

Several of the attributes for the IMG tag are deprecated with the HTML 4.0 draft specification. The following list contains the attributes currently supported for the IMG tag and a note as to whether the attribute is deprecated:

- ■ `src`: URL of image source file
- ■ `alt`: alternative text for text-based browsers
- ■ `align`: how image aligns with surrounding contents, deprecated
- ■ `height`: height to reserve for image, deprecated
- ■ `width`: width to reserve for image, deprecated
- ■ `border`: size of border surrounding image if image is contained within an anchor, deprecated
- ■ `hspace`: horizontal white space on either side of image, deprecated
- ■ `vspace`: vertical white space on either side of image, deprecated
- ■ `usemap`: URL of client-side image map, defined using tag MAP

- `ismap`: Set to specify that image is server-side image map
- `id`: image name, or named style sheet
- `class`: style sheet class
- `style`: style sheet information embedded directly into element specification
- `title`: element title which may be displayed as tips window

As you can see, all presentation and placement information about the image is now deprecated. This information is to be defined, instead, by the use of style sheets, and Internet Explorer provides support for image style sheet specifications. However, at this time Navigator provides limited support of style sheet information for images, so you should provide style sheet and attribute-based placement and presentation information for an image. Browsers that no longer support the attributes are ignored.

The IMG Width and Height Attributes

The width and height of the image define the area of the window the image occupies, not necessarily the size of the image itself. Listing 11.1 shows several different image specifications, each using the same image file and different widths and heights.

Listing 11.1. The same `image` object with different widths and heights.

```
<IMG src="Leaves.PNG" width=100 height=100>
<IMG src="Leaves.PNG" width=200 height=200>
<p>
<IMG src="Leaves.PNG" width=249 height=169>
<IMG src="Leaves.PNG" width=124 height=84>
<IMG src="Leaves.PNG" width=62 height=42>
```

The original image is 249 pixels wide and 169 pixels in height, as shown in the third `IMG` tag. Figure 11.1 shows the Web page containing all these image settings. Notice in the first two images that the browser applies a compression routine to display the entire image in the image space.

Also notice from Figure 11.1 that the last two images are half the original size and a quarter the original image size. These are identical representations of the image, though smaller. Instead of specifying exact pixels, you could also specify a percentage, which is based on the page size. Specifying a value of 25 percent for the width creates the image with a width equal to 25 percent of the page display space. There is some debate as to whether the use of page percentages for images will be supported in future versions of HTML, so you should use this sparingly. Using the percentage size technique is normally for images that act as horizontal bars within a Web page, and stretching the image does not degrade the image appearance too much.

It is important to include image sizing when creating an image. This helps the page display more quickly, as the browser does not need to hold the display of the page waiting on the image to be completely downloaded in order to determine the size to reserve for the image. Additionally, some browsers, such as Navigator, not specifying a size can have odd results if you use percentage sizes for any of the images within the page.

FIGURE 11.1.

This is the same image displayed with several differently sized IMG *tags.*

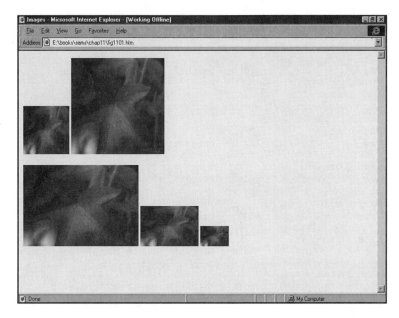

The alt Attribute

For text- or speech-based browsers that do not pick up images, using the alt attribute provides alternative descriptive text. If you have images representing a rock, a flower, and a bird in your page, you should use the associated alternative text, as follows:

```
<IMG src="rock.gif" width=100 height=150 alt="Smooth-sided rock">
<IMG src="flower.jpg" width=75 height=200 alt="Flower - rose">
<IMG src="bird.png" width=200 height=200 alt="Bird - robin">
```

With the alternative text, those who cannot see well and use speech-based browsers, or those who use a text-based browser can have an understanding of what is on the page.

The hspace, vspace, and align Attributes

COMPANION
Web site The whitespace attributes, hspace and vspace, have actually been used to control Web page placement prior to the use of CSS1. Web page authors used a 1-pixel transparent GIF and the hspace and vspace attributes to position other elements in a page. As an example, a 1-pixel non-transparent GIF image visually demonstrates how something like this would work. Listing 11.2 shows the source for the Web page, and you can try the page yourself by visiting the file img1.htm, which can be found on this book's Companion Web Site.

Listing 11.2. Using a 1-pixel image to control horizontal spacing.

```
<HTML>
<HEAD>
<TITLE> Images </TITLE>
</HEAD>
<BODY>
<img src="onepix.gif" width=1 height=1 hspace=200 vspace=10
    align=left>
Image One<p>
<img src="onepix.gif" width=1 height=1 hspace=180 vspace=10
    align=left>
Image Two<p>
<img src="onepix.gif" width=1 height=1 hspace=160 vspace=10
    align=left>
Image Three<p>
<img src="onepix.gif" width=1 height=1 hspace=140 vspace=10
    align=left>
Image Four<p>
<img src="onepix.gif" width=1 height=1 hspace=120 vspace=10
    align=left>
Image Five<p>
<img src="onepix.gif" width=1 height=1 hspace=100 vspace=10
    align=left>
Image Six<p>
<img src="onepix.gif" width=1 height=1 hspace=80 vspace=10
    align=left>
Image Seven<p>
<img src="onepix.gif" width=1 height=1 hspace=60 vspace=10
    align=left>
Image Eight<p>
<img src="onepix.gif" width=1 height=1 hspace=40 vspace=10
    align=left>
Image Nine<p>
<img src="onepix.gif" width=1 height=1 hspace=20 vspace=10
    align=left>
Image Ten

</BODY>
```

With each image and its associated text, the hspace attribute is set to an increasingly smaller amount, creating a semi-pyramid effect for the text. Figure 11.2 shows the result of using these images and their impact on the text aligned next to them. You probably won't be able to see the tiny image next to the text from the figure. If the image were transparent, you would not see it at all.

The sample listing also shows the align attribute, which determines how the image is positioned with respect to surrounding HTML elements. Acceptable values for this attribute are:

■ left—align image to left of other elements

■ right—align image to right of other elements

■ top—align image top to elements

■ center—align image to center of other elements

■ bottom—align image bottom to other elements

FIGURE 11.2.

Using a 1-pixel image to place text.

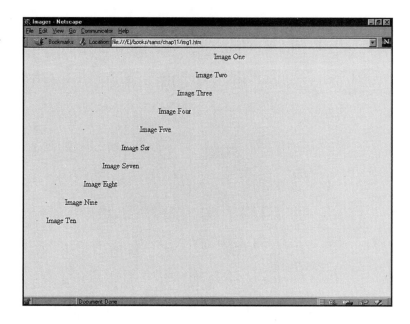

Applying Styles and Borders

By default, a border is created around an image when the image is surrounded by a hypertext link. This can be controlled by setting the border attribute to a value of zero (0). Conversely, if an image is created outside a link, you can create a border by setting the border value to an integer representing the size you want.

The source in Listing 11.3 creates two images within a Web page, both with borders. The first border is created automatically because the image is embedded within a link. The second image border is created by setting the border attribute to a non-zero value.

Listing 11.3. Two images with borders created using different techniques.

```
<HTML>
<HEAD>
<TITLE> Images </TITLE>

</HEAD>
<BODY>
<a href="" onclick="return false"><IMG src="photo1.jpg"
width=100 height=150 hspace=10></a>

<IMG src="photo1.jpg" width=100 height=150 border=6 >

</BODY>
```

 Figure 11.3 shows the two images and their associated borders. The border color for the link image is the same color as the link would be for a text-based rather

than an image-based link. The color of the image with the border that was deliberately created is black. The source code for this example can be found in `img2.htm`.

FIGURE 11.3.

Two bordered images.

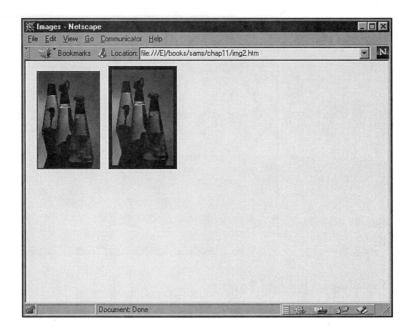

Instead of controlling the images' appearances using attributes, you can control them with CSS1 style sheets. As an example, the source in Listing 11.4, created specifically for Internet Explorer, embeds the same image several times within the Web page, and then alters the appearance of each image using different CSS1 style sheet settings.

Listing 11.4. Applying CSS1 style attributes to several images.

```
<HTML>
<HEAD>
<TITLE> Images </TITLE>
</HEAD>
<BODY>

<!-- image with green border -->
<IMG src="photo1.jpg" width=100 height=150
    style="border-width: 5; border-style: inset; border-color: lime">

<!-- image with horizontal space -->
<IMG src="photo1.jpg" width=100 height=150
    style="margin-left: 0.5in; margin-right: 0.5in">

<!-- image with style dimensions -->
<IMG src="photo1.jpg"
    style="width: 200; height: 300">

<!-- image with Internet Explorer Filter applied -->
```

```
<IMG src="photo1.jpg" width=100 height=150
    style="filter: alpha(opacity=50)">

<!-- clipped image -->
<IMG src="photo1.jpg" width=100 height=150
    style="position:absolute; left: 100; top: 350; clip: rect(75,50,auto,auto)">

</BODY>
```

The first style sheet sets a frame-like green border for the image and the second creates a horizontal margin around the image. In addition, the third image has its width and height increased, and the fourth image is set to 50-percent opacity using the Internet Explorer-only Alpha Visual filter.

> **NOTE**
>
> The Microsoft Visual Filter is discussed in more detail in the next chapter, "Merging Multimedia and Plug-Ins with HTML."

COMPANION Web site The last image is located within the page using absolute positioning and then clipped. You can read more about absolute positioning in Chapter 8, "Advanced Layout and Positioning with Style Sheets." You can try this example yourself by opening the file imgstyle.htm.

Figure 11.4 shows the page displayed in Internet Explorer. Note that this page does not display accurately with Navigator, which does not currently support style sheets for images.

FIGURE 11.4.

The same image with different style sheets creating different effects.

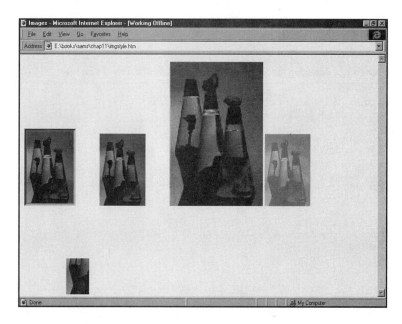

Once images are in a page, they can be used for client-side image maps or they can be altered dynamically in script, discussed later in the chapter.

The `image` Object and Accessing Images Within Script

Netscape exposed the `image` object to its scripting object model with version 3.0 of Navigator. Microsoft followed with support for the image object in version 4.0 of Internet Explorer. Exposing the image to script means that the image can be altered after the page loads, a handy technique for creating some interesting effects.

> **NOTE**
>
> For more details on scripting, and JavaScript in particular, see Part III, "Client-Side Scripting."

The `image` object is accessed by creating a new `image` object or by accessing the images embedded into the Web page via the `images` array. Each `IMG` tag within the Web page is associated with one entry in the `images` array. Entries to this array cannot be added or removed, but the image itself can be accessed and displayed.

As an example, Listing 11.5 implements a very simple application that changes an image each time the Web page reader presses the associated radio button. The first radio button is associated with the image that is first displayed, the second button with the second image, and so on. The radio button and image elements are centered using an HTML table, and the background of the document is set to an eye-tingling yellow.

Listing 11.5. Accessing the `images` array within script to alter the image.

```
<HTML>
<HEAD>
<TITLE> Images</TITLE>
<STYLE type="text/css">
    BODY { background-color: yellow }
</STYLE>
<SCRIPT language="javascript">
<!--
// change displayed image
function change_image(num) {
    var img = "";
    if (num == 1)
     img = "photo7.jpg";
    else if (num == 2)
     img = "photo8.jpg";
    else if (num == 3)
     img = "photo9.jpg";
```

```
    else
      img = "photo10.jpg";
    document.images[0].src = img;
}
//-->
</SCRIPT>

</HEAD>
<BODY>
<TABLE width=60% align=center border=0
    cellspacing=10>
<tr><td align=center>
<img src="photo7.jpg" width=100 height=150>
</td></tr><tr><td align=center>
<FORM name="form1">
<!-- radio buttons -->
<INPUT TYPE="radio" NAME="thegroup" VALUE="one" CHECKED
    onclick="change_image(1)"> One
<INPUT TYPE="radio" NAME="thegroup" VALUE="two"
    onclick="change_image(2)"> Two
<INPUT TYPE="radio" NAME="thegroup" VALUE="three"
    onclick="change_image(3)"> Three
<INPUT TYPE="radio" NAME="thegroup" VALUE="four"
    onclick="change_image(4)">Four
</FORM>
</td></tr></table>
</BODY>
```

Note a couple of things in the listing. First, the JavaScript built-in arrays always begin with zero (0) as the first entry. Additionally, the images are loaded into the images array in order of their position within the Web page document. As there is only one IMG element in the page, there is only one entry in the images array.

ACCESSING AN IMAGE BY ITS NAME

The image could also have been given a name and accessed by this name using the following type of code:

```
document.theimage.src=img;
```

The problem with using an image name is that the name attribute is deprecated with HTML 4.0, but is still the only way to name the image with Navigator. Browsers honoring the HTML 4.0 syntax use the attribute id to name the image, though most, at least for some time, should still honor name. In order to work with older and newer browsers, you can use the same value with both the NAME attribute and the ID attribute.

COMPANION
Web site Clicking one of the radio buttons sets the image's URL and alters the image's src attribute to the new URL. Figure 11.5 shows the page after the third radio button has been clicked. You can also try this page by opening the file radio.htm.

224

FIGURE 11.5.

Page showing image associated with third radio button.

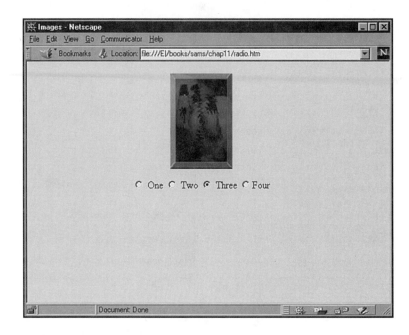

The src attribute is not the only image property that can be accessed from a scripting block. Table 11.1 shows the other image object properties. Note that all the properties, except the src property, are read only with Navigator 3.x and up. However, all of the properties can be modified with Internet Explorer 4.0.

Table 11.1. Image object properties, accessed via images array.

Property	Description
src	Image URL
width	Image width
height	Image height
lowsrc	lowsrc image's URL, first displayed when page is opened
hspace	Horizontal space
vspace	Vertical space
border	Border width
complete	Whether image has completed loading
name	Image name
prototype	Method of associating additional information with image

These same properties can be accessed with an image created using the Image constructor. This is described in detail in the next section, which also discusses image caching.

Images and Caching

COMPANION Web site In the previous example, when one of the radio buttons is pressed for the first time and the image loads, there was probably a very brief pause while the image loaded from your hard drive, if you copied the example from this book's Companion Web Site. If the page had been accessed from a Web server, the pause would be much more noticeable. Why? When you access an image for the first time, such as when assigning it to the src attribute of an existing image object, the image must be downloaded from the server. After the image is downloaded, though, it is cached on the client machine and subsequent accesses to the image pull it from the cache rather than the server. If image caching is turned off because of Web page reader preference, or is not supported by the browser, the image is accessed directly from the server each time the radio button is pressed.

> **NOTE**
>
> Both Netscape Navigator and Microsoft Internet Explorer support file and image caching.

A nice extension to the image-changing program would be having the images already cached by the time the reader presses the radio button. With this, the delay for the image loading occurs while the document is loading rather than after the reader presses the button.

There is a technique for caching images, and that is to construct a new image object to hold the image for use at a later time. The previous sample source is altered here to use image caching. Four image objects are created and assigned the src attribute. The code then references these when the reader presses any of the radio buttons, as shown in Listing 11.6.

Listing 11.6. Changing image source based on which radio button is pressed.

```
<HTML>
<HEAD>
<TITLE> Images</TITLE>
<STYLE type="text/css">
    BODY { background-color: yellow }
</STYLE>
<SCRIPT language="javascript">
<!--
// create cached images
image_array = new Array(4);
for (i = 0; i < image_array.length; i++)
   image_array[i] = new Image(100,150);

// load images
image_array[0].src = "photo7.jpg";
image_array[1].src = "photo8.jpg";
image_array[2].src = "photo9.jpg";
image_array[3].src = "photo10.jpg";
```

continues

Listing 11.6. continued

```
// change displayed image
function change_image(num) {
   document.images[0].src=image_array[num].src;

}
//-->
</SCRIPT>

</HEAD>
<BODY>
<TABLE width=60% align=center border=0
   cellspacing=10>
<tr><td align=center>
<img src="photo7.jpg" width=100 height=150>
</td></tr><tr><td align=center>
<FORM name="form1">
<!-- radio buttons -->
<INPUT TYPE="radio" NAME="thegroup" VALUE="one" CHECKED
   onclick="change_image(0)"> One
<INPUT TYPE="radio" NAME="thegroup" VALUE="two"
   onclick="change_image(1)"> Two
<INPUT TYPE="radio" NAME="thegroup" VALUE="three"
   onclick="change_image(2)"> Three
<INPUT TYPE="radio" NAME="thegroup" VALUE="four"
   onclick="change_image(3)">Four
</FORM>
</td></tr></table>
</BODY>
```

There's a four-element array in the listing, and each array entry is set to be an image object. A different image is assigned to each array entry. When creating the image object, the image width and height are also passed in, though these are both optional. The script to accomplish this is not enclosed within a function, which means it is parsed and run while the page is loading.

Notice from the code that I changed the numeric value of the parameter passed to the function? This numeric reference then becomes the cached image object array index.

If you have a chance, load both of these pages—radio.htm, which does not include caching, and imgche.htm, which does—onto a server and access them from a slower connection if possible. Note the differences in performance between the two when you click one of the radio buttons. A drawback to this technique is that the overall page contents load more slowly because of the image loading.

A DYNAMIC HTML IMAGE-CACHING TECHNIQUE

There is another technique for image caching that comes with the new Dynamic HTML capability. You can load the images using IMG tags, which are then inserted into a hidden DIV, or LAYER if you prefer, block. Placing this block at the end of the Web page document loads and displays the other page elements before beginning the image loading, meaning that your reader can see the page before all the images start loading. The image loading then occurs, more or less, in the background.

One of the most popular uses of altering an image and image caching is creating rollover effects for an image-based menu, discussed in the following section.

Creating Image Rollover Effects

The most popular use of changing images is to create a rollover effect for images that represent active links. When the reader moves his or her mouse over the image, the image takes on a different appearance, adding a highlight that provides feedback to the reader.

The rollover effect can also be applied by trapping the mouse down event, changing the image to one representing a highlighted image, and then changing the image back with the mouse up event, providing feedback for the clicking action. Both of these techniques are discussed in detail in the next two sections.

Rollover with Mouse Down and Mouse Up Events

A popular rollover technique is highlighting the image when the Web page reader clicks an image that is also a hypertext link.

To demonstrate this, three identical images are placed on a Web page using an HTML table for positioning. Each image is embedded within an anchor reference, and the onmousedown and onmouseup events are trapped for the anchor. A function named change_high is called with the mouse down event, and another function, change_low, is called for the mouse up event. The number representing the index of the image is passed as a parameter for both of these functions. Listing 11.7 contains the complete source for this page.

Listing 11.7. Three images, each of which becomes highlighted when clicked.

```
<HTML>
<HEAD>
<TITLE> Images </TITLE>
<STYLE type="text/css">
<!--
    background-color { white }
-->
</STYLE>
<SCRIPT language="javascript">
<!--

// cache images
highimage = new Image(106,157);
lowimage = new Image(106,157);
```

continues

Listing 11.7. continued

```
lowimage.src = "optnrm.jpg";
highimage.src = "opthigh.jpg";

// change to highlight image
function change_high(num) {
    document.images[num].src = highimage.src;
}

// change to normal image
function change_low(num) {
    document.images[num].src = lowimage.src;
}
//-->
</SCRIPT>
</HEAD>
<BODY>

<table width=350 cols=3 align=center border=0 cellspacing=10>
<tr><td>
<!-- image one -->
<a href="" onclick="return false" onmousedown="change_high(0)"
        onmouseup="change_low(0)">
        <IMG src="optnrm.jpg" width=106 height=157 hspace=10
            border=0></a>
</td><td>
<!-- image two -->
<a href="" onclick="return false" onmousedown="change_high(1)"
        onmouseup="change_low(1)">
        <IMG src="optnrm.jpg" width=106 height=157 hspace=10
            border=0></a>
</td><td>
<!-- image three -->
<a href="" onclick="return false" onmousedown="change_high(2)"
        onmouseup="change_low(2)">
        <IMG src="optnrm.jpg" width=106 height=157 hspace=10
            border=0></a>
</td></tr></table>
</BODY>
```

COMPANION
Web site When the change_high function is called, the source for the targeted image is changed to the highlighted image source. Conversely, when the change_low function is called, the source for the targeted image is changed to the normal image source. Both the highlighted and normal images are cached when the page is first loaded. You can try this example yourself by opening the file roll1.htm.

Notice from the example that the page is also trapping the onclick event. Because the hypertext link href attributes are not assigned URLs, the value of false must be returned at the end of the onclick event, or the browser attempts to load the empty URL.

Figure 11.6 shows the Web page from Listing 11.7 with the middle image clicked.

FIGURE 11.6.

Using the rollover effect with mouse down and up events.

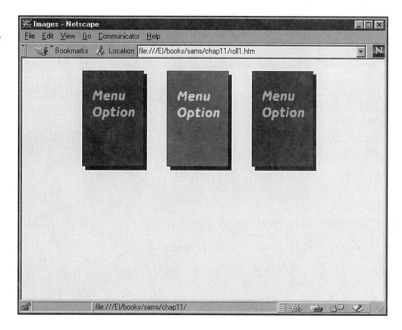

If the menu images are different, you can create an array of images to cache the highlighted and normal image sources. You would then use the code similar to the following to cache the images:

```
high_image = new Array(3);
for (i = 0; i < high_image.length; I++)
    high_image[i] = new Image();
high_image[i].src = "first_highlight.jpg";
...
function change_high(num) {
   document.images[num].src = high_image[num].src;
...
```

Rollover with Mouse Over and Mouse Out Events

Another popular use of the rollover technique is highlighting an image when the Web page reader's mouse is over it, and return it to normal when the mouse leaves the image area.

The Web page shown in Listing 11.7 is altered to trap the onmouseout and onmouseover events, instead of the onmousedown and onmouseup events. When the mouse is over the image, the function change_high is called. When the mouse leaves the image area, the function change_low is called. Listing 11.8 shows the Web page using this rollover technique.

Listing 11.8. Implementing image rollover with the mouse over and mouse out events.

```
<HTML>
<HEAD>
<TITLE> Images </TITLE>
```

continues

Listing 11.8. continued

```
<STYLE type="text/css">
<!--
    background-color { white }
-->
</STYLE>
<SCRIPT language="javascript">
<!--

// cache images
highimage = new Image(106,157);
lowimage = new Image(106,157);

lowimage.src = "optnrm.jpg";
highimage.src = "opthigh.jpg";

// change to highlight image
function change_high(num) {
    document.images[num].src = highimage.src;
}

// change to normal image
function change_low(num) {
    document.images[num].src = lowimage.src;
}
//-->
</SCRIPT>
</HEAD>
<BODY>

<table width=350 cols=3 align=center border=0 cellspacing=10>
<tr><td>
<!-- image one -->
<a href="" onclick="return false" onmouseover="change_high(0)"
        onmouseout="change_low(0)">
        <IMG src="optnrm.jpg" width=106 height=157 hspace=10
            border=0"></a>
</td><td>
<!-- image two -->
<a href="" onclick="return false" onmouseover="change_high(1)"
        onmouseout="change_low(1)">
        <IMG src="optnrm.jpg" width=106 height=157 hspace=10
            border=0"></a>
</td><td>
<!-- image three -->
<a href="" onclick="return false" onmouseover="change_high(2)"
        onmouseout="change_low(2)">
        <IMG src="optnrm.jpg" width=106 height=157 hspace=10
            border=0"></a>
</td></tr></table>
</BODY>
```

COMPANION **Web site** You can try this version of the rollover effect by opening the file roll2.htm.

11

NOTE

The onmouseover, onmouseout, onmousedown, and onmouseup events are defined in the HTML 4.0 draft specifications as intrinsic events for the IMG element. Internet Explorer 4.0 supports these events directly from the IMG tag, and future versions of Navigator should support them directly. This means that unless you want or need to provide this type of support for older browsers, you do not have to use the hypertext link to trap these events.

Summary

This chapter provides an in-depth look at the image object and the images array. All of the IMG element's attributes are also discussed.

In addition, you worked with a small application that changes the display images when you press the radio buttons. The chapter also discusses image caching, what it is and how you can use it to improve the performance of your application when working with images.

Finally, two different techniques for implementing the popular rollover effect are presented— one for the mouse down and mouse up events and one for the mouse over and mouse out events.

Chapter 12, "Merging Multimedia and Plug-Ins with HTML," continues the discussion of embedding objects into a Web page, and applying the multimedia effects Navigator 4.x and Internet Explorer 4.x build into their browsers. Be sure to check out the example of applying a rollover effect using the new Microsoft Filters attribute.

Merging Multimedia, Controls, and Plug-Ins with HTML

by Shelley Powers

IN THIS CHAPTER

No matter how practical Web pages become, the thing that still catches your eye, and bogs down the Internet, is multimedia. We are all attracted to vibrant, active pages full of sight and sound. These same qualities also tend to absorb bandwidth on an increasingly crowded Internet infrastructure.

As soon as HTML was extended to the point where you could embed external controls or plug-ins into a Web page, people immediately included video and sound clips, as well as other multimedia content. Now, newer technologies have improved the efficiency with which you can download sound and video files.

There are three methods currently supported for inserting external applications into a Web page: the <APPLET> tag, the <EMBED> tag, and the <OBJECT> tag. The use of applets is discussed in more detail in Part IV, "Web Publishing with Java," but this chapter discusses the use of the <EMBED> and <OBJECT> tags to include multimedia content.

Both Netscape Navigator and Internet Explorer support the scripting and plug-in or control interaction capabilities reviewed in this chapter. Each browser uses different techniques to include multimedia, and the chapter explores these techniques separately.

Finally, with Internet Explorer 4.0, Microsoft has integrated its DirectX animation and gaming technology directly into the browser, as well as into its Java implementation by class extensions. This chapter provides a brief introduction to the new technology that uses built-in ActiveX controls. The new filters that IE 4.0 supports by creating an imageless rollover effect are also demonstrated here.

Accessing Sound and Video in Web Pages

Multimedia was first used in Web pages to include sound. Both Netscape Navigator and Internet Explorer support the use of sound in a Web page, although both implement sound files in different ways.

Beginning with Netscape's Navigator version 3.x, the browser used the LiveAudio plug-in for sound, and the LiveVideo or QuickTime plug-ins for video. With Navigator 4.x, Netscape also supports a new streaming media technology called the Media Server. Media Server goes beyond the use of controls, so it's not included here.

THE NETSCAPE MEDIA SERVER

The Netscape Media Server and Media Player provide for streaming audio and synchronized multimedia. The Media Player is located on the client machine, and the Media Server on the Web server. Content is passed from the server using Real Time Streaming Protocol (RTSP), and is then converted for use on the client.

In Internet Explorer 4.0, Microsoft has provided a new and fairly complex ActiveX control it calls DirectShow, to control all forms of audio/visual media.

Using the <EMBED> Tag

The EMBED element is a simple-to-use technique that includes multimedia in a Web page. Both Netscape Navigator and Microsoft Internet Explorer support this element.

As an example, both IE and Navigator show a visible control in a Web page if the following embedded tag syntax is used:

```
<EMBED SRC="example.mid" controls=console
    width=144 height=60>
```

COMPANION Web site Each browser determines what plug-ins are currently installed to support files with the extension type of .mid (a MIDI file) and the browser then uses the associated plug-in. Netscape will most likely use the LiveAudio plug-in, and Microsoft will most likely use the DirectShow control. The midi1.htm file contains a Web page with the <EMBED> tag. Figure 12.1 shows what the page looks like with Navigator 4.0, and Figure 12.2 shows what the page looks like with IE 4.0.

12

MULTIMEDIA,
CONTROLS, AND
PLUG-INS

FIGURE 12.1.

Embedded sound file shown in Navigator.

The EMBED element can also be used to support video files, QuickTime files, and other multimedia, as demonstrated and discussed later in this chapter.

The EMBED element is very simple to use, but has one very major limitation: Because the attributes for the element are coded directly into the tag, modifications to the attributes of the embedded object require modifications to the underlying HTML rendering engine. In that case, if Netscape adds a new attribute for its LiveAudio plug-in to render the sound in stereo, a new attribute needs to be added to the <EMBED> tag just for the support of this one embedded control's attribute. This soon becomes insupportable. As you will see in the section titled "The <OBJECT> Tag and the Future," the use of the EMBED element is not supported in future specifications of HTML.

FIGURE 12.2.

Embedded sound file shown in Internet Explorer.

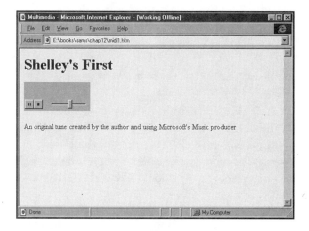

However, the <EMBED> tag remains the main technique used to integrate multimedia with Netscape Navigator and the following sections demonstrate this with both audio and video file content. The following sections also demonstrate how to control the playback of the multimedia content via the use of Netscape's LiveConnect scripting to object connectivity.

Netscape's LiveAudio Plug-In

Navigator uses the <EMBED> tag to include sound files and processes those files with the LiveAudio Sound plug-in (included as part of their installation). The following code shows how a sound file is included within a Web page with a console-like container to control how the sound plays and its volume:

```
<EMBED SRC="example.mid" controls=console
    width=144 height=60>
```

COMPANION Web site This sound control is visible, as shown previously in Figure 12.1, and includes controls to start, stop, pause, and adjust the volume. The sound itself is a MIDI format, electronic, 30-second tune created using Microsoft's Music Producer. You can try this embedded sound file by opening the file midi1.htm.

The LiveAudio plug-in plays files with extensions of .wav, .aiff, .au, and .mid. The LiveAudio plug-in attributes are given in the following list:

■ SRC—Audio source file URL

■ AUTOSTART—Whether file starts playing as soon as it is loaded

- ■ LOOP—Whether to loop sound file, and if so, whether to loop continuously, or to supply an integer for the number of times to loop
- ■ STARTTIME—Specifying a time in the source code to begin playing, specified in MINUTES:SECONDS
- ■ ENDTIME—Specifying a time in the source code to end playing, specified in MINUTES:SECONDS
- ■ VOLUME—A value between 0 and 100, representing percentage of sound volume
- ■ WIDTH—Width of display in pixels
- ■ HEIGHT—Height of display in pixels
- ■ ALIGN—Alignment of text surrounding console
- ■ CONTROLS—Type of console control to display: CONSOLE, SMALLCONSOLE, PLAYBUTTON, PAUSEBUTTON, STOPBUTTON, VOLUMELEVER
- ■ HIDDEN—Whether console is hidden
- ■ MASTERSOUND—Used with LiveConnect to designate true sound file
- ■ NAME—Name used to group several controls together to control the same sound

12

MULTIMEDIA, CONTROLS, AND PLUG-INS

NAME and MASTERSOUND are used when accessing a sound file from multiple controls or when using LiveConnect, the Netscape technology that supports accessing plug-in properties, methods, and events from script.

As an example of accessing a LiveAudio plug-in from script, Listing 12.1 contains an embedded audio plug-in, two form buttons that support starting and stopping audio play, and five radio buttons that control the audio volume.

Listing 12.1. Using LiveConnect to combine JavaScript and the LiveAudio plug-in.

```
<HTML>
<HEAD>
<TITLE> Multimedia </TITLE>

</HEAD>
<BODY onload="javascript:document.mysound.setvol(50)">
<H1> Shelley's First </H1>
<EMBED SRC="example.mid" hidden=true
    MASTERSOUND NAME="mysound" AUTOSTART=FALSE>
<FORM>
<INPUT type="button" value="Start Playing"
    onclick="javascript:document.mysound.play(false)">
<INPUT type="button" value="Stop Playing"
    onclick="javascript:document.mysound.stop()">
<p>
<INPUT type="radio" name="volume"
    onclick="javascript:document.mysound.setvol(50)" CHECKED>50 Percent
<INPUT type="radio" name="volume"
    onclick="javascript:document.mysound.setvol(60)">60 Percent
```

continues

Listing 12.1. continued

```
<INPUT type="radio" name="volume"
    onclick="javascript:document.mysound.setvol(70)">70 Percent
<INPUT type="radio" name="volume"
    onclick="javascript:document.mysound.setvol(80)">80 Percent
<INPUT type="radio" name="volume"
    onclick="javascript:document.mysound.setvol(90)">90 Percent
<INPUT type="radio" name="volume"
    onclick="javascript:document.mysound.setvol(100)">100 Percent
</FORM>
<p>
An original tune created by the author and using Microsoft's Music producer
</BODY>
```

COMPANION **Web site** The example uses the LiveAudio setvol, play, and stop methods to control the volume, start playing, and stop playing the audio file. To access the audio file plug-in from script, the MASTERSOUND and NAME attributes are set within the <EMBED> tag. You can try this file yourself by opening midi1ns.htm. Figure 12.3 shows the page with the form sound controls.

FIGURE 12.3.

The page has a hidden sound plug-in and form buttons to control sound.

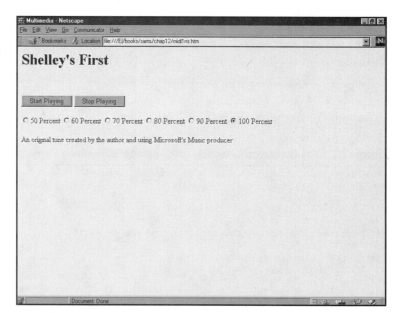

The methods that can be called from script for the LiveAudio plug-in are the following:

- play—Passing a Boolean value of false begins the sound playing. You can also pass a second parameter of the URL of the file to play.
- stop—Stops playing sound.
- pause —Pauses playing sound.

- start_time—Passes a parameter representing the number of seconds after the file starts to begin playing sound.

- end_time—Passes a parameter representing the number of seconds before the file ends to end playing sound.

- setvol—Passes parameter representing percentage of volume.

- fade_to—Passes a percentage value to fade volume to.

- fade_from_to—Passes two percentage values, one representing start volume, and the other representing end volume.

- start_at_beginning—Overrides start_time.

- stop_at_end—Overrides end_time.

- IsReady—Has file completely loaded?

- IsPlaying—Is sound playing?

- IsPaused—Is sound currently paused?

- GetVolume—Gets current volume.

Netscape also provides plug-in support for .avi files, as shown in the next section.

Netscape's LiveVideo Plug-In

Netscape's LiveVideo plug-in is very similar to the LiveAudio plug-in, except the LiveVideo plug-in processes files with the .avi extension. .avi files combine audio and visual output.

Listing 12.2 contains the source for a Web page that contains a combination of text and an embedded .avi file. The text and video are positioned using an HTML table, but the page title is positioned and altered using CSS1.

Listing 12.2. Source code for embedding an .avi file in a Web page.

```
<HTML>
<HEAD>
<TITLE> Multimedia </TITLE>
<STYLE type="text/css">
    H1 { color: red; text-align: center }
</STYLE>
</HEAD>
<BODY>
<H1>Video</H1>
<TABLE border=5 width=80% cols=2 align=center>
<tr><td>
<EMBED SRC="aria.avi" width=150 height=100 autostart=true
    align=right> ARIA Landing at Ascension Island </td>
<td>Apollo Range Instrumentation Aircraft
<a href="http://afftc.edwards.af.mil/452flts/aria/gall.htm">
Media Gallery</a> page.
</td></tr></table>
</BODY>
```

The photo caption is placed to the left of the photo using the LiveVideo ALIGN attribute, and the video is set to start playing as soon as the page is loaded by setting the AUTOSTART attribute to true. The video is one of several found at the Apollo Range Instrumentation Aircraft (ARIA) Gallery Web page located at the Edwards Air Force Base Web site at `http://afftc.edwards.af.mil/452flts/aria/gall.htm`.

COMPANION Web site You can try this page by opening the file avi1.htm. Figure 12.4 shows the page after the .avi video is finished playing.

.avi, .mpg, AND QUICKTIME

Because .avi files are really a Windows-based multimedia format, there can be problems playing these files on non-Windows platforms. They are popular to use because the largest percentage of Web page readers accessing a page are doing so from some form of Windows and because the files are fairly simple to create in a Windows environment. However, for audio-visual multimedia that works in multiple platforms, you need to use the QuickTime format (discussed in the section "Taking Advantage of Third-Party Plug-Ins and Controls") or .mpg if you want video only. You might want to provide variations of a file, providing both .avi and QuickTime versions and allowing the Web page reader to choose which format he or she wants.

FIGURE 12.4.

This page contains text and an .avi-embedded source, positioned using HTML table.

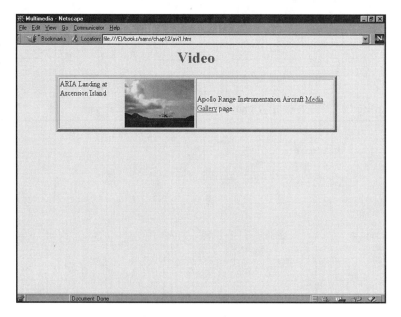

The other LiveAudio attributes are given in the following list:

- SRC—URL of .avi source file
- AUTOSTART—Set to true to begin playing video when page has loaded
- LOOP—Set to true to loop the video
- WIDTH—Plug-in width in pixels
- HEIGHT—Plug-in height in pixels
- ALIGN—How plug-in aligns with surrounding text

As with the LiveAudio plug-in, the LiveVideo plug-in also has exposed methods for access within a scripting block. Listing 12.3 shows the same page that was created in Listing 12.2, except two form buttons control the video playing, and the HTML table setup is a little different.

Listing 12.3. Embedded .avi file with form buttons to control playing.

```
<HTML>
<HEAD>
<TITLE> Multimedia </TITLE>
<STYLE type="text/css">
    H1 { color: red; text-align: center }
</STYLE>
<SCRIPT language="javascript">
<!--
var framenum = 0;

// hit once to play video
// hit again to pause video
function play_video() {
    document.embeds[0].play();
}

// hit once to stop or pause video
function stop_video() {
    document.theimage.stop();
}

//-->
</SCRIPT>
</HEAD>
<BODY>
<H1>Video</H1>
<TABLE border=0 width=80% cols=2 align=center
    cellpadding=10 cellspacing=10>
<tr><td width=70%>
<EMBED SRC="apo11h.avi" width=250 height=200
    autostart=false
    align=right NAME="theimage">
Apollo 11, planting the flag on the Moon </td><td>
NASA
```

continues

12

MULTIMEDIA, CONTROLS, AND PLUG-INS

Listing 12.3. continued

```
<a href="http://www.ksc.nasa.gov/shuttle/photos/">
Kennedy Space Center</a> Movie Archive
</td></tr>
<form>
<tr><td align=right >
<INPUT type="button" value="Play Video" onclick="play_video()">
</td><td align=left>
<INPUT type="button" value="Stop Video" onclick="stop_video()">
</td></tr>
</FORM>
</table>
</BODY>
```

One form button calls a function `play_video` to play or pause the video, the second calls the function `stop_video` to stop the video. The `.avi` file is not started automatically when the page loads, only after the Web page reader clicks the Play button. Figure 12.5 shows this Web page. Instead of a movie from the ARIA archives, the video clip featured in this page is from the Apollo 11 Mission. You can try the example directly by opening the file `avi1ns.htm`.

FIGURE 12.5.

The page has an embedded video file and two form buttons to control video playing.

As with the LiveAudio plug-in, Internet Explorer can process an embedded LiveVideo plug-in, as long as no scripting is applied to the object. Figure 12.6 shows the page from Listing 12.3 (from the file `avi1.htm`) as it would appear in Internet Explorer.

FIGURE 12.6.

The same page with the LiveAudio embedded plug-in file is shown as it would appear with Internet Explorer.

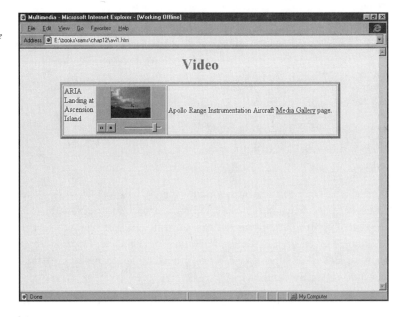

The use of the EMBED element never became an HTML standard, and is not mentioned in the HTML 4.0 draft specification for the reasons specified in the section "Using the <EMBED> Tag." The use of the <OBJECT> tag is the method currently under review by the W3C and most likely to become the recommended approach.

The <OBJECT> Tag and the Future

Microsoft introduced the use of the OBJECT element, and it is included in the HTML 4.0 draft specification as the element to use for embedding generic content into a Web page.

The OBJECT element has gained favor with the W3C because of its use of the PARAM element, embedded within the beginning and ending <OBJECT> tags, that provides name-value pairs as a method of passing attributes to the embedded element. With this approach, no change needs to be made to the underlying HTML rendering engine whenever the object creator wants to add or change attributes for the object.

The attributes specific to the OBJECT element and currently under review are given in the following list:

- CLASSID—Location of an object's implementation
- CODEBASE—Path used to resolve URL references
- CODETYPE—Internet Media type, optional if CLASSID is specified
- DATA—Location of data rendered by control

- ■ TYPE—Internet Media type of data
- ■ DECLARE—Object declaration only, instantiated by a later OBJECT
- ■ STANDBY—Message to display while control is downloading

The PARAM element is also included within the HTML 4.0 draft specification, with the following PARAM-specific attributes:

- ■ NAME—OBJECT attribute name
- ■ VALUE—OBJECT attribute value
- ■ VALUETYPE—Type of value attribute

Normally the CLASSID attribute contains the URL of the location of the control being embedded in the page. Microsoft uses a different approach for the CLASSID attribute, by downloading the OBJECT control, usually an ActiveX control, and then using the control's COM CLASSID in the location reserved for the OBJECT CLASSID. The COM CLASSID provides an identification of the location as well as type of control on the client machine by creating an entry in the client machine's Registry database.

As the following shows, the CLASSID Microsoft uses can be obscure. The Web page author either uses a tool to embed the OBJECT's CLASSID, or copies the CLASSID from documentation:

```
<OBJECT id="thename"
CLASSID="CLSID:05589FA1-C356-11CE-BF01-00AA0055595A">
<PARAM NAME="FileName" VALUE="multimediafile.avi">
</OBJECT>
```

Although I am not particularly fond of the CLASSIDs Microsoft supports in its implementation of ActiveX objects, they are within the guidelines established by the HTML 4.0.

The OBJECT element with associated PARAM elements is a good concept. This approach is superior to the use of the EMBED element in that object attributes do not have to be hard coded within the element definition, but can be added at the discretion of the object creator at any later time. To use the new attributes, the Web page author need only add the additional PARAM element for the new attribute.

The next sections demonstrate the use of Microsoft's DirectShow ActiveX control, providing demonstrations of its use within the EMBED element as well as the OBJECT element. You can use these examples to see some of the differences between the two object embedding techniques.

Handling Sound and Video with Microsoft's DirectShow

The DirectShow ActiveX control processes all forms of multimedia content such as .avi and .mpg video, .wav and .mid audio, and Apple QuickTime video for Internet Explorer.

This sophisticated control can be enabled in a variety of ways, as demonstrated in the next section. However, embedding the control into a Web page using the OBJECT syntax also provides for sophisticated manipulation of the control, its behavior, and its appearance, as well as what kind of control the Web page reader has over multimedia playback. This is demonstrated in the "The DirectShow Object Properties, Events, and Methods" section in this chapter.

Embedding Sound and Video into an HTML Page

With DirectShow, a multimedia file can be inserted into a page using a hypertext link, embedded into the page using the <EMBED> tag, or embedded as an ActiveX control using the <OBJECT> tag. For .mpg movies, the control can begin to play the movie while it is being downloaded using a progressive download approach. This doesn't work for QuickTime or .avi movies that include the frame index at the end of the file.

When using the DirectShow control with the <OBJECT> tag, you need to specify the class id (CLASSID) that Microsoft created for this object. The following code is the syntax necessary to embed the DirectShow object into a Web page:

```
<OBJECT id="thename"
CLASSID="CLSID:05589FA1-C356-11CE-BF01-00AA0055595A">
<PARAM NAME="FileName" VALUE="multimediafile.avi">
</OBJECT>
```

As an example of using DirectShow with .mid files, a Web page that uses three different techniques to include a sound file has been created. The first is a hypertext link to the sound file; the second is using the <OBJECT> tag and CLASSID for DirectShow; the third is using the <EMBED> tag. Listing 12.4 contains the source for this file, which you can also access from the file midi1ie.htm.

Listing 12.4. Three different techniques of using DirectShow to play a .mid file.

```
<HTML>
<HEAD>
<TITLE> Multimedia </TITLE>

</HEAD>
<BODY>
<H1>Shelley's First</H1>
<TABLE cols=3 border=0 width=90% align=center
    cellpadding=20>
<tr><td width=10%>
<a href="example.mid">Song</a>
</td><td width=50%>
<OBJECT id="themusic"
CLASSID="CLSID:05589FA1-C356-11CE-BF01-00AA0055595A">
<PARAM NAME="FileName" VALUE="example.mid">
</OBJECT>
</td><td width=40%>
<EMBED SRC="example.mid">
</td></tr>
<tr><td colspan=3>
A little tune I created using Microsoft's Music Producer
</td></tr>
</table>
</BODY>
```

The hypertext link results in a dialog box asking the Web page reader whether he or she wants to open this file and play it directly, or save it to the client. Opening the file and playing it directly results in a page similar to that shown in Figure 12.7. Note from the figure that all three .mid controls have started playing.

FIGURE 12.7.

This Internet Explorer page demonstrates three techniques for opening a MIDI sound file.

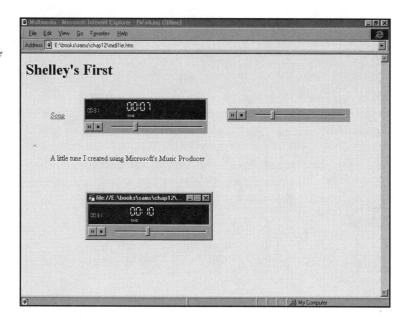

The same source code can be used to open an .avi or .mpg file. Listing 12.5 shows source using the three techniques to embed an .mpg file: a hypertext link, the <OBJECT> tag, and the <EMBED> tag. It also uses the <IMG> tag with the attribute of DYNSRC to represent loading dynamic content into the image.

Listing 12.5. Four techniques for embedding a video into a Web page using DirectShow.

```
<HTML>
<HEAD>
<TITLE> Multimedia </TITLE>
<STYLE type="text/css">
    H1 { color: red; text-align: center }
</STYLE>
</HEAD>
<BODY>
<H1>Discovery Shuttle Launch</H1>
<TABLE cols=3 border=0 width=90% align=center
    cellpadding=20>
<tr><td >
<a href="launch.mpg">Movie</a><p>
<img start=1 loop=0 dynsrc="launch.mpg">
</td><td>
<OBJECT
```

```
CLASSID="CLSID:05589FA1-C356-11CE-BF01-00AA0055595A">
<PARAM NAME="FileName" VALUE="launch.mpg">
</OBJECT>
</td><td>
<EMBED SRC="launch.mpg">
</td>
</tr></table>
</BODY>
```

COMPANION Web site Again, note there is no difference when using the `<OBJECT>` tag or the `<EMBED>` tag with an `.mpg` file, as with a `.mid` file. You can try this example yourself by opening the file `mpegie.htm`. Using the attribute `START` and setting it to a value of `1`, the image is set to start playing when it's first loaded. The movie only plays once because the attribute `loop` is set to a value of `0`. Figure 12.8 shows the page with all three movies displayed side by side and the external movie player displayed just below the embedded movies.

FIGURE 12.8.

Each of the four movies are embedded using a different technique.

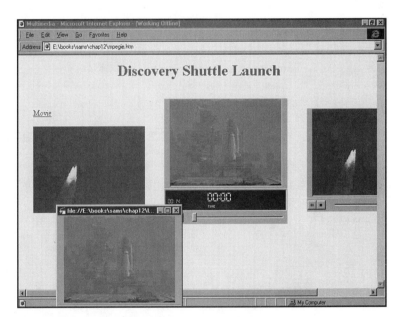

The DirectShow Object Properties, Events, and Methods

You can alter the default values for the properties for the DirectShow ActiveX control when you use the `<OBJECT>` tag syntax. You can also alter many of these same properties during runtime by accessing the control's menu with a right-click.

Several properties of the control can be altered at design time by using the `PARAM=` and `VALUE=` pairs. As an example, Listing 12.6 shows the source for a Web page that contains an `.avi` file that was embedded using the DirectShow object syntax. The object is also positioned absolutely within the Web page using CSS1 positioning.

12

MULTIMEDIA, CONTROLS, AND PLUG-INS

Listing 12.6. DirectShow embedded object with several properties set.

```
<HTML>
<HEAD>
<TITLE> Multimedia </TITLE>
<STYLE type="text/css">
    H1 { color: red; text-align: center}
</STYLE>
</HEAD>
<BODY>
<H1>Apollo 11 Flag Planting</H1>
<OBJECT CLASSID="CLSID:05589FA1-C356-11CE-BF01-00AA0055595A"
    style="position:absolute; left: 35%; top: 100">
<PARAM NAME="FileName" VALUE="apo11h.avi">
<PARAM NAME="DisplayBackColor" VALUE="&H00FF00">
<PARAM NAME="DisplayForeColor" VALUE="&H000000">
<PARAM NAME="Rate" VALUE="1.25">
</OBJECT>
</BODY>
```

COMPANION **Web site** The object is created with black writing on a green display background color. The playback rate for the movie is at 1.25, with authored speeds at 1. This means the playback will be faster than the video was authored. All other object properties are accepted with their default values. Figure 12.9 shows this Web page, which you can also try by opening the file dsprops.htm with Internet Explorer.

FIGURE 12.9.

This page used the DirectShow object syntax and altered the default values for control colors and playback speed.

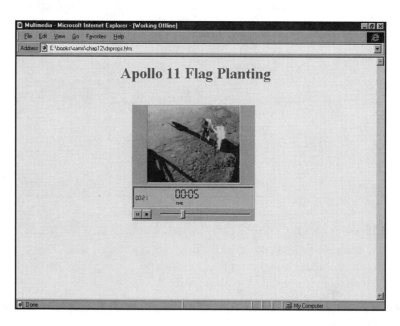

By default, this control has a property dialog box that can be accessed by right-clicking the control. Note that this property dialog box is also available if the <EMBED> tag was used with the multimedia file in addition to the `<OBJECT>` tag. Figure 12.10 shows the same Web page created in Listing 12.6, but with the properties dialog box displayed.

FIGURE 12.10.

The properties dialog box for the DirectShow embedded control.

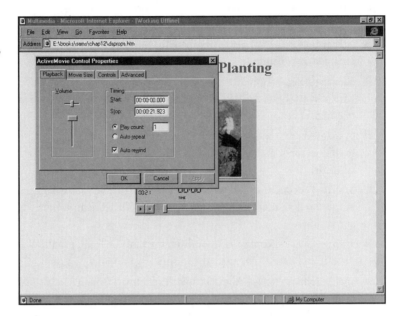

Note from Figure 12.10 that several properties can be changed by the Web page reader, such as how many times the video plays back, the start and stop points within the video, the colors, the size of the control, which controls to display, and other more advanced properties.

The DirectShow properties available when the control is used in a Web page, their default values, and whether they can be set at runtime are shown in the following list:

- `FileName`—URL of multimedia source file; this can be changed at design or runtime.

- `AllowChangeDisplayMode`—Whether the Web page reader can change between displaying time or frames. This is `true` by default and can be changed at runtime.

- `AllowHideControls`—Whether the Web page reader can hide or display controls. This is `true` by default and can be changed at runtime.

- `AllowHideDisplay`—Whether the Web page reader can hide or show control display This is `true` by default and can be changed at runtime.

- `Appearance`—Whether the control has an inset border (value of `1`) or flat border (value of `0`). This is inset by default and cannot be changed at runtime.

- `AutoRewind`—Rewinds the multimedia stream after playback is set to `true`. This is `true` by default and can be changed at runtime.

- `AutoStart`—Starts the multimedia stream play as soon as the control loads if `true`. This is `true` by default and cannot be changed at runtime.

- `Balance`—Long value representing sound balance. This is `0` by default with values from `-10,000` to `10,000` and can be changed at runtime.

- `BorderStyle`—Controls appearance of border. This is border (value of `1`) by default and cannot be changed at runtime.

- `CurrentPosition`—Current position in multimedia stream in seconds. This can be changed at runtime.

- `CurrentState`—Whether control is stopped, playing, or paused. This can be changed with the methods `Run`, `Pause`, and `Stop`. Value of `0` is stopped, `1` is paused, and `2` is playing.

- `DisplayBackColor`—Background color of display, set with hexadecimal value represented as `long`, using `&H000000` format, or RGB function. Property can be altered at runtime.

- `DisplayForeColor`—Color of the text of the display, set with hexadecimal value represented as `long`, using `&H000000` format, or RGB function. Property can be altered at runtime.

- `DisplayMode`—Display as seconds (value of `0`) or frames (value of `1`). This is seconds by default and can be changed at runtime.

- `EnableContextMenu`—Allow Properties menu. This is `true` by default and can be changed at runtime.

- `Enabled`—Whether control is enabled. This is `true` by default and can be changed at runtime.

- `EnablePostionControls`—Whether position controls are enabled. This is `true` by default and can be changed at runtime.

- `EnableSelectionControls`—Whether selection controls are enabled. This is `true` by default and can be changed at runtime.

- `EnableTracker`—Whether trackbar is enabled. This is `true` by default and can be changed at runtime.

- `FullScreenMode`—To display video fullscreen. This is `false` by default, and can be changed at runtime. Values are `0` for original size, `1` for double size, `2` for 1/16 screen size, `3` for 1/4 screen size, and `4` for 1/2 screen size.

- `PlayCount`—Number of times to loop playback. This can be changed at runtime.

- `Rate`—Playback rate for stream. This is set to `0` (authored speed) by default and can be changed at runtime. Values less than `0.5` or greater than `1.5` become difficult to understand.

- `ReadyState`—Controls readiness state. This cannot be changed at runtime. States are `-1` if file not initialized, `0` if control is a synchronously loading file, `1` if control has loaded enough file data to be playing, and `2` if all data has been downloaded.

■ SelectionEnd—Ending position of selection in seconds. This defaults to the length of the stream and can be changed at runtime.

■ SelectionStart—Beginning position of selection in seconds. This defaults to the beginning of the stream and can be changed at runtime.

■ ShowControls—Whether the controls panel is displayed. This is true by default and can be changed at runtime.

■ ShowDisplay—Whether display panel is displayed. This is true by default and can be changed at runtime.

■ ShowPositionControls—Whether position controls are displayed. This is false by default and can be changed at runtime.

■ ShowSelectionControls—Whether selection controls are displayed. This is false by default and can be changed at runtime.

■ ShowTracker—Whether trackbar is displayed or not. This is true by default and can be changed at runtime.

■ Volume—Controls sound volume. 0 is full volume. Acceptable values are -10,000 to 0, and it can be changed at runtime.

Each of these properties can be set at design time using the PARAM= and VALUE= pair, as shown previously in Listing 12.6. If the property has been set to be changeable at runtime, these same properties can also be set at runtime using script. All properties have read-only access at runtime.

Listing 12.7 shows a Web page with the embedded .avi file and a button. Clicking the button alters several of the object's properties including the multimedia source file, size, position, colors, and several others. Clicking the button again changes the DirectShow object back to what it was when the page first opened.

Listing 12.7. Altering several DirectShow object properties at runtime.

```
<HTML>
<HEAD>
<TITLE> Multimedia </TITLE>
<STYLE type="text/css">
    H1 { color: red; text-align: center}
    #mybutton { background-color: lime;
            font-size: 16pt; font-variant: small-caps;
            position:absolute; left: 35%; top: 400}
</STYLE>
<SCRIPT type="text/vbscript">
<!--

' track state
Dim mystate
mystate = 0
```

continues

Listing 12.7. continued

```
' change certain
' object properties
Sub change_object
   If mystate = 0 Then
      myobject.FileName = "aria.avi"
      myobject.DisplayBackColor = "&HFF00FF"
      myobject.DisplayForeColor = "&HFFFFFF"
      myobject.Rate = 1.0
      myobject.MovieWindowSize = 1
      myobject.style.posLeft=0
      myobject.style.posTop = 0
      myobject.ShowSelectionControls=True
      mystate = 1
   Else
      myobject.FileName = "apo11h.avi"
      myobject.DisplayBackColor = "&H00FF00"
      myobject.DisplayForeColor = "&H000000"
      myobject.Rate = 1.25
      myobject.MovieWindowSize = 0
      myobject.style.posLeft=250
      myobject.style.posTop = 100
      myobject.ShowSelectionControls=False
      mystate = 0
   End If
End Sub

' after file completely opened
' backwards compatibility only
' replace with ReadyStateChange
Sub myobject_OpenComplete
      myobject.run
      myobject.DisplayMode = 1
End Sub
'-->
</SCRIPT>
</HEAD>

<BODY>
<H1>Apollo 11 Flag Planting</H1>
<OBJECT CLASSID="CLSID:05589FA1-C356-11CE-BF01-00AA0055595A"
   id=myobject style="position:absolute; left: 250; top: 100">
<PARAM NAME="FileName" VALUE="apo11h.avi">
<PARAM NAME="DisplayBackColor" VALUE="&H00FF00">
<PARAM NAME="DisplayForeColor" VALUE="&H000000">
<PARAM NAME="AutoStart" VALUE="False">
</OBJECT>
<BUTTON id=mybutton
   onclick="change_object()">
Change Object
</BUTTON>
</BODY>
```

COMPANION Web site As you can see in the listing, altering the object's properties at runtime occurs through accessing the object by its name and setting the property to the appropriate value. You can access this example by opening the file dsprops2.htm.

The listing also demonstrates calling one of the DirectShow methods: the `Run` method. All the exposed methods are given in the following list:

- `AboutBox`—Version and copyright information about the control
- `IsSoundCardEnabled`—Whether sound card is installed and enabled
- `Pause`—Pause playback
- `Run`—Run multimedia stream
- `Stop`—Stop stream playback

Listing 12.7 also shows that an event for the object, `OpenComplete`, is trapped and gives the code to run the object when the object finishes loading. Other DirectShow events are as follows:

- `DisplayModeChange`—When `DisplayMode` property is changed
- `Error`—When an error occurs; particularly helpful to use if the multimedia file cannot be loaded
- `OpenComplete`—When source code has finished loading
- `PositionChange`—When media position is changed
- `ReadyStateChange`—When changes to an object's ready state occur
- `StateChange`—Player state changes
- `Timer`—For timing events

The DirectShow ActiveX control is a powerful object for controlling the playback of multimedia content such as `.mpg`, `.avi` videos, QuickTime videos, and audio files. Best of all, this control is installed with the minimum installation of Internet Explorer, so you know it will always be available.

A Brief Overview of Microsoft's DirectAnimation Technology

In addition to DirectShow, Microsoft has also built DirectX (their gaming, animation, and multimedia technology) into Internet Explorer with the DirectAnimation technologies.

DirectAnimation is a set of objects, a set of built-in controls, and an API that are accessible from script, Java, C++, or other code. With these sets you can integrate the use of scripting, Java, and controls to create interesting and download-friendly multimedia effects. Why download-friendly? With DirectAnimation you can use something like the Structured Graphics built-in control and function calls to create a complex graphic and animation, yet the function calls are nothing more than ASCII text downloaded from the server. Based on this, the page contents are smaller, download faster, and begin to display sooner than a Web page with a larger animated GIF file.

The DirectAnimation controls are:

- `Structured Graphics`—Creates a 2D image using several graphics functions
- `Path`—Controls the movement of any object

- ■ Sequencer—Controls and synchronizes the actions of several different elements
- ■ Sprite—Controls the animation frames and playback

Covering the DirectAnimation technology would take an entire book. In this chapter, the use of three of these controls is covered: Path, Structured Graphics, and Sequencer. These controls are used here to create a red circle that moves around the center of the page in a circle and that rotates on its X axis.

Listing 12.8 shows the complete source for the Web page. The first control created is the Structured Graphics control, and it uses several methods to create a circle shape, fill the shape with a solid color (red), and set the line color to black. The coordinate system being used sets the point of origin to the bottom of the control area and sets Y to increase as you move down the page. Based on this, to fully display the circle, I needed to set the beginning X and Y positions to a negative value so that they appear.

Listing 12.8. Example demonstrating three of the DirectAnimation controls.

```
<HTML>
<HEAD>
<TITLE> Multimedia </TITLE>
<SCRIPT language="jscript">
<!--
// Call rotate function to rotate
// around X axis
function RotateX() {
    circle.Rotate(15,0,0);
}

// call function to begin
// rotation around X axis and
// rotation around page
function rotate_circle() {
    circle.SetIdentity();
    seq.item('ActionSet1').at(1.000, 'RotateX',-1, 0.010, 1);
    seq.item('ActionSet1').Play();
    circle.SetIdentity();
    thepath.Target="circle";
    thepath.Play();
}
//-->
</SCRIPT>
</HEAD>
<BODY onload="rotate_circle()">

<!-- Stuctured Graphics Control - red circle -->
<OBJECT ID="circle"
STYLE="position:absolute; HEIGHT:200;WIDTH:200;TOP:200;LEFT:200"
CLASSID="CLSID:369303C2-D7AC-11d0-89D5-00A0C90833E6">
<PARAM NAME="Line0001" VALUE="SetLineColor(0,0,0)">
<PARAM NAME="Line0002" VALUE="SetFillColor(255,0,0,0,0,255)">
<PARAM NAME="Line0003" VALUE="SetFillSTYLE(1)">
<PARAM NAME="Line0004" VALUE="SetLineSTYLE(1,1)">
<PARAM NAME="Line0005" VALUE="Oval(-25,-50,100,100)">
 </OBJECT>
```

```
<!-- Path control - oval -->
<OBJECT ID="thepath"
CLASSID = "CLSID:D7A7D7C3-D47F-11D0-89D3-00A0C90833E6">
    <PARAM NAME="AutoStart" VALUE="0">
    <PARAM NAME="Repeat" VALUE="-1">
    <PARAM NAME="Bounce" VALUE="0">
    <PARAM NAME="Duration" VALUE="10">
    <PARAM NAME="Shape" VALUE="Oval(50,50,200,200)">
</OBJECT>

<OBJECT id=seq STYLE=""
    CLASSID=clsid:B0A6BAE2-AAF0-11d0-A152-00A0C908DB96>
</OBJECT>
<H1>Welcome to the DirectAnimation Demonstration</H1>
This example demonstrates that DirectAnimation
controls work with the regular HTML page contents.
These controls are windowless, meaning that they work directly on the web page
rather than within some arbitrary container.
</BODY>
```

The Path control is the next object created, and it is set to be loaded only, which means that the path must be programatically started. In addition, a parameter value is given to not reverse direction at the end of the path, and the path is given a timer value of 10 milliseconds. The shape used for the Path is the Oval shape and set to be a complete circle (the width and height, set with the values of "200", are the same). Following the Path object is the Sequencer object, and this control object is created without any parameters.

When the page loads, it calls a function called rotate_circle. This function uses the SetIdentity function to direct all future actions to the circle object. Then the at method is called for the ActionSet1 item of the Sequencer control to associate the rotateX function with a timer for the circle object. The Sequencer action is played next, followed by the Stop method call for the Path action. As the path's target is altered, the Stop method is called as a safety measure to ensure that the path is not playing when the target change is made. After the target's set, play the path.

COMPANION **Web site** The results of these three objects and the associated script are shown in Figure 12.11. You can also try this yourself by opening the file directa.htm in Internet Explorer.

As stated earlier, DirectAnimation—the controls, methods, and properties—and the associated DirectAnimation API are far too complex to cover in detail in this chapter, but Listing 12.8 should demonstrate some of this technology's capabilities. To learn more about DirectAnimation, consult the Client Internet SDK that comes with the Internet Explorer 4.0 CD-ROM, or download it directly from Microsoft at http://www.microsoft.com/ie.

Creating Interesting Effects with the Internet Explorer Built-In Filters

Microsoft created the CSS1-style Visual Filters to control the appearance of ordinary HTML elements. The Visual Filter effects can do such things as make an element semi-transparent, rotate an image, remove colors, or add specific lighting effects to a page.

FIGURE 12.11.

The Structured
Graphics *control creates
a red circle, the* Path
*control moves the circle
around a path, and the*
Sequencer *control spins
the circle.*

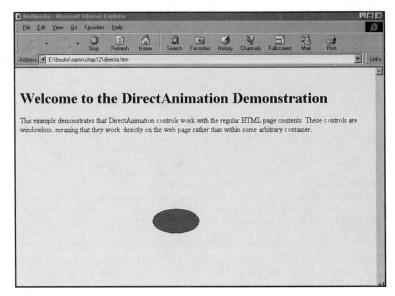

Covering this new filter style attribute in detail goes beyond the scope of this chapter, but an example of how it works gives you an idea of what these filter effects can do.

One very popular technique with Web page interaction is to use a rollover effect to alter an element when the Web page reader's mouse is over the element. One use of this is to display a highlighted image when the reader's mouse is over the base image. This is an effective feedback technique to let the reader know that an image is an active link to a process or another page. The downside to this technique, however, is that two images need to be loaded instead of just one.

With Dynamic HTML, you can also use a rollover effect for text and alter the color or font when the reader's mouse is over the text. This adds highlighting, but doesn't provide the "notice me" effect you might like to use with a rollover.

Combining the two techniques, a Web page that uses the Glow Visual Filter effect is created to add rollover highlighting to simple text. Listing 12.9 contains the source code for this page, which contains four menu items positioned using an HTML table. Each table cell traps the mouseover and mouseout events. The mouseover event calls the function highlight, which then applies the filter effect. The mouseout event calls the return_normal function, which returns the text to its previous state.

Listing 12.9. Using the Glow Visual Filter to create a rollover effect.

```
<HTML>
<HEAD>
<TITLE> Multimedia </TITLE>
<STYLE type="text/css">
```

```
      BODY { background-color: black }
      TD { font-size: 24pt; font-family: serif; color: red }
</STYLE>

<SCRIPT language="jscript">
<!--
// highlight menu item
function highlight(num) {
   var theelement = document.all.tags("TD").item(num);
   theelement.style.filter="Glow(color=#FFFF00,strength=5)";
}

// return menu item to normal text
function return_normal(num) {
   var theelement = document.all.tags("TD").item(num);
   theelement.style.filter=" ";
}
//-->
</SCRIPT>
</HEAD>
<BODY>
<table cols=4 border=0 width=80% align=center cellspacing=20>
<tr>
<td onmouseover="highlight(0)" onmouseout="return_normal(0)">
Menu 1</td>
<td onmouseover="highlight(1)" onmouseout="return_normal(1)">
Menu 2</td>
<td onmouseover="highlight(2)" onmouseout="return_normal(2)">
Menu 3</td>
<td onmouseover="highlight(3)" onmouseout="return_normal(3)">
Menu 4</td>
</tr>
</table>
</BODY>
```

As shown in the preceding listing, set the `Filter` property to the empty string in order to remove the filter.

NOTE

Note that instead of sending through the index number of the element that is receiving the mouseover or mouseout events, I could also use the event object srcElement attribute, as follows:

```
var theelement = window.event.srcElement;
```

The Event object is discussed and demonstrated in more detail in Chapter 30, "Using the HTML Object Model and Creating Dynamic HTML Pages."

The cost to this page is the ASCII for the script code as the page is downloading, which is trivial, and the slight time it takes to parse the scripting code when the page is loading. These extra efforts have virtually no impact on the Web page reader's perception of time for the page to load, compared to not having this extra code. However, the impact when the reader moves his or her mouse over any of the menu items is dramatic, as you can see from Figure 12.12. You can also try this yourself by opening the file `filtroll.htm`. Again, this technology only works with Internet Explorer 4.x.

FIGURE 12.12.

Notice the impact of using the Glow *Visual Filter effect for mouse rollover.*

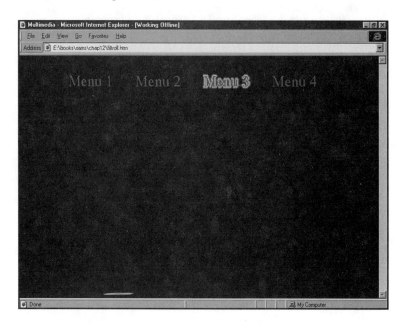

The other Visual Filter effects include the following:

- ■ `Alpha Effect`—Controls opacity of an element
- ■ `Blur Effect`—Adds motion blur to an element
- ■ `Chroma Effect`—Renders specified colors transparent
- ■ `Drop Shadow`—Adds an offset solid shadow
- ■ `FlipH`—Flips the element horizontally
- ■ `FlipV`—Flips the element vertically
- ■ `Glow`—Adds a glow outlining the element
- ■ `Gray`—Drops the element's color palette
- ■ `Invert`—Inverts the element's hue, saturation, and brightness
- ■ `Light`—Creates a light source on a page that can have several `Light` specific effects applied
- ■ `Mask`—Masks transparent pixels with a color
- ■ `Shadow`—Creates solid shadow in a specific direction

- Wave—Creates a wavelike effect
- Xray—Renders an object in black and white

Again, to learn more about these style filters, consult the Internet Client SDK located on the IE 4.0 CD-ROM, or download the SDK, at no charge, from Microsoft at http://www.microsoft.com/ie/.

Taking Advantage of Third-Party Plug-Ins and Controls

Only the browser-specific plug-ins and controls have been discussed so far in this chapter, yet there are hundreds of multimedia controls provided by third-party companies.

One of the most popular multimedia objects is Macromedia's Shockwave and the new Shockwave Flash multimedia players. These controls/plug-ins render content created with Macromedia's Flash, for streaming vector animations; Director, for streaming interactive multimedia including timing; and Authorware for streaming interactive multimedia. Prior to the use of dynamic HTML in the newest versions of IE and Navigator, Macromedia's Shockwave was probably the most widely used technique to include complex animations and other multimedia content within a Web page. You can find out more about Shockwave and download the players at the Macromedia Web site at http://www.macromedia.com.

Netscape provides access to an Apple QuickTime plug-in and Microsoft supports QuickTime files with the DirectShow ActiveX control. You can also find out more about QuickTime, as well as download the QuickTime plug-in, from http://quickTime.apple.com/dev/devWeb.html. This page also has instructions about creating QuickTime movies.

A new image format, called PNG, is gaining popularity. This royalty-free imaging format has an improved compression capability, as well as built-in support for Alpha-channel transparency and Gamma correction. It's seen as an eventual replacement for .gif format files, primarily because of limitations to the .gif format, and because .gif is a CompuServe proprietary technique. Internet Explorer 4.0 includes support for PNG directly within the use of the <IMAGE> tag, but you need to access a plug-in to include .png files viewable by Navigator. You can access this plug-in at http://www.siegelgale.com/png/index.html/.

Virtual Reality Modeling Language (VRML) files are becoming more popular to use within Web pages. You need a plug-in to view VRML files with Navigator, and Netscape currently supports the Cosmos player by SGI, which also works with Internet Explorer 4.0. You can download the Cosmos Player and read more about it at http://cosmo.sgi.com/. Microsoft has its own VRML 2.0 viewer, and you can read more on this at http://www.microsoft.com/vrml.

The Adobe Acrobat reader, which processes files with the extension of .pdf, is another very popular plug-in/control, as well as a separate utility for offline viewing. You can read more about Acrobat at the Adobe download site at http://www.adobe.com/supportservice/custsupport/

download.html/. Adobe provides a wide variety of plug-ins, controls, and applications for reading .pdf and other Adobe file formats such as Photoshop content, PageMaker, and others. In most cases the company has provided utilities and controls for a variety of platforms, including Windows, Macintosh, and UNIX, as well as DOS and OS/2. In the case of .pdf files, my preference has always been to download the files, which can be quite large, and then use the Adobe Acrobat utility to open the file for offline viewing.

For RealAudio or RealVideo, progressive multimedia content, Microsoft has provided a utility for viewing the content called RealPlayer, installed with the full installation of IE 4.0. RealPlayer also works with Navigator; you can read more about the player and the Real technologies, as well as download or order the player at the RealNetworks, Inc. Web site at http://www.real.com.

The best approach to take with both browsers is to view each browser's Web site for more information on plug-ins or ActiveX controls, and see what viewers are available. Before you download several viewers, you might want to restrict yourself to the ones mentioned in this section. If you need new viewers to access a page's contents, the page usually has a link to follow to download the control. With this approach you download only those players you are most likely to use.

Each of the multimedia viewers mentioned in this section has online documentation explaining how to embed the player within a Web page and how to control the player with scripting, if possible.

When and When Not to Use Multimedia

With Netscape Navigator 4.0 and Internet Explorer 4.0 you now have several types of multimedia that you can apply to a Web page. You can load images and sound, apply interesting effects with Dynamic HTML, and use visual filters, plug-ins, and controls. However, there are limitations to using multimedia.

Restrict Download Sizes

First, keep the total size of images that are downloaded with a page to a size in keeping with the page. If the page is associated with a graphics tool or other high-tech type of business, you are more justified in using more graphics or other multimedia content. If you are creating a Web site for a bank or insurance company or something similar, you might want to be more cautious with how many graphic images, or how much multimedia, you include.

If you want to include the use of video or sound, such as a company theme song or video message from the president of the company, you might want to consider placing these on a separate page so these bandwidth-hogging files do not impede your readers' access to other information. If the readers choose, they can access the page with the multimedia.

Consider including a .gif or .jpeg image that shows one of the frames of the video as the link to the video. This image then becomes a thumbnail of what the video contains.

Copyright Information

If you don't want your image, video, or song saved and used by another site, you must make sure that all copyright information on the multimedia file is displayed prominently on the same page the file is accessed from. You may legally be covered by posting copyright information in the main Web page of your site, and nowhere else, but this becomes confusing to those people who may access the page with the multimedia directly rather than entering from the main Web page. An approach many companies use is to provide a link to a copyright page at the bottom of all their site pages.

Speaking of copyright, do not ever copy and reuse images, videos, or sounds that are not public domain and that you do not have permission to use. This is unethical and could also get you sued. You can freely copy and use all public domain multimedia.

The videos used in this chapter were from government-based Web sites such as NASA. Government agencies cannot copyright their content, so you can copy and use multimedia from these sites freely as long as you do not, in any way, use any logos or other information from these sites that might cause confusion as to whether you represent these agencies.

If you are unsure of the copyright for a multimedia file, contact the Webmaster for the site and get clarification.

Cross-Browser Compatibility Issues

As demonstrated in this chapter, you can embed sound and video files in a Web page and have them opened equally with Navigator and Internet Explorer using the `<EMBED>` tag. Future generations of Navigator should also support the `<OBJECT>` tag.

If you want to use one browser's specific technique, but your page is accessed by both of these popular browsers, use the browser-specific technique to enhance an effect, not supply the entire effect. For the rollover example, you could have used two blocks of text, each located within a `DIV` block, and one placed on top of the other. The hidden block would then use a different, brighter color for the text. With the `mouseover` event, the script hides the original block, something both browsers can do, and then displays the hidden, highlighted block. This technique works with both browsers and has minimal impact on download times. To increase the visual impact of the highlight for Internet Explorer, you could also add the Visual Filter `Glow` effect, which Navigator should then ignore.

The point of this approach is that the Visual Filter then enhances the effect, but both browsers see highlighted text based on mouse movement.

Considering issues of accessibility, using something such as this rollover effect can be created in such a way as to be ignored in text only browsers, but these browsers will be able to access the original text, and from there the link the text represents. The rollover effect enhances the page but isn't the only method of navigation. You should be cautious in your use of newer multimedia technologies, especially if your page must be accessible by older browsers, or speech-only browsers.

Cross-Platform Compatibility Issues

As mentioned earlier in the chapter, not all multimedia files play equally well on all platforms. Non-Windows platforms do not render .avi files well, Apple systems only support 216 colors within the standard palette, while Windows supports 256 colors, and so on.

The rule of thumb is to deliver content to the lowest common denominator—what works for all platforms—or to provide different links to different multimedia types, and let the reader choose which format to use.

Summary

This chapter introduced the use of plug-ins to enable video and sound playback in both Navigator and Internet Explorer. For Navigator, the LiveConnect technique of accessing exposed methods and properties from plug-ins is demonstrated.

The new Microsoft DirectShow multimedia ActiveX control is also demonstrated. This control handles both sound and video, and has several properties that can be altered during design, at runtime, or both.

Microsoft also introduced a new DirectAnimation technology to include animation and sophisticated in-page multimedia techniques that don't rely on downloading images, video, or sound to create multimedia effects. You saw an example of using some of the DirectAnimation multimedia controls, although this technology is too extensive to cover in detail in this chapter.

Microsoft also exposed several Visual Filter effects that can add very noticeable effects to standard HTML elements. You saw how to use a Visual Filter to create a rollover effect that requires minimal download time or server resources.

Finally, some issues about using multimedia content, such as the multimedia file size or copyright issues, were covered, in addition to some cross-browser compatibility issues.

This chapter uses both JavaScript/JScript and VBScript, which are covered in more detail in Part III, "Client-Side Scripting." For the Microsoft Visual Filters and DirectAnimation technologies, you can get more information from the Internet Client SDK included with Internet Explorer 4.0, or it can be downloaded from http://www.microsoft.com/ie.

III

PART

IN THIS PART

Client-Side Scripting

Scripting Basics

by Robert McDaniel

CHAPTER 13

HTML is a powerful mechanism for laying out pages. However, with HTML alone, you are limited to static pages that may look nice, but do not provide for interactivity or interaction. Client-side scripting extends the static Web pages by providing a mechanism for Web page authors to create dynamic, interactive pages for their users.

Client-side scripting is not HTML in and of itself. The script, as it is commonly called, is written in one of the supported programming languages and then embedded in a Web page's HTML code. The script gets downloaded along with the rest of the Web page, and is run by the user's Web browser.

In this chapter you learn the basics about client-side scripting. You are introduced to what client-side scripting is, what programming languages you can use for your scripts, and how to create them. You also learn common tasks and limitations of client-side scripts.

What Is Client-Side Scripting?

Client-side scripting refers to creating scripts that are executed in the user's Web browser, the Web client, rather than on your Web server. A client-side script is typically a small program embedded within an HTML document. Whenever a Web browser that supports client-side scripting encounters one of these scripts, it executes the program by interpreting the commands. Listing 13.1 contains an example of a client-side script written in JavaScript. In the header section of the HTML, the example script places the user agent and version of the Web browser being used into two variables. Then, in the body section of the HTML, the values stored in these variables are written to the document, displaying them to the user. Figure 13.1 shows how this page is displayed when loaded into Netscape Navigator 4.0.

Listing 13.1. A simple JavaScript example.

```
<HTML>
<HEAD>
<TITLE>A Simple JavaScript Example</TITLE>

<SCRIPT LANGUAGE="JavaScript">
<!--

  var userAgent=navigator.appName;
  var browserVersion = navigator.appVersion;

//-->
</SCRIPT>

</HEAD>
<BODY BGCOLOR="#FFFFFF">
<CENTER>
<TABLE BORDER=0 WIDTH=300 HEIGHT=100%>
<TR>
<TD VALIGN=middle ALIGN=center>
```

```
<FONT SIZE=+2 FACE="COURIER">You are using</FONT> <FONT SIZE=+2><B>

<SCRIPT LANGUAGE="JavaScript">
<!--

  document.write(userAgent);

//-->
</SCRIPT>

</B></FONT> <FONT SIZE=+2 FACE="COURIER">version</FONT> <FONT SIZE=+2><B>

<SCRIPT LANGUAGE="JavaScript">
<!--

  document.write(browserVersion);

//-->
</SCRIPT>

</B></FONT> <FONT SIZE=+2 FACE="COURIER">as your Web browser.</FONT>
</TD>
</TR>
</TABLE>
</CENTER>
</BODY>
</HTML>
```

Figure 13.1.

The simple JavaScript example in Netscape Navigator 4.0.

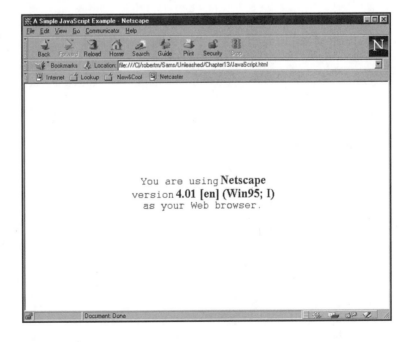

13

SCRIPTING
BASICS

> **NOTE**
>
> Web browsers are set up to ignore tags they do not recognize. Because of this, when you embed a script in your Web page, Web browsers that do not support scripting simply ignore the `<SCRIPT> </SCRIPT>` tags. The remaining script code will be ignored if the `<!--` and `//-->` tags are used.

Scripts and Programs

Client-side scripts are intended to be cross-browser and cross-platform compatible. Because users visiting your Web site use a variety of machines, such as PCs, Macintoshes, and UNIX Workstations, it is important that the script you embed in your Web page works properly on all the platforms.

This was the same challenge issued to the Java programming language. The intent with Java is to have a single code base that, when compiled to byte code, runs properly on all platforms. Byte code is a step between source code and executable code. Although no longer in the plain English text of source code, a file in byte code is not able to run independently. A byte code file must be interpreted.

Java, however, is a lot more challenging to learn than many Web designers would like. Therefore, client-side scripting languages were introduced. These languages are meant to have the same cross-platform compatibility, while being easy to learn.

Client-side scripts are referred to as scripts rather than programs. There is a subtle difference between these two types of applications. Scripts are typically code that is not compiled before being executed, whereas programs are compiled code that can be executed without the use of a command interpreter.

Compiled Programs

Whether you are writing your application in a programming language or a scripting language, you code statements in normal ASCII characters and save your results in a text file. This text file is your application's source code. It is where you write your statements and make any changes.

After you've written your source code, most high-level programming languages make use of a process called compiling to transform the statements you entered, such as conditional statements, loops, and variable assignments, into actual machine language executable code. Once the program has been compiled, you run that program on the platform for which it has been compiled without any other programs.

A compiled program no longer is a simple text file. It is now referred to as a binary file and opening the file in a text editor reveals strange characters rather than discernible statements. For example, Listing 13.2 contains the source code for a simple C program. When compiled and run, this program prints out the string `"Hello World"`. Figure 13.2 shows how the compiled version of that program looks when opened in the Notepad editor.

Listing 13.2. The "Hello World" source code.

```c
#include <stdio.h>

int main() {

  printf("\n\nHello World\n\n");

}
```

FIGURE 13.2.

The compiled Hello World program opened in Windows Notepad.

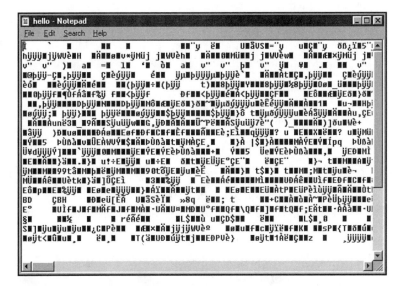

Compiled programs have some advantages. First, because the source code is changed into machine-dependent executable code, it executes much faster than an interpreted program. Because the compiled program does not have to worry about running on other platforms, the compiler can optimize the binary code specifically for that platform.

Another advantage of compiled programs is that you can distribute them without compromising your source code's integrity. Although the technology exists to disassemble executables back into source code, they do not always work well. Also, the majority of people using your programs do not have the skill or software necessary to disassemble your program. For the most part, you can be assured that your source code is safe with compiled programs.

Disadvantages come along with the advantages of compiled programs. For example, the process of compiling a program can take some time, depending on the speed of your machine. A simple change to your program can result in a lot of time coding and compiling.

13

SCRIPTING
BASICS

Perhaps the largest disadvantage, though, is the cross-platform compatibility problem. In general, code you write for one platform often does not work correctly on another platform, such as code written for a PC versus a Macintosh. To further complicate the situation, many compilers are also platform-dependent. In other words, a C compiler on Windows machines that compiles the code for execution on the Windows platform, will not always be able to produce executables for Macintosh or UNIX machines.

Interpreted Scripts

Scripts are similar to programs in that both use similar statement structures, depending on the language being used. However, instead of compiling, scripts are run through a command interpreter that interprets the commands at runtime.

The process of coding a script starts in a fashion similar to that of coding a program. You write the statements for your code and save them into a text file. However, after you have completed your source code, your script is finished. There is no compilation step.

You have a command interpreter process your source code file in order to run a script. A command interpreter is a compiled program. Like all compiled programs, it is specific to the platform for which it was compiled.

For example, with Perl, which is a common scripting language, you must have a Perl command interpreter on your machine in order to run Perl scripts. If you have a Windows machine, you must have a version of the Perl command interpreter for Windows platforms. This would be a different version of the Perl interpreter than someone who has a UNIX version of Perl. The key point is that the single script you wrote on your Windows platform usually runs without a problem on the UNIX platform also.

> **CAUTION**
>
> Cross-platform compatibility of scripts occurs because the commands are stored in a simple text file. If you code your script with statements that are only supported on a single platform, you get errors when you run it on other platforms.

The natural advantage to scripts over programs is the ability to write and distribute a single code base across many platforms. Scripts typically only need minor changes to run correctly on various machines. For example, the Perl script contained in Listing 13.3 runs on both Windows and UNIX platforms.

Listing 13.3. A simple Perl script.

```
#!/usr/bin/perl

print "\n\nHello World!\n\n";
```

The first line in Listing 13.3 is used only on UNIX platforms to specify the location of the Perl command interpreter on that machine. Because the line begins with the # symbol, which is the comment designator in Perl, Perl interpreters on other platforms ignore the line.

This is one of the strongest reasons for using a scripting language for client-side scripts. With the World Wide Web, users viewing your Web pages are on a variety of computer platforms. By using a scripting language, you can write your application in plain text and not worry about what computer is downloading and running it.

Another advantage of scripts is their ease of maintenance. Creating and maintaining a script is as easy as editing a text file. In fact, many people who write scripts using text-mode editors such as vi or Emacs on UNIX platforms and Notepad on Windows. When you make a change to your script, it is ready to be run as soon as you save the file; you do not have to compile it first. This enables you to quickly add a few lines of code and test your script. In general, because of the ability to make quick changes to scripts and test the results of your changes, you can code a script much faster than you can code a program.

There are some disadvantages to scripts as well, though. The biggest disadvantage is the speed at which scripts run. Scripts are run by processing the lines of code through a command interpreter at runtime. The command interpreter recognizes statements and executes the proper machine language code for that statement.

Sound familiar? Although not a direct translation of statements to machine-level code, the act of interpreting a script is not unlike compiling a program. The big difference is that the translation is done at runtime—the end user must endure the wait every time the program is run. With compiled programs, once the compilation is done, the time-consuming translation phase is completed.

Scripts run significantly slower than their program counterparts. With modern computers and with simple programs, this difference can almost be negligible to the user. However, when you start performing computationally intensive actions such as searches and sorts on large blocks of data, you will notice a difference.

The other common disadvantage of scripts over programs is the integrity of your source code. A script is just the source code file. There is nothing else you can distribute. Everyone who has an executable version of your script also has your source code. Depending on how important this code is to you, this may not be a viable option.

Java is the one example that borders the line between scripts and programs. Although the source code is compiled into byte code, the byte code must still be interpreted like scripts when it is run. However, by compiling the source code, the problem of code integrity can be diminished.

Client-Side Scripting Languages

Client-side scripting is relatively new, having only been around for about a year and a half. In that time, however, there are already a couple of scripting languages from which to choose.

The most important thing to remember in choosing a language for your client-side scripts is browser compatibility. Not all browsers support the same scripting languages. You should pick a language that is supported by the browsers the majority of your customers is likely to be using.

JavaScript

JavaScript was the first client-side scripting language. Because of its name, it's a common mistake to think that it is related to the Java programming language. Although it does contain some similar syntax, JavaScript is not Java.

Netscape Communications Corporation created JavaScript in early 1996. The purpose of JavaScript is to provide a true programming language for use by Web page authors to add more interactivity to Web pages. Netscape knew that not all Web page authors were strong programmers. Rather than requiring them to learn Java in order to build in interactivity, Netscape provided them a language that does not demand as much processor power as Java does and is easy to learn.

The first version of JavaScript contained most of the core functionality for the scripting language. It had the full range of data structures, control structures, and conditional statements. JavaScript 1.0 was supported by Netscape Navigator version 2.0.

With the release of Netscape Navigator version 3.0 came the release of JavaScript 1.1. This version of JavaScript contained more built-in functions and data types.

The current version of JavaScript is 1.2. It has a broader range of supported events and built-in functions, providing more flexibility and power to Web page authors. JavaScript 1.2 is supported in Netscape Navigator version 4.0 only.

Netscape also provides licensing for JavaScript, enabling developers to integrate JavaScript within other applications.

JScript

Around the time of JavaScript's introduction, Microsoft Corporation was beginning its own Web push with Internet Explorer. In true Microsoft fashion of embracing and extending, the intention was to support JavaScript in Internet Explorer. However, Netscape had copyrighted both the name JavaScript, and its implementation of the program. In order for Microsoft to integrate JavaScript within Internet Explorer, licensing fees would have to be paid to Netscape. Microsoft was unwilling to do this. So, in order for Microsoft to support this rising standard, it had to create its own implementation of JavaScript. The Microsoft implementation of JavaScript is JScript.

JScript contains the same syntax and structure JavaScript contains. There are a few JavaScript commands that are not supported in the current version of JScript, especially JavaScript 1.1

commands. These commands are supported in the next version of JScript released in Internet Explorer 4.0. For the most part, though, scripts written in JavaScript run properly in browsers that have implemented JScript rather than JavaScript. The current version of JScript is implemented in Internet Explorer 3.x only. Internet Explorer 2.0 does not have support for any client-side scripting.

In an attempt to standardize JScript and extend its uses, Microsoft provides for licensing of the JScript language within other applications.

VBScript

Around the time of JScript's release, Microsoft introduced another client-side scripting language called Visual Basic Scripting Edition, or VBScript. VBScript, unlike JavaScript, is based upon Microsoft's popular Visual Basic product. It uses the same syntax and structure as standard Visual Basic, allowing developers to use a language with which they are already familiar.

Because of the limitations of running within a Web browser, and because of security issues associated with running executable code downloaded with a Web page, VBScript does not contain all of the same commands that Visual Basic contains. Also, because of the unique environment for VBScript scripts, there are a few new built-in functions that are not a part of Visual Basic.

As with JScript, Microsoft allows for the licensing of VBScript for use within other applications.

Placing Scripts in Your Web Pages

The power of client-side scripts comes from their capability to be integrated within a Web page. Rather than having a separate page, application, or applet downloaded in order to run a script, client-side scripts are embedded within the HTML code of the Web page they work with. This makes the distribution of client-side scripts transparent and simple.

The <SCRIPT> Tag

In order to embed client-side scripts in your Web pages, you need an HTML tag to tell the browser that the following code is a script and not document text. This is done through the <SCRIPT> tag.

The <SCRIPT> tag has the syntax

```
<SCRIPT LANGUAGE=[scripting language]>
```

where you enter the scripting language you are using for that script. For example, if you wanted to embed a script written in JavaScript, the tag would be as follows:

```
<SCRIPT LANGUAGE="JavaScript">
```

13

SCRIPTING
BASICS

The <SCRIPT> tag has a closing tag, </SCRIPT>, to denote the end of the script.

You can embed multiple occurrences of the <SCRIPT> </SCRIPT> tags on a single Web page. You can also use different languages within your various script tags. For example, if you wanted to use VBScript as your primary scripting language, you could have a script with the following enclosing tags:

```
<SCRIPT LANGUAGE="VBScript">
</SCRIPT>
```

Because browsers that do not support that language ignore that script, only browsers supporting VBScript run your script. You could also have another script on the same page, using JavaScript to tell your users that your page contains some VBScript scripts that are not supported by their browser.

CAUTION

Internet Explorer will run all script tags that specify the language as JavaScript as JScript scripts. Since there are some features of JavaScript not supported by JScript, this could lead to errors. When using commands not supported by JScript in your scripts, you may want to check to see if the Web browser being used is Internet Explorer. If it is, you can skip the statements which are unsupported by JScript.

Hiding Scripts from Incompatible Browsers

Around 90% of people on the Internet use either Netscape Navigator or Microsoft Internet Explorer as their Web browser. This means that most people visiting your Web site use browsers that support Web page scripting. However, some users have browsers that don't support Web page scripting, or even older versions of Navigator or Internet Explorer that don't support scripting. If this is the case, your scripts are not run and may even appear as part of the document's text, depending on where you have placed them.

NOTE

Not all browsers support client-side scripting. Also, with the growth of a lot of other ways to browse the Web, such as with PDAs and Web TVs, there may be many users visiting your site who are not using a browser that supports scripting. If you are interested in supporting everyone who visits your site, you should be sure to properly hide your script code from all Web browsers that do not support client-side scripting.

To avoid this problem, Web browsers that support Web page scripts support a syntax style that enables you to hide your scripts from browsers that do not support client-side scripting.

This syntax style makes use of comment tags at the beginning and ending of the script, which make the script appear as a comment to incompatible browsers. The syntax style is as follows:

```
<SCRIPT LANGUAGE="JavaScript">
<!--

    Your script goes here.

//-->
</SCRIPT>
```

Notice the beginning comment characters on the line immediately after the <SCRIPT> opening tag. Browsers supporting client-side scripting ignore them and continue to execute the rest of the script code.

The syntax for hiding your scripts from incompatible browsers requires that you also place the closing comments characters before the closing </SCRIPT> tag. Notice that the closing comment characters are preceded by two slashes. These slashes denote scripting language comments in your code. By placing these slashes there, browsers supporting scripting ignore the closing HTML comments tag.

As for the <SCRIPT> tag itself, browsers that do not support scripting do not support the <SCRIPT> tag. Because of how HTML is interpreted, incompatible browsers simply ignore tags they do not support.

Placing Your Script in Your HTML Code

Client-side scripts can be placed anywhere in your HTML text. However, locate them in different places depending on what you want to accomplish. The most common place for scripts in the header section of your Web page is the section between the <HEAD></HEAD> tags. This location is ideal for all but a few scripts.

For example, you often want to create subroutines in your scripts to perform certain actions. Using a script tag in the header section is a good place to define all of your subroutines, whether you call them in the header section or somewhere else in the HTML document. Listing 13.4 contains a sample header section of an HTML document with a subroutine defined.

Listing 13.4. JavaScript embedded in the <HEAD> section.

```
<HEAD>
<TITLE>JavaScripting</TITLE>

<SCRIPT LANGUAGE="JavaScript">
<!--

  function display_message(string_message) {
    window.status = string_message;
  }
```

continues

13

SCRIPTING
BASICS

Listing 13.4. continued

```
//-->
</SCRIPT>

</HEAD>
```

The subroutine in Listing 13.4, which in JavaScript is called a function, takes a single string parameter. When called, the function places the contents of the string in the browser window's status bar.

You can also place your scripts within the body of your HTML document. Typically, you do this when you want to have your script write some dynamic code to your document as it's being parsed upon loading. Using a statement such as document.write accomplishes this. An example of this is shown in Listing 13.5.

Listing 13.5. JavaScript example for the HTML body section.

```
<SCRIPT LANGUAGE="JavaScript">
<!--

  if (userAgent == "Netscape") {
      document.write("Thank you for using Netscape!")
  }

//-->
</SCRIPT>
```

You can also place some scripts within certain HTML tags to handle events associated with those objects. For example, anchor tags have mouse events associated with them, specifically the mouseOver and mouseOut events. Listing 13.6 is a sample anchor tag with JavaScripted event handlers for these two events.

Listing 13.6. JavaScript example embedded in HTML tags.

```
<A HREF="toc.html" onMouseOver='window.status="Return to
the Table of Contents";return true'
onMouseOut='window.status="";return true'>
```

When the user moves the mouse pointer over the link created by this tag, the browser displays the following string in the status bar:

```
Return to the Table of Contents
```

When the user moves the mouse pointer away from the link, the string is removed by placing the empty string in the status bar.

Running Your Client-Side Scripts

Client-side scripts are run by loading the Web page in which they are embedded into a Web browser that supports that scripting language. Depending on how the script is to be run, the Web browser either executes the code immediately or waits until the user performs some action.

For example, the subroutine shown in Listing 13.4 is not run until the subroutine is called in another script. The code in Listing 13.5 on the other hand, is executed while the browser is parsing the HTML code. The event handler shown in Listing 13.6 is only executed when the user moves the mouse pointer onto and off of the link in the Web page.

What Can Client-Side Scripts Do?

Client-side scripts provide a mechanism for building more interactivity into your Web pages. Because HTML is not a programming language, you are very limited in what you can build with HTML alone. Client-side scripts, on the other hand, are full-featured programming languages with conditional statements, control structures, and data structures. You can use client-side scripts to perform a variety of tasks. Some of the more common tasks, such as validation of form data, status bar messages, image rollovers, and cookie manipulation, are described in the following sections.

Validation of Form Data

Before client-side scripting, the only mechanism for validation of form data was through the CGI script form handler. The user entered the data in the fields on the Web page and sent the data back to your server. The CGI script on your server would do any validation checking, and then return an error to the user if one occurred.

Because multiple errors can occur at one time, this process of sending back and forth between the client and server could happen several times. This adds more load to your Web server, which has to validate the form data every time it receives it from the user, and uses bandwidth.

Because form data is entered by the user in the Web browser, having the client perform any necessary validation is more efficient that having the server do it. Client-side scripts have this capability. You could have it do something as simple as verify that data is present in all the fields of the form, or as complex as checking that the data entered was within certain ranges.

Status Bar Messages

Another common application of client-side scripting is sending the user messages in the status bar. The status bar is the area at the bottom of the Web browser in which the status of actions is being shown. Typically, the browser uses this area to display messages such as Document Done, or the URL of a link to which the mouse is currently pointing.

13

SCRIPTING
BASICS

Client-side scripts have the capability to send messages to the status bar. These can be simple messages—such as "Welcome to our Web site!"—or they can be complex messages that scroll from right to left across the status bar. You can even have the status bar display descriptions of a Web page, rather than its URL, when the user has the mouse pointer over the link.

Image Rollovers

Image rollovers are a method of having a picture change, or *roll over*, to another image when the user moves the mouse pointer over the image. This action provides the user action feedback, adding another level of interaction and dynamics to the Web page.

A common use of rollovers is in navigational bars, which are composed of images. When the user moves the mouse pointer over one of the menu options, the image might change in some way, designating that the user is about to select that option. You could also have another image change to display a description of what the user would find on that linked Web page.

> **CAUTION**
>
> Most of the versions of Internet Explorer earlier than 4.0 do not support doing image rollovers.

Working with Cookies

Cookies are objects that enable Web page authors to save some state information about the user who just visited their site. In general, when a user requests a Web page from a server, that page is sent to the user's Web browser. After the page is sent, no record of the event is saved, except for the small mention in the access log file. Because the access log file is not set up for keeping track of and supplying this information to the Web server, there is no practical record kept of what page the user requested or any of the actions the user took.

A cookie is a simple record that is stored on the user's machine in a `cookie.txt` file. This file is created and maintained by the Web browser. Cookies are then created by the Web page authors, through either a CGI or a client-side script. Once the cookie has been created and sent to the Web browser, it is stored in the cookie file until it expires.

The real advantage to cookies is that the Web browser automatically sends the cookie as part of a certain Web page request. The Web page requests that the cookie gets sent will depend on the parameters of the cookie, as set upon its creation. When a script receives a cookie from the Web browser, it can decode the information about what happened in the previous session with the user. The script can then perform a different action, depending on what the Web page author wants to happen.

Before client-side scripting, the only way to work with cookies was through CGI scripts. Now, you can create, access, and modify scripts from within the Web page.

Limitations of Scripting

Client-side scripting provides a powerful tool for creating dynamic and interactive pages. However, it does have limitations. One of the biggest problems with client-side scripts is that your source code is embedded in your HTML page, making it available for viewing by everyone who downloads your Web page. This may be a problem for you, especially if you have spent time and effort developing a unique script. Of course, this may also be a benefit, because you can easily view the source code of other people's client-side scripts and see how they performed certain actions.

Another limitation of client-side scripts is the scope in which they can run. Because they are embedded in a Web page, that is the script's scope. When the user loads another Web page, the script for the previous page is no longer available. If you do want a script to be available on the majority of your Web pages, an easy work-around would be to use frames. For the most part, client-side scripts have access to elements and data in other frames. You could have a frame with your client-side script's main body in a frame that is always visible, thereby minimizing this limitation.

Client-side scripts are also somewhat limited in the actions they can perform. Because client-side scripts are embedded in Web pages, which are downloaded from a Web server somewhere on the Internet, there are many security issues related to running them. Because of these security issues, the client-side scripting languages do not have commands that would compromise the security of a user's machine, such as creating, accessing, or deleting files. By doing this, the scripting language authors have reduced the threat of malicious programmers creating harmful and destructive Web pages.

In addition to security issues, client-side scripts need to run on whatever platform the user accessing your pages has. These include a wide range of PC, Macintosh, and UNIX workstations. Therefore, client-side scripts must contain commands that are independent of the platform on which they are run. To accomplish this, the scripting languages do not contain commands that are platform-dependent.

Additionally, client-side scripts do not possess all of the power and flexibility of CGI scripts, making it necessary for you to have CGI scripts for your Web site. For example, you can validate form data using a client-side script, but you need a CGI script to handle the form data after it has been validated. You also need a CGI script to access information in a database or to perform keyword searches through the documents on your Web site. When possible, client-side scripts can alleviate the need for actions that were previously performed through CGI scripts alone, but not all CGI actions can be performed by client-side scripts.

Summary

This chapter introduces you to the basics of client-side scripting. You learned that client-side scripts are small applications embedded in your Web pages. When a user downloads a Web

13

SCRIPTING
BASICS

page containing a client-side script, the Web browser runs the script by interpreting the commands.

You also learned the difference between scripts and programs. Scripts are applications run through a command interpreter. Programs, on the other hand, are compiled. Compiling a program changes the source code into binary executable machine code. After a program is compiled, it can be run without the need for a command interpreter.

Client-side scripts are relatively new, having only been around for the last year or so. Already there are several choices of languages for use in your scripts. The most common and widely supported is JavaScript, which was developed by Netscape Communications. JScript is another common language, and is simply Microsoft's implementation of JavaScript.

VBScript is the other scripting language currently available. VBScript is based upon Microsoft's popular Visual Basic programming language. Although VBScript allows programmers to use a language with which they may be familiar, it is only supported in Microsoft's Internet Explorer browser.

Client-side scripts are easily placed in your Web pages by using the <SCRIPT></SCRIPT> tags. All of the code for your scripts is placed between these tags, and you can have multiple occurrences of the <SCRIPT></SCRIPT> tags in a single Web page. Because of how Web browsers interpret HTML, incompatible browsers simply ignore the <SCRIPT> </SCRIPT> tags. You should also place HTML comment tags around the body of your script code to hide the actual code from incompatible Web browsers.

Because client-side scripting languages are full-featured, with data structures, conditional statements, and control structures, there are many tasks you can use these scripts to perform. Some of the most common are form validation, status bar messages, image rollovers, and cookie manipulation.

Even though client-side scripts are full-featured, there are some limitations to scripting in Web pages: Your source code is available to everyone downloading your Web pages, and the scripts are limited in scope and functionality, partially because of the environment in which they run—the Web browser—and partially because of security reasons. Many of the practical uses of client-side scripting require the use of CGI programs as well, such as form handling. The client-side script can validate the user's entries into the fields of the form, but you still need a CGI script to handle the data once it's sent to the Web server.

Client-Side Image-maps: A Quick Demonstration of Client-Side Scripting

by Robert McDaniel

IN THIS CHAPTER

One of the earliest forms of client-side scripting came in the form of client-side imagemaps. You are probably familiar with imagemaps in general. Server-side imagemaps have been around since the early days of the World Wide Web. Client-side imagemaps have the same basic functionality as their server-side counterparts. However, instead of leaving all the work up to the server, you now have the choice of implementing your imagemaps in the Web browser.

In this chapter, you learn about client-side imagemaps. You examine the differences between server- and client-side imagemaps and learn how to make client-side imagemaps. You are also introduced to several imagemap editors, which greatly simplify your task of creating imagemaps. Finally, you learn how to enhance your client-side imagemaps with other client-side scripting, a feature not available to server-side imagemaps.

Server-Side Imagemaps versus Client-Side Imagemaps

In the world of client and server applications, having the client do as much of the processing as possible is a favorable situation. With modern computers, client machines are becoming much more powerful. Because there are typically many client machines connecting to a single server at a time, you could easily bottleneck your resources by having the server perform most of the work.

In the natural progression of the World Wide Web, more and more tasks previously performed by the Web server are starting to move to the Web browser. Imagemaps are one of the tasks that have no need to be performed on the server side. In fact, the only reason they have been in the past is because it was at one time easier to universally implement them on the server side than the client side.

This section explores both client- and server-side imagemaps. You learn what imagemaps are in general, and the difference between client- and server-side implementations.

What Are Imagemaps?

In the early days of the World Wide Web there were HTML documents. These documents could contain images and text, and, most importantly, links to other documents. Even at that early time, there was the choice of using text or images for links.

The idea of imagemaps came not long after these simple text or entire image links. Imagemaps are simple text descriptions of shapes and their related coordinates in an image file. The purpose of an imagemap is to define multiple hotspots or clickable points on a single image. Without an imagemap, you can either make the entire image a link, or break the image into several separate images, making each one a link.

Imagemaps are more flexible than the latter. With imagemaps, you can define polygons and circles for areas, whereas breaking down an image into smaller ones results in smaller, rectangular images. This may not always work well for the image you are using.

How Do Server-Side Imagemaps Work?

Server-side imagemaps were the first imagemap form. They're named for the fact that they reside on and are executed by the Web server, as opposed to the Web client. In the early days of Web servers, there was actually a separate CGI script called Imagemap used to interpret an imagemap. Some modern Web servers have server-side imagemap technology built in.

Server-side imagemaps function in a straightforward manner. On the client side, the Web page author includes the ISMAP attribute in the <IMG> tag of the image to be used with an imagemap. Then, in the <A> tag, the HREF attribute points to a map file on the server, which typically has a .map filename extension. This .map file contains shapes and coordinates for the imagemap's clickable areas.

When the user clicks an image that uses a server-side imagemap, the Web browser calculates the mouse click's coordinates and sends the coordinates to the Web server, along with the name of the imagemap file. The Web server opens the map file and finds the last area in which the coordinates lie. The corresponding URL is returned to the Web browser.

Listing 14.1 contains an example of a server-side imagemap file. All the lines that begin with a # symbol in this listing are comments; all other lines define an area of the image to be mapped to a URL. The first area is the default area. This acts as a catchall, to handle clicks on the image that are not in any of the mapped areas. The default for this imagemap is reloading the current page, which is the index.html page for the document root.

Listing 14.1. A server-side imagemap file.

```
# Imagemap file for circles on Casting Guild's home page
#
default /
#
# Union Circle
#
# Union Commercials
poly /union-commercials.html 35,27 43,46 69,44 94,63 98,85 117,86 116,60 96,34
➥71,23 45,23
#
# Union TV
poly /union-tv.html 77,107 92,95 106,107 87,122
#
# Union Stage
poly /union-stage.html 27,93 13,108 48,134 61,134 60,115 43,108
#
# Union Film
poly /union-film.html 5,83 23,83 29,56 29,51 19,46 8,61
#
# Union Default
poly /union-film.html 20,42 34,52 31,61 27,82 26,85 6,86 12,105 28,90 42,104
➥61,112 62,113 63,134 87,126 74,105 91,92 108,104 117,88 96,86 92,68 92,
➥64 68,46 42,48 34,27
#
```

14

CLIENT-SIDE
IMAGEMAPS

continues

Listing 14.1. continued

```
# Non-Union Circle
#
# Non-Union Commercials
poly /non-union-commercials.html 194,75 200,93 229,90 250,110 255,131 272,131
➥267,101 246,76 208,68
#
# Non-Union Film
poly /non-union-film.html 172,94 158,117 162,130 181,131 189,101
#
# Non-Union TV
poly /non-union-tv.html 234,155 250,142 262,156 242,170
#
# Non-Union Stage
poly /non-union-stage.html 185,141 168,154 202,179 217,180 218,162 197,155
#
# Non-Union Default
poly /non-union-film.html 175,93 193,100 184,133 163,133 167,151 186,137
➥197,152 222,159 221,181 241,174 231,153 250,139 264,152 270,133 252,
➥133 248,114 228,93 199,95 192,77
#
# Misc Circle
#
# Student Projects
poly /student-projects.html 46,233 60,230 60,209 77,187 92,179 123,189 133,181
➥117,163 74,164 49,187 42,209
#
# Technical
poly /technical.html 83,250 84,269 119,268 149,239 149,227 134,223 122,242
➥102,251
#
# Misc Default
poly /student-projects.html 135,183 123,192 93,181 77,190 63,208 63,232 47,235
➥51,253 80,267 81,246 100,247 120,238 131,220 153,225
```

All other areas in the listing start with the keyword `poly`. This specifies that the areas defined are polygons. The other available options are `rect` for rectangles, `circle` for circles, and `point` for single points. The URL to be mapped to the area is the second parameter in all of the area definitions. With server-side imagemaps, you need to use absolute URLs rather than relative URLs. Finally, the coordinates of the shape you are defining are supplied. For polygons, this is as many points as you want to specify.

The image being used with this imagemap file is shown in Figure 14.1. Notice that the mouse is pointing to the `Stage` option in the `Union` circle. Also, notice the destination URL in the Web browser's status bar. The URL is `http://www.castingguild.com/cgi-bin/imagemap/maps/ groups.map?38,125`.

The first part of the URL, up to `imagemap`, should look familiar. It is simply the URL to a program called `imagemap` in the cgi-bin directory. Everything after `imagemap` is a parameter to the program. The first parameter is the path information: `/maps/groups.map`.

This path information specifies the map file's location on the Web server machine. The second parameter, following the ? mark, is the x and y coordinates of the mouse pointer's location. The imagemap program uses these coordinates to determine in which area the point lies.

FIGURE 14.1.

The server-side imagemap example.

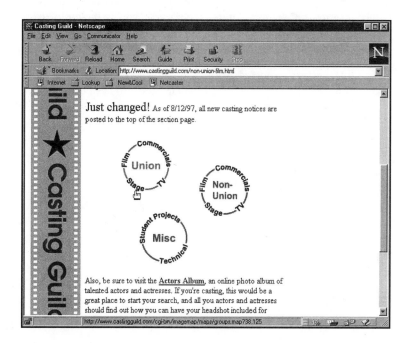

Because server-side imagemaps were the only option available to early Web page authors, they were a welcome change to linking entire images. However, every click on a server-side imagemap requires extra load on the Web server in order to determine the area in which the coordinates lie.

Also, users clicking an imagemap would see URLs similar to `http://www.castingguild.com/cgi-bin/imagemap/maps/groups.map?38,125` in the status bar. These URLs are not descriptive of where the user is actually navigating. Some users like to look at this information before actually following a link.

Another drawback to server-side imagemaps was their inaccessibility to users with text-only browsers. These could be traditional text browsers, such as Lynx, or a browser that has the displaying of inline images turned off. Server-side imagemaps were also inaccessible to some users with impairments, such as blindness, because the user would not know where to click.

To address some of these problems, Netscape Communications introduced client-side imagemaps.

How Do Client-Side Imagemaps Work?

Client-side imagemaps operate much more efficiently than their server-side counterparts. Rather than the Web browser sending only coordinates to the server for processing, the client machine performs the area matching for the coordinates of the mouse click. The map file on the server is no longer necessary. Instead, the coordinates for the area shapes and their related HREFs are listed in the body of the HTML document with which they are associated.

Naturally, there are some additional HTML tags you need in order to create client-side imagemaps: the <MAP> tag and the <AREA> tag. You also need to use the new USEMAP attribute for the <IMG>. The USEMAP attribute tells the Web browser you are using a client-side imagemap, in contrast to the ISMAP attribute used to designate server-side imagemaps. These attributes and tags are described in the following section.

Making Client-Side Imagemaps

Most of the steps to create a client-side imagemap are similar to the steps used to create your map file for server-side imagemaps. You need to start with the image for which you want to create a mapping. Then you need to use the client-side imagemap HTML tags, <MAP> and <AREA>, and the USEMAP attribute for the <IMG> tag. All these tags and their related attributes are described in the following sections.

The <MAP> Tag

The <MAP> tag is used to define a client-side imagemap, and has an associated closing </MAP> tag. There is only a single attribute for the <MAP> tag (NAME), which is used to specify the name of the imagemap you are creating. You can have multiple client-side imagemaps on the same page. The way you distinguish which map you want to use is by referring to it by the name you assign it. The syntax for the <MAP> tag is as follows:

```
<MAP NAME="map1">
...
</MAP>
```

The <AREA> Tag

The <AREA> tag defines an area on the image and what action takes place when the user clicks in that area. All <AREA> tags must go between the <MAP></MAP> tags. The <AREA> tag has the following six attributes:

- SHAPE
- COORDS
- ALT
- NAME
- TARGET
- HREF

You can also place client-side script event handlers such as onmouseover in the <AREA> tag. Using client-side scripting with client-side imagemaps is discussed in the section "Enhancing Your Imagemaps with Client-Side Scripting," later in this chapter.

The SHAPE attribute

The SHAPE attribute defines what type of shape the <AREA> tag is defining. There are four possible values for this attribute:

- rect
- circle
- poly
- default

rect

The rect shape is a rectangle and is defined by two sets of coordinates. This first x and y coordinate marks the rectangle's upper-left corner. The second x and y coordinate specifies the lower-right corner. If you do not specify a SHAPE explicitly, the <AREA> tag is treated as a rectangle.

circle

The circle shape is a standard circle. Similar to the rectangle, a circle is defined by two coordinates. The first x and y coordinate marks the center point of the circle. The second x and y coordinate specifies a point on the edge of the circle. Because a circle has a constant radius, it does not matter what point on the circle's edge you specify.

poly

The poly shape refers to a polygon, which is a more general shape than a rectangle. In fact, all rectangles are polygons. To define a polygon area, you simply supply the x and y coordinates for each point of the polygon. Polygons are useful for defining areas which are not simple rectangles or circles. The poly shape provides you the flexibility to be very specific about what section of the image you want for your <AREA> tag. You can specify up to 100 points for your polygon.

default

The default option for the SHAPE attribute is not like the other options. A SHAPE attribute set to default is used to designate the action for any mouse clicks made whose coordinates are outside all other areas you have defined. Because it acts as the default for all coordinates not defined in other <AREA> tags, you only need to have one <AREA> tag with the SHAPE attribute set to default.

COORDS attribute

The COORDS attribute is where you specify the actual numeric values for the x and y values of the area you are defining. The number of actual x and y coordinate values you supply for the COORDS attribute varies, depending on the corresponding value for the SHAPE attribute. For rectangles, the COORDS attributes have values similar to the following:

```
<AREA SHAPE=rect COORDS="19,20,49,40">
```

14

CLIENT-SIDE IMAGEMAPS

Polygons are similar to the rectangles, but usually contain many more x and y values, depending on how many points you define for your polygon. A typical polygon <AREA> tag would look like the following:

```
<AREA SHAPE=poly COORDS="19,20,17,25,21,35,23,25">
```

The values for the COORDS attribute for circles are similar to those used for rectangles. The co-ordinate value consists of the x and y values for the center of the circle, followed by a point on the edge of the circle. An example of a typical circle area tag is as follows:

```
<AREA SHAPE=circle COORDS="20,20,15,15">
```

Because default areas are defined as all space not covered in another <AREA> tag, there are no specific coordinates for a default area. Therefore, for your default <AREA> tag, you do not use the COORD attribute.

ALT Attribute

The ALT attribute is exactly like the ALT attribute for the <IMG> tag. With it, you can specify ALT text to be displayed for that section of the imagemap. Some browsers, such as Netscape Navigator 4.0, display the ALT text for an area when the user leaves the mouse pointer over an area for a short amount of time.

NAME Attribute

The NAME attribute for the <AREA> tag is an optional attribute not typically used. In this attribute, you specify the same name that is used in the USEMAP attribute of the <IMG> tag. Because you also specify this value in the NAME attribute for the <MAP> tag, which encloses all of the related <AREA> tags, it is rather redundant to use it in each <AREA> tag.

TARGET Attribute

The TARGET attribute is where you specify the window's or frame's name to which the referenced document is loaded. If this value is not specified, the default is the current window or frame in which the user clicked upon the link. You only need to use this value if you want to specifically target a different location.

HREF and NOHREF Attributes

The last attribute for the <AREA> tag is the HREF attribute. This is the same HREF attribute used in the <A> tag for defining links. The URL of the page that gets requested when the user clicks in that area of the imagemap is the value assigned the HREF attribute for an <AREA> tag. Unlike server-side imagemaps, these can be complete URLs in this form:

```
HREF="http://www.castingguild.com/non-union-film.html"
```

They can also be absolute URLs in this form:

```
HREF="/non-union-film.html"
```

Finally, they can be relative URLs, such as the following:

```
HREF="non-union-film.html"
```

As an alternative to HREF, you can specify NOHREF if you do not want an HTTP request sent when the user clicks in that imagemap area. This is often used if you want to define a script that occurs when the user moves over a section of an image with the mouse pointer, but do not want anything to happen if the user clicks in that area. NOHREF is most commonly used with default <AREA> tags, to explicitly instruct the browser not to perform any action when the user clicks outside all areas. An <AREA> tag to accomplish this would look like the following:

```
<AREA SHAPE=default NOHREF>
```

The USEMAP Attribute

After you create a client-side imagemap using the <MAP></MAP> tags, and have defined all the shapes using <AREA> tags, you need to tell the Web browser that your image has an associated client-side imagemap. This is done by using the USEMAP attribute in the <IMG> tag.

This is a new attribute that only Web browsers supporting client-side imagemaps recognize. It is similar to the ISMAP attribute used to declare that the image is using a server-side imagemap.

TIP

Because not all browsers support client-side imagemaps, it is a good idea to implement both a client-side and server-side imagemap to support all the users visiting your site. You can use the following syntax:

```
<A HREF="/cgi-bin/imagemap/maps/groups.map"><IMG BORDER=0
SRC="graphics/groups.gif" USEMAP="#groups" ISMAP></A>
```

Web browsers that support client-side imagemaps recognize the USEMAP attribute and look for a client-side imagemap named groups, ignoring the ISMAP attribute. Older Web browsers ignore the USEMAP attribute, because they don't recognize it; they treat it like a normal server-side imagemap.

The USEMAP attribute must be assigned the name of the client-side imagemap you want used for that image. This is the same value you assigned to the NAME attribute of the <MAP> tag. The name must be preceded with a #, such as in the following:

```
USEMAP="#map1"
```

This syntax instructs the Web browser to search for a client-side imagemap on the same page currently loaded, and is similar to the named anchor syntax used with the anchor tag <A>.

14

CLIENT-SIDE IMAGEMAPS

WYSIWYG Imagemap Editors

The most challenging task in creating client-side imagemaps is determining the coordinates for your areas. There are three ways you can do this:

- Take a guess.
- Determine the coordinates of each point, one at a time.
- Use a WYSIWYG imagemap editor.

The last choice is the best choice for creating imagemaps. WYSIWYG imagemap editors provide a graphical tool for creating your imagemaps. Simply select the shape you want and click around in the image. The editor converts your mouse clicks into the x and y coordinates and creates the <AREA> tag for you.

Three of the more popular WYSIWYG imagemap editors are:

- Map Edit
- Hotspots
- LiveImage

Map Edit

Map Edit was one of the first WYSIWYG imagemap editors available. It is written by Tom Boutell and originally supported only server-side imagemaps. Once client-side imagemaps were introduced, Map Edit was changed to support creating and editing both client- and server-side imagemaps.

To create a client-side imagemap in Map Edit, you need to create an HTML page with an image that you want to map. Then open up both the HTML file and the image in Map Edit.

For example, the HTML code shown in Listing 14.2 is currently using a server-side imagemap. The mapped image is about halfway down in the listing, and contains the ALT text "This is an imagemap. Use the text links below."

TIP

Some text-based browsers provide a way for users to navigate using a client-side imagemap, even without loading the image. The browser makes a list of all possible destinations from which the user can make a choice. To ensure that this list is as usable as possible, it's a good idea to make destination URLs as descriptive as they can be. For example, instead of uf.html, use union-film.html.

Listing 14.2. HTML for the Casting Guild home page.

```
<HTML>
<HEAD>
<TITLE>Casting Guild</TITLE>
</HEAD>
<BODY BACKGROUND="graphics/castingguild.gif" BGCOLOR="#FFFFFF"
TEXT="#000000" LINK="#000099" VLINK="#000084" ALINK="#000000">
<TABLE BORDER=0>
<TR>
<TD ROWSPAN=4 ALIGN=left VALIGN=top><IMG HEIGHT=1
WIDTH=105 SRC="graphics/dotclear.gif"></TD>
<TD ALIGN=right VALIGN=top WIDTH=400><IMG HEIGHT=60
WIDTH=310 ALT="All the World's a stage, And all the men and women
merely players: - William Shakespeare" SRC="graphics/shakes.gif">
</TR>
<TR>
<TD ALIGN=left VALIGN=top WIDTH=400>... some just seem to have better parts
than others!
<P>Are you casting a production, or trying to be cast? Either way, you're
in the right place.
Here at the Casting Guild, we freely post casting calls for Union and
Non-union productions.
For all you actors and actresses looking for parts, choose a section below
to begin viewing thecasting calls.  If you are casting a part, use this
<A HREF="post.html"><B>form</B></A>
to have it added to the Casting Guild. New notices are posted as soon as they
are received, so check back often!
<P><FONT SIZE=+2>NEW!</FONT> There are new listings under Union Film, Union
Stage, Non-Union Film, Non-Union TV, Non-Union Stage, Student Projects and
Technical.
<P><FONT SIZE=+2>Just changed!</FONT> As of 8/12/97, all new casting notices
are posted to the top of the section page.</TD>
</TR>
<TR>
<TD ALIGN=center VALIGN=center WIDTH=400><A
HREF="/cgi-bin/imagemap/maps/groups.map"><IMG BORDER=0 HEIGHT=285 WIDTH=273
ALT="This is an imagemap. Use the text links below." SRC="graphics/groups.gif"
ISMAP></A></TD>
</TR>
<TR>
<TD ALIGN=left VALIGN=top WIDTH=400>Also, be sure to visit the <A
HREF="actors-album/index.html"><B>Actors Album</B></A>, an online photo album
of talented actors and actresses. If you're casting, this would be a great
place to start your search, and all you actors and actresses should find out
how you can have your headshot included for <B>free</B>!
<P>Keep in mind that this site is best viewed with Netscape's browser. You can
download the latest version right now from <A
HREF="http://www.netscape.com/comprod/mirror/index.html"><B>Netscape's Web
Site</B></A>.
<P>Well, that's all for now. We are working on a few new things, which we will
announce soon. Until then, good luck with your search!
<P>The following links are for people who need text navigation.
<BR><IMG HEIGHT=1 WIDTH=80 SRC="graphics/dotclear.gif">
```

continues

Listing 14.2. continued

```
[ Union <A HREF="union-film.html">Film</A> / <A HREF="union-tv.html">TV</A> /
<A HREF="union-commercials.html">Commercials</A> /
<A HREF="union-stage.html">Stage</A> ]
<BR><IMG HEIGHT=1 WIDTH=80 SRC="graphics/dotclear.gif">
[ Non-Union <A HREF="non-union-film.html">Film</A> / <A
HREF="non-union-tv.html">TV</A> / <A
HREF="non-union-commercials.html">Commercials</A> / <A
HREF="non-union-stage.html">Stage</A> ]
<BR><IMG HEIGHT=1 WIDTH=80 SRC="graphics/dotclear.gif">
[ Misc. <A HREF="student-projects.html">Student Projects</A> / <A
HREF="technical.html">Technical</A> ]</TD>
</TR>
</TABLE>
</BODY>
</HTML>
```

When you open the image `groups.gif` and the HTML document in Map Edit, you see the screen shown in Figure 14.2. Now that your image is open in Map Edit, you are ready to create areas for your hotspots.

FIGURE 14.2.

Map Edit creating an imagemap.

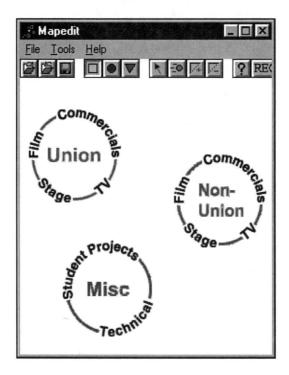

After creating several polygons for each option in the `groups.gif` image, Map Edit creates the <MAP> and <AREA> tags and saves your HTML document. The new HTML document, after being edited by Map Edit, is shown in Listing 14.3.

Listing 14.3. Casting Guild home page with client-side imagemap.

```
<HTML>
<HEAD>
<TITLE>Casting Guild</TITLE>
</HEAD>
<BODY BACKGROUND="graphics/castingguild.gif" BGCOLOR="#FFFFFF" TEXT="#000000"
LINK="#000099" VLINK="#000084" ALINK="#000000">
<TABLE BORDER="0">
<TR>
<TD ROWSPAN="4" ALIGN="left" VALIGN="top"><IMG HEIGHT="1" WIDTH="105"
SRC="graphics/dotclear.gif"></TD>
<TD ALIGN="right" VALIGN="top" WIDTH="400"><IMG HEIGHT="60"
WIDTH="310" ALT="All the World's a stage, And all the men and women merely
players: - William Shakespeare" SRC="graphics/shakes.gif">
</TR>
<TR>
<TD ALIGN="left" VALIGN="top" WIDTH="400">... some just seem to have better
parts than others!
<P>Are you casting a production, or trying to be cast? Either way, you're in
the right place. Here at the Casting Guild, we freely post casting calls for
Union and Non-union productions. For all you actors and actresses looking for
parts, choose a section below to begin viewing the casting calls.  If you are
casting a part, use this <A HREF="post.html"><B>form</B></A> to have it added
to the Casting Guild.  New notices are posted as soon as they are received, so
check back often!
<P><FONT SIZE="+2">NEW!</FONT> There are new listings under Union Film, Union
Stage, Non-Union Film, Non-Union TV, Non-Union Stage, Student Projects and
Technical.
<P><FONT SIZE="+2">Just changed!</FONT> As of 8/12/97, all new casting notices
are posted to the top of the section page.</TD>
</TR>
<TR>
<TD ALIGN="center" VALIGN="center" WIDTH="400"><A
HREF="/cgi-bin/imagemap/maps/groups.map"><IMG BORDER="0" HEIGHT="285"
WIDTH="273" ALT="This is an imagemap. Use the text links below."
SRC="graphics/groups.gif" ISMAP usemap="#groups"></A></TD>
</TR>
<TR>
<TD ALIGN="left" VALIGN="top" WIDTH="400">Also, be sure to visit the
<A HREF="actors-album/index.html"><B>Actors Album</B></A>, an online photo
album of talented actors and actresses. If you're casting, this would be a
great place to start your search, and all you actors and actresses should
find out how you can have your headshot included for <B>free</B>!
<P>Keep in mind that this site is best viewed with Netscape's browser. You can
download the latest version right now from <A
HREF="http://www.netscape.com/comprod/mirror/index.html"><B>Netscape's Web
Site</B></A>.
<P>Well, that's all for now. We are working on a few new things, which we will
announce soon. Until then, good luck with your search!
<P>The following links are for people who need text navigation.
<BR><IMG HEIGHT="1" WIDTH="80" SRC="graphics/dotclear.gif">
[ Union <A HREF="union-film.html">Film</A> / <A HREF="union-tv.html">TV</A> /
<A HREF="union-commercials.html">Commercials</A> / <A
HREF="union-stage.html">Stage</A> ]
<BR><IMG HEIGHT="1" WIDTH="80" SRC="graphics/dotclear.gif">
```

14

CLIENT-SIDE
IMAGEMAPS

continues

Listing 14.3. continued

```
[ Non-Union <A HREF="non-union-film.html">Film</A> / <A
HREF="non-union-tv.html">TV</A> / <A
HREF="non-union-commercials.html">Commercials</A> / <A
HREF="non-union-stage.html">Stage</A> ]
<BR><IMG HEIGHT="1" WIDTH="80" SRC="graphics/dotclear.gif">
[ Misc. <A HREF="student-projects.html">Student Projects</A> / <A
HREF="technical.html">Technical</A> ]</TD>
</TR>
</TABLE>
<map name="groups">
<area shape="polygon" alt="Union Commercials"
coords="36,26,45,43,99,83,113,85,116,54,76,16"
href="/union%2dcommercials.html">
<area shape="polygon" alt="Union Film"
coords="14,47,5,68,7,84,26,84,33,52" href="/union%2dfilm.html">
<area shape="polygon" alt="Union Stage"
coords="26,93,14,104,30,122,52,130,62,123,60,113" href="/union%2dstage.html">
<area shape="polygon" alt="Union TV"
coords="87,95,74,109,85,121,102,111,90,92" href="/union%2dtv.html">
<area shape="polygon" alt="Non-Union Commercials"
coords="194,73,198,92,256,132,268,132,270,108,247,75"
href="/non%2dunion%2dcommercials.html">
<area shape="polygon" alt="Non-Union Film"
coords="164,94,161,131,180,131,188,100,169,92" href="/non%2dunion%2dfilm.html">
<area shape="polygon" alt="Non-Union Stage"
coords="185,142,169,154,188,172,215,179,219,163,185,142"
href="/non%2dunion%2dstage.html">
<area shape="polygon" alt="Non-Union TV"
coords="244,144,232,158,243,171,261,157,253,141" href="/non%2dunion%2dtv.html">
<area shape="polygon" alt="Student Projects"
coords="46,191,39,237,62,232,137,182,104,154,60,166"
href="/student%2dprojects.html">
<area shape="polygon" alt="Technical"
coords="77,250,82,273,134,269,156,223,131,211" href="/technical.html">
</map>
</BODY>
</HTML>
```

Map Edit is available for UNIX, Windows, and Macintosh platforms. It is distributed as shareware from `http://www.boutell.com`.

Hotspots

Hotspots is another WYSIWYG imagemap editor. It has many of the same features Map Edit has, and can create either client- or server-side imagemaps. Figure 14.3 shows Hotspots with an example image loaded.

One of Hotspots' imagemap editor's best features is its ability to automatically create a combination client- and server-side imagemap. To do so, Hotspots creates the necessary HTML, as well as the client-side imagemap tags and the server-side map file. Listing 14.4 contains a sample HTML document generated by Hotspots with a client-side imagemap.

FIGURE 14.3.

The Hotspots imagemap editor.

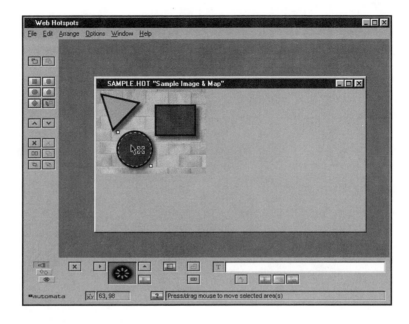

Listing 14.4. A Hotspots-generated client-side imagemap.

```
<html><head><title>New Page</title></head><body>

<MAP NAME="map.html">
<AREA SHAPE="CIRCLE" COORDS="70,106,30" HREF="circle.htm">
<AREA SHAPE="RECT" COORDS="110,30,178,79" HREF="rect.htm">
<AREA SHAPE="POLY" COORDS="75,25,31,69,12,11" HREF="poly.htm">
<AREA SHAPE="AREA" COORDS="75,25,31,69,12,11" HREF="poly.htm">
</MAP>
<!--Map by Web Hotspots 3.0  www.1automata.com -->
<!--Sample shipped with Hotspots 3.0 S-->

<center>
<img src="img.jpg" border=0 WIDTH="200" HEIGHT="150" USEMAP="#map.html"><br>

<font size=1>Media object created using
<a href="http://www.1automata.com/">Web Hotspots 3.0</a></font>
</center>

<p>
This page was created from <tt>NEWPAGE.HTM</tt> in the Hotspots
install directory.  Web Hotspots uses <tt>NEWPAGE.HTM</tt>
as a template for creating new pages.  <tt>NEWPAGE.HTM</tt>
can be customized.

</Body></html>
```

14

CLIENT-SIDE
IMAGEMAPS

Hotspots is available as shareware for Windows platforms. You can download the latest version at `http://www.concentric.net/~automata/hotspots.shtml`.

LiveImage

LiveImage, another imagemap editor, also supports both client- and server-side imagemaps. LiveImage's interface makes it extremely easy to add, delete, and modify areas in your image. The LiveImage editor contains many toolbar buttons and a listing on the left side of the window of all the areas defined in the currently open imagemap. The LiveImage editor is shown in Figure 14.4.

FIGURE 14.4.

The LiveImage imagemap editor.

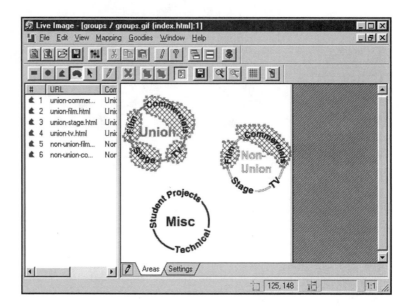

One of the best features of the LiveImage imagemap editor is the Define Smooth Polygon Area tool. This tool allows you to create a polygon by simply drawing around the area you want to use. It acts in a manner similar to that of a pencil tool in a paint program. After you have defined the area, LiveImage creates as many polygon points as necessary to approximate the drawn curve. An example of a client-side imagemap created by Live Image is shown in Listing 14.5.

Listing 14.5. HTML and client-side imagemap created by LiveImage.

```
<HTML>
<HEAD>
<TITLE>Casting Guild</TITLE>
</HEAD>
<BODY BACKGROUND="graphics/castingguild.gif" BGCOLOR="#FFFFFF" TEXT="#000000"
LINK="#000099" VLINK="#000084" ALINK="#000000">
<TABLE BORDER=0>
<TR>
<TD ROWSPAN=4 ALIGN=left VALIGN=top><IMG HEIGHT=1 WIDTH=105
SRC="graphics/dotclear.gif"></TD>
<TD ALIGN=right VALIGN=top WIDTH=400><IMG HEIGHT=60 WIDTH=310 ALT="All the
World's a stage, And all the men and women merely players: - William
```

```
Shakespeare" SRC="graphics/shakes.gif">
</TR>
<TR>
<TD ALIGN=left VALIGN=top WIDTH=400>... some just seem to have better parts
than others!
<P>Are you casting a production, or trying to be cast? Either way, you're in
the right place. Here at the Casting Guild, we freely post casting calls for
Union and Non-union productions. For all you actors and actresses looking for
parts, choose a section below to begin viewing the casting calls.  If you are
casting a part, use this <A HREF="post.html"><B>form</B></A> to have it added
to the Casting Guild.  New notices are posted as soon as they are received, so
check back often!
<P><FONT SIZE=+2>NEW!</FONT> There are new listings under Union Film, Union
Stage, Non-Union Film, Non-Union TV, Non-Union Stage, Student Projects and
Technical.
<P><FONT SIZE=+2>Just changed!</FONT> As of 8/12/97, all new casting notices
are posted to the top of the section page.</TD>
</TR>
<TR>
<TD ALIGN=center VALIGN=center WIDTH=400><A
HREF="/cgi-bin/imagemap/maps/groups.map">
<!-- Image tags modified by LiveImage for Client Side Imagemap insertion -->
<IMG SRC="graphics/groups.gif" USEMAP="#groups" WIDTH=273 HEIGHT=285 ALT="This
is an imagemap. Use the text links below." ISMAP BORDER=0></A></TD>
</TR>
<TR>
<TD ALIGN=left VALIGN=top WIDTH=400>Also, be sure to visit the <A
HREF="actors-album/index.html"><B>Actors Album</B></A>, an online photo album
of talented actors and actresses. If you're casting, this would be a great
place to start your search, and all you actors and actresses should find out
how you can have your headshot included for <B>free</B>!
<P>Keep in mind that this site is best viewed with Netscape's browser. You can
download the latest version right now from <A HREF="http://www.netscape.com/
comprod/mirror/index.html"><B>Netscape's Web
Site</B></A>.
<P>Well, that's all for now. We are working on a few new things, which we will
announce soon. Until then, good luck with your search!
<P>The following links are for people who need text navigation.
<BR><IMG HEIGHT=1 WIDTH=80 SRC="graphics/dotclear.gif">
[ Union <A HREF="union-film.html">Film</A> / <A HREF="union-tv.html">TV</A> /
<A HREF="union-commercials.html">Commercials</A> / <A
HREF="union-stage.html">Stage</A> ]
<BR><IMG HEIGHT=1 WIDTH=80 SRC="graphics/dotclear.gif">
[ Non-Union <A HREF="non-union-film.html">Film</A> / <A
HREF="non-union-tv.html">TV</A> / <A
HREF="non-union-commercials.html">Commercials</A> / <A
HREF="non-union-stage.html">Stage</A> ]
<BR><IMG HEIGHT=1 WIDTH=80 SRC="graphics/dotclear.gif">
[ Misc. <A HREF="student-projects.html">Student Projects</A> / <A
HREF="technical.html">Technical</A> ]</TD>
</TR>
</TABLE>
<!-- Start of Client Side Imagemap information -->
<MAP NAME="groups">
<!-- #$-:Created by LiveImage available at http://www.mediatec.com -->
<!-- #$-:Unregistered copy (robertm) -->
<!-- #$VERSION:1.26 -->
```

14

CLIENT-SIDE
IMAGEMAPS

continues

Listing 14.5. continued

```
<!-- #$DATE:Sun Sep 14 18:59:18 1997 -->
<!-- #$GIF:groups.gif -->
<AREA SHAPE=POLY
COORDS="42,22,39,28,39,34,39,41,43,47,51,50,57,52,63,55,69,59,75,65,80,71,86,
➥77,92,81,98,86,105,87,111,84,115,77,117,71,118,65,118,58,116,51,111,
➥44,105,39,98,34,92,32,84,31,76,28,70,25,61,22,51,21,42,22"
HREF="union-commercials.html" ALT="Union Commercials">
<AREA SHAPE=POLY
COORDS="12,50,4,84,7,90,14,92,20,92,26,88,31,82,32,75,32,69,33,63,33,57,33,50,
➥28,44,22,43,16,46,12,50" HREF="union-film.html" ALT="Union Film">
<AREA SHAPE=POLY
COORDS="31,94,25,94,19,98,16,104,16,110,16,116,18,122,24,128,30,131,36,133,43,
➥136,50,137,56,137,62,131,63,125,64,119,64,113,60,107,54,103,48,99,42,
➥96,36,95,31,94" HREF="union-stage.html" ALT="Union Stage">
<AREA SHAPE=POLY
COORDS="86,92,80,98,76,104,74,110,74,116,77,122,85,124,92,125,98,122,103,116,
➥105,110,105,104,103,98,97,93,91,91,86,92"
➥HREF="union-tv.html" ALT="Union TV">
<AREA SHAPE=POLY
COORDS="165,92,162,109,162,115,162,121,162,127,166,133,172,133,178,131,183,125,
➥187,119,189,113,189,107,188,101,185,95,179,92,173,91,167,93,165,92"
HREF="non-union-film.html" ALT="Non Union Film">
<AREA SHAPE=POLY
COORDS="213,66,207,66,199,66,193,67,187,67,186,73,187,79,191,85,198,89,204,89,
➥211,93,217,95,223,99,230,106,237,111,243,112,249,117,252,123,257,130,
➥263,132,268,126,271,120,273,114,273,108,272,101,268,95,262,88,256,82,
➥250,77,244,72,237,68,231,66,222,66,215,66,213,66"
HREF="non-union-commercials.html" ALT="Non-Union Commercials">
</MAP>
<!-- End of Client Side Imagemap information -->
</BODY>
</HTML>
```

As with the other WYSIWYG imagemap editors, LiveImage is distributed as shareware from its Web site: http://www.mediatec.com/.

There are versions available for Windows 95 and Windows NT.

Enhancing Your Client-Side Imagemaps with Client-Side Scripting

One of the biggest benefits of using client-side imagemaps over server-side imagemaps is the ability to add scripting to your <AREA> tags. Specifically, you have the ability to add event handlers, such as onmouseover and onmouseout, to your <AREA> tags to perform actions when the user moves the mouse pointer over that area in the image.

A common application is to replace the destination URL in the browser window's status bar with a more descriptive explanation. For example, the following <AREA> tag defines an area for the Casting Guild groups.gif graphic:

```
<AREA SHAPE="polygon" ALT="Union Stage"
COORDS="26,93,14,104,30,122,52,130,62,123,60,113"
HREF="union-stage.html">
```

When clicked, this hotspot loads the union-stage.html page.

Using the JavaScript onmouseover event handler, you could create a line of JavaScript that outputs the string "Union Stage Casting Calls" to the browser window's status bar. The JavaScript would be as follows:

```
onMouseOver='window.status="Union Stage Casting Calls";return true'
```

If you only trap for this event, the status bar retains this message even after the user moves the mouse pointer out of the hotspot area. You would also need to trap for the mouseout event with the JavaScript onmouseout event handler. The JavaScript would be as follows:

```
onMouseOut='window.status="";return true'
```

You would then place both of these JavaScript lines into the <AREA> tag, as in the following line:

```
<AREA SHAPE="polygon" ALT="Union Stage"
COORDS="26,93,14,104,30,122,52,130,62,123,60,113" HREF="union-stage.html"
onMouseOver='window.status="Union Stage Casting Calls";return true'
onMouseOut='window.status="";return true'>
```

Summary

In the early days of the World Wide Web, authors had two choices for creating links—text links or an entire image. Having only these choices did not provide much flexibility for creative Web pages. Server-side imagemaps were introduced to address this problem.

Server-side imagemaps provide a means to map areas on an image to a URL. The URL loads when the user clicks in one of the mapped areas. Web page authors could now take complex images and break the navigation into distinct areas, using circles, rectangles, and polygons. Although server-side imagemaps provided the desired functionality, the implementation was rather painful. The Web page author had to create a separate file, called a map file, to store the URL mappings for the image. In addition, every click on an imagemap results in a call to a server-side program, inflicting greater strain on the Web server.

Client-side imagemaps were introduced as a better solution to their server-side counterparts. Rather than using a CGI program and a separate map file, the mapping data is embedded in the HTML document containing the mapped image. When the user clicks in a client-side imagemap, the Web browser handles all of the processing.

In order to embed client-side imagemaps in an HTML document, new HTML tags had to be defined. The <MAP> tag, which also has a closing </MAP> tag, is used to specify the name of a client-side imagemap. These tags also enclose all the <AREA> tags, which are used to define the shapes to be mapped to URLs.

14

CLIENT-SIDE
IMAGEMAPS

To help you create client-side imagemaps, several companies have created WYSIWYG imagemap editors. WYSIWYG imagemap editors provide an easy-to-use tool where you simply point and click to create your areas. The editors will determine the coordinates of your mouse clicks, and create the necessary <MAP> and <AREA> tags for you.

With client-side imagemaps, you also have the ability to add scripted event handlers for the individual areas you have defined. Just like scripting mouse events for your anchor tags, you can add the onmouseover and onmouseout events for each <AREA> tag in your client-side imagemap. The most common application is to place descriptive explanations of the mapped URL in the browser window's status bar when the user moves the mouse pointer over the area.

In general, client-side imagemaps are a much better option then server-side imagemaps. They are easier to create and maintain, and they have less load on the Web server. With the advantages of client-side imagemaps, the only reason to continue to support server-side imagemaps is for backward compatibility with older browsers.

CHAPTER 15

Introducing JavaScript

by David Gulbransen

IN THIS CHAPTER

Scripting languages are not new to the World Wide Web. From the first days of the Web and CGI, scripting languages such as Perl have helped developers create CGI applications or have aided Webmasters in processing forms.

As the Web and techniques for building Web-based applications have matured, so have the scripting environments that developers have at their disposal. The latest versions of Netscape and Internet Explorer support client-side scripting, which allows developers to add a variety of functionality to pages without increasing the user's interaction with the server. Internet Explorer users can take advantage of Visual Basic Scripting Edition (VBScript) and JavaScript. Netscape Communicator also offers robust support for JavaScript, including JavaScript extensions geared toward Netcaster Channel creation.

Because JavaScript is supported across multiple browsers, it's an excellent choice for client-side scripting. It can be used to customize Web pages for individual users. It can be used by Webmasters to gather user data through cookies. It can also be used to generate and validate forms. JavaScript brings powerful, flexible scripting from the Web server to the Web client.

What Is JavaScript?

Simply put, JavaScript is a primarily client-side scripting language for the World Wide Web, that is similar to the syntax of the Java programming language.

What does that really mean? It means that JavaScript is similar to other scripting languages designed to provide limited programming functionality to a wide audience. For example, many people are intimidated at the thought of programming in a complex language like C++. In actuality, there are very few applications for the World Wide Web that require the power of a language like C++. It's a bit like the difference between a professional photographer's large format camera and the snapshot camera you might take on a picnic. While the complex camera can do things the snapshot camera can't, the snapshot camera still takes a picture good enough for capturing 90 percent or more of your photos.

Why JavaScript?

As Web browsers and the desktop computers on which they run have become more powerful, there has been a movement to make more Web functionality occur on the desktop, rather than on the server. This has several advantages for Webmasters and Web users alike.

First, by executing more Web functionality on the user's machine, Webmasters can optimize their servers to serve more pages. Because a server isn't bogged down with CGI processing or server-side includes, the same hardware can effectively serve more users—certainly a boon to any reasonably popular Web site. Additionally, the decrease in traffic from constant interaction with the server can also improve a server's performance.

From the user's perspective, client-side scripting is also a performance improvement. Because the scripts are executed on his or her local machine, the delay commonly associated with CGI applications can be greatly reduced. Because the local machine is doing the script processing, the user can view Web pages much faster, and elements such as animations or other multimedia effects can actually be entertaining and useful instead of slow and frustrating.

The first answer to "Why JavaScript?" is that it makes the Web experience better for producer and consumer alike.

Why an object-oriented scripting language? An object-oriented scripting language for the Web also makes sense, because many of the HTML elements you use to create Web pages can easily be thought of in an object model. By utilizing an object-oriented language such as JavaScript to manipulate HTML objects, the coding becomes much simpler and easier to support for multiple platforms. These are a few of the reasons why both Netscape and Microsoft support JavaScript for development in the Netscape Communicator and Microsoft Internet Explorer browsers.

Introducing JavaScript Syntax

Now that you understand why JavaScript is useful, take a look at how JavaScript functions. Here's an example of a very simple JavaScript program. Notice that the majority of this example is actually HTML, and that the script itself is only one line. That's how easy JavaScript can be. The example simply writes `Hello, World Wide Web` in a browser window:

```
<html>
<head>
<title>Hello World in JavaScript</title>
</head>
<body>

    <script language="JavaScript">
        document.write("Hello, World Wide Web");
    </script>

</body>
</html>
```

The first thing that you notice is the `<SCRIPT>` tag that sets apart the JavaScript example. Here the `LANGUAGE` attribute specifies what scripting language is used. Although some browsers may detect the language, it's a good habit to use the `language` parameter because many browsers today support multiple scripting languages, not to mention different versions of JavaScript itself.

There is actually only one line of JavaScript in the previous example:

```
document.write("Hello, World Wide Web");
```

This code produces the output shown in Figure 15.1.

What exactly is happening in this line of code? The script is simply instructing the browser to write into the current document whatever is inside the quotes. The `document.write` refers to the currently open document object, and the `write()` method is used to put information in the document. The example just contains text, but you could put literally any acceptable HTML inside the quotes and it would be rendered correctly. For example, if you change the line of code to read as shown here, you see the output shown in Figure 15.2, which reflects the changes made in the HTML:

```
document.write("<H2>Hello</H2><I>World</I> Wide Web");
```

FIGURE 15.1.

This is the output from a very simple JavaScript program.

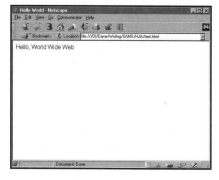

FIGURE 15.2.

JavaScript can be used to create HTML-formatted text in a browser window.

Statements

A statement is at the heart of JavaScript syntax. What is a *statement*? It is simply a line of code that contains some kind of instructions. This is from the previous example:

```
document.write("<H2>Hello</H2><I>World</I> Wide Web");
```

You should note that at the end of the line, or statement, there is a semicolon (;). JavaScript uses the semicolon to end a statement. If you don't end your statements with a semicolon, you may introduce unplanned errors in your code. The semicolon essentially lets the JavaScript interpreter in the Web browser know that the statement is finished, and that it can safely execute the commands in that line of the script.

Blocks

The statement is the smallest unit of JavaScript code, but it is rare for your scripts to only be one line long. In fact, there are many times when it is necessary for you to group several lines of code together for the sake of clarity (such as a function). This grouping of statements is a block:

```
{
    document.write("<H2>Each Line is a Statement</H2>");
    document.write("<P>These statements,<BR>");
    document.write("are part of a block");
}
```

This block denotes the beginning and ending of a block of code; you need to use the left and right curly braces ({}). They denote the start and end points of a block to the Java interpreter.

Comments

Like any other programming or scripting language, JavaScript provides you with a mechanism that can be used to place comments within your code. There are two types of comments that can be used with JavaScript: single-line and multi-line comments.

A single-line comment is denoted with two slashes (//):

```
//This is a comment, it will be ignored by the browser.
```

The comment is not read or interpreted by the browser. It can contain any type of text you would like, as long as there are no line breaks.

The single-line comment is very flexible. You can even use it on a line of code, after the statement:

```
document.write("Hello, World Wide Web"); //Here's a single-line comment in the code
```

This is a valid way to use the single-line comment. Because the statement has already been terminated, the comment text is simply ignored and should not interfere with the execution of the code in any way.

> **CAUTION**
>
> Although single-line comments can be used on the same line as a JavaScript statement, make sure they are only placed after the statement; otherwise the statement is ignored as a part of the comment.
>
> Also, be sure that a single-line comment does not continue onto a new line. Doing so causes an error in your code.

15

INTRODUCING JAVASCRIPT

Sometimes you may need to include a comment that spans more than one line. When that situation arises, you can use the multi-line comment format, which is similar to that in Java and C:

```
/*
This is a multi-line comment. It can be used to provide a higher level
of detail within a comment than a single line comment.
*/
```

These types of comments can be great for providing a detailed comment within your code, and can also be used for troubleshooting. For example, if you have a section of code that you suspect is causing an error, you can use the /* and */ to comment out the questionable section of code. Because the code is contained within the comment field markers, it is ignored as if it were a comment.

> **NOTE**
>
> All too often programmers ignore the important role that comments play in developing a good script. Remember that you might not always be the person in charge of maintaining your script, and any comments that you can provide to help explain your logic can be very useful to someone else reading your code.
>
> Comments are also important for yourself. After a script is written, it might be several days, weeks, or even months before you need to return to the script. When that happens, you might be thankful there are comments reminding you what you were thinking at the time you wrote the code. Deciphering uncommented code, even your own, can be quite a chore. All it takes are a few well-placed comments in the code to lend readability and good style. Developing the habit of commenting your code early in the stages of learning to program can pay off in the long run.

Data Types

Before you jump into the structure of JavaScript too deeply, it is important to understand the basics of the different types of information JavaScript can work with, and how it handles the information.

The information, or data, that you use in your JavaScripts can be in a wide variety of forms. For example, in the first JavaScript example, you wanted to write something to the browser window. The information that you wanted to display in the window was the data, and it was in the form of a string: Hello, World Wide Web. Keeping track of the type of data you use in your scripts is important because a number of factors concerning the data type come into play later. For example, you can combine two strings, much as you would add two numbers, but the methodology and syntax used to combine strings are different from combining numbers.

There are five basic data types in JavaScript: string, number, Boolean, object, and function. Take a look at the first three.

Strings

The string is probably one of the most commonly used data types. It's used in this chapter's opening example, and it's used in many examples in other chapters. A string is simply a character, or series of characters, such as "This is a string."

Strings can be any alphabetic characters, numbers, or combination. The following examples are all strings:

```
The quick brown fox.
January 1, 1999
S1mplepassw0rd
```

Even though the last two contain numerals, they are used as a part of a string, such as a date or password. Strings are contained within double quotes ("x") or single quotes ('x'):

```
"This is a string"
'This is also a string'
```

You can also use quotes as a part of a string:

```
"Fridays are a 'casual' dress day"
'he said, "Today, we will learn Javascript"'
```

Note that if you want to have the string contain one kind of quotation mark, single or double, then you can use the opposite type of quotation mark to enclose the string.

Numbers

JavaScript has a separate data type for numbers that allows you to perform arithmetic operations on the data. Some examples of numbers include the following:

```
-5
1
1.75
.125
```

If you have any programming or scripting experience, you notice that the number examples are different types of numbers. For example, -5 is a negative number, and 1 is an integer, while 1.75 and .125 are floating-point numbers. Programming languages many times have separate data types designed to deal with different types of numbers, such as int or float. JavaScript, however, treats all numbers the same, so there is no need to differentiate between the various types of numbers. A number is a number.

Booleans

There are many times during script-writing when it would be handy to have a data type that could be used to see if something has been done. For example, you might have a button on the page and you want to know if it has been clicked. That is where you could use a Boolean data type. A Boolean simply has two values: `true` or `false`.

It's that simple. `true` is the equivalent of a yes, so in the case of a button, the Boolean is set to `true` if the user has clicked the button. If the user has not clicked the button, the answer is no, and the Boolean value is `false`. The Boolean is a very simple, very useful data type.

For example, you might have a variable to determine whether a button has been clicked:

```
var button_has_been_clicked;
```

There are really only two states to keep track of: Has the button been clicked, or has it not? If it has, set the value to `true`:

```
var button_has_been_clicked=true;
```

If not, set the value to `false`:

```
var button_has_been_clicked=false;
```

That's one example of how you can use a Boolean to keep track of elements in your scripts.

Variables

Data types are methods of classifying data, but they don't create a way to keep track of the data or to store it. In order to do that, you need to create a storage container for information or a variable.

Variables can contain any type of data, from strings to Booleans. They are simply JavaScript's way of creating a simple name for more complex data. You can think of them as a nickname, or a storage container for your data types.

Creating a variable in JavaScript is very simple:

```
var Day = Thursday;
```

This would create a variable, called `Day`, that is set to `Thursday`. The var lets JavaScript know that you are creating a variable.

NOTE

When creating variables, it is important to note that JavaScript is a case-sensitive language. That means that day is not the same as Day. In fact, you could have the variables day, DAY, dAy, and DaY, and they would all be different! Of course, having variables with such similar names would be confusing, but the case sensitivity of JavaScript is a frequent source of errors due to typographical errors, so be sure to double-check the case of your variables, functions, and the like.

In the example, a variable called Day is created and its value is set to Thursday. You could also easily create a variable without assigning a value to it, for later use:

```
var month;
```

This creates a variable called month, which currently has no value. You can assign a value to it later. However, if you try to use it before you've assigned a value, you generate an error.

Creating and using a variable is quite simple. However, there are rules that cannot be violated:

1. The first character of a variable name must be an alphabetic letter or an underscore (_).
2. The variable name cannot be one of the JavaScript "reserved words."

There are a number of words that are reserved in JavaScript because they are used by the language for various functions. If these words are used for variables, they cause conflicts with other JavaScript functionality. Table 15.1 shows the JavaScript reserved words.

Table 15.1. The JavaScript reserved words.

Abstract	*Boolean*	*Break*	*Byte*	*Case*
Catch	Char	Class	Const	Continue
Default	Delete	Do	Double	Else
Extends	False	Final	Finally	Float
For	Function	Goto	It	Implements
Import	In	Instanceof	Int	Interface
Long	Native	New	Null	Package
Private	Protected	Public	Return	Short
Static	Super	Switch	Synchonized	This
Throw	Throws	Transient	True	Try
Typeof	Var	Void	While	With

Altering Variable Values

Of course, variables are called variables because the data they contain may be changed or altered by your script. For example, say you are going to create a variable to keep track of the number of items in inventory:

```
var inventory = 10;
```

You have a variable called inventory that has a value of 10. Now you can change the variable simply by using the = assignment operator:

```
inventory = 5;
```

Now the value of your inventory variable is set to 5. In fact, you can change the value of the inventory variable to anything you want, including another data type:

```
inventory = false;
```

The above line sets the `inventory` variable to a Boolean, with the value of `false`. You could use this to indicate that you are out of stock on an item. You could also just as easily increment the variable:

```
inventory = 7;
inventory = inventory + 5;
```

Now your inventory is set to 7 in the first assignment, and the value is increased by 5 in the second assignment. If you were to print the value of the following variable, it would display a value of 12, which is your original inventory value of 7 plus 5:

```
document.write(inventory);
```

That's all there is to changing the value of a variable. Take a look at another example:

```
<html>
<head>
<title>Altering Variable Values</title>
</head>
<body>

<script language="JavaScript">
    var myName="John Doe";
    var myAge=25
    document.write("My Name is: ");
    document.write(myName);
    document.write("<P>My Age is: ");
    document.write(myAge);
    myAge += 5 ;
    document.write("<P>In five years I'll be: ");
    document.write(myAge);
</script>

</body>
</html>
```

In this example, you first declare your variables:

```
var myName="John Doe";
        var myAge=25
```

You now have one variable that represents the name, and one that represents age. You can write these values to the screen, so you know what they are.

Next, add some years to the age. You can do that in a couple of ways, including the following:

```
myAge = myAge + 5;
```

This would add 5 to the current value of `myAge`. However, like many languages, JavaScript provides a shortcut for adding to the original value of the variable:

```
myAge += 5 ;
```

The shortcut of += allows you to automatically add 5 to the current value of the myAge variable without having to retype the variable name, which might cause confusion.

Now when you write the new variable value, it is increased by 5. The results of the script are shown in Figure 15.3.

FIGURE 15.3.

Manipulating JavaScript variables.

Expressions

Now that you have seen a very basic example of how you can manipulate variables, you can see how manipulating the data stored in the various data types can be useful. Now you need ways to alter the data used in your scripts. The methods that can be employed to manipulate the data are called *expressions*.

There are two types of expressions: numerical and logical. As the names imply, numerical expressions deal with the number data type and are principally mathematical expressions in the form of equations.

Logical expressions are a little more complex. Logical expressions might compare two data values, including strings, to see if they match. Logical expressions are very common in any language, JavaScript included. Take a closer look at each type of expression.

Numeric Expressions

Numeric expressions are very straightforward. They are the same types of statements you would use to perform basic mathematical functions. For example, the following is an expression that simply means "add the number 2 to the number 2." The result of this expression, of course, is 4:

2 + 2

Any type of arithmetic that occurs in your scripts is described by a numeric expression. Addition, subtraction, multiplication, and division are all types of numeric expressions.

Numeric Operators

There are several operators that can be used to perform numeric expressions. You're probably familiar with these symbols from other types of math, but you might not have thought of them as operators. An operator is simply the symbol that represents the type of mathematical operation you want your script to perform. Table 15.2 shows the JavaScript numeric operators.

Table 15.2. The JavaScript numeric operators.

Operator	Example	Uses
+	2 + 2	Addition, adds two numbers.
-	4 – 2	Subtraction, subtracts two numbers.
*	5 * 4	Multiplication, multiplies two numbers.
/	10 / 2	Division, divides two numbers.
%	23 % 4	Modulo, returns the remainder in the division of two numbers. This expression is evaluated to 3, because 4 divides into 23 five times, with a remainder of 3.
-	-(5 * 5)	Unary negation, sets an expression to a negative value. The result of the example would be -25.

The operators listed in Table 15.2 can be used to alter the value information stored in a number data type. As with mathematics, you can also specify the order in which numeric expressions are evaluated by placing them within parentheses (()):

```
4 - 5 + 3 * 5 / 2
```

The answer to this equation could be 10. The result could also be -10. The result could also be 5. Because you can perform each of the individual operations in any order—(4 - 5) first, or perhaps (5 / 2) first—there is no way to tell. However, you can use the parentheses to group expressions and set an order of precedence, so that the result you achieve suits your goals. For example, the correct answer is 5:

```
((4 - 5) + 3) * (5 /2)
```

This statement evaluates as the following:

```
((-1) + 3) * (2.5)
(2) * (2.5)
5
```

As you can see, setting the order in which your expressions are evaluated can be a very important task.

Logical Expressions

Another type of JavaScript expression is the logical, or Boolean, expression. These are expressions that, when evaluated, can return either a true or a false:

```
2 + 2 = 4
```

If you evaluate this expression, it returns a value of true, because 2 + 2 does, indeed, equal 4. There are several operators that exist simply for logical expressions, for example, the And operator &&:

```
(2 + 2 = 4) && (5 - 3 = 2)
```

In this expression, 2 + 2 equals 4, so it evaluates true. 5-3 is equal to 2, so it evaluates true, as well. Because both halves, each on either side of the And operator are true, then the entire expression is true. The And operator specifies that both sides of the expression need to evaluate true.

Another operator is the Equal operator ==. Unlike a mathematical equals, the logical Equal operator can be used to compare for an exact match, even for data types such as strings:

```
"The Same" == "The Same"
```

This expression would evaluate true because both sides of the expression are indeed the same. However, the following expression would return a false because the two sides of the expression are not the same:

```
"The Same == "Different"
```

Logical Operators

As with the numeric expression, there are a set of operators that can be used to evaluate logical expressions. These logical operators are shown in Table 15.3.

Table 15.3. JavaScript logical operators.

Operator	Name	Usage
&&	And	Evaluates two expressions and only returns true if they are both true.
¦¦	Or	Evaluates two expressions and returns true if one or the other is true.
!	Not	Returns the opposite value of the expression, for example, false if the expression is true, and true if the expression is false.

continues

Table 15.3. continued

Operator	Name	Usage
==	Equal	Evaluates two expressions and returns true if the expressions evaluate to the same value.
!=	Not Equal	Evaluates two expressions and returns true if the expressions do not evaluate to the same value.
>	Greater Than	Compares two expressions and returns true if the first expression is greater than the second expression.
>=	Greater Than	Similar to Greater Than, but returns true if the expressions are equal.
<	Less Than	Compares two expressions and returns true if the first expression is less than the second expression.
<=	Less Than or Equal To	Similar to Less Than, but returns true if the expressions are equal.

These operators can be used to evaluate a wide variety of expressions, and come in very handy for use with flow control methods and functions.

Flow Control

As you begin to write scripts to perform tasks in the client's Web browser, you find that you need to alter what happens in your scripts based on some value or some event. This decision-making process is called controlling the flow of your script, and there are several ways in JavaScript to influence the outcome of a script. For example, you could write an expression and instruct the script to perform an action only if the expression is true.

You could also write an expression that you want to occur repeatedly and place that expression inside a loop designed to evaluate the expression a set either number of times or indefinitely.

The possibilities are really endless, and combining the various methods of flow control can yield an amazing amount of precision with which your scripts can execute. However, even the most complex interactions are usually built on the basic flow control building blocks: if, if...else, for loops, and while loops.

Methods that determine how your script continues are known as *conditional expressions*, which simply means that you are evaluating a statement based on the logical expressions just discussed, and then using the results to determine the course of action for your script. Take a look at some of the basic types of conditional expressions.

if

The if statement is at the core of flow control. An if statement can be used to determine a course of action if a statement is true, or a different course of action if a statement is false. The statement itself is constructed in the following manner:

```
if(expression)
Do something;
```

The if keyword determines that if the parenthetical expression is true, then the script should perform the specified action. Otherwise, it should skip that action:

```
if(myAge < 18)
    document.write("You're too young to vote!");
```

In this if statement, the script compares the variable myAge to the number 18, and if its value were less than 18, it would print You're too young to vote! You could expand the example to offer another solution if the age were greater than 18:

```
if(myAge < 18) {
    document.write("You're too young to vote!");
}
if(myAge >= 18) {
    document.write("Welcome to the voting booth!");

}
```

Here, you have added another if statement that confirms whether myAge is greater than, or equal to, 18. If it is, the user is welcomed to the voting booth.

You can really use any combination of logical expressions with the if statement, and the actions to be performed can also be a block of code:

```
if(myAge < 18) || (registered == "no") {
    document.write("You're unable to vote!");
    document.write("Please see the attendant for assistance");
    }
    if(myAge >= 18) {
    document.write("Welcome to the voting booth!");
    document.write("Please cast your ballot");
    }
```

Here you have altered the original statement to also check the value of a registered variable, to make sure the voter is registered. Because you have used the logical or operator, your user won't be able to vote if he or she is either under 18, or not registered.

However, both if statements make use of multiple document.write statements, which have been placed inside blocks. This allows you to group many actions to a single event.

if...else

Another construct for creating conditional statements is the if...else statement. This conditional expression is used similarly to the if statement, but provides a mechanism for specifying actions to perform if the expression is false. Here's how it is constructed:

```
if(some expression)
    If the expression is true, do this;
else
    It the expression is false, do this instead;
```

Take a look at this in practice. You used two if statements in your voting example:

```
if(myAge < 18)
        document.write("You're too young to vote!");
    if(myAge >= 18)
        document.write("Welcome to the voting booth!");
```

First confirm whether the age is under 18, then check to see if it is greater than, or equal to, 18. Because you know that if myAge is not less than 18, it must be greater than 18, you could shorten this into one if...else statement:

```
if(myAge < 18)
    document.write("You're too young to vote!");
else
    document.write("Welcome to the voting booth!");
```

Whenever you are comparing data in that manner, the if...else statement can provide a short-cut to repeatedly writing if statements.

for Loops

The for loop is another basic conditional expression. A for loop can repeat an action a certain number of times, until the conditions you have set for the repeat have been met.

The structure of the for loop can seem a bit confusing at first, but it is really pretty straightforward:

```
for(some variable; A conditional; the counter) {
    The actions to be repeated;
}
```

The first part of the for loop is a variable of some kind that tracks how many times the action has occurred. Next, you need the statement that tests to see if the condition for stopping the loop has been met. You then need the mechanism to increase or decrease the variable toward the condition. Finally, you have the instructions that are to be carried out:

```
for(var count = 10; count >= 0; count--) {
    document.write("Countdown: ");
    document.write(count);
        document.write("<BR>");
}
```

In this example, you have a for loop that acts as a countdown, starting with the number 10 and counting down until it reaches 0. Here, you can see how the three components of the loop work; the following simply declares a variable called count that is equal to 10. You use that to keep track of your countdown:

```
var count = 10;
```

The following lets the `for` loop know that you want to keep looping as long as the count variable is greater than or equal to `0`. This way, your counter does not stop until it reaches `0`.

```
count >= 0;
```

The following statement subtracts 1 from the count variable each time you go through the loop. You could have also said `counter = counter - 1;`. However, this shorthand saves time and clutter.

```
count--;
```

Now you have a loop that executes 11 times (`10` through `0`) and displays the countdown on the screen. The final output is shown in Figure 15.4.

Figure 15.4.

Using a `for` *loop to provide a countdown.*

Keep in mind that although you used the `for` loop for a countdown, you could just as easily use it for another type of counter. You could make the counter increment instead of decrement, or even create some complex mathematical statement to manipulate the count variable.

while Loops

The `while` loop is another type of loop very similar to the `for` loop. A `while` loop simply takes a test case and then, as long as the test case is `true`, continues to perform an action. It is used in the following manner:

```
while(conditional statement) {
    Perform these actions;
}
```

Of course, that seems a little open-ended, so take your countdown example and turn it into a `while` loop instead of a `for` loop:

```
var count = 10
while(count >= 0) {
   document.write("Countdown: ");
   document.write(count);
```

```
    document.write("<BR>");
    count--;
}
```

Here you have a while loop that produces the exact same output as the for loop example. The difference between the loops is the structure:

```
while(count >= 0) {
```

With this statement you instruct the loop to evaluate the enclosed expressions while the counter variable is greater than or equal to 0. Of course, this functions the same way it does in the for loop. Because you have set the count variable to equal 10, the while loop checks; because the count is greater than 0, it executes the following lines:

```
document.write("Countdown: ");
document.write(count);
document.write("<BR>");
```

These lines are identical to the for loop. They simply write the countdown to the screen:

```
count--;
```

This is also the same as the for loop, except this instruction is contained within the block of action for the loop to perform. The result is that the counter variable decrements by one each time the loop is executed. Eventually, the count variable is equal to zero, and the loop exits.

Keep in mind that with a while loop, it is very important to include the mechanism for updating the variable within the loop itself. If you had failed to decrement the count variable within the loop, the test condition would never have been met, resulting in an endless, or infinite, loop.

Arrays

With the basic data structures and flow control expressions out of the way, take a look at a more complicated structure that can be used to keep track of the data in your script: the array.

An array is a very useful structure. For example, say you wanted to keep track of the seven days of the week. How would you do it with a variable? Having a different variable for each day is pretty silly, and changing a single variable to the day you need doesn't really keep track of all seven days—after all, you are still doing the work!

An array is simply a data structure designed to hold multiple values, or elements. For example, each day of the week would be an example of an array element. Here's how you could create an array:

```
days = new Array(6);
```

This statement results in a new array that contains seven elements being formed. This might seem a bit confusing; after all, six are showing. However, elements in an array are numbered starting with 0, not 1. The days array just created actually contains seven elements, from 0 to 6. This can become a bit confusing, so be careful when working with arrays—always count from 0.

Now that you have an array, how do you add the elements for the weekdays? Refer to each element by its number, appending the element number to the name of the array, while enclosing it in brackets:

```
days[0] = "Monday";
days[1] = "Tuesday";
days[2] = "Wednesday";
days[3] = "Thursday";
days[4] = "Friday";
days[5] = "Saturday";
days[6] = "Sunday";
```

That assigns each element a specific day of the week. Now you could refer to each element by the array number:

```
document.write(days[0]);
```

Take a look at how you could use a loop and an array to count down through the days of the week:

```
<html>
<head>
<title>Counting the Days</title>
</head>
<body>

<script language="JavaScript">

days = new Array(6);

days[0] = "Monday";
days[1] = "Tuesday";
days[2] = "Wednesday";
days[3] = "Thursday";
days[4] = "Friday";
days[5] = "Saturday";
days[6] = "Sunday";

var count = 0
while(count <= 6) {
   document.write(days[count]);
   document.write("<BR>");
   count++;
}

</script>

</body>
</html>
```

You are simply creating your days array as you did before, and using a `while` loop to print out the elements, one by one. You should note that even though you are printing seven days, your `while` loop stops when it reaches 6. Again, that's because the first element of your array is not 1, but 0, so the elements 0-6 actually consist of seven distinct items.

Functions

At this point you have all the tools you need to start writing your own JavaScript programs. However, there are some things that come in very handy as your programs become larger and more complex. The function is one of these elements.

A function is simply a block of code with a name, which allows the block of code to be called by other components in your scripts to perform certain tasks. Functions can also accept parameters or arguments that they use to complete their task. A function might have a simple task, such as printing something out to the screen, or a more complex task, like determining the square root of a number.

For example, say you had a function called `printDay`, and it accepted a day of the week and then printed out appointments for that day. You would call this function like this:

```
printDay(Monday);
```

where `printDay` is the name of the function, and the value is enclosed in the parentheses. Because this function takes care of all of the printing, it does not return a value; therefore, you don't have to deal with any new data. However, if you were using a function called `squareRoot`, you might get a value of 4 returned, and you would then have to write code to do something with that value:

```
squareRoot(16);
```

JavaScript actually comes with a number of built-in functions you can use to accomplish a variety of tasks. One of these functions is called `escape`. It can be used to process HTML so that it displays on the screen as plain text, tags and all. Here's how it is called:

```
escape(charstring);
```

The function name is `escape` and it accepts a data type of string, which it then converts to *escaped HTML*. Why would this be useful? You might want to provide an HTML tutorial for others, and you would need to show examples of the code in addition to how the code looked. You might be writing a guestbook and childproof it by escaping the text people have entered in order to prevent them from adding links to pornographic or adult sites.

NOTE

HTML makes use of certain symbols in the process of preparing text to be displayed in a Web browser. For example, the greater-than and less-than signs are used to denote HTML tags:

`<BODY>`

However, if you wanted to display code in a browser window as text, it would need to be escaped. That is, instead of using the symbols themselves, you would need to use a code in their place, so that the characters would be rendered on the screen, the following creates a level-one headline that reads Hello in the browser window:

`<H1>Hello</H1>`

If you use the escape codes for the brackets instead, as in the following, you would see `<H1>Hello</H1>` displayed as text in the browser window:

`&LT H1 &GT Hello &LT /H1 &GT`

Now use this function in a script:

```
<html>
<head>
<title>Using the Escape Function</title>
</head>
<body>

    <script language="JavaScript">
var ourText = "<H2>This is a level two headline</H2>";
ourText = escape(outText);
document.write(ourText);

    </script>

</body>
</html>
```

First, you define a variable that contains the string you want to escape. Place the string as the argument to your function and re-assign the variable with the following line:

```
ourText = escape(outText);
```

With the string escaped, you can write it to the document window without any problems.

Creating Custom Functions

In addition to using the functions provided automatically by JavaScript, you can also create and use your own functions. This is a perfect way to modularize your program into components that can be easily used in other programs, and at the same time make your application's organization much tighter.

For example, you previously built an array to keep track of the names of the days. It might be useful to build a function to print out a day, given the number.

To build this function, you need to define the function itself:

```
function printDay(theDay){
}
```

Do this by using the `function` keyword and then specifying, in parentheses, the variable that you will accept. In this case, it's a variable for the number called `theDay`.

Now, all you need to do is define what your function does. In this case, it takes a number and prints out the corresponding day. Your function takes shape as the following:

```
function printDay(theDay){

    days = new Array(6);

days[0] = "Monday";
days[1] = "Tuesday";
days[2] = "Wednesday";
days[3] = "Thursday";
days[4] = "Friday";
days[5] = "Saturday";
days[6] = "Sunday";

document.write("Today is ");
document.write(days[theDay]);
}
```

Now you have a function that prints the day of the week to the screen. You can call it like this:

```
printDay(3);
```

This results in `Thursday` being printed to the screen. That's it!

Your `printDay` function was self-contained; it accepted a value and performed an action, but it did not return any value. If you want to have the function return the name of the day, you could add a `return` statement:

```
return(days[theDay]);
```

This results in the value `Thursday` being returned to your program. By returning values, you can create functions that can be used inside other functions to perform some pretty complex tasks.

Summary

Believe it or not, you now have knowledge of all JavaScript's basic elements. With practice, and perhaps some help from the JavaScript reference, you can write your own JavaScripts that add functionality and interaction to your Web site.

In the following chapters, you take a look at some practical JavaScripts in order to help give you a head start on creating your own scripts and give you some examples of useful applications. You should feel free to modify and extend these examples; making them your own helps you learn more about the language.

15

INTRODUCING
JAVASCRIPT

Creating Simple JavaScripts

by David Gulbransen

IN THIS CHAPTER

Chapter 15, "Introducing JavaScript," introduced the JavaScript scripting language and provided you with the basic syntax that you need to begin constructing your own scripts. In this chapter you actually begin writing scripts to take care of some basic Web authoring tasks, such as creating confirmation boxes, date/time stamps, and changing status bars and other browser effects.

This chapter's purpose is to acquaint you with the techniques of good scripting and to aid you in developing your own scripts. Whenever possible, some other directions in which you might take the script examples are pointed out, and new resources are also suggested.

So now that you have the basics of JavaScript syntax under your command, take a look at scripting.

Formatting Scripts

If you recall from the last chapter, JavaScript scripts are set apart from the rest of the HTML in a Web page by using the `<SCRIPT>` tag, which marks the beginning and the ending of a script:

```
<SCRIPT>

    Here is some JavaScript.

</SCRIPT>
```

You might also recall that the script tag accepts a parameter called `Language`, which allows you to specify the type of scripting language that is being used. With several different versions of JavaScript available, and other scripting languages such as VBScript being supported by other browsers, it is important that you make use of the language parameter to ensure your scripts are optimally processed:

```
<SCRIPT LANGUAGE="JavaScript1.1">
</SCRIPT>
```

Using the language tag allows you to take advantage of features that are unique to that version of your scripting language, and help ensure that your scripts run smoothly. Although many scripts run properly without this parameter, using it is always a good habit to help ensure future compatibility in the ever-changing world of Web browsers.

In addition to thinking ahead for browser compatibility, it is also a good idea to consider users who might be using older versions of browsers, or those users who might be using browsers with special limitations, a text-only browser such as Lynx, for example.

Although you certainly don't want to limit the quality or creativity of your page, making your pages compatible with older browsers will only help you reach a wider audience, and annoy less people with errors generated by scripts their browsers can't run. Fortunately, HTML has a built-in mechanism for commenting HTML code which can be exploited for compatibility.

The HTML comment takes the form of `<!--` to mark the beginning of a comment and `-->` to mark the end of a comment:

```
<!-- This is an HTML Comment.
    It will be ignored by the browser -->
```

Even though the comment format is the same for all browsers, those browsers that can understand the `<SCRIPT>` tag have a special feature: They ignore HTML style comments within the tag.

Here's how it works:

```
<SCRIPT LANGUAGE="JavaScript1.1">
<!--

    Our JavaScript.
// -->
</SCRIPT>
```

Browsers that understand the script tag ignore the HTML comment and execute the script. The only trick is that you need to precede the HTML end comment with the `//` for a single line JavaScript comment. If you need to make comments inside the script tag, you can do so using the JavaScript comment format. However, older browsers won't understand the script tag, and therefore (in accordance with the HTML convention) ignore it. However, because the browser ignores the tag, anything between the tags would normally generate an error. That's why you place the HTML comments right inside the script tags. Older browsers then ignore both the tag and the script, which is commented out using the HTML comment format.

To maintain maximum compatibility, it is always a good idea to follow the preceding format for writing your scripts.

There are also some other ways that you can use some of JavaScript's built-in objects and functions to maintain compatibility of your scripts. The `navigator` object is designed specifically to return to you information about the browser, for example, `navigator.appName` and `navigator.appVersion`.

Using these two methods you can determine the browser and the browser version that someone is using to access your page. You can use this information to allow your scripts to execute different versions based on the browser. The following is an example.

First, just take a look at the information the functions return. If you were to call

```
navigator.appName();
```

while using Netscape, you would have the string `Netscape` returned. You could then determine the version by calling

```
navigator.appVersion();
```

which might return something like `4.02 - (Win95; I)`, indicating that you were using the 4.02 English version on Windows 95.

The same two functions called by a user running Internet Explorer would produce the following results:

```
Microsoft Internet Explorer
4.0 (compatible; MSIE 4.0; Windows 95)
```

These results could then be used to allow the browser to choose between two different versions of the same script, simply by making use of an `if` statement, as follows:

```
if (navigator.appName == "Netscape") {
    document.write("You're using Netscape!");
} else {
    document.write("You are not using Netscape!");
}
```

In this example, you could replace the contents of the `if` statement to contain two versions of the same script, one optimized for Netscape and one for any other browsers. If the script detected Netscape as the browser, it would use the first block; if not, it would use the second.

Of course, today many authors are concerned about compatibility between Netscape and IE. With a simple modification, the `if` statement can switch between the browsers as well:

```
if (navigator.appName == "Netscape") {
    document.write("You are Using Netscape");
} else if (navigator.appName == "Microsoft Internet Explorer") {
    document.write("You are using Internet Explorer");
} else {
    document.write("Sorry! You need Netscape or IE for this page!");
}
```

Now you have an `if` statement that allows you to write different scripts for a Netscape browser, Internet Explorer, and even to include a third script for any other browsers, such as Lynx. By using this technique and the `navigator` object, you can make sure that your scripts are truly visible by the widest possible audience.

Date and Time Entry

There are many instances where using a JavaScript can improve your Web page performance and help avoid security holes for your server. For example, say you want to provide a date and time stamp on a page when the user loads it. This information could then be used in filling out a form, or for setting a cookie on the user's machine.

There are a few methods you can use to display the current time on a user's machine with traditional CGI. One way is to have the entire contents of the page generated by a CGI script, such as a Perl script. This would allow you to update variables like a date/time stamp with the date and time of the server. Of course, converting it this way to the user's local time might prove more challenging. There is an increased response time and interaction with the server that make this method rather inefficient.

You could also employ server-side includes to simply add a date/time stamp to an existing page. Despite the remaining performance issue, it would still be faster than a complete CGI. However, as any Web tutorials inform you, enabling server-side includes on a Web server can open many security loopholes, and if you are not careful, could open your Web server up to attack. Further examination into SSI might reveal that the security risks for your site are not worth the trouble.

By eliminating the need to completely rely on server-based solutions for forms processing, JavaScript opens the door to more efficient forms and even the use of form validation. Much of what has been accomplished in the past now can be done with JavaScript. Text strings can be manipulated, calculations performed, the data the user has entered into the form can even be verified (although the verification is limited) to make sure it is not bogus information. For example, you could check the entry of a phone number to make sure it is in the format you desire and to make sure it contains the proper number of digits. This type of application with CGI would be extremely slow and rather painful. But with JavaScript, processing information on the user's machine increases efficiency for the user and the coder.

JavaScript can provide an easy, efficient way to get the local time onto a user's page. Take a look at how you can do that.

First, JavaScript has a number of built-in functions that you can take advantage of in situations like this. For a full list of the built-in functions available, check out the Netscape JavaScript reference at `http://www.netscape.com/eng/mozilla/3.0/handbook/javascript/index.html`.

It just so happens that there is a function called `Date()` that returns a value of the current date and time from the local system. You can begin your script by calling this function and getting the full date string:

```
<SCRIPT LANGUAGE="JavaScript">
<!--
    rightNow = new Date()
-->
</SCRIPT>
```

Of course the string that the function returns is very complete and longer than you really need for your script:

```
Wed Sep 04 14:31:46 US Eastern Standard Time 1997
```

Fortunately, JavaScript also provides a series of functions that allow you to grab the individual components that make up the date string, and reformat it as your own. First, format the time. To do this, use two functions—`getHours()` and `getMinutes()`—that return the hours and minutes for your time of day:

```
hour = rightNow.getHours();
minute = rightNow.getMinutes();
```

Because you have already stored the date string in your variable called `rightNow`, you can access the information by calling the functions for the right now variable, and assigning the value to your own `hour` and `minute` variables.

Now that you have the hours and minutes, you're almost ready to print them out, but first, do a little bit of formatting. You might have noticed that the time takes the form of 24-hour time, but you want to display the time in 12-hour time. You can do this by making use of the `if` statement to convert the `hour` variable from 24-hour time to 12-hour time:

```
if (hour > 12)
    hour = (hour - 12);
```

You are checking to see if the hour value is greater than 12. If it is, you can get the correct 12-hour time by subtracting 12. You can also make similar use of the `if...else` statement to append an AM or PM to the time value:

```
if (hour >= 13)
    status = "PM";
else
    status = "AM";
```

Here you simply check the value of the hour and set a new variable called `status` to AM or PM, depending on the value of the hour variable.

Once the hour and minutes are correct and you know if it is afternoon or morning, you're ready to write the time to the screen with the following code:

```
document.write(hour,":",minute, status);
```

Now, with the time printed out, you're ready to format your date. Formatting your date is simple, as well. You can make use of three built-in functions to get values for the `month`, `day`, and `year`:

```
month = rightNow.getMonth();
day = rightNow.getDate();
year = rightNow.getYear();
```

The values you have for each of these variables are almost ready for use. The month is the only problem. If you print out the value for the month as is, you notice that it is off by one. That is because the value comes from an array; if you recall from the previous chapter, the first element in the array is 0, not 1. Therefore, you need to add 1 to the month's value to make sure that the month is correct:

```
month = (month + 1);
```

With that formatting out of the way, the only thing left to do is to print out the date:

```
document.write(" ",month,"/",day,"/",year," ");
```

By combining all of these pieces into one script, you get the results shown in Listing 16.1. Your final script prints the time and the date to the window, in the short date format. You could easily list the month's or day's full name by comparing the value retrieved with an array containing the names of the months or days. The output from your script is shown in Figure 16.1.

16

Listing 16.1. A JavaScript to display the date and time.

```html
<HTML>
<HEAD>
<TITLE>Date and Time Example</TITLE>
</HEAD>
<BODY>

<SCRIPT LANGUAGE="JavaScript">
<!--
    rightNow = new Date()
    var status;

    hour = rightNow.getHours()
    minute = rightNow.getMinutes()

    if (hour >= 13)
        status = "PM";
    else
        status = "AM";

    if (hour > 12)
        hour = (hour - 12);

    document.write(hour,":",minute, status);

    month = rightNow.getMonth();
    month = (month + 1);
    day = rightNow.getDate();
    year = rightNow.getYear();
    document.write(" ",month,"/",day,"/",year," ");

-->
</SCRIPT>

</BODY>
</HTML>
```

FIGURE 16.1.

*The current local time
and date, produced
with a client-side
JavaScript.*

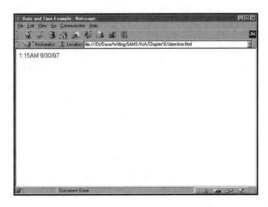

Using JavaScript to set the date and time on a page does raise one of the key issues developers sometimes face when using JavaScript to replace mechanisms previously performed by CGI.

This issue is that the local machine performs calculations. For example, with the date and time stamp a user stamping the page at the same moment in New York will likely have a different time stamped than a user stamping the page in California. If you are stamping the times to get them relative to your server, you should make note of this fact. However, in most instances you are likely to want the time based on the user's local time, so the technique is still useful. Just being aware that users can manipulate the date/time stamp by manipulating their machine's clock indicates why JavaScript might not be the most secure solution for sensitive scripts.

Determining Browser Information

Making use of the built-in objects and functions that are provided with JavaScript can be an invaluable way to make your scripting life easier. If you are unsure about what objects or functions might exist to make your life easier, check the documentation to see if there is one available for your task. Taking a few minutes to check the JavaScript reference for an existing function could save you hours of writing and debugging your own functions. Look at another example.

Say that you are developing a site that makes use of many different, cutting-edge technologies. You might even have special features on your site geared toward users that already have certain browser plug-ins installed—you might also want to guide users who don't have those plug-ins installed to the site where they can download them. Take a look at how you can use JavaScript to determine the plug-ins a user has installed.

First, check the reference to see if there are any built-in functions that could aid you in this exercise and, as it turns out, there are several. The `navigator` object contains functions that are designed to return information about the browser, including the name and version of the browser and even the installed plug-ins!

So now take a look at objects and properties to see how you might be able to use the `navigator` object in combination with its properties to get information about the user's installed browser plug-ins.

Objects

One very important, and often overlooked, advantage of JavaScript is that it is an object-oriented programming language. That means that elements within the language are treated as objects that can be used in different scripts, and manipulated to create other objects. Seem confusing? It really isn't.

Think of it this way: Suppose you have a vending machine that sells cola. The vending machine is really made up of a couple of different components—something to take the money, something to select the type of cola, and a mechanism for dispensing the cola. Each of these mechanisms is like an object. Take the cola-selection mechanism. This object is used to select an item. The selections for colas could easily be replaced with candy bars, and the selection object could still be used. That's the advantage of an object—it is interchangeable.

Another advantage of objects is that they have methods (or functions) and properties associated with them. For example, the change-counting object from the vending machine would have a method for counting coins. It would also keep track of how much money had been inserted. Imagine the following object:

Object	Methods	Properties
MoneyChanger	Count_Coins	Current_Amount
	Return_Change	Change_Due
	Reset	

If you want to know how much money had been inserted, you could use the `Count_Coins` method to calculate the `Current_Amount`. The value of the `Current_Amount` is called a property, and you can access the property of a method directly. In JavaScript, the syntax for using objects is this:

```
Object.Method.Property;
```

If you want to know how much money a customer had put in, assign the value of the `Current_Amount` property from your change mechanism to the variable `how_much`:

```
how_much = MoneyChanger.Count_Coins.Current_Amount;
```

This might seem confusing at first, but working with objects should soon become second nature to you. In fact, you have already been working with an object!

Whenever you have written something to the screen with a script, you have been using the `document` object:

```
document.write("Some Text");
```

This line of code is just the JavaScript's way of saying that you want to make use of the `write` method, or the `document` object to display the text onscreen. The `document` object is a predefined object that corresponds to the current opened document. Using the `document` object and the `write` method makes it much easier to write information to the browser widow. Now get back to your plug-in script.

CAUTION

The `document.write()` method will replace the current contents of the browser window. In essence, this creates an entirely new document. When you are creating a new page, the `document.write()` method works fine, however, if you want to write information to an existing page, you should consider using the `document.open()`, `writeIn()`, and `document.close()` methods.

Using the Navigator Object

Because you now know there are no functions available to query for plug-ins, you can explore some of JavaScript's other resources.

As it turns out, JavaScript has an object called navigator, which contains properties and methods that can be used to find information about the version, configuration, and features of the current browser, including the status of plug-ins.

By making use of the navigator object, the amount of code you need to review the plug-ins is surprisingly sparse. It begins with the following code:

```
var plug_count = navigator.plugins.length;
```

This line of code assigns the value of plugins.length plug-ins to your variable, called plug_count. This doesn't yield information about the plug-ins themselves, but the total number of plug-ins that you are going to be reviewing. To do this, use a for loop as follows:

```
for (var counter=0; counter < plug_count; counter++) {
}
```

This for loop allows you to step through the plug-ins one by one, until there are no more left. Within the for loop you could see if a certain plug-in is available, and load different data for different plug-ins. For this example, however, print the plug-in data to the screen with the following code:

```
var plugin_num = counter + 1;

document.write("<B>Plug-in Number" + plugin_num + "</B>");
document.write("<BR>"+navigator.plugins[counter].name);
document.write("<br>" + navigator.plugins[counter].filename);
```

Here you are using the document object and write method to display the plug-in information on the screen. You create a new variable called plug-in number, which acts as a placeholder for the current plug-in. Next, print the plug-in's name by accessing the navigator.plugin object using an array syntax to yield the plug-in name property. Since the plug-in values are stored in an array, you can access them using the counter variable from your for loop. The process is repeated for the filename property, which reveals where the plug-in is located on the local system. The final code for your script is shown in Listing 16.2.

Listing 16.2. Using JavaScript to determine information about the browser.

```
<HTML>
<HEAD>
<TITLE>Navigator Installed Plug-Ins</TITLE>


<H2>Navigator Installed Plug-Ins</H2>

<SCRIPT LANGUAGE="JavaScript">
<!--
```

```
var plug_count = navigator.plugins.length;

for (var counter=0; counter < plug_count; counter++) {

   var plugin_num = counter + 1;

   document.write("<B>Plug-in Number" + plugin_num + "</B>");
   document.write("<BR>"+navigator.plugins[counter].name);
   document.write("<br>" + navigator.plugins[counter].filename);

}

// -->

</SCRIPT>
</HEAD>
<BODY>
</BODY>
</HTML>
```

A surprisingly little amount of code can generate some impressive data. Using a similar technique, you could ensure that a user had installed a certain plug-in before loading a file that relies on a plug-in. The final results of this script are shown in Figure 16.2. Using so little code to accomplish such a useful task demonstrates how important it can be to exploit JavaScript's built-in resources. Making use of the tools provided within JavaScript can make your life much easier.

FIGURE 16.2.

A JavaScript that determines the number and type of plug-ins installed for Netscape.

Linking Scripts to Windows Events

In addition to JavaScripts that are executed immediately when a page loads, it might also be useful to have a script that executes when a specific task occurs.

For example, say you have a page that contains a form that adds users to your mailing list. You might want to check to make sure that these users want to be added to the mailing list before you have them fill out the form. One way to do this might be to have a check box on the form itself—but users might miss that if they aren't reading carefully. Another way might be to use a JavaScript alert box.

An *alert box* is simply a dialog box that opens to provide the user with some more information before allowing them to proceed with the current action. You've seen them many times when quitting applications: `"Are you sure you want to quit?"`

With JavaScript, it is possible to link actions, such as alert boxes, to specific windows events, such as clicking a button. To do so, you need to make use of the event properties of the element to which you are linking your script. Look at an example.

Suppose you have a line of code that produces an alert:

```
alert('Leave this page at your own peril!');
```

This produces a dialog box warning the user about the consequences of leaving your page. Now, how do you link it to execute when the user leaves your page? It's simple:

```
<HTML>
<TITLE>Alert on Leaving</TITLE>

<BODY onUnload="alert('Leave this page at your own peril!');">

<H2>Don't Leave This Page!</H2>
</BODY>
</HTML>
```

Notice that you have used a new parameter in the body tag called `onUnload`. This is a browser event that corresponds to leaving the currently loaded page. For the value of `onUnload` you have entered your script, which produces the dialog box. The results of the script are shown in Figure 16.3.

FIGURE 16.3.

Linking JavaScripts to windows events can be useful for producing effects such as dialog boxes.

Keep in mind that you could have just as easily used a script tag, and written the alert box as a function. Then, instead of placing the code itself in the value of `onUnload`, you could have simply called the function.

Alert Boxes and Confirmations

There are many times when you might want to present viewers of your site with an alert or a confirmation dialog box in order to make sure they understand what the consequences of their actions are.

For example, you might want to throw up an alert that lets users know they are leaving your site. Perhaps your site has sensitive material; you might have an alert that warns parents to keep children out.

Another place you might want to use a variant of the alert box, called a confirmation box, is with submitting forms. For example, if you have a form that allows users to sign up for your mailing list, you might want to confirm that they have signed up. Even more importantly, if you are taking product orders with credit card, you might want to give customers a warning about Internet security, and give them an option for canceling their submission. Take a look at how you could do that.

First, create a function that generates your confirmation box:

```
function double_check() {

    if (confirm ("Are you absolutely sure you want to do this?"))
        location="http://myserver.com/somepage.html";

}
```

This is a very simple function that uses an `if` statement and the `confirm` object. This function creates an alert box that includes an OK and a Cancel button when called. You can also change the alert's text by altering the string that is passed to `confirm`.

That's all that is required to create the confirmation dialog box. Now all you need to do is to link the function to the proper window event:

```
<FORM>
<INPUT TYPE="submit" onclick="double_check()" NAME="Submit" VALUE="Click Here">
</FORM>
```

By creating a form, and setting the `onclick` event to call your confirmation function, you have created a dialog that is automatically called when users click the Submit button. The code for this script is shown in Listing 16.3, and the final results are shown in Figure 16.4.

Listing 16.3. A JavaScript Confirmation dialog box.

```
<HTML>
<HEAD>
<TITLE>A Confirmation Alert Box</TITLE>
</HEAD>
<BODY>

<SCRIPT LANGUAGE="JavaScript1.1">
```

continues

Listing 16.3. continued

```
<!--

function double_check() {

    if (confirm ("Are you absolutely sure you want to do this?"))
        location="http://myserver.com/somepage.html";

}
// -->

</SCRIPT>

<H2>A Confirmation Dialog</H2>

<FORM>
<INPUT TYPE="submit" onclick="double_check()" NAME="Submit" VALUE="Click Here">
</FORM>

</BODY>
</HTML>
```

FIGURE 16.4.

JavaScript can be used to create confirmation boxes to allow users to double-check their decisions.

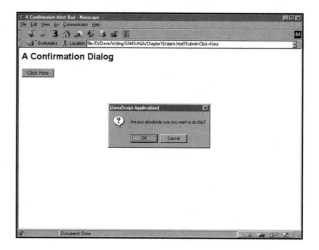

Altering the Status Bar

When using your browser, you may have noticed that messages, such as the location of a file, are occasionally displayed in the status bar JavaScript allows you to manipulate the text that appears in the status bar.

The JavaScript window object contains properties and methods for manipulating the text in the status bar. For example, you could use JavaScript to place a customized message in the status bar when the user passes over a link. Construct a function that accepts a string of text and places it in the status bar:

```
function msg(text) {

    window.status=text;
}
```

You have created a function called msg that requires a parameter called text. That parameter is the string of text you place in the status bar.

Next, you can change the value of the window.status property to that of your own text. It's that simple! Now, whenever this function is called, it replaces the status bar text with your own. Take a look at how you call the function from your link:

```
<A HREF="http://www.yahoo.com"
onMouseOver="msg('Click Here for Yahoo!'); return true;"
onMouseOut="msg(''); return true;">
Yahoo!</A>
```

All you are doing is creating calls to the function from the onMouseOver and onMouseOut events for your link, with the following code:

```
onMouseOver="msg('Click Here for Yahoo!'); return true;"
```

You are instructing the browser to call your message function with the string Click Here for Yahoo! as the value it places in the message bar. You use a similar call to return the message bar to an empty state, by replacing your text with a null string:

```
onMouseOut="msg(''); return true;">
```

With those events set to trigger your function, you're ready to place it in a page context. Listing 16.4 shows the complete script within the context of an HTML page. Figure 16.5 shows the results the user sees when he or she passes the mouse pointer over your new link.

Listing 16.4. Changing the text in the status bar.

```
<HTML>
<HEAD>
<TITLE>Changing the Status Bar Text</TITLE>
</HEAD>

<SCRIPT LANGUAGE="JavaScript1.1">
<!--

function msg(text) {

    window.status=text;
}

// -->
</SCRIPT>

<BODY>
<H2>Manipulating Text in the Status Bar</H2>
```

continues

Listing 16.4. continued

```
<A HREF="http://www.yahoo.com"
onMouseOver="msg('Click Here for Yahoo!'); return true;"
onMouseOut="msg(''); return true;">
Yahoo!</A>
<P>

Pass your mouse over the link above, and watch the status bar change.
</BODY>
</HTML>
```

FIGURE 16.5.

An example of using a JavaScript to update the text in the status bar.

Scrolling Text in the Status Bar

Now that you know how to display messages in the status bar, imagine adding some effects, such as scrolling text. This kind of effect could be used to create a welcome message for your page. It could also be used to provide status updates for any services that you offer.

Although it might seem very complicated, in reality it can be done with a relatively short script. The first order of business is to establish the function that you are going to use to write to the status bar and scroll your text:

```
function scrollStatus(counter) {
}
```

The function is called `scrollStatus`, and it accepts a value called `counter`, which you use within the function to keep track of how your message is displayed in the scroll bar. Now add a few variables to the function, so you can keep track of data:

```
var blank = "                               "
   var text = "Here is the message we will scroll…";
   var message = blank + text;
   var delay = 150;
```

The first variable is called `blank` and you use it to provide your text string with some leading spaces that you can scroll through; those spaces prevent the message from immediately scrolling off the screen. The `text` variable stores the actual message's text. Next, combine the two variables into the `message` string, which you actually use in the status bar. Finally, create a variable called `delay`, which controls the speed at which the text scrolls. A smaller value causes the text to scroll faster, a higher value scrolls slower. For example, it is set to `150`, which should provide a nice, smooth scroll.

Next, you need to have some way of scrolling the message. To accomplish this, you use a built-in function called `substring`, which allows you to trim your message by a certain number of characters—that's what you use the `counter` variable for. The substring function accepts two parameters, the number of characters to trim and the total length of the string:

```
message = message.substring(counter,message.length);
```

This statement passes your message string to the substring and trims it by the value of your `counter` variable. Now you can write the message to the status bar:

```
window.defaultStatus = message;
```

Now your message is displayed in the status window! Next, you need to write the JavaScript mechanism to scroll it. The first thing you need to do is increment your `counter` variable. You do this because you are looping the function to trim your message string one letter at a time; then you redraw your shortened message to the status bar. The effect is a scrolling message:

```
if (message.length > 0)
    counter++;
  else counter = 0;
```

Basically, the effect is created by adding 1 to your `counter` value each time the function is called, and then trimming the text by the `counter` number. So if you start with `Some Text`, on the next pass it becomes `ome Text`, followed by `me Text`, and so on.

Now that you have incremented the `counter` variable, you need to create a `newCounter` variable to keep track of the updated `counter` value:

```
newCounter = counter;
```

Use the `newCounter` value to seed your function, and call it again:

```
counter = setTimeout("scrollStatus(newCounter)", delay);
```

This line of code uses another built-in JavaScript function, called `setTimeout`, which provides your scrolling speed. `setTimeout` accepts two parameters: a function to be called and a delay in milliseconds. By using this function to call your own scrolling function, you have created a loop that repeats indefinitely, increasing your `counter` variable each time, until there are no characters left in the message string. Then the variable is reset, and the process starts over.

The last step in completing your scrolling status bar is to cause the scrolling function to be called when the page is loaded:

```
<BODY onLoad = "scrollStatus(0);" onUnload "window.defaultStatus = ''" >
```

This results in the function `scrollStatus(0)` being called when the page loads, and it also sets the status bar back to blank when the user exits the page. That's it! The complete code for the scrolling status bar is shown in Listing 16.5.

Listing 16.5. Scrolling the status bar text.

```
<HTML>
<HEAD>
<TITLE>Scrolling Status Bar Text</TITLE>
</HEAD>

<SCRIPT LANGUAGE="JavaScript1.1">
<!--
// Script modified by DLG
// Based on original code by Jason Schanker (jcheetah@orion.webspan.net)

function scrollStatus(counter) {

    var blank = "                                "
    var text = "Here is the message we will scroll…";
    var message = blank + text;
    var delay = 150;

    message = message.substring(counter,message.length);

    window.defaultStatus = message;

    if (message.length > 0)
        counter++;
    else counter = 0;

    newCounter = counter;

    counter = setTimeout("scrollStatus(newCounter)", delay);

}

// -->
</SCRIPT>

<BODY onLoad = "scrollStatus(0);" onUnload "window.defaultStatus = ''" >

<H2>Watch the Status Bar for Scrolling Information</H2>

</BODY>
</HTML>
```

Now you have a scrolling status bar that can easily be altered for your own use. You can customize the message that appears in the status bar by changing the value of the text variable.

You can control how fast the text scrolls along the status bar by altering the `delay` variable. The final output of the script is shown in Figure 16.6.

FIGURE 16.6.

Scrolling the status bar text with JavaScript.

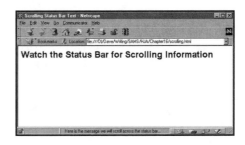

Summary

As you can see, scripting with JavaScript can be very flexible and powerful without becoming too complex. However, that doesn't mean that JavaScript is too limited. You have seen how it can be used to gather data about the user's environment and change virtually any type of element in the browser environment. Used correctly, JavaScript can increase the efficiency of page load times, execution of customized features, and improve the experience for your site's users.

As you continue to improve these scripts and build your own, be sure to check the reference documentation whenever possible, to see when the JavaScript creators have designed a built-in function or object method—they make your life easier. Becoming familiar with these resources can save you a great deal of time and effort.

Now you move on to Chapter 17, "Using JavaScript for Forms," where you take a look at how JavaScript is being used to replace HTML and CGI scripting for forms processing and forms validation.

Using JavaScript for Forms

by *David Gulbransen*

IN THIS CHAPTER

CHAPTER 17

There are as many reasons for having Web pages as there seem to be Web pages themselves. However, among all of the devices and features found on Web pages, the use of forms is perhaps one of the most common Web applications.

The ability to interact with the user and get feedback from visitors to your site are very appealing reasons to make use of forms. Developing forms themselves is pretty straightforward. By simply making use of the HTML form tags, you can easily create a form to do anything, such as mail you feedback, accept complaints, and order products.

The creators of JavaScript were well aware of the popularity of forms on the World Wide Web, and, as a result, there is a great deal of functionality built into JavaScript especially for forms. In this chapter, you will take a look at how you can use JavaScript to manipulate the data on your forms for client-side forms processing or to interact with a CGI script. You will also take a look at the mechanisms that JavaScript provides for Form Validation.

CGI versus JavaScript Forms

Creating forms with JavaScript doesn't vary that much from creating forms with CGI. You still make use of the same HTML tags you may have used before to create the form itself. Where JavaScript takes a drastic turn from traditional form development is the way in which data is entered and processed.

For example, say that you have a form to provide user feedback about your site. Within that form you might have a blank for the user to include his or her e-mail address. You might also have a checkbox that indicates the user doesn't want to be on your e-mail newsletter list. With traditional CGI, that's pretty much all that can be done with the form. The user enters his or her e-mail address and checks if he or she doesn't want to be on the list.

However, with JavaScript, it would be possible to link an event with the checkbox, so if the user clicked the option not to be included on the list, the e-mail address input field would no longer be available, or it might be replaced with a string such as No Thanks! Please don't include me on your list. This gives the user a clearer idea of what is being performed on the form, and gives you the ability to do some "pre-processing" before the form is submitted.

Another example of "pre-processing" might be the generation of an order number for a catalog form. After selecting the items the user wants to purchase, and entering billing information, you might want to assign the customer an order number to track the order. With traditional CGI you could generate the number on the server and then output the number back to the user, but that could be inefficient use of your server, and potentially be slow for the user. Imagine instead that you used a JavaScript to generate the order number, and then displayed in on the form for the user, ready to submit to your order processing CGI as well!

Finally, what if you have fields on your order form that are required for it to be processed? For example, you might require an e-mail address or phone number. How can you make sure that the user is aware of the required fields, and how can you make sure they are filled out before the form is submitted? This has been a big problem with CGI based-forms; often, Web sites have incomplete forms submitted from users who deliberately enter bogus information, or earnest users who missed a field.

One solution to the problem can be found in JavaScript. You can use JavaScript to partially check the integrity of the data entered into your forms so you might get better results.

The Form Object

Because JavaScript is an object-based scripting language, it should come as no surprise that there is a Form object that exists to allow you access to HTML form tags and properties through JavaScript.

The elements of a form are actually stored in the Forms[] array, which is property of the Document object. That means that all of your form elements are stored sequentially in the Forms array and can be accessed by their index number:

```
document.forms[0]
```

> **NOTE**
>
> Do not forget that when referencing items in an array, the first element of the array is always referred to by the number 0, rather than 1.

The preceding code represents the first form on the page (or the only one if the page contained only one form). Likewise, elements of each form are stored in their own Elements array. Sound confusing? It's not too bad. Take a look at a simple page:

```
<HTML>
<FORM NAME="firstform">
<INPUT TYPE="checkbox" NAME="ElementOne">
</FORM>

<FORM NAME="secondform">
<INPUT TYPE="radio" NAME="ElementOne">
<INPUT TYPE="text" NAME="ElementTwo">
</FORM>
</HTML>
```

This page actually contains two separate forms. If you wanted to use the object model to access the forms, then the following line refers to the first form:

```
document.forms[0]
```

This would refer to the second form:

```
document.forms[1]
```

If you wanted to access the first element in the second form on the page, you could use the following, which would correspond to the Radio Box called `ElementOne`:

```
document.forms[1].elements[0]
```

Allowing access to the elements of the form in this manner allows a great deal of flexibility for manipulating the data on a form and adding functionality such as alerts, notifications, or validating input fields.

The `Form` object also has a number of properties and methods that correspond to the features of an HTML form. The properties include:

■ ACTION

`Action` is the name of the CGI script or application on the server that handles your form input.

■ ENCODING

`Encoding` refers to any special data encoding that might be passed to the server from your script.

■ METHOD

`Method` refers to the method used to communicate your form data to the server, it can be either `get` or `post`.

■ TARGET

`Target` refers to the location where your form data is submitted. For example, you could host your script on one server while submitting it to another server.

You will find that these `Form` object properties are seldom used; however, it is a good idea to be aware of their presence. There are also two special methods that are associated with the `Form` object: `submit()` and `reset()`.

The `submit()` and `reset()` methods allow you to execute script functions when the user clicks your Submit or Reset buttons. For example, you could use the `submit()` function to call a customized function you have written called `validate()` that validates the user input before accepting the form.

form Elements

The `Form` object's elements conform to the elements that are created with the HTML form tags. These elements each have a number of associated properties, methods, and event handlers that can be used to customize your forms or to manipulate the data that is contained on the form. What follows is a summary of the `form` elements, complete with the properties, methods and event handlers for each element. The syntax for the HTML tag used to generate each element is also given.

Using JavaScript for Forms

CHAPTER 17

349

17

USING
JAVASCRIPT
FOR FORMS

button

The button element represents a button on the current form. The button is created using the `<INPUT TYPE="button">` tag, and can be used to represent any action the user can execute on a page. The `onclick()` event handler can be used to execute other functions or scripts when the button is depressed. Figure 17.1 shows some examples of buttons on a page.

FIGURE 17.1.

The HTML button
*element creates a push
button on the form.*

Here are the JavaScript properties, methods, and events associated with the button element, as well as its HTML usage:

> **Properties:** `form, name, type, value`
>
> **Methods:** `blur(), click(), focus()`
>
> **Event Handlers:** `onblur(), onclick(), onfocus()`
>
> **HTML:**
> ```
> <FORM>
> <INPUT
>         TYPE="button"
>         VALUE="label"
>         NAME="name"
>         onClick="handler"
> >
> </FORM>
> ```

checkbox Element

The checkbox element represents a checkbox in the current form. checkbox can be used to select a single value, and is created using the `<INPUT TYPE="checkbox">` tag. The `onclick()` event handler provides a mechanism for linking functions to the selection of a checkbox. Figure 17.2 shows two examples of a checkbox and the states they can represent.

FIGURE 17.2.

The checkbox *element
creates a checkbox on
the form that can be
used to select different
values.*

Here are the JavaScript properties, methods, and events associated with the `checkbox` element, as well as its HTML usage:

Properties: `checked, defaultChecked, form, name, type, value`

Methods: `blur(), click(), focus()`

Event Handlers: `onblur(), onclick(), onfocus()`

HTML:

```
<FORM>
<INPUT
        TYPE="checkbox"
        NAME="name"
        VALUE="value"
        CHECKED
        onClick="handler"
> label
</FORM>
```

radio

The `radio` box is a variation of the `checkbox`. It is invoked in a similar fashion, and can be manipulated with the same properties and methods. However, the appearance of the actual element to be checked is round, offering a different graphical representation, as shown in Figure 17.3.

FIGURE 17.3.

The radio box *functions like a* checkbox*, but offers a different visual style.*

Here are the JavaScript properties, methods, and events associated with the `radio` box element, as well as its HTML usage:

Properties: `checked, defaultChecked, form, name, type, value`

Methods: `blur(), click(), focus()`

Event Handlers: `onblur(), onclick(), onfocus()`

HTML:

```
<FORM>
<INPUT
        TYPE="radio"
        NAME="name"
        VALUE="value"
        CHECKED
        onClick="handler"
> label
</FORM>
```

select Element

The select element can take two forms: a single selection box or, by using the MULTIPLE keyword, a multiple selection box. A single selection box shows the current selection in the visible field. A multiple selection box accepts the SIZE attribute to determine the number of choices that are currently available. The list items for both types of selection boxes are specified using the <OPTION> tag. Figure 17.4 shows the two types of selection boxes side-by-side.

FIGURE 17.4.

The select element provides mechanisms that allows users to select items from pulldown menus and scroll boxes.

Here are the JavaScript properties, methods, and events associated with the select element, as well as its HTML usage:

Properties: form, length, name, options, selectedIndex, type

Methods: blur(), click(), focus()

Event Handlers: onblur(), onclick(), onfocus()

HTML:

```
<FORM>
<SELECT
    NAME="name"
    SIZE=integer
        MULTIPLE
        onChange="handler"
        onBlur="handler"
        onFocus="handler"
>
<OPTION VALUE="value" SELECTED>option label
<OPTION VALUE="value">option label
</SELECT>
</FORM>
```

text Element

The text element is used to create a one-line text input field on the form. The onchange() event handler can be used to invoke methods when text is entered into the field. The element also accepts a defaultValue, which pre-enters text into the field. Figure 17.5 shows a standard text box and a text box with a default value.

FIGURE 17.5.

The text *element provides a single-line text input field.*

Here are the JavaScript properties, methods, and events associated with the text element, as well as its HTML usage:.

Properties: defaultValue, form, name, type, value

Methods: blur(), focus(), select()

Event Handlers: onblur(), onchange(), onfocus()

HTML:

```
<FORM>
<INPUT
        TYPE="text"
        NAME="name"
        VALUE="default"
        SIZE=integer
        MAXLENGTH=integer
        onChange="handler"
        onBlur="handler"
        onFocus="handler"
>
</FORM>
```

textarea Element

The textarea element is similar to the text element, but allows the user to enter multiple lines of text. It accepts a ROWS and COLS parameter to determine the initial size of the textarea entry field, and it can also be seeded with a defaultValue. Figure 17.6 shows an example of a textarea.

FIGURE 17.6.

The textarea *element provides a flexible large input area for extended text entries.*

Here are the JavaScript properties, methods, and events associated with the textarea element, as well as its HTML usage:

Properties: defaultValue, form, name, type, value

Methods: blur(), focus(), select()

Event Handlers: `onblur()`, `onchange()`, `onfocus()`

HTML:

```
<FORM>
<TEXTAREA
    NAME="name"
    ROWS=integer
    COLS=integer
    WRAP= off ¦ virtual ¦ physical
onChange="handler"
    onBlur="handler"
    onFocus="handler"
>
default text
</TEXTAREA>
</FORM>
```

hidden Element

The `hidden` element exists to provide a mechanism for submitting data on a form without the data being visible to the form user. For example, you might have a form which produces a string to be written to a cookie, but you might not want to confuse the page viewer with such data. A `hidden` element could store the data in your form, and then submit it to your server without displaying it to the user.

Because there is no user interaction with the user, the `hidden` element has no built-in methods or event handlers.

Here are the JavaScript properties, methods, and events associated with the `hidden` element, as well as its HTML usage:

Properties: `form, name, type, value`

Methods: NONE

Event Handlers: NONE

HTML:

```
<FORM>
<INPUT
        TYPE="hidden"
        NAME="name"
        VALUE="default"
>
</FORM>
```

password Element

The `password` element provides a text entry field for entering passwords. The functionality is similar to that of the `text` element. However, data that is entered into the `Password` field will be masked from the viewer with the * character to prevent password theft. Figure 17.7 shows the `Password` field and the masking when the user enters data.

FIGURE 17.7.

The password *element
provides an input field
that is masked so the
input is not visible.*

Here are the JavaScript properties, methods, and events associated with the password element,
as well as its HTML usage:

> **Properties:** defaultValue, form, name, type, value
>
> **Methods:** blur(), focus(), select()
>
> **Event Handlers:** onblur(), onchange(), onfocus()
>
> **HTML:**

```
<FORM>
<INPUT
     TYPE="password"
     NAME="name"
     VALUE="default"
     SIZE=integer
>
</FORM>
```

submit Element

The submit element represents the Submit button on a form. This button is used to submit the
form data to a server application or CGI script for processing. A simple Submit button is shown
in Figure 17.8.

FIGURE 17.8.

The submit *element
creates a Submit button
on the page, while the
reset element creates a
Form Reset button.*

Here are the JavaScript properties, methods, and events associated with the submit element, as
well as its HTML usage:

> **Properties:** form, name, type, value
>
> **Methods:** blur(), focus(), click()
>
> **Event Handlers:** onblur(), onclick(), onfocus()

HTML:

```
<FORM>
<INPUT
    TYPE="submit"
    NAME="name"
    VALUE="default"
    onClick="handler"
>
</FORM>
```

reset Element

Most forms will contain a Reset button that corresponds to the reset element. This element provides users with a means of clearing any data they may have entered into a form, so they can either leave the session without leaving data in place or they can start filling out the form again. The Reset button is often found in conjunction with the Submit button, as shown previously in Figure 17.8.

Here are the JavaScript properties, methods, and events associated with the reset element, as well as its HTML usage:

Properties: form, name, type, value

Methods: blur(), focus(), click()

Event Handlers: onblur(), onclick(), onfocus()

HTML:

```
<FORM>
<INPUT
    TYPE="reset"
    VALUE="label"
    NAME="name"
onClick="handler"
>
</FORM>
```

form Element Properties

As you reviewed the different form elements, you might have noticed that many of them share similar properties. Because each of the properties represents the same type of data for each element, the properties are listed here for you to cross reference back to the element property listings.

form

The form property represents the name of the current form. For example, if you define a form using the following code, the value of the form property would be myForm:

```
<FORM NAME="myForm"> </FORM>
```

name

The name property represents the value of the name attribute specified in the HTML definition of the current form element. For example, if you define a text field such as the following,
the value for the name property would be address:

```
<INPUT TYPE="text" NAME="address">
```

This can be a very useful property, as it allows you to reference specific elements by their names,
a very convenient way to manipulate form data.

type

The type property represents the type of input element that has been defined in the current
form. For example, if you have a checkbox such as the following, the value of the type property
for this element would be checkbox:

```
<INPUT TYPE="checkbox">
```

value

For form elements that have a data value that is going to be submitted, the value property represents that data:

```
<INPUT TYPE="radio" NAME="Box1" VALUE="SendCatalog">Sign me up!
```

Here you have a radio button that evidently signs the user up to receive a catalog. The label on
the radio box is Sign me up! however, the value, and the information that would be sent to the
server is "SendCatalog".

checked

The checked property is a Boolean that indicates the current status of a checkbox element:

```
<FORM NAME="SignUp">
<INPUT TYPE="checkbox" NAME="SendIT">
</FORM>
```

If the user has selected the checkbox generated by the previous code, the value of the checked
property for the following would be true. If the user has not checked that checkbox, the value
would be false:

```
document.SignUp.SendIT
```

defaultChecked

This property is another Boolean, similar to the checked property. However, unlike the checked
property, the defaultChecked will return a true if the checkbox has been set to automatically be
checked by using the CHECKED keyword in the <INPUT> tag.

```
<FORM NAME="SignUp">
<INPUT TYPE="checkbox" NAME="SendIT" CHECKED>
</FORM>
```

The value for the `defaultChecked` property of `document.SignUp.SendIT` would be `true`.

options

The `options` property is very useful when working with selection elements on forms. The `options` property is actually an array that contains the values for all of the selection options that have been defined in the `<SELECT>` tag:

```
<FORM>
<SELECT NAME="UserThoughts" >
<OPTION VALUE="Yes" SELECTED>Absolutely!
<OPTION VALUE="No">No thank you!
<OPTION VALUE="Maybe">I'm not sure at the moment.
</SELECT>
</FORM>
```

In this example, the values of `option` would be the following:

```
option[0] = Absolutely!
option[1] = No thank you!
option[2] = I'm not sure at the moment.
```

This can be a useful property for reviewing or manipulating the options that are made available to your page viewers in selection boxes. There are also a few other properties that go hand-in-hand with the `options` property: `length` and `selectedIndex`.

length

The `length` property represents the number of elements that are contained in the options array, so the number is increased by one for each selection option that is defined:

```
<FORM>
<SELECT NAME="UserThoughts" >
<OPTION VALUE="Yes" SELECTED>Absolutely!
<OPTION VALUE="No">No thank you!
<OPTION VALUE="Maybe">I'm not sure at the moment.
</SELECT>
</FORM>
```

The value for `length` in this example would be 3, because the options array contains three elements, numbered 0 through 2.

selectedIndex

The `selectedIndex` property is another one that works hand-in-hand with the `options` property. Rather than returning the value of the array, this property represents the actual array index number of the selected `<OPTION>` element:

```
<FORM>
<SELECT NAME="UserThoughts" >
<OPTION VALUE="Yes" SELECTED>Absolutely!
<OPTION VALUE="No">No thank you!
```

```
<OPTION VALUE="Maybe">I'm not sure at the moment.
</SELECT>
</FORM>
```

In this form, the first `<OPTION>` element is selected. Assume, for this example, that the user just leaves this selected on the form as well. Because the first option is actually represented in the Option Property Array as the first element, which has an index number of zero, the `selectedIndex` is also now equal to zero. This can be a useful property for determining the selected string and reading it out of the Option Property Array.

defaultValue

The `defaultValue` property can be used to access the default text in elements such as the `<TEXTAREA>`, which allow you to set a default value for the text contained in the `Textarea`:

```
<FORM>
<TEXTAREA NAME="Comments" ROWS=40 COLS=5>
Hey, I love your site!
</TEXTAREA>
</FORM>
```

In this form, the `Comments Textarea` is seeded with the default text `Hey, I love your site!`. The `defaultValue` property represents this string, so you could conceivably alter it to any string you want.

form Element Methods

There are four `form` element methods that can be invoked to change the status of elements within your form. In order to understand how these methods work, keep in mind the following:

1. When an element is selected for input, such as placing the cursor inside a text box, that element is said to have *focus*. That is, the element has the attention of the user and the event-handling methods are currently focused on that element.

2. When a user leaves an element that currently has focus, that is called *blur*. The event-handling methods associated with receiving focus and blur are automatically called with the user's action.

3. Many of these functions have modified behavior in different browsers. Be sure to check the performance of your scripts in different browser versions before assuming how each function will behave.

blur()

The `blur()` method can be used to remove focus from a current element. Keep in mind, however, that this function does not assign the focus to any new element in particular, so when you are invoking this method, it should be done in conjunction with the `focus()` method.

The advantage of using the `blur()` method is that it removes focus from the `form` element without executing any event-handling calls. That is, if you have an event triggered to execute when the user leaves a text field, calling `blur()` leaves the text field without performing the action.

click()

The `click()` method simulates a mouse click on a button or another element that generates an `onClick` event. Similarly to the `blur()` method, it bypasses the call to the `onClick` event handler, effectively rendering the button useless. It can be used to bypass the functionality of a button but, because of its limited usefulness, it is rarely called.

focus()

The `focus()` method is the opposite of the `blur()` method. When called it passes the user interface focus to that element, allowing the element to accept user input. This method could be called to lead the user to filling out a particular field first, or it can be used in conjunction with the `blur()` method to remove focus from one element and pass it to another. Similar to the `blur()` method, the `focus()` method bypasses the `onfocus` event handlers.

select()

The `select()` method is used to select input elements that can be selected, such as text input fields, text areas, and so on. When called, it selects the text in the input box, just as if the user had selected the text with a mouse drag.

`form` Element Event Handlers

The event handlers are the methods that get called when a user interface event occurs. For example, clicking a button generates an `onClick` event for that button. By redefining what functions are called when an event occurs, you can alter the performance of elements on your page. For example, you could use event handling to display an image when a certain button is clicked. The event handlers that are associated with `form` elements follow.

onblur

`onblur` is the event handler called when the focus on a particular element is lost. This event handler can be used to alert the user that he or she is leaving a certain field, or it could be used to validate a field before progressing to the next.

onclick

The `onclick` event handler defines actions that should be performed when an element, such as a button, is clicked. This is a very useful event handler in form scripting because it is the primary mechanism for creating customized buttons.

onfocus

The `onfocus` event handler is called when a `form` element receives user interface focus, for example, when a user clicks inside a `textarea`. The `onfocus` event can be useful for generating ToolTips or status bar messages concerning an input field when the user enters that field.

onchange

The onchange event handler is similar to the onclick handler, but is used when the user enters data into a text field or other element that contains data that can be changed. This allows you to link events to the entry of new information into an element. This can also be a very flexible event handler.

Accessing form Elements with JavaScript

Now that you have all of the form elements, properties, functions, and event handlers at your disposal, take a look at how you can increase the functionality of your forms with JavaScript. Begin with a simple HTML form:

```
<FORM NAME="OrderForm">
<TABLE BORDER=0 WIDTH="75%" >

<TR>
<TD><I>First Name</I></TD>
<TD>
<INPUT TYPE=text NAME="FirstName" SIZE=30
 onfocus="window.status='Enter your first name please.';">
</TD>
</TR>

<TR>
<TD><I>Last Name</I></TD>
<TD>
<INPUT TYPE=text NAME="LastName" SIZE=30
 onfocus="window.status='Enter your last name please.';">
</TD>
</TR>

<TR>
<TD><I>Street Address</I></TD>
<TD COLSPAN="3">
<INPUT TYPE=text NAME="Address" SIZE=50
 onfocus="window.status='Enter your mailing address please.';">
</TD>
</TR>

<TR>
<TD><I>City</I></TD>
<TD >
<INPUT TYPE=text NAME="City" SIZE=30
 onfocus="window.status='Enter your city please.';">
</TD>
<TD><I>State</I></TD>
<TD>
<INPUT TYPE=text NAME="State" SIZE=3
 onfocus="window.status='Enter your state please.';"></TD>
<TD><I>ZIP</I></TD>
<TD>
<INPUT TYPE=text NAME="Zip" SIZE=11
 onfocus="window.status='Enter your zip code please.';"></TD>
</TR>
```

Using JavaScript for Forms

CHAPTER 17

361

17

USING
JAVASCRIPT
FOR FORMS

```
</TABLE>

<P>

<CENTER>
 <I>Would you like to be on our mailing list?</I>
<INPUT TYPE=checkbox NAME="List" CHECKED
 onClick="notify();"> <B>Yes</B>
</CENTER>

<P>
<HR WIDTH="50%" ALIGN=CENTER>
<P>


<SELECT NAME="OrderItem">
 <OPTION VALUE="8.95">Our Basic Item in Grey ($8.95)
 <OPTION VALUE="12.95">Our Basic Item in Color ($12.95)
 <OPTION VALUE="24.99">Our Mid-Range Color Item ($24.99)
 <OPTION VALUE="99.95">Our Super Deluxe Item! ($99.95)
</SELECT> <B>Select the Item You Want to Order</B>.

<P>

<SELECT NAME="Quantity">
 <OPTION VALUE="1">One
 <OPTION VALUE="2">Two
 <OPTION VALUE="3">Three
 <OPTION VALUE="4">Four
</SELECT> <B>Select the Quantity of Items to Order</B>.

<P>
<B>Total Due </B>
<INPUT TYPE=text NAME="Total" SIZE=11
 onfocus="totalOrder(this.form);">


<HR>
<P>
<INPUT TYPE=submit VALUE="Place Order"> <INPUT TYPE=reset VALUE="Clear the Form">

</FORM>
```

This example is going to be an order form, shown in Figure 17.9. This order form asks for the customer's name and address, gives him or her a chance to join the company mailing list, and allows him or her to pick from four different items, up to five units. There is also some special JavaScript-enhanced functionality:

1. When the customer enters a field, the status bar reflects the instructions for that field.

2. If the user decides not to join the mailing list, an alert box states the company's privacy policy, and asks him or her to reconsider.

3. After the customer selects the item and quantity, the total for his or her order is automatically generated in the Total Due field.

Now that you have your form, take a look at how it's done.

The first element of JavaScript functionality you wanted to add is the ability to update the status bar with instructions when you enter the input field. To do this, you can use the `form` element's event handler `onfocus`.

The `onfocus` event handler gets called whenever the user places the cursor within the input field. When that occurs, you can update the status bar. Here's the code:

```
<INPUT TYPE=text NAME="FirstName" SIZE=30
 onfocus="window.status='Enter your first name please.';">
```

What happens in this code is that the `onfocus` event handler for your `<INPUT TYPE=text>` form element is set to be `"window.status='Enter your first name please.'";`. This causes the status bar to update whenever this element receives the focus and, by simply repeating this event handler assignment for each of your elements, you can customize the instructions for the whole form.

You could have written a function to update the status bar for each function. However, since the code to update the status bar is so simple, it made more sense to enter it directly into the event handler, rather than deal with a separate function for each input field. One instance where you would opt for a separate function, though, was in creating the alert dialog that is linked to your mailing list checkbox.

With the Mailing List checkbox, you've created an automatically selected checkbox to indicate that the customer would be put on the company's mailing list. Because many customers do not join mailing lists because they are afraid their information will be sold, you know some users will unselect this option. However, when users click the checkbox to be removed from the mailing list, you want to give them another chance to sign up, after letting them know about the company privacy policy.

To create the checkbox dialog, you make use of another event, the `onclick` event handler, that is triggered when the checkbox is clicked (on or off):

```
<INPUT TYPE=checkbox NAME="List" CHECKED onClick="notify();">
```

Next, you needed to create the function called `notify()` that would display the alert dialog:

```
function notify() {

    alert ("Please be aware that our mailing list is for \n
internal use only, and your name will not \n
be sold or redistributed in any form. \n\n
Please Reconsider. Thanks!");
}
```

The results of the function are shown in Figure 17.9.

Realistically, you did not need a separate function to bring up the alert dialog either, but, because it contained so much text, moving it into a function made the code read much easier. Now take a look at some functionality that did require a separate function: your automatic total due.

FIGURE 17.9.

A form with JavaScript Functionality, including an Alert triggered with a checkbox.

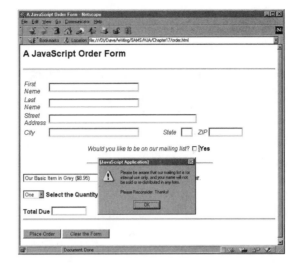

To create the `Total Due` field, you created a text field that used the `onfocus` event handler to call a function called `totalOrder()`:

```
<INPUT TYPE=text NAME="Total" SIZE=11
 onfocus="totalOrder(this.form);">
```

You've chosen to use a text field because it has a `value` property which can be updated, and it also has the `onfocus` event handler which will allow you to create your function to fill in the total due when the user enters the field. The function to calculate, `totalOrder()`, accepts a form as its argument, and when you call it from your field, you use the syntax `"totalOrder (this.form);"` to indicate that the form this function will be using for its data is the currently loaded form. Here's what the function looks like:

```
function totalOrder(form) {

    var x = form.OrderItem.options[form.OrderItem.selectedIndex].value;
    var y = form.Quantity.options[form.Quantity.selectedIndex].value;
    var due = (x * y);
    form.Total.value = due;
}
```

Although this looks like a complex function, it is really pretty straightforward. First, the function is defined to accept a form. In this case it will be the current form, or `"this.form"` as passed to the function from the `onfocus` event handler. Next, you needed to get the value of your `Selected Item`, as that corresponds to the price the user will pay.

Because the options for a `<SELECT>` element are stored in an array called options, you needed to use the `selectedIndex` property to access the element. You defined the cost of the item, or `x`, as:

```
var x = form.OrderItem.options[form.OrderItem.selectedIndex].value;
```

This simply translates to the current form, the `OrderItem` select field, and the options array element that is selected, as indexed by the `selectedIndex`. A similar technique is used to grab the `Quantity` and store it as y:

```
var y = form.Quantity.options[form.Quantity.selectedIndex].value;
```

Now you can calculate the total amount due, by multiplying the cost and the quantity, or (x * y):

```
var due = (x * y);
```

Finally, you write the amount due into the `Total` text field so the customer can see it:

```
form.Total.value = due;
```

The full code for the order form is shown in Listing 17.1.

Listing 17.1. A complete order form with JavaScript functionality.

```
<HTML>
<HEAD>
<TITLE>A JavaScript Order Form</TITLE>
</HEAD>

<BODY>

<H2>A JavaScript Order Form</H2>
<HR>

<FORM NAME="OrderForm">
<TABLE BORDER=0 WIDTH="75%" >

<TR>
<TD><I>First Name</I></TD>
<TD>
<INPUT TYPE=text NAME="FirstName" SIZE=30
 onfocus="window.status='Enter your first name please.';">
</TD>
</TR>

<TR>
<TD><I>Last Name</I></TD>
<TD>
<INPUT TYPE=text NAME="LastName" SIZE=30
 onfocus="window.status='Enter your last name please.';">
</TD>
</TR>

<TR>
<TD><I>Street Address</I></TD>
<TD COLSPAN="3">
<INPUT TYPE=text NAME="Address" SIZE=50
 onfocus="window.status='Enter your mailing address please.';">
</TD>
</TR>
```

```
<TR>
<TD><I>City</I></TD>
<TD >
<INPUT TYPE=text NAME="City" SIZE=30
 onfocus="window.status='Enter your city please.';">
</TD>
<TD><I>State</I></TD>
<TD>
<INPUT TYPE=text NAME="State" SIZE=3
 onfocus="window.status='Enter your state please.';"></TD>
<TD><I>ZIP</I></TD>
<TD>
<INPUT TYPE=text NAME="Zip" SIZE=11
 onfocus="window.status='Enter your zip code please.';"></TD>
</TR>

</TABLE>

<P>

<CENTER>
 <I>Would you like to be on our mailing list?</I>
<INPUT TYPE=checkbox NAME="List" CHECKED
 onClick="notify();"> <B>Yes</B>
</CENTER>

<P>
<HR WIDTH="50%" ALIGN=CENTER>
<P>


<SELECT NAME="OrderItem">
 <OPTION VALUE="8.95">Our Basic Item in Grey ($8.95)
 <OPTION VALUE="12.95">Our Basic Item in Color ($12.95)
 <OPTION VALUE="24.99">Our Mid-Range Color Item ($24.99)
 <OPTION VALUE="99.95">Our Super Deluxe Item! ($99.95)
</SELECT> <B>Select the Item You Want to Order</B>.

<P>

<SELECT NAME="Quantity">
 <OPTION VALUE="1">One
 <OPTION VALUE="2">Two
 <OPTION VALUE="3">Three
 <OPTION VALUE="4">Four
</SELECT> <B>Select the Quantity of Items to Order</B>.

<P>
<B>Total Due </B>
<INPUT TYPE=text NAME="Total" SIZE=11
 onfocus="totalOrder(this.form);">


<HR>
<P>
<INPUT TYPE=submit VALUE="Place Order"> <INPUT TYPE=reset VALUE="Clear the Form">

</FORM>
```

17

USING
JAVASCRIPT
FOR FORMS

continues

Listing 17.1. continued

```
<SCRIPT LANGUAGE="JavaScript1.1">
<!--

function notify() {

    alert ("Please be aware that our mailing list is for \n
internal use only, and your name will not \n
be sold or redistributed in any form. \n\n
Please Reconsider. Thanks!");
}

function totalOrder(form) {

    var x = form.OrderItem.options[form.OrderItem.selectedIndex].value;
    var y = form.Quantity.options[form.Quantity.selectedIndex].value;
    var due = (x * y);
    form.Total.value = due;
}

// -->
</SCRIPT>
</BODY>
</HTML>
```

After the customer has selected his or her item(s) and the number to order, clicking in the Total Due text box will generate a total, as shown in Figure 17.10. Of course, additional functionality could be added to account for multiple items, and so on. By using JavaScript to process and enhance form information, forms can be dynamic and useful to users without being unnecessarily slow.

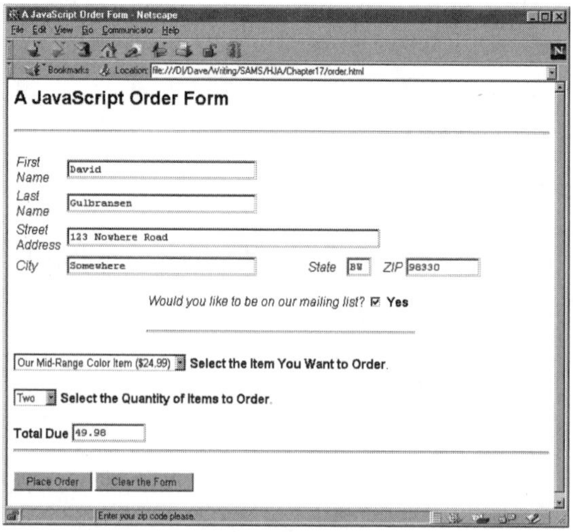

FIGURE 17.10.

A customized customer order form, complete with an automatically generated total due.

Form Validation

One of the benefits of using JavaScript in conjunction with your forms is the ability to perform form validation before submitting your forms. Form validation is simply checking the data users have entered, or making sure that they have entered all of the required information before the form is processed. It certainly can't eliminate people from incorrectly filling out forms, but it can aid you in getting the most accurate data from your users as possible. It can also help out the user filling out your form, in case he or she has missed a field, or incorrectly typed in an entry.

Take a look at an example of using JavaScript to perform form validation. For this example, you are going to use a form that asks a page viewer to submit his or her address, phone, and e-mail information. Because you can't really use the data if the entry is incomplete, you are going to use JavaScript validation to make sure all of the fields are filled in, and also to make sure that some of the data is close to the correct format.

First, start with a straightforward HTML form. The form is inside of a table to make it more readable in the browser window:

```
<FORM NAME="AddressForm" onsubmit="check(this.form);">
<TABLE BORDER=0 WIDTH="75%" >

<TR>
<TD><I>First Name</I></TD>
<TD><INPUT TYPE=text NAME="FirstName" SIZE=30></TD>
</TR>

<TR>
<TD><I>Last Name</I></TD>
<TD><INPUT TYPE=text NAME="LastName" SIZE=30></TD>
</TR>

<TR>
<TD><I>Street Address</I></TD>
<TD COLSPAN="3"><INPUT TYPE=text NAME="Address" SIZE=50></TD>
</TR>

<TR>
<TD><I>City</I></TD>
<TD ><INPUT TYPE=text NAME="City" SIZE=30></TD>
<TD><I>State</I></TD>
<TD><INPUT TYPE=text NAME="State" SIZE=3 onchange="verifyState(this.form);"></TD>
<TD><I>ZIP</I></TD>
<TD><INPUT TYPE=text NAME="Zip" SIZE=11 onchange="verifyZip(this.form);"></TD>
</TR>

</TABLE>

<I>Phone Number </I>
<INPUT TYPE=text NAME="Phone" SIZE=15> <I>(XXX) XXX-XXXX</I>

<P>
```

```
<I>E-Mail Address </I>
<INPUT TYPE=text NAME="Email" SIZE=20>

<HR>
<P>
<INPUT TYPE=submit VALUE="Submit">
<INPUT TYPE=reset VALUE="Reset the Form">

</FORM>
```

This form contains a number of fields, including fields for the name, address, city, state, zip code, phone number, and e-mail address of the user.

The first thing you need to do is create a function that checks to make sure a field is not left blank. You can do that by accessing the form element within the function, and making sure that the value for the element is not blank:

```
function verifyName(form) {
   if(form.LastName.value == "")
      alert("Please Enter Your Last Name.");
}
```

In this example, you have created a function called verifyName that accepts a form as the data passed into the function. Next, you check to make sure that the value of your element, in this case form.LastName.value, is not blank. If it is, then you pop up an alert window to notify the user.

You can then modify this function slightly to perform a check to see if the format of the data is correct as well. For example, look at the function you are going to use to verify the State field:

```
function verifyState(form) {

   if(form.State.value == "")
      alert("Please Enter Your State.");

   if(form.State.value.length > 2 || form.State.value.length < 2)
      alert("Please Use Your 2 Letter State Abbreviation");
}
```

This function performs a similar check to make sure that the value for form.State.value is not left blank, but then it also uses another if statement to check to make sure the data entered is actually a two-digit state abbreviation, by making use of the element's value length property.

Next, you can have this function called when the user enters the data, rather than checked later, so he or she can correct any errors before moving on. To do this, you make use of the form's onchange event handler, so that as soon as the user has entered the data into the State field, the data is checked for accuracy:

```
<INPUT TYPE=text NAME="State" SIZE=3 onchange="verifyState(this.form);">
```

You can write a similar function that checks for the accuracy of the zip code; here you simply check the length of `form.Zip.value` to make sure that the zip code complies with a five-digit or five-digit plus four-digit zip code length:

```
function verifyZip(form) {

   if(form.Zip.value == "")
      alert("Please Enter Your Zip Code");
   if(form.Zip.value.length < 5 ¦¦ form.Zip.value.length > 10)
      alert("Please Use Your Zip Code or Zip+4");
}
```

And again, you can call the function using the `onchange` event handler:

```
<INPUT TYPE=text NAME="Zip" SIZE=11 onchange="verifyZip(this.form);">
```

That's all there is to verifying a field. You can make the verification as simple or complex as you want. For example, anyone could easily enter a two-character state abbreviation in your form that did not correspond to an actual state. If you needed that kind of accuracy, you could enter all of the 50 state abbreviations into an array, and then compare the entered data to make sure it was found in the array. The level of complexity you can achieve for form validation is pretty astounding. But usually a simple validation to make sure data is entered and formatted somewhat correctly will yield the best results. That will keep users from forgetting important fields and submitting typos. Those who want to enter invalid information will generally find a way in spite of even the most complicated methods of validation.

Finally, before submitting the form, you actually want to check all of the fields to make sure they are not blank. You have created separate functions to check each field so they could be customized, and now you can create a function that checks the entire form by calling the individual verify functions:

```
function check() {
    verifyName(document.AddressForm);
    verifyAddress(document.AddressForm);
    verifyCity(document.AddressForm);
    verifyState(document.AddressForm);
    verifyZip(document.AddressForm);
    verifyPhone(document.AddressForm);
    verifyEmail(document.AddressForm);
}
```

The important thing to notice here is that you are passing the `document.AddressForm` object to your verify functions, so the `form` elements are available to the function to perform its checks. Now all you need to do is call your `check()` function when the form is submitted:

```
<FORM NAME="AddressForm" onsubmit="check(this.form);">
```

You have a validated form! The complete code for the form and all of the validation functions is shown in Listing 17.2.

Listing 17.2. A simple address form with JavaScript verification.

```
<HTML>
<HEAD>
<TITLE>Validating Forms</TITLE>
</HEAD>

<BODY>

<H2>Validating Forms with JavaScript</H2>
<HR>

<FORM NAME="AddressForm" onsubmit="check(this.form);">
<TABLE BORDER=0 WIDTH="75%" >

<TR>
<TD><I>First Name</I></TD>
<TD><INPUT TYPE=text NAME="FirstName" SIZE=30></TD>
</TR>

<TR>
<TD><I>Last Name</I></TD>
<TD><INPUT TYPE=text NAME="LastName" SIZE=30></TD>
</TR>

<TR>
<TD><I>Street Address</I></TD>
<TD COLSPAN="3"><INPUT TYPE=text NAME="Address" SIZE=50></TD>
</TR>

<TR>
<TD><I>City</I></TD>
<TD ><INPUT TYPE=text NAME="City" SIZE=30></TD>
<TD><I>State</I></TD>
<TD><INPUT TYPE=text NAME="State" SIZE=3
onchange="verifyState(this.form);"></TD>
<TD><I>ZIP</I></TD>
<TD><INPUT TYPE=text NAME="Zip" SIZE=11
 onchange="verifyZip(this.form);"></TD>
</TR>

</TABLE>

<I>Phone Number </I>
<INPUT TYPE=text NAME="Phone" SIZE=15> <I>(XXX) XXX-XXXX</I>

<P>

<I>E-Mail Address </I>
<INPUT TYPE=text NAME="Email" SIZE=20>

<HR>
<P>
<INPUT TYPE=submit VALUE="Submit">
<INPUT TYPE=reset VALUE="Reset the Form">

</FORM>
```

```
<SCRIPT LANGUAGE="JavaScript1.1">
<!--

function check() {
    verifyName(document.AddressForm);
    verifyAddress(document.AddressForm);
    verifyCity(document.AddressForm);
    verifyState(document.AddressForm);
    verifyZip(document.AddressForm);
    verifyPhone(document.AddressForm);
    verifyEmail(document.AddressForm);
}

function verifyName(form) {

    if(form.LastName.value == "")
        alert("Please Enter Your Last Name.");
}

function verifyAddress(form) {

    if(form.Address.value == "")
        alert("Please Enter Your Address.");
}

function verifyCity(form) {

    if(form.City.value == "")
        alert("Please Enter Your City.");
}

function verifyState(form) {

    if(form.State.value == "")
        alert("Please Enter Your State.");

    if(form.State.value.length > 2 || form.State.value.length < 2)
        alert("Please Use Your 2-Letter State Abbreviation");
}

function verifyZip(form) {

    if(form.Zip.value == "")
        alert("Please Enter Your Zip Code");
    if(form.Zip.value.length < 5 || form.Zip.value.length > 10)
        alert("Please Use Your Zip Code or Zip+4");
}

function verifyPhone(form) {

    if(form.Phone.value == "")
        alert("Please Enter Your Phone Number.");
}

function verifyEmail(form) {

    if(form.Email.value == "")
```

continues

Listing 17.2. continued

```
        alert("Please Enter Your E-Mail Address.");
}

// -->
</SCRIPT>

</BODY>
</HTML>
```

By creating separate validation functions, you can customize the type of validation performed, such as that shown in Figure 17.11 where the Zip Code field is checked.

FIGURE 17.11.

An address submission form for a mailing list, the ZIP field is verified when it is filled out.

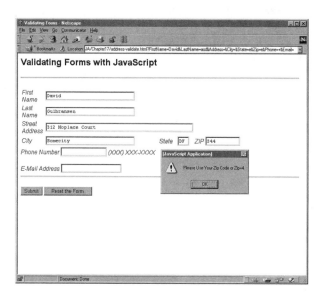

However, globally checking the form before submission, as shown in Figure 17.12, is a good way to ensure that all of the information is completed before the form is submitted to the server or processed further. As mentioned before, the only thing limiting the level of complexity you can bring to form validation is time and your imagination.

Summary

As you begin to explore JavaScript's interaction with forms, be sure to consult the JavaScript 1.2 reference at http://developer.netscape.com/library/documentation/index.html. Although this chapter has attempted to cover all of the elements, methods, properties, and events you will encounter, there are always unique cases that develop. This is a great resource for keeping up with the latest additions and changes to JavaScript.

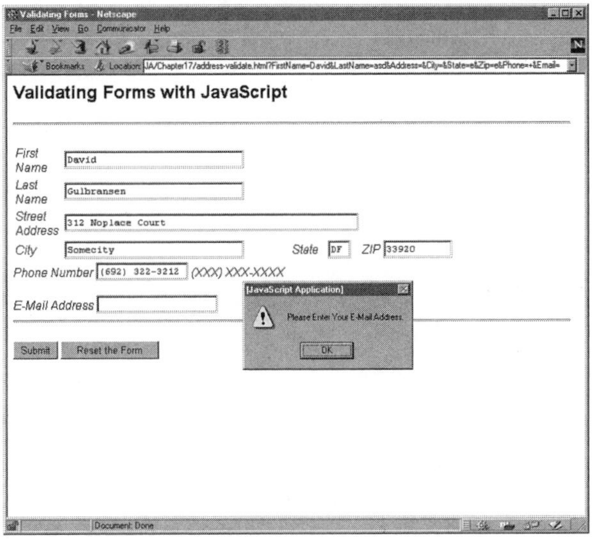

FIGURE 17.12.

Forms can also be verified before submission using JavaScript.

As you have learned, JavaScript provides you with an incredible level of flexibility for customizing your pages and adding functionality. You can create dynamic scripts that perform basic form processing on the client, increasing the usefulness of the form for you and the user. Now that you have JavaScript in your set of Web skills, you are ready to progress to the next section and begin learning how you can exploit Java to make the most of your Web development efforts.

Using JavaScript with Style Sheets

by Nana Gilbert-Baffoe

In this chapter you'll learn about how to add excitement to your Web pages by using JavaScript with style sheets. I will discuss what dynamic styles are, how to create browser friendly pages, events and event handling, and different ways to access the elements on your page.

Dynamic Style Sheets

For a long time HTML has lacked any capabilities for precise control of the layout and positioning of elements on a page. This meant that if you wanted your page to look exactly as you planned, you had to use tricks and other techniques to get what you wanted. Some of these included using graphics for text, resizing single-pixel GIFs to aid in the layout of pages, and using borderless tables. Just recently, two new technologies have been released that promise to put an end to all the extra work you have to do just to make your site look nice.

Cascading Style Sheets

First came CSS (Cascading Style Sheets), which gave designers the ability to fully lay out, position, and define pages, without the use of tables, single-pixel GIFs, and any other hacks. Using CSS, a designer could define the fonts each tag would use, its color, its margin, and many other properties. This was the beginning of true layout control for Web pages—instead of using a GIF for shadowed text, you could change the margins of two different text elements to create the same effect and cut download time in the process.

Using JavaScript to Control Style Sheets

That wasn't enough for Web designers—they wanted to change text properties on-the-fly. They wanted to animate text and HTML elements without the need for Java applets, plug-ins, or animated GIFs that could potentially increase a page's download time. With the release of the 4.0 browsers from Microsoft and Netscape, finally comes the capability to script style sheets using scripting languages such as JavaScript and VBScript.

What Are the Advantages?

What will this new technology enable you to do? Imagine that you could:

- Make the text on your page adjust its size to adapt to the user's browser size
- Create text rollover effects without the need for graphics
- Create an HTML-based menu that can expand and collapse to show its contents
- Change text properties on-the-fly without a full page refresh
- Fade in and fade out page elements

Web designers can create all this and more just by adding a few lines of code to a page. Unlike CGI, the script handles everything on the client side, making the Web pages load quickly, thus enhancing the interactive experience. Figure 18.1 shows how one popular Web site uses dynamic styles to enhance its pages.

FIGURE 18.1.

A Web site that uses JavaScript style sheets to highlight text.

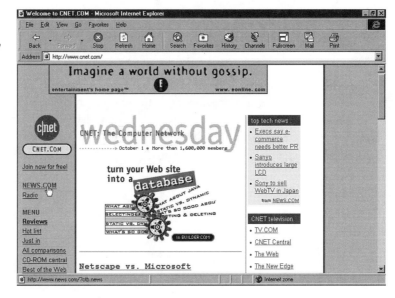

Getting Started

Working with dynamic styles is simple and fairly straightforward. You should be able to create your own dynamic styles in a very short time.

> **NOTE**
>
> Although this chapter uses JavaScript to create dynamic style sheets, you can also use VBScript. It's up to you to decide which scripting language you want to use. Obviously, if you have been programming in Visual Basic, you will probably feel more comfortable using VBScript. But, keep in mind that the only browser that supports VBScript is Internet Explorer. On the other hand, by using JavaScript you are guaranteed that your scripts will work with the majority of browsers being used.

The Changing of the Names

Before you start anything, there are a few things you should know. The naming conventions used in scripting are different from those in HTML. Basically, if you have an attribute name that is hyphenated, it must be changed to a nonhyphenated camel notation name. By *camel notation* I mean changing a CSS attribute name such as background-color to backgroundColor. Note that the first letter of the name is not capitalized. For an example for the distinction, note the following, which seems more like a subtraction statement written incorrectly than a statement to make the top margin of the blockquote element 34 pixels:

```
document.all.BLOCKQUOTE.style.margin-top = "34px";
```

Of course, that's not what you want, and it will surely cause errors when the browser runs the script. The correct way to write the previous example is to change it to this:

```
document.all.BLOCKQUOTE.style.marginTop = "34px";
```

Another thing to remember is that JavaScript is case sensitive, therefore `backgroundcolor`, `BackgroundColor`, and `backgroundColor` are all different. Always make sure to capitalize the right words. An easy way to remember correct capitalization is that, when changing a CSS property to its scripting property name, only the first letter after the hyphen is capitalized.

The following table shows some examples of CSS attributes and their scripting property names.

Attribute Name	*Property Name*
background-color	backgroundColor
font-size	fontSize
font-weight	fontWeight
list-style	listStyle
text-align	textAlign

Something New

The `<DIV>` and `<SPAN>` tags are two new tags that have been added to the already long list of tags available to you. Alone, they do almost nothing to the output of your HTML, but by setting their properties you can achieve some very powerful effects. The main properties that you'll be using are `Name`, `Id`, and `Style`. The `Name` and `Id` properties are used to provide unique names for each element. Look at the following example:

```
<DIV Id="text1">
This is a block of text, it is enclosed in DIV tags. It's id is "text1".
</DIV>
```

The `<DIV>` tag has been given an `Id` of `"text1"`; now when you want to write a script that only affects the text in the `<DIV>` tag, all you have to do is the following:

```
document.all.text1.style.color = "blue";
```

The previous line of code says to set the color of the HTML element identified by the id or name text1 to blue.

Using the style attribute, you can apply a set of CSS attributes to the element, and after that, you can use a script to manipulate it. For example, you could have a picture (maybe a menubar) that is hidden off screen that would, at the click of a mouse or when the page loads, slide into view.

```
<DIV Id="pic1" Style="position:absolute;left:-50;width:50">
<IMG Src="picture.gif">
</DIV>
```

```
Script:
<script language="javascript">
function move()
{
    if(document.all.pic1.style.left < 50)
    {
        document.all.pic1.style.left = document.all.pic1.style.posLeft + 5;
        setTimeout("move()", 15);
}
}
</script>
```

In the previous example there is an image that is hidden off screen by setting its left position to
-50. Because the picture is 50 pixels wide, it is not visible on the screen. The script has a function called move() that checks that the position of the left side (I'll call the x coordinate) of the
image is not greater than 50 pixels. If the x coordinate of the image is less than 50, the image
is moved 5 pixels to the right using the following statement:

```
document.all.pic1.style.left = document.all.pic1.style.posLeft + 5;
```

The whole process is repeated again until the image reaches its final position. The setTimeout()
function on the last line is used to call the move() function after 15 milliseconds.

Two Different Browsers, Two Different Object Models

The two most popular browsers are Netscape Navigator and Microsoft Internet Explorer. Because they are the browsers that most people use to surf the Web, they are also the browsers
that most people design their sites to look best on. Unfortunately, Microsoft and Netscape do
not have the same object models, and this makes creating scripts to work on both browsers
difficult. To add to your problems, Netscape Communicator 4.0 doesn't allow every style sheet
element to be scripted. In fact, you can't change any CSS attributes after the page is loaded.
Unless you want to make your pages support only one kind of browser, you need a way to
detect the browser being used. With that information, you can redirect users to a browser-
specific page, or take some alternative method to handle this situation. Listing 18.1 is an
example.

Listing 18.1. Allowing the page to determine a browser and serve up an appropriate page.

```
<HEAD>
<SCRIPT LANGUAGE="JAVASCRIPT"><!--
// Code by ©1997 Rob Falla, as used online at http://www.cwebdev.com;
// This code is public domain, just remember who wrote it;
// The code tests to see if the browser being used is IE or NN 3.x or 4.x;
var nav, brs
nav = navigator.appname
brs = navigator.appversion
if (nav == "MSIE"){
    if (brs == "4.0"){
        location.href= "index_ie4.html"
        }
    else if (brs == "3.0"){
        location.href= "index_ie3.html"
```

continues

Listing 18.1. continued

```
      }
   }
else if (nav == "Netscape"){
   if (brs == "4.0"){
      location.href= "index_nn4.html"
      }
   else if (brs == "3.0"){
      location.href= "index_nn3.html"
      }
   }
--></SCRIPT>
</HEAD>
```

With that problem out of the way, you can write your code to work with the browser viewing your page, and safely do what you want to do without leaving any viewers out.

> **TIP**
>
> It's always best to attempt to write code that is viewable by the largest audience possible; sometimes it means creating two separate pages. Other times it's not necessary because your pages are used in an intranet, where everyone uses the same browser.

The Events That Make It All Happen

Events are an important part of using JavaScript to create dynamic styles, so you need to understand and know how to deal with them. Most events in IE 4.0 are *bubbled*, which means that the event originates at an element and is passed up the hierarchy of elements until it reaches the window object. In the following, an event (such as a mouse click) that is generated inside the <I> tag would bubble up to the <DIV> tag:

```
<P>New technology:
<DIV>
Dynamic styles is <I>new</I> way to add life to your pages
</DIV>
</P>
```

Then it would bubble on up to the <P> tag, and continue bubbling till it reaches the end of the hierarchy.

While the event is being bubbled, it can be canceled at any time by using the following line of code:

```
window.event.cancelBubble = true;
```

A lot of what you do with dynamic styles deals with detecting an event and handling it in some interesting way. As a result of the event, you could flip over an image, make text larger, apply a CSS filter effect, or even play a sound. Listing 18.2 demonstrates one way to handle events.

Table 18.1 shows some of the main events you might be handling.

Table 18.1. Some of events you will most likely use.

Event Name	Description
onclick	Occurs when someone clicks an element
ondblclick	Occurs when someone double-clicks an element
onkeypress	Alerts you that a key has been pressed
onmousemove	Occurs when the mouse moves
onmouseout	Occurs when the mouse leaves the element
onmouseover	Occurs when the mouse enters an element

Listing 18.2. Example of event handling.

```
<HTML>
<HEAD>
<TITLE> Sample Event handling </TITLE>
<SCRIPT language="javascript">
<!--
function handlemouseover()
{
alert("You are over me");
}
-->
</SCRIPT>

</HEAD>
<BODY>
<DIV id="mytext" onmouseover="handlemouseover();"
style="background-color:white;text-align:center">
Here is some text
</DIV>
</BODY>
</HTML>
```

The sample code displays an alert box when the mouse goes over the text called `mytext`. It uses an event handler located in the `<DIV>` tag. Figure 18.2 shows the results of the code.

More Advanced Topics

Now that you know some of the basics, it's time for a longer example (see Listing 18.3). For this example you'll create an embedded style sheet. An embedded style sheet is enclosed in `<STYLE>` tags. It is usually defined at the top of the HTML document, between the `<HEAD>` tags. After the style sheet is defined, you'll write a script to access the text's `style` property to add a background color. The color changes only when the mouse is over the text. When the mouse exits the text, the background returns to its original color.

FIGURE 18.2.

*Here's an alert showing
that the mouse is over
the text.*

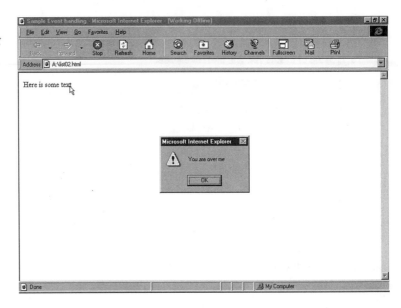

Listing 18.3. Creating a simple mouseover effect.

```
<HTML>
<HEAD>
<TITLE> Simple mouseover effect </TITLE>

<STYLE type="text/css">
A{text-decoration:none;color:brown;}
</STYLE>
<SCRIPT language="javascript">
<!--
function mOver(){
window.event.srcElement.style.backgroundColor = "orange";
}

function mOut(){
window.event.srcElement.style.backgroundColor = "white";
}

-->
</SCRIPT>

</HEAD>
<BODY>
<HTML>
<H1 style="color:orange;text-align:center;text-transform:uppercase;">
Simple mouseover sample</H1>
<A href="http://www.site1.com" onmouseover="mOver();" onmouseout="mOut();">
Site1</A><BR>
<A href="http://www.site2.com" onmouseover="mOver();" onmouseout="mOut();">
Site2</A><BR>
```

```
<A href="http://www.site3.com" onmouseover="mOver();" onmouseout="mOut();">
Site3</A><BR>
</HTML>
</BODY>
```

The previous example has the familiar `<STYLE>` tag with the style definition . The style sets the text decoration of all the anchor elements on the page to `none`, which means links won't be underlined when the page is rendered. It also sets the text color of all the anchor elements to `brown`. If you're not familiar with style sheets, read Chapter 6, "Style Sheets: Formatting for the Future," and you'll find everything you need to know about style sheets. The script part of Listing 18.3 has two functions called `mOver()` and `mOut()`. They are responsible for changing the background color of the text when the mouse enters or exits the link. The `mOver()` function finds the element that received the `mouseover` (by using `window.event.srcElement`) and then sets its background color to `orange` (`style.backgroundColor = "orange";`). The `mOut()` function returns the background color to its original color using the same technique. Figure 18.3 shows what the Web page looks like when the mouse is over a link.

FIGURE 18.3.

Selected text with orange background.

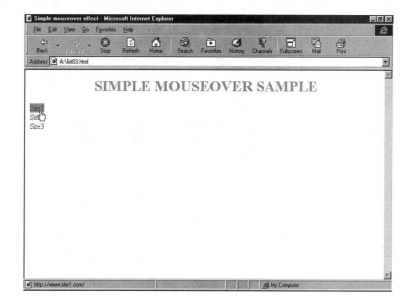

18

USING
JAVASCRIPT WITH
STYLE SHEETS

Accessing the Elements

Now that you know how to find what element has fired an event, you need to know how to access the elements on the page. After you know that you can do almost anything, from shrinking text to changing colors, making text bold, and more.

The all Collection

The all collection is used a lot when creating dynamic style sheets. The all collection is your ticket to all the elements on your page; you can use it to access any of the valid HTML tags on your page. When you use the all collection, it returns an array of the elements that you specified.

If you want to access a certain collection of tags on your page, for example the <B> tags, you can write the following:

```
document.all.tags("B")
```

Then follow it by the property that you want to access. In the following example, it is the font style property:

```
document.all.tags("B").style.fontStyle = "italic";
```

Here is the syntax for the previous code:

```
document.all.tags("tagname").style.property
```

tagname can be any of the valid tags on your page, and *property* is the property you want to access. Here are some more examples:

```
document.all.tags("H1").style.color = "green";
document.all.tags("P").style.fontFamily = "verdena";
document.all.tags("B").style.backgroundColor = "yellow";
```

Using the item() Method for More Control

What if you want only the second <B> tag to be affected? You are in luck, because there exists another method that does just that. It's similar to the first method described, but a little more fine-tuned.

In other words, it can access (if you wanted it to) all the <B> tags one by one. Because the all collection returns a collection of the tags you choose, you can select an individual <B> tag, and then apply a style rule to it. Listing 18.4 shows the code for this.

Listing 18.4. Using the item() method.

```
<HTML>
<HEAD>
<TITLE> Using item() to select the index of the element
➥you want to access</TITLE>
<SCRIPT language="javascript">
<!--
function mClick()
{
var b1 = document.all.tags("B").item(0);
b1.style.cursor = "hand";
var b2 = document.all.tags("B").item(1);
```

```
b2.style.color = "burlywood";
}
-->
</SCRIPT>
</HEAD>
<BODY onclick="mClick();">
<B> Here is some bold text</B><BR>
<B> Here is another line of bold text</B>
<BODY>
</HTML>
```

In this example, there is only one function in the script that handles everything. When the mouse is clicked anywhere on the page, the mClick() function is called. The first line sets the cursor of the first <B> element on the page to a hand, which is useful for telling users that clicking the element results in an action. The second line sets the second <B> element's color to burlywood; burlywood is one of the many user-defined colors available to you in IE 4.0.

The item() method is used to select the element you want from the collection. The first element has an index of 0; this is similar to how arrays are accessed in JavaScript and many other languages. Figure 18.4 shows the Web page before the mouse is clicked, and Figure 18.5 shows how the mouse cursor changes after the mouse is clicked.

FIGURE 18.4.

Picture of the Web page before the mouse is clicked.

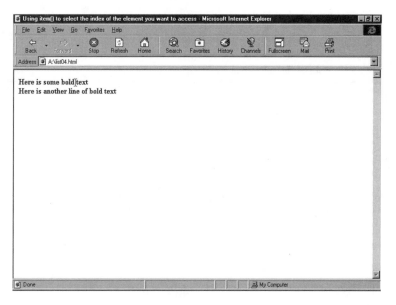

Assigning a Class to an Element

You can use a slightly different version of the previous example to assign a class to an element dynamically. It's a fast and easy way to apply a set of style rules to an element when you are scripting. For example, if you wanted to color the H1 element burlywood, make the background color `lemonchiffon`, change the font weight to `bold`, and change the font size to `30pt`. You could do this by using either the method in Listing 18.5 or Listing 18.6. Figure 18.6 shows the result of these listings.

FIGURE 18.5.

Picture of the Web page after the mouse is clicked.

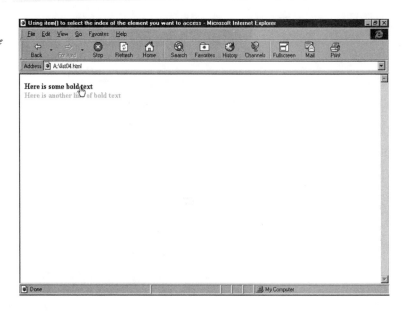

Listing 18.5. An inefficient way to apply a group of styles.

```
<HTML>
<HEAD>
<TITLE>Click and change</TITLE>

<SCRIPT language="javascript">
<!--
function mClick(){
document.all.tags("H1").item(0).style.color = "burlywood";
document.all.tags("H1").item(0).style.backgroundColor= "lemonchiffon";
document.all.tags("H1").item(0).style.fontWeight = "bold";
document.all.tags("H1").item(0).style.fontSize = "30pt";
}
-->
</SCRIPT>
</HEAD>
<BODY>
<HTML>
<H1 onclick="mClick();">Click me</H1>
</HTML>
</BODY>
```

Listing 18.5 sets the style sheet rules in the script part of the code, so it isn't as efficient as it could be. When it comes to the Internet, the smaller your files are, the faster your pages load. The faster your pages load, the happier your users are.

Listing 18.6 uses a predefined class to change the H1 element's attributes. It is 155 bytes smaller than the first example, and although it might not sound like much now, it adds up.

Listing 18.6. A more efficient way to apply a group of styles.

```
<HTML>
<HEAD>
<TITLE>Click and change</TITLE>
<STYLE type="text/css">
.change{color:burlywood;background-color:lemonchiffon;font-weight:bold;font-size:30pt;}
</STYLE>
</HEAD>
<BODY>
<HTML>
<H1 onclick=document.all.tags("H1").item(0).className ="change"> Click me</H1>
</HTML>
</BODY>
```

FIGURE 18.6.

Both Listing 18.5 and Listing 18.6 produce the same output, but Listing 18.6 loads faster.

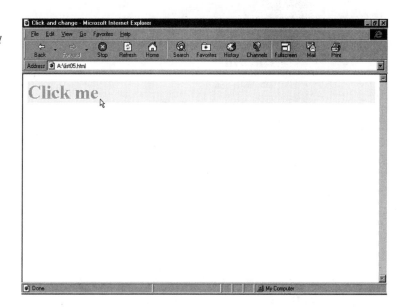

18

USING
JAVASCRIPT WITH
STYLE SHEETS

You cut down the amount of code you write and increase its efficiency at the same time when you use a predefined class. Now you can apply the class to any element without having to re-type the style rules. Listing 18.7 shows an example. Figures 18.7 and 18.8 show respectively the before and after results produced by this code.

Listing 18.7. Using a class to quickly set the attributes of more than one element.

```
<HTML>
<HEAD>
<TITLE> Using a class to set the attributes of more than one element </TITLE>
<STYLE type="text/css">
..theClass{color:chocolate;font-weight:bold;font-size:18pt;letter-spacing:24}
</STYLE>
</HEAD>
<BODY>
<HTML>
<H1 onclick=document.all.tags("H1").item(0).className="theClass"> Click me</H1>
<H2 onclick=document.all.tags("H2").item(0).
➥className="theClass"> Click me too</H2>
</HTML>
</BODY>
```

FIGURE 18.7.

Before clicking, both lines of text look different.

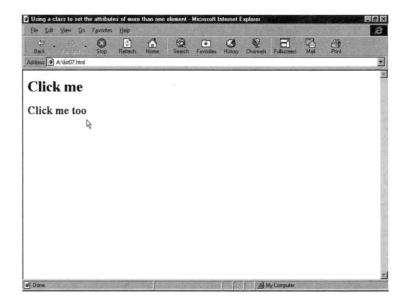

Where's Your id?

The id and name properties are usually used for scripting. They provide a way to give your elements a unique name that makes your code easier to read. This is how to access elements by their id or name when you are scripting:

```
document.all.elementId.style.property
```

elementId is the id or name of the element you want to access and *property* is the style property you are setting. Listing 18.8 shows an example of how to access elements by their id. You can see what the Web page looks like in Figures 18.9 and 18.10.

FIGURE 18.8.

After the text is clicked, both lines of text look the same because they have the same class.

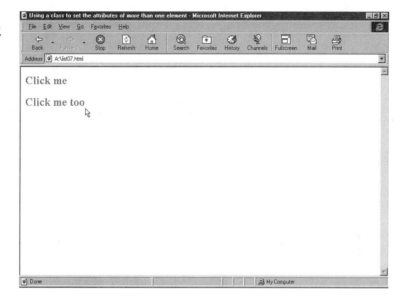

Listing 18.8. Using an `id` to access an element.

```
<HEAD>
<TITLE> Accessing elements by their id </TITLE>
<STYLE type="text/css">
span{color:orange;}
.hidden{visibility:hidden;color:green;}
</STYLE>
<SCRIPT language="javascript">
function mClick(){
if(document.all.hid.style.visibility!="visible"){
document.all.hid.style.visibility="visible";
document.all.hid.style.backgroundColor="yellow";
}

else{
document.all.hid.style.visibility="hidden";
document.all.hid.style.backgroundColor="white";
}
}
</SCRIPT>
</HEAD>
<BODY>
In the month of April there was a lot of
<SPAN onClick="mClick();"> precipitation </SPAN>

<SPAN class="hidden" id="hid">
<BR>
<B>Precipitation:</B> Water that falls on the earth's surface as rain, sleet, snow,
etc.
</SPAN>
</BODY>
</HTML>
```

18

USING
JAVASCRIPT WITH
STYLE SHEETS

FIGURE **18.9.**

The explanation is hidden before the word precipitation is clicked.

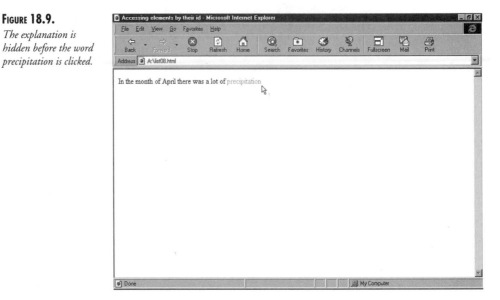

FIGURE **18.10.**

The explanation is set to visible *after precipitation is clicked.*

Listing 18.8 starts out by defining the style sheet rules for the document, and it is followed by the script. The function mClick() checks the visibility property of the element called hid. If it's not visible, it's set to visible. If it's already visible, it's set to hidden.

> **NOTE**
>
> Remember that when using the following, if there is more than one element with the same id, you get a collection of all the elements that have the id for which you were looking:
>
> ```
> document.all.name.style.property
> ```
>
> You can select which element you want by using the syntax item(*index*) after the id name, as in the following example:
>
> ```
> document.all.hid.item(1).style.visibility ="hidden";
> ```
>
> This sets the visibility of the second element to hidden.

The styleSheets Collection

The styleSheets collection is used to work with style sheets contained in your document. You can use it to collect information about and manipulate your style sheets.

Take a brief look at what you can do with the styleSheets collection:

- Find out how many style sheets are in your document.
- Add a style sheet.
- Replace a style sheet.
- Delete a style sheet.
- Disable a style sheet.
- Add a rule to the style sheet.

Finding the Number of Style Sheets in Your Document

Before you learn how to manipulate style sheets, it's important to know how to find the number of style sheets you have in your document. The styleSheets collection has a property called length, which you can use to find out how many style sheets are in your document:

```
document.styleSheets
```

The sample program in Listing 18.9 uses the styleSheets collection to print out how many style sheets are in your document. In Figure 18.11, the alert shows the number of style sheets in the document.

Listing 18.9. Using the length property to find the number of style sheets in your document.

```
<HTML>
<HEAD>
<TITLE>Finding the number of style sheets in your document</TITLE>
<STYLE type="text/css">
```

continues

Listing 18.9. continued

```
H1{font-size:30}
</STYLE>
<SCRIPT language="javascript">
<!--
function count()
{
alert("Did you know this document has" + document.
➥styleSheets.length + "style sheet(s).");
}
-->
</SCRIPT>
</HEAD>
<BODY onload="count();" >
<H1> A very simple document</H1>
</BODY>
</HTML>
```

FIGURE 18.11.

The alert box shows the number of style sheets in the document.

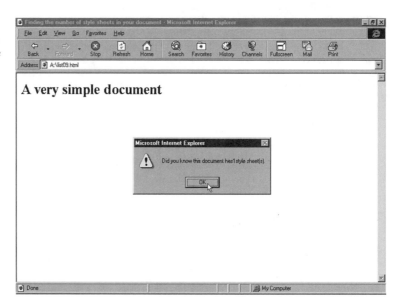

The length property tells you the total number of style sheets that are embedded (using the <STYLE> tag) and linked (using the <LINK> tag). If you want to know whether a style sheet is linked or embedded you can use this check:

```
document.styleSheets(index).href == "NULL"
```

index is the index of the style sheet you are checking (remember that indexing starts at 0 for the first style sheet, 1 for the second, and so on). The href property returns the URL of the style sheet. Because an embedded style sheet doesn't have a URL, the "NULL" return value of the href property lets you know that the style sheet is embedded. Here is an example of how to see whether your third style sheet is embedded:

```
<SCRIPT>
if(document.styleSheets(2).href == "NULL")
{
alert("The third style sheet in this document is an embedded style sheet");
}
</SCRIPT>
```

Adding a Style Sheet

You can add a style sheet to your document by using the following:

```
document.styleSheets(index).addImport("filename");
```

index is the index of the style sheet to which you are going to add a new style sheet. *filename* is the name of the file containing your style definitions.

You can't add another style sheet to an existing style sheet unless the existing style sheet is embedded. This is a good time to use the href property to make sure your style sheet is embedded. Here is an example:

```
if(document.styleSheets(0).href == "NULL")
{
    document.styleSheets(0).addImport("stylesheet.css");
}
```

The first part of the script checks to see whether the first style sheet is embedded; if it is embedded, a new style sheet is added to it. The new style sheet is added to the end of the old one. Having an external style sheet that is added to the document when needed is useful when you don't want to define new rules every time you want to change the look of your pages. For example, if you have a large site, you could have an external style sheet that is used to change the look of your text when a button is pressed. Instead of defining the rule on every page, you can use the addImport() method to add the new style sheet when the button is pressed. A few months down the road, if you want to change a rule in the style definition, you'll only have to change it in one file and the changes will affect your whole site.

Replacing One Style Sheet with Another

Using the styleSheets collection, you can also replace an existing style sheet with another. The only limitation is that the style sheet being replaced must either be linked (with the <LINK> tag) or imported into the document (with the @import statement). Listing 18.10 shows how it's done. Figures 18.12 and 18.13 show the before and after.

Listing 18.10. Replacing an existing style sheet with another.

```
<HTML>
<HEAD>
<TITLE> Replacing a style sheet</TITLE>
<LINK rel="stylesheet" href="stylesheet.css">
<SCRIPT language="javascript">
<!--
```

continues

18

USING
JAVASCRIPT WITH
STYLE SHEETS

Listing 18.10. continued

```
function replacesheet()
{
if(document.stylesheets.href != "NULL")
{
document.styleSheets(0).href = "newsheet.css";
}
}
-->
</SCRIPT>
</HEAD>
<BODY>
<DIV onclick="replacesheet();">Click me to replace my style sheet</DIV>
</BODY>
</HTML>

The old style sheet:
/*stylesheet.css*/
.spacedout{letter-spacing:30px}

The new style sheet:
/*newsheet.css*/
.spacedout{letter-spacing:15px}
```

FIGURE 18.12.

Before the new style sheet is applied.

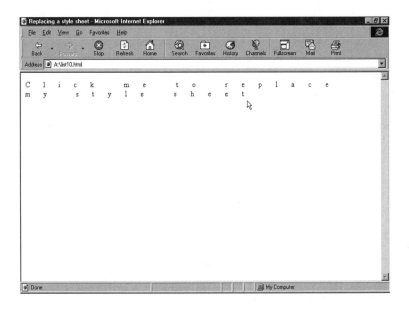

This simple example uses a linked style sheet, instead of the embedded style sheet used in the other examples. The <LINK> tag tells the browser to use the external style sheet called stylesheet.css. The file stylesheet.css has one class, spacedout, that sets the letter spacing to 30 pixels. In the script, the replacesheet() function checks to make sure the style sheet is linked. If it is linked, its href property is changed to newsheet.css, which replaces the old style sheet. When a style sheet is replaced, the rules in the new style sheet take effect immediately.

FIGURE **18.13.**
*After the new style sheet
is applied.*

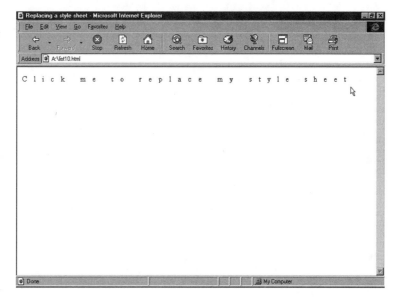

You can also delete a style sheet by setting its `href` property to `null`:

```
document.stylesheets(0).href = " "
```

Disabling and Enabling a Style Sheet

Style sheets can be disabled by setting the `disabled` property to `true`. Why would you disable a style sheet when you can delete it? When you delete a style sheet, the screen doesn't redraw. So even though the style sheet is no longer there, the elements on your page keep their properties. When you disable a style sheet the page is redrawn, causing your elements to lose their formatting. When it's enabled, the formatting comes back. Listing 18.11 demonstrates this, and the results are shown in Figure 18.14.

Listing 18.11. How to enable and disable a style sheet.

```
<HTML>
<HEAD>
<TITLE>Enabling and disabling a style sheet</TITLE>
<STYLE >
    BODY{background-color:white}
    H1{font-size:30pt;font-weight:bold;color:blue}
    H2{font-size:18pt;color:green;background-color:yellow}
    P{font-size:12pt;color:purple;text-indent:30px}
</STYLE>
<SCRIPT language="javascript">
<!--
function on()
{
```

continues

Listing 18.11. continued

```
    if(document.styleSheets(0).disabled)
    {
        document.styleSheets(0).disabled=false;
    }
    else
        document.styleSheets(0).disabled=true;

}
-->
</SCRIPT>
</HEAD>
<BODY>
    <H1>Title</H1>
    <H2>First paragraph </H2>
    <P>This is the first paragraph, it is very short.</P>
    <H2>Second paragraph </H2>
    <P>This is the second paragraph, it is short too </P>

<DIV id="state">
<button type="button" onclick="on();">Enable/Disable</button>
</DIV>
</BODY>
</HTML>
```

FIGURE 18.14.

A before and after picture of a page that demonstrates the effects of enabling and disabling a style sheet.

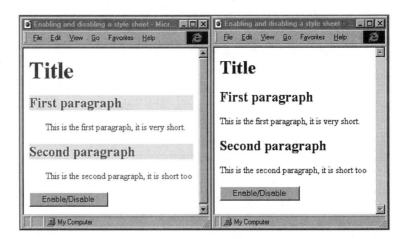

In this example, a button is used to toggle the style sheet's `disabled` property to `true` or `false`.

Adding a New Rule to a Style Sheet

If you have an embedded style sheet, you can also add rules to it with the addRule() method. You have to tell it what tag you want it to affect and the properties you want the tag to have. Type the following to add a new rule to make <BLOCKQUOTE> tags bold:

```
document.stylesheets.addRule("BLOCKQUOTE", "font-weight:bold");
```

Because you aren't limited to setting only one property, you can also do this:

```
document.styleSheets.addRule("BLOCKQUOTE", "font-weight:bold;color:black");
```

There is no way to remove a rule from a style sheet. Listing 18.12 shows how to add a rule to a style sheet.

Listing 18.12. A page with buttons that adds rules to the current style sheet.

```
<HTML>
<HEAD>
<TITLE> Adding a rule to a style sheet</TITLE>
<STYLE type="text/css">
BODY{background-color:white}
</STYLE>
<SCRIPT language="javascript">
function addarule(pick)
{
document.styleSheets(0).addRule("H1",pick);

}
</SCRIPT>

</HEAD>
<BODY>
<H1>ADD A NEW STYLE SHEET RULE TO ME</H1>
<FORM name="theform">
<BUTTON onclick=addarule("color:green");>Color:Green</button>
<BUTTON onclick=addarule("background-color:yellow");>
➥background-color:yellow</button>
<BUTTON onclick=addarule("letter-spacing:30");>
➥letter-spacing:30</button>
<BUTTON onclick=addarule("font-style:italic");>font-style:italic</button>
</form>
</BODY>
</HTML>
```

The <STYLE> block in the previous listing only defines one rule; new rules are later added by the script. When clicked, the buttons tell the script to add the rule passed to the script onto the style sheet. Figure 18.15 shows the results.

FIGURE 18.15.

*A Web page with some
of the style turned on.*

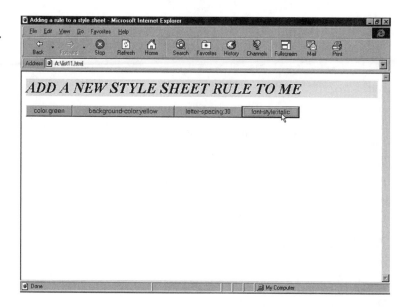

FIGURE 18.15.

*A Web page with some
of the style turned on.*

Summary

This chapter showed you how to create dynamic style sheets by using JavaScript to change their properties. You also learned how to manipulate and work with the styleSheets collection. You should now be able to create interesting interactive pages for your sites, without drastically lengthening the download time of your pages.

IV

Web Publishing with Java

Why Java?

by Corey Klaasmeyer

IN THIS CHAPTER

Java has created a huge amount of excitement within the Internet community. In essence, Java is to computers what HTML is to browsers: a standard, consistent, and predictable way of presenting or manipulating data. It also happens to run in browsers. Platform independence alone provides enough incentive for many people to choose Java over proprietary languages and tools. In addition to this alluring trait, a host of other language features give it cachet and smarts. Why consume house coffee when you can partake of a highly caffeinated espresso? As it turns out, sometimes a house coffee might be better than a mocha, but let's talk about the mocha first.

The mocha:

- **Platform independence**. Java runs on any browser with Java support and on any operating system with a virtual machine.

- **Industry standard/Standard APIs**. Java and its associated APIs are rapidly becoming an industry standard. Industry leaders have embraced the language and its APIs. In addition, Sun has applied to international standards bodies for acceptance of Java as an official standard.

- **Simple**. On paper Java looks a lot like its predecessors, but it certainly doesn't behave like its predecessors. A number of immodest traits such as exposing one's memory and pointing have been refined in this generation. The designers of Java chose not to include multiple class inheritance or templates for this reason.

- **Object oriented**. Everything in Java is represented as classes and objects.

- **Distributed**. Java supports client/server development with sockets and distributed objects.

- **Dynamic**. Java loads pieces of code as they are needed for a running application.

- **Interpreted**. Once compiled, the same Java code that runs on an AS/400 runs on a Macintosh, or a PC, or a Solaris....

- **Robust**. The Java language is designed with robustness in mind. Confusing and difficult-to-manage features of other languages have been removed from Java.

- **Secure**. Java security begins with the language and environment and ends with support for cryptographic APIs.

- **Architecture-neutral**. Where computers sometimes treat certain fundamental types differently, Java standardizes on a single policy.

- **Portable**. The language and APIs avoid relying on any sort of features or functionality of an operating system or piece of hardware that might reduce its portability.

- **High performance**. Native code written in C or C++ outperforms Java many times, but Java can approach these speeds by compiling to native code on-the-fly.

- **Multithreaded**. Java provides a simple and well-integrated method for creating applications that do many things at the same time.

A more complete description of each of these features follows.

Platform Independence

Software programs are traditionally written for a single computer because not all computers are alike. American National Standards Institute (ANSI) developed coding standards that allow source code to be compiled on a wide range of platforms without significant changes. Unfortunately, even in the case of ANSI-compliant code, it must still be recompiled for every platform. This is not the case for Java. Compiled Java code runs on any platform.

This platform independence is incredibly valuable to software developers, venders, and end users. For software developers, Java's platform independence eliminates the onerous task of writing code for each flavor of operating system. A Java developer can now write 100% Java code, compile it once, and watch it run on a wide variety of operating systems with no changes whatsoever. One company that has traditionally written software for the UNIX platform ported its code to seven different versions of UNIX for every application. Now developers write the code once and it will run on any UNIX flavor. As a bonus, this software can be distributed to users of Mac and Windows platforms without changes or recompilation. This vendor derives benefits from a wider market.

Industry Standard

Many leaders in the software industry support and invest in the Java language and its APIs, which is gradually making the Java APIs an industry-wide standard. Java is becoming more than a language.

In other words, the Java language really consists of two important standards that industry leaders are embracing. The first standard is the Java language, and it defines how Java programs can be written. This standard tells Java programmers how to pound out classes and for loops on the keyboard. The second standard is still evolving, and it defines what functional pieces of code are available for developers to build on and how to interact with them. Because the API is consistent, a Java programmer knows what class to instantiate to create a window on the screen, and she knows how the window will behave. These pieces of code make up the Java API.

Industry-wide standardization of the Java APIs will have another positive effect. Operated systems and browsers will embrace these APIs. As a result, the relatively bulky APIs will not have to be downloaded. In fact, Internet Explorer and Netscape Navigator already package the classes that make up the Java API. When the browser is downloaded, the API classes are downloaded along with it. This is already beginning to happen in some operating systems, as well. For instance, Windows, Macintosh, and Linux operating systems are distributed with the Java API.

As an ancillary effect, this industry support provides an insurance policy for any investment made in Java. Because of Java's wide acceptance, you can have confidence that the Java application built today will remain useful and valuable for a long period of time. Industry-wide support protects your investment. As leader and creator of the Java movement, Sun supports Java and has committed to rewriting many of its internal and end-user applications in Java. A diverse field of other companies has joined the Java movement, including notables Microsoft, IBM, Oracle, Netscape, and Apple. Each of these companies has committed to and invested in Java development efforts.

Finally, Sun is applying to ISO/IEC JTC1 for recognition as a Publicly Available Standards submitter. If accepted, Java will be eligible to become an ISO International Standard, which will give users an even greater degree of confidence in Java's long-term viability.

Simple

Java eliminates two major sources of confusion for programmers: pointers and memory management. Pointers are confusing, difficult to implement correctly, and easy to implement incorrectly. If implemented incorrectly, they can crash your application—or the entire computer. James Gosling once referred to Java as "C++–++" or "C++ without the guns and knives." "The guns" in this quote are almost certainly pointers. If pointers are the guns, memory management must be the knives, with the implication that if you forget to manage your memory, or manage it improperly, you will die a slow, painful death.

Because these two sources of hard-to-grasp concepts have been removed entirely from the language, Java is quickly the language of choice for introductory computer science courses all over the world. When developing in Java, it is possible to focus on understanding and implementing object-oriented software. Java's simplicity makes it the perfect choice for someone who is learning to program for the first time or for someone who is just learning to program in an object-oriented way. If the person is learning to program for the first time, there are real benefits, because there are no procedural habits or syntax to unlearn. Some of the object-oriented concepts referred to here are discussed in the following chapter, by way of introduction to the Java language.

The potential for time-consuming runtime debugging has also been reduced by catching some errors at compile time, such as the pernicious = or == syntaxes. The single equal sign assigns the variable on the left to the variable on the right, while == compares the value on the left with value on the right. The Java compiler requires that a conditional statement must result in a `boolean` value. When you make an assignment with the =, this is not usually the case. Instead of staring, bewildered, at a misbehaving program, you get a type mismatch error at compile time.

Some of the more controversial omissions made by the designers of the Java language include multiple class inheritance, templates, or parameterized types, and the `const` keyword. The omission of multiple class inheritance provides fodder for multipage rants on the `java.lang` group. Bearing this in mind, it wouldn't be prudent to say much more than this: A language without multiple class inheritance is less confusing than a language with multiple class inheritance. Keep in mind that Java does allow multiple interface inheritance, which is different from multiple class inheritance. Parameterized types are useful for generic programming, but Java offers a `meta` class, `oObject`, which superclasses all Java classes by default. Some items such as hash tables and vectors, which are often implemented as templates in C++, can be implemented in Java using the `Object` `meta` class.

Object Oriented

Implementing an application in Java means writing a number of classes. The class is a fundamental building block used by many object-oriented languages. Java refuses to let you develop in any other way. In other languages, such as C and C++, you are able to define global functions and variables, which are not a part of a class. Everything in Java is part of a class and the advantages of this approach quickly become apparent to the software programmers, engineers, and project managers.

Software programmers and engineers begin reaping the benefits of object-oriented design even at the initial stages of application development. Programmers and engineers use the Java API classes in their designs and implementations. They are effectively reusing classes that were developed with this reuse as a goal. This saves time and money. The combination of this flexible design, HTML-integrated documentation (Javadoc), and Java's one-class, one-file standard facilitates this process.

Down the road, the benefits of object-oriented design become more apparent to the project managers because classes that are reused rather than rewritten are less costly.

The benefits of object-oriented programming have been documented in stacks of books and proven in scores of applications. The primary advantages of object-oriented development include reuse, robustness, and scalability. Java does an especially good job of encouraging good object-oriented design by enforcing rules of the game, providing reusable classes from the start, and including tools, such as javadoc, which makes the process less painful.

Distributed

The Java team at SunSoft intended for Java to live in a networked environment from the beginning. Java was originally intended for use networked in smart appliances, and in fact, a number of smart appliances that run Java programs internally exist . Many of the features needed for a language to thrive on the Internet were also needed for Java-enabled intelligent consumer devices.

Most Internet applications must use some form of networking to connect to and communicate with servers running on distant computers. Java provides a full arsenal of networking functionality in the API to carry out these communications. The API includes classes for networked socket communications that utilize TCP/IP—the first language—of the Internet. Making TCP/IP socket connections and communicating over them can be accomplished as easily as saving or writing to a file. In fact, the same classes are used in both cases.

More recently, as part of the JDK 1.1, CORBA and RMI functionality has been integrated with the Java API. CORBA and RMI both provide a mechanism for two objects to communicate with each other, even though they may be located on entirely different machines. CORBA implementations written in Java may connect to and communicate with applications written in other languages, such as C++. RMI provides similar functionality, but the objects on both ends must be Java objects.

Dynamic

The Java virtual machine loads classes into the runtime environment as they are needed. In addition, the API allows this functionality to be overridden in order to implement custom class loaders, which load classes from a source other than the local file system. Java's dynamic architecture allows more flexibility in program design and development than can be achieved in a statically linked programming language.

Many Java programs currently use this dynamic capability of Java, but in the future its potential will be more fully exploited. The JavaServer and many browsers take advantage of this capability. The JavaServer is capable of dynamically loading classes into its environment by using a custom ClassLoader called the ServletLoader. Instead of loading classes from the classpath, the ServletLoader loads classes from a special directory called servlet. Servlets are really the server-side version of an applet that runs in a browser and is loaded in the same way. Applets are loaded by using a custom ClassLoader—usually called an AppletClassLoader—which makes HTTP requests for the class files needed to run the applet and loads them into the browser's environment. The process is the same on both the server and the client, except that on the client, the class files are loaded across the network, and on the server, the class files are loaded from a special directory.

In the future, more and more applications will use this feature as a means of distributing and componentizing software. At some point, your spread sheet will be able to display the phase-space of the non-linear equation by dynamically loading software components from the Santa Fe Institute in Santa Fe, New Mexico, even though you happen to be located at the South Pole. Although this feature is obscure and not widely needed, it will be available on demand across a global sea of objects without having to pay for the functionality up front. Sun's JavaSpaces research and development project is a harbinger of this future—yet another reason to use Java.

Interpreted

A compiled Java program executes within a virtual machine. The virtual machine must load all the pieces of the Java program, decipher them, put them back together, and turn them into a running program. This probably doesn't seem like a reason to use Java, but it makes Java's platform independence possible. This means every platform that runs a virtual machine may execute the architecture-neutral bytecode.

Aside from the issue of platform independence, the linking stage of a traditional development cycle is eliminated. As a result of this, Java development and prototyping can proceed more quickly than usual.

Robust

Largely as a result of Java's lack of pointers and memory management, Java applications tend to be more robust. Unfortunately, some of this robustness is offset by the simplicity with which threading can be incorporated into Java applications.

Aside from the lack of pointers and memory management, a number of other features within the language contribute to this robustness. Arrays always provide a length variable. The API includes a sString class, which provides a range of functionality, including a length() method. sStrings no longer exist as an array of char types unless it is necessary to work with them in this way.

The object-oriented nature of Java contributes to the robustness of applications. The sString class is just one example of this. Since the classes that are part of the API are fully tested and have a well-defined interface, this functionality does not have to reimplemented, creating the opportunity for another source of bugs.

The relative simplicity of implementing multithreaded applications in Java can replace some of the bugs lost by eliminating memory management and pointers from the language. Because threading is so simple, programmers use it more often in Java than in other languages. Writing multithreaded applications and avoiding deadlocks is a relatively difficult thing to do even though Java threading is easy to implement. This results in more bugs than would normally be found, because the responsibility of data synchronization rests squarely on the shoulders of the programmer in a multithreaded application.

Secure

Java provides security at the language level. This sort of security is not possible to implement in a language that compiles down to binary code, because native applications have direct access to memory locations. Java applications never have direct access to memory location. A reference to an object always represents an offset on the heap rather than a real memory address. Also at the language level, the System classes and other sensitive classes can be made final, which means they may not be subclassed and tampered with.

In addition to the these language features, all virtual machine implementations must verify classes every time into the environment. The virtual machine performs a test that verifies the authenticity of the compiled Java class. If the class doesn't pass these tests, it will not be loaded and a ClassFormatException is thrown.

The language also specifies the existence of a SecurityManager, which enforces a security policy. For instance, an applet that executes within a browser runs "in a sandbox." It cannot connect to any IP address, other than the IP of the host from which it was downloaded, or access any system resources local to the client machine where the applet is running. When a request for a socket connection to some other host is made from an applet, the SecurityManager refuses it. The JDK1.1 and later includes a range of cryptography interfaces and a default implementation provided by Sun. With this new functionality, trusted applets can be downloaded to a browser and run outside the sandbox with access to the hard drive and other system resources.

Architecture-Neutral

Although most computers differ in significant ways, the interpreted nature of Java allows it to run within the virtual machine, which always looks like the same architecture.

19

WHY JAVA?

For instance, the int type from one computer to the other may be defined as 16, 32, or 64 bits. Sometimes the order in which the bits are stored may be reversed. This is not the case in Java where an int has one length and one storage policy.

Portable

Java does not make use of any system-dependent functionality. For example, it does not rely on native print drivers to provide printing services.

Sun's "100% Java" initiative verifies this platform independence. Although the language and APIs are designed to run on any platform, platform-specific Java programs that do not run on multiple platforms can be written. To receive certification as a "100% Java" implementation, the application must not be written in a platform-dependent way.

The virtual machine that interprets Java bytecode is also designed to be as portable as possible. Although written in native code, the virtual machine is written in ANSI C, which means the code can be compiled on a wide range of platforms with relatively minor changes.

High Performance

According to Sun, Java written with the JDK 1.0 runs 20 times slower than C. Code written for the JDK 1.1 runs approximately twice as fast as JDK 1.0 code, so performance is constantly being improved. Other technologies, such as the just-in-time (JIT) compilation, provide even better performance.

JITs work by compiling Java code to native code as it runs. A Java program executing in a virtual machine that implements this feature begins running at normal Java speed, but speeds up as the program executes and the just-in-time compiler finds sections of code which can be optimized by compiling into native code.

Multithreaded

Writing threaded code in most languages entails using external libraries that implement this functionality. Few languages include threading, and fewer still interweave threads as simply and effectively as Java. Writing multithreaded code presents enough of a challenge without having to use a complex syntax during implementation.

Why Use Java for Distributed Internet and Intranet Applications?

Steve Jobs once publicly groused about the current Internet trend of moving from server-side smarts to client-side smarts. Jobs reasoned that the Internet works well because it is simple. Adding additional functionality to the browser on the client side would only make the Internet more complex and ultimately less useful and less appealing. This may prove to be true, but historically, the Internet has successfully culled ineffective technology and entrenched effective technology. Java applets and a host of other client-side technologies are entrenched, because it is sometimes more effective to perform complex tasks on the client side than it is to perform those same tasks on the server side.

As it turns out, Java also makes sense when used on the server side. A Java servlet, the server-side counterpart to an applet, provides a fast, efficient, and pleasant environment in which to develop distributed applications for the Internet.

Some of the more convincing reasons for using Java on the Internet include:

■ **State Awareness**. Because HTTP is a stateless protocol, keeping track of a chain of requests requires the passing of a unique identifier with each request like a baton in a relay race. This additional overhead and complexity is often avoided by implementing an applet or servlet in Java. In the applet case, state information can be maintained on the client side, while in the servlet case, state information can be maintained with relative ease on the server-side. Java offers a third, distributed approach—using RMI or CORBA—which eliminates the need to distinguish between the server and the client, and state information exists on both side of the equation.

An applet running on the client keeps track of its own state. For example, if someone uses a commerce applet to order a coffee mug, the transaction can be stored and retrieved when appropriate. If a traditional HTTP request had been made, this transaction would have been sent back to the client and stored in a file or database by a Common Gateway Interface program. If an umbrella were ordered after the coffee cup, the request would have to be sent to the server-side CGI program, the data from the last request would have to be located, and the new transaction would have to be appended. The data would then be saved again. In the case of the applet, the data would just be added to a list of transactions on the client side. When appropriate, this list would be sent back for processing. An applet simplifies Web applications by removing the burden of maintaining information about the state of this sequence of requests, which simplifies things.

Servlets must maintain the identity of the sequence of events as the CGI program was required to in the previous example, but it reduces complexity by allowing an object-oriented approach. Instead of storing state information about the session or sequence of requests, this information can now be stored in a collection of Session objects maintained by the servlet. As in the CGI approach, an ID must be passed from the client to the server and back, but the state information may be maintained in an object that lives throughout the sequence of requests. Effectively, this removes the burden of storing the state information externally in a database or file for data that does not need to be stored beyond a single session.

The RMI and CORBA solution allows an application to run seamlessly over the browser and server. When the coffee mug and umbrella are ordered in this case, the order data may be stored either within the application running on the browser or the server, and no external information must be shipped back and forth between requests.

19

WHY JAVA?

■ **Reuse**. The availability of the servlet API allows Java functionality developed for the client side to be effectively reused on the server side. If Java classes are designed generically, this provides an advantage over distributed Internet applications, which make use of server-side languages that cannot be used on the client, or vice-versa.

■ **Input validation**. Parsing a user's input on the client side often makes more sense than passing the input back to the server for validation and re-prompting the user to correct an invalid input. For example, rather than prompting for a monetary value in an HTML form input, that value could be entered into a form in an applet that validates the input amount as the user enters it on the client side. The data never has to make the extra trip back to the server.

■ **Efficiency**. Applets can display data without information about how the data should be formatted. For this reason, applets can sometimes perform tasks more efficiently than HTML, once the applet code has been downloaded. For example, an Internet banking application that allows a user to inquire about account balances, make transfers, or make payments, would require fewer data packets to be sent than the same application written in HTML. The HTML-based application must send information with every response about how the data should be formatted. An applet only requires the raw data and displays this data within a pre-designed GUI.

Servlets, discussed in Chapter 29, "Server-Independent Technologies—The Java Servlet API," provide an even greater performance advantage when used in place of the traditional CGI mechanism.

■ **Agents**. Software agents roam throughout computer networks delivering messages or gathering information. Because Java runs on any platform, agents implemented in Java can roam further afield and across more varied digital terrain than agents implemented in other languages.

■ **Commerce applications**. The Java language supports the level of security required by commerce applications and provides an excellent dynamic infrastructure on which to build the distributed commerce applications of the future.

■ **Concurrent applications**. Java provides a highly integrated, multithreaded programming environment that is relatively easy to use. Distributed Internet applications usually must do more than one thing at the same time. For instance, an Internet banking application may read from a socket and receive user input simultaneously.

Why Use Java for Database Connectivity?

Java provides an excellent tool for database connectivity. Almost any application, whether on the client or server side, needs to access a database at some point. Java abstracts a database into a series of classes and interfaces, that effectively hide the implementation of the database drivers. The specification is called Java Database Connectivity (JDBC), and drivers already exist for most applications. The advantage of this is twofold. Not only is the code platform independent, but also database independent if SQL queries conform to the SQL-92 specification.

As a result, Java code written to access a database runs on any platform and with any database. An investment in code that used JDBC lives through operating systems and new databases.

Why Use Java When You Could Use ActiveX?

Although ActiveX is often mentioned in the same breath with Java, these technologies differ in fundamental ways. In a nutshell, Java runs on any machine with a Java virtual machine or a Java-enabled browser. ActiveX runs on any 32-bit Windows machine, in Microsoft's Internet Explorer, in a Netscape Browser with an ActiveX-enabling plug-in on a 32-bit Windows machine, or on an operating system with a DCOM implementation. ActiveX controls are usually larger than compiled Java bytecode. ActiveX is less secure than Java in an untrusted environment. Finally, Java's component model, JavaBeans, is gaining industry-wide acceptance.

ActiveX Is Not yet Platform Independent

In theory, ActiveX will someday be able to run on any platform, but before that happens, all target operating systems must run a 32-bit windows emulator. These emulators are not yet available for many platforms. MVS, Sun Sparc, and Digital Alpha versions are under development as this goes to press.

Size

Java applets and applications are much smaller than their ActiveX counterparts. When sending an applet over the Internet, size determines whether the user chooses to wait for code to download. Until 38.8 modems are supplanted by faster hardware on a wide scale, the amount of data to download is an extremely important consideration.

Security

ActiveX makes no security claims in an untrusted context. In other words, an ActiveX control is downloaded as a trusted control, or no security assumptions can be made. The Java applet security policy delineates itself from this model by running in a sandbox by default. While running in a sandbox, the applet has no access to system resources, such as the client's hard drive.

JavaBeans Is Gaining Industry-Wide Acceptance

Microsoft's Component Object Model (COM) outdates the relatively new upstart, JavaBeans, by many years. In some respects, this maturity is an asset because of the extensive period of testing it has been put through—in some other respects it's unwanted baggage. However, many software development organizations have voiced their approval of JavaBeans as a new component model standard.

For years, Microsoft has been singing the praises of the component model of development. Instead of thinking in terms of applications, developers and designers think in terms of components. Components may encapsulate an algorithm or an entire application, but they always expose a well-documented range of services and can either exist on their own or as a part of some other application or component. The industry has yet to embrace the component model as fully as Microsoft has, but many have taken the first steps and chosen JavaBeans over COM.

Companies that have chosen JavaBeans over COM did so primarily because JavaBeans are platform independent. Although COM has weathered the test of time and proven its viability, this is not a good enough reason for many to commit to a model built for a single platform. JavaBeans also has the advantage of not being tied to a system-level registration architecture. Because of this freedom, the designers of the Java language were able to design them in a more abstract way. JavaBeans are Java classes that conform to certain rules and expose their services via a standard set of classes.

Why Not Use Java When You Could Use ActiveX?

There are many compelling reasons, listed previously, to use Java on the Internet and within a corporate intranet—especially if the Intranet is a sufficiently heterogeneous mixture of platforms. What if the Intranet consists of all Microsoft platforms? What about using Java on the server side? In both of these cases, there might be good reasons to use ActiveX.

A Homogeneous Windows Network

If the entire intranet is made up of Microsoft platforms and will always be made up of Microsoft platforms, using ActiveX for development purposes may be the right decision. Transfer speeds over a LAN are much higher than transfer speeds over the Internet, so size considerations are less important in this environment.

VB Developers

If there is a large staff of trained developers, which may be the case for many IS departments, they could be put to work building functionality for the intranet immediately. This may justify the decision to use ActiveX over Java. Although it is possible to script ActiveX controls in Java, it would probably make more sense to write components as JavaBeans, because they could easily be reused in other contexts. If written as beans, at some later date, they could easily be exposed to business partners or clients as an extranet, no matter what kind of operating system they happened to be using.

The Server Software Is Internet Information Server

IIS provides support for active-server page scripting. Because of the large number of ActiveX controls available, this may make development proceed more swiftly, especially if there are a large number of VB-proficient developers on staff. ASP scripting can be included directly in the HTML page, eliminating the need for compilation or scripting of CGI programs. Interpretation of the ASP script does not require the creation of a separate process on the server machine that makes Active Server Pages more efficient than CGI.

ActiveX controls can be scripted in Java, as well as a number of other scripting languages. As before, if Java is chosen as the language of implementation for the project, developing servlets would probably make more sense, because they do not lock you into any one platform or server software.

Summary

There are many reasons to choose Java for any development project—whether on the server side or the client side. One of the most compelling reasons to make this choice is Java's platform independence. The "write once, run anywhere" approach represents an incredible amount of value for developers, businesses, and venders. Many languages run on multiple platforms without changes, but Java offers this feature in addition to a dynamic, distributed, object-oriented environment and APIs designed with security, performance, and multithreading in mind. Few languages can make claim to all of these features, as well as industry-wide acceptance and a component model.

It is also important to note that Java is becoming more than a language; it is a language and a set of APIs. As those APIs gain acceptance as standards, most platforms and browsers will include them as part of their package, so they will not have to be downloaded when Java makes use of them.

As an alternative to Java, ActiveX may be the language of choice for a homogeneous network of Microsoft windows clients and servers. Because of the large numbers of VB scripters and the availability and relative maturity of COM and OLE Components, the path from development to deployment may be a shorter one.

Ideally, with the possibility of Java-to-COM communication, or vice versa, these two technologies will not provide alternative solutions to a problem, but a synergistic solution. In some ways, ActiveX and Java are complementary. This chapter should have given you enough information to make a decision about whether to use Java or ActiveX or both.

In this chapter, the question "Why Java?" was addressed, but the next chapter takes you on a whirlwind tour of Java wherein you are introduced to Java language concepts and to the process of coding in Java.

19

WHY JAVA?

CHAPTER 20

The Java Language:
A Crash Course

by Corey Klaasmeyer

IN THIS CHAPTER

This chapter introduces fundamental object-oriented and Java language concepts. After reading this chapter, you should understand the steps necessary to develop small applications and applets in Java.

Classes and Objects

Java applications and applets are built on classes and objects. If you can understand these two concepts, you will have a solid foundation for developing in Java or any other object-oriented language.

Classes—Designing an Application: JMAIL

When writing an object-oriented software application, a design is developed based on concepts rather than algorithms or specific tasks. In the procedural software of the past, programs were designed by finding all the procedures needed to accomplish some task or set of tasks. In the object-oriented paradigm, the tasks are just members of a *class*, or a group of tasks that have related functionality. Developing in Java takes a different approach, which involves analyzing the concepts associated with a particular project or problem. When you approach the project from this perspective, some aspects stand out as fundamental concepts, whereas other aspects appear relatively less important or peripheral to the system.

For example, you can discover classes from the following description of an e-mail application by isolating central concepts:

REQUIREMENT FOR THE APPLICATION JMAIL

The user should be able to compose an e-mail message through a graphical user interface. The interface should have fields for the sender's address, the recipient's address, the subject, and the message text itself. There should also be Send and Clear buttons on the screen. When the user clicks the Send button, the current date and time should be added to the message, and the composed message should be sent to an e-mail server using the SMTP protocol. When the user clicks the Clear button, all the fields in the user interface should be cleared.

This paragraph describes requirements that will be satisfied by a Java application called JMAIL. Before writing any code, you must think about the problem and how to structure JMAIL to provide an effective solution.

An e-mail message probably stands out to you as fundamental to the system in this description. This might represent a class in the project. Other elements are necessary to fill these requirements. The user interface described in the paragraph must be created, and the message must be sent somehow. After you understand the functioning and the system's general behavior, you can write classes to model those central concepts. To fulfill the requirements for this project, two classes might be enough. One would model the e-mail message and a second would encapsulate the send functionality.

In the next chapter, "Introduction to Applet Programming," you build the user interface as part of an applet.

The EMail class consists of smaller elements. It might be appropriate to also model these elements as classes. For instance, classes could describe the addresses, date, subject, and message. Fortunately, Java already has classes that can provide all the functionality needed to represent these additional items. This is good, because it gets you closer to the ultimate goal of writing an e-mail client rather than focusing on the smaller details. The classes that represent the address, subject, date, and body of the e-mail are already part of the Java Application Programming Interface, or API. They are designed with enough flexibility so that you can use them in a wide variety of Java applications.

It was a simple exercise to discover the central classes of the e-mail application, but as the development proceeds, you'll probably find more classes or the existing classes will need to be redesigned. However, it's important to spend enough time initially designing the classes even though they may change. If the classes are well-designed, they can easily be reused in other applications or extended and enhanced. Ideally, when the programming begins, the process should involve filling in pieces of the design. This process in and of itself is complex enough to fill an entire book. In fact, many books deal with this process in depth. (If you are serious about engineering software, you may want to take some time to do some additional research on object-oriented design.) Meanwhile, continue with the crash course.

What are classes? *Classes* are objects that have certain *attributes* and *behaviors*. A good way to understand what a class describes is to know what a class does not describe. A class does not describe a piece of e-mail from Bill that was sent Sunday from Redmond, Washington. Instead of describing the specifics of a particular e-mail, a class describes e-mail in general as having a sender, a recipient, a date, and some message. These are the message's attributes. The message's behavior is described by a number of actions the class must perform in order to do its job. For instance, the EMail class should have methods for storing and retrieving the sender's address, the recipient's address, the date of the e-mail creation, and the message. In this era of multimedia e-mail, the class should probably define quite a few other methods, but these were not specified in the requirements.

Functionality is needed to send the e-mail on its way. This class has to implement a method that knows how to send an e-mail. It also needs to know which server the e-mail should be sent to.

Now that a rough design of the classes needed for the JMail application has been established, how is a particular e-mail represented? The class is a general description, but how do you represent an e-mail from Bill that was sent on Sunday from Redmond, Washington?

Objects

If a class is a general description of a range of items, an object is a description of a concrete item. In object-oriented languages, an *object* is an instance of a class. Whereas the EMail class answers the question "What is an e-mail?" the object answers questions about an e-mail message, such as, "Who is this particular e-mail from?" or "When was this particular e-mail sent?" In other words, an object represents a specific instance of what is described in general by the class.

An object differs from a class in its life cycle. An object is created and exists until it is no longer needed or destroyed. For example, an instance of the EMail class is created after a message has been written or received. After the mail has been sent or read, the object may be destroyed.

Classes and Types

You may be accustomed to using variables that contain numbers or characters. For instance, an int is a simple variable type in Java, which may contain a positive or negative number:

```
int i;
i = 3000;
```

The type of i is int. In Java, it's possible to define variables as class types:

```
EMail mail;
```

The variable mail can be used to point to an object of type EMail. In other words, classes are used just like other types of data, such as numbers and characters. Variables can be defined to store an integer, but in an object-oriented language, they can also be defined to store a certain type of object that has some behavior. A variable defined as type EMail can store instances of the EMail class or EMail objects. The methods defined within the EMail class can then be invoked on this object.

> **NOTE**
>
> Java has two kinds of variables: primitives and object types. Primitive type variables have no behavior, only values. There are eight primitive types in Java:
>
> - Boolean
> - char
> - byte
> - short
> - int
> - long
> - float
> - double

Object types can include behavior. Methods may be invoked on a variable, which is an object type. Here are some examples of classes that can be used as variable types:

- `String`
- `Integer`
- `EMail`

When the program is running, most of what the program does is implemented by a number of objects working together in some predetermined way.

Creating Classes and Objects

This description of classes and objects may seem too abstract, but this section presents a more concrete picture of how classes and objects are actually implemented within the Java language.

Creating Classes

Classes provide the basis for Java programs, which may take the form of applications, applets, or servlets. All three of these types of Java programs are also classes. You define a class in the following way:

```
public class EMail { ... }
```

The first word in the definition is a modifier that dictates where the class may be accessed. The `public` keyword means this class may be used by anyone, like a public telephone. (Modifiers are discussed in greater detail later in this chapter's "Access Modifiers.") The second word, `class`, defines `EMail` as a class. `Email`, the last word before the first curly brace, is the name of the class.

> **TIP**
>
> When you're naming classes, capitalize the first letter of every word. This is a widely used convention in Java and many other object-oriented languages.

Finally, everything within the curly braces defines either an `EMail` attribute or behavior.

Class Behavior—Writing Methods

You define behavior of the `EMail` class by writing methods for the class. Because an `EMail` object contains information about a sender, you could add a method to set a sender's e-mail address and return that value. If you add such a method to the `EMail` class definition, the class looks like this:

```
public class EMail {
    public void setSenderAddress( String anEMailAddress ) { ... }
    public String getSenderAddress( ) { ... }
}
```

The first word of a method definition is similar to a class definition; it dictates from where the method may be called. In this case, as in the case of the class, the method may be called from anywhere because it is public. The next word that differs in each of the method definitions defines the return type for the method. The `setSenderAddress()` method returns `void` because this method isn't asking for any information.

> **NOTE**
>
> Return types must be specified for all methods or a compile-time error results.

Instead, information about the sender's e-mail address is passed to the `EMail` object. In this case, the type of this information is `String`. The `String` class is built into the standard Java language or the API. After the type declaration, the name of the variable is added. The name of the variable passed to the `EMail` object is `anEMailAddress`.

> **TIP**
>
> When you're naming variables, capitalize only the first letter of every word after the first word. This is another widely used convention in Java and many other object-oriented languages.

Variables passed to a method in this way are referred to as *parameters*. The methods themselves are often referred to as *member methods*, because they are considered members of the `EMail` class.

In some respects, the class's behavior is its most important feature, because all the public methods of a class make up the interface to that class. The interface is used repeatedly by other programmers, so it should be well thought-out and easy to use. An interface defines all the ways in which a class can be used. In the preceding example, two methods store a sender's e-mail address within an object of type `EMail` or retrieve a sender's e-mail address from an object of type `EMail`.

Class Attributes

The variable where this data is stored is called an *attribute*. Attributes are added to this class by adding a variable to the block defined by the class. If an attribute describing the name of the sender is added to the `EMail` class, each of the methods `setSenderAddress()` and `getSenderAddress()` can be implemented to modify or access this attribute. Here's a look at the new class definition:

```
public class EMail {
    public void setSenderAddress( String anEMailAddress ) {
        senderAddress = anEMailAddress;
    }
    public String getSenderAddress( ) { return senderAddress; }
    private String senderAddress;
}
```

Because a `senderAddress` attribute has been added to the `EMail` class, each of the methods can now be implemented. In the previous class definition, there was no place to store the sender's address, but now that information can be stored in the `senderAddress` variable. The `senderAddress` variable is referred to as a member variable of the `EMail` class, because it is part of that class and not part of a method of the class.

> **NOTE**
>
> Methods come in "set and get" pairs so often that they are commonly referred to by the names *mutator* and *accessor* methods. A set (mutator) method mutates the state of an object, whereas a get (accessor) method only provides access to data within the object.

If the `senderAddress` variable had been defined within the method, it would not have been considered a member of the class. It would not have been accessible within any of the other methods of the class. For example, the following code would not compile:

```
public class InvisibleVariable {
    public void setVariable( String aVariable ) {
        String v = aVariable;
    }
    public void getVariable( ) {
        return v;
    }
    // v should be defined here...
}
```

This code would not compile because v is defined within the `setVariable()` method. Because of this, it is not considered to be a part of the class. When `getVariable()` compiles, the compiler does not know what v is. A *method* is a block of code defined by curly braces. A *class* is also a block of code defined by curly braces. If a block is defined within some other larger block, it has access to all the identifiers defined within that block. For this reason, a method of a class has access to variables defined as part of that class.

Two methods of the same class do not have access to variables defined within each other's blocks. They will only have access to the variables defined within the class or within their own blocks.

As in the case of the class, the definition includes a modifier that defines where the variable can be used. In this case, the variable can only be used within the `EMail` class because it is defined as `private`.

20

THE JAVA LANGUAGE: A CRASH COURSE

The variable senderAddress is of type String. As mentioned before, the Java API includes a ready-to-use String class, so this functionality does not have to be built. The method setSenderAddress() sets the value of senderAddress to the value of the anEMailAddress parameter, which is also of type String. In the getSenderAddress() method, the value of this variable is returned. Any object of type EMail can now store and retrieve a sender's address when the appropriate method is called.

The EMail class doesn't yet define all the functionality it needs, but the additional behavior and attributes are also added as member methods and member variables of the class.

Creating Objects

EMail describes one of the central classes in the e-mail project developed in this chapter; however, it does not describe a specific e-mail. A specific e-mail is described by an instance of the EMail class. Remember, the class definition is only a template that describes the general behavior of objects of that class. In order to create a new object of type EMail, enough space must be allocated for it. The new keyword does this work for you. In Java, if the name of the EMail class is EMail, you can create a new object in this way:

```
EMail eMailObject = new EMail();
```

Several things are going on in this line. First, a variable of type EMail is defined. Second, a new object of type EMail is created and stored in this variable. This statement could have been expressed in two lines:

```
EMail eMailObject;
eMailObject = new EMail();
```

This technique is used within the EMail class when it defines the senderAddress variable within the class block. It is later assigned an object when the setSenderAddress() method is called.

Special Methods—Constructors

Whenever an eMailObject is created, a special method called a constructor is invoked. A *constructor* sets the initial state of the object. It constructs the object.

Although a constructor is similar to a method in many respects, it differs from a method in two ways. First, a constructor must have the same name as the name of the class. In this example, the constructor for the EMail class must be named EMail. Second, the constructor defines no return type.

To illustrate this, a date attribute is added to the EMail class definition along with a pair of set and get methods and a constructor. The constructor's job is to initialize the state of the object. For EMail, the date is the only thing that needs to be initialized upon creation. The constructor EMail() initializes this date to the current date and time:

```
public class EMail {

    // Default constructor
```

```
    public EMail() {
            date = Calendar.getDate();
    }
    public void setSenderAddress( String anEMailAddress ) {
            senderAddress = anEMailAddress;
     }
            return senderAddress;
     }
    public void setDate( Calendar aDate ) {
            date = aDate;
     }
    public Calendar getDate( ) {
            return (Calendar)date.clone();
     }

    // EMail attributes
    private String senderAddress;
    private Calendar date;
}
```

Now, when an object of type EMail is created, the constructor EMail() will be called and the date variable will be set to the current date and time. This date can be reset by the setDate() method or accessed by the getDate() command. In other words, when you write the following statement, it calls the EMail() constructor:

```
EMail anEMailObject = new EMail();
```

You may have been confused by the Calendar.getDate() call from the preceding code. All the method calls in the preceding example are invoked on an object with the exception of the getDate() method. The Calendar.getDate() method is a static method of the Calendar class. That is, no object of type Calendar is necessary in order to be able to call this method. When you see a method being invoked this way, it means that the method has been defined as a static method. A special static method that turns the EMail class into an application is defined in "Putting It All Together: A Java Application."

NOTE

The java.util.Calendar class has been added in the JDK 1.1 in order to handle internationalization issues. Although the Date class still exists as in the JDK 1.0, most of its methods are deprecated—no longer recommended for use. A Calendar object is never created using the new keyword, but through static methods of the Calendar class.

Using Objects

In order to invoke methods of an object, the . operator is used. You can now get the date from this new EMail object the following way:

```
anEMailObject.getDate();
```

The first part of the method call, before the period, indicates which object the method should be called on, whereas everything after the period specifies which of the methods to call. This method returns the date of this EMail object's creation. You could store this in a separate variable called theDate:

```
Calendar theDate = anEMailObject.getDate();
```

You could also reset the date to a new value by calling the setDate() method.

```
anEMailObject.setDate( Calendar.getDateTimeInstance( FULL,LONG ) );
```

Inside the method, this value is assigned to the private variable, date. This value remains the same for the life of the object or until that value is changed again.

If getSenderAddress() had been called and a sender address had never been set for this object, the method would return a null value. The null value indicates the lack of an object. In particular, it indicates that senderAddress variable was never assigned to a new String object.

Putting It All Together—A Java Application

Before you go further, test the EMail class in an application. Java has a nice feature that allows a class to become an application with the addition of a single method. The method is a little more complicated than the two methods from the preceding example, but it follows the same pattern:

```
public class EMail {
      public static void main(Sring[] args) {...}
}
```

Notice that the main() method is a static method.

If the rest of the methods necessary to implement an e-mail class are added, and the main() is added, it is possible to test the class from the command line. Here's what the EMail class definition now looks like:

```
import java.util.Calendar;
import java.text.DateFormat;

public class EMail {

    public static void main( String[] args ) {
        EMail anEMailObject = new EMail();
        anEMailObject.setSenderAddress( "bill@ms.org" );
        anEMailObject.setRecipientAddress( "bill@whitehouse.com" );
        anEMailObject.setSubject( "What are we doing today?" );
        anEMailObject.setMessage(
            "Dear Bill, blah, blah, blah, Sincerely, Bill" );
        System.out.println( anEMailObject );
    }

    public EMail() {
        date = Calendar.getInstance();
    }
```

```
    public void setSenderAddress( String anEMailAddress ) {
            senderAddress = anEMailAddress;
    }
    public String getSenderAddress() {
            return senderAddress;
    }
    public void setRecipientAddress( String anEMailAddress ) {
            recipientAddress = anEMailAddress;
    }
    public String getRecipientAddress() {
            return recipientAddress;
    }
    public void setDate( Calendar aDate ) {
            date = aDate;
    }
    public Calendar getDate() {
            return date;
    }
    public void setSubject( String aSubject ) {
            subject = aSubject;
    }
    public String getSubject() {
            return subject;
    }
    public void setMessage( String aMessage ) {
            message = aMessage;
    }
    public String getMessage() {
            return message;
    }

    // Format the message.
    public String toString() {
            DateFormat dateFormat =
                DateFormat.getDateTimeInstance(
                    DateFormat.FULL,DateFormat.LONG );
            return "From: " + senderAddress + "\n" +
                "To: " + recipientAddress + "\n" +
                "Subject: " + subject + "\n" +
                "Date: " + dateFormat.format( date.getTime() ) + "\n\n" +
                message; }

private String senderAddress;
private String recipientAddress;
private Calendar date;
private String subject;
private String message;

}
```

Several things should be explained in this EMail class. The main() method is nothing new to most procedural and C++ programmers. An instance of EMail is created with the sender's address, the recipient's address, and the subject of the message, and then the message is sent. The System.out.println() method prints the object.

When you run the EMail application by typing java EMail from the command line, the Java virtual machine looks for this method within EMail and executes it.

20

THE JAVA
LANGUAGE: A
CRASH COURSE

The `println()` method doesn't know how to print an `EMail` object. It only knows that it must call the `toString()` method on the `EMail` object. This method has been added to the new `EMail` definition. Because `System.out.println()` calls `toString()`, and the `toString()` method knows how to print the `EMail` object, an e-mail message that looks like this should be printed out:

```
From: bill@ms.org
To: bill@whitehouse.com
Subject: What are we going to do today?
Date: Thursday, September 10, 1997 10:37:02 PM PDT
Dear Bill, blah, blah, blah, Sincerely, Bill.
```

Go ahead and give it a try. Install the JDK 1.1 and type the `EMail` class as listed in the preceding code lines into a text editor. The file name must be the same name as the name of the class, in addition to a `.java` extension. After the `EMail.java` file has been created, use the Java compiler to compile it. Type **javac EMail.java** from the command line. If your environment has been properly set up and the class has been entered with no errors, you should receive no message and a new file called `EMail.class` should have been added to the directory. In the same directory, type **java EMail** in order to run the program.

Take a closer look at the `toString()` method, because it makes use of the + operator. In Java, the + operator has a special purpose. In addition to adding two numbers, it concatenates `String` types if there happens to be a `String` somewhere in the expression. If the expression contains other types, everything in the expression is converted to a `String`. Everything in the return statement is of type `String`. It took some work to get the date to format correctly!

Notice that when the `EMail` object is printed, the output includes a line with the current date and time. The date was never set in the `main()` method. How does the class know the current date? The answer lies in the special `EMail()` constructor discussed in more detail earlier. A constructor such as this one, which takes no parameters, is called the default constructor. Storing the current date and time in the date attribute is the only responsibility of the `EMail()` default constructor.

Instance and Class Variables and Methods

The `FROM`, `TO`, `DATE`, `SUBJECT`, and `MESSAGE` attributes are associated with a particular object. They are said to be instance variables, because an object is an instance of the class. In the example, a variable called `anEMailObject` refers to an instance of the class `EMail`. However, even though `main()` is declared as a method of `EMail`, it is running before the `EMail` object is created!

The solution lies in the definition of the `main()` method. One of the modifiers for this method is `static`. When a method or variable is declared as `static`, it indicates to the compiler that the member belongs to the class rather than the instance. A class member has no allegiance to any particular object; it belongs only to the class. Instance variables and methods are accessed by referring to an object, but class variables and methods are accessed by referring to a class. For example, in order to keep track of the number of instances of a class, a static counter could be added to the class:

```
public class TestCounter {
    public static void main( String[] args ) {

        // Create 3 instances of InstanceCounter.
        InstanceCounter firstInstance = new InstanceCounter();
        InstanceCounter secondInstance = new InstanceCounter();
        InstanceCounter thirdInstance = new InstanceCounter();
            System.out.println(
            "Number of instances: " + InstanceCounter.getNumberOfInstances() );
    }
}
public class InstanceCounter {
    public InstanceCounter() {
            numberOfInstances++;
        }
    public static int getNumberOfInstances() {
            return numberOfInstances;
        }
    private static int numberOfInstances;
}
```

This code outputs the following line:

```
Number of instances: 3
```

Notice that there are two static members of `InstanceCounter`—the `getNumberOfInstances()` method, and the `numberOfInstances` variable. Because it is a class method, the method must be called by referring to the `InstanceCounter` class. Every time a new `InstanceCounter` object is created, the `numberOfInstances` variable is incremented by one. Because `numberOfInstances` is part of the class, its value is the same for all objects of type `InstanceCounter`. In this code, three instances are created; therefore, the method `numberOfInstances()` returns the integer 3.

The `EMail` class uses static methods in two different places. The default constructor of `EMail` calls a static method of calendar, `getDate()`, in order to get a new `Calendar` object, and the `EMail` class includes a `main()` method, which is also static.

Packages

Where did the `Calendar` class used in the `EMail` class come from? At the top of the file, the line `import java.util.Calendar` tells Java where to look for the `Calendar` class. It's not a class that you wrote; `Calendar` comes as part of the Java API. A separate package contains this class. A package in Java has a larger scope than a class. Although it is similar to a class, because it defines a scope, rather than containing member methods, a package contains member classes. `Calendar` belongs to a package by the name of `java.util`, which contains utility classes—surprise!

> **NOTE**
>
> Java specifies a naming convention that prevents your package names from accidentally being named the same name as other packages. When naming a package, use your domain name backwards and capitalize the COM. For instance, a package developed by a company with ownership of the domain name MacDonalds would use the package name COM.MacDonalds, which may be divided into any number of subpackages.

Overloading Constructors

It is possible to write constructors that do entirely different things, yet have the same names. This practice is referred to as *overloading*.

Instead of creating an instance of the EMail class that just initializes the date attribute with the current date and time, it would be possible to define another constructor that would create an instance of the EMail class and initialize the from, to, subject, and body. The constructor would have to take parameters as in set methods of the class. The new EMail() constructor would look like this:

```
public class EMail{
    ...
    public EMail( ) {
        date = Calendar.getDateTimeInstance( FULL,LONG );
    }
    public EMail( String aMessage ) {
        date = Calendar.getDateTimeInstance( FULL,LONG );
        message = aMessage;
        }
    ...
}
```

Notice that the two constructors have the same name. The compiler can differentiate between the two constructors based on the parameters that are passed to the constructor. The number, type, and order of the parameters make up a unique signature for the constructor. The default constructor takes no parameters, so in order to create a default instance of the EMail object, use the following syntax:

```
EMail anEMailObject = new EMail();
```

In order to create a new EMail object and specify a body for the EMail simultaneously, create a new instance and pass a String to the method as the message body:

```
EMail anEMailObject = new EMail(
        "Dear Bill," +
        "\nConcerning the software necessary for every computer... " );
anEMailObject.setSender( "bill@ms.org" );
anEMailObject.setRecipient( "bill@whitehouse.com" );
anEMailObject.setSubject( "A Computer in Every House!" );
```

When the second object is created, Java knows to use the constructor that takes a `String` parameter. The other attributes may be set later using the set methods.

> **NOTE**
>
> The combination of method name, number, type, and order of parameters make up a method's *signature*. The return type does not contribute to this signature. Therefore, writing two methods with the same name and the same number, type, and order of parameters but differing return types will result in a compilation error.

In Java, these two constructors can be written in a more concise form by using the `this` keyword.

The `this` Keyword

The `this` keyword refers to the current object when used within a method. When used within a constructor, it can be used as the first item in the constructor to call a different constructor defined within the class. For instance, it could be used in the default constructor of the `EMail` class to call the constructor that takes a body `String`:

```java
public class EMail{
    ...
    public EMail( ) {
        this( null );
    }
    public EMail( String aBody) {
        date = Calendar.getDate();
        body = aBody;
    }
    ...
}
```

In the preceding code, the default constructor of `EMail` calls the second constructor and sends a `null` value, which will be assigned to the body attribute. Rather than writing the line `date = Calender.getDateTimeInstance( FULL,LONG )` within each of the two constructors, the default constructor just calls the second constructor and accomplishes the same thing with less redundancy.

Methods can be overloaded in a similar way. The method `println()` of `System.out.println()` is a good example of this. It's possible to send any type to this method, and the method will know how to print it. `println()` is capable of doing this, because it has a method for every possible type. When an integer is passed in, the `println()` method of the `out` object, which handles integers, is called:

```java
public void println( int anInteger ) { ... }
```

When an object is passed to the `println()` method, the out object knows to call the method that takes an object type:

```
public void println( Object o ) { ... }
```

The `println()` method is able to print the object by calling its `toString()` method. If a `toString()` method is not defined within the object that is passed in, Object's `toString()` method is called. Everything is a subclass of the `Object` class. The next section discusses inheritance and the `Object` class in more detail.

Inheritance and Overriding Methods

Most object-oriented languages—Java included—implement the concept of *inheritance*. Use inheritance to express the relationship between classes when one of those classes is a special kind of the other class.

A 2D shape and a square or an animal and an aardvark are sets of general things and more specific types of those general things. A checking account is a special type of account. In an inheritance relationship, one class is defined as a subclass, and the other class is defined as the superclass. The keyword `extends` expresses this relationship. In these examples, a 2D shape is the superclass of a square, and a square is its subclass. An aardvark is a subclass of animal, and a checking account is a subclass of an account.

In the simple `EMail` example, there is no `extends` keyword, so you would probably guess that no is inheritance used. However, an inheritance relationship does exist, because of the design of the Java language.

The Java language includes the concept of a *metaclass*, which is implicitly the superclass of all Java objects. The name of this metaclass is, appropriately enough, `Object`. So, `EMail` subclasses `Object` implicitly even though the `extends` keyword was never typed.

Because `EMail` extends `Object`, the `toString()` method of `EMail` overrides Object's `toString()` method. It makes sense to do this, because the `EMail` class needs to have a certain format when converted to a `String` of characters. Specifically, it should look like an e-mail message. The `toString()` method of Object looks something like this:

```
public class Object {
    ...
    public String toString() {
      return getClass().getName() +
            "@" + Integer.toHexString(hashCode());
    }
    ...
}
```

There are some unfamiliar methods in this code, but the method essentially creates a generic string representation of the `Object`, which looks something like this when printed out:

EMail@23412f

By overriding toString() in the EMail subclass of Object, a formatted e-mail message is output when an EMail object is printed.

Overriding is not the same thing as the concept of overloading methods and constructors discussed in the last section. Overloaded methods are methods with different signatures in the same class, whereas overridden methods are methods with the same signature within two classes in an inheritance tree.

Abstract Methods and Interfaces

Object-oriented languages include the concept of classes that cannot be represented as objects. Classes of this type represent concepts that are too abstract to represent in terms of concrete objects. Some of the examples from the last section are sufficiently abstract to fall into this category. For instance, what is a 2D shape? How is a 2D shape represented graphically? It's not, because the concept is too abstract. What about an animal? How is an animal represented? It's not. An animal is also too abstract a concept to represent as a concrete item. In the language, Java provides support for this powerful concept. Classes from which objects cannot be created are called *abstract classes*. At least one method of such a class must be an abstract method. Some classes have all abstract methods, and these are not referred to as classes, but as interfaces in Java.

Abstract Classes and Abstract Methods

If a class is abstract, at least one of its methods is defined as abstract. An abstract class cannot be instantiated.

Consider an Animal class mentioned earlier. An Animal class might define a speed attribute and a speak() method. The method speak() would have to be defined as abstract within the Animal class. What kind of sound does an animal make when it speaks? It's impossible to say unless the question is asked about a specific animal.

You could create a LeggedAnimal and declare it as a subclass of the Animal class. The LeggedAnimal class may define another attribute that represents the number of legs belonging to an animal, but it still cannot implement the speak() method. Thus, the Animal class is made up of a combination of concrete and abstract methods. Because it has a single abstract method, it is still an abstract class, which cannot be instantiated:

```
public class LeggedAnimal extends Animal {
    public LeggedAnimal() {
}
    public LeggedAnimal( int legs ) {
        numberOfLegs = legs;
}
public abstract void speak();
public void setNumberOfLegs( int legs ) {
    numberOfLegs = legs;
}
public int getNumberOfLegs( ) {
    return numberOfLegs;
```

```
}
protected int numberOfLegs;
}
```

The concrete methods of the `LeggedAnimal` class include `setNumberOfLegs()` and `getNumberOfLegs()`. Because you don't know how a legged animal speaks, it's impossible to implement the `speak()` method.

Notice that there are no curly braces after the `speak()` method—just a semicolon. This method probably should not be implemented for `LeggedAnimal`, because not all animals with legs make the same sounds. As a consequence, this class is an abstract class and cannot be instantiated.

```
LeggedAnimal animal = new LeggedAnimal(); // Not allowed!
```

On the other hand, a `Dog` class could implement a method called `speak()` and be correct, because dogs make a barking sound.

A class such as `Dog` can implement the abstract method of `LeggedAnimal`, which means that the `Dog` class is concrete and can be instantiated.

```
public class Dog extends LeggedAnimal {
    // Number of meters moved in a second.
    public Dog() {
        super( 4 );
    }
    public Dog( String aName ) {
        super( 4 );
        name = aName;
    }
    public void speak() {
        bark.play();
    }
    public setVoice( AudioClip aBark ) {
        bark = aBark;
    }
    private AudioClip bark;
}
```

Because your dog, Spot, has a certain number of legs and makes a barking sound, it will be possible to create an object out of him and play with him:

```
Dog spot = new Dog( "Spot" );
spot.speak();
spot.setNumberOfLegs( 3 );
System.out.println( "See " + spot.getName() +
    "running on " + spot.getNumberOfLegs() " legs." );
```

An object of type `Dog` can be instantiated, because `Dog` overrides the abstract `speak()` method from the `LeggedAnimal` class. If `Dog` could not override this method, it would still be an abstract class.

Notice that `Dog` also inherited attributes from the `LeggedAnimal` class. In particular, he inherited the `numberOfLegs` variable. Unfortunately, `Spot` does not have as many legs as most other dogs. He only has three. The preceding program would print the following message:

```
See Spot running on 3 legs.
```

Interfaces and Implementation

Java includes a Shape interface with all abstract methods. Because a Shape has an abstract method, it cannot be instantiated like an EMail object or a Dog object:

```
Shape s = new Shape()    // Not possible!
```

In fact, all the methods of Shape are abstract. In the Java language, when a class has all abstract methods, it is declared to be an *interface*. Here is the entire definition of the Shape interface:

```
public interface Shape {
        public Rectangle getBounds();
}
```

The idea is that anything that is a shape—a polygon of some sort—should be able to provide information about what size box it can fit. Thus any class that implements the Shape interface must be able to calculate its bounding rectangle and return it. Think about how this differs from the inheritance example earlier. In the inheritance example, Dog inherited implementation from the superclass. In other words, because it was possible to set and get the number of legs a legged animal possessed, it was possible to do that with a Dog also. This is not the case for a class that implements an interface. There is an advantage in this, because any object can implement the Shape interface. Only Animals can implement the speak() method from the inheritance example.

If you wrote a Square class, and it implemented the Shape interface, it would look something like this:

```
public class Square implements Shape {
    public Square( int aLength ) {
        x = 0;
        y = 0;
        length = aLength;
    }
    public Rectangle getBounds( ) {
        return new Rectangle( x,y,length,length );
    }
    private int x;
    private int y;
    private int length;
}
```

Because the Square class provides an implementation of the Shape interface, it can be instantiated as normal:

```
Square s = new Square( 5 );
System.out.println( s.getBounds() );
```

This would print a String representation of the Rectangle object returned by the getBounds() method:

```
java.awt.Rectangle[x=0,y=0,width=5,height=5]
```

If you really wanted to create a Square class, you would probably use the Rectangle class as a superclass. A square is a special sort of rectangle, right?

```
public class Square extends Rectangle {
    public Square( int aLength ) {
        super( 0,0,aLength,aLength );
    }
}
```

If you run the following code again, the output will be the same, because `Rectangle` implements the `Shape` interface as was done in the original `Square` class:

```
Square s = new Square( 5 );
System.out.println( s.getBounds() );

java.awt.Rectangle[x=0,y=0,width=5,height=5]
```

The keyword `super` is an unfamiliar one. It refers to the immediate superclass of the `Square` class. In fact, every time a constructor is written, as in your `EMail` class, there is an implicit call to the superclass. A class always has a superclass, because of the `Object` metaclass. So, the `EMail` constructor could also be written in this way:

```
public class EMail {
    —
    public EMail() {
        super();
        date = Calendar.getDateTimeInstance( FULL,LONG )
    }
    —
}
```

The `Square` class now has access to all protected variables and methods of the `Rectangle` class. It has inherited both attributes and behavior from the `Rectangle` class.

Access Modifiers

Up to this point in the chapter, only three types of access have been used, but there are four different levels of access in Java. The modifiers are listed following from most visible to least visible.

- ■ `public`   All classes have access to public attributes and behavior.
- ■ `default`   Only classes within the package have access to default attributes and behavior.
- ■ `protected`   Only classes within the same package or classes from different packages have access to protected attributes and behavior.
- ■ `private`   Private attributes and behavior are only accessible within a single class.

The modifiers in the preceding list are listed from most public to most private.

Streams, Sockets, and Sending the E-Mail Message

Because the EMail class now encapsulates the attributes and behavior of an e-mail message, half of the requirements have been met. The paragraph of requirements for the application also stipulated that there must be some means of sending the message using the SMTP protocol.

Writing the code to do this is more simple than you might guess, and along the way, you will encounter Java classes that do Java input and output, and exception handling. The java.io classes and exception handling will be discussed only briefly.

Communicating with an SMTP Server

The protocol an e-mail client uses to communicate with an e-mail server is called SMTP. Like the e-mail format, this protocol is specified in an Internet RFC. The server is called an SMTP server. You could write an SMTP client class that knows everything about the SMTP protocol and pass it an EMail object. An EMail object already knows how to format the message to be sent to the server.

SMTPClient is a good descriptive name for the class. All you need to know about the protocol itself is what to say to the SMTP server in order for it to do its job, and what kind of information it might return. Your goal is really just to send a simple e-mail message. The SMTPClient will not even process responses from the server. Here is an example session between an SMTP client and an SMTP server:

```
HELO ms.org
MAIL FROM:bill@ms.org
RCPT TO:bill@whitehouse.com
DATA
From: bill@ms.org
To: bill@whitehouse.com
Subject: What are we going to do today?
Date: Thursday, September 10, 1997 10:37:02 PM PDT
Dear Bill, blah, blah, blah, Sincerely, Bill.
..
QUIT
```

Everything after DATA should look familiar. It will be necessary to do some networking in order to get this class to do what it needs to do, but once the connection is made, it won't be too much harder than printing the e-mail message to the console by means of the System.out.println() call.

The next step is to write the SMTPClient class to handle this protocol. Of course, the client will have to make a connection to an SMTP server. Luckily these are fairly easy to come by. There might already be one you can use from your Internet service provider. There is also some shareware available for Windows, but you will have to make sure you are connected to the Internet in some fashion if you expect other people to receive the mail.

SMTPClient connects, sends a message, and disconnects, so it might make sense to create a class that has a method capable of sending an EMail object. Because SMTPClient must know where to connect, the host name to connect to should be passed in by the constructor. Here is the code:

```java
public class SMTPClient {

    /**
     * Constructs an instance of the SMTPClient class. This method requests
     * the name of a host running a sendmail server on port 25.
     *
     * @param smtpServerHost The host name of the SMTP server.
     */

    public SMTPClient( String smtpServerHost ) {
        server = smtpServerHost;
    }

    /**
     * Makes a connection to the SMTP server and sends the message
     * contained by the EMail object.
     *
     * @param anEMailMessage The name of the EMail object to be sent.
     */

    public void send( EMail anEMailMessage ) {
        anEMail = anEMailMessage;
        String sender = anEMail.getSenderAddress();

        // Get the host name from the sender's EMail address.
        client = sender.substring(
            sender.indexOf( "@" ) + 1,sender.length() );

        // Send the message using private utility methods.
        sendMessage( anEMail.toString() );
    }

    // Makes a connection, initiates a dialog with the server,
    // sends the message, ends the dialog, and closes the socket.

    private void sendMessage( String message ) {
        connect();
        initiate();
        output.print( message );
        output.flush();
        end();
        disconnect();
    }

    // Connects to the SMTP server.
    private void connect() {

        try {

            // Connect to the sendmail port 25 on the host
            Socket socket = new Socket( server,25 );
```

```java
        // Get the streams.
        input = new BufferedReader( new InputStreamReader(
            socket.getInputStream() ) );
        output = new PrintWriter(
            new BufferedWriter(
                new  OutputStreamWriter(
                    socket.getOutputStream() ) ));

    } catch( IOException e ) {
        System.out.println(
            "Error connecting to the SMTP server: " + server );
        e.printStackTrace();
    }
}

// Closes the socket.
private void disconnect() {

    // Close the connection
    try {
        input.close();
        output.close();
    } catch( IOException e ) {
        System.out.println(
            "Error closing connection to the SMTP server: " + server );
        e.printStackTrace();
    }

}

// Initiates the dialog with the SMTP Server
private void initiate() {
    String response = null;

    try {
        output.print( "HELO " + client + "\r\n" );
        output.print(
            "MAIL FROM:" + anEMail.getSenderAddress() + "\r\n" );
        output.print(
            "RCPT TO:" + anEMail.getRecipientAddress() + "\r\n" );
        output.print( "DATA\r\n" );
        output.flush();
        response = input.readLine();
    } catch( IOException e ) {
        System.out.println(
            "Error initializing connection to the SMTP server: "
                + server );
        System.out.println( "Error from server: " + response );
        e.printStackTrace();
    }
}

// Ends the dialog with the SMTP Server
private void end() {
    String response = null;

    try {
        output.print( "\r\n.\r\n" );
        output.print( "QUIT\r\n" );
```

```
            output.flush();
            response = input.readLine();
        } catch( IOException e ) {
            System.out.println(
                "Error disconnecting from the SMTP server: " + server );
            System.out.println( "Error from server: " + response );
            e.printStackTrace();
        }
    }


    // Instance variables of SMTPClient.
    private BufferedReader input;
    private PrintWriter output;
    private EMail anEMail;
    private String server;
    private String client;

}
```

The SMTPClient class uses a number of private utility methods to implement the communication protocol. The connection() method connects to the SMTP server on the host running on port 25. SMTP servers listen for connections on port 25 by convention. The PORT constant defines this port number. Java does not allow global constants to be defined because everything must be defined within a class. The keywords static and final make PORT a constant. The static modifier indicates that one PORT variable exists for all instances of a class. The final keyword ensures that the value of PORT can never be modified. The initiate() method starts the dialog between SMTPClient and the SMTP server by sending the first part of the protocol beginning with HELO and ending with DATA. The DATA message signals to the SMTP server that the next data up to the <CRLF>.<CRLF> mark is the message header and body. The EMail class takes care of all this formatting within its toString() method, so you just print the output of this method to the socket. Finally, the dialog is ended in the end() command with the QUIT message, and the socket is closed in the disconnect() method. The final keyword means that it cannot be changed.

Several new classes and concepts are used in this class: Socket, PrintWriter, and BufferedWriter.

Sockets

The socket makes a TCP/IP connection to a server and specifies the host machine to connect to. In the JMAIL application, the host can be any machine with an SMTP server. In the next chapter, the SMTPClient class will be used within an applet context, which means that it will only be able to connect back to the host that it came from. From the JMAIL application, mail can be sent to any host.

Streams

PrintWriter and BufferWriter turn this socket into something SMTPClient can print to just as System.out.println() was used to print an e-mail message. An InputStream is returned from the Socket. This could be used to communicate with the server directly, but it is less convenient than using `PrintWriter`, because `PrintWriter` contains methods that take more complex information than just bytes. The out object of `System.out.println()` is a `PrintWriter` object. `BufferWriter` just makes sure that information sent to `PrintWriter` is sent out in the most efficient way.

Now you have all the pieces needed to write the JMAIL application:

```java
import java.io.*;

/**
 * JMail reads an e-mail message from the
 * command line, and sends it to the host specified below.
 *
 * @see EMail
 * @see SMTPClient
 * @author Corey Klaasmeyer
 */
public class JMail {

    // The main method.
    public static void main( String[] args ) {

        DataInputStream input = null;
        String sender = null;
        String recipient = null;
        String subject = null;
        String server = null;
        String message = "";
        String line = "";

        try {
            input = new DataInputStream( System.in );

            // Read in the email message from the command line
            System.out.println( "Enter the host of the SMTP Server: ";
            System.out.flush();
            server = input.readLine();
            System.out.println( "Enter the sender's e-mail address: " );
            System.out.flush();
            sender = input.readLine();
            System.out.println(
                "Enter the recipients's e-mail address: " );
            System.out.flush();
            recipient = input.readLine();;
            System.out.println( "Enter the subject: " );
            System.out.flush();
            subject = input.readLine();
            System.out.println(
                "Enter the message and type a '.'" +
                "on a separate line when done: " );
            System.out.flush();
            while( !( line = input.readLine() ).equals( "." ) )
                message += line + "\n";

        } catch( IOException e ) {
            System.out.println(
                "Error reading input in JMail application." );
```

```
            e.printStackTrace();
        }

        // Store the message in an EMail object.
        EMail anEMailObject = new EMail();
        anEMailObject.setSenderAddress( sender );
        anEMailObject.setRecipientAddress( recipient );
        anEMailObject.setSubject( subject );
        anEMailObject.setMessage( message );
        System.out.println( anEMailObject );

// Send the message.
SMTPClient smtpClient = new SMTPClient( server );
smtpClient.send( anEMailObject );
    }

}
```

When the new instance of SMTPClient is constructed, the host passed in from the command line is used as the host address. This means there must be an SMTP server running on that host, and the computer running JMAIL must be connected to the Internet in some way for the e-mail message to be successfully sent. If you have a TCP/IP stack installed on your machine, and an SMTP server running on port 25, the local loopback host can be specified: 127.0.0.1. The message will then be sent to the SMTP server running locally. This is enough information for SMTPClient to make a connection to the SMTP server when sendMail() is called.

The JMAIL application is very short. All the complexity is hidden in the EMail and SMTPClient classes. That's the power of object-oriented programming at work.

Summary

By designing classes and objects and taking advantage of the networking pieces of the Java API, it is a relatively simple exercise to build e-mail functionality into an application. Java's object-oriented design makes it possible to create an EMail and SMTPClient class on your own. Because these classes were designed in a flexible way, they can easily be used in other Java programs, which may be applets, servlets, or applications.

All the complicated functionality that goes on behind the scenes in the SMTPClient is hidden from the programmer. Everything necessary to communicate with an SMTP server, including Sockets and an implementation of the SMTP protocol, is encapsulated within the class. Existing networking and input/output classes take care of all the pesky details. Instead of encapsulating protocols and Sockets as is done in the case of the SMTPClient, the EMail class stores an e-mail message and formats it for output within the toString() method. The toString() method of EMail overrides the toString() method of Object. The Object class is the superclass of all Java objects.

Along the way, you got a crash course in classes, objects, constructors, inheritance, interfaces, scope, sockets, streams, and applications within the context of a useful Java application. You created three reusable objects for the JMAIL application, two of which will be put to work in

Chapter 21, "Introduction to Applet Programming." In Chapter 29, "Server-Independent Technologies—The Java Servlet API," instead of writing an applet that sends e-mail using sockets, you'll write a servlet. The servlet will process an HTML form on the server side and send the e-mail using the `SMTPClient` class.

Introduction to Applet Programming

by Corey Klaasmeyer

IN THIS CHAPTER

CHAPTER 21

Java applets are programs written in Java, loaded as part of a Web page, and run within a browser or some other program that provides a context for the applet. Sun's AppletViewer provides a context in which the applet can run, but it is not really a browser. The applet can access a number of resources by accessing URLs and has access to a limited amount of context information, such as the URL of the document containing the applet.

Applet Security

It seems like a new story about hostile applets appears every day. In reality, they enjoy very little freedom while running in most browsers. However, Java applets represent an alluring target for hackers because of the challenge. Java was designed from the beginning with security in mind. Applets, by default, run in a sandbox with very little, if any, access to system resources. This used to be the only option for an applet, but browser security policies with regard to applets are constantly evolving. In some of the more recent versions of browsers such as Internet Explorer 4.0 and Netscape Communicator, it is possible to run trusted applets with different types of access to system resources.

Writing Applets

Instead of writing a program that has a `main()` method as in the case of an application, applets are any class that subclasses the Applet class and override some of its methods. The `HelloWorld` class from this chapter is an applet, because it subclasses the Applet class.

A Simple Applet

You wrote a `HelloWorld` application in the previous chapter. In this chapter, you write a `HelloWorld` applet:

```
public class HelloWorld extends Applet {
    public void paint( Graphics g ) {
        g.drawString( "Hello World!",10,10 );
    }
}
```

Notice the two extra words at the end of the `HelloWorld` class declaration. The words, `extends Applet`, declare the `HelloWorld` class a subclass of `Applet`. The `paint()` method overrides the `paint()` method of the superclass `Applet`. When the Web page containing `HelloWorld` is loaded in a browser, this `paint()` method is called, and the words `"Hello World!"` are painted to the applet window.

The <APPLET> Tag and the <OBJECT> Tag

The <APPLET> tag defines the size of this window:

```
<APPLET CODE="HelloWorld.class" WIDTH="200" HEIGHT="20" >
</APPLET>
```

The WIDTH parameter defines the horizontal size of the applet window in pixels. The HEIGHT parameter defines the size of the applet vertically. The CODE parameter specifies which Java class file should be loaded by the browser. All three of these parameters must be present in order for the browser to successfully load the applet. The CODE attribute may be replaced by the OBJECT attribute described later. It looks in the directory from which the HTML file was loaded.

You can run the HelloWorld applet by using the AppletViewer utility, which comes with the JDK. If you are using the JDK 1.1, it is probably necessary to use the AppletViewer, because only Sun's browser, HotJava, currently runs Java compiled under 1.1. HelloWorld can also be run in a browser with no problem, as long as you have compiled it in 1.02, or you happen to have a browser that supports the JDK 1.1 version.

NOTE

No browsers run the JDK1.1 as this goes to print. The only Web browser that supports the full range of features implemented in the new version of the JDK is Sun's HotJava browser. Netscape Communicator 4.x supports some features of the JDK1.1. Version 4.03 supports everything but the new event delegation model, which is used in this chapter.

The following lists all the <APPLET> tag's possible attributes:

- WIDTH and HEIGHT. The width is the horizontal size of the applet in pixels. The height is the vertical size of the applet in pixels.

- CODE. The name of the class file to be loaded. The browser tries to load the class file by looking in the same directory as the HTML file.

- CODEBASE. If the applet class file is located in some other directory, the browser looks for the path of the class file relative to the URL of the HTML file.

- ARCHIVE. Zipped or jarred archives of all the classes necessary to run an applet are specified via this attribute. Normally used when an applet is loaded. All of the necessary classes are loaded one by one. Because opening and closing a connection back to the server adds a lot of overhead, download times suffer. Netscape Navigator version 3.x loads classes from a zipped archive with no compression. In order to take advantage of this feature, all the packages and classes used by the applet must be placed in an archive. The ARCHIVE attribute is set to the name of this ZIP file. Later versions of the Netscape browser, such as Communicator, allow multiple jar files to be specified. *Jar files* are compressed archives. This is also the packaging scheme for JavaBeans. In order to store an applet in a CAB file for use with Internet Explorer, a <PARAM> tag must be included within the <APPLET> tag. The <PARAM> tag is discussed later in this chapter.

> **TIP**
>
> When using ZIP files with Netscape Navigator 3.x make sure the `.zip` extension is lowercase; otherwise, the browser will not load the applet classes properly.

- OBJECT. The OBJECT attribute contains a reference to a serialized applet object. The browser loads the serialized applet and calls its `start()` method rather than its `init()` method.

- ALT. As with `<IMG>` tags, an alternate textual content defined by the ALT attribute if the browser cannot run Java for some reason.

- NAME. If a name is specified for this applet, other applets on the same page may communicate with this applet by referring to its name.

- ALIGN. Align defines how the applet should be aligned with respect to other elements in the Web page.

- VSPACE and HSPACE. If the applet needs space around its window within the Web page, the vertical and horizontal spacing in pixels can be specified using these two attributes.

The `<OBJECT>` tag replaces `<APPLET>` in HTML 4.0. This tag is intended to replace `<IMG>`, `<DYNSRC>`, and `<EMBED>`. This tag is used to insert media types and code. Data can be specified by a URL, inline, or by a set of properties.

In this example, the CLASSID attribute is used to specify the name of the Java code to execute:

```
<OBJECT CLASSID="java:HelloWorld.start" HEIGHT=100 WIDTH=100>
</OBJECT>
```

Notice that the `.class` extension is no longer specified here.

In the next example, the new `<OBJECT>` tag CODEBASE is used to specify where the browser should look for the Java code. CODETYPE specifies the mime type of the object.

```
<OBJECT CODETYPE="application/java-vm" CODEBASE="http://host/somepath/"
➥CLASSID="java:program.start" HEIGHT=100 WIDTH=100></OBJECT>
```

The `<PARAM>` Tag

`<PARAM>` tags can be placed within the `<APPLET>` or the new `<OBJECT>` tag to send additional information to the applet. For instance, you could change your HelloWorld program to Salutation and specify the salutation in the HTML file. The modified code would use the `getParameter()` method of applet in order to retrieve the message from the Web page:

```
public class Salutation extends Applet {
    public void init() {
        salutation = getParameter( "salutation" );
    }
    public void paint( Graphics g ) {
        g.drawString( salutation,10,10 );
```

```
    }
    private String salutation;
}
```

The `Salutation` class gets its message from the browser's HTML file. In order to have the Salutation applet display `Greetings and Salutations`, add it as a parameter within the `<APPLET>` tag:

```
<APPLET CODE="Salutation.class" WIDTH="200" HEIGHT="20">
    If you are reading this, your browser does not
➥support Java or Java is not currently
    enabled in your browser preferences.
    <PARAM NAME="salutation" VALUE="Greetings and Salutations"></PARAM>
</APPLET>
```

When this HTML page is loaded into a browser, the browser displays the message `Greetings and Salutations`. Each `<PARAM>` tag has a name and value, and the `<APPLET>` tag can contain any number of parameters with its body.

If text is added to the `<APPLET>`, that tag appears in any browser that does not support Java or any browser that has Java disabled in preferences.

Applet Methods

The `Applet` class defines a number of methods overridden in subclasses. Up to this point in the chapter, the example code has overridden two methods from applet—`init()` and `paint()`. These two methods are probably the most commonly overridden methods, but there are four other methods which are sometimes also overridden. The `init()` method is called once when an applet is loaded into a browser. The `paint()` method is called whenever the applet needs to repaint something on the screen. A complete list of the applet methods that can be overridden follows:

- ■ `init()`. This method is called after the Web page containing an applet is loaded into a browser. The `init()` method is not called on an applet loaded as a serialized applet. Serialized applets are loaded using the `OBJECT` attribute rather than the `CODE` attribute.

- ■ `start()`. This method is called every time the user comes back to the Web page containing the applet. This method should be overridden if the applet uses resources released in the `stop()` method when the user leaves the applet's HTML page. Some things that might need to be re-initialized in this method include `Socket` and `Thread`. If your applet implements the `Runnable` interface, it can be multi-threaded. The `start()` method should start the thread for the first time, and every time the user returns to the applet's Web page.

- ■ `stop()`. This method is called every time the user leaves the Web page containing the applet. This method should be overridden to release any resources that are held and stop any running threads.

NOTE

Unfortunately, the `Applet` class defines the two methods `start()` and `stop()` with the same name as those found in the `Thread` class. These `start()` and `stop()` methods in the `Applet` class do not start and stop the applet's thread.

- `paint()`. This method is called any time the applet's `repaint()` method is called. `paint()` takes a `Graphics` context as its parameter. The `Graphics` context belongs to the applet's panel on the Web page. Anything drawn within this graphics object is visible within the applet's panel on the Web page.

- `update()`. This method is called every time the applet is repainted. By default, it erases the entire screen, which often makes the screen flicker during repaints. Double buffering can remedy this problem.

- `getAppletInfo()`. The `getAppletInfo()` method is usually called by the browser when information about the applet is requested by the user. Usually the returned information indicates the applet's version number, author, and date of creation.

- `getParameterInfo()`. This method is called to find out what kind of parameters the applet can handle. This should be overridden by applets that make use of parameters specified in the HTML. It returns a multi-dimensional array of `Strings`.

TIP

By default, the `update()` method erases the entire applet every time it receives a `repaint()` call. This causes flickering. By overriding the `update()` method and calling `paint()` within the overridden method, double buffering can eliminate the flicker associated with erasing and redrawing directly on-screen. This is accomplished by doing the erasing and redrawing off-screen, invisible to the user.

Resources Available to Applets

A number of resources are available to applets. An applet can get audio clips, images, and information about the URL where the HTML document it is contained within was loaded from.

The methods that provide access to resources are listed:

- `AudioClip getAudioClip()`. The `getAudioClip()` method can be used to load an audio clip from a URL.

- `Image getImage()`. The `getImage()` method is commonly used to load images from an URL.

- `void play( URL url )`. The `play()` method plays a loaded audio clip. It must be an `.au` file.

Methods that provide access to information about an applet and its context are listed:

- `URL getCodeBase()`. This method returns the URL from which the applet's class files were loaded.

- `URL getDocumentBase()`. This method returns the URL from which the applet's HTML document was loaded.

- `AppletContext getAppletContext()`. This method returns an object of type `AppletContext`. An `AppletContext` object is useful for loading and viewing Web pages.

- `showStatus( String message )`. This method displays the message parameter `String` in the browser's status bar. The `showStatus()` method must be invoked on an `AppletContext` object.

- `resize()`.This method resizes the applet's bounds. A `resize()` call is usually ignored by the browser, because HTML objects are not resized according to specification after they have been laid out.

Other Applet Class Functionality

Some of the applet methods listed are illustrated in this example. The `Dawg` class takes advantage of an applet's capability to display images and play sounds. The informational methods of applet—`getAppletInfo()` and `getParameterInfo()`—are also implemented.

```
import java.applet.*;
import java.awt.*;
import java.awt.event.*;

public class Dawg extends Applet implements ActionListener {

    // Get the images and audio files, create two buttons
    public void init() {
        setLayout( new BorderLayout() );

        // getDocumentBase() returns the URL of the HTML file
containing the applet
        dawg = getImage( getDocumentBase(),getParameter("image") );
        bark = getAudioClip( getDocumentBase(), getParameter("audio") );
        statusButton = new Button( "Status" );
        statusButton.addActionListener( this );
        add( "North",statusButton );
barkButton = new Button( "Bark" );
barkButton.addActionListener( this );
add( "North",barkButton );
imageCanvas = new Canvas();
imageCanvas.setSize( 150,150 );
add( "South", imageCanvas );
    }

    public void start() {
            bark.play();
    }
```

```
    // Paints an image in the imageCanvas
    public void paint( Graphics g ) {
      imageCanvas.getGraphics().drawImage( dawg,0,0,this );
    }

    // Information about what kind of
// parameters the applet expects
    public String[][] getParameterInfo() {
       return info;
    }

    // Information about the author of the applet
    public String getAppletInfo() {
       return "A dawg.";
       }

       // Handle button events, implement the ActionListener interface
       public void actionPerformed( ActionEvent e ) {
          Object source = e.getSource();
          if( source == barkButton ) {
             bark.play();
    } else if( source == statusButton ) {
       getAppletContext().showStatus( "Woof!" );
    }
}

    // Dawg attributes
    private Image dawg;
    private AudioClip bark;
    private Button statusButton;
    private Button barkButton;
    private Canvas imageCanvas;
    private static final String[][] info = {
            { "image", "url", "A Dawg." },
            { "audio", "bark", "A Dawg Bark." }
    };
}
```

The init() method of Dawg loads an image and audio file. A canvas is created on which to paint the image. Two buttons are created and the Dawg applet is added as a listener to both of the buttons. One button plays an audio file of a dog barking, while the other button writes the word Woof! to the browser's status window.

If the info option is selected from the menu in AppletViewer, a window pops up with the following information about the author of the applet and the type of parameters it expects:

```
A dawg.
image -- url -- A Dawg.
audio -- bark --  A Dawg Bark.
```

The HTML page contains the name of the image and audio file:

```
<HTML>
<BODY>
<APPLET CODE="Dawg.java" WIDTH=300 HEIGHT=200>
    NAME="audio" VALUE="bark.au"></PARAM >
    </APPLET>
```

Introduction to Applet Programming

CHAPTER 21

451

21

INTRODUCTION
TO APPLET
PROGRAMMING

```
</BODY>
</HTML>
```

Both of these values are included directly in the HTML within parameter tags.

Graphics and Double Buffering

Most programmers will, at one time or another, use the Graphics context to draw images on the screen—whether part of a GUI component or part of an application that must render images in a window. The paint() method takes a Graphics object as one of its parameters. In fact, the first applet in this chapter uses the paint() method to write a simple message to the screen. At some point, you probably need to do more than draw text to the screen. This section describes the functionality of the Graphics objects and how to prevent flicker when drawing by using double buffering.

Here is a list of some of the more commonly used methods of the Graphics class:

- ■ void drawString(String string, int x, int y) Draws a string to the screen at the x, y coordinates.

- ■ void clearRect(int x, int y, int width, int height) Clears a rectangle on the screen with its top-left corner located at x,y and the specified width and height.

- ■ void fillRect(int x, int y, int width, int height) Fills a rectangle on the screen with its top-left corner located at x,y and the specified width and height.

- ■ void drawRect(int x, int y, int width, int height) Draws a rectangle on the screen with its top-left corner located at x,y and the specified width and height.

- ■ void Graphics create() Creates a new graphics context. This is often used to create an off-screen space for drawing when implementing double buffering.

- ■ void dispose() Frees resources associated with a graphics context.

The following code draws a circle within the applet, which follows the pointer around the screen. When the Follower applet receives a mouse click within the boundary of the applet, the circle travels to that point. The applet uses double buffering to prevent flickering when the circle is erased and redrawn.

```
import java.awt.event.*;
import java.applet.*;
import java.awt.*;

public class Follower extends Applet implements MouseListener {

    public void init() {

    // Place the polygon in the middle of the screen
    dimension = getSize();
    x = dimension.width/2;
    y = dimension.height/2;

    // Create the offScreen image.
```

```java
        offScreenImage = createImage( dimension.width, dimension.height );
        offScreenGraphics = offScreenImage.getGraphics();

    // Size of the image.
    size = 5;

    // Register for mouse events.
    addMouseListener( this );

    }

    public void paint(Graphics g) {

        // Clear the screen
        offScreenGraphics.setColor( getBackground() );
        offScreenGraphics.fillRect( 0, 0, dimension.width, dimension.height );
        offScreenGraphics.setColor( Color.black );

     offScreenGraphics.drawOval( x,y,size,size );

        // Paint the image onto the screen
        g.drawImage( offScreenImage, 0, 0, null );

    }

    /**
     * Invoked when the mouse is pressed. Changes the polygon's shaped.
     *
     * @param event The MouseEvent.
     */

    public void mousePressed( MouseEvent event ) {
    int pointerX = event.getX();
    int pointerY = event.getY();

    // Move to the mouse
    while( x != pointerX || y != pointerY ) {
       if( x != pointerX )
          if( x < pointerX )
             x++;
          else
             x--;
          if( y != pointerY )
             if( y < pointerY )
                y++;
             else
                y--;
       paint( getGraphics() );
          try {
             Thread.currentThread().sleep( 10 );
          } catch( InterruptedException e ) { }
    }

    }

    /**
     * Invoked when the mouse is pressed and released.
     * Must be overridden although we don't use it.
     *
```

Introduction to Applet Programming

CHAPTER 21

453

21

INTRODUCTION
TO APPLET
PROGRAMMING

```
    * @param event The MouseEvent.
    */

    public void mouseClicked( MouseEvent event ) {}

    /**
    * Invoked when the mouse enters the applet.
    * Must be overridden although we don't use it.
    *
    * @param event The MouseEvent.
    */

    public void mouseEntered( MouseEvent event ) {}

    /**
    * Invoked when the mouse exits the applet.
    * Must be overridden although we don't use it.
    *
    * @param event The MouseEvent.
    */

    public void mouseExited( MouseEvent event ) {}

    /**
    * Invoked when the mouse is released. Must be overridden
➥ although we don't use it.
    *
    * @param event The MouseEvent.
    */

    public void mouseReleased( MouseEvent event ) {}

    private Image offScreenImage;
    private Graphics offScreenGraphics;
    private Dimension dimension;
    private int x;
    private int y;
    private int size;
}
```

This code introduces a number of new things, but the important thing to look at here are Graph-ics and Image objects involved in the double buffering. The buffering is implemented within the paint() method. The fillRect() method erases everything that has been drawn to the offScreenGraphics object by drawing over the image with the same color as the background color. The color is then set to black, so that images drawn to after that point will be visible. The drawOval() method draws an off-screen image of the circle at its new location. This image is then drawn directly over the contents of the visible screen. Because the erasing and drawing goes on off-screen, there is no noticeable flickering.

Here, you are trapping an event when the mouse button is pressed. When you click within the applet, the circle moves to the x,y position of the mouse click. This animation is handled in the mousePressed() method. In order to receive these types of events, the Follower applet had to declare itself as a MouseListener and register itself with the source of mouse events. Component, the superclass of Applet, is the source of mouse events in this case. Because the interface defines four methods for handling different types of mouse events, you had to implement all of them. Because you were able to add a pair of empty curly braces at the end of each of these methods, it wasn't that much work.

An EMail Applet

Because the EMail class from the previous chapter has been written and tested, why not create an applet that sends e-mail, so everyone can use it? Reuse, already! Your object-oriented approach is paying off. However, writing the Email applet requires a little more work. In order to write an applet, it is necessary to inherit some behavior from the Applet class and override some methods in order to make the applet work as an e-mail client.

Applet belongs to the package java.applet. The java.applet package is a set of classes that provide functionality for an applet. This package contains the Applet class. A line such as the following has to be added to the top of the source file:

```
import java.applet.applet;
```

Now you can get to work.

Applets must inherit from the Applet class in order to run in a browser. An applet inherits behavior from the Applet class, such as methods, which can be used to load and play images and audio files. The inheritance relationship between EMailApplet and Applet is expressed with the keyword extends. For the EMailApplet, the class is declared like this:

```
import java.applet.Applet;

public class EMailApplet extends Applet {
    //Member methods
    //Member variables
}
```

Because EMailApplet is defined as a "special kind" of applet, you can do anything an applet can do. In other words, the EMailApplet class acquires all the behavior of the inherited class. For example, an applet can paint itself on the screen using the paint() method, or it can initialize itself using the init() method. After you define what these methods do in your EMailApplet class, you have a custom applet. None of the methods of the class Applet have to be implemented in order to create an applet, but it won't be very interesting unless it paints something to the screen.

The process of defining what methods do when they are inherited from a superclass is called *overriding*. Technically, you are re-defining applet's methods, but in this case, in the methods of the Applet class they weren't actually instructed to do anything. There is no implementation defined with the Applet class for the init(), start(), stop(), and destroy() methods. For a more complete discussion of inheritance and overriding methods refer to the previous chapter.

Creating a User Interface Using the AWT

You first need to create some way for the user to write an e-mail. When this is done, the user interface (UI) for EMailApplet has been defined. In order to create the interface, EMailApplet uses classes from the Java API, which already does most of what EMailApplet's user interface needs to do.

Labels, TextField, TextArea, and Button

Luckily, it's not necessary to make the pieces of the EMailApplet's user interface from scratch— these classes already belong to the java.awt package: Label, TextField, and TextArea.

In order to use them, EMailApplet creates an instance of each of these classes and places them on the page. For instance, it's almost as easy to create a Label object as it is to create an EMail object. There is an additional twist to instantiating a Label object, because the Label must know what to display. This is done by passing a String to Label via its constructor:

```
Label subjectLabel = new Label( "Subject: " );
```

This displays the text "Subject:" somewhere within the applet. Here's more code from the EMailApplet class:

```
public EMailApplet extends applet {
    public void init() {
        senderLabel = new Label( "Sender: " );
        add( senderLabel );
        senderField = new TextField( 20 );
        add( senderField );
        recipientLabel = new Label( "Recipient: " );
        add( recipientLabel );
        recipientField = new TextField( 20 );
        add( recipientField );
        subjectLabel = new Label( "Subject: " );
        add( subjectLabel );
        subjectField = new TextField( 20 );
        add( subjectField );
        messageArea = new TextArea( 20,10 );
        clearButton = new Button( "Clear" );
        add( clearButton );
        submitButton = new Button( "Submit" );
        add( submitButton );
    }
    private Label senderLabel;
    private TextField senderField;
    private Label recipientLabel;
    private TextField recipientField;
    private Label subjectLabel;
    private TextField subjectField;
    private TextArea messageArea;
}
```

The init() method is the first method called when an applet begins running in a Web page. Because the user interface needs to be created before the applet can be used, this code should be added to the init() method.

The first line of the init() method shown in the previous code creates a Label object with the string "Sender: ". The second line in init() paints the "Sender: " string to the applet screen in the Web page. When EMailApplet is displayed for the first time, the applet automatically knows to draw this label within its boundary. An object of type TextField is created on the next line, and it is added to the screen as well. The Label to the left of this component indicates that the recipient address for the e-mail should be entered in this field.

Organizing Things on the Screen

It's not clear from the code how all these components will be arranged on the screen. There was no information in the init() method that explicitly told the applet where to draw the Label object in x, y coordinates. This lack of instruction is the result of that applet having a particular strategy it uses to draw interface components on the screen.

Java takes a different approach to laying out user interfaces than most other GUI toolkits out there. Most other windowing toolkits use absolute positioning or x, y coordinate positioning. With absolute positioning, the user interface component keeps track of its x/y coordinate position on the screen. Java designers decided that the burden of laying out the interface should be the responsibility of the container that holds user interface components. In your case, because it is a subclass of the Container class, the applet holds all the user interface components. The motivation for taking this approach was twofold. First, this approach is preferable in terms of object-oriented design. Second, Java runs on multiple platforms with multiple screen sizes and dot pitches. As a result, applets have enough layout flexibility to accommodate a variety of display screen environments. Some HTML elements, tables for instance, take a similar approach, allowing the table to resize to fit the browser window as it changes size. In other words, each table knows how to lay out its contents.

The applet's strategy for laying out its interface isn't explicitly coded in the EMailApplet example; FlowLayout, the default strategy, is used. The words on that page are positioning themselves on the screen as they are being entered. When a word does not fit on the current line, it is wrapped to the next line. In a nutshell, this describes the FlowLayout strategy. EMailApplet wraps its components as words are wrapped in a word processor. They can even be centered, left-justified, or right-justified.

FlowLayout is easy to use, but not very powerful. In most cases, a user interface needs to be designed so that designers have more control over how it is displayed, regardless of the window's size. In order to make the EMailApplet lay out correctly, it needs to be just the right size. Because the different layouts are not discussed at length here, a sufficient size is chosen.

Creating an HTML File and Running the Applet

The applet is ready to run at this point—but one piece of the puzzle is lacking. Because applets are intended to run in Web pages, you need to enter the code into a Web page.

Because this doesn't have to be integrated within a complex HTML page, it can just be added to a small test HTML page. The following HTML serves this purpose well:

```
<HTML>
<TITLE><HEAD>EMailApplet</HEAD></TITLE>
<BODY>
<APPLET code="EMailApplet.class" WIDTH=250 HEIGHT=350>
</APPLET>
</BODY>
</HTML >
```

Save this code in a file called test.html. After the EMailApplet has been compiled, it should be placed in the same directory as the test.html file; it can either be viewed through the browser or through an AppletViewer. AppletViewer creates a browser-like environment in which the applet can run.

Event Handling

Although the user interface has been created, the EMailApplet doesn't really do anything. It is possible to enter values into the input fields, but nothing very exciting happens. Event handling allows the applet to respond to user input and make something more exciting happen.

A user interface component, such as a TextField or Button, creates events whenever a user takes some significant action. When text is entered into a TextField component, nothing needs to be done, because this type of event is only significant to the text field itself. In other words, the text field consumes most keystroke events. The text entered into that text field is stored within the TextField object, until it is cleared or the object is destroyed. On the other hand, when the Submit button is selected, something needs to happen; the e-mail message must be sent.

There are a couple of ways the EMailApplet can know the Submit button has been selected. When the button is clicked, an action event is created. EMailApplet uses the least mysterious of the two options: It listens directly to the button for an ActionEvent by registering with that Button object. This approach is new to the JDK 1.1.x and is referred to as an *event delegation model*.

The other approach to event handling is a hierarchical event delivery mechanism similar to the JDK 1.0.x model. Hierarchical refers to the method of passing events from superclass to subclass. Because the EMailApplet subclasses, or inherits from, Applet, it can potentially receive all the events received within the applet screen. It is necessary to add another line to the init() method in order to enable EMailApplet to receive events that way:

```
enableEvents( ActionEvent.ACTION_EVENT);
```

This method call tells the superclass to send any events of ActionEvent type down EMailApplet. The source/listener event delegation model is more flexible, efficient, and simpler than the hierarchical delivery mechanism, so you do not use this model.

Before writing any code, you need to understand some of JDK 1.1's concepts. In the JDK 1.1, user interface components, such as the button used in this example, can create any number of events. The events are described by separate classes. For instance, the EMail class describes an EMail class's attributes and behavior, while an ActionEvent class describes an ActionEvent's attributes and behavior.

A button creates an `ActionEvent` that the `EMailApplet` must receive and react to. The mechanism that handles this process in the JDK 1.1 is based on sources and listeners, and it is the same event architecture used for JavaBeans. In fact, JavaBeans required the event-handling model to be redesigned in order to accommodate its component architecture. The source of the events this example is concerned with is the `submitButton` and the `clearButton`. If the `submitButton` is the source, then the `EMailApplet` is the listener. Somehow, the `submitButton` must be told that the `EMailApplet` is listening for events. This is accomplished by adding the `EMailApplet` as a listener to the `submitButton` by registering the applet via the `addActionListener()` method:

```
submitButton.addActionListener( theEMailApplet );
```

In this case, the button is contained by the `EMailApplet` and there is no variable referring to the `EMailApplet`. You can add `EMailApplet` as a listener without specifying a user-defined variable.

A special variable is used for just this reason—`this`. The `this` keyword refers to whatever object in which it is used. In your `EMailApplet`, it refers to the `EMailApplet`. That provides a neat way to add the applet as a listener to the `submitButton`:

```
submitButton.addActionListener( this );
```

There is one more concept you must be aware of in order to understand the new JDK 1.1 event-handling mechanism. The listeners for events must implement the appropriate interface. In Java, it is possible for a class to implement an interface by declaring that it is implementing the interface, and by implementing all the methods within that interface. For instance, in order to receive `ActionEvent`-type action events, the `ActionListener` interface must be implemented. You are already using another fundamental type of relationship between objects in the `EMailApplet` called inheritance. Implementation of an interface differs from inheritance of a superclass because the interface has no behavior. In other words, no implementation is inherited as in the last example when `EMailApplet` is inherited from `Applet`. When inheriting from `Applet` in `EMailApplet`, the behavior of the `Applet` class is available to `EMailApplet`. When implementing the `ActionListener` interface, there is no behavior. The methods of an interface are not defined at all! Instead of using curly braces to enclose code that makes the method do something, a method defined in an interface ends with a semicolon. The `ActionListener` interface looks like this:

```
public interface ActionListener {
    public void actionPerformed( ActionEvent e ); //
➥In a class, there would be curly braces and code here!
}
```

If an object behaves like an action listener, it implements the `ActionListener` interface, which means it has some code that makes `actionPerformed()` do something. Its definition has curly braces and code:

```
public class EMailApplet extends applet
implements ActionListener {
    public void actionPerformed( ActionEvent e ) {
```

```
            // Code which does something in response to an action.
      }
}
```

When a class implements another class, the special keyword `implement` has to be added to the class declaration. The preceding code defines `EMailApplet` both as a subclass of `Applet` and an implementation of `ActionListener` by adding four words: `extends Applet implements ActionListener`. This means that somewhere within `EMailApplet` there is a method called `actionPerformed()`, whose behavior is defined a certain way. The following code puts all these pieces together to create a functioning client:

```java
import java.applet.*;
import java.awt.*;
import java.awt.event.*;

public class EMailApplet extends Applet implements ActionListener {

    // Create the GUI.
        public void init() {
        host = getParameter( "host" );
        senderLabel = new Label( "Sender: " );
        add( senderLabel );
        senderField = new TextField( 20 );
        add( senderField );
        recipientLabel = new Label( "Recipient: " );
        add(recipientLabel );
        recipientField = new TextField( 20 );
        add(recipientField );
        subjectLabel = new Label( "Subject: " );
        add( subjectLabel );
        subjectField = new TextField( 20 );
        add( subjectField );
        messageArea = new TextArea( 15,35 );
        add( messageArea );
        clearButton = new Button( "Clear" );
        clearButton.addActionListener( this );     // Listen to this button!
        add( clearButton );
        submitButton = new Button( "Submit" );
        submitButton.addActionListener( this );    // Listen to this button!
        add( submitButton );
    }

    public void actionPerformed( ActionEvent e ) {
        Object source = e.getSource()          // Where did this
 ➥ event come from?

        // Is it the same object as the "Submit" button?
        if( source == submitButton ) {

            // Create a new EMail object.
            EMail eMail = new EMail();

            // Set the from,to,subject, and message for the object
            eMail.setSenderAddress( senderField.getText() );
            eMail.setRecipientAddress(recipientField.getText() );
```

```java
        eMail.setSubject( subjectField.getText() );
        eMail.setMessage( messageArea.getText() );

        // Print it out.
        System.out.println( eMail );

        // Send the EMail object to the SMTP Server
        SMTPClient client = null;
        if( host == null )
            client = new SMTPClient( getCodeBase().toString() );
        else
            client = new SMTPClient( host );
        client.send( eMail );

    } else

    // Is it the same object as the "Clear" button?
    if( source == clearButton ) {

        senderField.setText( "" );
        recipientField.setText( "" );
        subjectField.setText( "" );
        messageArea.setText( "" );

    }

}

private Label senderLabel;
private TextField senderField;
private Label recipientLabel;
private TextField recipientField;
private Label subjectLabel;
private TextField subjectField;
private TextArea messageArea;
private Button submitButton;
private Button clearButton;
private String host;
}
```

Three changes have been made in order to handle events: listeners were added, EMailApplet was declared to implement ActionListener, and the ActionListener interface was implemented by adding the actionPerformed() method and defining its behavior.

The class definition has been changed to indicate that EMailApplet is an ActionListener, as described earlier. The EMailApplet is then added as a listener for action events to the submitButton and the clearButton. Whenever one of these two buttons are pressed, the EMailApplet's actionPerformed() method is called and information about the event is sent as a parameter of type ActionEvent. Inside this method, the source of the event must be determined by requesting the source from the ActionEvent object parameter. The getSource() method of ActionEvent returns an Object type, which refers to the source of the ActionEvent. The ActionEvent source refers to the component that received the event. This value is then compared to the submitButton and clearButton variables. The == operator tests whether the source object is the same object as the submitButton or clearButton objects. If the event's source is the submitButton, an EMail object is constructed and printed. If the event was created by the `clearButton`, all the fields in the `EMailApplet` are cleared by setting the value to `""`.

> **TIP**
>
> The `getActionCommand()` method of `ActionEvent` returns a value representing the button's `String` label. For instance, calling the `getActionCommand()` on the `ActionEvent` after the `submitButton` has been pushed would return the value `Submit`. This value could be tested for in the `actionPerformed()` method of `EMailApplet`, but this isn't a good approach. The text associated with the `submitButton` may change in the future. It's much better to keep a reference to the object and compare it when differentiating between user interface components.

It may seem strange to compare a button with an `Object`. The `ActionEvent` object's `getSource()` method returns an `Object`. In order to understand how this comparison works, it's necessary to know that a `Button` is an `Object`. In fact, everything in Java is an `Object`. `Object` is the superclass of all Java objects. `Button` is a special type of `Object`—these two things can be compared without any problems. In general, any class can be referred or compared to an object or variable of its superclass type.

Notice that the host name specified is sent to the `SMTPClient` by calling the `getCodeBase()` method of the `Applet` class. This method returns the name of the host from which the applet was loaded. `SMTPClient` sends the e-mail message back to this host via the SMTP protocol. Because of the type of security enforced by a browser, no other host can be specified. An `Applet` can only make socket connections back to the host of origin.

If the `EMailApplet` is running within AppletViewer, it might connect to any host, so an optional `host` parameter is checked in the `init()` method. If it's necessary to specify a different host running an SMTP server—there are probably a couple million out there—add a line to the HTML file, so that it looks like this:

```
<HTML>
<TITLE><HEAD>EMailApplet</HEAD></TITLE>
<BODY>
<APPLET code="EMailApplet.class" WIDTH=250 HEIGHT=350>
    <PARAM NAME="host" VALUE="www.myhost.com">
</APPLET>
</BODY>
</HTML>
```

If you have an Internet connection through an Internet service provider, you can probably connect to his or her SMTP server by specifying his or her host name in the value of the `<PARAM>` tag.

Running the `EMailApplet`

The `EMailApplet` now incorporates both a user interface and the `EMail` object. It's possible to write an e-mail message with `EMailApplet` and send it if an SMTP server is running on port 25 of the host where the applet came from. In order to test the applet, use the HTML file, modify the `EMailApplet` class to incorporate the new behavior, and run it from the AppletViewer or within a browser that supports JDK 1.1 features (including the AWT enhancements).

If you are running within an AppletViewer type the following in the same directory as the `EMailApplet.class` file:

```
appletviewer EMailApplet
```

You should be able to enter the sender's e-mail address, the recipient's e-mail address, a subject, and the message. You can erase the entire message by clicking the Clear button. Once the message is written, just click on the Send button to send it on its merry way.

When the Send button is clicked, the information entered into the user interface should be printed to the DOS Window if running in an AppletViewer context or to the Java Console if running in a Netscape browser. The message should be a properly formatted e-mail message that can be sent over the Internet.

Showing an HTML Document

One common task for an applet is to get a URL and show a Web page. For example, ImageMap applets make use of this functionality. You create an applet that displays any URL typed into a text field.

This process of getting and displaying a Web page involves creating a `URL` object that refers to the desired Web page. This URL is then sent as a parameter to the `showDocument()` method of the `AppletContext` object.

Depending upon whether the Web page's target is specified, one of two overloaded `showDocument()` methods in `AppletContext` is invoked. If the `showDocument()` method, which takes a URL and a target, is called the Web page is sent to the frame with that `target` attribute. If there is no frame with the same target, the Web page is shown in a new browser window.

For example, there are three different frames. The left frame contains the `Applet`, and two other empty frames are created to the right. The one on the top-right is called `A` and the one on the bottom-right is called `B`.

Write the HTML pages first. Here are the frames:

```
<HTML>
<HEAD><TITLE>BrowseApplet Frame</TITLE></HEAD>
<FRAMESET COLS="50%,50%">
    <FRAME NAME="BrowseApplet" SRC="BrowseApplet.html">
    <FRAMESET ROWS="50%,50%">
        <FRAME NAME="A" SRC="A.html">
```

```
        <FRAME NAME="B" SRC="B.html">
    </FRAMESET>
</FRAMESET>
</HTML>
```

Each of the frames has a NAME attribute. The BrowseApplet uses those names to refer to the various frames on the page. The BrowseApplet frame is listed here:

```
<HTML>
<BODY>
<APPLET code="BrowseApplet.class" WIDTH=250 HEIGHT=350>
</APPLET>
</BODY>
</HTML>
```

Frame A is listed here:

```
<HTML>
<BODY>
This is Frame A.
</BODY>
</HTML>
```

Frame B is listed here:

```
<HTML>
<BODY>
This is Frame B.
</BODY>
</HTML>
```

BrowseApplet uses a Label and a TextField for the URL field and the target field. For variety, use a new layout in this applet called BorderLayout. The BrowseApplet code follows:

```
import java.awt.event.*;
import java.net.*;

public class BrowseApplet extends Applet implements ActionListener {

    // Create the GUI.
public void init() {

    // Specify a new layout for the Applet
    setLayout( new BorderLayout() );

    // Create a new Panel and add it to the North
    // frame of the BorderLayout.
    Panel p = new Panel();
        urlLabel = new Label( "URL: " );
        p.add( urlLabel );
        urlField = new TextField( 20 );
        p.add( urlField );
        add( p, "North" );

    // Create a new Panel and add it to the North
    // frame of the BorderLayout.
    Panel p1 = new Panel();
        targetLabel = new Label( "Target: " );
        p1.add( targetLabel );
```

```
        targetField = new TextField( 20 );
        p1.add( targetField );
        add( p1, "Center" );


        // Add the buttons to clear and show.
        Panel p2 = new Panel();
        clearButton = new Button( "Clear" );
        clearButton.addActionListener( this );      // Listen to this button!
        p2.add( clearButton );
        showButton = new Button( "Show" );
        showButton.addActionListener( this );    // Listen to this button!
        p2.add( showButton );
        add( p2,"South" );

    }

    public void actionPerformed( ActionEvent e ) {
        Object source = e.getSource();        //
➥Where did this event come from?

        // Is it the same object as the "Submit" button?
        if( source == showButton ) {

            URL url = null;

            // Get the url from the urlField
            String urlString = urlField.getText();

            // Get the target from the targetField
            String targetString = targetField.getText();

            // Create an URL.
            try {
                url = new URL( urlString );

                // Get the AppletContext object, and show the URL.
                if( targetString != "" )
                    getAppletContext().showDocument( url,targetString );
                else
                    getAppletContext().showDocument( url,"A" );


            } catch( MalformedURLException exception ) {
                getAppletContext().showStatus( "Invalid url!" );
                return;
            }

        } else

        // Is it the same object as the "Clear" button?
        if( source == clearButton ) {

            urlField.setText( "" );
            targetField.setText( "" );

        }

    }
```

```
        private Label urlLabel;
        private TextField urlField;
        private Label targetLabel;
        private TextField targetField;
        private Button showButton;
        private Button clearButton;

}
```

The user interface components are added to the panel. Because BrowseApplet uses the BorderLayout strategy to lay out its components, the container's add() method, which takes a Component and a String parameter, is used. This is an overloaded version of the add() method that takes only the Component as a parameter. The tag for this particular layout refers to where the components are placed within the applet. Everything placed to the North is situated at the top of the screen. Everything placed to South is situated at the bottom of the screen.

The actionPerformed() method actually creates a URL object from the string entered into the URL field. If a target has been entered into the target field, the Web page is sent to this target. If A is entered as a target, the selected Web page should be shown in the top-right frame. If B is entered into the target field, the Web page should be shown in the bottom-right frame. If neither A nor B is entered, an entirely new browser window is created, and the Web page is shown there.

Summary

This chapter introduced applets. Applets provide a convenient way for distributing Java code over the Internet. Applets will run in any Web page, as long as a Java-supporting browser is available.

Applets are added to HTML by using the <APPLET> tag. The <APPLET> tag specifies what applet to load, the applet's size and position on the Web page, and any parameters that need to be passed in. The ARCHIVE attribute was added to the <APPLET> tag, allowing browsers to handle archived class files. This approach reduces download times—especially if the archive is a compressed archive.

You used Java AWT components to build a user interface for an e-mail client. In order to make the e-mail client functional, the new delegation event model captured and handled events from Send and Clear buttons. The EMail and SMTP classes developed in the previous chapter were reused here to format and send the new e-mail message.

JavaBeans, JARs, and Safe Computing

by Rob Falla, Mike Fletcher, and Michael Morrison

IN THIS CHAPTER

CHAPTER 22

NOTE FROM THE AUTHORS

The contents of this chapter might at times seem a bit odd. Each of the major areas of the chapter—JavaBeans, JARs, and Java Security—are thoroughly covered, but they don't necessarily seem to belong in a single chapter. Well, that's one way to look at it. Another, more preferable view is that with this chapter of miscellaneous topics the book is a complete reference tool for any serious developer.

In Chapter 19, "Why Java?" you learned about Java. Chapter 20, "The Java Language: A Crash Course," and Chapter 21, "Introduction to Applet Programming," taught you how to use the Java language to develop applications and applets for your Web site. Now you will learn how to make components of those applications reusable.

JavaBeans are actually just components of a Java application. An example of Java components is the code for a Java menu bar, a text field, a button, or anything else that is reusable. The JavaBean contains the code for that component and you have only to associate the component with the applet for which it is needed. Several beans can be used on a single applet using the new `innerClass` methods.

The JavaBeans Developers Kit (BDK 1.0) is used for creating these Java components. The bean source code must have a `.java` extension, and the prefix must be the name of the class to which the bean belongs. Your compiled bean will be packaged into a .jar compressed file so it can be distributed over the net. Once compiled, beans can be used with any Java application. This chapter will show you how.

In addition to the discussion on JavaBeans in general, a substantial portion of this chapter is devoted to JARs and security issues. The information provided here is intended to assist you in understanding many of the issues involved with JavaBeans, JARs, and security, it is not, however a complete manual; if you require additional information, there are several URLs listed throughout this chapter that point you to very helpful online resources. Also, several books have been written that focus exclusively on these topics.

JAVABEANS—ACTIVEX BRIDGE

Near the end of September 1997, JavaSoft announced the release of the ActiveX Bridge. This program is used to make your JavaBeans work in ActiveX environments. At the time the API was released, several ActiveX containers have been tested and are supposed to be supported.

The following is a list of tested ActiveX containers:

- Visual Basic 4.0 Standard Edition
- Visual Basic 5.0 CCE

■ Microsoft Office 95 (Word, Excel, PowerPoint)

■ Microsoft Office 97 (Word, Excel, PowerPoint)

■ In-place Document or ActiveX component

■ Lotus SmartSuite

■ Internet Explorer 3.02, 4.0 (preview 2 without shell integration)

■ Microsoft ActiveX ControlPad

■ Microsoft FrontPage 97

■ Delphi 2.0

■ MFC 4.2 or 5.0

The ActiveXBridge 1.0 program will create an OLE from the JavaBean. Methods are supported for converting a GIF format image into a BMP. You do not need to code the JavaBeans differently to use the ActiveX bridge.

One thing to remember about the new JavaBeans ActiveX bridge is that the old JAR files will not work. You need to repackage your beans with the new bean packager.

What Are JavaBeans?

JavaBeans are reusable components of a Java application. Once a JavaBean is created it may be used with several Java applications at the same time. The benefit of having code that can simply be applied to any application is the reduction in your work load. You will still have to develop the core application, though. Beans are added to the application with the ARCHIVE attribute of the APPLET tag.

```
<APPLET CODE="javaApp.class"
ARCHIVES="jarfile.jar">
```

Imagine yourself creating a large corporate Web site that requires several Java applications to give it that extra touch management has asked for. What you will notice immediately is that several portions of the Java code are the same in content and functionality throughout all the applications. As you write out these applications, you will start to wonder why you are typing the same portion of code time after time. It will occur to you that maybe you should start using short cuts like cut and paste to eliminate the task of actually rewriting the code for each application.

With JavaBeans, it's about as simple as cut and paste. The difference is that you must search through an application's code to locate all those components, whereas with JavaBeans you only write the code once and pass the component to any application.

> **COMPONENT**
>
> A *component* is a reusable piece of software that can be assembled easily to create applications with much greater development efficiency. The idea is to build small, reusable components once and then reuse them as often as necessary, thereby streamlining the entire development process.

Components make sense because they can be used again and again in as many Java applications as needed. When you modify a JavaBean, you are only changing the code for that one component, other components of the Java application remain unchanged. Also, the modifications will be applied to the component on each application in which it is used. Another somewhat obvious benefit of beans is that, by targeting a specific component of an application and editing only the code for that component, you reduce the risk of contaminating an already proven application.

Often JavaBeans will be used in distributed environments in which entire components may be transferred across a low-bandwidth Internet connection. The JavaBeans API, coupled with the platform-independent Java system on which it is based, creates the platform-independent component solution. As a result, developers don't have to worry about including platform-specific libraries with their Java applets.

The existing Java architecture already offers a wide range of benefits easily applied to components. One of the more important, but rarely mentioned, features of Java is its built-in class-discovery mechanism, which enables objects to interact with each other dynamically at runtime, similar to the way a Java application interacts with a JavaBean at runtime. Another example of JavaBeans inheriting existing Java functionality is *persistence* (the capability for an object to store and retrieve its internal state). Persistence is handled automatically in JavaBeans by way of the serialization mechanism already present in Java. Alternatively, developers can create their own customized persistence solutions whenever necessary.

The Basic Structure of a Bean

First, let me clarify some terminology that is sometimes used for JavaBeans: A JavaBeans component can also be referred to as a *bean* or a *JavaBean*. Therefore, from here on, note that *bean*, *JavaBeans component*, and *JavaBean* all refer to the same thing. Also keep in mind that the word *JavaBeans* usually refers to the component technology itself, as opposed to multiple components.

A bean, like an object in any object-oriented environment, is comprised of two primary things: data and methods that act on the data. The data part of a bean completely describes the state of the bean; the methods provide a way for the bean's state to be modified and for actions to be taken accordingly. Figure 22.1 shows the two fundamental parts of a bean.

FIGURE 22.1.

The fundamental parts of a JavaBeans component.

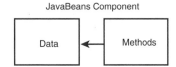

JavaBeans Component

A bean can have methods with different types of access. For example, `private` methods are accessible only within the internals of a bean, but `protected` methods are accessible both internally and in derived beans. The methods with the most accessibility are `public` methods, which are accessible internally, from derived beans, and from outside parties such as applications and other components, like JavaScript and VBScript. *Accessible* means that an application can call any of a component's `public` methods. `public` methods have unique importance to beans because they form the primary way a bean communicates with the outside world.

> **NOTE**
>
> A bean also communicates with the outside world through events, which are generated when the internal state of the bean changes. Events are handled and responded to by interested outside parties (event listeners), such as applications.

A bean's `public` methods are often grouped according to function. Functionally, similar groups of `public` methods are also known as *interfaces*. A bean exposes its functionality to the outside world through these interfaces. Interfaces are important because they specify the protocol by which a particular bean is interacted with externally. A programmer only has to know a bean's interfaces to be able to successfully manipulate and interact with the bean. Figure 22.2 shows how interfaces expose a bean's functionality to the outside world.

Although beans are expected to provide support for facilities such as persistence and application builder tool integration, all beans ultimately boil down to data and methods. These facilities are supported in the form of additional methods, data, and interfaces, which are themselves groups of methods. Therefore, no matter how complex a bean looks on the outside, just keep in mind that it is ultimately a combination of data and methods deep down. That brings you to the next section, the technical aspects of JavaBeans are more clearly defined in the following sections.

The JavaBeans API

JavaBeans is ultimately a programming interface. What that means is that all its features are implemented in the java.beans package, which is also known as the JavaBean(s) API. The java.beans package is provided as part of the standard Java 1.1 class library. The API itself is merely a suite of smaller APIs devoted to specific functions, or services. Following is a list of the main component services in the JavaBeans API that are necessary to facilitate all the features that make JavaBeans such an exciting technology:

- Property management
- Introspection
- Event handling
- Persistence
- Application builder support

By understanding these services and how they work, you'll have much more insight into JavaBeans.

Figure 22.2.

The relationship between interfaces and methods in a JavaBeans component.

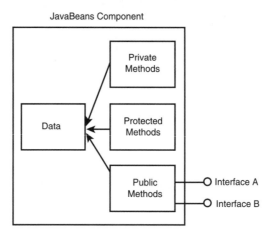

Property Management

The property management facilities in the JavaBeans API are responsible for handling all interactions relating to bean properties. Properties reflect the internal state of a bean and constitute the data part of a bean's structure. More specifically, properties are discrete, named attributes of a bean that determine its appearance and behavior. Properties are important in any component technology because they isolate component state information into discrete pieces that can be easily modified.

Properties come into play in a variety of ways when it comes to bean access and manipulation. Notice the flexibility properties provide: You can access them through scripting languages such as JavaScript, through full-blown programming languages such as Java, and through visual builder tools. This freedom to access and manipulate beans in a variety of ways is one of the critical design goals of the JavaBeans technology, and it is fulfilled by the property management facilities in the JavaBeans API. The next few sections discuss some of the major issues addressed by the JavaBeans API property management facilities.

■ Accessor Methods

The primary way properties are exposed in the JavaBeans API is through accessor methods. An accessor method is a public method defined in a bean that directly reads or writes the value of a particular property. Each property in a bean must have a corresponding pair of accessor methods: one for reading the property and one for writing. The accessor methods responsible for reading are known as getter methods, because they get the value of a property. Likewise, accessor methods responsible for writing are known as setter methods, because they set the value of a property.

■ Indexed Properties

The JavaBeans API also supports *indexed properties*, which are properties that represent an array of values. Indexed properties work very similar to arrays in traditional Java programming: You access a particular value using an integer index. Indexed properties are very useful for situations in which a bean must maintain a group of properties of the same type. For example, a container bean that keeps track of the physical layout of other beans might store references to them in an indexed property.

■ Bound and Constrained Properties

The JavaBeans API supports two mechanisms for working with properties at a more advanced level: bound and constrained properties. *Bound properties* are properties that provide notifications to an interested party based on changes in the property value. An interested party is an applet, application, or bean that wants to know about changes in the property. These properties are called bound properties because they are bound to some type of external behavior based on their own changes. Bound properties are defined at the component level, which means that a bean is responsible for specifying which components are bound. An example of a bound property is a visibility property; a bean's container might be interested in knowing the status of this property because the container has to graphically reorganize other beans based on a bean's visibility.

The other interesting property feature provided by the JavaBeans API is support for *constrained properties*, which are properties that enable an interested party to perform a validation on a new property value before accepting the modification. Constrained properties are useful in providing interested parties with control over how a bean is altered. An example of a constrained property is a date property for which the application containing the bean wants to limit the valid date property values to a certain range.

Introspection

The introspection facilities in the JavaBeans API define the mechanism by which components make their internal structure readily available to the outside world. These facilities consist of the functional overhead necessary to enable development tools to query a bean for its internal structure, including the interfaces, methods, and member variables that comprise the bean. Although the introspection services are primarily designed for use by application builder tools, they are grouped separately from the application builder services in the API because their role in making a bean's internal structure available externally is technically independent of builder tools. In other words, you may have other reasons for querying a bean about its internal structure beyond the obvious reasons used in builder tools.

The introspection services provided by the JavaBeans API are divided into two parts: low-level services and high-level services. These two types of services are distinguished by the level of access they provide to bean internals. The low-level API services are responsible for enabling wide access to the structural internals of a bean. These services are very important for application builder tools that heavily use bean internals to provide advanced development features. However, this level of access isn't appropriate for developers who are using beans to build applications because it exposes private parts of a bean that aren't meant to be used by developers at the application level. For these purposes, the high-level API services are more appropriate.

The high-level services use the low-level services behind the scenes to provide access to limited portions of a bean's internals (typically, the bean's public properties and methods). The difference between the two levels of services is that the high-level services don't enable access to internal aspects of a bean that aren't specifically designed for external use. The end result is two distinct services that offer bean introspection capabilities based on the level of access required by the interested party, be it an application builder tool or a user. The next few sections cover several of the major functions supported in the JavaBeans API introspection facilities.

Reflection and Design Patterns

The JavaBeans API has a very interesting technique of assessing the public properties, methods, and events for a bean. To determine information about a bean's public features, the bean's methods are analyzed using a set of low-level reflection services. These services gather information about a bean and determine its public properties, methods, and events by applying simple design patterns. *Design patterns* are rules applied to a bean's method definitions that determine information about the bean. For example, when a pair of accessor methods are encountered in the analysis of a bean, the JavaBeans introspection facilities match them based on a design pattern and automatically determine the property they access.

The whole premise of design patterns is that method names and signatures conform to a standard convention. There are a variety of different design patterns for determining everything from simple properties to event sources. All these design patterns rely on some type of consistent naming convention for methods and their arguments. This approach to introspection is not only convenient from the perspective of JavaBeans, it also has the intended side effect of encouraging bean developers to use a consistent set of naming conventions.

Explicit Bean Information

Even though the design-pattern approach to introspection is very useful and encourages a consistent approach to naming, you may be wondering what happens if bean developers don't follow the convention. Fortunately, design patterns aren't the only option for introspection, meaning that obstinate developers are free to ignore the suggested naming conventions if they so choose. The developers who opt to cast convention to the wind must use another introspection facility in the JavaBeans API: They must explicitly list the public information about their beans. They must "spill the beans," to inject a painfully bad pun.

The explicit introspection facility in the JavaBeans API to which I'm referring involves creating a bean information class that specifies various pieces of information about a bean including a property list, method list, and event list. This approach isn't automatic like the design-pattern approach, but it does provide a way to explicitly describe your bean to the world, which might be advantageous in some situations.

The Introspector

Just in case you're wondering how two different introspection approaches can possibly coexist to describe a single bean, you should know about another service that consolidates the whole introspection process. The introspection facilities provide an introspector used to obtain explicit bean information for a bean. The introspector is responsible for traversing the inheritance tree of a bean to determine the explicit bean information for all parent beans. If, at any point, explicit information is not defined, the introspector falls back on the reflection services and uses design patterns to automatically determine external bean information.

This two-tiered solution to assessing bean functionality is very nice because it first attempts to use information explicitly provided by a bean's developer and relies on automatic design patterns only if the explicit information isn't there. The other nice thing is that it supports a mixture of the two approaches, which means that methods for a bean can be explicitly defined in a provided bean information class, but the properties and events can be determined automatically using design patterns. This gives bean developers a lot of flexibility in deciding how they want their beans exposed.

Event Handling

The event-handling facilities in the JavaBeans API specify an event-driven architecture that defines interactions among beans and applications. If you're familiar with the Java AWT, you know that it provides a comprehensive event-handling model. This existing AWT event model forms the basis of the event-handling facilities in the JavaBeans API. These event-handling facilities are critical in that they determine how beans respond to changes in their state, as well as how these changes are propagated to applications and other beans.

The event-handling facilities hinge on the concepts of event sources and listeners. A bean capable of generating events is considered an event *source*; an application or bean capable of responding to an event is considered an event *listener*. Event sources and listeners are connected by an event registration mechanism that is part of the event-handling facilities. This registration mechanism basically boils down to an event listener being registered with an event source through a simple method call. When the source generates an event, a specified method is called on the event listener with an event state object being sent along as its argument. Event state objects are responsible for storing information associated with a particular event. In other words, event state objects carry with them any information related to the event being sent. The next few sections cover some of the major issues dealt with by the JavaBeans API event-handling facilities.

Unicast and Multicast Event Sources

Although most practical event sources support multiple listeners, the event-handling facilities provide for event sources that choose to limit their audience to a single listener. These sources are called *unicast event sources*; their more liberal counterparts are called *multicast event sources*. The primary functional difference between the two is that unicast event sources throw an exception if an attempt is made to register more than one listener.

Even though the JavaBeans API supports both unicast and multicast event sources, keep in mind that multicast event sources are much less limiting in terms of practical use. In other words, developers should avoid designing beans as unicast event sources whenever possible.

Event Adapters

Even though many bean events follow the standard source/listener model about which you just learned, the JavaBeans API provides a mechanism for dealing with more complex situations for which this model doesn't quite fit the bill. This mechanism is based on event *adapters*, which act as intermediaries between event sources and listeners. Event adapters sit between sources and listeners and provide a way of inserting specialized event-delivery behavior into the standard source/listener event model. Event adapters are important to the event-handling facilities because they open the door for the implementation of a highly specialized event-handling mechanism tailored to the unique challenges sometimes encountered in applications or application builder tools.

Persistence

The persistence facilities in the JavaBeans API specify the mechanism by which beans are stored and retrieved within the context of a container. The information stored through persistence consists of all the parts of a bean necessary to restore the bean to a similar internal state and appearance. This generally involves the storage of all public properties and, potentially, some internal properties, although the specifics are determined by each particular bean. Information not stored for a bean through persistence is references to external beans, including event registrations. These references are expected to be stored somehow by an application builder tool or through some programmatic means.

By default, beans are persistently stored and retrieved using the automatic serialization mechanism provided by Java, which is sufficient for most beans. However, bean developers are also free to create more elaborate persistence solutions based on the specific needs of their beans. Like the introspection facilities, the JavaBeans persistence facilities provide for both an explicit approach and an automatic approach to carrying out their functions.

Application Builder Support

The final area of the JavaBeans API deals with application builder support. The application builder support facilities provide the overhead necessary to edit and manipulate beans using visual application builder tools. Application builder tools rely heavily on these facilities to enable a developer to visually lay out and edit beans while constructing an application. These facilities fulfill a major design goal of the JavaBeans API: They enable beans to be used constructively with little or no programming effort.

One issue with which the JavaBeans architects wrestled is that application builder support for a specific bean is required only at design time. Consequently, it is somewhat wasteful to bundle this support code into a runtime bean. Because of this situation, the application builder facilities require that builder-specific overhead for a bean must be physically separate from the bean itself. This separation enables beans to be distributed by themselves for runtime use or in conjunction with the application builder support for design-time use. The next few sections cover some of the major issues dealt with by the JavaBeans API application builder support facilities.

Property Editors and Sheets

One of the ways in which the JavaBeans API supports the editing and manipulation of beans with application builder tools is through property sheets. A *property sheet* is a visual interface that provides editors for each public property defined for a bean. The individual editors used in a property sheet are called *property editors*. Each type of exported property in a bean must have a corresponding property editor if it is to be edited visually by a builder tool. Some standard property editors are provided by the JavaBeans API for built-in Java types, but user-defined properties require their own custom editors. The property editors for all the exported properties of a bean are presented together on a property sheet that enables users to edit the properties visually.

Customizers

The other way in which the JavaBeans API enables beans to be visually edited in an application builder tool is through *customizers*. Customizers are user interfaces that provide a specialized way of visually editing bean properties. Because customizers are implemented entirely by bean developers, there are no firm guidelines about how they present visual property information to the user. However, most customizers probably will be similar in function to "wizards," those popular user interfaces on the Windows platform that use multiple-step questionnaires to gather information from the user.

What Are JAR Files?

In versions of the JDK before 1.1, if an applet was made up of several different class files or had resources such as GIFs or audio files, you had to download each resource individually. In addition to forcing the user of the applet to wait while the applet's pieces downloaded, this arrangement put an extra load on the HTTP server. To address this problem, Sun introduced JAR files. Based on the widely used ZIP file format developed by PKWare, a JAR file allows multiple resources (Java class files, graphics files, and others) to be bundled into a single, compressed archive file. In addition to making the server's job easier, applets and resources download quicker when they are compressed. A new package, `java.util.zip`, contains classes to manipulate JAR files (as well as normal ZIP files). You can simply store files in a JAR file, or you can compress them before storing to save space.

JAR files include a manifest file in the archive. This manifest (named `META-INF/MANIFEST.MF`) gives message digests of the component files in the archive. Additionally, digital signatures of component files can be included in the `META-INF` directory of the archive. Code signed by a trusted entity can be granted extra privileges such as writing files.

Manipulating JAR Files with jar

Included with the JDK 1.1 is a tool to create and manipulate JAR files. This tool is called, logically enough, `jar`. The `jar` tool runs from the DOS command line or UNIX shell prompt (represented in the following examples by the `%` character). The following examples show how to use `jar` to create a JAR file, how to list the contents of an archive, and how to extract a file from an archive. In all cases, two extra options can be used with `jar` to change how it operates.

Option	Description
v	Tells `jar` to generate verbose output about the actions it is performing.
f	Specifies the filename to manipulate. If this option is not given, `jar` writes to standard output.

If you happen to forget how to use `jar`, you can run it with no arguments to generate a usage listing.

> **NOTE**
>
> Because JAR files are stored in the standard ZIP format, you do not have to use `jar` to create JAR files. You can use any application that can create ZIP files—as long as you generate your own manifest file and name it correctly (`META-INF/MANIFEST.MF`). You can find information about the manifest and signature file formats at this site:
>
> `http://www.javasoft.com/products/JDK/1.1/docs/guide/jar/manifest.html`

Free ZIP and unZIP programs are available from the Info-ZIP group. Source code and binaries for many platforms are available from this site:

`http://www.cdrom.com/pub/infozip/Info-Zip.html`

Creating a JAR File

To create an archive, you use `jar` with the `c` flag. Suppose that you want to create a JAR file with three files: `sampleApplet.class`, a Java class file; `sampleGraphic.gif`, an image file; and `sampleSound.au`, an audio file. The following command places these three files into an archive named `sample.jar`. The options `cvf` specify that you want to **c**reate an archive, you want **v**erbose output, and the archive **f**ilename should be `sample.jar`.

```
% jar cvf sample.jar sample.jar sampleApplet.class
➥sampleGraphic.gif sampleSound.au
```

Here's what `jar` shows you as it's creating the archive:

```
adding: sampleApplet.class in=4480 out=2065 deflated 53.0%
adding: sampleGraphic.gif in=506 out=419 deflated 17.0%
adding: sampleSound.au in=5529 out=1088 deflated 80.0%
```

For each file, `jar` specifies the input size before compression and the output size after compression, as well as a ratio showing how well the file was compressed.

Listing the Contents of a JAR File

Next, list the contents of the archive file you just created. The `t` option tells `jar` that you want a **t**able of contents for the JAR file; the `vf` options specify **v**erbose mode and the **f**ilename for which you want information:

```
% jar tvf sample.jar
```

Here's the output from `jar`:

```
 402 Tue Feb 18 23:12:10 EST 1997 META-INF/MANIFEST.MF
4480 Mon Feb 17 02:03:46 EST 1997 sampleApplet.class
 506 Tue Feb 18 22:24:52 EST 1997 sampleGraphic.gif
5529 Mon Feb 17 00:16:02 EST 1997 sampleSound.au
```

Notice that there is an extra file named `META-INF/MANIFEST.MF` in the JAR archive file. This is a manifest of all the files contained in the archive and a message digest of the contents of each file. The `jar` tool automatically generates a manifest file; alternatively, you can generate one yourself and pass the `m` flag to `jar` when you create the archive.

Extracting a File from a JAR File

Now you'll extract `sampleGraphic.gif` from the `sample.jar` file. In the following command, the `vf` options are the same as they were in the preceding section (**v**erbose mode and the **f**ilename from which you want to extract a file). The x option specifies that you want to extract files. If no extra arguments are given, jar extracts the entire contents of the archive. If arguments are given after the archive name, jar takes those as the names of the files to extract.

```
% jar xvf sample.jar sampleGraphic.gif
```

Here's the response from jar concerning the extraction request:

```
extracted: sampleGraphic.gif in=419 out=506 inflated 17.0%
```

An Overview of `java.util.zip`

The `java.util.zip` package contains several classes that facilitate the manipulation of compressed files.

The `ZipFile` Class

The `ZipFile` class provides a way to read the contents a ZIP archive. There are two constructors: one that takes a string specifying the filename of the archive to open and one that takes a `java.io.File` object. The `getName()` method returns the path name of the ZIP file represented by the `ZipFile` object.

Two methods are provided to obtain `ZipEntry` objects representing the contents of the ZIP file. The `getEntry()` method takes a string and returns a `ZipEntry` for the corresponding file; it returns `null` if no such file exists in the archive. The `entries()` method returns a `java.util.Enumeration` of `ZipEntry` objects for all the entries in the ZIP file. The `getInputStream()` method is used to obtain an `InputStream` for the entry represented by the `ZipEntry` given as a parameter.

The `ZipEntry` Class

Each file in a ZIP archive can be represented by a `ZipEntry` object. `ZipEntry` objects can be obtained for an existing file from a `ZipFile` or `ZipInputStream` object; they can also be created when you make a new ZIP archive with a `ZipOutputStream`. The `ZipEntry` class provides methods to retrieve information about the entry (for example, the filename, the compressed and uncompressed size of the file, and the compression method used for the file). The `isDirectory()` method is provided to determine whether the entry in question is a normal file or a directory.

ZIP Stream Classes

In addition to the `ZipFile` class, the `java.util.zip` package has two stream classes that handle compressed data. The stream classes in `java.util.zip` extend either `InflaterInputStream` or `DeflatorOutputStream` as appropriate. These two filtered streams provide a generic interface for handling compressed data.

`ZipInputStream` reads data in the ZIP format from an `InputStream`. The `getNextEntry()` method returns a `ZipEntry` for the next component in the ZIP file and places the stream at the beginning of the data for that component. The `closeEntry()` method closes the current entry and advances the stream to return the next entry in the archive. Both methods throw a `ZipException` if a ZIP-related exception occurs.

The `ZipOutputStream` provides `OutputStream` functionality for writing compressed data. The `putNextEntry()` method takes a `ZipEntry` as a parameter. A new entry is created in the ZIP file and any data written to the stream goes to the current entry. Two methods are provided to control the compression used to store entries: `setMethod()` takes as a parameter either `ZipOutputStream.DEFLATED` (to specify that the next entries should be compressed) or `ZipOutputStream.STORED` (to specify that any subsequent entries should simply be stored with no compression). The `setLevel()` method takes an integer from 0 to 9, inclusive, with higher numbers indicating more compression (which takes longer to compress). The `setComment()` method allows the ZIP file comment to be set.

GNU Zip Stream Classes

In addition to classes for the ZIP compression format, the `java.util.zip` package provides two classes that support reading and writing files in the GNU Zip format. GNU Zip is a widely used compression format for UNIX. Unlike the ZIP format, the GNU Zip format handles only one file at a time, rather than multiple files and a directory structure. GNU Zip is most often used as a replacement for the UNIX `compress` utility, so there is no `getNextEntry()` method for the `GZIPInputStream` class. In addition, the `GZIPOutputStream` has no way to specify filenames for entries.

Using JAR Files

A new attribute has been added to the HTML `<applet>` tag: `archives`. This tag specifies one or more JAR files that should be downloaded with the applet (obviously, these JAR files contain components needed by the applet). You should still specify the `code` attribute, even if you give the archives attribute, because `code` is used as the name of the applet class to load. Whenever the applet requests a class, image, or sound file, the archives specified are searched first. If the necessary resource is not contained in one of the JAR files downloaded the applet contacts the server and searches for the resource as it did with the JDK version 1.0.2. You can specify multiple archive files by separating the filenames with + (a plus sign). A sample applet tag is shown in Listing 22.1.

Listing 22.1. A sample `<applet>` tag using JAR files.

```
<applet code="sampleApplet.class"
    archives="sample.jar + icons.jar + commonClasses.jar"
    width="550"
    height="300">
<param name="animal" value="lemur">
<param name="server" value="qa.nowhere.com">
</applet>
```

Code Signing and JAR Security

Before delving into the details of signed applets, you may find it useful to know how digital signatures work. Digital signatures provide a way to indicate that some piece of information was generated by some entity (for Java digital signatures, this "entity" would usually be either a programmer or a company) and that the information has not been altered. Methods for generating signatures are designed so that it is mathematically impossible to create two different documents with the same signature in any reasonable period of time.

Public key cryptography differs from what is referred to as *conventional* or *secret key cryptography*. In public key cryptography, you have one key to encrypt a message and a different key to decrypt the message. For a well-designed algorithm, it is mathematically impossible to determine the secret key given the encrypting key. The encrypting key (usually referred to as the *public key*) can be given to anyone who wants to send an encrypted message to the holder of the corresponding secret key (usually referred to as the *private key*). Anyone can use the public key to encrypt, but only the secret key can decrypt the message and recover the original text.

Some public-key encryption algorithms can also be used to create digital signatures. Instead of the sender using the public key to encrypt a message to the private key holder, the private key holder encrypts the message using his or her private key. Anyone who has the public key can decrypt this message and verify that it did in fact come from the private key holder (because that person should be the only person with access to the private key). The signature algorithm used by the default JDK security package is known as DSA (Digital Signature Algorithm). DSA was created by the U.S. government's National Institute of Standards and Technology (the standard is FIPS 186, if you are interested) and the National Security Agency. The DSA has public keys that use anywhere from 512-bit to 1024-bit prime numbers and a 160-bit private key. Rather than using DSA to generate a signature of the entire document (a possibly time-consuming operation), a one-way hash of the document is generated using the MD5 algorithm; this hash is signed. MD5 generates a 128-bit string that is unique for a given input document. To verify the signature, the one-way hash of the received document is generated and checked against the signed 128-bit string from the sender. If the two match, the document has not been tampered with.

> **NOTE**
>
> For more information on digital signatures and public key cryptography, check out *Applied Cryptography*, Second Edition, by Bruce Shneier (published by John Wiley & Sons, ISBN 0-471-11709-9). This book is a very good introduction to cryptography in general, as well as an excellent reference for the details on specific algorithms. On the Web, the NIST's Computer Security Resource Clearing house (http://csrc.ncsl.nist.gov/) provides copies of the Federal Information Processing Standards for DSA and SHA. The sci.crypt newsgroup and its Frequently Asked Questions posting is another good starting place for cryptography resources.

The `java.security` API

The `java.security` package implements the new Java security API. This API is intended to give developers access to security functionality in a standard, cross-platform way. In addition to the digital signatures, key management, and access control lists provided in the 1.1 release, future releases of `java.security` will provide support for exchanging digital keys and data encryption. For more information on the `java.security` package.

The Signature Class

The `Signature` class represents a digital signature algorithm. The constructor takes as its parameter a string representing the name of the signature algorithm desired. Once a `Signature` reference has been obtained, it must be initialized with either the private key (for signing) or the public key (for verifying a signature). To generate a signature, call the `update()` method with the contents of the document to be signed. The `update()` method takes either a single `byte` argument or a `byte[]` array with optional offset and length. After the contents of the document have been given to `Signature()`, the `sign()` method can be called to obtain a `byte[]` representing the signature. Verifying a signature is very similar to creating one: After calling the `initVerify()` method with the `PublicKey`, the contents of the document are passed to `update()`. Once the entire contents have been given, the `verify()` method is called with the `byte[]` representing what the signature should be. The `verify()` method returns a `boolean` specifying whether the signature was valid or not; the `Signature()` method is reset and ready to verify another signature by the same `PublicKey`.

The KeyPairGenerator and KeyPair Classes

These classes are used to generate a pair of public and private keys for use with other security packages. The `KeyPairGenerator` class's static method `getInstance()` returns a reference to an object, which in turn may be used to generate public and private keys for the algorithm specified. The `initialize()` method sets up the generator to provide a key of a specific *strength* (that is, a key of a certain length, such as 512 bits or 1024 bits). The `generateKeyPair()` method returns a `KeyPair` object. The `KeyPair` class provides two methods, `getPrivateKey()` and `getPublicKey()`, which return the corresponding key reference.

The PrivateKey and PublicKey Interfaces

These two interfaces represent key material for various algorithms. Each algorithm returns objects implementing these interfaces, which then behave as appropriate for the algorithm. For example, the DSA algorithm has the `DSAPrivateKey` and `DSAPublicKey` interfaces. In general (unless you are implementing an algorithm), you do not manipulate keys directly, only give them as parameters.

The Identity, IdentityScope, and Certificate Classes

The `Identity` class represents an entity that can be authenticated by a public key. The entity represented can be a person, a company, or even a particular computer. `Identity` objects have a name associated with them; this name should be unique within a given scope. An IdentityScope represents a scope for an Identity, giving the context in which the Identity object exists. Both Identity and IdentityScope objects can have one or more Certificate objects associated with them. A Certificate represents a guarantee by some entity that the Identity and its associated public key actually belong to the owner represented by the Identity.

For example, a programmer can be represented by an Identity object, which he or she uses to sign code he or she produces. The IdentityScope for this Identity object could be set to Acme Software, the company for which the programmer works. The programmer's Identity would have a Certificate signed by Acme Software. The IdentityScope for the company might have a Certificate signed by an entity providing certification of signatures (such as VeriSign or the U.S. Post Office). The Certification object can then be used to verify that the Identity is valid and belongs to the programmer.

Signing Code with javakey

The javakey utility included with the JDK provides facilities for managing identities and certificates, and for signing code. Along with the jar utility used to generate JAR files, javakey allows you to sign code and place the class files (and other resources used by an applet) into a single archive. Identities are stored in a database file named identitydb.obj, which is stored in a location specified in the java.security properties file in the JDK lib/security directory. When the applet is run in a properly configured browser, the signed code is granted privileges beyond those given to unsigned code. For example, a department can develop a signed applet for its intranet that stores its preferences in a local file on the user's computer. All the members of the department then set their browsers to allow code signed by the department to read and write files from their hard drive.

Creating an Identity and Key Pair

The first step in signing applets is to generate an identity and a public/private key pair for the identity. This is done with the following command:

```
% javakey -cs "MySigner" true
```

> **NOTE**
>
> In this section, all the examples that show javakey commands use the % character to represent your command or shell prompt.

The -cs "MySigner" part of the preceding command tells javakey that you want to create an identity in your identitydb.obj database for a signer with the name MySigner. The true parameter indicates that you will trust code signed by this particular signer. If the last argument is omitted, signatures from this signer can be verified but the code signed is not granted extra privileges. Now that you have an identity in your database, you must have `javakey` generate a key pair for your identity.

The following command is used to have `javakey` create a key pair:

```
% javakey -gk "MySigner" DSA 512 MySigner.public MySigner.private
```

This command tells `javakey` to generate a key (`-gk`) for the signer named `MySigner`. The next two arguments specify that you want a key for the DSA algorithm that is 512 bits long. The last two arguments are optional; they specify that you want `javakey` to store a copy of the public and private keys in the files named `MySigner.public` and `MySigner.private`, respectively.

> **CAUTION**
>
> Be careful with your private keys. Anyone who can get a copy of a private key can generate signatures for the corresponding identity.

Generating an X.509 Certificate

Before you can sign code, `javakey` must generate a certificate for your identity. To do this, you have to create a text file containing the parameters for the certificate, such as the identity to create the certificate for and what period of time the certificate is valid for. For this example, the last line of the text file specifies that you want a copy of the certificate saved into the file named `MySigner.x509`. This certificate file can be distributed to people who want to verify signatures from your example identity. You can embed comments in the directive file by preceding the comment with a # character. Listing 22.2 shows the contents of the directive file for your example.

Listing 22.2. The certificate directive file.

```
# This is a comment
issuer.name=MySigner

issuer.cert=1

subject.name=MySigner

subject.real.name=Example Signer
subject.org.unit=Bogus Organization
subject.org=Bogus Corporation
subject.country=US

start.date=15 Feb 1997
end.date=15 Feb 1998
serial.number=2000
out.file=MySigner.x509
```

Once you have the certificate directive in a file, you can use the `javakey -gc` options to generate the actual certificate. The following command assumes that the certificate directive in Listing 22.2 was placed in a file named `cdirective`:

```
% javakey -gc cdirective
```

Signing the JAR File

Now you are ready to sign a JAR file with your `MySigner` identity. Assume that a JAR file named `example.jar` has already been created, and that this JAR file contains an applet. The next step is to create a signing directive file that tells `javakey` what identity to use to sign the file, what certificate to use, and what to name the signature file. The `signer` parameter in the directive file specifies which identity you want to use to create the signature. The `cert` directive specifies which certificate the identity is to use (for this example, you'll use 1 because your signer has only one certificate). The next parameter, `chain`, is not used in JDK 1.1 and should be set to zero. The final parameter gives the name of the signature file that will be generated and included in the JAR file. Listing 22.3 shows the complete signing directive file.

Listing 22.3. The signature directive file.

```
# This is a comment
signer=MySigner
cert=1
chain=0
signature.file=MySig
```

The last step is to have `javakey` sign the JAR file. The signed version of the JAR file has `.sig` appended to its name. Here is the command line to use to have `javakey` sign our example JAR file:

```
% javakey -gs sdirective example.jar
```

Distributing Signed Code

You now should have a JAR file named `example.jar.sig` which contains your applet resources and a signature by the `MySigner` identity. This JAR file can be manipulated with the `jar` utility the same way as any other file. If you extract the contents of the JAR file, the `META-INF` directory contains the signature file just created. To grant trusted status to signed code, you must make available to users the X.509 certificate file created when the certificate was generated (this file is called `MySigner.x509` in the preceding example). Once a user has a copy of the certificate file, he or she can use `javakey` to add the identity to his or her own database.

The first step in verifying a signature is similar to creating the identity—but instead of using the `-cs` flags, you use only the `-c` flag, as shown here:

```
% javakey -c MySigner true
```

After creating the identity, you must import the actual information about the identity from the certificate file. This is done using the `javakey -ic` options, which take the identity name and the filename containing the certificate as parameters:

```
% javakey -ic MySigner MySigner.x509
```

Now any code signed by the `MySigner` identity that is loaded over the network is given full access, just as if it had been loaded from a local disk.

Other javakey Operations

The `javakey` utility controls your database of identities and certificates. It can be used to list or remove identities as well as create them. The `-l` option allows you to list a summary of all the identities contained in `identitydb.obj`. You can use the `-ld` option to list detailed information for all entities in the database; use `-li` to limit the detailed display to a specific identity. Listing 22.4 shows what an identity listing looks like.

Listing 22.4. An identity listing.

```
% javakey -ld

Scope: sun.security.IdentityDatabase, source file: \fletch\identitydb.obj

MySigner[identitydb.obj][trusted]
        public key initialized
        certificates:
        certificate 1   for  : CN=Example Signer, OU=Bogus Organization, O=Bogus
  Corporation, C=US
                        from : CN=Example Signer, OU=Bogus Organization, O=Bogus
  Corporation, C=US

        No further information available.
```

If you want to remove an identity from the database, you can use the `-r` option with the name of the identity to delete:

```
% javakey -r MySigner
```

Summary

This chapter introduced you to JavaBeans, JavaSoft's software component technology. You learned how JavaBeans relates to Java, which is an interesting topic because of the way the JavaBeans technology is built on top of Java. From there, you moved on to the basic structure of a JavaBeans component, which was probably familiar to you from the structure of Java classes. You learned that JavaBeans components are internally composed of data and methods—which is to be expected because JavaBeans is fundamentally an object-oriented technology. You finished up the section by learning about a couple of development scenarios involving JavaBeans components, which gave you some insight into the options developers have in how they use JavaBeans.

Then you had a look inside the JavaBeans technology by exploring the JavaBeans API. This API is ultimately responsible for delivering all the functionality of JavaBeans. You learned that the API has several major functional areas, each of which is devoted to a particular JavaBeans service. You covered the basics of each of these areas and looked at the kinds of problems they address and the different solutions they provide.

JAR files provide a way to simplify applet and JavaBean distribution. Along with the new code-signing facilities, JAR files should greatly increase the usefulness of applets by making them easier to distribute and allowing trusted code to step outside the narrow limits of the sandbox. Additionally, the `java.util.zip` package provides support for manipulating ZIP and GNU Zip archives in any Java program.

You should now have an idea how the code-signing facilities in the JDK 1.1 extend the capabilities of applets. The new `java.security` API provides a framework for manipulating digital signatures in general, as well as for creating signed code. You now understand how to use `javakey` to create and manage identities and certificates for distributing and verifying signed code.

In the next chapter, you will be introduced to some of the issues involved in using Java with JavaScript. Basically, you will be shown how JavaScript can be used to control a Java applet, and how a Java applet can take advantage of some of the JavaScript features. After that, you will move into the area of server-side programming. All too often server-side programming and the benefits of using it are ignored or simply overlooked. After you read through the server-side scripting section you should feel much more at ease with those programs.

Integrating Java and JavaScript

*by Rob Falla and
Rick Darnell*

IN THIS CHAPTER

CHAPTER 23

Chapters 15 through 23 discuss either Java or JavaScript; you learned how to use JavaScript and Java and were presented with several practical applications for them—applications that you can basically cut and paste into your editor.

Alone, Java and JavaScript represent significant developments in the online world. They enable you to stretch the behavior of your pages far beyond what was ever imagined for the World Wide Web.

Together, they become even more powerful. As you'll recall, although Java is powerful enough to add animation, sound, and other features within the confines of an applet, it's very cumbersome to directly interact with an HTML page. JavaScript isn't big or powerful enough to match Java's programming power, but it is uniquely suited to work directly with the elements that comprise an HTML document.

By combining the best features of both, your applet can interact with your Web page, or vice versa, offering a new level of interactivity for both Java and JavaScript.

An understanding of the following terms will help you with the discussion in this chapter:

Element	An element is an HTML tag, a style sheet, a script, or an applet. Basically, anything in the code of the HTML document is an element.
Ordinal position	This is the order in which an element is included in the document. The first element is the first item in the ordinal position of elements. This is represented by a zero-based array of elements.

The Browsers Role

In order for Java and JavaScript to interact on your Web pages, both have to be active and enabled in the user's browser. Netscape Navigator and Internet Explorer both provide an interface for controlling how Java and JavaScript are received. There are many users who don't understand Java and JavaScript, and consequently, do not have these features turned on in their browsers. If you are going to put the time in to develop a dynamic HTML document with scripts and Java applets, you should consider explaining, somewhere on your site, how the user can configure his or her browser (including screen size) in order to take advantage of the excellent features you included.

Take a few minutes to review the procedures for setting up both the IE and NN browsers for Java and JavaSript.

Internet Explorer

The user interface is very straightforward and makes turning the language on a snap. The scripting languages available in Internet Explorer, JScript, and VBScript are automatically enabled each time the browser starts. There is no security risk associated with using a scripting application, so there is no point in providing a means for disabling them. Follow these steps to make sure Java is active in Microsoft Internet Explorer:

1. From the IE menu bar, choose View | Options.
2. Select the Advanced tab (see Figure 23.1).

FIGURE 23.1.

Internet Explorer Options dialog box allows you to customize many aspects of your browser. Enabling the Java VM is done from the Advanced tab in the Options dialog box.

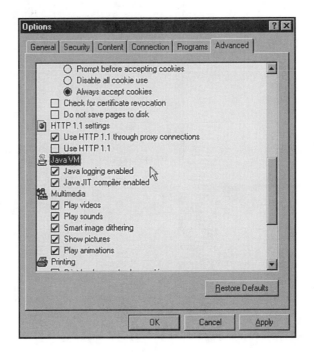

3. Scroll down the list of advanced options to Java VM. Select the Java JIT compiler enabled check box. This tells Internet Explorer that it should create all Java applets automatically using the internal Java JIT compiler.
4. Internet Explorer can log all Java activity, which includes displaying any systems messages (such as error messages). Select the Enable Java logging check box if you want a log file created for Java applets.

Netscape Navigator

To make sure both features are active in Netscape Navigator, follow these simple steps:

1. Choose Edit | Preferences.
2. The Preferences box is split into two frames. Select the Advanced category from the left frame (which contains the categories).
3. You see the Java and JavaScript check boxes in the right frame. These options are automatically set when you install Navigator. If they have been disabled you can re-enable them by checking the boxes—it's that easy (see Figure 23.2).

23

INTEGRATING JAVA
AND JAVASCRIPT

FIGURE 23.2.

FIGURE 23.2.

The Preference's Advanced category controls whether Java applets and JavaScript commands are processed for HTML documents.

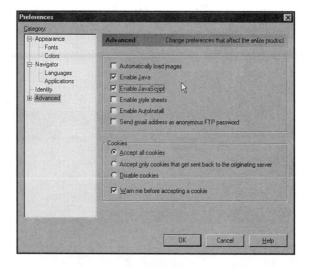

> **NOTE**
>
> Netscape Navigator also includes a Java Console for displaying applet-generated messages. In addition to system messages, the console is where any messages generated by the applet using the `java.lang.System` package, including `System.out.println`, are displayed. To display the console, select Window | Java Console.

Accessing a Java Applet with JavaScript

JavaScript can be used to modify applet behavior by creating a bridge between the Java applet and the HTML object model. Any programmable HTML element can control the applet with the help of JavaScript. Keep in mind that there are inherent differences in the way Java is treated by IE and NN. While Netscape supports a direct access model for JavaScript and Java interaction, Explorer treats Java applets like ActiveX controls.

> **ACTIVEX CONTROLS**
>
> An ActiveX control is actually an application control that can be shared across a networked environment. ActiveX's roots are in OLE. As a matter of fact, cut and paste is OLE in it's simplest form.
>
> ActiveX controls are based on the COM model. Applications are broken down into their components and shared across the network on an as needed basis. No component ever needs to be called upon unless it is actually needed. If you want to find out more about ActiveX controls, you can consult a book called *Internet Explorer Plug-in and ActiveX Companion*, written by Krishna Sankar and published by Que.

The bridge is created in a JavaScript function using the Java keyword `Packages`, which is supported only in Netscape. This keyword is used by the JavaScript application to invoke the Java method directly, as if the method were a member of the JavaScript language. For example, the following code invokes the Java class `System` of the `Java.lang` package and display the string as an error message in the Java Console:

```
function tryit(){
var Java = packages.java.lang.System.err
Java.println("Error Messages can be sent directly to Java")
}
```

While the IE browser doesn't support a direct access connection like that described for Netscape Navigator, it does provide a much broader HTML element base from which the Java applet may be accessed by JavaScript. These elements, known as *programmable elements,* can have an event assigned to them that activates an applet and control the applet's functionality. See Chapter 30, "Using the HTML Object Model and Creating Dynamic HTML Pages" for more information on programmable HTML elements.

JavaScript to Java syntax is identical to other JavaScript object syntax, so if you're familiar with this scripting language, adding Java control is an easy step. Here's an example:

```
<HTML>
<HEAD>
<STYLE><!--
.hand {cursor:hand} // tells the user to click the element.
--></STYLE>
<SCRIPT><!--
function aunapp() {
document.applets.sampleapp.start()
// starts the Java Applet
}
--></SCRIPT>
</HEAD>
<BODY>
<APPLET ID="sampleapp" CODE="sampleapp.class">
<PARAM ID=pict NAME="image" VALUE="somepic.gif">
</APPLET>
<H1 CLASS="hand" ID="init" onclick="runapp()" TITLE="start the application">
</H1>
<INPUT TYPE=BUTTON VALUE="STOP" onclick="document.applets.sampleapp.stop()">
</BODY>
</HTML>
```

Calling Java Methods

Groups of related classes are combined in a construct called a *package*. Classes from a package are usable by outside classes via the `import` command.

An example in all applets is the `java` package. One section of the package, `java.awt.Graphics`, is imported into every applet to give the `paint` method the additional methods it needs to add items to the applet screen. Because all applets are outside of the `java` package, its classes, or subsets of those classes, are imported into the applet for local use.

The syntax to call a Java package directly follows:

```
[Packages.]packageName.className.methodName
```

The object name is optional for the three default packages—java, sun, and netscape. These three can be referenced by their package name alone:

```
java.className.methodName
sun.className.methodName
netscape.className.methodName
```

Together with the package name, the object and class names can result in some unwieldy and error-prone typing. This is why you can also create new variables using the package product.

```
var System = Packages.java.lang.System;
System.out.println("Hello from Java in JavaScript.");
```

Controlling Java Applets

Controlling an applet with a script is a fairly easy matter, but it does require a knowledge of the applet you're working with. Any public variable, method, or property within the applet is accessible through JavaScript. There are two public methods common to all applets which you can always use—start and stop. These provide a handy means to control when the applet is active.

> **TIP**
>
> If you're changing the values of variables within an applet, the safest way is to create a new method within the applet for the purpose. This method can accept the value from JavaScript, perform any error checking, then pass the new value along to the rest of the applet. This helps prevent unexpected behavior or applet crashes.

There are five basic activities common to all applets, as opposed to one basic activity for applications. An applet has more activities to correspond to the major events in its life cycle on the user's browser.

None of the activities have any definitions. You must override the methods with a subclass within your applet.

- Initialization—This occurs after the applet is first loaded. This can include creating objects, setting state variables, and loading images.
- Starting—After initialization or stopping, an applet is started. The difference between initialization and starting is that initialization only happens once, while starting can occur many times.
- Painting—This is how the applet actually gets information to the screen, from simple lines and text to images and colored backgrounds. Painting can occur a lot of times in the course of an applet's life.

Stopping—This method suspends the applet execution and stops it from using system resources. This can be important because an applet continues to run even after a user leaves the page.

Destroying—This is the extreme form of stop. Destroying an applet begins a clean-up process in which running threads are terminated and objects are released.

With this information in hand, getting started begins with the applet tag, `<APPLET>`. Giving your applet a name makes JavaScript references easier to read. See the following code for an example of naming an applet:

```
<APPLET CODE="UnderConstruction" NAME="AppletConstruction" WIDTH=60 HEIGHT=60>
</APPLET>
```

Naming the applet isn't absolutely necessary however, because JavaScript creates an array of applets when the page is loaded. Including it does make for a much more readable page, which is easier to edit.

To use a method of the applet from JavaScript, use the following syntax:

```
document.appletName.methodOrProperty
```

Using the Applets Array

An array is created (in both browsers) that contains a reference to every instance of the `<APPLET>` tag. It is used to reference all the applets on a page. Use the following syntax when writing your own code:

```
document.all.appletID.MethodOrProperty
document.all(n).MethodOrProperty
document.applets[index].methodOrProperty
document.applets[appletName].methodOrProperty
```

The first two methods work only in Internet Explorer, which has added the `all` collection to the object model. The `all` collection is an array of every element on the HTML document. This collection allows the developer to access its members by their ID value or as a reference to the element's ordinal position in the collection. The ID and ordinal position are valid syntax for both browsers. They allow you to get properties and methods for the applet by way of the applet's array. The same rules hold true for the applets array—it is a collection of every applet on the HTML document. Once again, you may access the properties and methods of this collections members using `ID`, `NAME`, or by making a reference to the applet's ordinal position within the applets collection.

Starting and Stopping an Applet with JavaScript

One of the easy methods of controlling applet behavior is starting and stopping its execution. This can be accomplished using the `start` and `stop` methods common to every applet. Use a form and two buttons to add the functions to your Web page (see Figure 23.3).

```
<FORM>
<INPUT TYPE="button" VALUE="Start" onClick="document.appletName.start()">
<INPUT TYPE="button" VALUE="Stop" onClick="document.appletName.stop()">
</FORM>
```

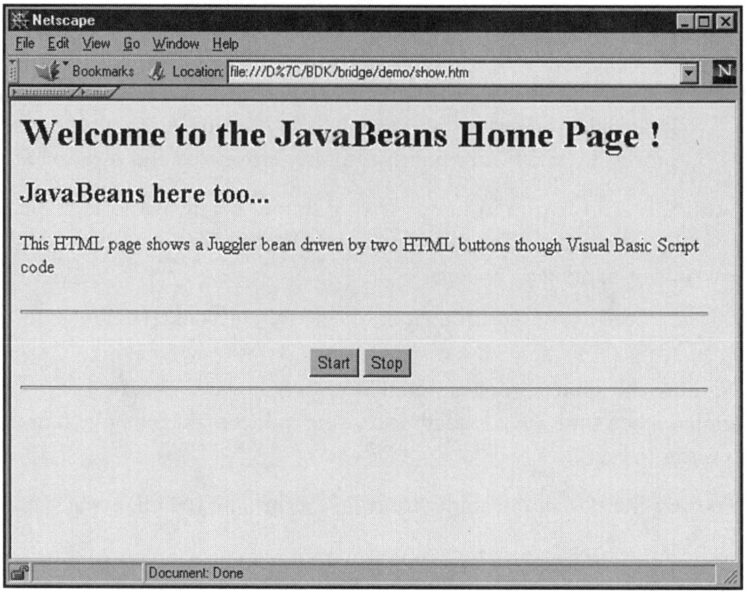

FIGURE 23.3.

One of the simplest methods of controlling an applet is to use buttons to start and stop it.

Remember the Public in Java

You can also call other methods, depending on their visibility (public or private) to the world outside the applet. Any method, or variable with a public declaration can be called by JavaScript.

> **TIP**
>
> Any variable or method within the applet that doesn't include a specific declaration of scope is protected by default, it's private. If you don't see the public declaration, it's not. In other words, you must explicitly declare a method as being public, otherwise it is considered to be a private method.

The syntax to call applet methods from JavaScript is simple and can be integrated with browser events such as the previous button code snippet:

```
document.appletName.methodName(arg1,arg2,arg3)
```

Accessing JavaScript from a Java Applet

Java can take a direct look at your HTML page through JavaScript objects. This requires the use of the `netscape.javascript.JSObject` class when the applet is created.

To include the `JSObject` class as part of your applet, use the `import` command as you would normally include any other class package:

```
import netscape.javascript.JSObject;
```

Another important feature also necessary in the applet tag—MAYSCRIPT. This is a security feature that gives specific permission for the applet to access JavaScript objects.

```
<APPLET CODE="colorPreview.class" WIDTH=50 HEIGHT=50 NAME="Preview" MAYSCRIPT>
```

Without it, any attempt to access JavaScript from the applet results in an exception. If you want to exclude an applet from accessing the page, simply leave out the MAYSCRIPT parameter.

TIP

netscape.javascript.JSObject is included with the other class files under the Netscape directory. In Windows, this is \Program Files\Netscape\Navigator\Program\java\classes\java_30.

In order for your Java program to compile, create a folder set called \netscape\javascript elsewhere on your hard drive, such as under the \java\lib folder. Copy the file to the new folder and make sure your CLASSPATH variable includes C:\java\lib\ in its list. After you restart the computer, the Java compiler should be able to find the new classes. This new package extends the standard Java Object class, so the newly created JSObjects are treated the same way other Java objects are treated.

CLASSES IN THE java PACKAGE

There are five subsets of classes within the java package:

lang These classes and interfaces are the core of the Java language. This subset includes the Runnable interface (used for threading) and the basic data types (Boolean, character, class, integer, object, string, and so on). It also includes the System class, which provides access to system-level behaviors.

util This group of utility interfaces and classes aren't crucial to running Java, but they provide ways to make programming easier. This includes utilities to generate random numbers, stacks, hash tables, and dates.

awt The Abstract Windowing Toolkit (also known as Another Windows Toolkit) contains the graphical items to help create user interfaces and other graphical items. It includes interfaces for a layout manager and menu container, along with classes for form elements, colors, keyboard and mouse events, fonts, images, menus, and windows.

io Used for passing information in and out of applets and applications, this subset includes classes for sending and receiving input streams and files, not including networking activity.

net This subset of classes has the tools and operations for working over a network. This group includes methods and interfaces to handle URLs, URL content, and socket connections.

Java and JavaScript Values

JSObject gives Java the capability to look at and change objects defined through JavaScript. This requires certain assumptions, especially when passing or receiving values from Java. Every JavaScript value is assigned some form from `java.lang.Object` to ensure compatibility. The following list identifies the assumptions:

- Objects—Any object sent or received from Java remains in its original object wrapper.

- Java numbers—Because JavaScript doesn't support the variety of numerical types as Java (`byte`, `char`, `short`, `int`, `long`, `float`, and `double`), they lose their specific type and become a basic JavaScript number.

NOTE

A *Java float* is a 32-bit floating point number. A version for larger numbers or greater precision behind the decimal point is the double, which is 64 bits long. `bytes`, `shorts`, `ints`, and `longs` are all integers of various bit lengths, beginning with 8 bits for the byte and going up to 64 bits for the `long`. A char is a 16-bit number representing a single Unicode character.

- JavaScript numbers—There's no way to tell what kind of number Java may be receiving from JavaScript. All JavaScript numbers are converted to Java floats.

- Booleans and Strings—These are passed essentially unchanged. Java Booleans become JavaScript Booleans and vice versa. The same occurs with strings.

Looking at the JavaScript Window

In order to get a handle on JavaScript objects, including form items and frames, you must create an object to hold the current Navigator window first. `getWindow` provides the means.

First, you need to create a new variable of type `JSObject`:

```
JSObject jsWin;
```

Then, using the `JSObject` class, assign the window to the variable:

```
jsWin = JSObject.getWindow(this);
```

This type of work is typically accomplished within the applet's `init()` method.

After you have a handle on the window, you can start breaking it into its various components with `getMember`. This method returns a specific object from the next level of precedence. For example, to access a form on a Web page, with a form called `response`, the following set of statements can be used:

```
jsWin = JSObject.getWindow(this);
JSObject jsDoc = (JSObject) jsWin.getMember("document");
JSObject responseForm = (JSObject) jsDoc.getMember("response");
```

In JavaScript, this form is referred to as `window.document.response`. Note that each JavaScript object is assigned to its own variable in Java and is not a property of a parent object. The form in Java is contained in `responseForm`, not `jsWin.jsDoc.responseForm`.

> **NOTE**
>
> All parts of an HTML document exist in JavaScript in set relationships to each other. This is called *instance hierarchy*, because it works with specific items on the page rather than general classes of items. The `window` object is at the top of the pyramid. It is the parent of all other objects.
>
> The Java `netscape` package recognizes and uses this hierarchy through its `getWindow` and `getMethod` methods. `getWindow` gets the window object (the highest object), while `getMethod` returns individual members of the next level.

So far, you've only retrieved broad objects, such as windows and forms. Getting a specific value from JavaScript follows the same principles, although now you need a Java variable of the proper type to hold the results instead of an instance of `JSObject`.

> **TIP**
>
> Don't forget about passing numbers between JavaScript and Java. All JavaScript numbers are converted to a float. You can cast it to another Java type if needed after it's in the applet.

Using the previous form, say there's a text field (`name`), a number (`idNum`), and a check box (`member`). Each of these values is retrieved from JavaScript using the following commands:

```
jsWin = JSObject.getWindow(this);
JSObject jsDoc = (JSObject) jsWin.getMember("document");
JSObject responseForm = (JSObject) jsDoc.getMember("response");
JSObject nameField = (JSObject) responseForm.getMember("name");
JSOBject idNumField = (JSObject) responseForm.getMember("idNum");
JSOBject memberField = (JSObject) responseForm.getMember("memberField");
String nameValue = (String) nameField.getMember("value");
Float idNumValue = (Float) idNumField.getMember("value");
Boolean memberValue = (Boolean) memberField.getMember("checked");
```

This chunk of code becomes a bit unwieldy, especially when there are several values needed from JavaScript. If you need to access more than several elements on a page, it helps to create a new method to handle the process:

```
protected JSObject getElement(String formName, String elementName) {
    JSObject jsDoc = (JSObject) JSObject.getWindow().getMember("document");
    JSObject jsForm = (JSObject) jsDoc.getMember(formName);
    JSObject jsElement = (JSObject) jsElement.gerMember(elementName);
    return jsElement;
}
```

V

PART

CGI and Controlling the Web from the Server

Putting Your Server to Work

by Robert McDaniel

IN THIS CHAPTER

CHAPTER 24

Many applications and features get their start through implementation on the server side. Several of the first interactive features of Web sites were introduced through server-side programming, either through CGI programs or through server-side plug-ins.

Initially, this was done for a few reasons. First, client machines at the time were not nearly as powerful as their server machine counterparts. Many tasks simply took too long to accomplish on the slower client machines. Also, in general, many of the programming tasks were easier to program on the server than on the clients.

As client/server technology has progressed and client machines have become much more powerful, features are moving off the server to the client machines. This is done to distribute the load to the many client machines, rather than having a bottleneck with the server machine.

This new push for clients performing the majority of the work has shifted the focus to development on the client side. For the World Wide Web, this means fatter and more complex Web browsers that perform more and more processing. With most of the focus on the Web browser, server-side applications are often overshadowed and overlooked.

Naturally, distributing processing load to the client side makes sense most of the time. However, there are some Web applications that need the help of the server in order to function.

This chapter's focus is on when and how to put your server to work. You learn about:

- Server-side programs and scripts
- Advantages to server-side scripting
- Common servers-side applications
- Placing server programs in your Web site

Server-Side Programs and Scripts

The first form of programming and scripting for Web pages was on the server side. As a way to add functionality to the Web server, you could extend it through writing CGI programs. Because of some performance issues with CGI programs, most Web server developers created an open API for their programs, so you could write server-side plug-ins, which further enable you to extend the functionality of your Web server.

In this section, you are introduced to server-side programs and scripts. You learn the difference between these two types of programming, and some common applications for each. You also find out what programming languages are available for writing your server-side applications.

What Are Server-Side Scripts and Programs?

Server-side programs and scripts are applications that run on a Web server machine rather than on the user's machine. The server-side applications run in conjunction with the Web server software, which handles the HTTP requests for documents.

Server-side applications can perform a variety of functions, such as working with databases, searching for keywords in documents, and creating custom log files. To some degree, your only limits for server-side applications are the bounds of your imagination and programming abilities.

Unlike client-side scripting, which is introduced in Chapter 13, "Scripting Basics," server-side applications can be either scripts or programs. The difference between these two types of applications lies in a process called compiling. Programs are compiled applications, whereas scripts are interpreted. The differences between compiling and interpreting applications are discussed in "Compiled Programs and Interpreted Scripts" in Chapter 13.

Compiling versus Interpreting

As you already learned in Chapter 13, there are various advantages to using both types of applications, compiled and interpreted. With compiled programs, you have the benefits of faster execution because of the compiled code having been optimized for the platform on which it is running; there is no runtime parsing of source code. Also with compiled programs, you also can have source code integrity if you distribute your executables to other people.

There are disadvantages to compiled programs, too. First, the time it takes to code, test, and debug a compiled program is typically much longer than the time to program the same application in a scripting language. This is because of the time involved in actually compiling the source code.

The other major disadvantage is cross-platform compatibility. Because compiled programs have been changed into machine-dependent binary code, you cannot run a compiled program on a machine of a different platform. You would have to recompile the program for that other machine, often changing a large amount of your program.

You also have advantages and disadvantages with scripts. The first advantage of scripts over programs is their ability to run on other platforms, with few or no changes. Most commands in scripting languages are machine-independent. It is up to the command interpreter, which is a compiled program, to know how to execute the command for a given platform.

Scripts also beat out programs when it comes to maintenance. Making quick changes to a script is no more difficult than editing a text file. You are ready to run and test your script as soon as you save your changes—you don't have to spend any time compiling first. This is a major benefit, especially if you like to do a lot of trial-and-error type programming.

The two major disadvantages of scripts versus programs are a script source code's lack of integrity and the speed at which scripts run. Because a script is just a text file, if you distribute your script, you are distributing your source code! Also, scripts can be significantly slower than programs. All of the time you spent compiling gets added to the execution time every time your run the program. Scripts are noticeably slower if you are performing computationally intensive tasks such as sorting and searching through a lot of records.

Now, with programming applications for the server side, some of these advantages and disadvantages are discounted. Mostly, the advantages gained from cross-platform compatibility of scripts and code integrity of programs are not that important. Typically, you run your application on a single machine, maybe changing platforms once, if ever. You probably do not distribute your applications to anyone else. Therefore, you don't need to take these factors into consideration.

Instead, you should be greatly concerned with performance factors, such as speed. Because the server has to run an application for many clients at the same time, you want these applications to be as swift as possible. This does not preclude you from using a scripting language—keep performance in mind if you are coding a processor-intensive function, such as a search or a sort.

Which Programming Language Should You Use?

When creating applications to run on the Web server, you have many choices as to the programming language you use. Naturally, the task you want to accomplish can narrow your choices. For example, if you wanted to create some plug-ins for the Web server, you would need to work in a programming language that can access the necessary API calls for the server. For most Web servers, the API language of choice is C. However, this may not always be the case.

There are also several choices when it comes to writing server-side scripts. CGI applications have more choices than any other server-side application. The only real limitation is whether the language you want to use works on the machine running your Web server. There are some practical choices you should make. If you are writing an application that performs a lot of computations, such as sorting or searching, you probably want to use a compiled language such as C or C++. Compiled programs give you much better performance. However, compiled languages often require more programming time than an interpreted language. Perl, which is an interpreted language, is very popular for writing CGI scripts because of its ease of use.

Some Web servers are starting to develop built-in scripting interfaces. Different than the API, the scripting interface allows you to do simple scripts for your Web pages that are executed by the Web server, with the results sent to the Web browser. LiveWire is an example of this type of scripting interface. It is developed by Netscape Communications Corporation for its Web server, and enables you to write JavaScript programs executed by the Web server. Naturally, the limitation of language choice with these interfaces depends on what languages the company producing the Web server software supports. With LiveWire, you can only use JavaScript, not VBScript or Perl.

In general, a good starting place for a choice of programming language is one with which you are familiar. It is much easier to program an application if you don't have to spend the time learning the programming language. From there, narrow your choice by the task you have to accomplish. In other words, choice the best tool for the job.

Advantages to Server-Side Applications

In Chapter 13, you are introduced to client-side scripting, and the many advantages and applications of programming on the client side. In general, it's a good idea to distribute as much of the processing load to the individual clients rather than relying on the server. With more powerful and feature-rich Web browsers being introduced at a blazing speed, you might come to think that client-side programming will eventually replace server-side programming.

However, this is not the case. Server-side applications have unique benefits that will keep them around for years to come. Many of these benefits are features that are not even available to your client-side programs and scripts. Specifically, server-side programming provides the following advantages:

- Cross-platform/cross-browser support
- More options for applications
- Increased power
- Code integrity

Cross-Platform/Cross-Browser Support

A major concern when programming for the client side is that you do not know the type of machine, configuration, or Web browser with which the user is visiting your Web site. These large unknowns are the environment in which your program must be able to run. You have to program for all the possibilities—or as many as you care to support—and make sure your software is working as expected.

Also, although most Web browsers in use today do support client-side scripting, they don't all support the same languages or even the same implementation of the same language. You will run into many inconsistencies and bugs, which result in your Web pages being seen entirely different in each browser, if it even gets displayed at all. Some browsers even return scripting error messages depending on what you have programmed.

On the other hand, with server-side applications, you only have one machine to worry about—your Web server machine. When you get the application to run correctly on your server machine, you are ready to put it into production. This is because you are not sending a program to the user's Web browser. You are only sending the results of an application after it has been run. As long as the data you send to the user's Web browser is in standard HTML or another displayable format, you have cross-platform/cross-browser compatibility with only having one version of the program.

More Options for Applications

As you saw in Chapter 13, client-side scripts are fairly limited in the actions they can perform. In fact, some of the common tasks of client-side scripts require a server-side application with which to work in conjunction. For example, when performing form input validation with client-side scripts, you need a server-side CGI program to handle the form input when it has been validated and sent to the Web server.

Server-side programming offers more control and flexibility as to the tasks you can perform. On the server, you have the ability to access outside information, such as data in databases. You can run complex programs in high-level programming languages, or perform an electronic payment transaction to fulfill online orders. The only restriction is that you return your results to the user's Web browser in formatting that can be properly displayed in a Web browser.

This is not to say that server-side programming should be used to the exclusion of client side. In fact, many of the applications you perform in a client-side environment, such as image rollovers and dynamic status bar messages, cannot be done on the server side. At the same time, most server-side applications could not be done on the client side, either. Server-side applications do have limitations, but in general, the number of possibilities on the server side far exceed the possibilities on the client side.

Increased Power

In the early days of the client/server distribution model, server machines were significantly more powerful than their client machine counterparts. Because of this, the majority of applications were written on the server side. Writing these applications for the client side was not a viable option, because it would take too long to run them on the slower machines.

Over the last several years, the performance level of client machines has risen dramatically, and the gap in performance between these two machines has narrowed. As a result, more and more functionality is being distributed to these more powerful client machines, easing the load on the server machine. Because the server machine doesn't have to do as much work, it is no longer as big of a bottleneck for information flow.

With the World Wide Web, there are some complex applications that could be programmed to run in a user's Web browser. However, even though most users' machines are fairly powerful, you don't know exactly how powerful. Specifics about the user's machine, such as the amount of memory, the processor, or the clock speed, are a mystery to you. By creating processor-intensive applications, you are gambling that the majority of your users can run your program in a reasonable amount of time.

This issue has been one of the largest barriers for widespread adoption of Java programming. From one machine to the next, Java can run either really well or really poorly. Unfortunately, as a Web page author, you cannot determine beforehand which case it will be.

Because you cannot always count on the performance level of the user's machine, you want to code your processor-intensive applications for the server side. In general, high performance Web server machines are still more powerful than the average computer being used for Web browsing. Even at high loads, the Web server can quickly run your program and send the results back to the user's Web browser.

You also get the advantage of seeing exactly how quickly your program runs for every user. Because the server is running the program for every user, the results you see when accessing it are the same as the results your end user experiences.

Code Integrity—Hide What Is Really Happening

With all client-side scripts, your source code is available within the HTML code for your document. Anyone with the ability to view the source code of a Web page can view your script. That is not a big deal for many client-side applications. Rollovers, status bar messages, and validating form data are not exactly proprietary information. Chances are, you learned how to do some of your HTML or client-side scripting from looking at others' source code.

However, there are some applications that provide a competitive advantage over your competition, or that simply cost you some money. You would not want the source code to these applications to be available to other people. The advantage to coding these applications on the server side is that the source code is not available to other users. Even if you use a scripting language such as Perl, which is stored in a simple text file, your source code is not available for inspection. As long as you have configured your Web server properly, any request to a CGI script results in the Web server executing the program on the server and only returning the results to the requesting Web browser. And, as for server-side plug-ins or server-side scripts like LiveWire, the user most likely does not even know they exist, nor does he or she have the ability to gain access to their source code.

Common Server-Side Applications

Server-side programming is a powerful way to extend the functionality of your Web site. As you learned in the previous section, there are many advantages for creating applications on the server side, mostly in terms of performance and cross-platform compatibility.

Some applications implemented on the server side could instead be implemented on the client side. Imagemaps, for example, are one such application. Early image maps could only be implemented on the server side, through the use of the image map CGI program. However, with the introduction of client-side imagemaps, you now have the ability to implement your imagemaps entirely in the Web browser, bypassing all server-side programming.

Although the ability to implement some server-side applications on the client side exists, this is not commonly the case. Most of the applications implemented on the server need to be there for some reason, usually because of access to server-side resources. In this section, you explore a few common applications for server-side programming. Specifically, the server-side applications you look at are as follows:

- Search engines
- Database access
- Chat and bulletin board services
- Form handlers

Search Engines

A search engine is the program that enables users to search through documents on your Web site. Search engines have varying functionality. Simple search engines may only have some predefined categories for which you can search for matches. For example, a Web site that features used cars for sale might have a search engine that allows you to search the vehicle manufacturer returning only the listed make and model.

Complex search engines allow keyword searches, returning all the documents that contain the supplied keywords. Keyword searches are much more powerful from the user's perspective, because they allow users to define what the search engine should look for. However, a keyword search is much more difficult to implement for a programmer, and can be much more time-consuming for the machine performing the search.

In general, two of the most computationally intensive tasks a computer can perform are searching and sorting. These two topics alone are the subject of many computer science courses. A basic search engine contains both tasks. When a search is performed, all of the documents, or a compiled index, are first checked for the search string supplied by the user. The resulting matches are then sorted after the keywords search, displaying first the document most likely to match the user's criteria.

Because search engines contain both of these computationally intensive tasks, the code needs to be highly optimized in order to run efficiently. A search feature is of little use and will be rarely used if it takes too long to return results.

Search engines must be implemented on the server side. The documents or the document index reside on the server machine. The search engine must look through these items on the Web server in order to find matches to the user's search string. Also, because searching is so intensive, you need a powerful machine to run the program, again making the server side the correct platform for the application. For highly trafficked sites where the search feature is used frequently, a dedicated machine running the search engine is a good idea.

If you have a relatively small site and are not that interested in supporting keyword searches, you could write your own search engine program. Rather than spending the time and effort creating something for your site, you may want to simply license the technology that someone else has already optimized for the task.

Excite, Incorporated has an excellent search engine designed for a Web site. It is called Excite for Web Servers and supports complex keyword searches. In fact, they have integrated technology that enables related documents that do not contain the user's keywords to be returned.

Excite for Web Servers is an excellent choice for a Web site search engine. Beyond the technical capabilities of the product lies the low cost for licensing. With their current license, Excite for Web Servers is free for download!

The quality of their product and the attractive cost structure make Excite for Web Servers the search engine of choice for many top-rated Web sites, such as the following:

- *Forbes* Magazine (`http://www.forbes.com`)
- Hotwired (`http://www.hotwired.com`)
- Woman's Wire (`http://www.women.com`)
- Mr. Showbiz (`http://www.mrshowbiz.com`)
- Gamespot (`http://www.gamespot.com`)

Figure 24.1 shows the Excite for Web servers search engine interface implemented on JavaSoft's Web site. Figure 24.2 shows how Excite for Web Servers displays the results for a keyword search.

FIGURE 24.1.

The Excite for Web Servers interface on JavaSoft's Web site.

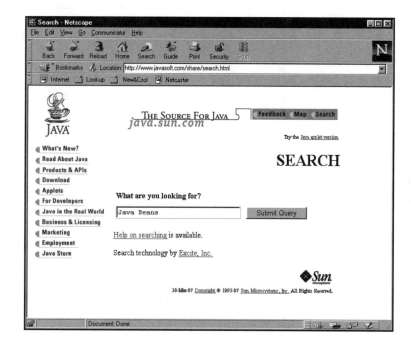

You can view the complete license and download the software from Excite's Web site at `http://www.excite.com/navigate/`.

Database Access

Databases are a powerful way to store information. When data is stored in a database, it is relatively easy to maintain by adding, deleting, and modifying records. Through database access systems, viewing the information is also relatively simple, and the data being viewed is as up-to-date as the information in the database.

FIGURE 24.2.

Search Results generated by Excite for Web Servers.

Used by permission of Sun Microsystems, Inc. Copyright 1997, Sun Microsystems, Inc. 901 San Antonio Road, Palo Alto, CA, 94303-4900, USA. All rights reserved.

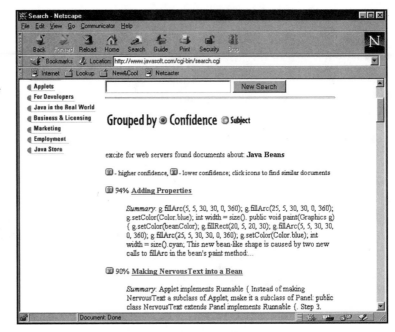

In a broad sense, the World Wide Web can act as a database access system. The front end, where the user sends the request for data and then views the results, is the Web browser. The user could be requesting a Web page that contains some data from a database. Another way the user could access database information would be by submitting a form. The form could be a query requesting information from the database, or the form data may be information to be added to the database. Either way, the request is sent on the Web server.

After the request reaches the Web server, which requires data retrieval from a database, a server-side application must handle the request. The server-side program, usually a CGI script, then queries the database for the necessary information, formats the results for display in a Web browser, and sends the information back to the user's Web browser.

Integrating database systems with Web servers is a powerful way to maintain a current Web site with dynamic, up-to-date information. The Web site administrator can easily maintain data in the database without having to recreate Web pages every time a change needs to be made. In addition, as soon as a change is made to the database, the updated information is immediately available to the Web site users.

Databases for use with a Web site can be as simple as a comma-delimited text file, with each record taking a single line in the file. A CGI script is able to open the database file, search through it if necessary, and return the results to the user's Web browser.

Naturally, for larger databases, a full-featured, relational database is a better solution. Relational databases store data in related tables. A specific database's creator defines the relationship between records in different tables. Commercial relational database systems are highly optimized for performing database queries. A database query is the act of searching through the database for matches to specific search criteria, which can be computationally intense for large databases. If you plan on having a large database for your Web site, look into commercial database packages such as the following:

- Oracle (`http://www.oracle.com`)
- Sybase (`http://www.sybase.com`)
- Informix (`http://www.informix.com`)

Whether with a text file database or a commercial relational database system, you need server-side programming to interface the database with your Web server. Client-side scripting does not have the ability to integrate with a server-side database.

For simple text-based databases, your CGI script acts as both the database management program and as the interface between the Web server and the database. You need a CGI script to handle the interaction between the Web server and the database for the commercial relational database systems. An advantage to the systems mentioned earlier is that there are many server-side CGI packages already available, which eases the job of writing custom CGI scripts for interfacing these databases with your Web server.

Chat and Bulletin Board Services

Creating a community around your Web site is a strong way to retain your existing customer base and increase the amount of traffic your Web site gets. Although community itself does not revolve around a single technology, two features that help build communities are chat and bulletin board services.

Chat is the act of communicating with other people online in real-time. This can be done with text chat, graphical chat, or voice chat. Text chat is simply scrolling text messages. Typically, text chat programs have a single window in which all messages are displayed. You follow conversations by reading the messages as they scroll by. Ichat (`http://www.ichat.com`), one of the most popular text chat programs currently available, is shown in Figure 24.3. It contains a scrolling message window along with an input line for you to type your own messages.

Graphical chat adds another dimension to the interaction. A graphical chat program consists of an environment in which you and everyone else are represented by avatars. An *avatar* is a graphical representation of yourself, similar to the characters in video games. In graphical chat environments, the challenge is in displaying the messages from other users. Many graphical chat programs use a separate text window, making the chat interface seem like text chat with a separate graphical component. Other graphical chats incorporate the messages in thought balloons around the individual avatars.

FIGURE 24.3.

Ichat text chat.

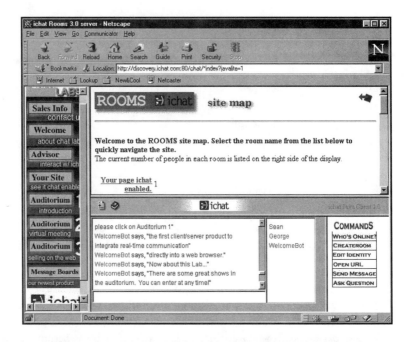

> **NOTE**
>
> Avatar (Sanskrit *avatara*, "descent"), in Hinduism, means the descent of a god into the world of humanity for the duration of a human life span.

One of the most popular graphical chat programs, The Palace (http://www.thepalace.com), is shown in Figure 24.4. Each of the images in the room with a name beneath it is an avatar of the various room users. The messages appear as bubbles around the avatars.

Voice chat goes a long way in helping the awkward displaying of messages in a graphical chat environment. Most voice chat programs are a combination of a graphical chat environment and a voice party line—you can actually hear the other participants speaking in the environment.

Most of these chat solutions are far too complicated for the Web browser and Web server to handle alone. A full-featured chat program requires client-side plug-ins, a Java applet, or a separate, stand-alone application. However, they also require a server-side application in order to keep all the users up-to-date,

There have been some simple chat environments written with forms on the client side and with CGI scripts on the server side. The client periodically refreshes the current page, updating any new messages. In strict terms, this type of solution is more like a bulletin board than a chat application. Chat applications need to be in real-time. As soon as a user posts a message, all other people in the chat room must see it. Having to reload a Web page in order to receive updates removes the real-time component.

FIGURE 24.4.

The Palace graphical chat.

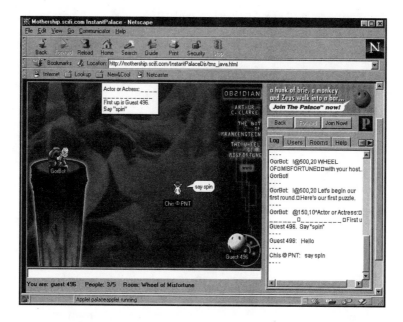

Bulletin boards are structures that allow users to read messages from other users, and post their own messages. Simple bulletin boards list the messages in the order they were received. More complex bulletin boards *thread* the messages by subject. In other words, if you reply to someone else's message, your reply appears underneath the message to which you were replying. Figure 24.5 shows a bulletin board on Time Warner's Pathfinder Network (`http://pathfinder.com`).

Unlike chat, bulletin boards are easily implemented with a CGI script. You could have the script maintain the Web pages that display your bulletin board, or you could have the script place the messages in a database. If you choose to use a database, you can dynamically generate the bulletin board Web page that gets sent to the user.

24

PUTTING YOUR SERVER TO WORK

CAUTION

Bulletin Boards allow users visiting your site to add content to your site in the form of messages. These messages can contain material that is inappropriate for your site. If you plan on implementing a Bulletin Board on your Web site, plan to monitor it frequently for postings that should be removed.

FIGURE 24.5.

A CGI bulletin board.

© 1997 Time Inc. New
Media. All rights reserved.
Reproduction in whole or in
part without permission is
prohibited. Pathfinder is a
registered trademark of Time
Inc. New Media.

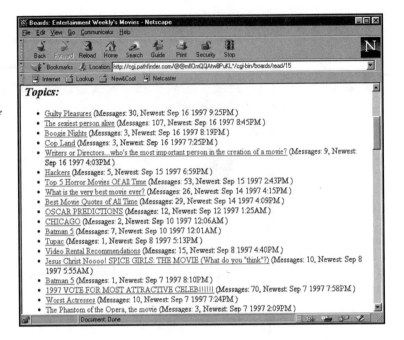

Form Handlers

Although not explicitly stated, your form handling has already been touched on briefly in the database and bulletin board sections. In order for a user's data to be sent to a database, form data must be sent to the Web server. You need a CGI script to decode the data and place it in the database. Likewise, with the bulletin board, you need to handle the incoming messages from users posting to your site. Your form handler in this case decodes the data and either adds it directly to a Web page, or places it in a database.

Form handlers are the most common application of server-side programming. With the exception of Java applets that accept and send data back to the Web server, HTML forms are the only way in which users can send information back to the Web server. After the Web browser has encoded the form data and sent it to the Web server, you must have a CGI program receive the data and decode it before you can work with it. Additionally, any action you want to take based on the data you received must be done in a CGI script.

Placing Server Programs in Your Web Site

Before you can start developing a server-side application, you need to decide how it is going to be integrated into your Web site. There are several options available with client-side programming. The first is embedding the script code directly into your HTML document. The other options involve programming plug-ins, ActiveX controls, or Java applets.

You also have several options available for integrating server-side programming on the server side. The most common of these options is through the Common Gateway Interface. By using CGI, you have the following integration options available to you:

- Direct linking to the program
- Server-side includes
- Handling form actions
- Calling from client-side scripts

Apart from using the CGI, there are limited choices for integrating server-side programming. In fact, all the choices available can be summed up as integrating your program directly into the Web server software. The possible implementations of doing this are discussed in the section "Integrating Directly into the Web Server."

Direct Linking to the Program

A convenient CGI scripts feature is that they can be directly referenced in a link from an HTML page. When the Web server receives a request for a CGI script, it runs the script and returns the results to the user's Web browser. You can use a relative URL, such as the following:

```
<A HREF="/cgi-bin/myscript.pl">
```

You can also use an absolute URL like the following:

```
<A HREF="http://www.somedomain.com/cgi-bin/myscript.pl">
```

A common way to use this feature is to use a CGI program to generate dynamic content for a Web page. Rather than linking to a static Web page, you code your links with the URL for your CGI script. Then, when your users click the link, the CGI program is executed and returns the latest information to the Web browsers.

Server-Side Includes

Server-side includes are actually an HTML feature that allows you to embed other items in an HTML file. The following is the syntax for a server-side include:

```
<!--#command name="value1" name2="value2" ...-->
```

The most interesting server-side includes feature is the ability to include a call to a CGI program. The syntax for a server-side include that calls a CGI program makes use of the `exec` command and looks like the following:

```
<!--#exec cgi="/cgi-bin/cgi-script.pl"-->
```

Server-side includes work through a process known as server parsing. For normal Web pages, the Web server receives the request and returns the requested Web page without looking through the file's contents. With server parsing, the Web server skims through your HTML file's contents looking for server-based commands, such as server-side includes. When the Web server finds one, it performs the requested action and places the results of the action in the place of the server-side include statement.

With server-side includes, you could have a CGI program provide part of the Web page's contents. A common application is to call a CGI script that inserts a page counter, displaying the number of times that Web page has been requested.

Handling Form Actions

Perhaps the most common method of integrating a CGI script into your Web site is by setting it up to handle form data. This is done by using the ACTION attribute in the <FORM> HTML tag. For example, the following <FORM> tag sends any form data entered by the user to the CGI script form-handler.pl when the form is submitted.

```
<FORM METHOD=post ACTION="/cgi-bin/form-handler.pl">
```

Calling from Client-Side Scripts

CGI scripts can also be called from a client-side script. This method is similar to direct linking to a CGI script. The only difference is that the client-side script is requesting the URL rather than the user clicking a link with a CGI script in the URL.

For example, JavaScript can load other URLs into the user's Web browser by assigning a URL to the location property of the document object. To call a CGI script, you could use a JavaScript statement similar to the following:

```
document.location = "http://www.somedomain.com/cgi-bin/myscript.pl"
```

Integrating Directly into the Web Server

CGI applications are a powerful way to add functionality to your Web server. However, there are some disadvantages to using the CGI. First, CGI applications are not run as part of the Web server. Whenever a Web server receives a request for a CGI application, it must launch a separate application—the CGI application. This can cause a slight performance drain on some systems, especially when many users are simultaneously accessing CGI applications.

An alternative to the CGI is integrating your application directly into the Web server. This is done in one of two ways. The first way is to program your application as a server plug-in, utilizing the Web server's API. The other method is to make use of server-side scripting, a new feature of the more popular Web servers.

Server Plug-Ins

You are probably already familiar with the concept of plug-ins from the client side. The most popular Web browsers have support for other developers to integrate their own applications into the Web browser. These client-side plug-ins extend the Web browser's functionality. In the same manner, server-side plug-ins can extend the functionality of the Web server. By writing your application as a plug-in, your application actually becomes part of the Web server.

Plug-ins in general are made possible through the Application Programming Interface, or API. The API contains a set of functions and procedures, which you can call from your applications. The advantages to using an API is that you don't have to do all the work. For example, when programming an application for a Web server plug-in, a simple task, such as determining the values of the HTTP request headers, is rather difficult. The Web server has received that information and stored it somewhere—but you don't know where. This is where the API comes in. The API contains functions that retrieve the information for you.

Server-side plug-ins operate more efficiently than CGI applications because plug-ins are initialized when the Web server is started. There is also less overhead, because the Web server does not have to launch a separate application nor save important data to environment variables. However, writing server-side plug-ins requires more programming skills than writing CGI applications. Also, you are limited to programming languages that can access the API functions. Because most APIs are written in C or C++, those are the languages of choice.

Server-Side Scripting

Because server-side plug-ins are more efficient than CGI applications, but more challenging to program, there has been a recent push to support server-side scripting. Server-side scripting is similar to its client-side counterpart, with the exception that the server-side script is parsed and run by the Web server before the Web page is sent to the Web browser.

In order for server-side scripting to work, you must be using a Web server that supports it. Also, not all Web servers that support server-side scripting also support the same languages, or even the same implementation. Two server-side scripting methods have emerged from two of the more popular Web servers. LiveWire is Netscape Communications Corporation's server-side scripting solution, and Active Server Pages is Microsoft's.

LiveWire

LiveWire is the name associated with server-side scripting for Netscape's Web server. LiveWire enables you to embed JavaScript in your HTML pages, which gets parsed by the Web server before the document is sent to the Web browser. Because the JavaScript is parsed on the server side, you can code statements that connect to server-side resources, such as databases.

A major difference between server-side JavaScript with LiveWire and client-side JavaScript is that the server-side scripts are actually compiled into bytecode before being placed on the Web server. This process is contrary to the normal execution process of scripts, and is different from compilation of programs.

The bytecode generated by this compilation of JavaScript and HTML source code does not produce a stand-alone executable. You still need the Web server to run the bytecode you generated. However, the compilation to bytecode process saves execution time by removing the need to interpret the script every time the Web server receives a request for a Web page containing server-side JavaScript. Also, because the Web server handles the running of the JavaScript bytecode, there is no launching of a separate application to handle the request, as with CGI applications.

Active Server Pages

Active Server Pages, or ASP, is Microsoft's implementation of server-side scripting. ASP operates in a manner similar to LiveWire, except that ASP pages are not to be compiled to bytecode. When the Microsoft Web server receives a request for an ASP page, it parses the code, executing any server-side commands. After it has finished parsing the page, the results are sent to the user's Web browser.

At its most basic level, ASP provides native support for combining HTML, VBScript, and JScript. Developers can combine code from either of the scripting languages into the HTML code of an active server page. On a more advanced level, you can integrate server-side ActiveX components, which can be programmed in virtually any programming language, such as C, C++, Java, Cobol, or Visual Basic.

Summary

With much of Web application development focus being on the Web browser, server-side options can often be overlooked. However, there are many applications that work better, if not exclusively, on the server machine. As a Web developer, you need to be open to server-based solutions when the opportunity arises.

In this chapter, you learned about server-side applications, comprising both programs and scripts. A program is typically an application compiled into an executable before being run. Scripts, on the other hand, are not compiled, but are interpreted at runtime by a command interpreter. Whether you use a program or a script to accomplish your task depends on the application you are creating and the programming language you need to use. For example, when creating server-side plug-ins, you need to use a programming language that executes quickly and be able to access the API functions. This leads you to creating a program in C or C++.

There are many advantages to creating applications on the server side versus the client side. One of the biggest advantages is the ability to support all browsers and platforms with a single application that runs on the server. You also have more application options available to you with the other server-side resources available to your applications, such as databases. Also, even though client machines are becoming more powerful, your server machine is better able to handle processor-intensive tasks, such as searches and sorts. Finally, you don't have to be as concerned with the integrity of your source code, because both the source and executable, if they constitute a program, reside on the server machine and are not distributed to the clients.

Because of server-side programming's advantages, there are several common server-side applications. Perhaps the most used are CGI form handlers, because most HTML forms need a CGI script to handle the data when it is sent to the Web server. However, other common server-side applications are search engines, database integration, and chat and bulletin board services. All of these applications require resources on the server-side of the connection in order to operate, making it necessary to develop them on the server side.

Determining how you plan to integrate in your server-side application into your Web site plays a large role in how you develop the application. If you plan on using the CGI, you have a large number of programming language from which to choose. You also have several options for how to run your CGI application. You could have it called by linking to the CGI application from a URL in one of your Web pages, using a server-side include, placing it in the ACTION attribute of an HTML form, or using a client-side script.

Many Web servers also enable you to integrate your application directly into the Web server. This is most commonly done through the Web server's API. Through the API, you can write server-side plug-ins that have access to most of the resources of the Web server. Server-side plug-ins can handle a variety of tasks and are very efficient in the amount of resources necessary to run them.

Server-side plug-ins can be very challenging to program. As an alternative, some Web servers offer the ability to do server-side scripting. Similar to client-side scripting, server-side scripts are relatively easy to write. Server-side scripts also have access to other server-side resources, such as databases, making it easy to integrate these resources into your Web site.

CHAPTER 25

Traditional CGI Programming

by Robert McDaniel

IN THIS CHAPTER

CGI programming is one of the ways you can integrate server-side applications with your Web site. CGI has been around since the early days of the World Wide Web. With the introduction of some of the newer server-side application programming interfaces, such as server-side plugins and active server pages, CGI doesn't get as much attention as it used to. However, through the use of the CGI, you can create powerful applications that extend the functionality of your Web server.

This chapter is all about CGI programming. It takes you through the beginner phase of CGI with an explanation about what CGI is and how to use it.

What Is the CGI?

A common misconception is that CGI programming and scripting refer to a specific language for creating Web applications. This is not the case. CGI stands for Common Gateway Interface and is a set of standards around the communication between your Web server and your server-side applications. These standards provide the gateway through which data can pass between the Web server and your CGI application.

At a basic level, the CGI specification defines how Web servers will make information available to CGI applications and how CGI applications will return data to the Web server. So, when you think of the terms CGI programming or CGI scripting, you should think of them as a methodology to programming and scripting, not a specific language.

Programming Language Choices

Because CGI programming and scripting don't refer to a specific language for coding applications for Web sites, you will need to choose a language with which to work. The good news is that you could use almost any programming or scripting language that will run on your Web server's machine. However, there are some points to consider when choosing a language.

You should first consider the languages with which you are familiar. Although some of the languages, such as BASIC or FORTRAN, may not be the best choice, many other commonly used languages are. Using a language you are already familiar with will save you the time and effort of learning a new language to code CGI applications.

Another consideration when choosing a CGI language is to choose one that is commonly used by other CGI developers. The most common languages used for CGI applications are Perl, C, C++, TCL, UNIX shells, Java, Visual Basic, and AppleScript. By choosing one of these languages you may leverage the support and experience of existing developers and CGI applications. When you have a coding problem with one of these languages, there are numerous bulletin boards, Web sites, and chat rooms where other developers can help you answer your question. However, if you are working in an obscure language that most other people are not using, you may have more difficulty obtaining help when you need it. The first time you seek help when writing a CGI application in one of the more common languages, you may be surprised by the amount of suggestions and responses you receive.

Choosing one of these common languages may also save you some coding time. There are many Web sites containing free code listings for CGI applications that you can download and use on your Web site. Many of these will run with little or no changes on your part. And, if you need the application to work slightly differently, you can modify it to suit your needs. There are also CGI libraries available that have functions you can call from your own application. These functions are common tasks you have to perform in CGI applications, such as creating valid headers, decoding user data, and returning results to the Web server.

Typically, the only requirement for using these code samples is that you retain some copyright information in the source code of the script, or give the author credit on your Web site. These CGI application archives are great starting points for enhancements to your Web site. You can find the most popular of these archives on Yahoo!'s site at `http://www.yahoo.com/ Computers_and_Internet/Internet/World_Wide_Web/CGI_Common_Gateway_Interface/`.

You must also make sure the language you choose can yield the necessary performance for the task at hand. For example, searches and sorts are two of the most processor-intensive tasks you can code in an application. If you code your search algorithm in Perl, your performance may suffer, because Perl is an interpreted language. A compiled language, such as C or C++, may be a better choice because it will run significantly faster. Keep in mind that not all languages work the same on all platforms. Java is the most notable example. It runs fairly well on UNIX platforms, making it an acceptable choice for those systems. However, on most Macintosh machines, Java tends to bog down and run slowly.

HTTP Connections and Headers

To fully understand the CGI, you need to have some idea of how HTTP connections work. An HTTP connection is the communication channel between the Web browser and the Web server. Most HTTP connections begin on the client side, with the Web browser sending an HTTP request to a Web server for a document.

At the beginning of the request is a section referred to as the *request header*. The request header contains information about the request and about the Web browser requesting the information. The fields in the request header are described in Table 25.1.

Table 25.1. HTTP request headers.

Request Header Field	Meaning
ACCEPT	Contains a list of media types in MIME format that the Web browser can accept from the Web server.
ACCEPT_ENCODING	Specifies to the Web server the document encoding methods the Web browser supports.

continues

Table 25.1. continued

Request Header Field	Meaning
ACCEPT_LANGUAGE	Specifies to the Web server the Web browser's preferred language for a response.
AUTHORIZATION	The authentication information sent by the Web browser to identify itself to the Web server.
CHARGE_TO	Not currently implemented.
FROM	The e-mail of the user whose Web browser sent the HTTP request. Most current Web browsers do not supply a value for this header.
IF_MODIFIED_SINCE	Date value that specifies to the Web server to only return the document if it has been modified since the given date.
PRAGMA	Contains any special instructions for the Web server. For example, the no-cache PRAGMA directive instructs Web servers not to send cached versions of the requested document.
REFERER	The URL of the previous document on which the user clicked a link to navigate to the current document.
USER_AGENT	The name and version of the Web browser making the request. For example, Mozilla/4.01–(Win95; I) is the user agent for Netscape 4.0 on Windows 95.

After the Web server receives an HTTP request from a Web browser, it evaluates the request, returning the requested document if it exists, and then shuts down the HTTP connection. Immediately preceding the document, the Web server sends an HTTP response header to the Web browser. The Web browser parses the response header for information about displaying the document being returned by the Web server. The fields of the HTTP response header are described in Table 25.2.

Table 25.2. HTTP response headers.

Response Header Field	Meaning
ALLOWED	Tells the Web browser what request methods are allowed, such as the GET method.
CONTENT-ENCODING	Notifies the Web browser of the encoding method used on the returned document.

continues

Response Header Field	Meaning
CONTENT-LANGUAGE	Specifies the language of the returned document.
CONTENT-LENGTH	Contains the size, in bytes, of the document being returned.
CONTENT-TRANSFER-ENCODING	Contains the encoding of the data between the Web server and the Web browser, such as binary or ASCII.
CONTENT-TYPE	Specifies to the Web browser the MIME type of the data being returned.
COST	Not currently implemented.
DATE	Contains the date the returning document was created.
DERIVED-FROM	Not currently implemented.
EXPIRES	Specifies a date when the returning document is expired.
LAST-MODIFIED	Specifies the date when the returning document was last modified.
LINK	Contains information, such as the URL, of the document being returned.
MESSAGE-ID	A unique identification number for the HTTP connection.
PUBLIC	Contains allowed request methods. It is similar to the ALLOW field, but applies to all Web browsers, not just the one the header is being sent to.
TITLE	Specifies the title of the returning document.
URI	Contains the URI of the returning document.
VERSION	Not currently implemented.

When a Web browser sends an HTTP request for a CGI application from a Web server, the Web server starts the CGI program or script, and then passes on most of the HTTP request information to the CGI application. Most of this information is placed in environment variables. Some of the information may be accessible via standard input to the program or script, depending on the request method used. Accessing the HTTP request information is discussed in more detail in the next section, "Sending Data to Your CGI Application."

Sometime during a CGI application's execution, it needs to send output back to the Web server. The Web server than takes the output, forms an HTTP response header and sends the HTTP response back to the user's Web browser. You have the option of forming the HTTP response header in your CGI application and sending the data back to the Web browser directly. Both methods will be discussed in detail in the section "Returning Data from Your CGI Application," later in this chapter.

Sending Data to Your CGI Application

When started by the Web server, CGI programs and scripts run as separate applications on the Web server machine. They are not integrated within the Web server environment. Because of this, your CGI application does not have native access to the data sent from the Web browser in the HTTP request. This includes both the HTTP request headers and any user-supplied data, such as in an HTML form.

To work with this data from the Web browser, your CGI application needs to have access to the data. Fortunately, you don't have to do anything on the Web server or in your CGI application to make sure this data is available for your CGI application. The Web server will make this available to you automatically.

Remember that the CGI specification defines how information passes between your Web server and your CGI applications. Part of this definition is how the Web server will make available the data coming from the user. All this data, including both the HTTP request headers and user-supplied data, is sent to your CGI application through either environment variables, or through standard input. The actual location of these two varies, depending on the request method used. All that is left for your CGI application to do is to retrieve the data from one of these two locations.

> **NOTE**
>
> Standard input is the default location defined by your application from which it will receive data. For example, for most computer applications, such as word processors, standard input is the keyboard.

The GET and POST Request Methods

You may already be familiar with the GET and POST request methods. These are the same request methods that you specify in the METHOD attribute of the <FORM> tag. These are the two ways in which a request can be sent to the Web server.

A GET request is the most common request method. It is used to specify a request for a document from the Web server. POST methods, on the other hand, are used when form data is being sent from the user's Web browser to the Web server. Form data is only sent with the POST method. However, you can append additional data to the end of a URL with the GET method.

Appending Information to URLs

Two forms of additional information can be appended to a URL with the GET method. The first form is additional path information. Path information is usually the path to a resource on the server machine, and is usually used only with CGI applications. For example, with server-side image maps, the URL sent by the browser is in the following form:

```
http://www.castingguild.com/cgi-bin/imagemap/maps/groups.map?201,118
```

The URL to the CGI application is as follows:

```
http://www.castingguild.com/cgi-bin/imagemap
```

The remaining part of the URL is the additional information being discussed. The first part of this additional information is as follows:

```
/maps/groups.map
```

This is some extra path information being sent to the CGI script. In the case of this example, this specifies the path to the map file on the server machine.

The second part of the additional information is as follows:

```
?201,118
```

The question mark in any URL designates the beginning of the second form of additional information appended to a URL. This second form is referred to as a *Query string*, and it is typically used only with CGI applications. It is used to supply additional data that the application may need. For this example, the Query string contains x and y coordinates of the user's mouse click on the image map.

The POST Method and Standard Input

Earlier in this chapter you learned that Web servers send data to your CGI applications through either environment variables or standard input. The only time standard input is used is when the request method used by the Web browser is the POST method. The POST method is only used when the user is submitting form data. Although the user data is supplied to the CGI application through standard input, the Web server sends the rest of the available information via environment variables.

> **CAUTION**
>
> The GET method can also be used with the METHOD attribute in the <FORM> tag, but it's better to use the POST method. Some browsers limit the amount of characters that will be sent using the GET method, which could result in truncated data being sent to your CGI application. Because this limit varies from browser to browser, it's best to just use the POST method.

Through Environment Variables

No matter which method is used to request your CGI application, the Web server will set some environment variables for your application. These environment variables contain useful information about the HTTP request, the Web browser, and the Web server. Unless the POST method was used to send data to the Web server, the environment variables will be the only source of information available to your CGI application. Table 25.3 contains all the CGI environment variables set by the Web server.

Table 25.3. CGI environment variables.

Environment Variable	Meaning
AUTH_TYPE	Specifies the authentication method, such as username/password, used by the Web browser, if any.
CONTENT_LENGTH	Contains the length, in characters, of the user-supplied data, if any.
CONTENT_TYPE	Specifies the MIME type of the user-supplied data.
GATEWAY_INTERFACE	Designates the version of the CGI specification being used. The current version is 1.1.
PATH_INFO	Contains any additional path information appended to the requesting URL.
PATH_TRANSLATED	Contains the Web server's translation of the virtual path information, appended to the URL, to the actual path on the server machine.
QUERY_STRING	Contains any information appended to the URL with a question mark.
REMOTE_ADDR	Contains the IP address of the client machine.
REMOTE_HOST	Contains the domain name, if available, of the client machine.
REMOTE_IDENT	Contains the user's login name, if one was used for authentication with the Web server.
REMOTE_USER	Contains the remote username, as supplied to the Web server.
REQUEST_METHOD	Specifies the request method used by the browser (GET or POST).
SCRIPT_NAME	Contains the virtual path and filename of the CGI script.
SERVER_NAME	Contains either the domain name or IP address of the Web server machine.

Environment Variable	Meaning
SERVER_PORT	Contains the port being used by the Web server.
SERVER_PROTOCOL	Specifies the protocol being used between the Web server and Web browser, typically HTTP.
SERVER_SOFTWARE	Contains the name and version of the Web server software.

In addition to the CGI environment variables, the Web server also sets environment variables for all the HTTP request headers listed previously in Table 25.1. The actual environment variable set by the Web server is the prefix HTTP_ followed by the name of the HTTP request header field. For example, the HTTP environment variable for the REFERER header is HTTP_REFERER.

As you can see, there are a lot of environment variables available to your CGI application. For the most part, you will only make use of a few of them. Many of these variables that the Web server makes available to your CGI application do not even contain values, because they are not currently implemented. Figure 25.1 shows an example of a CGI application that displays all the available environment variables. The code for this application is shown in Listing 25.1.

FIGURE 25.1.

The environment variables available to your CGI application.

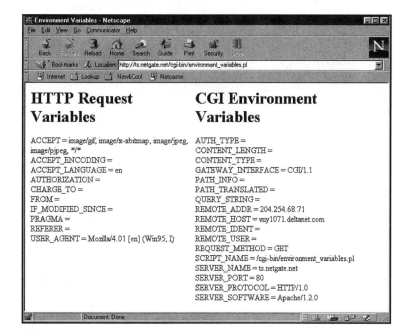

25

TRADITIONAL CGI
PROGRAMMING

Listing 25.1. A CGI script for displaying the environment variables.

```perl
#!/usr/bin/perl

print "Content-type: text/html\n\n";
print "<HTML><HEAD><TITLE>Environment Variables</TITLE></HEAD>\n";
print "<BODY BGCOLOR=\"#FFFFFF\">\n";
print "<TABLE BORDER=0><TR><TD VALIGN=top>\n";
print "<H1>HTTP Request Variables</H1>\n";
print "ACCEPT = $ENV{'HTTP_ACCEPT'}<BR>\n";
print "ACCEPT_ENCODING = $ENV{'HTTP_ACCEPT_ENCODING'}<BR>\n";
print "ACCEPT_LANGUAGE = $ENV{'HTTP_ACCEPT_LANGUAGE'}<BR>\n";
print "AUTHORIZATION = $ENV{'HTTP_AUTHORIZATION'}<BR>\n";
print "CHARGE_TO = $ENV{'HTTP_CHARGE_TO'}<BR>\n";
print "FROM = $ENV{'HTTP_FROM'}<BR>\n";
print "IF_MODIFIED_SINCE = $ENV{'HTTP_IF_MODIFIED_SINCE'}<BR>\n";
print "PRAGMA = $ENV{'HTTP_PRAGMA'}<BR>\n";
print "REFERER = $ENV{'HTTP_REFERER'}<BR>\n";
print "USER_AGENT = $ENV{'HTTP_USER_AGENT'}<BR>\n";
print "</TD></TR><TR><TD VALIGN=top>\n";
print "<H1>CGI Environment Variables</H1>\n";
print "AUTH_TYPE = $ENV{'AUTH_TYPE'}<BR>\n";
print "CONTENT_LENGTH = $ENV{'CONTENT_LENGTH'}<BR>\n";
print "CONTENT_TYPE = $ENV{'CONTENT_TYPE'}<BR>\n";
print "GATEWAY_INTERFACE = $ENV{'GATEWAY_INTERFACE'}<BR>\n";
print "PATH_INFO = $ENV{'PATH_INFO'}<BR>\n";
print "PATH_TRANSLATED = $ENV{'PATH_TRANSLATED'}<BR>\n";
print "QUERY_STRING = $ENV{'QUERY_STRING'}<BR>\n";
print "REMOTE_ADDR = $ENV{'REMOTE_ADDR'}<BR>\n";
print "REMOTE_HOST = $ENV{'REMOTE_HOST'}<BR>\n";
print "REMOTE_IDENT = $ENV{'REMOTE_IDENT'}<BR>\n";
print "REMOTE_USER = $ENV{'REMOTE_USER'}<BR>\n";
print "REQUEST_METHOD = $ENV{'REQUEST_METHOD'}<BR>\n";
print "SCRIPT_NAME = $ENV{'SCRIPT_NAME'}<BR>\n";
print "SERVER_NAME = $ENV{'SERVER_NAME'}<BR>\n";
print "SERVER_PORT = $ENV{'SERVER_PORT'}<BR>\n";
print "SERVER_PROTOCOL = $ENV{'SERVER_PROTOCOL'}<BR>\n";
print "SERVER_SOFTWARE = $ENV{'SERVER_SOFTWARE'}<BR>\n";
print "</TD></TR></TABLE></BODY></HTML>\n";
```

Name/Value Pairs

Whether sending form data via the GET method or the POST method, the Web browser will always perform two actions on the data before it is sent. The first action is placing the data from each form element into a name/value pair. These name/value pairs are used to identify on the server side which data came from which form element. The second action performed by the Web browser, is a process called URL encoding, which is discussed in the next section.

The name portion of a name/value pair is taken from the NAME attribute of the form element. When you create form elements, with <INPUT>, <SELECT>, and <TEXTAREA> tags, you supply the NAME attribute, giving the element a name. When the form is submitted, the Web browser takes the name, appends an equal sign and the data entered by the user, if any. The data entered by the user is the value portion of the name/value pair.

Not all `form` elements have unique names. When you use the `MULTIPLE` attribute with the `<SELECT>` tag, a user can choose multiple options from the list. Each option the user selects is associated with the same name. For example, using the following `<SELECT>` tag:

```
<SELECT NAME="language" MULTIPLE>
<OPTION>English
<OPTION>French
<OPTION>German
<OPTION>Spanish
</SELECT>
```

when the user selects the options `English`, `French`, or `German` and submits the form, the Web browser creates three name/value pairs:

```
language=English
language=French
language=German
```

The Web browser sends all the name/value pairs in a single, long string. Each name/value pair is separated by an ampersand (&). At the start of your CGI application, you will want to break apart the name/value pairs so you can work with the individual values.

URL Encoding

The other process performed by the Web browser on all user-supplied form data before sending it to the Web server is URL encoding. *URL encoding* is the act of changing all spaces in the name/value pairs string to plus signs (+) and changing other reserved characters into their hexadecimal equivalents.

The primary purpose for URL encoding is to remove any characters with which the Web server or CGI application will have trouble. Specifically, this means removing all spaces. Naturally, spaces are important to the data being sent, and you don't want to permanently remove them. So, spaces are replaced with the plus sign, which acts as a placeholder for where the spaces belong.

This introduces a new problem. Suppose the user enters a plus sign in the data being sent to the Web server. How will your CGI application distinguish between that plus sign and the plus signs used as space placeholders? Additionally, other characters, such as the equal and ampersand signs, are used to separate names and values and the name/value pairs. Your CGI application will need some way to distinguish the difference between these characters and the ones entered by the user as part of the form data.

To address these issues, certain special characters, including the three described previously, are converted to their hexadecimal equivalent value. Only special characters entered by the user in the form data are converted. The plus, ampersand, and equal signs inserted by the Web browser as placeholders and separators are not converted.

Because hexadecimal values consist of numbers and letters between A and F, your CGI application also needs a way to designate which values are hexadecimal values, and which are simply normal characters. To designate the beginning of a hexadecimal value, rather than normal characters, the Web browser inserts a percent sign (%). This adds another character that must be URL encoded when entered by the user. In all, the characters that get changed to hexadecimal include the following:

Character Name	Character Hexadecimal	Equivalent
percent sign	%	25
slash	/	2F
single dot	.	2E
double dots	..	2E2E
pound sign	#	A6
question mark	?	3F
plus sign	+	2B
ampersand	&	26
equal sign	=	3D
asterisk	*	2A
exclamation mark	!	21

Before working with form data in your CGI applications, you need to decode any URL encoding. This consists of changing all hexadecimal values back into their equivalent signs, and swapping plus spaces for plus signs.

TIP

When decoding form data, you should first split apart name/value pairs, then change plus signs into spaces, and lastly return hexadecimal values to their respective signs. If you don't do the hexadecimal conversion last, you may make splitting name/value pairs or replacing spaces more difficult. Remember that the user could have included ampersands or plus signs in the form data. After you decode the hexadecimal values, you will have no easy way to distinguish which ampersands and plus signs are being used as placeholders and which are part of the form data.

Returning Data from Your CGI Application

After your CGI application is finished executing, it needs to return a result to the user's Web browser. This result will typically be HTML-formatted text. Most of the time, the result from the CGI application is sent through the Web server. However, this is not always the case. Regardless of whether the result returns through the Web server, your CGI application must return a valid header before returning any other data.

Whether returning the header or returning other data, CGI applications typically return results by sending data to standard output. Standard output is the counterpart of standard input. Standard output is the location that output from a program is sent by default. For example, most Windows applications use the monitor as standard output. The information you see on your monitor is the output of various programs.

The CGI specification has been set up so that the Web server listens for results from a CGI application via the applications standard output. When the Web server receives results from a CGI application, it checks for a partial HTTP response header with server directives. The Web server parses the header and forms a complete HTTP response header, before sending the results back to the browser.

Creating the Response Header

There are two types of response headers your CGI application can return, parsed and non-parsed. A parsed header is a partial HTTP response header. With parsed headers, the Web server must parse the response from the CGI application and form a complete HTTP response header, before sending the data on to the Web browser. Non-parsed headers, on the other hand, are valid HTTP response headers that do not require any action by the Web server.

Parsed headers can contain any of the HTTP response headers shown previously in Table 25.2, and always must be followed by a blank line. As part of your parsed header, you must include at least one server directive. Server directives are commands, interpreted by the Web server when it parses the header, that give special instructions to the Web server. The currently defined server directives are shown in Table 25.4.

Table 25.4. Web server directives.

Directive	Meaning
Content-type	Designates the MIME type of the data being returned
Location	Designates the virtual or absolute URL to which the Web browser is to be redirected
Status	Contains an HTTP status code, such as 404 Not Found

Content-type is the most commonly used server directive. It instructs the Web server that the application is returning data of the specified MIME type. The Web server uses this directive to form the Content-type HTTP response header. The Location directive asks the Web server to redirect the Web browser to a different URL. This new URL is then loaded in the user's Web browser. The Status directive is used to specify a status code to the Web server, such as the 404 status code, designating Not Found. The Status directive is the least used of these three.

When the Web server parses the header returned from a CGI application, it looks for server directives and performs the associated action. All other HTTP response header fields a CGI application returns as part of a parsed header become part of the HTTP response header the Web server forms and sends to the Web browser. The following parsed header is the most common one for CGI applications to return:

```
Content-type: text/html
```

> **CAUTION**
>
> Don't forget to include a blank line after your parsed and non-parsed response headers. If you don't, you receive error messages!

Bypassing the Server with Non-Parsed Headers

Most Web servers enable you to use Non-Parsed headers when returning data from your CGI application. Non-parsed headers are HTTP response headers that you create in your CGI application. The header and data are then sent directly back to the user's Web browser, without further processing by the Web server. Typically, you have to somehow identify your CGI applications that contain non-parsed headers to your Web server. For the Netscape Communications Corporation's server, you accomplish this by prefixing the name of the CGI application with nph-.

When you use non-parsed headers, you have to create a complete HTTP response header in your CGI application. You don't use the server directives shown previously in Table 25.4 because the server will not be parsing the header. You also do not have to use all the HTTP response header fields shown earlier in Table 25.2. For example, the following is a valid non-parsed HTTP response header that you can return from your CGI applications:

```
HTTP/1.0 200 OK
Server: Netscape-Communications/3.0
Content-type: text/html
```

> **NOTE**
>
> Do not confuse the use of the Content-type HTTP response header field in the non-parsed HTTP response header example with the Content-type server directive. Although they are named the same, the HTTP response header field is sent directly to the Web browser, without the server seeing it. The server directive, on the other hand, is used to inform the Web server of the type of data to be returned.

Redirecting to Another URL

Rather than returning a complete Web page from your CGI application, you could simply return a redirection command to the user's Web browser. The Web browser will then load the URL sent by your CGI application.

To send a redirection command, you need to return the location directive from your CGI application. For example, you would return the following server directive from your CGI application to redirect the user's browser to Netscape Communications Corporation's home page:

```
Location:http://www.netscape.com
```

Calling CGI Applications

As you learned in Chapter 24, "Putting Your Server to Work," there are several ways that you can call your CGI applications. Typically, the method you use will be dictated by the task you are accomplishing. For example, the most common way CGI applications are called is from the ACTION attribute in the <FORM> tag. If your task is to create a CGI application to handle a form submission, then it must be placed in the ACTION attribute.

You can also call your CGI applications by directly linking to them in the <A> tag. When you have a link set up in this manner, the CGI application will be called when the user clicks the link. When using this method, keep in mind that the CGI application will be called with the GET request method. You can use this to your advantage and add query string data to be sent to the user by appending a question mark and the data, such as:

```
<A HREF="/cgi-bin/banner.pl?link=17">
```

When this link is clicked, it sends the name/value pair link=17 to your CGI application. In most cases, this is not very useful. However, you have your Web pages generated dynamically, thereby creating unique query strings for each user. For example, you could use the query string as an identification number to track the user's movement on your Web site.

Server-side includes are another common way to call your CGI applications. Server-side includes are actually HTML code that is parsed by the Web server before being sent to the Web browser. The syntax for server-side includes is:

```
<!--#command tag1="value1" tag2="value2" -->
```

One of the available commands for server-side includes is the #exec command. With the #exec command, you can specify a CGI application that runs when the Web server parses the HTML. The results are then placed in the location of the server-side Include statement. A server-side Include that calls a CGI application is

```
<!--#exec cgi="/cgi-bin/counter.pl" -->
```

The most common CGI applications that are called from server-side includes are Web page counters. However, you could also set up your default home page to be an HTML file containing a single server-side include. This server-side include would then call a CGI application to generate a dynamic page depending on the user's Web browser and machine platform.

One method for calling CGI applications that wasn't discussed in Chapter 24 is in the SRC attribute of the <IMG> tag, such as:

```
<IMG SRC="/cgi-bin/image.pl">
```

Placing a CGI application call in this location is similar to using a server-side include. When the Web browser parses the HTML, it loads all the images referenced in <IMG> tags. To do so, it must open a separate HTTP request for the document listed in the SRC attribute.

Because a reference to a CGI application is a URL, placing it here results in the Web browser sending a request to run the application. The results will then be displayed for that image. You can use this technique to dynamically create custom images for your users. However, make sure your CGI application returns the data for a binary image. Otherwise, the browser won't be able to display it.

The newest method for calling CGI applications is by calling them from a client-side script. Client-side scripts have the capability to reference other URLs and load them in the current window, or another window or frame. Although this method is similar to the direct linking method described earlier, in this case the client-side script has control over when the CGI application is called. Here is a JavaScript statement that would call the reply.pl CGI script:

```
document.location = "http://www.somedomain.com/cgi-bin/reply.pl
```

Summary

The Common Gateway Interface is a standard by which Web servers and server-side CGI applications communicate. Through the CGI, you are able to program a wide variety of applications, and have them work seamlessly with your Web site. As newer technologies arise for integrating applications into your Web site, CGI gets less attention. However, it is still a viable solution for many tasks.

To fully understand the workings of the CGI, you need to have a basic understanding of how HTTP connections work. An HTTP connection is divided into two portions. The first portion is the HTTP request, typically initiated by a Web browser. The HTTP request is made up of an HTTP request header, that contains information about the requesting machine and browser and the document being requested.

When the Web server receives a request, it creates an HTTP response header, returning both the header and the requested item, if available. If the requested item is not available, or if access to it is refused, the HTTP response header will contain an error code associated with the appropriate problem.

When an HTTP request comes in for a CGI application, the Web server executes the application. Most of the HTTP request headers are placed in environment variables for the CGI application. User data, if any, is either placed in an environment variable as well, or sent to the application via standard input. Regardless of the way the user data gets to the CGI application, the data will be URL encoded and grouped together as a long string of name/value pairs. It's up to your CGI application to decode the data before you work with it.

After your CGI application has finished performing its task, it can send results back to the user's Web browser. Typically, the resulting data will pass through the Web server first. This method requires your CGI application to create a partial HTTP response header, complete with a server directive to instruct the Web server as to what to do with the data. The Web server then creates a complete HTTP response header and returns the data to the Web browser.

You CGI application has the option of returning the results directly to the user's Web browser without going through the Web server. If this is the case, the application will need to create a valid HTTP response header to precede the data. Because the Web server will not be parsing this header, the response header your application generates must be complete, without any server directives.

Because of the close integration of CGI and HTML, you have many options available to you for how your CGI application is called. You can embed it in anchor tags, image tags, form tags, and server-side includes. You can also call it from client-side scripts. For the most part, the option will be driven by the task you want to perform, such as with form handlers. In such a case, you would have to place the call to your CGI application in the ACTION attribute of the <FORM> tag.

The Anatomy of a CGI Application

by Robert McDaniel

CHAPTER

26

Chapter 25, "Traditional CGI Programming," introduced you to the Common Gateway Interface (CGI). You learned about how data is passed between the Web server and your CGI applications. There is a wide variety of tasks that can be accomplished with CGI applications. You can create Web page counters, dynamically generate Web pages, track users through your Web site, and create bulletin boards. The most common task for which you will use CGI applications is handling form input.

In this chapter, you implement a form handler CGI application. Your CGI application accepts form input from an HTML page, decodes and formats the input, and places it in a text file database. Here are the steps you need to take to complete your application:

1. Create the HTML page.
2. Handle the form input.
3. Put the data in a simple database.
4. Return a response to the user.

Creating the HTML Page

The first step in creating a CGI application to handle form data is to set up the HTML page and the form elements. You should do this step first because you need to know the values of the NAME attributes for each of the form elements before doing any programming. You use these values in your programs to identify the data entered by the user.

In this section, you assemble a Web page form used on the unGROOM'd Web site (http://www.ungroomd.com). This form is used to gather demographics and interests of the users reading the online magazine.

Planning Your Form

As you begin planning your form, you should think about what questions you want to ask your users and what kind of answers you should accept. Carefully planning your form and the elements it contains makes your programming task much easier.

For example, if you want to find out the gender of your users, you can simply put in a simple text input field, such as the following:

```
<INPUT TYPE="text" NAME="gender" VALUE="" SIZE=10>
```

This generates a text box in which the user can type a response. What kind of response will be entered? If the user is a male, he could enter any one of these:

```
m

M

male
```

```
Male

MALE
```

You might even get a few users who like to be unique and will enter responses such as these:

```
man

guy

masculine

of the male persuasion

unknown

neutral
```

Of course, any of these entries is accepted. However, when your application receives this data, compiling summary statistics becomes a nightmare. You have to check for every possibility, or, more likely, when your CGI application receives the form data, convert it to a standard before entering it in the database.

The point of this example is to restrict the amount of freedom your users have in entering responses. When you have a question for which you want the user to respond with one of only a few possible responses, use either radio buttons or select list boxes. Both of these enable the user to choose from predefined choices. Therefore, when your CGI application receives the form data, it knows the range of possible responses.

For example, with the gender question presented earlier, a better way would be to use a `<SELECT>` statement, such as this:

```
<SELECT NAME="gender">
<OPTION>Male
<OPTION>Female
</SELECT>
```

No matter how much a user wants to enter a creative response, the only value that gets sent from this form element is one of the following:

```
Male

Female
```

Creating the Form

After you have planned the questions you want to ask and the form elements used to receive the responses, you are ready to create your HTML form. For the CGI application you construct in this chapter, use the unKNOW'n survey response form from the unGROOM'd Web site. This form (see Listing 26.1) has text input fields, radio buttons, check boxes, and a text area. Figure 26.1 shows how a portion of the form looks in Netscape.

Listing 26.1. The unKNOW'n survey.

```
<HTML>
<HEAD>
<TITLE>unGROOM'd: unKNOW'n</TITLE>
</HEAD>
<BODY BACKGROUND="../background2.gif" BGCOLOR="#000000" TEXT="#FFFFCC"
LINK="#FFA500" VLINK="#F7007B">
<TABLE BORDER="0" CELLPADDING="0" WIDTH="100%">
<TR>
<TD ALIGN=LEFT VALIGN=TOP>

<IMG SRC="../1pixel.gif" ALIGN=TOP WIDTH="165" HEIGHT="75" BORDER="0"><BR>
<MAP NAME="upperbar">
<AREA SHAPE="rect" COORDS="-6, 178, 133, 201" HREF="../../unarchivd.html">
<AREA SHAPE="rect" COORDS="6,127,135,178" HREF="../columns/columns.html">
<AREA SHAPE="rect" COORDS="6,103,135,127" HREF="../hiscastle/hiscastle.html">
<AREA SHAPE="rect" COORDS="6,75,135,103" HREF="../incout/incout.html">
<AREA SHAPE="rect" COORDS="6,53,135,75" HREF="../mom/mom.html">
<AREA SHAPE="rect" COORDS="6,29,135,53"
HREF="../tyingtheknot/tyingtheknot.html">
<AREA SHAPE="rect" COORDS="6,2,135,29"
HREF="../nowfeaturing/nowfeaturing.html">
<AREA SHAPE=DEFAULT HREF="../toc.html">
</MAP>

<IMG SRC="../upperbar.gif" ALT="navigation bar" ALIGN=TOP WIDTH="135"
HEIGHT="229" BORDER="0" USEMAP="#upperbar"><BR>

<MAP NAME="level1bar">
<AREA SHAPE="rect" COORDS="6, 146, 131, 174" HREF="mmg_pr/pr.html">
<AREA SHAPE="rect" COORDS="6,124,135,147" HREF="mmg_pr/mmg.html">
<AREA SHAPE="rect" COORDS="6,99,135,125" HREF="staff/credits.html">
<AREA SHAPE="rect" COORDS="6,73,135,99" HREF="unlinkd.html">
<AREA SHAPE="rect" COORDS="6,52,135,74" NOHREF>
<AREA SHAPE="rect" COORDS="6,28,135,53" HREF="unlistd/unlistd.html">
<AREA SHAPE="rect" COORDS="6,3,135,28" HREF="uneditd/unedited.html">
<AREA SHAPE=DEFAULT HREF="../toc.html">
</MAP>

<IMG SRC="../level1bar.gif" Alt="alternate navigation bar" ALIGN=top
WIDTH="135" HEIGHT="208" BORDER="0" USEMAP="#level1bar">

</TD>

<TD ALIGN=LEFT VALIGN=TOP>

<TABLE BORDER="0" CELLPADDING="0" WIDTH="400">
<TR>
<TD ALIGN=LEFT VALIGN=TOP >
<IMG SRC="unknown.gif" ALIGN=MIDDLE WIDTH="200" HEIGHT="50" BORDER="0">
<BR><BR>
</TD>
<TD ALIGN=LEFT VALIGN=TOP ></TD>
<TD ALIGN=RIGHT VALIGN=TOP >
<A HREF="../toc.html"><IMG SRC="../150plogo.gif" ALIGN=TOP WIDTH="150"
HEIGHT="63" BORDER="0"></A><SMALL><SUP>TM</SUP></SMALL></TD>
</TR>
```

```
<TR>
<TD ALIGN=LEFT VALIGN=TOP COLSPAN="3"><BR><HR>
<IMG SRC="../1pixel.gif" ALIGN=TOP WIDTH="400" HEIGHT="1" BORDER="0">
<B>unGROOM'd<SMALL><SUP>TM</SUP></SMALL></B> is dedicated to providing men
with an on line service to help with your "engagement, marriage, and what
follows......"  Please take the time to fill out our survey so we can better
understand our readers and what topics are most important to you.  We thank
you for your time and support!<BR>
<P><HR>
</TD>
</TR>
<TR>
<TD ALIGN=LEFT VALIGN=TOP COLSPAN="3">
<A NAME="top"></A>
<FORM ACTION="/ungroomd/cgi-bin/survey.pl" METHOD="POST">
<P><INPUT TYPE="text" NAME="name" VALUE="" SIZE=40>Name
<P><INPUT TYPE="text" NAME="email" VALUE="" SIZE=30>E-mail address
<P><B>Are You:</B>
<P><B>Married?</B> <INPUT TYPE="radio" NAME="married" VALUE="Yes">Yes
<INPUT TYPE="radio" NAME="married" VALUE="No">No
<P>If yes, how many years? Years:<INPUT TYPE="text" NAME="yearsmarried"
VALUE="" SIZE=3 MAXLENGTH=3>
<P><B>In a relationship?</B> <INPUT TYPE="radio" NAME="relationship"
VALUE="Yes">Yes <INPUT TYPE="radio" NAME="relationship" VALUE="No">No
<P>If yes, how many years? Years:<INPUT TYPE="text" NAME="yearsrelationship"
VALUE="" SIZE=3 MAXLENGTH=3>
<P><B>Are your parents still married?</B>
<P><INPUT TYPE="radio" NAME="parents" VALUE="yes">Yes
<INPUT TYPE="radio" NAME="parents" VALUE="no">No
<P><B>Would you rather?</B>
<P><INPUT TYPE="radio" NAME="howmarried" VALUE="elope">Elope
<INPUT TYPE="radio" NAME="howmarried" VALUE="have wedding">Have Wedding
<P><B>Do you read any books on marriage/relationships?</B>
<P><INPUT TYPE="radio" NAME="readbooks" VALUE="yes">Yes
<INPUT TYPE="radio" NAME="readbooks" VALUE="no">No
<P>If no, any interest in them? <INPUT TYPE="radio" NAME="booksinterest"
VALUE="yes">Yes <INPUT TYPE="radio" NAME="booksinterest" VALUE="no">No
<P><B>Have you ever cheated sexually on your partner?</B>
<P><INPUT TYPE="radio" NAME="cheated" VALUE="yes">Yes
<INPUT TYPE="radio" NAME="cheated" VALUE="no">No
<P><B>For those who have taken the plunge:</B>
<P><B>How long were you engaged for?</B>
<P><INPUT TYPE="radio" NAME="timeengaged" VALUE="less than a year">Less than
a year <INPUT TYPE="radio" NAME="timeengaged" VALUE="1-2">1-2 Years <INPUT
TYPE="radio" NAME="timeengaged" VALUE="2+">2+ Years
<P><B>Did you feel part of the wedding planning process?</B>
<P><INPUT TYPE="radio" NAME="planning" VALUE="yes">Yes
<INPUT TYPE="radio" NAME="planning" VALUE="no">No
<P><B>Did you attend bridal events?</B>
<P><INPUT TYPE="radio" NAME="bridalevents" VALUE="yes">Yes
<INPUT TYPE="radio" NAME="bridalevents" VALUE="no">No
<P><B>How much did you spend on the engagement ring?</B>
<P><INPUT TYPE="radio" NAME="ring" VALUE="1-3">$1,000 -3,000
<INPUT TYPE="radio" NAME="ring" VALUE="3-5">$3,000 -5,000
<INPUT TYPE="radio" NAME="ring" VALUE="5-8"> $5,000 - 10,000
<INPUT TYPE="radio" NAME="ring" VALUE="10+">$10,000 +
```

continues

Listing 26.1. continued

```
<P><B>How much did you/are you spending on your wedding?</B>
<P><INPUT TYPE="radio" NAME="weddingcost" VALUE="1-5">$1,000-5,000
<INPUT TYPE="radio" NAME="weddingcost" VALUE="5-8">$5,000-10,000
<INPUT TYPE="radio" NAME="weddingcost" VALUE="10-15">$10,000-15,000
<INPUT TYPE="radio" NAME="weddingcost" VALUE="15-25">$15,000 - 25,000
<INPUT TYPE="radio" NAME="weddingcost" VALUE="25+">$25,000+
<P><B>Who organized the Honeymoon Details?</B>
<P><INPUT TYPE="radio" NAME="honeymoondetails" VALUE="her">Her
<INPUT TYPE="radio" NAME="honeymoondetails" VALUE="you">You
<INPUT TYPE="radio" NAME="honeymoondetails" VALUE="both">Both
<P><B>Did you see a travel agent?</B>
<P><INPUT TYPE="radio" NAME="travelagent" VALUE="yes">Yes
<INPUT TYPE="radio" NAME="travelagent" VALUE="no">No
<P><B>How long was your honeymoon?</B>
<P><INPUT TYPE="radio" NAME="honeymoonlength" VALUE="1 week">1 week or less
<INPUT TYPE="radio" NAME="honeymoonlength" VALUE="2-3 weeks">2-3 Week
<INPUT TYPE="radio" NAME="honeymoonlength" VALUE="4 weeks+">4 weeks or more
<INPUT TYPE="radio" NAME="honeymoonlength" VALUE="none">No honeymoon
<P><B>How much was your honeymoon?</B>
<P><INPUT TYPE="radio" NAME="honeymooncost" VALUE="less than 1000">$1,000 or
less
<INPUT TYPE="radio" NAME="honeymooncost" VALUE="2,000-4,000">$2,000 - 4,000
<INPUT TYPE="radio" NAME="honeymooncost" VALUE="4,000-6,000">$4,000 - 6,000
<INPUT TYPE="radio" NAME="honeymooncost" VALUE="7,000">$6,000 or more
<P><B>Did you have any marriage counseling prior to marriage or now that you
are married?</B>
<P><INPUT TYPE="radio" NAME="counseling" VALUE="yes">Yes
<INPUT TYPE="radio" NAME="counseling" VALUE="no">No
<P><B>A little about yourself:</B>
<P><B>Age:</B><INPUT TYPE="radio" NAME="age" VALUE="18-24">18-24
<INPUT TYPE="radio" NAME="age" VALUE="25-30">25-30
<INPUT TYPE="radio" NAME="age" VALUE="31-35">31-35
<INPUT TYPE="radio" NAME="age" VALUE="36-40">36-40
<INPUT TYPE="radio" NAME="age" VALUE="40+" CHECKED>40+
<P><B>Sex: </B><INPUT TYPE="radio" NAME="sex" VALUE="male">Male
<INPUT TYPE="radio" NAME="sex" VALUE="female">Female
<P><B>Estimated yearly income?</B>
<INPUT TYPE="radio" NAME="income" VALUE="0-20">0-$20,000
<INPUT TYPE="radio" NAME="income" VALUE="20-40">$20,000-$40,000
<INPUT TYPE="radio" NAME="income" VALUE="40-60">$40,000-60,000
<INPUT TYPE="radio" NAME="income" VALUE="60-100">$60,000-$100,000
<INPUT TYPE="radio" NAME="income" VALUE="100+">$100,000+
<P><B>Education:</B>
<INPUT TYPE="radio" NAME="education" VALUE="High School">High School
<INPUT TYPE="radio" NAME="education" VALUE="Some College">Some College
<INPUT TYPE="radio" NAME="education" VALUE="College Degree">College Degree
<INPUT TYPE="radio" NAME="education" VALUE="Graduate Degree">Graduate Degree
<INPUT TYPE="radio" NAME="education" VALUE="other">Other
<P><B>Weekly internet usage:</B>
<INPUT TYPE="radio" NAME="internet" VALUE="less than an hour">1 Hour or less
<INPUT TYPE="radio" NAME="internet" VALUE="2-3">2-3 Hours
<INPUT TYPE="radio" NAME="internet" VALUE="3-5">3-5 Hours
<INPUT TYPE="radio" NAME="internet" VALUE="5+">5 Hours or more
<P><B>What do you use the web for?</B>
<INPUT TYPE="checkbox" NAME="webusage" VALUE="business">Business
<INPUT TYPE="checkbox" NAME="webusage" VALUE="Entertainment">Entertainment
```

```
<INPUT TYPE="checkbox" NAME="webusage" VALUE="Research">Research
<P><B>Favorite types of magazines (you may check more than one box):</B>
<P><INPUT TYPE="checkbox" NAME="magazines" VALUE="music">Music
<INPUT TYPE="checkbox" NAME="magazines" VALUE="entertainment">Entertainment
<INPUT TYPE="checkbox" NAME="magazines" VALUE="business">Business
<INPUT TYPE="checkbox" NAME="magazines" VALUE="adult entertainment">Adult
Entertainment
<INPUT TYPE="checkbox" NAME="magazines" VALUE="sports">Sports
<INPUT TYPE="checkbox" NAME="magazines" VALUE="mens">Men's Publications
<INPUT TYPE="checkbox" NAME="magazines" VALUE="financial">Financial
<INPUT TYPE="checkbox" NAME="magazines" VALUE="computer">Computer
<P><B>Favorite types of Internet sites (you may  check more than one
box):</B>
<P><INPUT TYPE="checkbox" NAME="internetsites" VALUE="music">Music
<INPUT TYPE="checkbox" NAME="internetsites"
VALUE="entertainment">Entertainment
<INPUT TYPE="checkbox" NAME="internetsites" VALUE="business">Business
<INPUT TYPE="checkbox" NAME="internetsites" VALUE="adult">Adult Entertainment
<INPUT TYPE="checkbox" NAME="internetsites" VALUE="sports">Sports
<P><B>What section of unGROOM'd<SMALL><SUP>TM</SUP></SMALL> is of most
interest to you? (you may check more than one box):</B>
<P><INPUT TYPE="checkbox" NAME="ungroomdsection" VALUE="now featuring">Now
Featuring
<INPUT TYPE="checkbox" NAME="ungroomdsection" VALUE="tying the knot">Tying
the Knot
<INPUT TYPE="checkbox" NAME="ungroomdsection" VALUE="mind over marriage">Mind
Over Marriage
<INPUT TYPE="checkbox" NAME="ungroomdsection" VALUE="the income's
outcome">The Income's Outcome
<INPUT TYPE="checkbox" NAME="ungroomdsection" VALUE="his castle">His Castle
<INPUT TYPE="checkbox" NAME="ungroomdsection" VALUE="last bachelor/MM">The
Last Bachelor/The Marrying Man
<P><B>What topics related to marriage would you like to see covered in
unGROOM'd<SMALL><SUP>TM</SUP></SMALL>? (you may check more than one box):</B>
<P><INPUT TYPE="checkbox" NAME="topics" VALUE="financial">Financial Issues
<INPUT TYPE="checkbox" NAME="topics" VALUE="Psychology">Psychology Issues
<INPUT TYPE="checkbox" NAME="topics" VALUE="Wedding Day">Wedding Day Issues
<INPUT TYPE="checkbox" NAME="topics" VALUE="Becoming a father">Becoming a
father Issues
<INPUT TYPE="checkbox" NAME="topics" VALUE="Infidelity">Infidelity Issues
<INPUT TYPE="checkbox" NAME="topics" VALUE="Religious">Religious Issues
<P><B>How did you hear about unGROOM'd<SMALL><SUP>TM</SUP></SMALL>?</B>
<P><INPUT TYPE="checkbox" NAME="hearaboutus" VALUE="internet search">Internet
Search
<INPUT TYPE="checkbox" NAME="hearaboutus" VALUE="Followed a link"> Followed a
link
<INPUT TYPE="checkbox" NAME="hearaboutus" VALUE="Print article">Print article
<INPUT TYPE="checkbox" NAME="hearaboutus" VALUE="Word of mouth">Word of mouth
<INPUT TYPE="checkbox" NAME="hearaboutus" VALUE="Radio">Radio
<INPUT TYPE="checkbox" NAME="hearaboutus" VALUE="Advertisement">Advertisement
<INPUT TYPE="checkbox" NAME="hearaboutus" VALUE="Flyer/hand out">Flyer/hand
out
<P><B>Any Additional Comments?</B>
<TEXTAREA NAME="comments" ROWS=4 COLS=40></TEXTAREA>
<P><INPUT TYPE="submit" NAME="Submit" VALUE="Submit"><INPUT TYPE="reset"
VALUE="Reset">
<P><CENTER><B>THANK YOU FOR YOUR TIME &amp; INPUT TO
```

continues

Listing 26.1. continued

```
unGROOM'd<SMALL><SUP>TM</SUP></SMALL>!!!</B>
</CENTER>
</FORM>
</TD>
</TR>
</TABLE>
</TD></TR></TABLE>
</BODY>
</HTML>
```

FIGURE 26.1.

The unKNOW'n survey.

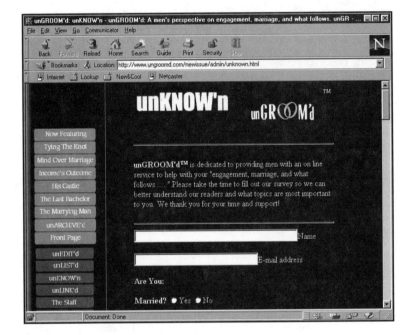

Handling the Form Input

Now that you have an HTML form, you are ready to begin constructing your CGI application. Your CGI application needs to perform the following tasks:

1. Receive the form data.
2. Decode the form data.
3. Insert the data into the database.
4. Return a result to the user.

For this example, you construct your CGI script in Perl. You do not need to know Perl to follow this example. The actual syntax used is not the important part. The logic behind the syntax, which will be explained for each task, is what's important.

Receiving the User's Data

As you learned in Chapter 25, a CGI application receives its data from two sources. One source is environment variables, which the Web server sets when it starts the application. The second source is available only when form data is being sent with the POST request method. This form data is the data you are interested in when creating a form handler CGI application.

In Listing 26.1, you used the opening <FORM> tag:

```
<FORM ACTION="/ungroomd/cgi-bin/survey.pl" METHOD="POST">
```

In this <FORM> tag, the request method is set to POST. Because you explicitly set this in your <FORM> tag, you expect the form data to come to your CGI script via standard input. Because you expect data to be available via standard input, it is a good idea to verify that the CGI script is being called with the correct request method before starting to process the data. In Perl, you can easily do this with the following lines:

```perl
if ($ENV{"REQUEST_METHOD"} ne "POST") {
    &Print_Error("This script can only be used with the POST method.");
    exit(1);
}
```

The first line is an if statement that checks whether the request method, which is stored in the environment variable REQUEST_METHOD, is a value other than POST. If so, the subroutine Print_Error is called, and the program exits. In other words, this code causes the script to exit if the POST method is not being used.

This code segment contains a call to the Print_Error subroutine. The Perl code for the Print_Error subroutine is shown in Listing 26.2.

Listing 26.2. The Print_Error subroutine.

```perl
sub Print_Error {
    local($error) = @_;

    open(ERROR,"$path/unknown-error.tmpl") || die
    "Content-type: text/html\n\nCannot open error template.";
    @error = <ERROR>;
    close(ERROR);

    for($i=0;$i<@error;$i++) {
      if (substr($error[$i],0,4) eq "XXXX") {
          $error[$i] =~ s/XXXX/$error/e;
      last;
      }
    }

    print "Content-type: text/html\n\n";
    print @error;

}
```

This subroutine's purpose is to report an error message to the user's Web browser. The subroutine's first line places the string parameter in the $error variable. Next, a template file named unknown-error.tmpl is opened. This file is a simple template for an HTML document from the unGROOM'd Web site. The code for the unknown-error.tmpl file is shown in Listing 26.3.

Listing 26.3. The `unknown-error.tmpl` file.

```
<HTML>
<HEAD>
<BASE HREF="http://www.ungroomd.com/newissue/admin/unknown-error.html">
<TITLE>unGROOM'd: unKNOW'n survey submission error</TITLE>
</HEAD>
<BODY BACKGROUND="../background2.gif" BGCOLOR="#000000" TEXT="#999966"
LINK="#FFA500" VLINK="#F7007B">
<TABLE BORDER="0" CELLPADDING="0" WIDTH="100%">
<TR>
<TD ALIGN=LEFT VALIGN=TOP>

<IMG SRC="../1pixel.gif" ALIGN=TOP WIDTH="165" HEIGHT="75" BORDER="0"><BR>
<MAP NAME="upperbar">
<AREA SHAPE="rect" COORDS="-6, 178, 133, 201" HREF="../../unarchivd.html">
<AREA SHAPE="rect" COORDS="6,127,135,178" HREF="../columns/columns.html">
<AREA SHAPE="rect" COORDS="6,103,135,127" HREF="../hiscastle/hiscastle.html">
<AREA SHAPE="rect" COORDS="6,75,135,103" HREF="../incout/incout.html">
<AREA SHAPE="rect" COORDS="6,53,135,75" HREF="../mom/mom.html">
<AREA SHAPE="rect" COORDS="6,29,135,53"
HREF="../tyingtheknot/tyingtheknot.html">
<AREA SHAPE="rect" COORDS="6,2,135,29"
HREF="../nowfeaturing/nowfeaturing.html">
<AREA SHAPE=DEFAULT HREF="../toc.html">
</MAP>

<IMG SRC="../upperbar.gif" ALT="navigation bar" ALIGN=TOP WIDTH="135"
HEIGHT="229" BORDER="0" USEMAP="#upperbar"><BR>

<MAP NAME="level1bar">
<AREA SHAPE="rect" COORDS="6, 146, 131, 174" HREF="mmg_pr/pr.html">
<AREA SHAPE="rect" COORDS="6,124,135,147" HREF="mmg_pr/mmg.html">
<AREA SHAPE="rect" COORDS="6,99,135,125" HREF="staff/credits.html">
<AREA SHAPE="rect" COORDS="6,73,135,99" HREF="unlinkd.html">
<AREA SHAPE="rect" COORDS="6,52,135,74" NOHREF>
<AREA SHAPE="rect" COORDS="6,28,135,53" HREF="unlistd/unlistd.html">
<AREA SHAPE="rect" COORDS="6,3,135,28" HREF="uneditd/unedited.html">
<AREA SHAPE=DEFAULT HREF="../toc.html">
</MAP>

<IMG SRC="../level1bar.gif" Alt="alternate navigation bar" ALIGN=top
WIDTH="135" HEIGHT="208" BORDER="0" USEMAP="#level1bar">
</TD>
<TD ALIGN=LEFT VALIGN=TOP>

<TABLE BORDER="0" CELLPADDING="0" WIDTH="400">
```

The Anatomy of a CGI Application

CHAPTER **26**

553

26

THE ANATOMY
OF A CGI
APPLICATION

```
<TR>
<TD ALIGN=LEFT VALIGN=TOP >
<IMG SRC="unknown.gif" ALIGN=MIDDLE WIDTH="200" HEIGHT="50" BORDER="0">
<BR><BR>
</TD>

<TD ALIGN=LEFT VALIGN=TOP ></TD>
<TD ALIGN=RIGHT VALIGN=TOP >
<A HREF="../toc.html"><IMG SRC="../150plogo.gif" ALIGN=TOP WIDTH="150"
HEIGHT="63" BORDER="0"></A><SMALL><SUP>TM</SUP></SMALL>
</TD>
</TR>
<TR>
<TD ALIGN=LEFT VALIGN=TOP COLSPAN="3"><BR><HR>
<IMG SRC="../1pixel.gif" ALIGN=TOP WIDTH="400" HEIGHT="1" BORDER="0">
XXXX
<P>
</TD>
</TR>
</TABLE>
</TD></TR></TABLE>
</BODY>
</HTML>
```

Notice XXXX in Listing 26.3. These characters are placeholders for the error message. The
Print_Error subroutine looks for these characters and replaces them with the error message
sent to the subroutine as a parameter. @error = <ERROR>; follows the open statement in Listing 26.2.

In Perl, this is an easy way to read in the contents of a file and place them in an array. Each
array element contains one line from the file. By placing the entire contents in an array, you
can then check the contents of each array element until you find the placeholder. After you
find the placeholder, you replace the XXXX characters with the contents of the $error variable.
This is done with the following Perl code:

```
for($i=0;$i<@error;$i++) {
  if (substr($error[$i],0,4) eq "XXXX") {
      $error[$i] =~ s/XXXX/$error/e;
      last;
  }
}
```

Now that the placeholder has been replaced with the actual error code you want to use, you
can output the entire contents of the @error array to the user's Web browser. Remember, you
have to send a parsed header to the Web server before sending any data back to the Web browser.
In this case, all you need is a server directive. The two print statements in Listing 26.2 send the
server directive and contents of the @error array to the Web server for parsing. After parsing,
the Web server sends the data on to the user's Web browser.

> **NOTE**
>
> Creating a subroutine to output error messages can save you a lot of code writing. Because you might need to output error messages periodically throughout your program, you can simply make a call to the subroutine with an appropriate error message for that location in your code.

Decoding the User's Data

Now that you know the request method used by the Web browser, you know where the Web server has placed the user data for your CGI script. You can now retrieve the data and decode it. The Web browser encodes some of the characters in the user's data before sending it to the Web server. Before you can store the data in the database, you need to decode it.

Decoding user data is a fairly common task. You need to do it for every CGI application you write that accepts form input. Because of this, you should write a generic subroutine that will decode user data. You can then reuse this subroutine in any of the other CGI applications that need it. Listing 26.4 contains the Perl code for a subroutine that decodes form data.

Listing 26.4. A decoding subroutine.

```perl
sub User_Data {
  local (%user_data, $user_string, $name_value_pair,
         @name_value_pairs, $name, $value);

  # If the data was sent via POST, then it is available
  # from standard input. Otherwise, the data is in the
  # QUERY_STRING environment variable.
  if ($ENV{'REQUEST_METHOD'} eq "POST") {
    read(STDIN,$user_string,$ENV{'CONTENT_LENGTH'});
  } else {
    $user_string = $ENV{'QUERY_STRING'};
  }

  # This line changes the + signs to spaces.
  $user_string =~ s/\+/ /g;

  # This line places each name/value pair as a separate
  # element in the name_value_pairs array.
  @name_value_pairs = split(/&/, $user_string);

  # This code loops over each element in the name_value_pairs
  # array, splits it on the = sign, and places the value
  # into the user_data associative array with the name as the
  # key.
  foreach $name_value_pair (@name_value_pairs) {
    ($name, $value) = split(/=/, $name_value_pair);

    # These two lines decode the values from any URL
    # hexadecimal encoding. The first section searches for a
```

The Anatomy of a CGI Application

CHAPTER 26

555

26

THE ANATOMY
OF A CGI
APPLICATION

```
     # hexadecimal number and the second part converts the
     # hex number to decimal and returns the character
     # equivalent.
     $name =~
       s/%([a-fA-F0-9][a-fA-F0-9])/pack("C",hex($1))/ge;
     $value =~
       s/%([a-fA-F0-9][a-fA-F0-9])/pack("C",hex($1))/ge;

     # If the name/value pair has already been given a value,
     # as in the case of multiple items being selected, then
     # separate the items with a ":".
     if (defined($user_data{$name})) {
       $user_data{$name} .= ":" . $value;
     } else {
       $user_data{$name} = $value;
     }
  }
  return %user_data;
}
```

You use this subroutine by calling it with a line similar to the following:

```
%data_received = &User_Data;
```

The line calls the `User_Data` subroutine and places the returned data into the `%data_received` associative array.

In the `User_Data` subroutine, the first block of code consists of these lines:

```
if ($ENV{'REQUEST_METHOD'} eq "POST") {
  read(STDIN,$user_string,$ENV{'CONTENT_LENGTH'});
} else {
  $user_string = $ENV{'QUERY_STRING'};
}
```

These Perl statements read in the user's form data from either standard input or from the `QUERY_STRING` environment variable, and place it in the `$user_string` variable. For this example, you know the form data is coming from standard input. However, because this subroutine is meant to be a generic one that you can use with other CGI applications, you should handle both cases.

With the form data now in the `$user_string` variable, the `User_Data` subroutine begins to decode the data. The first step is to change all plus signs into spaces. This is easily accomplished with this Perl statement:

```
$user_string =~ s/\+/ /g;
```

Next, all name/value pairs should be separated. Recall from Chapter 25 that each name/value pair is separated by the ampersand. So, the following Perl statement splits the `$user_string` string into separate name/value pairs:

```
@name_value_pairs = split(/&/, $user_string);
```

Each pair is placed as a separate element in the @name_value_pairs array.

The next block of code in Listing 26.4 is the following foreach loop, which performs several actions at the same time:

```
foreach $name_value_pair (@name_value_pairs) {
  ($name, $value) = split(/=/, $name_value_pair);

  $name =~
    s/%([a-fA-F0-9][a-fA-F0-9])/pack("C",hex($1))/ge;
  $value =~
    s/%([a-fA-F0-9][a-fA-F0-9])/pack("C",hex($1))/ge;

  if (defined($user_data{$name})) {
    $user_data{$name} .= ":" . $value;
  } else {
    $user_data{$name} = $value;
  }
}
```

This foreach loop executes the statements in the body of the loop for each element in the @name_value_pairs. The current element, upon any loop iteration, is stored in the $name_value_pair variable.

Once inside the foreach loop, the name and value are separated and placed into separate variables. Then, both variables are checked for any hexadecimal values. If they contain any, the hexadecimal value is converted to its character equivalent.

At the end of the loop is an if statement that checks whether there has already been a name/value pair having the same name. Remember that select statements and check boxes can return multiple name/value pairs with the same name. If there was a previous name/value pair with the same name, a colon and the new value are appended to the existing entry. Otherwise, a new associative array element is created with the name as the index and the value as the contents of that new array element.

The final line in the User_Data subroutine appears as the following:

```
return %user_data;
```

This line returns the %user_data associative array constructed in the previously described foreach loop.

As a security precaution, whenever you process user-supplied form data, you should check the data for any server-side includes that might have been inserted in one of the fields. Keep in mind that some server-side includes are actual directives to the Web server to execute a program. If the user has included any and you send the form data to a Web browser for display, the server-side includes will get processed. In most cases, if a user has done this, the server-side include will have some malicious effect. Therefore, you should look for and remove any server-side includes in form data.

The Anatomy of a CGI Application

CHAPTER 26

557

26

THE ANATOMY
OF A CGI
APPLICATION

As with the decoding form data, removing server-side includes is a task that you probably will need to do frequently. Therefore, you should write a subroutine that can be reused in other CGI applications. Listing 26.5 contains the No_SSI subroutine, which looks for and removes any server-side includes. You call this subroutine with a line similar to

```
&No_SSI(*data_received);
```

You should call the No_SSI subroutine after you have called the User_Data subroutine. Pass the same associative array to the No_SSI subroutine that you had returned from the User_Data subroutine.

Listing 26.5. The No_SSI subroutine.

```
sub No_SSI {
  local (*data) = @_;

  foreach $key (sort keys(%data)) {
    $data{$key} =~ s/<!--(.¦\n)*-->//g;
  }

}
```

Putting the Data in a Simple Database

So far you have received the form data sent by the Web browser and decoded it. Now you are ready to work with the data, performing any related tasks that you wanted to accomplish.

For this example, you place the data into a text file database. This involves the following:

- Formatting the data for the database
- Opening the database
- Locking the database
- Appending the new record
- Unlocking the database
- Closing the database

Formatting the Data For the Database

When you add form data to a database, you often need to do some special formatting of the raw data before inserting it. This formatting could include adding additional fields based on user input, changing other fields based on some standards, or removing any special characters the data might contain.

On the unKNOW'n survey form, there are a few text input fields and a textarea element, in which the user can freely type. Because the database is a simple text file database, with each line representing a different record, you need to make sure the user has not entered any return or newline characters in any of these text fields.

An easy way to eliminate these characters is to first store them in some variables. This is accomplished by using the associated ASCII value for the characters. The ASCII value of a return character is 10, and the ASCII value of a newline character is 13. The following two lines place these characters in their respective variables:

```
$ASCII_ten = pack("c", 10);
$ASCII_thirteen = pack("c", 13);
```

After you have these characters stored, you can loop over each of the elements in your %data_received array, checking for either one of these values. The following Perl loop performs this task, removing any occurrences of these characters:

```
foreach $key (keys(%data_received)) {

    $data_received{$key} =~ s/$ASCII_ten//ge;
    $data_received{$key} =~ s/$ASCII_thirteen/$space/ge;

}
```

Opening the Database

With all the fields formatted for the database, you are ready to combine the fields into a database record and append it to the database file. The first step is to open the database file. This is done with the following Perl statement:

```
open(DATABASE,"$database_file") ||
    die "Content-type: text/html\n\nCannot open database.";
```

Earlier in your program, the variable $database_file has been set to the path and filename of the database file on the Web server.

The second part of this Perl statement uses the die command. This command causes the contents of the string to be printed to the standard error stream and program execution to halt. For many systems, standard error will be the same as standard output, and this message will be sent on to the user's Web browser. For systems where standard error is not sent to the same location as standard output, you need to change this to contain print and exit statements.

Locking the Database

Whenever you develop CGI applications, you need to keep in mind that there might be several instances of the application running at the same time. This is because multiple users can be accessing the CGI application on your Web site at the same moment. You must make sure your CGI applications do not interfere with each other.

In the case of this application, you are writing to a file on the Web server machine. If another user is writing to it at the same time, only one of the new records is saved—whichever one finishes editing the file last. To avoid this, you can place a file lock on the database files to keep any other application from editing the file at the same time. With the open Perl statements used in the examples in this chapter, if the file being opened is locked, it continues trying to open the file for editing until it does so successfully.

The Anatomy of a CGI Application

CHAPTER 26

559

26

THE ANATOMY
OF A CGI
APPLICATION

In order to lock the database file, you must use a file system function that can modify access permissions to the file. In Perl, you can use the `flock` statement, such as:

```
flock(DATABASE, 2);
```

The first parameter is the stream associated with an open file. You must use the same filestream name as you use in the `open` statement you created in the previous section. In this case, the filestream name is `DATABASE`.

The number being sent as the second parameter is a code to the `flock` function. The number 2 denotes locking the file. You will see an example of another code being used with `flock` in the section "Unlocking and Closing the Database," later in this chapter.

Because locking is another process that you might do frequently throughout various CGI applications, you might want to create a subroutine that calls the `flock` function for you. You could create the following subroutine:

```
sub Lock_File {
  flock(DATABASE, 2);
}
```

You would then use the following statement to call it:

```
&Lock_File();
```

Appending the New Record

At this point in the development, the form data is decoded and formatted for your database, the database file is open, and you have locked other applications from editing the database. You are now ready to place the new database record in the database file. In Perl, you do this by using the filestream name for the open database file and the `print` statement. The following lines print all the fields of the unKNOW'n survey form into the database:

```
print DATABASE $quote . $data_received{"name"} . $quote . "," .
     $quote . $data_received{"email"} . $quote . "," .
     $quote . $data_received{"married"} . $quote . "," .
     $quote . $data_received{"yearsmarried"} . $quote . "," .
     $quote . $data_received{"relationship"} . $quote . "," .
     $quote . $data_received{"yearsrelationship"} . $quote . "," .
     $quote . $data_received{"parents"} . $quote . "," .
     $quote . $data_received{"howmarried"} . $quote . "," .
     $quote . $data_received{"readbooks"} . $quote . "," .
     $quote . $data_received{"booksinterest"} . $quote . "," .
     $quote . $data_received{"cheated"} . $quote . "," .
     $quote . $data_received{"timeengaged"} . $quote . "," .
     $quote . $data_received{"planning"} . $quote . "," .
     $quote . $data_received{"bridalevents"} . $quote . "," .
     $quote . $data_received{"ring"} . $quote . "," .
     $quote . $data_received{"weddingcost"} . $quote . "," .
     $quote . $data_received{"honeymoondetails"} . $quote . "," .
     $quote . $data_received{"travelagent"} . $quote . "," .
     $quote . $data_received{"honeymoonlength"} . $quote . "," .
     $quote . $data_received{"honeymooncost"} . $quote . "," .
     $quote . $data_received{"counseling"} . $quote . "," .
```

```
$quote . $data_received{"age"} . $quote . "," .
$quote . $data_received{"sex"} . $quote . "," .
$quote . $data_received{"income"} . $quote . "," .
$quote . $data_received{"education"} . $quote . "," .
$quote . $data_received{"internet"} . $quote . "," .
$quote . $data_received{"webusage"} . $quote . "," .
$quote . $data_received{"magazines"} . $quote . "," .
$quote . $data_received{"internetsites"} . $quote . "," .
$quote . $data_received{"ungroomdsection"} . $quote . "," .
$quote . $data_received{"topics"} . $quote . "," .
$quote . $data_received{"hearaboutus"} . $quote . "," .
$quote . $data_received{"comments"} . $quote . "\n";
```

The $quote variable is used to make the code more readable. Somewhere near the beginning of your script, you would have this line:

```
$quote = "\"";
```

This line assigns a quotation mark to the $quote variable.

The preceding print statement prints each element from the %data_received associative array, enclosed in quotes and separated by commas. This results in lines similar to the following being added to the database:

```
"Joe Reader","joe@somewhere.com","No","","Yes","1","yes","have wedding",
"no","yes","no","less than a year","no","no","1-3","15-25","you","yes",
"2-3 weeks","4,000-6,000","no","31-35","male",
"20-40","Some College","5+","business: Entertainment:Research",
"entertainment:sports:mens:financial:computer",
"entertainment:business:sports","mind over marriage:the income's outcome:his
castle:last bachelor/MM","financial:Psychology:Wedding Day:Becoming a father",
"Print article","I enjoyed reading the articles on your site."
```

Unlocking and Closing the Database

With the new record appended to the database, you are finished working with the database file. You can now release the lock you have on the file and close the database.

As with locking the database, you should place the flock command to unlock a file in a reusable subroutine, such as this:

```
sub Unlock_File {
    flock(DATABASE, 8);
}
```

The number 8 designates to the flock function to remove an existing lock from the file pointed to by the DATABASE filestream. You would then call the function with the following statement:

```
&Unlock_File();
```

Closing the database file is even easier and is done with the following intuitive statement:

```
close(DATABASE);
```

Returning a Response to the User

At this point, your CGI application has accomplished all the tasks you need it to perform. The only thing left that it must do before finishing is return a result to the user's Web browser. If you do not return any results, the user will most likely receive an error message similar to Docu-ment contains no data.

For the unKNOW'n survey, the best thing to return to the user would be a response, thanking the user for filling out the survey. There is no need for the CGI script to contain all the HTML tags for this response. So, rather than having your CGI application return data to be displayed in the user's Web browser, the CGI application will redirect the Web browser to the URL of the response document. To do so, you must use the Location *server* directive, described in the section "Creating the Response Header" of Chapter 25. In Perl, this is done with the statement

```
print "Location:http://www.ungroomd.com/newissue/admin/unknown-success.html\n\n";
```

Putting It All Together

In the previous sections, you developed all the pieces for the CGI script to receive the form data from the unKNOW'n survey and place the data in a text file database. You now have to put them all together to have a finished CGI script. Listing 26.6 contains the entire CGI script for handling the unKNOW'n survey. Notice how all the components you developed are integrated into a complete application.

Listing 26.6. The survey.pl file.

```perl
#!/usr/local/bin/perl5

# *******************************************************
# This Script maintains a flat-file database of
# ungroomd.com survey responses.
# *******************************************************

$HOME = (getpwnam("www03640"))[7];
$path = "$HOME/survey";
$database_file = ">>$path/unKNOWn.dat";
$quote = "\"";
$ASCII_ten = pack("c", 10);
$ASCII_thirteen = pack("c", 13);
$space = " ";

# Make sure this script is being used via
# a web page form with the Post method.
if ($ENV{"REQUEST_METHOD"} ne "POST") {
    &Print_Error("This script can only be used with the POST method.");
    exit(1);
}

# Format the web data received and make sure
```

continues

Listing 26.6. continued

```perl
# it does not contain any Server Side Includes
%data_received = &User_Data;
&No_SSI(*data_received);

# Make sure all mandatory fields are full and
# truncate all strings to a maximum of 255 characters
# Also make sure no new-line characters.
foreach $key (keys(%data_received)) {

    $data_received{$key} =~ s/$ASCII_ten//ge;
    $data_received{$key} =~ s/$ASCII_thirteen/$space/ge;

}

open(DATABASE,"$database_file") ||
    die "Content-type: text/html\n\nCannot open database.";

# Lock the database file now.
&Lock_File();

print DATABASE $quote . $data_received{"name"} . $quote . "," .
        $quote . $data_received{"email"} . $quote . "," .
        $quote . $data_received{"married"} . $quote . "," .
        $quote . $data_received{"yearsmarried"} . $quote . "," .
        $quote . $data_received{"relationship"} . $quote . "," .
        $quote . $data_received{"yearsrelationship"} . $quote . "," .
        $quote . $data_received{"parents"} . $quote . "," .
        $quote . $data_received{"howmarried"} . $quote . "," .
        $quote . $data_received{"readbooks"} . $quote . "," .
        $quote . $data_received{"booksinterest"} . $quote . "," .
        $quote . $data_received{"cheated"} . $quote . "," .
        $quote . $data_received{"timeengaged"} . $quote . "," .
        $quote . $data_received{"planning"} . $quote . "," .
        $quote . $data_received{"bridalevents"} . $quote . "," .
        $quote . $data_received{"ring"} . $quote . "," .
        $quote . $data_received{"weddingcost"} . $quote . "," .
        $quote . $data_received{"honeymoondetails"} . $quote . "," .
        $quote . $data_received{"travelagent"} . $quote . "," .
        $quote . $data_received{"honeymoonlength"} . $quote . "," .
        $quote . $data_received{"honeymooncost"} . $quote . "," .
        $quote . $data_received{"counseling"} . $quote . "," .
        $quote . $data_received{"age"} . $quote . "," .
        $quote . $data_received{"sex"} . $quote . "," .
        $quote . $data_received{"income"} . $quote . "," .
        $quote . $data_received{"education"} . $quote . "," .
        $quote . $data_received{"internet"} . $quote . "," .
        $quote . $data_received{"webusage"} . $quote . "," .
        $quote . $data_received{"magazines"} . $quote . "," .
        $quote . $data_received{"internetsites"} . $quote . "," .
        $quote . $data_received{"ungroomdsection"} . $quote . "," .
        $quote . $data_received{"topics"} . $quote . "," .
        $quote . $data_received{"hearaboutus"} . $quote . "," .
        $quote . $data_received{"comments"} . $quote . "\n";

&Unlock_File();
close(DATABASE);
```

```perl
# Output success message
print
"Location:http://www.ungroomd.com/newissue/admin/unknown-success.html\n\n";

# Print_Error
# This procedure takes a string as input. It then opens
# the error template file and outputs the string as the
# error message.
sub Print_Error {
    local($error) = @_;

    open(ERROR,"$path/unknown-error.tmpl") ||
     die "Content-type: text/html\n\nCannot open error template.";
    @error = <ERROR>;
    close(ERROR);

    for($i=0;$i<@error;$i++) {
      if (substr($error[$i],0,4) eq "XXXX") {
          $error[$i] =~ s/XXXX/$error/e;
      last;
      }
    }

    print "Content-type: text/html\n\n";
    print @error;

}


# Lock_File
# Places a lock on the file. Used to lock
# a file before making changes.
sub Lock_File {
    flock(DATABASE, 2);
}

# Unlock_File
# Removes a lock on the file. Used to unlock
# a file after making changes.
sub Unlock_File {
    flock(DATABASE, 8);
}

# User_Data
# This procedure receives form input from a web
# page form and formats it into an associative
# array. The keys of the associative array are
# the Names of the form elements. The associative
# array is returned from the procedure.
sub User_Data {
  local (%user_data, $user_string, $name_value_pair,
        @name_value_pairs, $name, $value);

  # If the data was sent via POST, then it is available
  # from standard input. Otherwise, the data is in the
  # QUERY_STRING environment variable.
  if ($ENV{'REQUEST_METHOD'} eq "POST") {
    read(STDIN,$user_string,$ENV{'CONTENT_LENGTH'});
```

continues

Listing 26.6. continued

```perl
  } else {
    $user_string = $ENV{'QUERY_STRING'};
  }

  # This line changes the + signs to spaces.
  $user_string =~ s/\+/ /g;

  # This line places each name/value pair as a separate
  # element in the name_value_pairs array.
  @name_value_pairs = split(/&/, $user_string);

  # This code loops over each element in the name_value_pairs
  # array, splits it on the = sign, and places the value
  # into the user_data associative array with the name as the
  # key.
  foreach $name_value_pair (@name_value_pairs) {
    ($name, $value) = split(/=/, $name_value_pair);

    # These two lines decode the values from any URL
    # hexadecimal encoding. The first section searches for a
    # hexadecimal number and the second part converts the
    # hex number to decimal and returns the character
    # equivalent.
    $name =~
      s/%([a-fA-F0-9][a-fA-F0-9])/pack("C",hex($1))/ge;
    $value =~
      s/%([a-fA-F0-9][a-fA-F0-9])/pack("C",hex($1))/ge;

    # If the name/value pair has already been given a value,
    # as in the case of multiple items being selected, then
    # separate the items with a ":".
    if (defined($user_data{$name})) {
      $user_data{$name} .= ":" . $value;
    } else {
      $user_data{$name} = $value;
    }
  }
  return %user_data;
}

# No_SSI
# This procedure checks form data entered by
# a user, and removes any SSI fields. (Server
# Side Includes). It receives an associative
# array as the input.
sub No_SSI {
  local (*data) = @_;

  foreach $key (sort keys(%data)) {
    $data{$key} =~ s/<!--(.|\n)*-->//g;
  }

}
```

Summary

Web page forms and their associated CGI applications are a good medium for users of your Web site to interact with you. From the user's perspective, the form is a nonintrusive item that is simply part of the Web site. For you, you can have a CGI application receive the form data and place it in a database, from which you can generate real-time, up-to-date reports.

After you have decided to add a form to your Web site, the first step in creating it is to develop the HTML for your Web page. You need the values you specify in the NAME attributes of the form elements in your CGI application, so it is best to create the form before coding the application.

You start development of your CGI application after your form is complete. Your CGI application needs to perform several tasks. First, it needs to retrieve the form data from the Web server. Next, it must decode the data, removing all hexadecimal conversions and special character replacements. Following these two tasks, the data is ready to be added to your database. For text file databases, this entails formatting the data for your database, opening and locking the database file, printing the new record to the database file, and unlocking and closing the file. When all these tasks are completed, the CGI application should return a result to the user's Web browser.

Server-Specific Technologies: Netscape ONE Versus Microsoft WindowsDNA

by Shelley Powers

IN THIS CHAPTER

Netscape and Microsoft both have established platforms that define their technical philoso-phies, supported standards, client and server tools, and technical integration. Netscape calls its platform Netscape ONE, and Microsoft terms its platform WindowsDNA.

This chapter provides an overview of the technologies that make up each company's platform. This includes their implementation and support of technologies such as Java, Scripting, and Dynamic HTML, mentioned elsewhere in this book. The rest of the chapter then focuses on each company's server and the technologies used specifically with the servers, which are not detailed anywhere else.

This chapter provides examples of some of these technologies as they relate to the focus of this book, concentrating on Web development. The chapter also provides some links to more in-formation on each server's capabilities. Note that the chapter does not provide all the detail you need to create complex server-side applications; an entire book is needed for that topic alone. It does, however, provide enough information for you to understand what the technologies are, and how they work.

Netscape and Microsoft both provide powerful Web servers, and both have extended these products to handle a variety of technologies. The Microsoft server is called the Internet Infor-mation Server (IIS), and this chapter covers the beta release of version 4.0 of this product. The Netscape server covered in this chapter is the Enterprise server, version 3.0. Both servers were installed in Windows NT.

The technologies these servers support range from server-side plug-ins (incorporating the new JavaBeans technology), to extending the server capability through exposed API functions and embedding server-side capability into an HTML page using scripting.

With these technologies you can extend your Web server to access data from a database and present it to your Web page readers, or alter the appearance and text of a Web page, dynami-cally, without requiring the use of client-side Dynamic HTML.

With the ability to extend the server's functionality, you can fine-tune the server to fit your company's specific needs without sacrificing performance and general access.

Technology Components of Netscape ONE

Netscape ONE is a group of technologies packaged under one corporate philosophy. The philosophical basis of these products is crossware support—providing the tools to build appli-cations that can run in many environments—on many different types of machines.

The main page to find out about Netscape ONE is at `http://developer.netscape.com/one`, shown in Figure 27.1. This page lists all the major Netscape technologies in the side frame, each with an active link to take you to more detailed information pages.

FIGURE 27.1.

The main information page for the Netscape ONE platform.

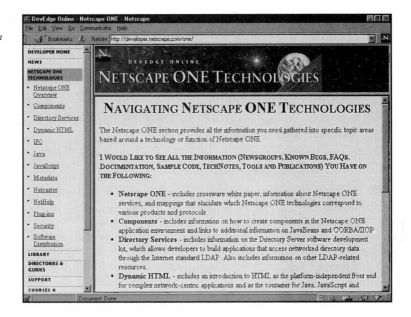

The Netscape ONE technologies listed at this page are:

- Components —Application objects built using a variety of languages such as Java, JavaScript, or C++, and interfaced with each other using CORBA/IIOP (Common Object Request Broker Architecture/Internet Inter-Orb Protocol) and the JavaBeans model.

- Directory Services—Provide techniques to programmatically access directory-based information.

- Dynamic HTML—Covered elsewhere in this book, Dynamic HTML is the capability to modify or position traditional HTML elements using a combination of style sheets and scripting. Dynamic positioning is currently supported, but alterations of CSS1 attributes of an element after the page loads are not currently supported.

- IFC—Internet Foundation Classes that were a set of classes for working with interface components, and are now integrated into the Sun JFC (Java Foundation Class) effort.

- Java—Netscape supports Java, both from the client application, Navigator, and from the server. It currently supports JDK 1.1 and promises support of JDK 1.2 when it releases.

- JavaScript—Netscape's scripting language, which is the first scripting language to be used with client-side browsers. It's a key component of server-side scripting covered later in this chapter.

- Metadata—Not to be confused with XML, the Extended Markup Language specification currently being reviewed, metadata is associated with W3C's RDF (Resource

Description Framework) efforts. Metadata controls things such as the base location of a Web page for the resolution of relative URLs and other information.

- Netcaster—Netscape's Channel technology.
- Nethelp—Based on the capability to create HTML-based help files, viewable online and based on open standards.
- Plug-ins—Netscape's capability of embedding external software components into Web pages for client-side or server-side access.
- Security—Netscape actually has several security components, such as object signing, SmartCards, and digital certificates.
- Software Distribution—Netscape also supports several techniques for software publication, such as publishing to the server (demonstrated later), the SmartUpdate feature, and the use of Marimba Castanet technology.

As you can see, Netscape's ONE is a very comprehensive approach to Internet and intranet development using a variety of technologies; some are homegrown, and some are incorporated from outside sources.

As an example of one of these technologies, the following code uses Dynamic HTML technology to place a block of HTML elements into a specific position in the Web page:

```
<DIV style="position:absolute; left: 100; top: 100">
<img src="someimage.gif" width=100 height=180 alt="Some Image">
<H1>Welcome to the site</h1>
</DIV>
```

Dynamic HTML is the component of Netscape's technology that alters and moves traditional HTML elements within a Web page. The following code, on the other hand, uses IFC to create a button with an image in a Java applet:

```
Button     thebutton;
Bitmap     image;
...
image = Bitmap.bitmapNamed("buttonimage.gif");
thebutton = New Button (0,0, image.width(), image.height());
thebutton.setType(Button.TOGGLE_TYPE);
thebutton.setImage(image);
```

The IFC, and the JFC currently under development, extend the traditional windowing components of the standard Java classes, adding components such as the button, 2D and 3D image methods, and other techniques to enable more sophisticated interface development. These classes also provide the capability to access other objects within the Web page. If you create one object using Java, you can reference it within a page using a standard hypertext link, and this same object is accessible by other Java classes that are also included within the page. The referenced Java classes don't need to be accessed directly from the referencing Java file. This definitely facilitates a modular development environment.

The metadata concept covers technology such as W3C's RDF, and Netscape currently uses the Apple MCF (Meta Content Framework), although the company will support RDF as soon as a recommendation from the W3C is issued. RDF provides a framework for metadata that is used by search engines, site cataloging tools, and other information tools that are interested basically in "information about the information," which is the loose translation of *meta*. Currently, with Apple's implementation of this technology there are tools that display the pages of a Web site in a 3D format, which you can then traverse using VRML-like techniques. Search engines also use this technology with HTML tags, such as the <META> tag, to determine how to classify a page. This will lead to better results from search engines. Additionally, the <META> tag assists you in making sure your page is included when a search is made on a topic you are covering. Netscape proposed a hybrid MCF/XML specification for RDF. XML then becomes the syntax used to create the framework specification.

JavaScript is Netscape's scripting language and can be used in client-based and server-based applications. The server-based application use of JavaScript, server-side scripting, is currently termed *LiveWire* from Netscape.

WORKING WITH LIVEWIRE

The first server-based Web task is creating a Web interface application for online banking software. The application was created to run with the Netscape server, and used LiveWire, the Netscape server-side scripting technique. The primary use of the LiveWire capability was to invoke C functions to access and update data from a supporting database. The page coding for this project was fairly simple, but the setup caused problems. Now that LiveWire is an integral component of Netscape's Enterprise Server 3.0, you may have considerably fewer problems installing and setting up the environment.

Plug-ins are embedded into the page using the <EMBED> tag, although this is likely to change when HTML 4.0 becomes a recommendation. The HTML 4.0 draft specification supports the use of the <OBJECT> tag for embedded content.

Again, for more information on these technologies, you can review them in more detail at the Netscape site. Examples of using LiveWire, the server-side scripting technique, are given later in the chapter. Part III, "Client-Side Scripting," discusses the various client-side scripting techniques, and Part IV, "Web Publishing with Java," covers the various Dynamic HTML techniques.

What are the Technology Components of Microsoft WindowsDNA?

Microsoft also has its own platform—WindowsDNA or Distributed interNet Applications Architecture—and with it Microsoft lists its key technologies, Internet and other. For the most part, the Internet-related technologies map directly to the Netscape technologies, although the mapping may not be a one-to-one correspondence.

The main page to begin to learn about the DNA technologies is located at `http://www.microsoft.com/sitebuilder/dna`, as shown in Figure 27.2.

FIGURE 27.2.

The main Web page to begin to learn about the DNA technologies.

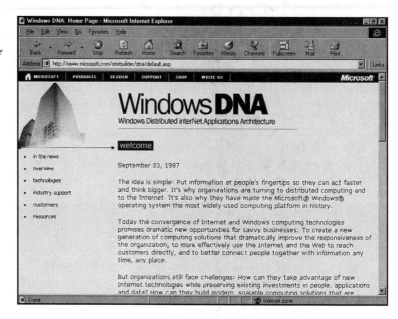

The following list contains the Microsoft DNA groupings:

- Windows Platforms—Includes the Windows operating systems and the Win32 technologies
- Common Object Model (COM)—Contains the object development structure that forms the framework of all the DNA technologies
- Internet Technologies—Including Internet Explorer, Dynamic HTML, Internet Information Server, the Microsoft Site Server, and Java technologies
- Windows DNA Services—Including security, directory, transaction, message queuing, database management, data access, e-mail, scripting, and systems management
- Windows DNA Tools—Includes the company's visual tools such as Visual Basic and Visual C++; component creation, such as ActiveX controls; team development with Visual SourceSafe; content creation, such as FrontPage; and Web site development with Visual InterDev
- Other Windows DNA server applications—Includes Office

Prior to the new DNA name, Microsoft had what it termed Active Platform, which listed in more detail the technologies Microsoft considers key. The following list contains the key technologies of Active Platform:

- Cascading Style Sheets (CSS1)—CSS1 is used to define the presentation of traditional HTML elements.

- Dynamic HTML—Microsoft has exposed all HTML 4.0 supported elements to scripting, including the capability to modify CSS1 presentation attributes as well as dynamically position elements after the Web page is displayed.

- HTML Authoring—This technology has to do with traditional Web page structural elements, based on the HTML 4.0 draft specification.

- Internet Explorer 4.0 Technologies—This could be considered to include many of the other technologies described in this list, such as CSS1 and Dynamic HTML.

- Intranets—This really isn't a specific technology as much as it is an explicit statement of support. Microsoft includes its FrontPage tool in this listing, so you could also classify it as software distribution within an Internet context.

- Java—Microsoft has promised support for Java and has provided its own framework classes—the Application Framework Classes (AFC)—as well as access to the Windows-based services through J/Direct. Microsoft also has its own Java development tool, called Visual J++.

- SDKs (Software Development Kits)—Microsoft has a slew of SDKs, covering everything from multimedia to Java to the Internet.

- Security—Microsoft supports several security technologies such as the Personal Information Exchange (PFX), Smart Card, Digital IDs, SSL (Secure Sockets Layer), and Authenticode.

- Server technologies—This includes Active Server Pages (ASP) and Internet Server API (ISAPI), which is exposure of server methods through an accessible API.

- Typography—This technology addresses embedding fonts into a Web page, as well as the TrueType and OpenType fonts.

- Web Content Management—This covers the use of the Microsoft Visual SafeSource tool to manage Web page content.

- Other Technology—This section seems to include all the other technologies that Microsoft didn't include elsewhere. These technologies include Cabinets—the Microsoft archive resource format—the Common Object Model and its distributed component (COM/DCOM), and Point-to-Point Tunneling Protocol (PPTP).

Microsoft DNA, and the previous Active Platform, represent Microsoft's diversified interests in client/server, Web, and distributed development.

As an example of the CSS1 style sheet technology, the following alters the presentation of a Web page to have a red background, white letters, and an inch margin surrounding the page contents:

```
<STYLE TYPE="text/css">
    BODY { background-color: #FF0000; color: #FFFFFF; margin: 1.0in }
</STYLE>
```

27

SERVER-SPECIFIC TECHNOLOGIES

Another example, this time of Dynamic HTML and the Microsoft Scripting object model, is to alter the appearance of a header:

```
<H1 id=header1 style="color: blue; font-family: Arial; font-size: 24pt"
    onmouseover="document.header1.style.color='red'"
    onmouseout="document.header1.style.color='blue'">The Header</H1>
```

This example creates a mouseover effect that changes the color of the header when the Web page reader's mouse is over it.

Microsoft has numerous SDKs, which can usually be downloaded from their site for no charge. The following SDKs are available:

- ActiveX SDK for the MAC and PC
- Design Time Control SDK
- DirectX SDK
- Internet Client SDK
- JAVA SDK
- Microsoft Platform SDK
- Netmeeting SDK
- Web Wizard SDK

The ActiveX SDK is for creating ActiveX controls, and the DirectX SDK is used for controlling multimedia for uses such as creating games. An extension to the DirectX is DirectAnimation, which adds DirectX capabilities that are accessible via scripting or Java as well as via traditional programming languages such as C++.

The Internet Client SDK really encompasses many of the technologies already mentioned separately as Active Platform technologies, such as Dynamic HTML and ActiveX. The Web Wizard SDK enables developers to create their own wizards for Visual InterDev, the Microsoft Visual Development environment.

Microsoft Java support includes a development tool, Visual J++, Application Framework Classes (AFC), and the company's own Virtual Machine (VM) for Java. Microsoft also provides classes that allow access to the operating system services through its J/Direct technology.

MICROSOFT AND THE JAVA FOUNDATION CLASSES

Microsoft has provided its own foundation classes with AFC. Sun and Netscape support the Java Foundation Classes (JFC). Microsoft doesn't explicitly state it won't eventually support JFC, but does imply from a Java Q&A located at `http://www.microsoft.com/java/issues/techsupfaq.htm` that they will probably stay with their support of AFC because to Microsoft, the JFC is late. Sun's promised delivery of JFC functionality has caused some users problems, but some are concerned about creating applets for Web pages that work with Navigator as well as Internet Explorer. I don't agree with Sun that its foundation classes are the only standard classes because Sun provides them. This violates the company's own stated policy of Java being an open standard. However, Sun's issue of "write once, run anywhere" is violated with operating system-specific framework classes such as the JFC. The issue is hot and becoming hotter. You can see Sun's viewpoint on these issues at http://www.javasoft.com.

Microsoft has had support for object development with COM (Common Object Model) and for distributed object development with DCOM. Although not compatible with CORBA, many tools that support CORBA also provide some form of a COM/CORBA bridge to interface the two technologies.

Unlike Netscape, Microsoft WindowsDNA covers other forms of development and systems other than just Internet or intranet applications, as you would expect from an operating system and development tool company. More of the differences between the two platforms are discussed in the next section.

Differences Between the Netscape and Microsoft Platforms

The differences in platforms between Netscape and Microsoft have more to do with each company's perspective than with what each company considers as the key technologies. Microsoft is first and foremost an operating system and tools development company; Netscape's first emphasis is Web browsers and Web servers. This isn't to say that one company's support of the technology is somehow more complete than the other. As an example, Netscape mentions Directory Services specifically as a key technology, and it's also a key technology for Microsoft. However, Microsoft also implements operating systems and includes Directory Services as a component of its Windows NT Server product, rather than necessarily splitting it out as separate technology. Netscape also has support for tools and provides HTML authoring with Netscape Navigator Professional Edition, and its new tool Visual JavaScript.

The key differences tend to rely on focus, and previous commitments. For example, Microsoft primarily supports COM/DCOM as its main interoperability technology rather than CORBA and its Web component, Internet Interface Operability Protocol (IIOP). This is because Microsoft and third party vendors that support Microsoft technologies have too much invested in the COM/DCOM technology, and a stated preference for it as well. Netscape has no real commitment to any previous component technology, so it's a simple matter for it to support CORBA/IIOP and JavaBeans for this type of technology.

That's not to say you can't use both technologies together. Sun has provided a JavaBeans to ActiveX bridge to provide OLE/COM/ActiveX support for JavaBeans components to work within an OLE/COM/ActiveX environment. For more information on this, see `http://www.javasoft.com/beans/bridge`.

Another differences between the two companies is that Netscape is a close partner with Sun in creating the JFC, and supports this framework as it encompasses its own framework class set (IFC). Microsoft started creating its own framework classes (AFC) before the JFC began, and is resistant to any use of the JFC in its own products. Unlike the JavaBeans to ActiveX bridge, this difference won't be as easily solved, unfortunately.

Web Server Extensions

COMPANION Web site Netscape has two Web server products: Enterprise Server and Fast Track. Enterprise Server is the full-featured server and Fast Track is an easier to install and simpler to work with version of the main Web product. The Companion Web Site contains the download location for accessing either of these servers.

The Netscape Enterprise Server is relatively easy to install, and once installed it has online documentation and application administration tools accessible via Navigator. Figure 27.3 shows the server with the main administration page open. From this page the Web administrator can access each individual Web installed locally or remotely.

FIGURE 27.3.

Netscape Enterprise Server 3.0 main administration page.

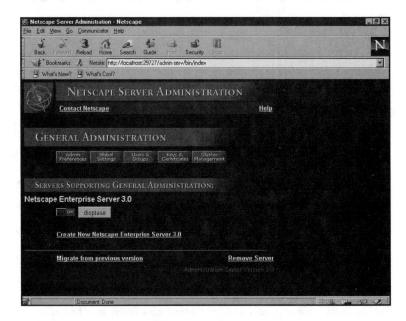

Microsoft has one server, the Internet Information Server (IIS), and it is usually accessible as a component of the Windows NT Server operating system product. However, in this chapter's examples, a new 4.0 beta version of IIS is used, which is accessible from a separate CD-ROM or downloadable from the Microsoft Web site.

IIS 4.0 has two techniques for administrating not only the default Web server, but also the administration Web server and the FTP server, if one is created. One technique is not Web-based, and Figure 27.4 shows this administration tool.

FIGURE 27.4.

This is Internet Information Server's non-Web administration tool.

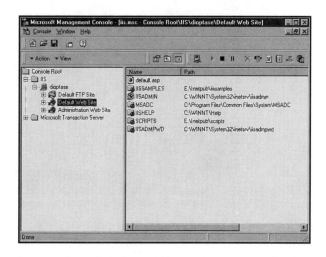

27

SERVER-SPECIFIC
TECHNOLOGIES

The Web-based administration tool is shown in Figure 27.5. As shown in the figure, the administration, default, and FTP servers have all been started and are running.

You can modify parameters such as accessible MIME types, security, logging frequency, file location, and other Web-server features according to the fairly comprehensive documentation each server provides.

After you have installed the server and set all the server properties to fit your needs, you can begin to add Web page content. Most of the content will probably be standard HTML files, so you'll just need to move them to the server site and make sure that any hypertext links reflect the page locations accurately. However, you could and probably will have some server application pages in the Web site also. The next two sections discuss one type of server extension for both Netscape and IIS: server-side scripting. Netscape terms its extension LiveWire, and Microsoft has the Active Server Pages (ASP).

Server-Side JavaScript with Netscape's LiveWire

Netscape's server-side scripting was created as a separate product—LiveWire and the associated LiveWire Pro—but the company has since integrated this capability into Enterprise Server 3.0.

FIGURE 27.5.

Here is the Internet Information Server's Web administration tool.

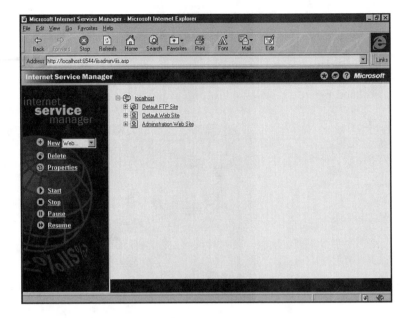

With LiveWire you can embed server-side scripting into a Web page, and the server processes these scripting blocks before the page is sent to the browser. The scripting can create new Web page content, process a form submission, call external functions created in programming languages such as C or C++, and access a database.

For the most part, the scripting language you can use with Enterprise Server 3.0 is JavaScript 1.2. Some features, such as alert boxes that require user input, are, of course, not supported because these server-side applications must run without user intervention.

Enabling Server-Side JavaScript Applications

To use server-side JavaScript applications, you need to activate the application environment and decide whether an administration password is required for those in the group that need to access the Application Manager tool. To do this, access the Programs menu item of the tool, and then select the Server Side JavaScript sidebar item. Figure 27.6 shows the resulting Web page.

In this example, the server-side JavaScript application environment is used, and did not require an administration password.

After the environment is enabled, you are ready to create an application. This is detailed in the following sections.

FIGURE 27.6.

The administration Web page controls the running of server-side JavaScript applications.

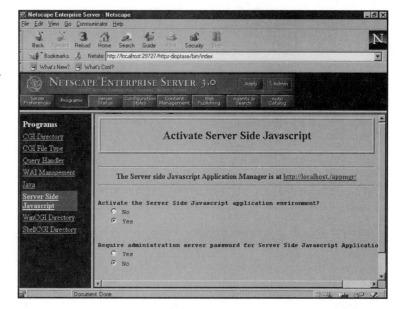

Creating a LiveWire Application—Time of Day

To demonstrate the components of LiveWire, a small application is created on the server that alters the page color, header, and image based on what time of day it is. It's based on a previous example that uses client-side scripting to alter these same components. That example uses the images array (only supported in Navigator 3.x and Internet Explorer 4.x and up) for changing the image and an input element for the message. Using LiveWire, you can create a better edition of this page and one that works with Navigator 2.x and up and Internet Explorer 3.x and up. This example demonstrates how Web pages can be dynamically altered based on external information without having to use Dynamic HTML.

COMPANION **Web site** First, the Web page is created and included in the server-side scripting block or blocks. This script is enclosed within special tags that denote server-side scripting, <SERVER> and </SERVER>. Listing 27.1 contains the contents of the page, which you can also examine in the file timeday.html.

Listing 27.1. Server-side JavaScript application to alter the page's color, image, and greeting.

```
<!--
// Server-side time of day - Netscape
//
// author: shelley powers
//
// (c) 1997, 1998 shelley powers and SAMS
-->
<HTML>
```

continues

27

SERVER-SPECIFIC
TECHNOLOGIES

Listing 27.1. continued

```
<HEAD>
<TITLE> Server-Side Time of Day </TITLE>
</HEAD>
<SERVER>

// get time in hours
var dateObj = new Date();
var iDay = dateObj.getDay();
iTime = dateObj.getHours();

// set stub images to image objects
var iBright = "";
var img1 = "blank.gif";
var img2 = "blank.gif";
var img3 = "blank.gif";

// set hue/saturation based on time of day
if (iTime > 4 && iTime <= 11) {
    iBright = "FF";
    img1 = "sunrise.gif";
    }
else if (iTime > 11 && iTime <= 19) {
    iBright = "CC";
    img2 = "sun.gif";
    }
else     {
    iBright = "99";
    img3 = "moon.gif";
    }

var icolor = "#" + iBright + "0000";

</SERVER>
<BODY bgColor='icolor'>
<CENTER>
<H1> Time of Day</H1>
<SERVER>
if (iBright == "FF")
    write("<H1>Good Morning!</H1>");
else if (iBright == "CC")
    write("<H1>Good Afternoon!</H1>");
else
    write("<H1>Good Evening!</H1>");
</SERVER>

<table width=90% cols=3 cellspacing = 20>
<tr><td align=left colspan=3>
<img src='img1'></td></tr>
<tr><td align=center colspan=3>
<img src='img2'></td></tr>
<tr><td align=right colspan=3>
<img src='img3'></td></tr>
</table>
</center>
</BODY>
</HTML>
```

The code in Listing 27.1 demonstrates the two techniques necessary to include server-side scripting. The first technique is to create a separate scripting block and surround it with the <SERVER> and </SERVER> tags. Within that block can be any JavaScript 1.2 or earlier compatible script, except that you cannot use message windows or open new windows, and the comparison operations work differently, with the server-side JavaScript using JavaScript 1.1 behavior. Other differences are detailed in the documentation provided by Netscape.

The second technique is used to assign the image source filename to the embedded image, using an inline approach. To use this technique, you surround the inline server-side scripting with backquotes. This latter approach is best reserved for simple conditional checks or assignments, such as the one demonstrated. Otherwise, the code becomes a bit difficult to read.

The block of code to create the date object and set the color and image parameters is JavaScript 1.2 and would work equally well as client-side scripting. The main difference is that this code is processed before the page is sent. The `write` method is used to create HTML content to be displayed when the Web page is displayed.

After the page is created, it needs to be compiled and the resulting application added to the server, which is all detailed in the next section.

Compiling and Installing a Server-Side JavaScript Application

After one or more source files are created, you create the application by running the compiler. Source files can be any HTML or JavaScript source code (.js). The compiler runs from a command line, and the following is an example of how the Time of Day example can be compiled:

```
jasc -o timeday.web timeday.html
```

This line creates a server-side JavaScript application called `timeday.web` that consists of one source code file, `timeday.html`. If more than one source file was needed, they would be listed, one after the other, with spaces between. Again, the Netscape documentation has more details on running the compiler. The application created ends with a `.web` extension.

After the application is created, it must be added to the Application Manager by clicking the Add Application menu item. Figure 27.7 shows the contents of the page used to add the Time of Day application.

The `timeday.html` file is identified as the start-up page. With multiple HTML pages, you need to identify whichever page to display when the application is accessed. The Web File Path has the path and name of the application name, which is the file just compiled with the `.Web` extension. The application is not connecting to a database, so the Built-In Maximum Database Connections text box is set to zero (0). Client-side cookies are used as the preferred persistence technique. This is covered in more detail in the next sections.

After the application is installed and started using the buttons in the left side of the page, a Web page reader can access the application from the server. Figure 27.8 shows the Time of Day page, opened in the afternoon.

FIGURE 27.7.

The Add Application page for the Time of Day server-side JavaScript application.

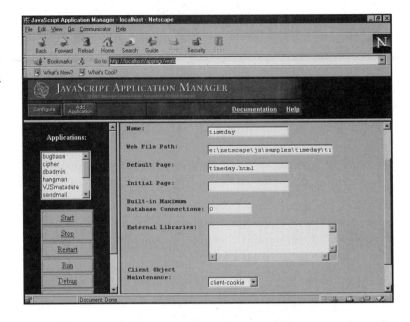

FIGURE 27.8.

The Time of Day application has been opened in the afternoon.

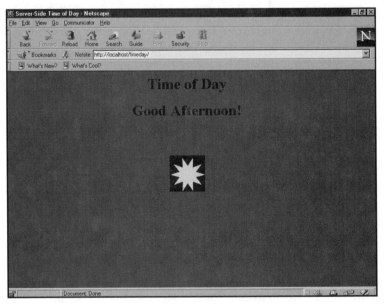

Note that the time used to determine the greeting, image, and color is based on server time. Client time could have been accessed by a preceding Web page and then passed to the server in a cookie or as part of a form submission, and then the page would reflect the client's time zone. Using Netscape cookies and using server-side JavaScript with form submissions is covered in the next example.

Using Server-Side JavaScript to Process Form Submissions

Let's look at another example to demonstrate using multiple-page server-side JavaScript applications that use Netscape cookies for persistence. The example also demonstrates processing an HTML form.

The first page of the application is a small page to get the customer's name. It contains a form with two text elements, one for the first name and one for the last name. The only JavaScript the page contains is client-side script, which checks to make sure both the first and last name are supplied before submitting the form. Listing 27.2 contains the source for this Web page.

Listing 27.2. The first page of the LiveWire shopping cart example.

```
<!--
//
// Netscape Shopping Cart
//
// author: shelley powers
//
// (c) 1997 - shelley powers and SAMS
-->
<HTML>
<HEAD>
<TITLE>The Shopping Cart</TITLE>
<SCRIPT language="javascript">
<!--
// validate presence of data
// before submitting form
function submit_form() {

  // validate that all values are in
  var oktosend = 1;
  if (document.forms[0].lastname.value == "")
    oktosend = 0;
  if (document.forms[0].firstname.value == "")
    oktosend = 0;

  // send or give message
  if (oktosend == 0)
    alert("You must provide your first and last name");
  else {
      document.forms[0].submit();
    }
}
//-->
</SCRIPT>
</HEAD>
<BODY>
<FORM action="cart.html" method="post">
Last Name: <INPUT name="lastname" value="" type=text><p>
First Name: <INPUT name="firstname" value="" type=text><p>
<INPUT type=button onclick="submit_form()" value="Enter Store">
  
```

continues

Listing 27.2. continued

```
<INPUT type=reset>
</FORM>
</BODY>
</HTML>
```

Notice from the code that the ACTION attribute for the form is set to another HTML page. This page contains the server-side JavaScript that processes the current page's form information. Figure 27.9 shows the page with information entered into the fields.

FIGURE 27.9.

The first HTML page of the server-side JavaScript shopping cart example.

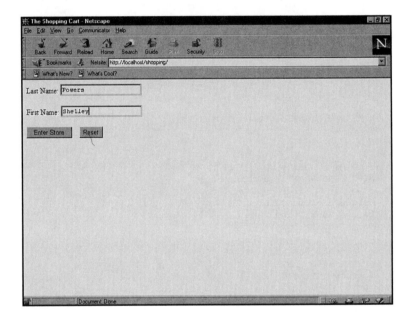

Not entering information in either of the fields results in an error, the result of running the client-side script when the form is submitted.

The next page of the application uses two predefined server-side JavaScript objects: the client object and the request object. You can access this page directly as cart.html. All the objects and their purposes are in the following list:

- request—This object is created whenever the server processes a client request, such as opening a new page. It contains information such as the IP address of the client or which type of client software accessed the page. Its properties are read only.
- client—This object is created for each client-application association, and is re-created with each client request. If no properties are assigned to the client object, it's not saved between client requests. This object provides a technique to store information between client requests.

- project—This object is created for each application and is accessible by multiple clients. It can be used to store a customer identifier that is incremented for each new client, and maintain the information while the application is still running.

- server—This object contains information about the server and is a method to share information between all applications running on that particular server. Stopping the server destroys the object.

The application doesn't use the project or server objects, but does use the request and client objects. The request object is used to access the information submitted from the form, and the client object is used to maintain a persistent connection between form submissions.

Listing 27.3 contains the source code for the second shopping cart page. Notice that the page uses both client-side and server-side scripting blocks. When the page is processed and sent through to the client browser, the server-side scripting block won't be visible, because it has been processed on the server, but the client-side scripting will show up in the page source. The server-side script processes the persistent information and creates the top of the page that contains the greetings and current customer total; the client-side script adds up the checked items and assigns the value to a hidden form element.

Listing 27.3. Source code for the second page of the server-side shopping cart application.

```
<!--
// Shopping cart - page 2
//
// author: shelley powers
//
// (c) shelley powers and SAMS
-->
<HTML>
<HEAD>
<TITLE>Shopping Cart</TITLE>
<SCRIPT language="javascript">
<!--
// add values of checked items
// set into hidden form field
function submit_form() {
   var total = 0.0;
   for (i = 0; i < 3;i++)
    if (document.forms[0].elements[i].checked)
       total+=parseFloat(document.forms[0].elements[i].value);
   document.forms[0].total.value = total;
   document.forms[0].submit();
}
//-->
</SCRIPT>
<BODY>
<SERVER>

// check to see if client info set
// if not, set from request object
```

continues

Listing 27.3. continued

```
var thetotal = 0.0;
if (client.lastname == null) {
   client.lastname = request.lastname;
   client.firstname = request.firstname;
   }


if (client.calctimes == null)
   client.calctimes = 1;
else {
   client.calctimes++;
   thetotal = request.total;
}

// create individual greeting, write current total
var strng = "<h3>Hello " + client.firstname + " " + client.lastname;
if (client.calctimes == 1)
   strng = strng + " Welcome to the Shopping Cart</h3>";
else
   strng = strng + " Please verify your new charges</h3>";
write (strng);
write ("<p><BOLD>Current Total is: $" + thetotal + "</BOLD><p>");
</SERVER>

<FORM method=post action="cart.html">
Item 1 (12.00) <INPUT type="checkbox" name="cart1" value=12.00><br>
Item 2 (15.00) <INPUT type="checkbox" name="cart2" value=15.00><br>
Item 3 (20.00) <INPUT type="checkbox" name="cart3" value=20.00><p>
<input type=hidden name=total>
<input type=button value="Calculate Total"
    onclick="submit_form()">  <input type=reset>
</FORM>
</BODY>
</HTML>
```

Again, the write method is used to generate the greeting based on the number of times the second shopping cart page has been accessed. Figure 27.10 shows the contents of the page when it is first opened.

Notice that the total amount is set to a dollar amount of zero (0), and that the greeting is set to "Welcome to the Shopping Cart." The only time this greeting is used is when the Web page reader accesses the page from the customer name page. Figure 27.11 shows the page after it has been submitted a couple of times.

Notice from the figure that the greeting has been changed, and the total amount reflects the previous charges. As an extension to this application, I could also have created three properties on the client object to reflect the checked property of the radio buttons, and set them after each form submission. Or, I could have created one property and sent it through the state of all three buttons, as one to-be-parsed line. If you have access to a LiveWire-enabled Netscape server, you might want to experiment a bit with this application by adding this new functionality.

FIGURE 27.10.

The second shopping cart application page when it is first opened looks like this.

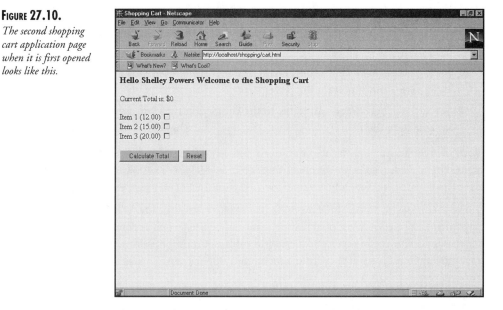

FIGURE 27.11.

The second shopping cart application page when it has been accessed a couple of times looks like this.

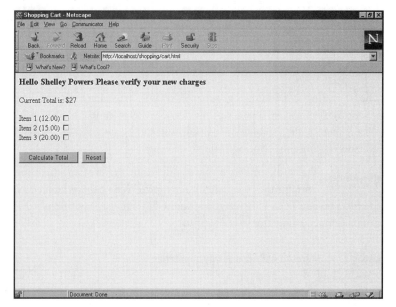

After the second page is created, the new application is installed and shopcust.html is used as the initial page of the application. Client-side cookie is set as the method of maintaining persistence. Other methods that could have been used are:

- Client URL encoding—Client information is appended to the URL.
- Server IP address—This only works with clients that have fixed IP addresses; the IP address acts as an index to a database of information stored on the server.
- Server cookie—The Netscape cookie protocol is still used, but maintains an index to the information stored on the server.
- Server URL encoding—An index to the cookie information, stored on the server, is appended to the URL.

Each of these techniques has its limitations and advantages. You'll find this information described in detail in the document on writing server-side JavaScript applications, found at `http://developer.netscape.com/library/documentation/enterprise/wrijsap/index.htm`.

This section provided a very brief overview of creating a Netscape LiveWire server-side JavaScript application. There are additional features that can be used, such as connecting to one or more databases and processing query requests and information submissions. You can also make direct calls to C or C++ routines from a server-side application.

Next, creating applications using Microsoft's Active Server Pages is demonstrated.

Server-Side Scripting with Active Server Pages

Active Server Pages (ASP) do not require any special compilation or installation, because the page extension (`.asp`) triggers Internet Information Server to parse the page for server-side scripting first.

The beginning and ending tags for an ASP Web page are angle-bracket and percent sign combinations of `<%` and `%>`. The scripting can occur as complete blocks, or be interspersed throughout the page. Values defined using scripting can be assigned to HTML elements by using `<% =` and then listing the scripting variable or value.

COMPANION Web site   The Time of Day server application is re-created, this time for ASP. Listing 27.4 contains the complete source for the Web page, which you can access directly from the file `timeday.asp`. This file is a straight HTML page with embedded ASP directives, and can be opened using any HTML editor.

Listing 27.4. Microsoft ASP Time of Day application.

```
<%@ LANGUAGE = javascript %>
<HTML>
<HEAD>
<TITLE> Server-Side Time of Day </TITLE>
</HEAD>
<%
var dateObj = new Date();
var iDay = dateObj.getDay();
```

```
iTime = dateObj.getHours();

var iBright = "";
var img1 = "blank.gif";
var img2 = "blank.gif";
var img3 = "blank.gif";

// set hue/saturation based on time of day
if (iTime > 4 && iTime <= 11) {
    iBright = "FF";
    img1 = "sunrise.gif";
    }
else if (iTime > 11 && iTime <= 19) {
    iBright = "CC";
    img2 = "sun.gif";
    }
else     {
    iBright = "99";
    img3 = "moon.gif";
    }

var icolor = "#" + iBright + "0000";

%>
<BODY bgColor=<% = icolor %>>
<CENTER>
<H1> Time of Day</H1>
<% if (iBright == "FF") %>
    <H1>Good Morning!</H1>
<% else if (iBright == "CC") %>
    <H1>Good Afternoon!</H1>
<% else if (iBright == "99") %>
    <H1>Good Evening!</H1>
<% %>

<table width=90% cols=3 cellspacing = 20>
<tr><td align=left colspan=3>
<img src=<% = img1 %>></td></tr>
<tr><td align=center colspan=3>
<img src=<% = img2 %>></td></tr>
<tr><td align=right colspan=3>
<img src=<% = img3 %>></td></tr>
</table>
</center>
</BODY>
</HTML>
```

Notice that the first line of the listing is a directive to use JavaScript as the language for all server-side scripting blocks. By default, VBScript is the scripting language of choice for ASP pages.

The image and greeting parameters are created in a separate block, and then are embedded throughout the page. The background color and the source of the image are set using the set to server-side scripting technique of <% =, which says to supply the value following the equal sign to the HTML element. A conditional statement determines which greeting to present and then writes out the greeting. Notice that I end the conditional statement with an empty scripting block to specify that the conditional statement is finished. If I had used VBScript, the last statement would have included the End If text as you will see demonstrated when I create the shopping cart application.

After the page is created, it is moved to the IIS server and accessed as any other HTML page would be accessed. No other processing is required. Figure 27.12 shows the page loaded into IE 4.0, although the page would also appear the same with Netscape Navigator.

FIGURE 27.12.

The Time of Day server application is shown as an ASP application.

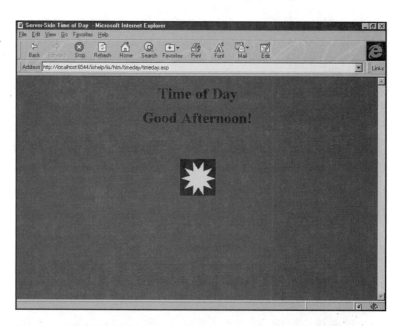

> **NOTE**
>
> One real advantage to using server-side techniques is that you can create content that works with any browser and still be dynamic. Both the Time of Day and the Shopping Cart examples created for Netscape LiveWire and Microsoft ASP can be viewed with any browser and JavaScript-capable browser.

Using ASP to Process Form Submissions

The two-page form application is created originally with LiveWire into an application using ASP technology. The first page is identical to the original LiveWire page, except that it calls a page with an .asp extension. The page also has more hidden fields, one for the number of times the second page is called, set to 1, and the other showing a total, set to 0. Hidden fields are used as a method of persistence in this version of the application, and the server-side scripting in the second page expects these fields to exist. Otherwise, the rest of the source is identical, as shown in Listing 27.5.

Listing 27.5. The first page for the shopping cart application based on ASP.

```
<HTML>
<HEAD>
<TITLE>The Shopping Cart</TITLE>
<SCRIPT language="javascript">
<!--
// validate presence of data
// before submitting form
function submit_form() {

  // validate that all values are in
  var oktosend = 1;
  if (document.forms[0].lastname.value == "")
    oktosend = 0;
  if (document.forms[0].firstname.value == "")
    oktosend = 0;

  // send or give message
  if (oktosend == 0)
    alert("You must provide your first and last name");
  else {
      document.forms[0].submit();
  }
}
//-->
</SCRIPT>
</HEAD>
<BODY>
<table style="text-align: center" width=60% border=5 cellpadding=5>
<FORM action="cart.asp" method="post">
<tr><td align=right>
Last Name: </td>
<td align=left><INPUT name="lastname" value="" type=text></td></tr>
<tr><td align=right>First Name:</td>
<td align=left><INPUT name="firstname" value="" type=text></td></tr>
<tr><td colspan=2 align=center>
<INPUT type=button onclick="submit_form()" value="Enter Store">
<INPUT type=reset>
<input type=hidden name="calctimes" value=0>
<input type=hidden name="total" value="0">
</td></tr></table>
</FORM>
</BODY>
</HTML>
```

The JavaScript used to check whether the reader has filled in both fields is the same for both servers, as neither server will process this code.

To add a little formatting magic to the page, the form was spaced using an HTML table. Figure 27.13 shows the page as it is displayed with IE 4.0. You can access the page, using IIS, from the file `shopcust.asp`.

FIGURE 27.13.

The customer name page for the shopping cart application.

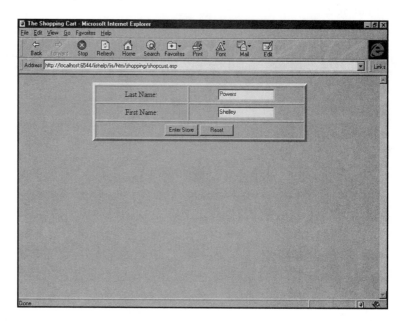

The next page that contains form processing actually uses VBScript to process the server-side scripting, but JavaScript for the client-side processing. The page also differs in that it doesn't use Netscape style cookies to maintain information between page submissions, but instead uses hidden fields to hold all the persistent information. This information is then accessed from an IIS predefined object called the `Request` object.

> **NOTE**
>
> Active Server Pages have access to two built-in objects: the `Request` object and the `Response` object. The `Request` object contains information moving from the client to the server, and the `Response` object contains information moving from the server back to the client. More on these objects a little later.

Listing 27.6 contains the source for this page. The `Request` object contains all the form elements from a previous submission in the `Form` collection, which is an array of like elements.

Listing 27.6. The second page of the ASP version of the shopping cart.

```
<HTML>
<HEAD>
<TITLE>Shopping Cart</TITLE>
<STYLE type="text/css">
    BODY { margin: 0.5in }
</STYLE>
<SCRIPT language="javascript">
<!--
function submit_form() {
   var total = 0.0;
   for (i = 0; i < 3;i++)
    if (document.forms[0].elements[i].checked)
       total+=parseFloat(document.forms[0].elements[i].value);
   document.forms[0].total.value = total;
   document.forms[0].submit();
}
//-->
</SCRIPT>
<BODY>
<%
Dim thetotal, name
Dim lastname, firstname, calctimes
thetotal = Request.Form("total")
firstname = Request.Form("firstname")
lastname = Request.Form("lastname")
calctimes = Request.Form("calctimes")
calctimes = calctimes + 1

name = firstname + " " + lastname
%>
<h3>Hello <% = name %>
<% If calctimes = 1 Then %>
   Welcome to the Shopping Cart</h3>
<% Else %>
   Please verify your new charges</h3>
<% End If %>

<BOLD>Current Total is: $ <% = thetotal %> </BOLD><p>

<FORM method=post action="cart.asp">
Item 1 (12.00) <INPUT type="checkbox" name="cart1" value=12.00><br>
Item 2 (15.00) <INPUT type="checkbox" name="cart2" value=15.00><br>
Item 3 (20.00) <INPUT type="checkbox" name="cart3" value=20.00><p>
<input type=hidden name=total>
<input type=hidden name="firstname" value=<% = firstname %>>
<input type=hidden name="lastname" value=<% = lastname %>>
<input type=hidden name="calctimes" value=<% = calctimes %>>
<input type=button value="Calculate Total"
    onclick="submit_form()">  <input type=reset>
</FORM>
</BODY>
</HTML>
```

Note that you could also have used a Netscape cookie by referencing the Cookie collection of the Request object. The Request object has information about the client request, such as the form information, client cookies, and the URL query string, if one exists. Another of the collections used in the example is the Form collection. A cookie can be set by the server-side of the application by using the Cookie collection of the Response object, which contains information about the response returned to the client. The cookie can be set on the client-side of the application using the Cookie collection associated with the Request object.

COMPANION **Web** site You can access the second shopping cart page by opening the file cart.asp. Figure 27.14 shows the second page when it is first brought up in the browser, and Figure 27.15 shows the page after it has been submitted a couple of times.

FIGURE 27.14.

The second shopping cart page when it is first opened.

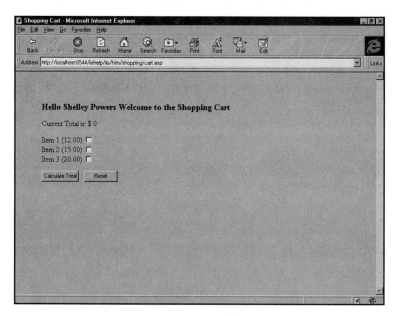

As with Netscape's LiveWire technique, the server directives are processed before the page is returned, and all that is returned are the results and any client-side scripting. Listing 27.7 shows the second shopping cart page after it is returned from IIS.

Listing 27.7. The second shopping cart page after being returned from IIS.

```
<HTML>
<HEAD>
<TITLE>Shopping Cart</TITLE>
<STYLE type="text/css">
    BODY { margin: 0.5in }
</STYLE>
<SCRIPT language="javascript">
<!--
function submit_form() {
```

```
   var total = 0.0;
   for (i = 0;  i < 3;i++)
    if (document.forms[0].elements[i].checked)
        total+=parseFloat(document.forms[0].elements[i].value);
   document.forms[0].total.value = total;
   document.forms[0].submit();
}
//-->
</SCRIPT>
<BODY>

<h3>Hello Shelley Powers
   Please verify your new charges</h3>


<BOLD>Current Total is: $ 27 </BOLD><p>

<FORM method=post action="cart.asp">
Item 1 (12.00) <INPUT type="checkbox" name="cart1" value=12.00><br>
Item 2 (15.00) <INPUT type="checkbox" name="cart2" value=15.00><br>
Item 3 (20.00) <INPUT type="checkbox" name="cart3" value=20.00><p>
<input type=hidden name=total>
<input type=hidden name="firstname" value=Shelley>
<input type=hidden name="lastname" value=Powers>
<input type=hidden name="calctimes" value=4>
<input type=button value="Calculate Total"
    onclick="submit_form()">  <input type=reset>
</FORM>
</BODY>
</HTML>
```

FIGURE 27.15.

The second shopping cart page when it has been submitted a couple of times.

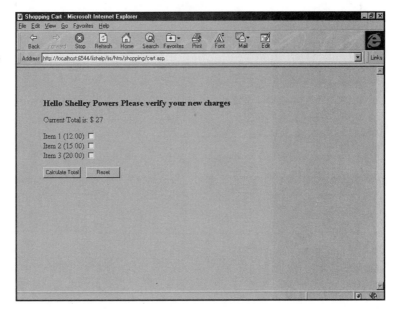

Note that the number of times the form has been submitted is four, as the `calctimes` hidden field is set to a value of 4.

As with LiveWire, ASP can connect to databases and process reader queries and format results. It can also make use of ActiveX server objects. External language access usually occurs through the Information Server API (ISAPI) functions. More about this technology can be read at the IIS Web site at `http://www.microsoft.com/iis`.

Summary

This chapter provides a listing of the components each company deems significant for its own platform strategy. Netscape includes technologies such as Dynamic HTML, Directory Services, Java, and LiveWire in its Netscape ONE platform. Microsoft includes Dynamic HTML, CSS1, Java, SDKs, and other technologies in its Active Platform.

Additionally, this chapter explains that the main difference between the platforms of the two companies has to do with focus, with Netscape focused solely on Web applications, and Microsoft focused on Web, traditional development, and operating system technologies.

Finally, demonstrations of the server-side scripting techniques each company supports were provided, with one example altering the appearance, image, and greeting based on the time of day, and another application processing form results. The examples were first implemented in LiveWire, and then implemented using Active Server Page (ASP) technology.

Serious Applications for Serious Web Publishing

by Leena Prasad

IN THIS CHAPTER

The Next Generation of Web Tools

In terms of dramatic changes, ten months in the life of the Internet can be likened to ten years in the life of an average human being. Ten months ago, businesses were rushing to add their electronic billboards to the electronic equivalent of the yellow pages. Now they are competing just to get noticed. Getting noticed involves more than shouting the loudest. Getting noticed also means providing valuable services like Internet commerce, account management, communication, and many other functionalities (for tasks like shopping, banking, bill-payment, research, social/professional networking). The list can go on and on (without even mentioning leisure activities like games and other entertainment) and includes a lot of the activities people previously accomplished via traveling, phone, or use of conventional software.

The frenzy to activate Web pages gave life to Java, ActiveX, and JavaScript, and gave a CGI twist to conventional languages like Perl, C, Objective-C, and C++. With an array of technologies to choose from and an explosion of ready-made tools that can be plugged into Web pages, serious developers are able to reduce the time to market from months to days by using serious Web software tools like WebObjects and Cold Fusion. These tools are much more evolved than design-biased publishing tools like Microsoft FrontPage or Adobe PageMill. Tools like Cold Fusion and WebObjects don't simply generate HTML, provide hooks for plug-ins, or throw in some existing and popular code for good measure; they also provide the next step beyond page design by facilitating the complex process of software engineering to accomplish tasks like database management, state management (cookie creation, for example), creation of dynamic/interactive pages, and any and all nonstatic demands of Web pages.

Rapid Web Application Development

Cold Fusion and WebObjects are both server-side solutions for rapid application development. Cold Fusion is usually available via NT-based Internet service providers and is used by small and mid-sized businesses; WebObjects is a high-end tool available on most server platforms and is used by small and large corporations like Cybermeals, Disney, Dell Computers, and The Sharper Image. Both tools are browser independent.

Cold Fusion and WebObjects are based on an open architecture to simplify integration with legacy database systems, and contain hooks for including code developed using other Web technologies like CGI, ActiveX, Java, and JavaScript. Both tools allow code-reusability and use familiar software development methodologies to reduce the learning curve.

The seamless database integration inherent in these technologies means that they can connect with databases like MS-Access, Oracle, Sybase, and others that are currently popular with many companies. This means that when a company's internal database is updated, the change can automatically show up on the Web site. The SQL-based database connection is easy to generate in WebObjects with its WYSIWYG WebObjects Builder, and in Cold Fusion with its text and form-based SQL generator HomeSite and development environment Cold Fusion Studio (released with Cold Fusion 3.1).

In addition to exploiting existing database systems, any serious Web publishing/programming tool must be capable of exploiting existing technologies in order to be useful, by not reinventing the wheel, but by using the existing wheel for newer applications. CGI tools, written in Perl, C, Objective-C, C++, ActiveX, and Java, are usually the intelligence behind many non-static Web pages. There are also many non-CGI Java, JavaScript, ActiveX, and VBScript applications that are popularly used for activating a Web page. Both Cold Fusion and WebObjects either already support all the current technologies or plan full support in the near future.

Tying in neatly with existing technologies is not enough; new tools should also be in synch with state of the art methodologies. Among software developers, the methodology of writing reusable code has gained currency in recent years. Being able to use the same code many times saves time and money Cold Fusion provides code reusability by the methods of file inclusion, by allowing calls similar to subroutine calls in conventional programming languages and by making it possible for third-parties to create Cold Fusion extensions. Code reusability is inherent in WebObjects because of its object-oriented architecture, where different types of objects (a Shopping Cart object, for example) can be simply plugged into the code and used.

A new tool must also be relatively easy to learn. Based on the theory that familiarity with a new tool decreases the learning curve, Cold Fusion provides language tags, which look similar to HTML tags but provide high-level programming possibilities like conditional processing and looping. Cold Fusion also includes handy built-in math functions and state management capabilities, such as global variables and the capability to pass variables (similar to a CGI POST and GET) from one application page to another. WebObjects provides the choice of using the WYSIWYG development tool or WebObjects-specific WebScripts, Objective-C, Java, or JavaScript for programmers who find the WYSIWYG environment too cumbersome.

Cold Fusion 3.0

Although Cold Fusion 3.1, released in November 1997 and supported on Solaris, will most likely become the new standard soon, Cold Fusion 3.0 is one of the most popular rapid application development tools used for Web database implementation on NT machines.

What Is Cold Fusion?

It is a Web site development solution that is picking up popularity, along with the recent surge in the use of NT-based servers by small to mid-size businesses. Its seamless database integration and an HTML look-alike language with the power of programming languages make it popular with developers who are already familiar with HTML and SQL.

Who Is It For?

It can be used by someone who only knows HTML or by software engineers to develop complex applications. It is also ideal for HTML experts with aspirations of learning to write software code. It's a bit like combining HTML with the power of CGI languages. Any Web application, including electronic commerce, intranets, technical support, games, publishing, and business

28

APPLICATIONS FOR
WEB PUBLISHING

systems, can be developed using Cold Fusion. It's a cost-effective solution for small-to-medium size businesses that rely on ISPs or on dedicated NT servers for Web space support.

Why Use Cold Fusion?

For database management on an NT server, Cold Fusion is easier to use than the Microsoft ISAPI—it's all-in-one. You don't need to use the MS-ISAPI and CGI programs because you can do a lot of the CGI work by using Cold Fusion's built-in CGI-type functionalities. Because Cold Fusion is fully integrated with other Internet technologies, it's also easy to extend.

Getting Started

Take an HTML file, change the extension to .cfm and place the file in the /scripts directory of a NT server with Cold Fusion support. Voilá! You are using Cold Fusion. Using your HTML expertise as a foundation, you can easily learn to use Cold Fusion tags to develop CGI functionalities like sending mail, validating and manipulating form input, formatting dates, and more without having to write or use CGI code. If you are familiar with SQL, you are ready to start doing database management with Cold Fusion by adding tab-based queries. If you don't know SQL, you can pick up the basics in a few minutes or use tools like Microsoft Access query builder or the Microsoft Query applet bundled with Microsoft Office or the Crystal Reports Query Builder. If you know any high-level programming language, you can do a lot more by exploiting the programming constructs of Cold Fusion.

An Application Page

An application page is a Cold Fusion page, which is similar in concept to an HTML page but resides in an executable directory, usually the NT scripts directory. The Cold Fusion Markup Language (CFML) source code on that page is not visible via the browser, unlike HTML. Do not confuse this with the page named Application.cfm. Application.cfm is a special Cold Fusion application framework for maintaining state variable information and for managing the appearance of error messages. This file contains details on the look and feel of dynamically generated error messages and a list of globally defined variables that can be used instead of cookies to maintain state.

Language Notes

Variables can be passed between pages and state information can be maintained with cookies or with global variables. There are over 150 built-in functions including date, time, math, list, and string functions. Flow control is possible via if...then...else and all the conventional looping expressions. Boolean operators like AND, OR, and so on, provide conditional logic, and multi-dimensional arrays simplify list processing. Complete code reusability is achieved by the combination of including a page inside another page, passing variable parameters from one page to another, and using custom tags.

The Cold Fusion application server integrates with most major Web servers (http://www.allair.com contains a comprehensive list), and it is the engine behind the server-side markup language, Cold Fusion Markup Language (CFML) tags. CFML tags are similar to HTML tags and integrate seamlessly with HTML tags.

For example, CFML database query tags can be used with HTML-defined tables or with CFML-defined tables. The building blocks of CFML are tags, functions, and expressions. Cold Fusion offers over thirty tags and allows for creation of custom tags. Unlike HTML, CFML code is not visible via a browser and can be further encrypted for security. Similar to other programming languages, Cold Fusion expressions are a combination of data, variables, operators, functions, and other expressions created to manipulate data and return results.

CGI Functionalities

Many common functionalities used by CGIs are included and passed to application pages or the database via hidden fields in a manner similar to HTML forms:

```
<INPUT TYPE="hidden" NAME="DateRegistered" VALUE="CurrentDateTime()">
<INPUT TYPE="hidden" NAME="ClientAddress" VALUE="CGI.REMOTE_ADDR">
<INPUT TYPE="hidden" NAME="ClientBrowser" VALUE="CGI.HTTP_USER_AGENT">
<INPUT TYPE="hidden" NAME="ClientReferrer" VALUE="CGI.HTTP_REFERER">
```

Built-in data validation makes it unnecessary to write additional CGI code:

```
<INPUT TYPE="hidden" NAME="UserName_required"
      VALUE="Please enter a user name.">

<INPUT TYPE="hidden" NAME="Email_required"
      VALUE="Please enter an e-mail address.">
```

OR

```
<INPUT TYPE="text" NAME="UserName" REQUIRED="Yes"
      MESSAGE="Please enter a user name.">
<INPUT TYPE="text" NAME="Email" REQUIRED="Yes"
      MESSAGE="Please enter an e-mail address.">
```

The fields UserName and Email are automatically validated by Cold Fusion, and the message in the VALUE/MESSAGE parameter is written to the browser screen.

Security

There are several levels of security available for Cold Fusion. The application pages are not visible from the browser, but there's an additional level of security achieved by encrypting the pages. The datasource for the database can also be secured by adding a password requirement for accessing the data. Access to Cold Fusion directories can be restricted.

Developing Cold Fusion Application Pages

Cold Fusion works with any ODBC-compliant relational database. Existing HTML forms can be upgraded to use Cold Fusion for inserting, updating, and deleting records and for many

28

Applications for Web Publishing

other advanced functionalities, such as creating dynamic HTML pages based on information stored in the database. Reports can also be generated by using HTML or the report generating application, Crystal Reports. Managing files on the server is enabled with CFML commands to copy, rename, move, read, write, append, upload, and delete files using a simple server-side tag. Distributed queries and intelligent agents can also be developed using Cold Fusion. Standard Web server authentication and SSL encryption are supported. CFML tags provide comprehensive e-mail functionalities. The Cold Fusion Application Programming Interface (CFAPI) is used to create extensions (CFXs) for interacting with legacy codes, OLE automation servers, or any third-party software. One of the most useful extensions is CFX_Cybercash, which simplifies the integration of the popular net-commerce software, cybercash (http://www.cybercash.com), without too much fuss.

For example, the CGIs that are normally supplied by Cybercash for implementing the Cybercash Cash Register can be completely replaced with the following code, which sends all the required information like server ID, password, credit card information, and so on to the Cybercash verification server. CFX_Cybercash processes the credit card transaction and returns a status message that contains a success or failure message that can be immediately displayed on the page.

```
<CFX_CYBERCASH
      SERVER="666.666.666.6"
      MERCHANTPASSWORD="ItIsASecret"
      TRANSTYPE="mauthonly"
      ORDERID="9999"
      AMOUNT="99.99"
      CCNUMBER="1234-5678-9101-1121"
      CCEXP="12/99"
      CCNAME="Forrest Gump"
      CCADDRESS="666 Lost Street"
      CCCITY="Somewhere"
      CCSTATE="LA"
      CCZIP="00000"
      CCCOUNTRY="USA"
>
```

Custom tags written using CFML provide code reusability by technology similar to subroutines and functions in many high-level programming languages.

Anatomy of a Cold Fusion Shopping Cart

The basic concepts in a shopping cart application are to record the order information in a temporary structure, allow the client to confirm the order, process and authorize credit card transactions, and save the information to a database. As in any Internet application, the user interface layout is important. The following shopping cart implementation achieves its functionalities via the use of cookies, variables, conditional processing, loops, and database management.

Creating and Deleting the Cookies Application Page

This page is loaded via an action command connected to an HTML page. The FORM.* variables are the form input fields. The <CFSET> tag is used to assign values. The <CFCOOKIE NAME=

"#FORM.Item#" VALUE="#Value#"> command creates a cookie, whereas the <CFCOOKIE NAME="#Item#" EXPIRES="now"> command deletes a cookie. The <CFINCLUDE> tag appends the ShoppingCart.cfm page here, effectively loading that page into the browser:

```
<!-- Delete cookies -->
<CFIF #ParameterExists(FORM.Delete)# IS "YES">
    <CFSET Count = 1>
     <CFSET Item = GetToken(#FORM.Delete#,#Count#,",")>
    <CFLOOP Condition = "Item IS NOT ''">
        <CFCOOKIE NAME="#Item#" EXPIRES="now">
        <CFSET Count += 1>
        <CFSET Item = GetToken(#FORM.Delete#,#Count#,",")>
    </CFLOOP>
</CFIF>

<!-- Create cookies -->
<CFIF #ParameterExists(FORM.Quantity)# IS "YES">
        <CFSET Value = "#FORM.Quantity# #FORM.Price#">
        <CFCOOKIE NAME="#FORM.Item#" VALUE="#Value#">
</CFIF>
<CFINCLUDE TEMPLATE="ShoppingCart.cfm">
```

ShoppingCart.cfm

The ShoppingCart.cfm reads the information in the cookie and dynamically creates an HTML page to display the items in the cart. This file has been defined separately because it is executed independently of creating the cookies, if the user simply wants to view the cart. The cookies contain purchase information and are persistent until the user deletes the information, makes a purchase, or exits from the browser session.

This slice of code skips unwanted cookie contents like username, CFTOKEN, CFID (these two are created by Cold Fusion):

```
<CFSET Count = 0>
<CFINCLUDE TEMPLATE="cookie_test.cfm">
```

cookie_test.cfm

The GetToken function gets the #Count# element in #Cookie# (CF internal variable name) using the token; and returns the result into the variable Item. The <CFSET Count += 1> could also have been written as <CFSET Count = IncrementValue(#Count#)>, where IncrementValue is a CF internal function. The operator IS is a decision operator:

```
<!-- Skip unwanted cookie contents -->
<CFSET Count = Count + 1>
<CFSET Done = 0>
<CFLOOP Condition = "#Done# IS 0">
    <CFSET Item = GetToken(#Cookie#,#Count#,"; ")>
    <CFIF Item IS ''>
        <CFSET Done = 1>
    <CFELSE>
        <CFSET Temp = GetToken(#Item#,1,"=")>
        <CFIF #Temp# IS "USERNAME" OR #Temp# IS "CFTOKEN" OR #Temp# IS "CFID">
```

```
                <CFSET Count = Count + 1>
            <CFELSE>
                <CFSET Done = 1>
            </CFIF>
        </CFIF>
    </CFLOOP>
```

An HTML form and action statement, `<form action="CartItems.cfm" method="post">`, is used to load the `CartItems.cfm` page to request deletion of an item in the cart.

The labels for items in the cart are displayed by printing the cooking contents using HTML tags:

```
<table border=1 width=90%>
<tr><th align=left>Item</th><th>Quantity</th><th>Price</th><th>Total</th></tr>
```

Database tables are accessed to replace code words with the actual names, that is, R gets translated to Red based on a database table entry, TS gets translated to T-Shirt with a company logo, and X gets translated to Xtra-Large:

```
<CFQUERY NAME="GetItem" DATASOURCE="MontageProductionsTestDB">
    SELECT * FROM ShoppingItem
</CFQUERY>

<CFQUERY NAME="GetColor" DATASOURCE="MontageProductionsTestDB">
SELECT * FROM Color
</CFQUERY>

<CFQUERY NAME="GetSize" DATASOURCE="MontageProductionsTestDB">
SELECT * FROM Size
</CFQUERY>
```

The datasource, once set up (using the Cold Fusion Administrator tool), is accessed by database queries. The NAME field is required to identify the query in order to use the results and the SELECT, FROM, and WHERE conform to SQL standards. The `<CFQUERY></CFQUERY>` mark the beginning and end of a query.

Each cookie is tokenized and the information is used to print item details. The function Lcase changes the item name to lowercase. This particular code assumes that information is being sent in the format tshirt_r_1, where tshirt is the item name, r is the item color, and 1 is the item size:

```
<CFLOOP Condition = "#Item# IS NOT ''">
    <CFSET Name = LCase(GetToken(#Item#,1,"="))>
            <CFSET NameID = GetToken(#Name#,1,"_")>
            <CFSET ColorID = GetToken(#Name#,2,"_")>
            <CFSET SizeID = GetToken(#Name#,3,"_")>
            <CFSET Value= GetToken(#Item#,2,"=")>

<CFSET SubTotal = 0>
<CFSET Quantity = 0>
<CFSET Price = 0>
<CFSET Total = 0>
<CFSET Quantity = GetToken(#Value#,1,"+")>
<CFSET Price= GetToken(#Value#,2,"+")>
```

The <CFLOOP> reiterates through each item in the list retrieved by the query GetItem, and <CFOUTPUT> is needed to print the contents of the table field:

```
<CFLOOP QUERY="GetItem">
    <CFIF #ID# EQ #NameID#>
        <font color=FF0000><CFOUTPUT>#Name#</CFOUTPUT></font>,
        </CFIF>
</CFLOOP>
```

```
<input type=checkbox name="Delete" Value="<CFOUTPUT>#Name#</CFOUTPUT>">

<CFINCLUDE TEMPLATE="cookie_test.cfm">

</CFLOOP> <!-- end of  Condition = "#Item# IS NOT ""--->
```

Once the purchase button is pressed, the code must inform registered users that their credit card will be charged, and give new users an opportunity to sign up:

```
<form action="NamePassword.cfm" method="POST">Please review your order before
hitting the purchase button. If you've already registered your credit card
with us, you will be automatically charged for the purchase.
Otherwise, you'll be asked to fill out a credit card information form.
<input type=submit value="Purchase!"></form>
```

NamePassword.cfm

This page validates registered users and loads the Purchase.cfm page. This page fills in the user name from a cookie, if a cookie exists using conditional logic:

```
<!-- These templates set up the consistent page layout -->
<CFINCLUDE TEMPLATE="ShoppingCartSetup.cfm">
<CFSET #Header# = "Name/Password">
<CFINCLUDE TEMPLATE="header.cfm">

<!-- Validate user and load the purchase module -->
<FORM ACTION="Purchase.cfm" METHOD=POST>
        Username <INPUT TYPE="text" NAME="User"
            <CFIF #ParameterExists(Cookie.Username)# IS "Yes">
                VALUE="<CFOUTPUT>#Cookie.Username#</CFOUTPUT>"
        <CFELSE>
        VALUE="Visitor">
            </CFIF>
Password <INPUT TYPE="password" NAME="Pass">
<INPUT TYPE="submit" VALUE="Charge purchase to Credit Card">
</FORM>

<!-- OR -->
<!-- Take the user to a sign up application page -->

I would like to sign up to make purchases.
<FORM ACTION="StoreOrder.cfm" METHOD=POST>
```

```
<INPUT TYPE="submit" VALUE="Sign Up">
</FORM>
<CFINCLUDE TEMPLATE="footer.cfm">
```

Maintaining Layout Consistency

Cold Fusion includes SSI capabilities for inclusion of variables in a page, but takes the concept a bit further, making it easy to use templates to maintain the look and feel of pages across a Web site and saving hours by eliminating the need to change individual pages at a site. The following header and footer pages illustrate the use of variables to maintain a consistent appearance on all the Web pages by updating pages dynamically.

Header Template/Application Page

All the variables are enclosed within the pound (#) sign and are replaced by the values passed to the page when the page is displayed:

```
<html>
<head>
<title><CFOUTPUT>#PageTitle#</CFOUTPUT></title>
<HEAD>
</head>
<body background="../images/<CFOUTPUT>#BackgroundGIF#</CFOUTPUT>"
bgcolor=<CFOUTPUT>#Color#</CFOUTPUT>
LINK="663300" VLINK="663300" ALINK="FFCC00">
<H1>CFOUTPUT>#Header#</CFOUTPUT</H1>
```

A sample call to the header file (header.cfm) looks like this:

```
<CFSET #PageTitle# = "Shopping Cart">
<CFSET #Header# = "Shopping Cart">
<CFSET #Color# = "00FFFF">
<CFSET #BackgroundGIF# = "b_cart.gif">
<CFINCLUDE TEMPLATE = "header.cfm">
```

The names of variables in the calls must match the names in the header file and all the variables that are used in the header files must be passed to it before it is called. For example, an error occurs if the #Background# variable is not defined before header.cfm is called.

Any changes in the general look and feel of the site can be made by making the changes in the header file.

Footer Template/ Page

The footer of every page can be made generic by a template page as follows:

```
<table bgcolor =<CFOUTPUT>#FooterColor#</CFOUTPUT>>
<tr><td>Copyright &copy; 1997 Montage Productions.
All rights reserved.</td></tr>
</table>
</body></html>
<CFABORT>
```

A sample call to the header file (footer.cfm) looks like this:

```
<CFSET #FooterColor# = "B5FFF7">
<CFINCLUDE TEMPLATE = "footer.cfm">
```

COMPANION
Web site Listing 28.1 contains the complete code. An implementation of this can be seen at `http://www.xword.com`. The complete set of code is included in the book's Companion Web Site and a copy can also be downloaded from `http://www.montageproductions.com/ColdFusion`.

Listing 28.1. Source code listing for the Shopping Cart.

```
<!----------------------------------------------------------------
ShoppingCartSetup.cfm
---------------------------------------------------------------->
<CFSET #PageTitle# = "Shopping Cart">
<CFSET #Color# = "00FFFF">
<CFSET #BackgroundGIF# = "b_cart.gif">


<!----------------------------------------------------------------
cookie_test.cfm
---------------------------------------------------------------->
<!-- Skip unwanted cookie contents -->
<CFSET Count = Count + 1>
<CFSET Done = 0>
<CFLOOP Condition = "#Done# IS 0">
    <CFSET Item = GetToken(#Cookie#,#Count#,"; ")>
    <CFIF Item IS ''>
        <CFSET Done = 1>
    <CFELSE>
        <CFSET Temp = GetToken(#Item#,1,"=")>
        <CFIF #Temp# IS "USERNAME" OR #Temp# IS "CFTOKEN" OR #Temp# IS "CFID">
            <CFSET Count = Count + 1>
         <CFELSE>
            <CFSET Done = 1>
        </CFIF>
    </CFIF>
</CFLOOP>


<!----------------------------------------------------------------
ShoppingCart.cfm
---------------------------------------------------------------->
<CFINCLUDE TEMPLATE = "ShoppingCartSetup.cfm">
<CFSET #Header# = "Shopping Cart:  current contents">
<CFINCLUDE TEMPLATE = "header.cfm">

<CFIF #ParameterExists(Cookie)# IS "YES">
    <!-- Skip unwanted cookie contents -->
    <CFSET Count = 0>
    <CFINCLUDE TEMPLATE="cookie_test.cfm">
    <CFIF Item IS "">
        <form action="CartItems.cfm">
<p><font color=FF0000 size=3>Shopping Cart is Empty! Please
<strong>reload/refresh</strong> if you've added something recently
and it is not here.</font></p>
</form>
<CFELSE>
                <font color=FF0000 size=4>Please reload/refresh if you do not
                immediately see your changes.</font><br><br><br>
```

continues

Listing 28.1. continued

```
<form action="CartItems.cfm" method="post">
  <table border=1 width=90%>
      <tr>
      <th align=left>Item</th>
      <th>Quantity</th>
      <th>Price</th>
      <th>Total</th>
      </tr>

  <!-- Begin: print cart contents -->

      <CFQUERY NAME="GetItem" DATASOURCE="MontageProductionsTestDB">
          SELECT * FROM ShoppingItem
      </CFQUERY>

      <CFQUERY NAME="GetColor" DATASOURCE="MontageProductionsTestDB">
          SELECT * FROM Color
      </CFQUERY>

      <CFQUERY NAME="GetSize" DATASOURCE="MontageProductionsTestDB">
          SELECT * FROM Size
      </CFQUERY>


   <CFSET SubTotal = 0>
  <CFLOOP Condition = "#Item# IS NOT ''">
  <!-------- Print each item -------->
          <CFSET Name = LCase(GetToken(#Item#,1,"="))>
          <CFSET NameID = GetToken(#Name#,1,"_")>
      <CFSET ColorID = GetToken(#Name#,2,"_")>
      <CFSET SizeID = GetToken(#Name#,3,"_")>
        <CFSET Value= GetToken(#Item#,2,"=")>

      <CFSET Quantity = 0>
      <CFSET Price = 0>
      <CFSET Total = 0>
       <CFSET Quantity = GetToken(#Value#,1,"+")>
       <CFSET Price= GetToken(#Value#,2,"+")>

     <tr>
       <td>
       <CFLOOP QUERY="GetItem">
           <CFIF #ID# EQ #NameID#>
               <font color=FF0000><CFOUTPUT>#Name#</CFOUTPUT></font>,
           </CFIF>
       </CFLOOP>

       <CFLOOP QUERY="GetColor">
           <CFIF #Code# EQ #ColorID#>
               <CFOUTPUT>#Color#</CFOUTPUT>,
            </CFIF>
       </CFLOOP>

       <CFLOOP QUERY="GetSize">
```

```
                    <CFIF #Code# EQ #SizeID#>
                        <font color=0000FF><CFOUTPUT>#Size#</CFOUTPUT></font>
                      </CFIF>
                </CFLOOP>
                </td>

        <CFSET Total = '#Price#' * '#Quantity#'>
                <CFSET SubTotal = '#SubTotal#' + '#Total#'>

            <td align=right><CFOUTPUT>#Quantity#</CFOUTPUT></td>
                <td align=right>$<CFOUTPUT>#Price#</CFOUTPUT>.00</td>
                    <td align=right>$<CFOUTPUT>#Total#</CFOUTPUT>.00</td>
<td align=center><input type=checkbox name="Delete"
Value="<CFOUTPUT>#Name#</CFOUTPUT>"></td>
                    </tr>

<CFINCLUDE TEMPLATE="cookie_test.cfm">

            <!------------------------------->
        </CFLOOP>

    <!-- End:  print cart contents -->

    <tr>
<th colspan=3>Subtotal (Tax, Shipping&Handling will be added)</th>
        <td align=right>$<CFOUTPUT>#SubTotal#</CFOUTPUT>.00</td>
        </tr>

        </table>
    </center>
    <br><br>
        <table width=90%><tr><td>
        <font size=3>Press this button
<input type=submit value="Update Cart">
and reload/refresh if you've changed quantities in the cart.
An item can be deleted by selecting 0 quantity.
</form>

        <form action="NamePassword.cfm" method="POST">
Please review your order before hitting the purchase button.
If you've already registered your credit card with us,
you will be automatically charged for the purchase.
Otherwise, you'll be asked to fill out a credit card information form.
<input type=submit value="Purchase!">
 </form>
</font>
 </td></tr></table>
</CFIF>
<CFELSE>
    <p><font color=FF0000 size=3>Shopping Cart is Empty!
    Please <strong>reload/refresh</strong>
    if you've added something recently and it is not here.</font></p>
</CFIF>
<CFINCLUDE TEMPLATE="footer.cfm">
```

Purchase.cfm

`Purchase.Cfm` looks identical to `ShoppingCart.cfm`, except tax and total is calculated, the Cybercash Register is invoked via the CFX_Cybercash tag, item purchase information is saved in the database, and cookies for the shopping cart items are deleted.

You can insert or update fields in the table with one line of code:

```
<CFINSERT TABLE="ShoppingCart" DATASOURCE="MontageProductionsTestDB">
```

You can also use this following code:

```
<CFUPDATE TABLE="ShoppingCart" DATASOURCE="MontageProductionsTestDB">
```

Field-specific insertion is also possible using this code:

```
<CFQUERY></CFQUERY>.
```

Debugging

Debugging can be turned off and on for specific application pages or queries and debug mode parameters are provided. All the parameters and CGI environment variables of an application page can be viewed by adding a `mode=debug` parameter:

```
http://www.myserver.com/scripts/foobar.cfm?mode=debug.
```

For a query, debug information can be viewed with a `DEBUG` attribute:

```
<CFQUERY NAME="ThisQuery" DATASOURCE="MontageProductionsTestDB" DEBUG>
```

The default behavior is to show general information stating that there were some problems with a query, variables, or syntax. A list of helpful environment variables like browser and referrer name are also displayed. These error displays can be customized via the administrator and the `Applications.cfm` page.

Integration with Advanced Web Technologies

Cold Fusion works with all browsers and all ODBC-compliant databases.

There are Java applet classes included with Cold Fusion that provide a pie, bar, multibar, area, line, and 3D multiyear chart with options for changing the parameters values. A CFML tag, `<CFFORM>`, can be used for adding Java-based form controls. No Java knowledge is necessary. Special support including JavaScript-based form validation is also included.

There are special tags included for supporting industry-standard search methods. The Verity search engine is included for complex indexing and searching capabilities of documents, databases, and Verity collections. The Lightweight version of the X.500 Directory Access Protocol (LDAP) is included in Cold Fusion via a `<CFLDAP>` tag, and provides the capability to create Internet white pages.

Integration with industry standard is achieved by COM and DCOM support for integrating with ActiveX, Visual Basic, Delphi, C/C++, or Java. The content type for documents can be set to VRML and MIME document types (MS Office products, for example).

Looking to the future, the Cold Fusion HDML SDK can be used to build Handheld Device Markup Language (HDML) applications.

WebObjects

WebObjects is ideal for software engineers, especially if they are already familiar with object-oriented concepts. It is not a tool for nonprogrammers.

What Is WebObjects?

WebObjects is a high-end Web site development solution based on Apple's famous object-oriented framework. Its prepackaged set of Web objects, comprehensive set of Web development tools, database support, and open architecture make it possible to implement business logic independent of the underlying software implementation.

Who Is It For?

Unlike Cold Fusion, which is only supported on NT, Windows 95, and Solaris (Cold Fusion 3.1), WebObjects is supported on Solaris, Windows NT/95, HP-UX, MACH (NextStep) and is soon to be supported on Apple's Rhapsody. It is currently only available through some ISPs, but is mostly bought and used by small and large companies to integrate their current application to a Web interface or to build new Web sites from the ground up. Nonprogrammers can use the drag-and-drop GUI to create active Web pages, and programmers can use the object-oriented architecture to add sophisticated software technology. Nonprogrammers, however, will have difficulty in exploiting the potentials of this highly sophisticated object-oriented Web page programming tool.

Why Use WebObjects?

Its suite of graphical tools have the potential to greatly reduce the time-to-market, especially for connecting existing legacy database systems to the Net. It is object-oriented, and thus designed for maximum ease in integration with existing technologies and for hooking in third-party products. For developers familiar with the concept of object-oriented programming, it is simple to understand the underlying principles of WebObjects. A newbie to object-oriented programming might have to spend some time understanding it to fully exploit the potentials of WebObjects. Learning object-oriented programming, however, is not conceptually difficult, and it is a useful skill in general, as many new Internet technologies, like Java, are also object-oriented.

Getting Started

WebObjects is not as simple as Cold Fusion when it comes to getting started, despite the WYSIWYG development tool.

A WebObjects Application

Applications that consist of an HTML template, a script file, and a declaration file are the programming core of WebObjects. The HTML template uses an <WEBOBJECT> tag to indicate a connection request. The declaration file contains the mapping of variables and actions between the script and the HTML file. The script file, written using Apple's WebScript, Objective-C, Java, or JavaScript, contains the programming logic for generating the dynamic HTML file.

Language Notes

The WebObjects Builder is a drag-and-drop WYSIWYG tool used for developing a WebObjects Application. For the serious programmer who wants to go beyond the GUI environment, the HTML template, the script, and the declaration files can all be generated outside the GUI editor to create an application. There is also no need to learn WebObjects's WebScript (similar to JavaScript) or Objective-C, however; the script can be written in Java or JavaScript.

Objective-C is based on similar concepts to Smalltalk and it is an Apple product for developing object-oriented software. The WebScripts language is a WebObjects-specific scripting language. WebScripts does not look like HTML (as compared to CFML for Cold Fusion), but it is a fairly simple language with object-oriented properties and it is similar to Objective-C.

In a completely different strategy than Cold Fusion, both HTML and SQL are invisible to the programmer. A software engineer with no knowledge of HTML or SQL could use WebObjects to perform HTML and SQL tasks. For the following code, WebObjects generates the SQL necessary to fetch the data, and update it when objects change:

```
"Find me all the Dealership objects"
    allDealerObjects = dealershipController.fetchAllObjects();

"Give me the list of Customer objects corresponding to this
dealer object"
    customerList = dealer.customers();

"Set this customer's Credit limit to 10,000"

    aCustomer.setCreditLimit(10000)
```

Objects also generate their own HTML as needed.

Scalability/Performance

The application server architecture and load-balancing capability make it possible to distribute processing across many servers. Additional servers can be plugged in, if needed, without requiring code change. This also implies fault tolerance because if a server goes down, the application can be accessed from the other server.

Security

Because the business logic is contained in the WebObjects application server, it's self contained and, thus, secure. Also, the HTML, SQL, and code are independently stored, which adds another level of security.

Developing Applications

WebObjects simplifies Web site creation by facilitating the organizing and connection of applications developed using existing Web technologies and by providing full programming power to site creation.

Objects Available

The are at least twenty HTML-specific classes that are packages with WebObjects. There are also just as many objects that are packaged with the software and many more can be found at the Apple sites and via third-party vendors. It is also possible for developers to create and reuse their own objects. Any object used by WebObjects is called WebObject.

Model Building

The Enterprise Objects Modeler (EOModeler) tool is used to access existing databases and for generating new database schemas. It supports legacy database systems like Informix, Microsoft, Oracle, Quickbase, Sybase database servers, and even raw 3270. Third-party support is also available for DB2 and Interbase, and a set of EOModeleer API (Application Programming Interface) can be used to connect to any other database systems. This tool contains a Database Wizard that can generate SQL on-the-fly and can help get a company database on the Web in a matter of minutes with the help of the graphical WebObjects Builder tool for creating applications.

Implementation Independence

The Enterprise Objects Framework (EOF) provides a layer between the database management code and the database itself. This means that the database can be changed without having to change the business logic inherent in the front-end code. Additional behavior can also be added. For example, queries like, "What is this customer's credit limit?" or "Is this student eligible to graduate?" can be added by writing Java or Objective-C methods that extend the behavior of the data-bearing objects created by EOF.

Maintaining State

Storing states (using cookies or passing variables between pages, for example) can be achieved by the WOSessionsStore object, which stores states in applications, in HTML pages by using the hidden field mechanism, in memory on the server, or in cookies. It is also possible to create customized storage mechanisms by modifying methods in the WOApplication object.

28

APPLICATIONS FOR
WEB PUBLISHING

Graphical Application Development Tool

The *Project Builder* is used for editing, compiling, and debugging code written in WebScript, Objective-C, or Java. There are also third-party tools available for developing WebObjects applications.

Sample Application

This sample WebObjects code shows what goes in the various files. Note that the only thing that needs to go into the HTML is a little tag giving the name of a specific WebObject; when the application runs, this <WEBOBJECT> tag will be replaced with some dynamically generated HTML code. WebObjects pages, or reusable components (bits of pages, maybe a header that appears on every page), are stored in .wo directories, containing html, wod and (sometimes) wos files. The starting page of a WebObjects application is kept in Main.wo, which might look like this:

```
Main.wo/Main.html
    <WEBOBJECT NAME=MyHeader></WEBOBJECT>
    <P>
    The date today is
        <WEBOBJECT NAME=DateString></WEBOBJECT>
    Please log in.
        <WEBOBJECT NAME=MyInputForm>
            <WEBOBJECT NAME=NameField></WEBOBJECT>
            <WEBOBJECT NAME=PasswordField></WEBOBJECT>
        </WEBOBJECT>

    Main.wo/Main.wod  - this file declares the types of the object defined
in the HTML, and how they are to be initialized.
        # MyHeader is a custom reusable component that appears on every page.
  It may contain some graphics or navigation buttons.
We only need to maintain it in one spot,
however we can include it on every page really easily, just like this:

    MyHeader: MyCustomHeaderComponent {};

    # Create an NSDate object containing the current date/time
    DateString: WOString {
        Value = NSDate.date;
    }

    # MyInputForm is a form object; here we can say what method should be
invoked when the user hits "return" or clicks the submit button.
    MyInputForm: WOForm {
        Action = checkLogin;

    # NameField and PasswordField are text fields; let's decide what we want
    # to do with the data the user types there.  Keep the user name in a
    # "session" object, where it will be available to all WebObjects components

    nameField: WOText {
        Value = session.userName;
    };
        # Keep the password in an object that's local to this page,
and use a WOPasswordField
```

```
    # so the password isn't displayed
    passwordField: WOPasswordField {
        Value = password;
    };
```

Now, if you were writing a scripted page, you might create a
Main.wo/Main.wos file in JavaScript or WebScript that implements the
"checkLogin" method and decides what to do next.
You could also create a Main.java or Main.m file if you wanted this
to be a compiled class implemented inJava or Objective-C.
Here's a JavaScript version.

```
Main.wo/Main.wos
    id password;          # the password the user types will go here
    function checkLogin()
    {
        id theNextPage;
        # check the password - a trivial example
        if ( password.isEqualToString("TopSecret") ) {
          # find the page named "MyNextPage.wo" and transfer control to it,
          # so that page will come up next.  We do this by asking the
          # Application object to find a particular component.

            theNextPage = self.application.pageWithName("MyNextPage");
            return theNextPage;
        }
        # Bad password - arrange that we'll stay on this page
        return self;
    }
```

Integration with Advanced Web Technologies

WebObjects is fully integrated with other Internet technologies and also with standard, non-Internet technologies. For example, Apple's technology called D'OLE allows Objective-C clients/servers and OLE Automation client/servers to talk to each other, making it possible to import Excel spreadsheet information into an HTML page, and export data from an HTML page to a Delphi or VB application.

Viability and Directions

For an expert Internet programmer with a comprehensive knowledge of CGI languages (Perl, C, C++), Java, ActiveX, and JavaScript, either Cold Fusion or WebObjects would serve the programming purpose. Cold Fusion incorporates many of the popular uses of CGI—creating forms, form input validation, e-mail, built-in Java applets, JavaScript form validation, and creating cookies. WebObjects allows seamless integration with existing CGI code. For a nonprogrammer or someone with very little programming background, the WebObjects development environment is a way to organize existing objects (software code, database) into a working site. However, advanced programmers can take advantage of WebObjects' object-oriented architecture, Objective-C support, and underlying script to push the tool to its limit. WebObjects relies on the pre-existence of objects that it can put together and allows for extension by allowing a programmer to modify the WebScript or to write his or her own script in a

28

APPLICATIONS FOR
WEB PUBLISHING

language of choice. Cold Fusion allows similar flexibility but with a procedural/interpretive language that's easy to learn (because it looks similar to HTML). Whether the tool proves to be a RAD tool depends much on the user of the tool.

Cold Fusion is superior to WebObjects in its easy-to-use built-in functions/tags, which are normally implemented via CGIs, and WebObjects is superior to Cold Fusion in its scalability, platform independence, and use of object-oriented technology. Some may argue that the object-oriented nature of WebObjects makes it easier to maintain. The code-reusability structure, the collection of built-in functionalities, and the custom tags available in CFML make it easy to maintain, as well. In WebObjects, maintainability is inherent in the nature of this object-oriented tool, whereas the onus of writing maintainable code in Cold Fusion is on the software developer.

Cold Fusion has been adding features with each new release. In version 3.0, application pages are stored on the server in p-code for increased performance. Version 3.1, released in mid-November 1997, includes Solaris support, scheduling, support for European time/date/currencies, tags for FTP and directory functions, Cold Fusion Studio 1.0 for development, and many database features. In performance, which can sometimes be the deciding factor on the Internet, WebObjects is ahead of the game—and it remains to be seen whether Cold Fusion will catch up.

Cold Fusion costs much less than WebObjects, and that could very well be a deciding factor for many small to mid-size businesses. If many ISPs decide to partner with Apple to make WebObjects accessible to smaller businesses, these two tools might compete for market share; they are currently far apart enough not to be in direct competition. Of course, these are not the only such tools on the market. There's also LiveWire, NetDynamics, and so on, and probably more being developed.

Sample Sites

Trying out some sample sites might give you an idea as to how these products can be used.

Cold Fusion

A crossword game site where all the database management, state management, and dynamic pages are generated with Cold Fusion can be found at http://www.xword.com.

WebObjects

The Apple site contains links to many businesses (Nissan, Club Med, Dell, The Sharper Image, and so on) that use WebObjects. See http://software.apple.com/webobjects/test_drive.html. A fun site developed almost completely with WebObjects is http://www.cybermeals.com.

Resources

There are, of course, many resources available for further information on Cold Fusion and WebObjects. Only a few are listed here.

Cold Fusion

A list of useful URLs, newsgroups, and mailing lists is provided here.

URL

The Cambridge, Massachusetts-based company that invented Cold Fusion has a site at `http://www.allaire.com`, which is constructed entirely with Cold Fusion and HTML. It contains information on products and services, technical support, education services, and list of Cold Fusion developers, among other resources. This is the best place to start for learning Cold Fusion, because you'll find sample code, demos of sites using Cold Fusion, free third-party tools, comprehensive technical documents, and much much more.

Newsgroups

These newsgroups discuss everything from business to technical details.

```
comp.infosystems.www.authoring.site-design
comp.databases
alt.html
comp.infosystems.www.authoring.html
```

Mailing Lists

There is a Cold Fusion mailing list; it is allegedly managed by `listproc@hawaii.edu`, but seems to be inoperable. There's an upcoming list at `cf-talk@smokescreen.org`, with details and sign-up information at `http://www.smokescreen.org/list/listdir.cfm`.

WebObjects

A list of useful URLs, newsgroups, and mailing lists is provided here.

URLs

The Apple Enterprise pages, `http://enterprise.apple.com` and `http://www.stepwise.com/Resources/WebObjects`, contain general product information. FAQs can be found at `http://www.omnigroup.com/MailArchive/WebObjects/`.

Newsgroups

A search for WebObjects in `http://www.dejanews.com` turns up at least a dozen postings for people looking for someone with WebObjects experience.

28
APPLICATIONS FOR WEB PUBLISHING

WebObjects hasn't quite made the rounds in the authoring groups, but there are lots of discussions at the Apple-centric groups:

```
comp.sys.next.advocacy
comp.sys.mac.advocacy
comp.sys.next.software
```

Mailing Lists

Archives and subscription information are available at `http://www.omnigroup.com/MailArchive/WebObjects/`.

Summary

This chapter covers details on using Cold Fusion for rapid application development. It also presents a functionality summary of WebObjects for RAD. You learned about Web/database integration using these tools. You also learned about the usefulness of integrating the various existing programming techniques for creating interactive and dynamic Web sites. You learned that Cold Fusion is easy to learn and can be used to accomplish many of the tasks achieved by CGI programs. I showed that WebObjects is a very powerful tool and can be used by experienced programmers to build scalable Web sites. Both of these tools are very powerful and do not need to be used exclusively, but can be used together depending on the site requirements. I hope this chapter will help you make a decision as to whether you need to use both or just one and what you'd need to do to get started.

Server-Independent Technologies—The Java Servlet API

by Corey Klaasmeyer

IN THIS CHAPTER

Servlets are the server-side counterpart of applets. Servlets play the same role on the server side as applets do on the client side. Typically, an HTTP server dynamically loads a servlet to build dynamic Web pages or process input of some type—usually both. However, servlets are not restricted to HTTP-based Web servers; they will cooperate with any kind of server software that can provide them with an environment in which to run. This chapter primarily discusses how to write servlets intended to work within a Web server.

Why Servlets?

Servlets provide an attractive alternative to writing directly to a server's API or writing Common Gateway Interface (CGI) programs. Java servlets execute more efficiently than CGI programs, and they are easier to develop than programs that use a server's API. As an added bonus, like applets, servlets will run within any server that provides the proper support.

Because a servlet is loaded and executes as part of a server, the host machine does not have to start another process, as in the case of CGI. Starting an entirely new process separate from the Web server degrades performance considerably on machines that receive many thousands or millions of requests. Instead of starting a new process, a servlet is initialized as a separate thread within the server. Whenever that servlet is requested, the server knows to pass it some information. The servlet then processes the data sent from the client and returns a document.

In addition to running as efficiently as programs written directly to the server API, servlets can usually be developed more quickly in Java than in native languages. They enjoy the additional advantage of platform independence, which other languages cannot promise. An application written directly to a server API, such as NSAPI or ISAPI, will execute more quickly than a Java servlet, but an application of this type written for one server cannot easily be changed to run in another server or on another computer. A Java servlet that runs on one machine and in a single Web server will run without changes on any other machine and Web server that supports the servlet API.

The HelloWorld Servlet

Let's jump right in and write a HelloWorld servlet:

```
import java.io.*;
import javax.servlet.*;
import javax.servlet.http.*;

public class HelloWorld extends HttpServlet {
        public void doGet( HttpServletRequest request,
➥HttpServletResponse response ) throws
                ServletException, IOException {

        // Set the content type
        response.setContentType("text/html");

        // Get an output stream to the client.
        ServletOutputStream out = response.getOutputStream();
```

```
        // Create the html page
        out.println("<html>");
        out.println("<head><title>Hello World</title></head>");
        out.println("<body>");
        out.println("<h1>Hello World</h1>");
        out.println("</body></html>");

    }

    public String getServletInfo() {
            return "A HelloWorld Servlet";
    }
}
```

If you have read some of the chapters on Java, this example should be fairly straightforward. If not, you might want to turn back to the whirlwind tour of Java in Chapter 20, "The Java Language: A Crash Course."

The import statements at the top of the example load all the classes necessary to create a servlet. In particular, the servlet must declare itself as a subclass of HttpServlet from the javax.servlet.http package. The servlet may extend another class called GenericServlet, but this will be discussed later in the chapter. The line after the import statements declares the class HelloWorld as a subclass of HttpServlet.

Because the HelloWorld class is a subclass of HttpServlet, it can redefine a number of important methods, such as service(). The server calls the service() method every time a browser requests the HelloWorld servlet by name. Usually, the browser calls this service() method in the servlet using the following syntax:

```
http://www.host.com/servlet/HelloWorld
```

The next section describes the steps necessary to configure your environment to enable a servlet to respond to a browser request.

The service() method takes two parameters and must throw two exceptions. The two parameters are streams that enable you to read information from the browser request and pass back information to the browser. The first parameter in this method, HttpServletRequest, contains any name value pairs passed from a form. It also contains other information, such as what type of browser made the request and what IP address the request was made from. The HttpServletResponse parameter provides a way to communicate information back to the client. For instance, in this servlet, a simple HTML page that says nothing but HelloWorld is sent back by printing directly to the request variable. Every time a browser makes a request that is sent to the servlet, the service() method is called, and these streams are passed into the method.

If something goes wrong within the method, a ServletException or an IOException might be thrown. These exceptions are then handled by the server, which called the method in the first place. A server might send an internal error message back to the browser or take some other action in the event of a problem. These exceptions formally declare what might go wrong at runtime.

The first line of the method sets the content type for the response. In this case, because the method will be sending back an HTML page, the content type is set to text/html. A ServletOutputStream is then requested from the HttpServletResponse parameter. The HTML page is written to this OutputStream. This method sends the HTML page back to the browser. None of the formatting comes free, which means all the necessary HTML tags must be specified. However, the response does take care of constructing a valid MIME type header for the returned Web page.

The last method, getServletInfo(), provides information about the servlet's intended function to an administrative interface. The JSDK does not really support this feature, but administrative tools packaged with other servers might provide a way to access this data.

Executing the HelloWorld Servlet

In order to run this servlet, you need to install the JDK if you haven't already done so and download and install the Java Servlet Development Kit (JSDK). Now that you know something about how this servlet works, you can compile it using the JDK and run it using the srun utility included with the JSDK. In order to view the output, you can access the servlet from the browser of your choice.

The srun utility looks for servlets in the servlets directory, using a special ServletLoader class. The servlets directory can be set on the command line when srun is executed, but defaults to the current directory. Thus, you can just change to the servlets directory and type srun.

Add the JSDK's bin directory to the PATH. Make sure the compiled HelloWorld file is in the servlets directory. Change to this directory and type the following:

```
srun -p 80 -v
```

The -v option ensures that you get as much information as possible. The -p option sets the port to 80. By convention, Web servers communicate with browsers via this port.

> **NOTE**
>
> In order for srun to execute properly, your computer must have a TCP/IP stack installed and be connected to a network.

If everything went well, srun should have given you information about what port it is running on, the servlet directory, the document directory, and so forth. You should be able to access the HelloWorld servlet by typing this URL into the browser:

```
http://127.0.0.1/servlet/HelloWorld.
```

The 127.0.0.1 IP address is a special address called the *local loop-back address*. It tells the browser to make a connection back to the same computer.

If everything has been configured correctly, the servlet should return a simple Web page that says Hello World.

Servlet Classes

The servlet API defines two classes that provide servlet functionality. A servlet must declare itself as a subclass of one of these two classes. Servlets that are not necessarily intended to work with a Web server declare themselves a subclass of the more general type of servlet: GenericServlet. Servlets that are intended to work with a Web server declare themselves as subclasses of the more specific servlet API class: HttpServlet. Servlets described in this chapter will primarily be subclasses of HttpServlet in order to have access to all the functionality associated with the HTTP protocol.

The GenericServlet Class

The GenericServlet class provides some functionality that makes writing servlets easier. Among other things, it provides simple logging and implements the ServletConfig interface.

GenericServlet implements the following methods:

- **void init(ServletConfig config)**. This method initializes the servlet when it is loaded into the server. GenericServlet logs any calls to this method.
- **abstract void service(ServletRequest req, ServletResponse res)**. This method must be implemented by a subclass of GenericServlet, because it is not implemented by GenericServlet. It is declared as an abstract method within GenericServlet.
- **destroy()**. The destroy() method is called when the server removes a servlet from memory. GenericServlet logs any calls to this method. This method should be overridden to release any valuable system resources held by the servlet upon destruction.

In order to take advantage of the automatic logging implemented by GenericServlet, any subclasses should call the superclass methods before any other code.

The HttpServlet Class

The HttpServlet class extends GenericServlet and adds HTTP-specific behavior for use within a Web server context. A servlet of this type usually overrides the doGet() or the doPost() methods from HttpServlet rather than either of the two service() methods.

The following are the more important methods of the HttpServlet class:

- **void doGet (HttpServletRequest req, HttpServletResponse resp)**. do handles HTTP GET requests. The HttpServletRequest parameter encapsulates information about the request sent from the client. This class is described in more detail.
- **void doPost(HttpServletRequest req, HttpServletResponse resp)**. The doPost() method handles HTTP POST requests. Often, these requests are sent from a form. The

servlet can read parameters sent in from the form via the HttpServletRequest parameter. This class is also described in more detail.

■ **void service(HttpServletRequest req, HttpServletResponse resp).** Typically, a servlet overrides one or both of the previous two methods instead of the service method. However, if a servlet overrides this method, it can handle both GET and POST operations.

■ **void service(servletRequest req, ServletResponse res).** This method overrides the service method of GenericServlet, and it will be called for both GET and POST operations. The additional HTTP functionality available via the parameters of the last method is not available here, because both are just plain request and response parameters.

Most of the rest of this chapter deals with the request and response parameters, and examples will implement the service() method.

Communicating with the Browser

A servlet communicates with a browser via response and request objects. Information passed into the servlet is read from the request object. Any information sent back from the servlet must be sent to the response parameter. Two interfaces define the methods that make this possible: ServletRequest and ServletResponse.

ServletRequest and ServletResponse each define special functionality associated with reading or writing to a browser. A servlet can read parameters or information about the client through an object that implements the ServletRequest interface. The ServletResponse interface defines a set of methods that enable information to be sent back to the client. In addition to sending information back to the client, the content type and length associated with the information can be manipulated via methods in the ServletResponse object.

The HttpServletRequest and HttpServletResponse are concrete classes that implement the ServletRequest and ServletResponse interfaces. The server passes objects of this type into the methods doGet(), doPost(), and service(). The servlet may set status codes for the browser or add a number of different types of header fields to the HTTP header.

The ServletRequest Interface

The ServletRequest interface defines methods that return information about parameters sent with the request, the type of client making the request, the remote host, the protocol, and any attributes attached to the header. It also defines a method, getInputStream(), which returns a ServletInputStream object. The body of the request can be read from the ServletInputStream object.

The methods of ServletRequest are as follows:

■ **int getContentLength( ).** Returns the length of the body attached to this request in number of bytes.

- **String getContentType( )**.Returns the media type of the request. This is similar to the CGI variable CONTENT_TYPE.

- **String getProtocol( )**.Returns the protocol of the request.

- **String getScheme( )**. Returns information about the scheme that is being used—for example, HTTP, FTP, HTTPS, and so forth.

- **String getServerName( )**. Returns the host name of the server that received the request.

- **int getServerPort( )**.The port number that received the request.

- **String getRemoteAddr( )**. The IP address of the client that sent the request.

- **String getRemoteHost( )**. Returns the name of the remote host as in the REMOTE_HOST variable.

- **String getRealPath(String path)**. Returns a real path based on an alias sent in as a parameter. If a slash (/) is sent in, the path to the document root will be returned.

- **ServletInputStream getInputStream( )**. Returns a ServletInputStream, which can be used to read a request body.

- **String getParameter(String name)**. Returns the value associated with the specified name. If there is no parameter with this name, the method will return a null.

> **NOTE**
>
> This method should be used only if a single parameter by this name exists. For instance, if an HTML form on the client might send back multiple values, the getParameters() method should be used instead.

- **String[ ] getParameterValues(String name)**. Returns an array of values for this named parameter. If there are no parameters with this name, the method will return a null. This method provides a way of dealing with multiple-value parameters, such as an HTML list box that enables multiple selections.

- **Enumeration getParameterNames( )**. Returns an enumeration of all the parameters contained within this request. If there are no parameters, an empty Enumeration object will be returned.

- **Object getAttribute(String name)**. Returns a value for a named attribute.

In order to see the output of these methods, take a look at the SnoopServlet.java source file included with the JSDK. Run it in a browser to see what information this servlet returns.

The ServletResponse Interface

The ServletResponse interface defines a number of methods that are useful when sending information back to the client. ServletResponse defines fewer methods than ServletRequest.

29

THE JAVA
SERVLET API

They enable a servlet to set the content length of the response being sent back, set the content type, and get a `ServletOutputStream` to which to write. The `ServletOutputStream` supports an interface similar to the `PrintStream` interface of `System.out`, which enables the servlet to use `println()` to send back Web pages. The following list defines and explains methods of the `ServletResponse` class:

- **void setContentLength(int len)**. Sets the length of the information sent back to the client in bytes.

- **void setContentType(String type)**. Sets the content type of the information being sent back to the client. Usually, this type will be a MIME type, such as `text/html`.

- **ServletOutputStream getOutputStream( )**. Returns a `ServletOutputStream` attached to the client. Anything written to this stream will be redirected to the client. Typically, a Web page is sent back via a `ServletOutputStream` object.

Two of these methods are used in the HelloWorld example. The content type of the response is set to `text/html`, and the `getOutputStream()` is called to get a stream back to the client. This `ServletOutputStream` is then used to send an HTML page back to the client that says `Hello World`.

The `HttpServletRequest` and `HttpServletResponse` Methods

`HttpServletRequest` and `HttpServletResponse` methods offer extended HTTP functionality. `HttpServletRequest` supports GET, POST, and HEAD methods. The `HttpServletResponse` response object can be used to redirect requests to a different location or send HTTP-specific error messages. In addition, `HttpServletRequest` inherits the methods defined in `ServletRequest` for reading parameters sent to the servlet as part of a request from a Web page with a form.

`HttpServletRequest` methods provide the same information available to a CGI program via environment variables sent by the server. The following methods are defined in the `HttpServletResponse` interface:

- **String getMethod( )**. Returns the HTTP request method GET, HEAD, or POST. This method is equivalent to the CGI REQUEST_METHOD environment variable.

- **String getServletPath( )**. Returns the name of the servlet being invoked.

- **String getPathInfo( )**. Returns the path information if any has been appended to the request. If none has been appended, the method returns `null`. This is equivalent to the CGI PATH_INFO environment variable.

- **String getPathTranslated( )**. Returns a real path translation of the path information. This method also returns `null` if no path is specified. This is equivalent to the CGI PATH_TRANSLATED environment variable.

- **String getQueryString( )**. Returns the query string part of the URI. This method returns `null` if no query string has been sent. This is equivalent to the CGI QUERY_STRING environment variable.

- **String getRemoteUser( )**. Returns the name of the user on the client side. The method returns `null` if no user name is provided. This is equivalent to the CGI `REMOTE_USER` environment variable.

- **String getAuthType( )**. Returns the authentication scheme of the request. The method returns `null` if no scheme is being used. This is equivalent to the CGI `AUTH_TYPE` environment variable.

- **String getHeader(String name)**. Returns a header field associated with this name or `null` if no header with the name exists.

- **String getIntHeader(String name)**. Returns an integer header field associated with this name or `-1` if no header with the name exists.

- **long getDateHeader( )**. Returns the date specified in the header field. A `-1` is returned if no date is specified in the header.

- **Enumeration getHeaderNames( )**. Returns all the names included in the header.

`HttpServletResponse` methods provide extended support not usually conveniently available to CGI programs. A combination of methods and constants enable standard HTTP error codes to be sent back easily to the client. For a description of the codes, read RFC 1945. The following methods are defined in the `HttpServletResponse` interface:

- **boolean containsHeader(String name)**. Tests for the presence of a header within the response object with the specified name.

- **void setStatus(int statusCode, String statusMessage)**. Sets a code and message for the response. The first parameter or status code can be set by using one of 15 constants defined within the `HttpServletResponse` class.

- **void sendError(int statusCode, String message)**. Sets an error code and message for the response.

- **void sendError(int statusCode)**. Sets an error code for the response.

- **void setHeader(String name, String value)**. Adds a field to the header with the specified name and `String` value.

- **void setDateHeader(String name, long date)**. Adds a date to the header.

- **void sendRedirect(String location)**. Redirects the browser to some other location. This method will take only an absolute URL.

`HttpServletRequest` and `HttpServletResponse` are powerful tools for building server-side functionality on the Internet. They provide easy-to-use methods for building dynamic applications on the Web.

Reading Form Parameters

Servlets can easily read form parameters sent from a Web page by calling methods in the `ServletRequest` interface. The methods of `ServletRequest` are inherited by `HttpServletRequest`,

29

THE JAVA
SERVLET API

```
<td></td><td><input type="submit"></td>
</tr>
</table>
</form>
</body>
</html>
```

The following HTML file uses the POST method:

```
<html>
<head>
<title>Test EchoServlet using the POST method</title>
</head>
<body bgcolor="FFFFFF">
<form action="http://127.0.0.1:8080/servlet/EchoServlet" method="POST">
<table>
<tr>
   <td>Name:</td><td><input name="Name"></td>
</tr>
<tr>
   <td>Multiple:</td>
   <td><select name="Multiple" multiple>
    <option>Choice 1</option>

 <option>Choice 2</option>
    <option>Choice 3</option>
    <option>Choice 4</option>
   </select></td>
</tr>
<tr>
<td></td><td><input type="submit"></td>
</tr>
</table>
</form>
</body>
</html>
```

Notice that EchoServlet can handle multivalued parameters because it uses the getParameterValues() method, which returns a String array for a parameter name. Had EchoServlet used the getParameter() method, it would not have been able to return the multivalued parameters, because getParameter() would return only the first value for a given parameter name and ignore the rest.

Creating and Returning Dynamic HTML

In each of the previous examples, dynamic HTML was generated by the servlet and returned to the client. Creating dynamic HTML is a powerful technique, but it is difficult to make changes to code that contains HTML, because the code must be recompiled. This can result in a lengthy cycle of editing, recompiling, and testing. Ideally, the HTML should be disconnected as much as possible from the code.

It's not always possible to completely disconnect server-side processing from dynamic HTML code, but there are a number of ways to approach the problem. One way is to store the HTML in a database. Another approach is to create a markup language that can be parsed and replaced by server-side output. A server-side include is a simple example of this sort of approach.

For instance, the last example, EchoServlet, created code dynamically based on the values passed in from the form. In order to change the color of that page, the source for EchoServlet would have to be edited and then recompiled.

Although the servlets in this chapter are dynamic, they are simple and specific enough that the hard-coded HTML is not a problem.

An E-Mail Servlet

This example uses the e-mail classes developed in Chapters 20, "The Java Language: A Crash Course," and 21, "Introduction to Applet Programming," to implement an e-mail client that is HTML-based rather than applet-based. In essence, it creates a much thinner client and moves the processing to the server side. This approach often makes more sense than writing an applet for the client side and distributing it with a Web page, because of the time it takes to download an applet. In general, there should be a good reason to use processing on the client side, such as security or functionality. Most of the functionality needed for a simple e-mail client is easily implemented with an HTML form.

A simple e-mail form is not especially helpful, because e-mail functionality is already built into most browsers. However, responses to HTML forms are often e-mailed via the server to a company or individual. The SMTPClient can be used to connect to an SMTP server on the same machine or on some other machine in order to resend the contents of a form. The EMailServlet needs to be changed only to handle form data other than e-mail.

The EMailServlet

The EMailServlet reads e-mail data from an HTML e-mail form and resends the message by using the SMTPClient developed in Chapter 20. It reads each of the relevant parameters, including sender, recipient, subject, and body. An EMail object is constructed from this data and passed on to an SMTP server via SMTPClient.

The code looks like this:

```
import java.io.*;
import javax.servlet.*;
import javax.servlet.http.*;
import java.util.*;

public class EMailServlet extends HttpServlet {

   public void service( HttpServletRequest request,
►HttpServletResponse response ) throws
        ServletException, IOException {

      // Set the content type
      response.setContentType("text/html");

      // Get the message sent with the request
      String sender = request.getParameter( "from" );
      String recipient = request.getParameter( "to" );
      String subject = request.getParameter( "subject" );
```

```
        String body = request.getParameter( "body" );

        if( sender == null |¦ recipient == null ) {
           resendPage( response.getOutputStream() );
           return;
        }

        // Create the e-mail object
        EMail mail = new EMail();
        mail.setSenderAddress( sender );
        mail.setRecipientAddress( recipient );
        mail.setSubject( subject );
        mail.setMessage( body );

        // Send the e-mail object via SMTPClient
        SMTPClient smtp = new SMTPClient( "127.0.0.1" );
        smtp.send( mail );

        // Get an output stream to the client.
        ServletOutputStream out = response.getOutputStream();

        // Create the html page
        out.println("<html>");
        out.println("<head><title>Message Sent</title></head>");
        out.println("<body bgcolor=FFFFFF>");
        out.println("Your message was successfully sent!");
        out.println("</body></html>");

        // Close the SMTPClient connection

    }

    public String getServletInfo() {
       return "An Echo Servlet";
    }

    // Either the from or to fields were not specified, so resend the
    // the page with the same data.
    private void resendPage( ServletOutputStream out ) throws IOException {

        // Create the html page
        out.println("<html>");
        out.println("<head><title>Message Incomplete</title></head>");
        out.println("<body bgcolor=FFFFFF>");
        out.println("Both sender and recipient fields must be filled in.");
        out.println("</body></html>");

    }

}
```

This code looks simple, because it re-uses on the EMail and SMTPClient classes. The EMail object is created from the data entered on the client. This EMail object is then sent via the SMTPClient object.

NOTE

In order for SMTPClient to be able to send the message, there must be an SMTP server running on the same machine, or the host name must be changed to a machine that is running an SMTP server. Alternatively, this host could be specified via the ServletConfig properties.

The EMailServlet tests to see whether both the sender and recipient addresses are entered. If not, the servlet calls the method resendPage(), which sends an HTML page back to the client reporting that the message is incomplete.

The HTML Form

The HTML form used to send data to the EMailServlet includes fields for all the EMail information:

```
<HTML>
<HEAD>
    <TITLE>EMail Form</TITLE>
</HEAD>
<BODY BGCOLOR="#FFFFFF">

<FORM ACTION="http://127.0.0.1:8080/servlet/EMailServlet" METHOD="POST">
<TABLE>
<TR>
<TD>Sender Address:</TD>
<TD><INPUT TYPE="text" NAME="from" SIZE="25"></TD>
</TR>
<TR>
<TD>Recipient Address:</TD>
<TD><INPUT TYPE="text" NAME="to" SIZE="25"></TD>
</TR>
<TR>
<TD>Subject:</TD>
<TD><INPUT TYPE="text" NAME="subject" SIZE="25"></TD>
</TR>

<TR>
<TD>Message:</TD>

<TD>
<TEXTAREA NAME="body" ROWS="10" COLS="21"></TEXTAREA>
</TD>
</TR>

<TR>
<TD><INPUT TYPE="submit" NAME="Send!" VALUE="Send!"></TD>

<TD><INPUT TYPE="reset" NAME="Clear" VALUE="Clear"></TD>
</TR>
```

29

THE JAVA
SERVLET API

```
</TABLE>
</FORM>

</BODY>
</HTML>
```

Again, the ACTION attribute of the form sends data to a servlet running on the same machine. When the Send! button is clicked, the EMailServlet is invoked, and the message is sent.

Servlet Lifecycle and Writing Thread-Safe Servlets

Servlets differ from CGI programs in one very important way—lifecycle. Every request after initialization spawns a new thread instead of running a new program, as when invoking a CGI program. Although spawning a new thread requires less work and takes less time, there are some additional issues that a servlet programmer must be aware of in order to write safe code. Any member-instance variables belonging to the servlet must be synchronized.

The Servlet Lifecycle

Servlets are loaded, initialized, and destroyed.

Loading

Servlets are loaded after the first request for that service is made by a client. Typically, the server can also be configured to load servlets on startup.

Servlets may be loaded locally or remotely. If loaded remotely, the server must be configured to load the servlet from a URL. The examples in this chapter load servlets from the local file system in the servlets directory.

Initialization

Like an applet, a servlet may implement an init() method. This method initializes the servlet when it is first loaded. This method is called only once, because a servlet is loaded only once. Any requests sent to the servlet after this point invoke either a doGet(), doPost(), or service() method and create a new thread.

> **NOTE**
>
> A servlet may be loaded a second time if the class servlet is located in the servlets directory under the home directory of the JSDK. Servlets loaded from this directory are loaded using a special ServletLoader, which tests to see whether the class file has changed and loads it again if the file has changed. Thus, servlets may be loaded more than once when located in the servlets directory. This method is convenient, because it does not require that the server be restarted after recompilation.

During initialization, the servlet also has access to some initialization information passed in as a `ServletConfig` object. This would be useful in the `EMailServlet` for specifying the SMTP server to use.

In order to specify initialization parameters, you must create a file called `servlet.properties` and place it in the servlets directory. Alternatively, the location of this file can be specified when `srun` is invoked, using the `-s` option.

Two lines should be added to this file for each servlet. The first line names the servlet and assigns a class file to this name. In the case of `EMailServlet`, the line looks something like this:

```
servlet.mail.code=EMailServlet.class
```

The second line specifies any initialization arguments. You will probably want to pass in a host name for the SMTP server. This line takes this format:

```
servlet.mail.InitArgs=host=smtp.com
```

This property is sent to the `EMailServlet` as part of the `ServletConfig` object. Additional properties can be appended to the end of the `InitArgs` line if comma-delimited.

In order to access this property from `EMailServlet`, an additional `init()` method has to be added to the class:

```
public class EMailServlet extends HttpServlet {

    ...

    // Initialize the EMailServlet. Get an SMTP host.
    public void init( ServletConfig config ) {
        host = config.getInitParameter( "host" );
            if( host == null ) {
                host = "127.0.0.1";
            }
    }
    ...          // The host     private String host;
}
```

The method `getInitParameter()` returns the value of the host variable to the `EMailServlet`. If `null`, the host defaults to local loopback. Notice that this variable was added as an instance variable of the class, which means that it will be accessible to all the threads. If this variable is altered after initialization, it is important to synchronize any code blocks that access it. In this case, you don't have to worry about synchronization, because the `init()` method is called only once for the servlet.

Destruction

The servlet stops processing requests when the server calls its `destroy` method.

Summary

In this chapter, the main servlet classes of the `javax.servlet` package are described in detail. Servlets can be used as a more efficient alternative to CGI, because they run as part of the Web server rather than as separate processes. However, writing servlets poses some interesting problems regarding synchronization of data. Because a servlet is loaded once and every request thereafter creates a new thread of execution, the servlet must be written in a thread-safe way.

A servlet that responds to HTTP requests should extend `HttpServlet` one or more methods of the appropriate type. Three main methods defined in `HttpServlet` are used to implement GET and POST methods: `doGet()`, `doPost()`, and `service()`. The `service()` method works for both POST and GET methods.

The classes `HttpServletRequest` and `HttpServletResponse` provide convenient HTTP-specific functionality. They give a servlet access to parameters sent from a form, and CGI information such as the identity of the client, the query string, and path information. `HttpServletResponse` provides functionality for setting the returned document's content type, sending a redirect, setting header attributes, or sending back status-code and error-code information.

VI
PART

Putting It All Together: Engineering a Web Site

Using the HTML Object Model and Creating Dynamic HTML Pages

by Shelley Powers

IN THIS CHAPTER

Dynamic HTML enables Web page developers to alter a page's presentation by adjusting a style sheet, and accessing properties, methods, and events for traditional HTML elements in order to dynamically or statically position these elements, or modify their appearance. With DHTML, you can alter the look and behavior of the Web page without forcing a page reload, having the page return to the Web server, or relying on outside objects, plug-ins, controls, or applets.

Netscape implemented DHTML in Navigator 4.0, and Microsoft implemented the technology in Internet Explorer 4.0. Both browsers share some common DHTML functionality, such as support for CSS1 and CSS1 positioning. However, the browsers differ in their implementation of DHTML, including their handling of HTML element modification, their event models, and the dynamic access of HTML elements.

This chapter provides an overview of DHTML's major components and briefly covers the scripting object models for both Navigator and IE. Following the object models, the chapter discusses the compatibility issues exposed with the models, and helps you create a cross-browser DHTML Web page.

What Are the Major Components of Dynamic HTML?

The very words "Dynamic HTML" imply that the technology has to do with the dynamic alteration of a Web page after the page is loaded. However, both Netscape and IE consider that DHTML also covers Web page presentation and static positioning in addition to the livelier aspects of the technology. DHMTL's major components are:

- Web page presentation using CSS1 and JASS
- HTML element exposure to the scripting object models
- Dynamically altering the appearance of HTML elements
- Hiding, displaying, moving, or clipping HTML elements
- Trapping events for traditional HTML elements
- Multimedia enhancements such as interesting transition and filter effects and downloadable fonts

Web page presentation, the scripting object models, the event models, and the dynamic alteration of HTML elements are covered in this chapter. In addition, this chapter covers some of the issues with creating cross-browser DHTML Web pages, and a technique that helps you work around these by creating a cross-browser DHTML Web page is demonstrated.

CSS1 positioning—which covers the movement and visibility of an element—and Web page interaction are covered in Chapter 31, "Manipulating Objects and Responding to User Interaction." Additionally, this chapter contains a quick review of some of the fun multimedia enhancements each browser provides. Chapter 32, "Saving User Preferences: Cookies and OPS," covers using Netscape-style cookies to store information about Web page presentation preferences, and restoring DHTML effects when a Web page loads. The chapter also discusses the differences between cookies and the new Open Profiling Standard (OPS).

Web Page Presentation Using CSS1 and JASS

Web developers and authors use CSS1 style sheets to define style rules for all elements of a certain type, for a class of elements, or for a specifically identified element.

As an example, Listing 30.1 contains the style sheet for a Web page that sets the background color to ivory, the background image to `redbar.jpg`, and repeats this image along the y axis, which means the image repeats vertically, not horizontally.

Listing 30.1. Impact of CSS1 on a simple HTML document.

```
<HTML>
<HEAD><TITLE>Example 1</TITLE>
<STYLE type="text/css">
<!--
    BODY { background-color:ivory;
        background-image: url(redbar.jpg);
        background-repeat: repeat-y;
        margin-left: 220px; margin-right: 50px;
        font-family: Courier }
    H1 { color: firebrick; font-family: Fantasy }
//-->
</STYLE>
</HEAD>
<BODY>
<H1>This is the first example</H1>
This is the first example in Chapter 30, covering Dynamic HTML. This
chapter reviews CSS1 and covers the scripting object model for
Netscape Navigator and Microsoft Internet Explorer. Additionally,
the chapter also provides demonstrations of CSS1 Positioning.
</BODY>
</HTML>
```

In addition to the background image and color, the style sheet also creates a margin 200 pixels from the left and 50 pixels from the right, and redefines the overall font to Courier. Finally, the style sheet changes the H1 header font to Fantasy, and sets its color to firebrick.

Netscape also provides its own style sheet technique, which it refers to as JavaScript Accessible Style Sheets or JASS. JASS is a way to alter CSS1-like attributes for a Web page from a scripting block as well as a style block. Based on this, you could query for information about the screen resolution and alter the font size, or query for information on the color-depth and alter the colors of HTML elements.

JASS attributes can be applied to all HTML elements with the use of the `tags` object, or they can be applied to a class of elements with the `classes` object. Attributes can also be adjusted for specific elements using the identifier, or `ids` object. The following code provides a demonstration of how each of these works:

```
document.tags.H1.fontSize="18pt";
document.tags.P.backgroundColor="yellow";
...
document.classes.someclass.all.color="red";
document.classes.someclass.P.color="blue";
...
document.ids.someid.marginLeft="0.1in";
document.ids.someid.textDecoration="none";
```

The first pair of style rules sets the H1 headers font size to 18pt, and the background color of all paragraphs to yellow. The second pair of style rules sets the font color to red for all elements that belong to the class `someclass`, except for paragraphs, which are set to the color blue. The final pair of style rules sets a margin of 0.1 inches on the left, and removes any text decoration of an element or elements identified by `someid`.

As you can see by this last code, there are several attributes that can be changed using JASS, and they are listed in Table 30.1.

Table 30.1. JASS attributes.

Attribute	Description
fontSize	Font size, such as 18pt
fontWeight	Font weight, such as 700 or bold, which are equivalent
fontFamily	Font family, such as Courier or Times New Roman
fontStyle	Font style, such as italic or small caps
lineHeight	Height of line between two adjacent lines
verticalAlign	Vertical alignment of element contents within block
textAlign	Horizontal alignment of element text within block
textTransform	Transform text in some manner, such as capitalize, which capitalizes the first letter of every word in block
margins	Function to specify one or more margins at a time
marginLeft	Left margin of element
marginRight	Right margin of element
marginTop	Top margin of element
marginBottom	Bottom margin of element
paddings	Function to specify one or more paddings at a time
paddingTop	Top padding between block border and element contents
paddingLeft	Left padding between block border and element contents
paddingRight	Right padding between block border and element contents

Attribute	Description
`borderWidths`	Function to specify one or more border widths at a time
`borderTopWidth`	Width of top border of block
`borderLeftWidth`	Width of left border of block
`borderRightWidth`	Width of right border of block
`borderBottomWidth`	Width of bottom border of block
`borderStyle`	Style of border, such as 3D or solid
`borderColor`	Color of border
`width`	Width of block
`height`	Height of block
`align`	How element aligns with surrounding elements, with a value such as `left` or `right`
`clear`	Whether other elements are allowed on either side of element
`color`	Text color
`backgroundImage`	Image used for background of block
`backgroundColor`	Color used for background of block
`display`	Whether element displays inline, as block, or a list
`listStyleType`	Controls formatting of lists and type of list bullets

JASS styles can be applied within a script block. Listing 30.2 has the contents of a Web page that checks the color depth of the screen as the page is loaded, and alters the colors based on that depth.

Listing 30.2. Testing screen color depth and using JASS to alter colors to match depth.

```
<HTML>
<HEAD><TITLE>Example 1</TITLE>
<STYLE type="text/javascript">
    with (document.tags) {
        BODY.marginLeft="0.5in";
        BODY.marginRight="0.5in";
        BODY.marginTop = "1in";
        P.fontSize="14pt";
        }
</STYLE>
<script language="javascript">
<!--
    if (screen.colorDepth <= 8) {
    document.tags.backgroundColor="white";
    document.tags.H1.color="red";
```

30

USING THE HTML
OBJECT MODEL

continues

Listing 30.2. continued

```
        document.tags.P.color="black";
        }
      else {
        document.tags.BODY.backgroundColor="honeydew";
        document.tags.H1.color="indianred";
        document.tags.P.color="lightseagreen";
        }
//-->
</SCRIPT>
</HEAD>
<BODY>
<H1>This is the Second example</H1>
<P>
This is the Second example in Chapter 30, covering Dynamic HTML. This
chapter reviews CSS1 and covers the scripting object model for
Netscape Navigator and Microsoft Internet Explorer. Additionally,
the chapter also provides demonstrations of CSS1 Positioning.
</P>
</BODY>
</HTML>
```

In the JavaScript block, the color depth is checked and if it is less than 8 (representing 256 colors or lower), the background color is set to white, the header to red, and the paragraph text is black. All colors will show true, meaning that they will show the same regardless of operating system, video card, or monitor, at this color depth. However, with color depths of over 8, such as 16- or 24-bit colors, you are freer to become a little more subtle with the coloring and feel relatively confident that the colors will show true.

Notice also in Listing 30.2 that JASS is used in a style block as well as the script block. The style block sets those attributes that aren't dependent on script to check the screen resolution, or anything else for that matter, though you can use JavaScript in this block. Curly brackets and the keyword with are used to avoid having to repeat the words document.tags. Additionally, as this style sheet is within a block, you don't have to use the document specifier, as you do when accessing style sheets within a script block.

In addition to specifying style sheets within the Web page, you can also link external JASS style sheets using the same techniques that you used for CSS1 style sheets, except the type of style sheet is JavaScript, as shown in the following code:

```
<LINK REL=STYLESHEET TYPE="text/JavaScript"
    HREF="somestyles.jss" TITLE="sometitle">
```

The style sheet in the external file is declared in the same manner as the style sheet within the document is declared, except you don't need to specify the <STYLE></STYLE> tags.

How styles combine using JASS is similar to how they combine with CSS1 in that a style that is defined last for an element takes precedence over another style for the same element declared earlier.

COMPANION Web site The best way to learn about JASS is to take a look at a document that uses most of the JASS attributes, and try changing the attributes' values and seeing what happens to the document. I created a Web page document that contains most types of JASS attributes. These attributes redefine the presentation of several HTML elements used within the page. Listing 30.3 shows only the style sheet for the example, as the entire sample is too large to be shown in this chapter. However, you can access the sample by opening the file home.htm on this book's Companion Web Site.

Listing 30.3. Styles Sheets for example.

```
<STYLE type="text/javascript">
    with (tags.BODY) {
        margins("20px","50px","10px","220px");
        backgroundColor="ivory";
    }
    with (tags.H1) {
        color="gold";
        marginLeft="-200px";
    }
    with (tags.UL) {
        borderWidth=5;
        borderStyle="3D";
        borderColor="darksalmon";
        width=150;
        height=200;
        paddings("5","5","5","5");
        backgroundColor="black";
        color="orange";
    }
    ids.strong1.fontSize="larger";
    ids.strong2.color="darkseagreen";
    ids.strong3.textDecoration="overline";
    ids.strong4.textTransform="uppercase";
    tags.STRONG.color="salmon";
    with (tags.A) {
        textDecoration="blink";
        color="sienna";
    }
    classes.para1.all.textIndent="10px";
    classes.para1.all.fontFamily="Arial";
</STYLE>
<STYLE type="text/css">
    BODY { background-image: url(redbar.jpg);
           background-repeat: repeat-y }
</STYLE>
```

Again, most of the JASS attributes are used in this example, including creating new versions of the STRONG tag and changing the anchor's text decoration to blinking text rather than underlined. Borders and padding are used, and the list's colors are altered to make it stand out more; CSS1 style sheets are used, include the sidebar image as JASS does not provide attributes to control background image repetition. Figure 30.1 shows the Web page's list portion.

30

USING THE HTML OBJECT MODEL

FIGURE 30.1.

List portion of Web page containing an extensive example using JASS.

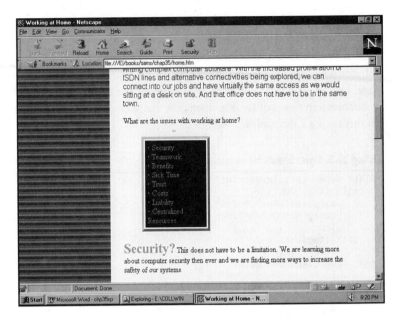

Again, to gain familiarity with JASS, you should open `home.htm`, alter the properties, and see what the impact is on the document's presentation.

The Scripting Object Models

Scripting languages can iterate through a block of code a given number of times, or can check for conditions, or set and get values from form elements. However, a scripting language is nothing more than functionality without substance, and scripting object models are the substance.

You can run the following code in IE 4.0, and the code alters the color and font family of the specified header, and hides the paragraph under it, all based on the Web page reader clicking the header:

```
function alter_contents() {
    document.all.header1.style.color="red";
    document.all.header1.style.fontFamily="Arial";
    document.all.para1.style.visibility="hidden";
    }
...
<H1 id="header1" onclick="alter_contents()">The Header</H1>
<p id="para1" style="visibility:inherit">
Some paragraph
</P>
```

This code block's language components are the function and assignment statements. However, the other components, such as the `onclick` event, the `header`, paragraph, `document`, and `all` objects, and the `style` object/property are all exposed to the Microsoft scripting object model, meaning that you can access them directly via a scripting language.

When addressing issues of browser compatibility, the differences between browsers has less to do with the scripting language and more to do with the disparity between the scripting object models. Taking the same example, a second block of code uses the Navigator scripting object model:

```
function alter_contents() {
    document.para1.visibility="hidden";
    }
...
<H1 id=header1 style="position:absolute; left:10; top:10">
<a href="" onclick="alter_contents();return false">The Header</a></H1>
<P id=para1 style="position:absolute; left:10; top:50">
Some paragraph
</P>
```

First, Netscape does not currently expose the CSS1 attributes of HTML elements such as color or font, but does expose the elements for CSS1 positioning. You cannot change the color or font of the header, but you can hide the paragraph. Additionally, Microsoft has exposed HTML elements to their event model, a move that Netscape matches, but in a more limited sense. Whereas with IE you can trap most events directly within an element, Netscape allows you to only trap certain events, such as the `mouseover` event, but not other events, such as `click`. That's not to say you can't work around the differences. Navigator won't allow you to trap the clicked event for an element such as a header; you can use an empty link anchor to enclose the text of the header element. The anchor element can trap the `click` event, allowing you to indirectly trap this event for the header. This workaround's limitation is that you have to return `false` at the end of the clicked event to prevent the Web page from attempting to load the empty reference. Also, you may have to change the anchor's style setting to eliminate the normal underline and link colors.

Overviews of both browsers' models are included in the next two sections.

The Microsoft Scripting Object Model

Microsoft has made the most extensive changes to its scripting object model with the release of IE 4.0. In addition to new filter and transition properties, the company also exposed all HTML elements to its scripting object model. For each HTML element you can trap an event, alter a CSS1 property, or move, layer, or hide the element.

The Basic Model Objects

The following list contains the basic objects Microsoft exposed in its model prior to IE 4.0. Except for some new attributes or methods, these objects have changed very little from IE 3.0 to IE 4.0.

- Window object—Owns most elements within the browser window, including the document object.
- Document object—Controls access to most elements within the browser page.
- Location object—Contains information about the page currently loaded.

- History object—Contains information about previously viewed Web pages, and maintains a history of recently visited URLs.
- Navigator object—Contains information about the type and version of the browser.

The list doesn't include the form or input elements, but again, these have changed little from IE 3.x to IE 4.0. Because most of the objects listed existed prior to IE 4.0 and are not necessarily associated with Dynamic HTML, there's not too much detail about them here. However, there are some new features for the window object worth mentioning.

The window owns most everything within a Web page, and isn't usually referenced when an element is referenced. As an example, either of the following lines of code provide access to the same element:

```
document.all.theelement = ...;
window.document.all.theelement = ...;
```

The window object also has a couple of functions to open new browser windows. The first, open, is used to open a new fully functioning browser window. The syntax for the command is the following:

```
windowvar = window.open("URL","title","features");
```

The variable windowvar is optional, as is the window's URL, title, and feature list. If no feature is given, the default values are used, which for the most part means a window with no status bar, toolbar, menubar, or scrollbars. One new window feature handy for use with DHTML applications is opening a window full screen, without any *chrome* on the window—things like toolbars, titlebar, menu bar, and the like. The Web page in Listing 30.4 shows an example of opening a full-screen window. The content for the window is a page from a Web site that discusses some images used in a menu bar for the month of January; functionality has been added to close the window when the Web page reader clicks the logo.

Listing 30.4. Window browser opened using the full-screen window attribute.

```
<HTML>
<HEAD><TITLE>Window Open Example</TITLE>
<STYLE type="text/css">
    BODY { background-color: aqua }
    H1 { position:absolute; left: 20; top:20;
        color: red }
</STYLE>
<SCRIPT language="javascript">
<!--
// open window fullscreen
function open_window() {
    window.open("menu.htm", "Menu", "fullscreen=yes");
}
//-->
</SCRIPT>
</HEAD>
<BODY>
<H1 onclick="open_window()">Click here to open window</H1>
```

```
</BODY>
</HTML>
```

Figure 30.2 shows the full screen window. Note that there is no titlebar or menu bar. You must provide some form of exit for your visitors. In the example, the logo's `onclick` event is trapped and used to close the window, as shown in the following code:

```
<img onclick="window.close()" align=top src="yasd.gif"

alt="logo" border=0 width=104 height=152>
```

FIGURE 30.2.

Results of opening a Web page using full-screen window open *attribute.*

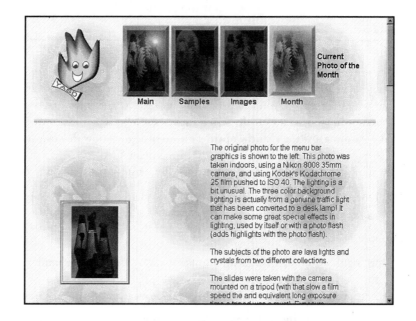

Table 30.2 contains the attributes that can be used with the window's open method.

Table 30.2. Window Open method attributes.

Attribute	Description
fullscreen	Create full screen browser window without any title, status, or scrollbars
channelmode	Create window in channel mode for displaying as a channel
toolbar	Toggles toolbar display
location	Toggles location bar display
directories	Toggles directory buttons display

continues

Table 30.2. continued

Attribute	Description
status	Toggles status bar display
scrollbars	Toggles scrollbars display
resizeable	Controls whether window can be resized
width	Window width
height	Window height
top	Window top position
left	Window left position

There are also a couple of new window methods, showHelp and showModalDialog, that are of interest. The showHelp method opens a Web page document that contains information to help the Web page reader. You can pass arguments to the newly opened window that can be processed within the window to do such things as scroll the window's contents to a particular topic. The showModalDialog window opens a modal dialog window that can access information from the reader and return the information to the main Web page. The dialog window is *modal*, meaning that it receives all events for the browser until the window is closed.

For the example demonstrated in Listing 30.4, opening the same Web page using the showHelp function is included in the following code:

```
window.showHelp("menu.htm");
```

Opening the same window using the showModalDialog could be similar to the following code:

```
var ret_value = window.showModalDialog("menu.htm", "Menu",
    "border:thick;dialog-width:300; dialog-height:300;help:no;center:yes");
```

Figure 30.3 shows the image menu bar page, but this time opened as a modal dialog window.

Table 30.3 shows the attributes you can specify when using the showModalDialog function.

Table 30.3. ShowModalDialog function attributes.

Attribute	Description
dialogHeight	Dialog's height
dialogWidth	Dialog's width
dialogTop	Dialog's top position
dialogLeft	Dialog's left position
center	Whether window is centered on desktop
font-family	Font family used in dialog

Attribute	Description
font-size	Font size used in dialog
font-weight	Font weight used in dialog
font-style	Font style used in dialog
font-variant	Font variant used in dialog
border	Determines window border thickness
help	Controls appearance of Help icon
minimize	Whether minimize button is added to title bar
maximize	Whether maximize button is added to title bar

Note that some of the showModalDialog attributes, such as font-family or font-size, are overridden within the dialog Web page, if these same styles are set using CSS1 directly in the dialog page.

FIGURE 30.3.

Results of opening image menu bar Web page using the showModalDialog window method.

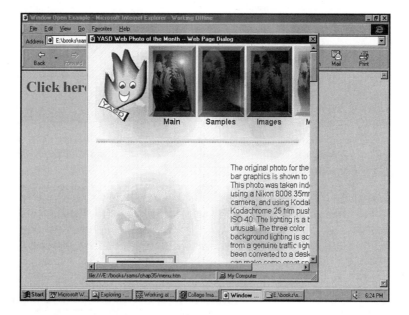

The New Microsoft Dynamic HTML Objects

Microsoft added several new objects to its scripting object model with IE 4.0. These objects contain information about the Web page events, the screen resolution and color depth, or can assist in examining the Web page contents in closer detail. One object is used specifically to alter the existing CSS1 attributes for an HTML element. These objects are, respectively, the event object, the screen object, the textrange object, and the style object.

The event Object

The event object is accessible anywhere within code, and contains information about the most recent Web page event. Here's an example demonstrating the use of the event object. The file home.htm is converted to use CSS1 styles instead of JASS, as the page is opened in IE. The converted style sheet is shown in Listing 30.5.

Listing 30.5. File home.htm style sheet, converted from CSS1 to JASS.

```
<STYLE type="text/css">
    BODY { margin: 20px 50px 10px 220px;
            background-image: url(redbar.jpg);
            background-repeat: repeat-y }
    H1     {color:gold; margin-left:-200px}
    UL { border-width:5; border-style:groove;
        border-color:darksalmon;width:150;
        height:200;paddings: 5 5 5 5;
        background-color:black;
        color:orange}
    #strong1 {font-size:larger}
    #strong2 {color:darkseagreen }
    #strong3 {text-decoration:overline};
    #strong4 {text-transform:uppercase};
    STRONG {color:salmon}
    A   {text-decoration:overline; color:sienna}
    .para1 {text-indent: 10px ; font-family:Arial)
</STYLE>
```

Both Navigator and IE should be able to process this style sheet. Note that the main differences between the CSS1 rules and the JASS assignments, is that CSS1 separates attribute and value with a colon (:), and JASS uses an equal sign (=). Also, the attributes use dashes instead of capitalizing the second part of the attribute, so that for CSS1 the attribute text-decoration becomes textDecoration with JASS.

Next, a function that traps all onclick events for the Web page document is added. The event object is accessed to retrieve the element that receive the event and to retrieve information about the element's position relative to the its parent element, the Web page, and the screen. This information builds a new block of HTML, which is used to replace the element within the page, as shown in Listing 30.6.

Listing 30.6. Function to trap the onclick event and replace clicked element with information

```
<SCRIPT FOR=document EVENT=onclick language="jscript">
    var theelement = window.event.srcElement;
    if (theelement.tagName == "BODY") return false;
    var thecontents="<strong style='color:red'>" +
        theelement.tagName + "</strong><br>";
    thecontents+="<strong style='color:blue'>x position=" +
        window.event.x + "</strong>";
    thecontents+="<strong style='color:lime'> y position=" +
        window.event.y + "</strong><br>";
    thecontents+="<strong style='color:magenta'>client x position=" +
```

```
        window.event.clientX + "</strong>";
    thecontents+="<strong style='color:aqua'> client y position=" +
        window.event.clientY + "</strong><br>";
    thecontents+="<strong style='color:yellow'>screen x position=" +
        window.event.screenX + "</strong>";
    thecontents+="<strong style='color:orange'> screen y position=" +
        window.event.screenY + "</strong><br>";
    theelement.outerHTML=thecontents;
</SCRIPT>
```

COMPANION
Web site

Several of the event properties are accessed, such as the `srcElement` which is the element that received the event, and event location information such as `clientX` and `clientY`. This information is used to create a string of HTML; the new `outerHTML` element property, discussed in the later section covering the `TextRange` object, replaces the element. You can try the example yourself by opening the file `ieevent.htm`. Figure 30.4 shows the page after `STRONG` and paragraph elements have been clicked.

FIGURE 30.4.

Contents of Web page after a couple of the elements have been clicked and then replaced with event information.

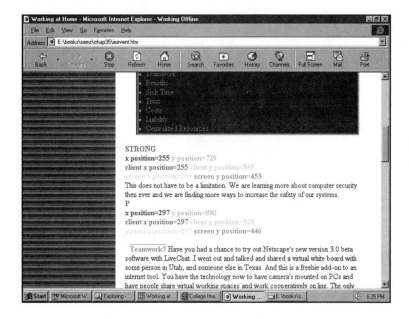

Figure 30.5 shows the page after the paragraph that contains the previously clicked `STRONG` element has been clicked.

30

USING THE HTML OBJECT MODEL

NOTE

The new HTML used to replace both the `STRONG` element and the paragraph contents have been replaced in Figure 30.5. This happened because the original `STRONG` element was

continues

continued

contained within the paragraph, so when the STRONG element was replaced, the replacement element is also contained within the paragraph. In turn, replacing the paragraph replaced both elements.

FIGURE 30.5.

Contents of Web page after paragraph containing previously clicked STRONG element has itself been clicked and replaced.

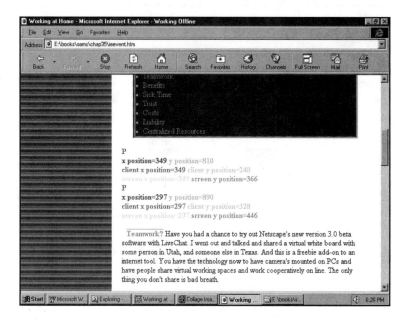

The example just discussed accessed some of the event properties. Table 30.4 shows all of the properties.

Table 30.4. Event object properties.

Property	Description
AltKey	Alt key state
Button	Mouse button pressed, if any
CancelBubble	Whether to continue passing event through element hierarchy
ClientX	Horizontal location of event relative to document
ClientY	Vertical location of event relative to document
CtrlKey	Ctrl key state
fromElement	For mouse move or drag, element being moved
keyCode	ASCII value of key pressed, if any

Property	Description
offsetX	Event horizontal offset from element container
offsetY	Event vertical offset from element container
reason	For data binding only
returnValue	Return value from modal dialog only
screenX	Horizontal location of event in screen units
screenY	Vertical location of event in screen units
srcElement	HTML element that received event
toElement	Element being dragged to with mouse drag event
type	Type of event
x	Horizontal location of event relative to parent element
y	Vertical location of event relative to parent element

The cancelBubble property is particularly important. If you have a Web page with a paragraph, layered on an image, which is, in turn, layered on the Web page document, any event such as a clicked event to the paragraph triggers the same event for the image and the document, in a top-down order. To prevent this, you can assign a false value to the cancelBubble property, and the event stops at that specific event handler.

A new HTML element property called outerHTML is used in the last example. It is discussed in more detail in the next section, which covers the TextRange object.

The TextRange Object and the Text/HTML Element Properties

The TextRange object contains the text of whatever element is used to create the object. You can create an instance of this object by using the createTextRange method with the BODY, BUTTON, and TEXT, and TEXTAREA INPUT elements. Additionally, you can create a TextRange element using one of the TextRange methods with an existing TextRange object.

There are only a few TextRange object properties:

■ htmlText
■ text

The first property, htmlText, returns the HTML source of the element, the second property, text, only returns the text itself.

One use of this object is to search for some text within the Web page, and replace the text when it is found. The file ieevent.htm is opened and the existing scripting block removed. The STRONG tag style sheet is modified to increase the font size and weight. Next, a new scripting block is created to produce a TextRange object from the document body. The code accesses some text from a text input field, and searches for the text within the TextRange object. If the code finds the text, it replaces it with an emphasized version, using a STRONG tag; otherwise it prints out a message that it could not find the text. The scripting block and modified STRONG tag are shown in Listing 30.6.

Listing 30.6. Code to create a `TextRange` object and use it to find and replace text within the Web page.

```
STRONG {color:salmon; font-size: 14pt; font-weight: 800}
...
<SCRIPT language="jscript">
<!--
// create TextRange and search and
// replace block of text
function FindAndReplace() {
    var bodyText = document.body.createTextRange();
    if (bodyText.findText(tofind.value))
        bodyText.pasteHTML("<strong>" + tofind.value + "</strong>");
    else
        alert("Could not find " + tofind.value);
}
//-->
</SCRIPT>
```

The input text field provides a location for the reader to input the text and a button to press when the reader wants the text searched for and replaced, as shown in the following block of code:

```
<p style="margin: 0.5in">
Enter text to find and replace:
<input name="tofind">
<input type="button" value="Find"
onclick="FindAndReplace()">
</p>
```

COMPANION **Web site** The modified file is saved as `iefind.htm`; you can open this file and try the example yourself. Figure 30.6 shows the Web page after several words have been replaced using the `TextRange` object.

Listing 30.6 demonstrates several `TextRange` methods, and Table 30.5 contains some of the most useful `TextRange` methods. The Microsoft client SDK contains documentation on the other methods.

Table 30.5. Some of the `TextRange` methods.

Method	Description
duplicate	Duplicates `TextRange`
execCommand	Executes command on `TextRange`
expand	Increases `TextRange` to include component
findText	Searches for text within `TextRange`

Method	Description
inRange	Compares one range to see if it is contained within another
isEqual	Compares one range to see if it is equal to another
move	Moves TextRange a given unit, such as character, word, sentence, or TextRange start/end
moveEnd	Changes size of TextRange object by moving the end
moveStart	Changes size of TextRange object by moving the beginning
moveToElementText	Moves TextRange to enclose element text
moveToPoint	Moves TextRange to given point
pasteHTML	Replaces contents of TextRange with new HTML block
scrollIntoView	Scrolls TextRange into view
select	Selects the TextRange
setEndPoint	Sets end point of TextRange based on another TextRange object's end point

FIGURE 30.6.

Web page with several words replaced by their equivalent, but enclosed within STRONG begin and end tags.

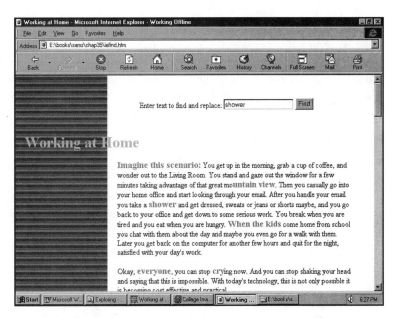

The TextRange object is not the only method to access and replace the text or HTML of an element. Each HTML element has four properties:

■ innerHTML—The HTML block contained within the element's enclosing tags

■ innerText—The text block contained within the element

- outerHTML—The HTML block of the element, including the enclosing tags
- outerText—The element text

Listing 30.6 has an example of using the outerHTML property to replace the element with another HTML block when the element is clicked. These properties can be used to retrieve either the HTML or the element text, and can be used to replace the element text or HTML. Other HTML element properties are discussed in more detail in the next section, which discusses the elements, and specifically, the style object.

The HTML Elements and the Style Object

As discussed earlier in this chapter, Microsoft exposed all the standard HTML elements to their scripting object model. Based on this, you can trap events for an element, as was demonstrated in the section on the basic model objects, when the onclick event is trapped for an image. You can also replace the object, demonstrated in Listing 30.6 in the section on the event object.

There are several methods you can use to access an HTML element. You can access it through the all collection, which contains all the HTML elements in the page. The following code demonstrates this with a paragraph named theelement:

```
document.all.theelement...
document.all.item("theelement")...
document.all.tags("P")...
```

The first technique references the element name or identifier directly, the second technique uses the items function and searches for it by element location index, and the final technique searches for the element by using the tags function and looking for all paragraphs in the page. The techniques can be used together, such as finding all paragraphs in the page, using the tags function, and then accessing a specific one by using the items function:

```
document.all.tags("P").item("theelement")...
```

You can also access the element directly:

```
theelement...
```

To access an element directly by name, you must assign a value to the item's id attribute rather than the item's name attribute.

The style object is used to access or alter the CSS1 attribute of an element. For instance, the code in Listing 30.7 alters the style setting for whatever element is clicked, if the element's background color has been set to red or lime.

Listing 30.7. Altering the CSS1 attributes of elements using the style object.

```
<HTML>
<HEAD><TITLE>Example</TITLE>
<SCRIPT LANGUAGE="JSCRIPT" FOR=document EVENT=onclick>
    var theelement = window.event.srcElement;
    if (theelement.style.backgroundColor == "red") {
        theelement.style.backgroundColor="lime";
```

```
            theelement.style.color="red";
            theelement.style.fontFamily="Cursive";
            theelement.style.marginLeft="0.5in";
            theelement.style.fontVariant="small-caps";
            theelement.style.textTransform="lowercase"
            }
        else if (theelement.style.backgroundColor == "lime") {
            theelement.style.backgroundColor="red";
            theelement.style.color="lime";
            theelement.style.fontFamily="Arial";
            theelement.style.marginLeft="0in";
            theelement.style.fontVariant="normal";
            theelement.style.textTransform="capitalize";
            }
</SCRIPT>
</HEAD>
<BODY>
<H1 id=header1 style="background-color: red; color:lime">
This is the header
</H1>
<P id="para1" style="background-color: lime; color:red">
This is another example in Chapter 30, covering Dynamic HTML. This
chapter reviews CSS1 and covers the scripting object model for
Netscape Navigator and Microsoft Internet Explorer. Additionally,
the chapter provides demonstrations of CSS1 Positioning.
</P>
<OL>
<LI style="background-color: red; color:lime">First list item
<LI style="background-color: red; color:lime">Second list item
<LI> Third Item
</OL>
</BODY>
</HTML>
```

COMPANION Web site Clicking the header, paragraph, or the first two list items generates a change in the style settings, altering the background color, font color, font variant and family, and text transform. Clicking the document body itself, or the third list item does not generate any change in the document. You can try the example yourself by opening the file style.htm.

Any CSS1 attribute can be altered dynamically for any HTML element using the style property/object in IE. The following is a list of the attributes as they are defined within the CSS1 recommendation, and the syntax used to access the attribute directly in order to alter the property dynamically:

background	background
background-color	backgroundColor
background-attachment	backgroundAttachment
background-image	backgroundImage
background-position	backgroundPositionXbackgroundPositionY
background-repeat	backgroundRepeat

30

background	background
border	border
border-bottom	borderBottom
border-bottom-color	borderBottomColor
border-bottom-style	borderBottomStyle
border-bottom-width	borderBottomWidth
border-color	borderColor
border-left	borderLeft
border-left-color	borderLeftColor
border-left-style	borderLeftStyle
border-left-width	borderLeftWidth
border-right	borderRight
border-right-color	borderRightColor
border-right-style	borderRightStyle
border-right-width	borderRightWidth
border-top	borderTop
border-top-color	borderTopColor
border-top-style	borderTopStyle
border-top-width	borderTopWidth
border-width	borderWidth
clear	clear
clip	clip
color	color
float	styleFloat
font	font
font-family	fontFamily
font-style	fontStyle
font-variant	fontVariant
font-weight	fontWeight
height	height
letter-spacing	letterSpacing
line-height	lineHeight
list-style	listStyle
list-style-image	listStyleImage

list-style-position	listStylePosition
list-style-type	listStyleType
margin	margin
margin-bottom	marginBottom
margin-left	marginLeft
margin-right	marginRight
margin-top	marginTop
padding-bottom	paddingBottom
padding-left	paddingLeft
padding-right	paddingRight
padding-top	paddingTop
text-align	textAlign
text-decoration	textDecorationBlink
	textDecorationUnderline
	textDecorationOverline
	textDecorationLineThrough
	textDecorationNone
text-indent	textIndent
text-transform	textTransform
vertical-align	verticalAlign

The style object has additional properties, specifically for CSS1 positioning. However, these are covered in more detail in Chapter 31, "Manipulating Objects and Responding to User Interaction."

The Netscape Scripting Object Model

Netscape also has added new objects, properties, events, and methods to its scripting object model with the release of Navigator 4.0. They have also added a new element, called the LAYER element, delimited by <LAYER></LAYER> tags.

Netscape's Basic Model Objects

The basic scripting objects are the same for Navigator and IE: the window, document, navigator, location, and history objects. Also, there is little or no change to the form or form element object. Any differences are in the properties or methods used with each of these objects, and are covered in detail in the documentation Netscape released with Navigator 4.0.

One real difference are the attributes you can use when opening a new browser window. IE had attributes such as channelmode, fullscreen, width, and height. Netscape has attributes such as alwaysraised and hotkeys. Table 30.6 has the Navigator-specific open window attributes.

30

USING THE HTML
OBJECT MODEL

Table 30.6. Navigator `window` `open` method attributes.

Attribute	*Description*
`alwaysLowered`	Whether window is opened in a minimized state
`alwaysRaised`	Window is opened in a maximized state
`dependent`	Window is created as a dependent window
`hotkeys`	Can disable hotkeys in window
`innerWidth`	Client area width of window
`innerHeight`	Client area height of window
`screenY`	Top position of window
`screenX`	Left position of window
`z-lock`	Locks window into position, and doesn't raise it above others when activated
`titlebar`	Whether window has a titlebar

Netscape also shares the following window attributes with IE: `toolbar`, `menubar`, `scrollbars`, `status`, `resizeable`, `scrollbars`, and `location`.

Several of the attributes only work if the script is digitally signed, such as setting the titlebar to `no` and using the `alwaysRaised` attribute. Using digital signatures is beyond the scope of this chapter and book, but Netscape has documentation and tools for this at its site. Using these attributes outside of a digitally signed scripting block negates their effect.

COMPANION **Web site**   The example located in the file `ieopen.htm` is converted to use the Navigator open attributes and is renamed `nsopen.htm`. The opened file, `menu.htm`, has been adjusted to work with Navigator and renamed it to `nsmenu.htm`. Listing 30.8 contains the contents of `nsopen.htm`.

Listing 30.8. Opening a window using the Navigator `window` `open` method attributes.

```
<HTML>
<HEAD><TITLE>Window Open Example</TITLE>
<STYLE type="text/css">
    BODY { background-color: aqua }
    H1 { position:absolute; left: 20; top:20;
        color: red }
</STYLE>
<SCRIPT language="javascript">
<!--
// open window fullscreen
function open_window() {
    window.open("menu.htm", "Menu", "dependent=yes,scrollbars=yes");
}

//-->
```

```
</SCRIPT>
</HEAD>
<BODY>
<H1><a href="" style="text-decoration:none;color:red"
    onclick="open_window();return false">Click here to open window</a></H1>
</BODY>
</HTML>
```

Figure 30.7 shows the Netscape-specific page, opened with the `dependent` and `scrollbars` attributes set to yes, and all other values set to their defaults.

FIGURE 30.7.
Dependent Web page, with scrollbars, opened in separate Navigator window.

The New Netscape Dynamic HTML Objects

Information about the screen resolution and color depth can be accessed from the new screen object. Also, event information can be found by accessing the new event object. Finally, as stated earlier, Netscape has the LAYER element, an element that has several properties and methods that can be accessed dynamically.

The event Object

Netscape's event object is actually quite similar to Microsoft's. Each browser's event object contains information about the event and the event's receiver. The main differences between the browsers, though, are how the event is accessed and the event object's properties.

IE allows access to its event object from virtually anywhere in the scripting block. Navigator only allows access directly from within an event handler, or passed to an event handler function. This means that you can pass the event as a parameter when using inline event handlers,

30

USING THE HTML
OBJECT MODEL

or access it as a parameter, by default, when an event handler is assigned to an event. The following code block demonstrates passing the event object to a function:

```
Function some_function(e) {
    // do something with event object 'e'
<a href="" onclick="some_function(Event);return false">...
document.onclick=some_function;
```

Not all elements can access all events. A traditional HTML element such as a header or list can receive events only if it is positioned using absolute positioning. Layers can also receive events. Anchors have always been able to receive most events, such as mouseover, mousedown, and mouseup, and click events. Layers and non-anchor-specific traditional HTML events can only receive these events if you use event capturing to trap these events for the object, as the following code demonstrates:

```
document.header1.captureEvents(Event.MOUSEDOWN);
document.header1.onmousedown=eventhandler;
```

When you use event capturing you can specify more than one event at a time:

```
document.header1.captureEvents(Event.MOUSEDOWN ¦ Event.MOUSEUP);
document.header1.onmousedown=mouse_down;
document.header1.onmouseup=mouse_up;
```

A handy technique for trapping a wide variety of events is to enclose the element within an empty anchor tag. An empty anchor tag is one that does not reference an URL or NAME, as shown in the following code:

```
<H1><a href="" onclick="some_function();return false">The Header</a></H1>
```

To remove the anchor link colors and text decoration, assign a style sheet to the anchor tag. You must return a value of false at the end for the clicked event handler, onclick, or the clicked event is processed by the anchor element. As the document references an empty URL, the directory the document is contained in is displayed.

Listing 30.9 contains the Web page contents for a demonstration of the three event-trapping techniques just mentioned. The first technique assigns an event handler to the mouseover event for the header when the page loads; the second technique references the onmouseover event handler inline within the tag; the third technique uses an empty anchor tag to access the onmouseover event handler inline.

Listing 30.9. Trapping the mouseover event using three different techniques for three different elements.

```
<HTML>
<HEAD><TITLE>Example 1</TITLE>
<STYLE type="text/css">
<!--
    BODY { background-color:ivory;
        background-image: url(redbar.jpg);
        background-repeat: repeat-y;
```

```
          margin-left: 220px; margin-right: 50px;
          font-family: Courier }
   H1 { color: firebrick; font-family: Fantasy}
   #astyle { text-decoration:none; color:black }
//-->
</STYLE>
<SCRIPT language="javascript">
<!--
// print out event type and location
function event_type(e) {
    var msg = "The type of event is " + e.type +
    " located at " + e.pageX + " " + e.pageY + " " +
    " at " + e.target.id;
    alert(msg);
    }

// assign header1 mouseover events to handler
function setup() {
    document.header1.onmouseover=event_type;
    }
//-->
</SCRIPT>
</HEAD>

<BODY onload="setup()">
<H1 id=header1 style="position:absolute;left:220;top:0">
➥This is the first example</H1>
<LAYER name=layer1 left=220 top=50
    onmouseover="event_type(event)">
This is the first example in Chapter 30, covering Dynamic HTML. This
chapter reviews CSS1 and covers the scripting object model for
Netscape Navigator and Microsoft Internet Explorer. Additionally,
the chapter also provides demonstrations of CSS1 Positioning.
</LAYER>
<p style="position:absolute;left:220;top:150">
<a href="" id=astyle onclick="return false"
    onmouseover="event.target.id='para1';event_type(event)">
This is a paragraph, surrounded by an anchor reference in order to trap events.
</a></p>
</BODY>
</HTML>
```

COMPANION **Web site** The event_type function accesses several properties from the event object, creates a message from these properties, and prints the message out using an alert message box. Notice the value assigned to the id property of the event target object for the empty anchor technique. It's assigned because the id value is not set when this technique passes the event object, regardless of whether you set the name or the id of either the paragraph element or the anchor element. Figure 30.8 shows the Web page with the mouse over the paragraph element. You can try out the example by opening the file nsevent.htm.

This last example also uses the Layer tags to create a layer object. Layers are a new Netscape-specific element released in version 4.0 of Navigator, and discussed in the next section.

FIGURE 30.8.

Alert message with event object properties with mouseover *paragraph element.*

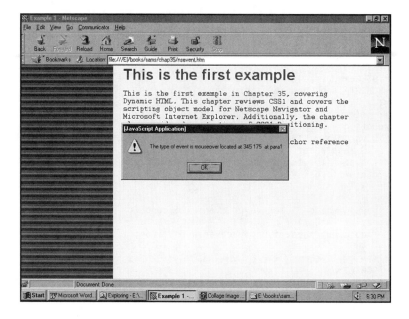

The Layer Object

Netscape created a new element with the release of Navigator 4.0—the Layer element. Layers are container elements, meaning that they can enclose one or more HTML elements, and whatever you do to the layer impacts all the elements the layer contains. The Layer element also has its own attributes, methods, event handlers, and layers array.

THE Layer ELEMENT AND HTML 4.0

Netscape created the Layer element as a means of statically and dynamically positioning HTML elements. However, with the introduction and general acceptance of CSS-P (Cascading Style Sheet Positioning), co-authored by Netscape and Microsoft, even Netscape promotes the use of CSS-P over the layer element. There is functionality associated with the layer element that's not available with CSS-P, which is why I included it in this chapter, for completeness.

To create a Layer element, you use the begin-end <LAYER> tags as you would any other HTML element:

```
<LAYER><P>A paragraph</p><img src="some.gif"></LAYER>
```

There are actually two different types of layers. The one just shown is the positioned layer, and it has attributes that determine where the contents are positioned within the Web page. The inflow layer is delimited with the tags <ILAYER></ILAYER> and does not have positioning attributes. It is used to embed contents into the Web page using the page's natural flow, similar to most HTML elements. I don't use ILAYER because the main reason I use the layer element is to control the exact positioning of an element or elements. To include elements within the natural flow of the document, I don't really need a layer element at all.

The LAYER attributes are listed in Table 30.7.

Table 30.7. LAYER attributes or properties.

Attribute	Description
name	Layer's name
left	Layer's name
	Layer's leftmost position
top	Layer's name
	Layer's topmost position
pageX	Layer's name
	Layer's horizontal position relative to the Web page
pageY	Layer's name
	Layer's vertical position relative to the Web page
zIndex	Layer's name
	Layer's z-order position
visibility	Layer's name
	Whether layer is visible
clip.top	Top clipping position
clip.left	Left clipping position
clip.right	Right clipping position
clip.bottom	Bottom clipping position
clip.width	Clipping width
clip.height	Clipping height
background	Layer's name
	Background image for layer
bgColor	Layer's name
	Background color for layer
siblingAbove	Layer's name
	For layers that share a common parent element (such as the document), the layer above the current layer, if any

continues

30

USING THE HTML
OBJECT MODEL

Table 30.7. continued

Attribute	Description
siblingBelow	For layers that share a common parent element (such as the document), the layer below the current layer, if any
above	Layer above current layer regardless of containing element, or window if current layer is top layer
below	Layer below current layer regardless of containing element, or document is current layer is lowest in stack
parentLayer	Layer containing current layer, if any, or window if none
src	HTML source file used for layer

COMPANION
Web site To demonstrate how to use some of these properties, I created a fun little clipping and hiding layer demo page. Listing 30.10 contains the Web page contents, and you can also access the page directly by opening layer.htm. The page contains several layers, some with text, one with an image, and one using the src attribute to load in the file css1smpl.htm.

Listing 30.10. Showing the `clipping` and `hiding` properties of the LAYER object.

```
<HTML>
<HEAD><TITLE>Example</TITLE>
<STYLE type="text/javascript">
    ids.layer1.fontSize="48pt";
    ids.layer1.backgroundColor="blue";
    ids.layer1.color="yellow";
    ids.layer2.color="red";
    ids.layer2.fontSize="16pt";
</STYLE>
<SCRIPT language="javascript1.2">

layer3_width = 0;
layer3_height = 0;
layer4_width = 0;
layer4_height = 0;

// start element hiding
function hide_elements() {
    layer3_width = document.layer3.clip.width / 10;
    layer3_height = document.layer3.clip.height / 20;
    layer4_width = document.layer4.clip.width / 20;
    layer4_height = document.layer4.clip.height / 20;
    document.layer2.visibility="hidden";
    setTimeout("hide_layer3()",200);
    setTimeout("hide_layer4()",300);
}

// clip layer 3
function hide_layer3() {
    document.layer3.clip.width-=layer3_width;
    document.layer3.clip.height-=layer3_height;
```

```
        if (document.layer3.clip.width > 0)
            setTimeout("hide_layer3()",200);
}

// clip layer 4
function hide_layer4() {
    document.layer4.clip.width-=layer3_width;
    document.layer4.clip.height-=layer3_height;
    if (document.layer4.clip.width > 0)
        setTimeout("hide_layer4()",300);
    else
        setTimeout("hide_layer1()", 1000);
}

// hide layer 1
function hide_layer1() {
    document.layer1.visibility="hidden";
}
</SCRIPT>
</HEAD>
<BODY>

<layer name=layer3 left=20 top=10 zIndex=2>
<img src="image1.jpg" width=301 height=400>
</layer>

<layer left=25% top=15% id=layer2 width=200 height=250 zIndex=1>
Bye
</layer>
<layer name=layer1 id=layer1 left=25% top=15% width=200 height=250 zIndex=3>
Move
</layer>

<layer name=layer2 id=layer2 left=35% top=20% width=40 height=30 zIndex=4
    onmouseover="hide_elements()">
here
</layer>
<layer name=layer4 left=370 zIndex=1 top=10 clip.width=220
    clip.right=600 clip.bottom=400 src="css1smpl.htm">
</layer>

</BODY>
</HTML>
```

Several of the layers are actually layered on top of each other, as shown in Figure 30.9 when the page is first loaded.

Moving the mouse over the "here" text begins the process of hiding or clipping the layers.

When the element hiding process begins, the layer named "layer2" is hidden, and two separate timers are created to be clipping layers "layer3" and "layer4". Different time increments are used to stagger the clipping times. Clipping occurs by decrementing each layer's width and height each time the timer fires, until the width of the layer is 0. For the layer named "layer4", that is a signal to set the final timer, which then hides the layer named "layer1". At the end, only the small little layer with the word "bye" is showing. Figure 30.10 shows the page when it's about halfway through the hiding process.

FIGURE 30.9.

Layers example after Web page is first loaded.

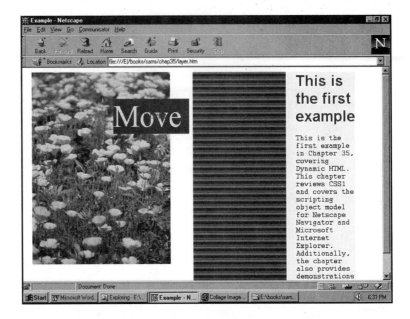

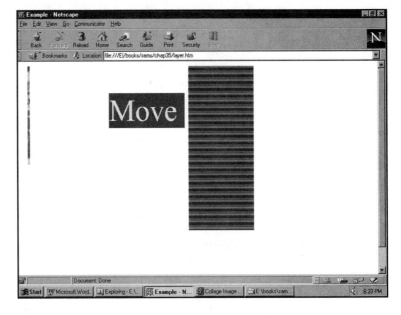

The clipping is performed by setting the clip properties directly. However, you could also use the `resizeBy` layer method, which is equivalent to setting the clip width and height properties. Converting the clipping for `layer3` to use this method is in the following code:

```
document.layer3.resizeBy(layer3_width, layer3_height);
```

Table 30.8 contains the `layer` methods.

Table 30.8. The Layer methods.

Method	Description
moveBy	Moves layer a given distance
moveTo	Moves layer to absolute position relative to container
moveToAbsolute	Moves layer to absolute position regardless of container
resizeBy	Resizes layer by a given amount
resizeTo	Resizes layer to given dimensions
moveAbove	Moves target layer above higher layer in stack, if any
moveBelow	Moves target layer below lower layer in stack, if any
load	Loads source file

Note that any block-level element, such as a `DIV` block or a header, can also use the same properties and methods of the layer element, if the HTML element is positioned using absolute positioning. Chapter 31, "Manipulating Objects and Responding to User Interaction," goes into more detail about CSS1 positioning and applying these techniques to general HTML elements.

Creating Cross-Browser Dynamic HTML Pages

Except for the CSS1 demonstration, the examples in this chapter have been explicitly created for Navigator or IE—not both. However, you can apply DHTML techniques to a cross-browser Web page, you just have to be aware of some of the issues of cross-browser compatibility.

Cross-Browser Issues

Microsoft and Netscape both support the HTML, CSS1, and CSS1 positioning standards as they are defined by the W3C, and they support the scripting language standard known as ECMAScript (from the European standards organization, ECMA). Regardless of this, there will always be differences in how each browser implements these standards.

As an example, the ECMAScripting standard defines a compliant browser as one that implements the minimum data types and functions defined within the standard. However, the standard also goes on to say that a compliant browser can also extend the language to include any new objects, properties, and functions not listed in the standard. This leaves open a pretty wide door for incompatibilities.

Also, browsers can conform to either the level 1 CSS1 standard, or to just the core CSS1 specification. For instance, IE does not support the `white-space` attribute, which prevents the collapse of whitespace, and Navigator does, but the attribute is not part of the core standard and doesn't have to be supported. Both browsers are in compliance, but a Web page's presentation can differ between the two.

Both browsers support HTML 3.2 and will most likely support HTML 4.0 when it is released. However, how the browsers implement many of the elements is independent of the standard itself. As an example, a BLOCKQUOTE element can be surrounded by quotation marks, indented, or both, and the individual browser is still in compliance, regardless of which implementation approach they use.

The biggest issue of all for cross-browser compatibility is the scripting object model, or Document Object Model (DOM), as it is referred to by the W3C. At this time, effort is underway to create a DOM standard. At issue are differences such as Microsoft exposing the CSS1 attributes for dynamic change through the style object, and Navigator only exposing these same attributes through change via JASS, and only when the page loads. It is doubtful that the W3C will ever solve all cross-browser differences—other standards have not ensured compatibility within the scope of the standard, and there's no reason the DOM standard will be any different.

Cross-Browser Compatibility Workarounds

You can create cross-browser pages, however, with a few tweaks and tricks.

First of all, you can use nonstandard HTML elements, such as the LAYER tag, and non-Navigator browsers, such as IE, should ignore it. Better yet, both Navigator and IE support the DIV block, and both support static CSS1 Positioning with these types of elements. Based on that, you will probably use DIV blocks instead of LAYER elements.

IE has a wider range of events for HTML elements than Navigator has, but using the empty anchor reference discussed earlier in the chapter can equalize the two browsers. Additionally, event capturing and trapping, though different, can also be accomplished in separate code blocks, or within the same code block as long as you conditionally check for the type of browser. The following is an example of how this can work:

```
if (navigator.appName == "Microsoft Internet Explorer") {
    ...
    }
else {
    ...
    }
```

Both browsers support the majority of CSS1 attributes, making this a more appropriate choice than JASS for Navigator. However, JASS and IE's dynamic alteration of CSS1 attributes can work together in an application that tests the screen resolution and color depth and alters the document accordingly.

As an example of this, an earlier example in the section covering JASS, "Web Page Presentation Using CSS1 and JASS," demonstrates altering a Web page based on screen resolution and color depth. Microsoft and Netscape both support the screen object, so I use this object in the final example for this chapter, which uses JASS and the screen object to adjust the Web page for Navigator, and the style and screen objects and dynamic CSS1 attribute alteration with IE. Listing 30.11 contains the Web page contents, including the JASS section for Navigator and the scripting block for IE.

Listing 30.11. A cross-browser compatible page that adjusts to fit the Web page reader's monitor resolution and color depth settings.

```
<!-- screen.htm
//
// author: shelley powers
//
// demonstration of cross-browser page
// and screen object
//
// copyright: shelley powers and SAMS publishing, 1997
//
-->
<HTML>
<HEAD><TITLE>Example</TITLE>
<STYLE type="text/javascript">
    if (screen.width >= 800) {
        tags.H1.fontSize="48pt";
        tags.P.fontSize="12pt";
        }
    else {
        tags.H1.fontSize="24pt";
        tags.P.fontSize="10pt";
        }

    if (screen.colorDepth <= 8) {
        tags.H1.color="red";
        tags.P.color="black";
        tags.BODY.backgroundColor="white";
        }
    else {
        tags.H1.color="firebrick";
        tags.P.color="forestgreen";
        tags.BODY.backgroundColor="ivory";
        }
</STYLE>
<SCRIPT language="jscript" FOR=window EVENT=onload>
<!--
    var h1size="";
    var psize="";
    var h1color="";
    var pcolor="";
    if (screen.width >= 800) {
        h1size="48pt";
        psize="12pt";
        }
    else {
        h1size="24pt";
        psize="10pt";
```

continues

Listing 30.11. continued

```
        }

    if (screen.colorDepth <= 8) {
        h1color="red";
        pcolor="black";
        document.body.style.backgroundColor="white";
        }
    else {
        h1color="firebrick";
        pcolor="forestgreen";
        document.body.style.backgroundColor="ivory";
        }
    var theheaders = document.all.tags("H1");
    var theparagraphs = document.all.tags("P");
    for (i = 0; i < theheaders.length; i++){
        theheaders[i].style.color=h1color;
        theheaders[i].style.fontSize=h1size;
        }
    for (i = 0; i < theparagraphs.length; i++) {
        theparagraphs[i].style.color=pcolor;
        theparagraphs[i].style.fontSize=psize;
        }
//-->
</SCRIPT>
</HEAD>
<BODY>
<H1>
This is the header
</H1>
<P>
This is another example in Chapter 30, covering Dynamic HTML. This
chapter reviews CSS1 and covers the scripting object model for
Netscape Navigator and Microsoft Internet Explorer. Additionally,
the chapter also provides demonstrations of CSS1 Positioning.
</P>
</BODY>
</HTML>
```

COMPANION Website The Navigator JASS block adjusts the color and font size for all the given elements, and the IE scripting block section creates a collection of elements based on tag type and then adjusts each member, one at a time. IE ignores the JASS section because IE doesn't process style blocks with `"text/javascript"` type. Navigator ignores the scripting block because it doesn't recognize blocks with the `"jscript"` language type. You can try the example yourself with either browser and at whatever resolution and color depth by accessing the file `screen.htm`.

Summary

This chapter provides demonstrations and discussions on JavaScript Accessible Style Sheets and Cascading Style Sheets. Additionally, it overviews the Microsoft scripting object model, and including the new `style` object, the new event model, and the exposure of all HTML elements to CSS1 attribute modification, in addition to demonstrating some of the changes to the win-dow open method.

The chapter also overviews the Netscape scripting object model, including the new window open method attributes, the new event model, and the Layer element.

Some of the cross-browser compatibility issues are discussed, and a cross-browser Web page is created using the new screen object from both the Netscape and Microsoft scripting object models.

Chapter 31, "Manipulating Objects and Responding to User Interaction," continues with the demonstration of DHTML techniques by providing a more detailed look at CSS1 positioning and Web page interaction. Chapter 32, "Saving User Preferences: Cookies and OPS," covers storing and retrieving the Web page reader's DHTML preferences.

The preceding chapter introduces the concept of Dynamic HTML and reviews the major components. This chapter follows by providing a more detailed look at three aspects of Dynamic HTML: Dynamic Positioning, event handling, and user interaction.

CSS1 Positioning is based on a draft recommendation co-created by Netscape and Microsoft and covering the static positioning of elements within a Web page. Both companies have also extended their scripting object models to expose the CSS1 Positioning attributes to scripting languages. Among the attributes are those that can hide or display an HTML element, move elements dynamically after the page is loaded, layer elements, and move the individual elements through the layers. The attributes can also be used to clip the element's height or width.

The chapter also discusses Microsoft's and Netscape's event models and then uses this information to demonstrate techniques to capture the Web page reader's actions and respond interactively.

Dynamic Positioning—Browser Differences

Chapter 8, "Advanced Layout and Positioning with Style Sheets" provides a detailed explanation of CSS Positioning, which covers static positioning of elements. The rest of this chapter provides some demonstrations of dynamic positioning for IE and Navigator. First, however, you should be aware of how each browser implements its dynamic positioning, and this is briefly covered in this section.

First, IE provides dynamic support for positioning via the `style` object. As an example, the following code moves an element's top-left corner to a coordinate of 100,100:

```
document.all.some_item.style.posLeft = 100;
document.all.some_item.style.posTop = 100;
```

Microsoft supports several properties for positioning, as listed in Table 31.1.

Table 31.1. Microsoft positioning properties.

Property	Description
clip	Clipping region of element
height	String containing element height, including units
left	String containing left position of element, including units
overflow	How to handle element overflow
pixelHeight	Height of element in pixels
pixelLeft	Left position in pixels
pixelWidth	Width of element in pixels
posHeight	Height of element as an integer

Property	Description
posLeft	Left position as an integer
position	Whether element is positioned relatively or absolutely
posWidth	Width of an element as an integer
styleFloat	Whether text flows around element
top	String containing top position of element and units
visibility	Whether element is visible
width	Width of element including units
zIndex	Number representing z-order for element

All of the CSS1 positioning properties for IE are simple values—except for the strings for the position, width and height of the element (which also includes size units), and the clip property that includes the clipping shape as well as the dimensions. As an example of using the clip property, the following code clips the image horizontally:

```
var wdth = document.all.the_element.style.pixelWidth;
var rectstrng = "rect(auto," + wdth-10 + ",auto," + 10 + ",auto)";
document.all.the_element.style.clip=rectstrng;
```

All the dimensions for the clipping area need to be specified, but you can use auto to maintain the existing value for those values that are unchanging.

Navigator supports CSS Positioning properties directly from the element. In addition, it supports a simplified set of CSS Positioning properties, as well as splitting the clipping properties into separate values. Table 31.2 contains the Navigator dynamic CSS1 Positioning properties.

Table 31.2. Navigator dynamic CSS1 Positioning properties.

Property	Description
clip	Clipping region of element
height	Height of element
left	Left position of element
overflow	How to handle element overflow
top	Top position of element
visibility	Whether element is visible
width	Width of element
zIndex	Z-order of element

Unlike IE, Navigator accesses each clipping property individually, as the following code demonstrates:

```
incr = 20;
document.div1.clip.left+=incr;
document.div1.clip.right-=incr;
```

The sections later in this chapter that demonstrate creating a sliding menu, "Adding a Slide-In Menu or Tip," and "Clipping an Image," use these IE and Navigator CSS Positioning properties.

The Microsoft Event Model

Chapter 30, "Using the HTML Object Model and Creating Dynamic HTML Pages," discussed the Microsoft event object and its properties. The object can be accessed anywhere in code, and contains information about the last event received by the Web page.

Event Trapping and Assigning Event Handlers

Microsoft supports several different techniques for binding an event, such as the onclick event handler, which can be used to bind the click event to a function or some other code. The oldest technique, and the one most commonly used, is capturing an event by assigning an event handler to an event inline within the tag of the element. As an example, the following code assigns the onclick event to a function called process_click with a header:

```
<H1 onclick="process_click()">The Header</H1>
```

As you can see from this last line of code, Microsoft also supports events for the majority of HTML elements.

Another technique for trapping events and processing them is to use the FOR= and EVENT= attributes that Microsoft supports for a script block. Using these two attributes means that the event, specified in the event attribute, is captured for the specific element or element type, specified in the for attribute. This technique is demonstrated in the following code:

```
<SCRIPT language="jscript" FOR=some_object EVENT="onclick">
...
</SCRIPT>
```

Another event-handling technique is only available with VBScript. With this technique, the event-handling procedure is named with the syntax object_onevent, where object is the event's target and onevent is the event. This technique is demonstrated next:

```
<SCRIPT language="vbscript">

Sub header1_onclick
   ...
End Sub
</SCRIPT>
```

A final event-handling technique is to assign the event handler function pointer directly to the event for the object. This technique does require that the script block be located after the element is created, or that the event handler assignment occurs within a function that is called after the Web page is loaded. The following code shows an event handler assignment from a function called after the page is loaded:

```
<SCRIPT language="javascript">

function post_load() {
    document.all.the_header1 = header1_event;
}
...
<BODY onload="post_load()">
```

With all of these techniques, parameters can be passed to the function by enclosing the function within parentheses. Also, VBScript does not work with function pointers and the function needs to be enclosed within parentheses regardless of whether there are parameters or not. Applying this to the last code block, I re-create the header1_event function and pass to it three parameters:

```
<SCRIPT language="javascript">

function post_load() {
    document.all.the_header1 = "header1_event(param1,param2,param3)";
}
...
<BODY onload="post_load()">
```

To demonstrate these event-handling techniques, a simple example traps the onmouseover events for several different elements and uses the different techniques. All the event handlers perform the same action, which is to output information about which element received the event. You can see the code for this example in Listing 31.1, and try it by accessing the file ieevent.htm.

Listing 31.1. Exploring different techniques for handling events.

```
<HTML>
<HEAD><TITLE>Event Sampler</TITLE>
<SCRIPT language="jscript" FOR=header1 EVENT=onmouseover>
<!--
    document.all.results.innerHTML=
      "<STRONG> Over " + window.event.srcElement.tagName + "</STRONG>";
//-->
</SCRIPT>

<SCRIPT language="vbscript">
<!--
Sub para1_onmouseover
    document.all.results.innerHTML= _
      "<STRONG> Over " + window.event.srcElement.tagName + "</STRONG>"
```

continues

Listing 31.1. continued

```
End Sub
'-->
</SCRIPT>

</HEAD>
<BODY>
<H1 id=header1>Move your mouse over this header</H1>
<P id=para1>Paragraphs are also capable of generating events that
can be trapped within code and used to respond to the reader
</p>
<H3 id=header3> You can assign event handlers to events by:</H3>
<UL id=list1 onmouseover="over_element()">
<LI> Embedded an event handler directly into the element
<LI> Trapping the event using the script block attributes
<LI> Using the VBScript syntax of "object_event"
<LI> Assign an event handler directly to the objects event
</UL>
<SCRIPT language="jscript">
<!--
function over_element() {
   document.all.results.innerHTML=
     "<STRONG> Over " + window.event.srcElement.tagName + "</STRONG>";
     }
document.all.header3.onmouseover=over_element;
//-->
</SCRIPT>

<DIV id=results>
</DIV>
</BODY>
</HTML>
```

Event Bubbling

There is actually a hierarchy of events that can occur from one action. As an example, if the Web page reader clicks a Web page, the document receives the onclick event. However, if the person clicks a header within the document, both the header and the document receive the event. If more elements are layered, each element in the stack receives the event.

To prevent an event from moving up, or bubbling up, the element hierarchy, you can assign a value of true to the event's bubbleCancel property.

As an example, if a STRONG tag is used within a paragraph and the paragraph is enclosed within a DIV block, clicking the STRONG contents triggers the onclick event for the STRONG tag, the paragraph, the DIV block, and the page document, in that order. The elements receive the events from the inside out:

■ The STRONG tag receives the clicked event.

■ The paragraph receives the clicked event.

■ The DIV block receives the clicked event.

■ The document body receives the clicked event.

Though all of these elements may receive the event, you may be coding an event handler for just one, such as the DIV block or the paragraph. However, if you trap the clicked event for several of the items, such as the paragraph and the document body, and you only want the document body to receive events that are not triggered from the paragraph, you need to set the bubbleCancel property. Setting this property to true from the event handler for the paragraph clicked event prevents the event from being passed to the document body element.

COMPANION Web site In addition to using the bubbleCancel property, you can also cancel an event action, or alter it in some way by returning a specific value from the event, or setting the returnValue property. Be aware that this does not prevent the event from bubbling up the element hierarchy. As an example, if you have an anchor element enclosed within the STRONG tag, and it is then enclosed with the paragraph, the DIV block, and the document body, clicking the anchor fires the clicked event. In addition, IE also attempts to load the URL specified in the anchor tag as part of the clicked action. If you return a value of false from the event handler for the anchor clicked event, the browser does not attempt to load the URL. This won't stop the event from continuing to bubble up the element hierarchy, and being passed, in turn, to the STRONG element, the paragraph, the DIV block, and finally the document body. An example of this can be found in the file iebubble.htm, and is also shown in Listing 31.2.

Listing 31.2. Providing event handler for `clicked` event for nested elements.

```
<HTML>
<HEAD><TITLE>Event Hierarchy</TITLE>
<SCRIPT language="jscript">
<!--
function clicked(elem) {
   alert("You originally clicked " +
   window.event.srcElement.tagName + " and this is " + elem);
   window.event.returnValue = false;
}
//-->
</SCRIPT>
</HEAD>
<BODY onclick="clicked(this.tagName)">
<DIV id=div1 onclick="clicked(this.tagName)">
<p id=para1 onclick="clicked(this.tagName)">
This is the paragraph that contains the
➡<strong onclick="clicked(this.tagName)">
<a href="" onclick="clicked(this.tagName)">
anchor reference</a></strong> that actually contains no URL.
</p>
</DIV>
</BODY>
</HTML>
```

Clicking the anchor element generates a clicked event, resulting in the onClick event handler being invoked and the function assigned to the event handler being called. From this function, a message is output that the function was called from a clicked event to the strong element, the paragraph, the DIV block, and, finally, the document body. What won't happen is an attempt by the browser to load the empty URL.

The Netscape Event Model

Chapter 30 also describes the Netscape event object and its properties. Unlike the Microsoft event object, the Netscape event object can only be accessed from within the event handler call, or by assigning an event handler function pointer to an event.

Event Trapping and Assigning Event Handlers

Netscape has exposed most HTML elements to events, except that for the majority of HTML elements, they only support a limited number of events. Events such as the mousedown or clicked events only apply to elements, such as a hypertext link or input elements, such as the buttons. However, the mouseout and mouseover events work for most elements. You need to specifically assign an event handler to an element event for most elements. Only elements such as links, layers, and input elements actually have event attributes you can trap inline. If you haven't had a chance to work with layers yet, you can read about them in Chapter 30.

To trap an event inline, you use the following code:

```
<a href="" onclick="some_function();return false">the link</a>
```

Clicking the link calls the function some_function. Returning false from the event handler stops the browser from trying to load the empty document URL.

You can capture events for a specific element, and then all events of that type for the page are directed to the event handler from that time. With this technique, you can trap an event such as the mousedown event for an element such as a header, as demonstrated in the following code:

```
document.header1.captureEvents(Event.MOUSEDOWN);
document.header1.onmousedown=mouse_down;
```

This code also demonstrates assigning an event handler directly to an object's event.

As an example, the code in Listing 31.3 traps all the mousedown events for the page and assigns them to the specific event handler. In addition, the mouseover event is trapped and assigned to an event handler for the layer object layer1, and an inline event handler is created for the mouseover event for the list element.

Listing 31.3. Capturing and handling events using three different techniques.

```
<HTML>
<HEAD><TITLE> NS Event Sampler</TITLE>
<SCRIPT language="javascript1.2">
<!--
//page clicked event handler
function clicked(e) {
    alert("clicked page");
    document.header1.handleEvent(e);
}

// header clicked event handler
function clicked_header(e) {
```

```
      alert("header received click too");
      document.releaseEvents(Event.MOUSEDOWN);
}

// moved mouse over list
function mouse_move(e) {
      alert("moved mouse at " + e.x + " " + e.y);
}

//setup event capturing
function setup() {
      document.captureEvents(Event.MOUSEDOWN);
      document.header1.onmousedown=clicked_header;
      document.onmousedown=clicked;
      document.list1.onmouseover=mouse_move;
}
//-->
</SCRIPT>

</HEAD>
<BODY onload="setup()">
<H1 id=header1 style="position:absolute; left:20; top:20">
This is a header</H1>
<layer name=layer1 left=20 top=50
      onmouseover="alert('over layer')" onmouseout="alert('leave layer')">
Layers are also capable of generating events that
can be trapped within code and used to respond to the reader
</layer>
<H3 id=header3 style="position:absolute; left:20; top:100">
You can assign event handlers to events by:</H3>
<UL id=list1 style="position:absolute;left:20;top:150">
<LI> Embedded an event handler directly into the element
<LI> Capturing the events for the page and assigning to the element
<LI> Assign an event handler directly to the objects event
</UL>
</BODY>
</HTML>
```

When the mousedown event occurs within the document page, it uses the event handleEvent method to route the event to the header event handler. This method and others that have to do with routing and canceling an event are discussed in the next section.

Event Routing and Canceling

The window, document, and layer objects have methods to determine what to do with an event or events. These methods are:

- captureEvents—Captures one or more events and routes to object
- releaseEvents —Releases the capture of the specific event or events
- routeEvent —Routes event further along the hierarchy to other elements that may have the same event handlers
- handleEvent —Passes the object's event to process, bypassing the normal event hierarchy

Within an event handler, returning a value of `true` results in the browser handling the event but not passing the event up the element hierarchy. Returning a value of `false` from an event handler prevents the event from being handled.

As said earlier, the `clicked` event is only available for certain input elements, such as a button and hypertext link. It can be handy at times to trap this for other elements; a workaround is to enclose the element within an `anchor` element, and set the URL to an empty string. The following code uses this approach with a header:

```
<H1><a href="" style="text-decoration:none; color:black"
    onclick="some_function();return false">The header </a></H1>
```

Notice from the code that the clicked event handler returns `false` at the end. If it didn't, the browser would attempt to process the clicked event and load an empty document. This, in turn, would display the subdirectory within which the original document is contained. The hypertext link's style is set to remove the normal link underline, and to change the color to match other headers within the document. If it weren't, the text would show the link's text decoration (underline) and color.

Adding a Slide-In Menu or Tip

In this chapter, you have had a chance to explore dynamic positioning, and see how Microsoft and Netscape trap and handle events. This section starts combining these techniques to create dynamic effects in response to the Web page reader's actions.

COMPANION Web site The first effect is also probably one of the more common uses of Dynamic HTML, which is to create a sliding menu and hidden tips that display if the reader clicks a button or label, or moves the mouse over an element. These effects use event trapping and element movement and display. You can try the example page by opening the file `sliding.htm` on the Companion Web Site.

The page has a menu area that is positioned to the left of the Web page. When the Web page reader clicks a displayed image, or types in the letter "m" or "M," the menu slides to the right, covering the page. The menu contains four buttons representing four separate submenus, but for this example, clicking the buttons does not bring up any other element or Web page. When the mouse is over each of the button images, a tip describing the menu option is displayed under the menu button. As an alternative to using the mouse, the Web page reader can also type the letter of the menu option, displaying the tip. Typing the letter again causes the tip to hide. The reader can type "m" or "M" again, or click the menu opener image, to close the menu.

The first section of the page is the CSS1 style sheet, which defines the positions and appearance for several of the elements, and is shown in the following code:

```
<STYLE type="text/css">
    #menu1 { position:absolute; left: 10; top: 10 }
    #menu2 { position:absolute; left: 200; top: 10 }
    #menu3 { position:absolute; left: 10; top:  200}
```

```
       #menu4 { position:absolute; left: 200; top: 200 }
       #tip1 { position:absolute; left: 10; top: 100;
           width: 100; height: 40; visibility:hidden }
       #tip2 { position:absolute; left: 200; top: 100;
           width: 100; height: 40; visibility:hidden }
       #tip3 { position:absolute; left: 10; top: 300;
           width: 100; height: 40; visibility:hidden }
       #tip4 { position:absolute; left: 200; top: 300;
           width: 100; height: 40; visibility:hidden }
       A { text-decoration: none }
       H3 { color:yellow }
       #div1 { position:absolute; z-index: 5; left:-400;
           top:0; width:400; height:400; background-color:red }
</STYLE>
```

The scripting code sections for the document follow the style sheet, but are listed after all the elements have been placed in the page. DIV blocks enclose the images because Navigator does not support positioning for images; a layer provides the menu background because Navigator does not entirely fill a DIV element, the way it will a layer element. Listing 31.4 contains the Web page element contents.

Listing 31.4. Web page contents for sliding menu example.

```
<BODY>
<LAYER name=layer1 left=-400 top=0 width=400 height=400
    bgColor="red">
</LAYER>

<DIV id=div1>
<DIV id=menu1>
<a href="" onclick="return false" onmouseover="show_tip('tip1')"
    onmouseout="hide_tip('tip1')">
<img src="buttona.jpg" border=0 width=133 height=86></a>
</DIV>
<DIV id=tip1>
<H3>This is the tip for menu A</H3>
</DIV>
<DIV id=menu2>
<a href="" onclick="return false" onmouseover="show_tip('tip2')"
    onmouseout="hide_tip('tip2')">
<img src="buttonb.jpg" border=0 width=133 height=86></a>
</DIV>
<DIV id=tip2>
<H3>This is the tip for menu B</H3>
</DIV>
<DIV id=menu3>
<a href="" onclick="return false" onmouseover="show_tip('tip3')"
    onmouseout="hide_tip('tip3')">
<img src="buttonc.jpg" border=0 width=133 height=86></a>
</DIV>
<DIV id=tip3>
<H3>This is the tip for menu C</H3>
</DIV>

<DIV id=menu4>
```

continues

Listing 31.4. continued

```
<a href="" onclick="return false" onmouseover="show_tip('tip4')"
    onmouseout="hide_tip('tip4')">
<img src="buttond.jpg" border=0 width=133 height=86></a>
</DIV>
<DIV id=tip4>
<H3>This is the tip for menu D</H3>
</DIV>
</DIV>
<DIV id=div2 style="position:absolute; left:0; top:0">
<a href="" onclick="start_menu();return false">
<img src="image4.jpg" border=0></a>
</DIV>

</BODY>
```

Notice from the example code that empty or stub anchors trap the mouse events for the page. The keypress events for the page are trapped within the code.

The scripting blocks are the last component for the example, and they are included in Listing 31.5. The code checks the navigator object to determine how to process the movement, because IE uses the style object and Navigator does not. Also, both browsers use different processes to trap events and the browser-specific event objects themselves have different properties.

Listing 31.5. Code for the CSS1 Positioning example.

```
<SCRIPT language="javascript">
<!--
counter = 0;
incr = 0;

// setup increment size
function start_menu() {
    if (incr == 0)
      incr = 20;
    else if (incr == 20)
      incr = -20;
    else
      incr = 20;
    move_menu();
}

// move menu by increment
function move_menu() {
    if (navigator.appName == "Microsoft Internet Explorer") {
      document.all.div2.style.posLeft+=incr;
      document.all.div1.style.posLeft+=incr;
      }
    else {
      document.div2.left+=incr;
      document.layer1.left+=incr;
      document.div1.left+=incr;
```

```
      }
    counter++;
    if (counter < 20)
     setTimeout("move_menu()", 200);
    else
     counter = 0;
}

function show_tip(tip_name) {
    if (navigator.appName == "Microsoft Internet Explorer")
     document.all.item(tip_name).style.visibility="inherit";
    else
     document.div1.document.layers[tip_name].visibility="inherit";
}

function hide_tip(tip_name) {
   if (navigator.appName == "Microsoft Internet Explorer") {
     document.all.item(tip_name).style.visibility="hidden";
     }
   else
       document.div1.document.layers[tip_name].visibility="hidden";
}
//-->
</SCRIPT>

<SCRIPT language="javascript1.2">
<!--
function keypress(e) {
    if (e.which == 77 || e.which == 109)
       start_menu();
    else {
     tip_name = "";
     if (e.which == 65 || e.which == 97)
        tip_name = 'tip1';
     else if (e.which == 66 || e.which == 98)
        tip_name = 'tip2';
     else if (e.which == 67 || e.which == 99)
        tip_name = 'tip3';
     else if (e.which == 68 || e.which == 100)
        tip_name = 'tip4';
     if (tip_name != "") {
        document.div1.document.layers[tip_name].visibility =
        document.div1.document.layers[tip_name].visibility ==
           "hide" ? "inherit" : "hide";
       }
    }
}

if (navigator.appName != "Microsoft Internet Explorer") {
    document.captureEvents(Event.KEYPRESS);
    document.onkeypress = keypress;
    }
//-->
</SCRIPT>

<SCRIPT FOR=document EVENT=onkeypress language="jscript">
if (event.keyCode == 77 || event.keyCode == 109)
```

continues

Listing 31.5. continued

```
    start_menu();
else {
    tip_name = "";
    if (event.keyCode == 65 ¦¦ event.keyCode == 97)
        tip_name = 'tip1';
    else if (event.keyCode == 66 ¦¦ event.keyCode == 98)
        tip_name = 'tip2';
    else if (event.keyCode == 67 ¦¦ event.keyCode == 99)
        tip_name = 'tip3';
    else if (event.keyCode == 68 ¦¦ event.keyCode == 100)
        tip_name = 'tip4';
    if (tip_name != "" )
        document.all.item(tip_name).style.visibility =
        document.all.item(tip_name).style.visibility == "hidden" ? "inherit" :
"hidden";
    }

</SCRIPT>
```

Walking through the code from the top, the first function, start_menu, tests to see if the menu should be slid out into the page, or returned to the side. It then calls move_menu to perform the movement, testing for browser type first, and using the browser-specific technique to move the menu objects.

The next two functions are the show_tip function, called when the mouse is over the menu item image, and the hide_tip function, called when the mouse leaves the image area.

The next script block is Navigator-specific code, which traps the keypress event for the page and determines which action to take based on which key is pressed. The scripting block that performs the same action for IE follows. For both of these blocks, the key code that is checked is the ASCII value of the pressed key.

Figure 31.1 shows the Web page when the menu is not displayed. All that is visible is a small image, discretely located in the upper-left corner of the Web page.

Figure 31.2 shows the Web page when the menu is fully displayed. Also, the page shows the appearance of the tip for the first menu item.

COMPANION
Web site
Again, this example can be found in sliding.htm, and demonstrates trapping Web page readers' actions and displaying content using CSS1 Positioning techniques. The example also demonstrates adding alternative keyboard-based event handling to supplement the mouse events. Supporting keyboard events is important for accessibility for voice-based browsers, and for Web pages accessed via hand-held pocket computers.

Only one technique is not demonstrated in this section, and that's clipping, which is covered in the following section.

FIGURE 31.1.
Web page with menu hidden and only menu pull image displayed.

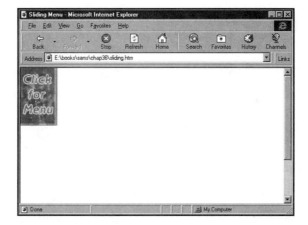

FIGURE 31.2.
Wed page with menu fully displayed, and tip for first menu item displayed.

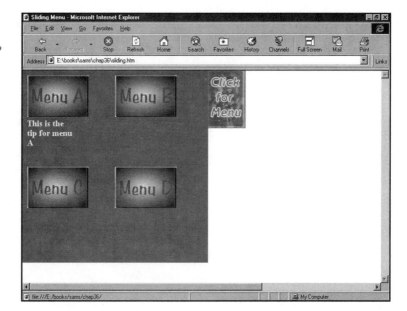

Clipping an Image

Every element within a Web page has a rectangular, usually non-visual area surrounding it called the *clipping region*. This region is normally large enough to support the element contents. However, the clipping region can be resized smaller or larger than the element's contents. When the clipping region is smaller than the element's contents, they are clipped and hidden from view.

COMPANION
Web site A simple clipping example has been created by shrinking the clipping region for the image and resizing it to fit the image's original size, based on the Web page reader clicking the image. You can try the example yourself by opening the file `clip.htm`.

IE and Navigator support different techniques for clipping, so the code needs to be kept separate. Listing 31.6 contains the complete Web page contents.

Listing 31.6. Using CSS1 Positioning to clip image based on browser.

```
<HTML>
<HEAD>
<TITLE> Clipping Example</TITLE>
<STYLE type="text/css">
    BODY { background-color: white }
</STYLE>
<script language="javascript">
<!--
// Begin timer for clipping
function clip_image() {
    if (navigator.appName == "Microsoft Internet Explorer")
      setTimeout("ie_shrink()", 200);
    else
      setTimeout("ns_shrink()", 200);
}

// global variables
var incr = 10;
counter = 0;
wdth = 200;
left = 0;

// test for browser
// and call browser specific function
function ie_shrink() {
    left+=incr;
    wdth-=incr;
    var rectstring = "rect(auto," + wdth + ",auto," + left + ")";
    document.all.div1.style.clip=rectstring;
    counter++;
    if (counter < 5)
    setTimeout("ie_shrink()",200)
    else {
    counter=0;
    setTimeout("ie_grow()",200)
    }
}

// IE specific function to
// resize image back to original clipping region
function ie_grow() {
    left-=incr;
    wdth+=incr;
```

```
    var rectstring = "rect(auto," + wdth + ",auto," + left + ")";
    document.all.div1.style.clip=rectstring;
    counter++;
    if (counter < 5)
    setTimeout("ie_grow()",200)
    else
    counter = 0;
}

// Navigator function to
// shrink image
function ns_shrink() {
    document.div1.clip.left+=incr;
    document.div1.clip.right-=incr;
    counter++;
    if (counter < 5)
    setTimeout("ns_shrink()", 200);
    else {
    counter = 0;
    setTimeout("ns_grow()", 200);
    }
}

// IE specific function to
// resize image back to original clipping region
function ns_grow() {
    document.div1.clip.left-=incr;
    document.div1.clip.right+=incr;
    counter=0;
    if (counter < 5)
     setTimeout("ns_grow()", 200);
    else
     counter = 0;
}
//-->
</SCRIPT>
</HEAD>
<BODY>
<DIV id=div1 style="position:absolute; left:150; top:100">
<a href="" onclick="clip_image();return false">
<img src="image3.jpg" width=200 height=136 border=0></a>
</DIV>
</BODY>
</HTML>
```

The example uses a timer to call the browser-specific function to shrink the image by decreasing the clipping region size. This is accomplished by increasing the clipping value of the left side of the region and decreasing the clipping value of the right side of the region. Clipping can also occur by increasing the top value of the clipping region while decreasing the bottom value. The IE-specific function is called `ie_shrink` and the Navigator-specific function is called `ns_shrink`. Figure 31.3 shows the image at about its smallest size.

FIGURE 31.3.

Image after clipping region has been shrunk.

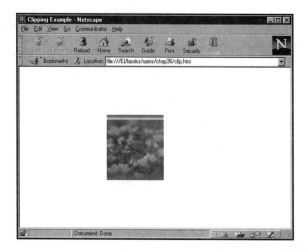

CREATING CROSS-BROWSER OBJECTS

You can create cross-browser objects instead of creating separate code sections for handling the differences between browsers. As an example, the simplest approach is the following, which creates an object with a `style` property for use with Navigator specific objects:

```
function iens_object(obj) {
    this.style = obj;
}
...
// creating object
var the_element = new iens_object(document.div1);
...
// using the object within both IE and Navigator
iens_object.style.left = 100;
```

After working with the CSS1 Positioning elements, you might want to try your hand at creating cross-browser objects. There are examples of these objects at http://www.yasd.com.

After the image is shrunk, it is resized to the original size by using timers to call growth functions, which are again specific to each browser. To increase the size of the clipping region, the left clipping value is decreased and the right clipping value is increased. Figure 31.4 shows the image after it has been resized to its original size.

FIGURE 31.4.

*Image restored to
original size.*

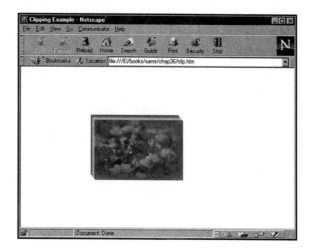

Summary

This chapter provides demonstrations of dynamic positioning. In addition, a discussion and examples of event-trapping techniques applicable for both browsers are presented.

A sliding menu Web page, also using hidden/displayed tips, is used to demonstrate these techniques.

A simple clipping example is shown, demonstrating how to perform element clipping using each browser's unique clipping properties.

Chapter 32, "Saving User Preferences: Cookies and OPS," continues the use of Dynamic HTML to present Web page display options for the reader to choose from, and then storing those options using Netscape cookies. In addition, Netscape cookies are also used to restore the dynamic HTML page status when the reader resizes or reloads the page.

Saving User Preferences: Cookies and OPS

by Shelley Powers

IN THIS CHAPTER

CHAPTER 32

In Chapters 30, "Using the HTML Object Model and Creating Dynamic HTML Pages," and 31, "Manipulating Objects and Responding to User Interaction," you had a chance to try out some Dynamic HTML (DHTML) techniques. Those include altering the appearance of the Web page and moving or hiding Web page elements.

This chapter provides a discussion of Netscape cookies—what they are and how you can use them. The chapter also provides two in-depth examples of using cookies to store DHTML information, such as Web page presentation information and the state of a Web page in case the Web page reader reloads the document.

The last section of this chapter provides a brief discussion of Open Profiling Standard (OPS), and whether OPS is considered a cookie's replacement, or a cookie's complementary technology.

Setting and Retrieving Cookies

When Netscape first released JavaScript, it assured its clients that the scripting language would not be a threat to the security of their machines because information cannot be stored or retrieved from the client machine. However, the problem with this type of security is that there is no way to maintain a persistent line of communication between the Web page(s) and the Web page reader, either within one Internet session, or over a period of time. Additionally, the Web page request mechanism, Hypertext Transport Protocol (HTTP), is normally *stateless*, meaning that persistent information cannot be maintained between the client and the server.

To work around this lack of persistence, the Web developer used CGI (discussed in detail in Part V, "CGI and Controlling the Web from the Server") and maintained information on the server about any choices or options that the Web page reader had selected. However, this seemed to defeat the purpose of a client-side scripting language such as JavaScript, which was to provide processing that could reside on the client and did not require visits back and forth from the Web page server.

Netscape solved the problem of not being able to store or retrieve any information on the client by creating *cookies*. Cookies are small bits of information stored for a specified period of time, and retrievable by name and by Web page location.

What Are Netscape Cookies?

This is how cookies work: a file, named `cookies.txt`, contains all the cookies located on the client machine. Cookie access is restricted to this file, preventing the devious Web developer from creating script code that wanders all over the client's machine. As an additional security, cookie access and storage also includes the Web page's domain and URL information in addition to the cookie name. When a Web page is accessed, any cookie information for the Web page (based on location and URL) is retrieved and stored by the browser.

The browser also checks to see if any cookie has expired, in which case it is removed from the client cookie file. This prevents old cookies from cluttering the file.

Netscape Navigator 4.0 still uses a file called `cookie.txt`, and it can be found on your machine, in a subdirectory within the Netscape Communicator directory. Microsoft's IE, on the other hand, uses the registry database to install the location of the cookie subdirectory, and the subdirectory contains several little files, each one a cookie.

There are limitations to the size and number of cookies a site can create on the client's machine. The limitations per Netscape are as follows:

■ Only three hundred cookies can be in the cookie file.

■ Each cookie can only be 4K in size, for both the name and content combined.

■ Each server/domain can only have 20 cookies. This means that for each subdirectory in your server, you only have 20 cookies, for each explicit URL you have only 20 cookies, and so on.

Can Netscape cookies become a client-side database? No, that's not their purpose. However, they are handy for maintaining persistent information between pages, or between page downloads. This makes them ideal for use with Dynamic HTML, which dynamically alters a Web page after the page is loaded. With cookies, DHTML state information, which is information about the exact state of the page as created with DHTML, can be saved and used to restore the Web page's appearance.

Creating a Cookie

A cookie is a property of the document object. Setting the value for a specific name overwrites what existed when the cookie was previously set.

Netscape has two example functions—`get_cookie` and `set_cookie`—located within its JavaScript programming guide (which can be found from the Netscape developer site at `http://developer.netscape.com/`). These functions are adapted for use with a sample Web page. The page, which can be found in `cookies.htm`, has a form with fields for the cookie name, value, and the number of days before the cookie expires. To use the page, type in the cookie's name, the value you want the cookie to have, and the number of days to keep the cookie. Select the button labeled Set Cookie. To re-retrieve the cookie, type in the cookie's name and select the button labeled Get Cookie, as shown in Figure 32.1.

The Web page contents can be found in Listing 32.1. The two functions to set the cookie and retrieve it are called `get_cookie` and `set_cookie`. Unlike the Netscape versions of these functions, you access the values from and output the cookie results to the form.

Listing 32.1. Creating and retrieving a Netscape cookie.

```
<!--
//
// cookies.htm
//
```

continues

Listing 32.1. continued

```
// author: shelley powers
//
// (c) 1997, shelley powers and SAMS Publishing
//
-->
<HEAD>
<title>test</title>
<STYLE type="text/css">
    BODY { background-color: aqua; color: #3333cc }
</STYLE>
<SCRIPT language="javascript">
<!--

// set_cookie
// retrieves information from form
// and uses it to create cookie
function set_cookie() {
    var cookieDate = new Date();
    var thename = document.forms[0].elements[2].value;
    var thetext = document.forms[0].elements[3].value;
    var thedays = document.forms[0].elements[4].value * 24;
    cookieDate.setTime (cookieDate.getTime() + (1000 * 60 * 60 * thedays));
    var content = document.forms[0].elements[2].value;
    document.cookie = thename + "=" + escape (thetext) +
        "; expires=" + cookieDate.toGMTString();
    document.forms[0].elements[2].value = "";
    document.forms[0].elements[3].value = "";
    document.forms[0].elements[4].value = "";


    }

// get_cookie
// gets cookie based on name
// and displays in form
function get_cookie() {
    var results="";
    var thename = document.forms[0].elements[2].value;
     var search = thename + "=";
     if (document.cookie.length > 0) {
        offset = document.cookie.indexOf(search)
        if (offset != -1) { // if cookie exists
            offset += search.length
            // set index of beginning of value
            end = document.cookie.indexOf(";", offset)
            // set index of end of cookie value
            if (end == -1)
                end = document.cookie.length
                results= unescape(document.cookie.substring(offset, end))
                }
        }
    document.forms[0].elements[3].value = results;
}
//-->
</SCRIPT>

</HEAD>
```

```
<BODY>
<FORM>
<TABLE cellspacing=10 width=40% border=0
    style="background-color: ivory">
<TR><TD colspan=2>
<INPUT type=button value="Set Cookie" onClick="set_cookie()">
<INPUT type=button value="Get Cookie" onClick="get_cookie()"><p>
</TD></TR>
<TR><TD align=right>
Name:</TD><TD><INPUT type=text name="cookie_name">
</TD></TR>
<TR><TD align=right>
Text:</TD><TD> <INPUT type=text name="cookie_text">
</TD></TR>
<TR><TD align=right>
Days:</TD><TD> <INPUT type=text name="cookie_days">
</TR></TD>
</TABLE>
</FORM>
</BODY>
```

32

SAVING USER
PREFERENCES

FIGURE 32.1.

*Web page showing
retrieved cookie value
for specific cookie name.*

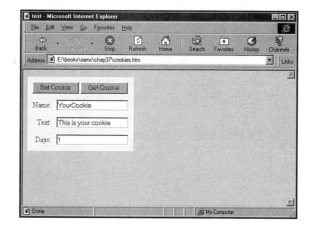

The Web page layout is a combination of CSS1 positioning, page presentation, and using an HTML table to control the layout of the form elements.

The full cookie format is:

```
name=value;expires=date;
```

Notice that the expiration date, which is optional, is set by creating a date object and using the toGMTString method to create a GMT date, with the format of:

```
Wdy, DD-Mon-YY HH:MM:SS GMT
```

If the date is not used, the cookie expires when the browser session is ended. Also, notice the use of the escape and unescape functions. The functions convert and then unconvert special characters such as the colon (:) or a space, which cannot be included within a cookie value.

Storing Web page reader preferences would be an effective use of Netscape cookies. The next time the reader accesses the page, it can be converted back to the presentation style matching the reader's preferences. An example of this is shown in the following section.

Creating a DHTML Preferences Window

A Web page can be dynamically altered while it is loaded, either to have a specific Web page color or to use a certain size and type of font. A next step is using some method of storing page characteristics based on the reader's preferences, and then retrieving this information to re-create the page when he or she next accesses the page.

COMPANION **Web site** A Web page application that opens a profile window to set and save Web page presentation preferences is shown in Listing 32.2. The reader can choose from options to change the Web page colors, to set the font size for headers and the page, and to set the size and resolution of any images within the page. The application can be accessed by opening the file `maindoc.htm`.

Listing 32.2 contains the complete Web page for the profile window. The page contains two buttons, one to close the window without saving the preferences, and one to save the preferences and then close the window. It also contains two drop-down lists, one that contains several color combinations, and one that contains several font sizes. The page also contains radio buttons to control the size and resolution of the images. The resolution is the amount of compression used with the image, and hence the image file size.

Listing 32.2. Form to access and store Web page reader's preferences.

```
<!--
// profile.htm
//
// author: shelley powers
//
// (c) 1997 by shelley powers and SAMS publishing
//
-->
<HEAD>
<title>test</title>
<STYLE type="text/css">
    BODY { background-color: #993333 }
</STYLE>
<SCRIPT language="javascript">
<!--

// set cookies for new formats
function set_cookie() {
   var thefont, thecolors, theimage, theimagesize;
   if (navigator.appName == "Microsoft Internet Explorer") {
    thefont = document.forms[0].font;
    thecolors = document.forms[0].colors;
    theimage = document.forms[0].imageon;
    theimagesize = document.forms[0].imagesize;
```

```
      }
      else {
       thefont = document.formdiv.document.forms[0].font;
       thecolors = document.formdiv.document.forms[0].colors;
       theimage = document.formdiv.document.forms[0].imageon;
       theimagesize = document.formdiv.document.forms[0].imagesize;
       }
      var thefontvalue = thefont.options[thefont.selectedIndex].value;
      var thecolorsvalue = thecolors.options[thecolors.selectedIndex].value;
      if (theimagesize[0].checked)
       theimagesizevalue = 0;
      else
       theimagesizevalue = 1;
      if (theimage[0].checked)
       theimagevalue = 0;
      else
       theimagevalue = 1;
      set_long_cookie("colors", thecolorsvalue);
      set_long_cookie("font", thefontvalue);
      set_long_cookie("images", theimagevalue);
      set_long_cookie("imagesize",theimagesizevalue);
      window.close();
      }


// for Navigator and IE set component values
function setup() {
    if (navigator.appName != "Microsoft Internet Explorer") {
     document.layers["layerinset"].bgColor=inset_color;
     }
    else {
     document.body.style.backgroundColor=other_color;
     document.body.style.color=inset_color;
     document.body.style.fontSize=font_size;
     document.body.style.fontFamily=font_type;
     document.all.item("inset").style.backgroundColor=inset_color;
     var thegroup = document.all.tags("H1");
     for (i = 0; i < thegroup.length; i++)
         thegroup[i].style.fontSize=header_size;
     document.all.item("formdiv").style.color=other_color;
     document.all.item("formdiv").style.fontSize=font_size;
     document.all.item("formdiv").style.fontFamily=font_type;
     }
}
//-->
</SCRIPT>

<SCRIPT language="javascript" src="present.js">
</SCRIPT>

</HEAD>
<BODY onload="setup()">

<DIV id=inset
style="position:absolute; left:2%; top:2%; width:100%; height:100%;
➥background-color:ivory">
</DIV>
```

continues

Listing 32.2. continued

```
<LAYER width=92% height=92% top=2% left=2% name=layerinset
    bgColor="ivory">
</layer>

<DIV id=formdiv
style="position:absolute; left: 5%; top: 5%; width:95%; height:95%;">
<FORM>
<input type=button value="Set Profile" onclick="set_cookie()">
<input type=button value="Close Window" onclick="window.close()">
<p>
<SELECT name="colors">
<OPTION VALUE="ig">ivory/dark green
<OPTION SELECTED VALUE="ir">ivory/rust
<OPTION VALUE="wl">white/black
<OPTION VALUE="wb">white/blue
<OPTION VALUE="ar">aqua/rust
</SELECT>

<SELECT name="font">
<OPTION VALUE="A8">Arial 8/16pt
<OPTION SELECTED VALUE="A10">Arial 10/20pt
<OPTION VALUE="A2">Arial 12/28pt
<OPTION VALUE="C8">Cursive 8/16pt
<OPTION VALUE="C1">Cursive 10/20pt
<OPTION VALUE="C2">Cursive 12/28pt
</SELECT>
<p>
Low Resolution Images:
    <INPUT TYPE="radio" NAME="imageon" VALUE="Low Res" CHECKED>
High Resolution Images:
    <INPUT TYPE="radio" NAME="imageon" VALUE="Hi Res">
<p>
Small Images:
    <INPUT TYPE="radio" NAME="imagesize" VALUE="Small Images">
Large Images:
    <INPUT TYPE="radio" NAME="imagesize" VALUE="Large Images" CHECKED>

</FORM>
</DIV>

</BODY>
```

With this application, the set_cookie function actually calls another function, set_long_cookie, to save the preferences as cookies. These cookies are set to last 30 days. The Profile window not only sets the profile cookies, it uses them in order to present a consistent look among all the pages of the application.

Any page-specific settings that must occur after the page loads, and when all the elements have been created, are located in the function called setup. Layers and DIV blocks are not accessible from script until after the page is fully loaded. The Microsoft page settings and the element-specific settings for Navigator are included within setup. The cookie-retrieving and -setting functions and some code to pull out values used with all the Web pages are located in a JavaScript code file named present.js. Listing 32.3 contains the code from this file. This is included within all the Web pages that use the presentation cookies.

Listing 32.3. JavaScript source code file containing preference-storing functionality.

```
//
// present.js
//
// author: shelley powers
//
// (c) 1997 by shelley powers and SAMS publishing
//

// globals
thecolors="";
thefont="";
theimage="";
theimagesize="";
inset_color = "ivory";
other_color = "firebrick";
font_size = "12pt";
header_size = "28pt";
font_type = "Arial";

// find document cookie values
function find_values() {

    // find colors
    thecolors = get_cookie("colors");
    // find font
    thefont = get_cookie("font");
    // find images
    theimage = get_cookie("images");
    // find image size
    theimagesize = get_cookie("imagesize");

}

// for name, return cookie value
function get_cookie(name) {
   var results = "";
   if (document.cookie.length > 0) {
      var search = name + "=";
      offset = document.cookie.indexOf(search)
      if (offset != -1) { // if cookie exists
          offset += search.length
          // set index of beginning of value
          end = document.cookie.indexOf(";", offset)
          // set index of end of cookie value
          if (end == -1)
              end = document.cookie.length
              results= unescape(document.cookie.substring(offset, end))
              }
      }
```

continues

Listing 32.3. continued

```
    return results;
}

// set 30 day cookie
function set_long_cookie(name, value) {
    var cookieDate = new Date();
    cookieDate.setTime (cookieDate.getTime() + (1000 * 60 * 60 * 30));
    document.cookie = name + "=" + escape (value) +
        "; expires=" + cookieDate.toGMTString();
}

// pull out values for setting page
// these are attribute settings shared across pages
find_values();
if (thecolors.substring(0,1) == "w")
    inset_color="white";
else if (thecolors.substring(0,1) == "a")
    inset_color="aqua";

if (thecolors.substring(1,2) == "l")
    other_color="black";
else if (thecolors.substring(1,2) == "b")
    other_color="blue";
else if (thecolors.substring(1,2) == "g")
    other_color="darkgreen";

if (thefont.substring(0,1) == "C")
    font_type = "Arial";

if (thefont.substring(1,2) == "8") {
    font_size = "8pt";
    header_size = "16pt";
    }
else if (thefont.substring(1,2) == "1") {
    font_size = "10pt";
    header_size = "20pt";
    }

// for Navigator use JASS to set document formats
if (navigator.appName != "Microsoft Internet Explorer") {
    document.tags.BODY.backgroundColor=other_color;
    document.ids.inset.backgroundColor=inset_color;
    document.tags.BODY.color=other_color;
    document.tags.BODY.fontSize=font_size;
    document.tags.BODY.fontFamily = font_type;
    document.tags.H1.fontSize=header_size;
    }
```

A set of global variables is created to hold the presentation values, and these are updated as soon as the page starts loading. Because Navigator does not allow modification of CSS1 attributes after the page loads, code is included in this file and parsed as soon as the script is processed to apply the Navigator formatting, using JavaScript Accessible Style Sheets (covered in detail in Chapter 30).

The colors and fonts are coded to ensure they take up as little space as possible within the cookie. The values are then decrypted for use in setting the CSS1 attributes. Another technique could be to create arrays of values and use the encrypted values as array access values, as shown in the following block:

```
Colors = new Array();
Color["b"] = "blue";
Color["a"] = "aqua";
```

With this approach it is fairly simple to add new colors. The decrypted value is then accessed as follows:

```
Inset_color = Color[thecolors.substring(0,1)];
```

The get_cookie function is very similar to the one created by Netscape.

To use the profile window and the new cookie-based DHTML preferences, there's an example Web page that calls the profile window when a button is pressed. The page also contains an image and some associated text, both of which are altered by whatever preferences are set by the profile window. The page can be found in maindoc.htm, which is on the companion Web site. Figure 32.2 contains the page when it first opens with the default values.

Figure 32.2.

Main window when first opened, using default values.

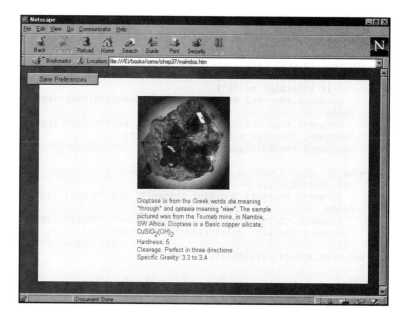

Listing 32.4 contains the complete contents from the main Web page. The page contains two functions: open to open the profile window and setup to set presentation attributes for the page.

Listing 32.4. continued

```
Dioptase is from the Greek words <em>dia</em> meaning "through"
and <em>optasia</em> meaning "view". The sample pictured was
from the Tsumeb mine, in Nambia, SW Africa.
Dioptase is a Basic copper silicate,
 CuSiO<sub>2</sub>(OH)<sub>2</sub>.<br>
Hardness: 5<br>
Cleavage: Perfect in three directions<br>
Specific Gravity: 3.3 to 3.4<p>
</DIV>

</BODY>
```

Navigator and IE have different window open method attributes and each are used to create a small profile window, with a minimum of window chrome. Also, based on the image preferences, one page element or another is displayed. Navigator does not support image resizing after the page is loaded, otherwise only one layer would be needed and the image could be resized.

Running the application, the profile settings are changed to use the aqua and rust color combination, the larger Arial font setting, and the smaller image, with the lower image resolution. Figure 32.3 shows the main page with these new preferences, and Figure 32.4 shows them applied to the profile window.

FIGURE 32.3.

The main Web page with new reader-based presentation preferences.

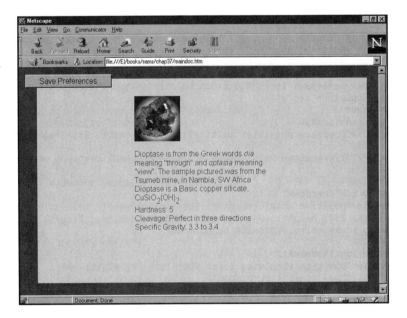

The same techniques can be applied fairly easily to your own Web pages—but be forewarned that the maintenance of these changes can become complicated. To demonstrate this, the next section extends this example to include a second image and associated text and information about the state of the page is stored in case the reader reloads or resizes the Web page.

FIGURE 32.4.

The profile window with the same reader-based presentation preferences.

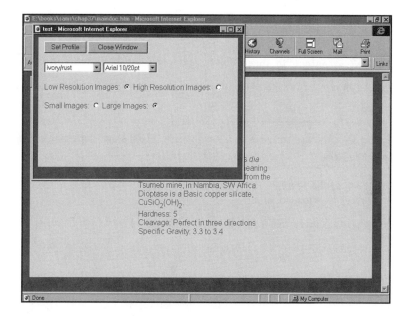

Adding Persistence to DHTML

One problem with DHTML is that if the Web page reader reloads or resizes the page, it usually returns to its originally loaded state. However, cookies can be used to maintain DHTML state information, which can then be used to restore a Web page to the same layout and look just prior to the page being reloaded.

The example Web page from the last section is extended to maintain state information. A second image and associated text are added to the main Web page, along with a second button to switch between the two images. Each time the image is switched, a short-term cookie stores information regarding which image is currently displayed in the page. The short-term cookie is only maintained for 10 minutes, which should be long enough for most uses such as this. Another option would be to avoid using an expiration date, in which case the cookie is not stored when the browser session is ended.

A new function, `set_short_cookie`, is added to the `present.js` file and shown in the following code block:

```
// set 10 minute cookie
function set_short_cookie(name, value) {
   var cookieDate = new Date();
   cookieDate.setTime (cookieDate.getTime() + (1000 * 60 * 10));
```

```
        document.cookie = name + "=" + escape (value) +
            "; expires=" + cookieDate.toGMTString();
}
```

COMPANION
Web site A duplicate of the maindoc.htm file is created and the setup function is modified to handle the second set of images and text. A new function, set_short_cookie, is created; it determines which image needs to be hidden, and which is then displayed. The function also calls the short-term cookie function to set the state information.

Four functions are created, two for Netscape and two for IE, to handle displaying the requested image and text. Listing 32.5 contains the code for this modified Web page.

Listing 32.5. The modified main Web page, storing DHTML state information and handling two images and associated text.

```
<!--
//
// maindoc2.htm
//
// author: shelley powers
//
// (c) shelley powers and SAMS publishing
//
-->
<HEAD>
<SCRIPT language="javascript">
<!--

// open profile window
function open_window() {
    if (navigator.appName == "Microsoft Internet Explorer")
        window.open("profile.htm","Preferences",
        "width=450,height=300,menubars=yes,resizable=no,toolbars=yes");
    else {
        newwin=window.open("profile.htm","Preferences",
        "innerWidth=450,innerHeight=300,menubars=yes,
➥resizable=no,toolbars=yes");
        }
}

// which image and description is showing
imagenum = 0;

// switch images and description
function switch_images() {
    if (navigator.appName == "Microsoft Internet Explorer")
    if (imagenum == 1) {
        document.all.item("therock1").style.visibility="hidden";
        document.all.item("therock2").style.visibility="hidden";
        document.all.item("thetext").style.visibility="hidden";
        imagenum=2;
        ie_show2();
        }
    else {
        document.all.item("therock3").style.visibility="hidden";
        document.all.item("therock4").style.visibility="hidden";
```

```
                document.all.item("thetext2").style.visibility="hidden";
                imagenum=1;
                ie_show1();
                }
        else
         if (imagenum == 1) {
                document.therock1.visibility="hidden";
                document.therock2.visibility="hidden";
                document.thetext.visibility="hidden";
                imagenum=2;
                ns_show2();
                }
         else {
                document.therock3.visibility="hidden";
                document.therock4.visibility="hidden";
                document.thetext2.visibility="hidden";
                imagenum=1;
                ns_show1();
                }
        set_short_cookie("imagenum",imagenum);
}

// for Navigator and IE set component values
function setup() {
    imagenum = get_cookie("imagenum");
    if (imagenum == "" ¦¦ imagenum == "1")
     imagenum = 1;
    else
     imagenum = 2;
    if (navigator.appName != "Microsoft Internet Explorer") {
     document.layers["layerinset"].bgColor=inset_color;
     if (imagenum == 1)
        ns_show1();
     else
        ns_show2();
    }
    else {
     document.body.style.backgroundColor=other_color;
     document.body.style.color=inset_color;
     document.body.style.fontSize=font_size;
     document.body.style.fontFamily=font_type;
     document.all.item("inset").style.backgroundColor=inset_color;
     document.all.item("thetext").style.color=other_color;
     document.all.item("thetext").style.fontSize=font_size;
     document.all.item("thetext").style.fontFamily=font_type;
     document.all.item("thetext2").style.color=other_color;
     document.all.item("thetext2").style.fontSize=font_size;
     document.all.item("thetext2").style.fontFamily=font_type;
     var thegroup = document.all.tags("H1");
     for (i = 0; i < thegroup.length; i++)
        thegroup[i].style.fontSize=header_size;
     if (imagenum == 1)
        ie_show1();
     else
        ie_show2();
    }
}
```

32

SAVING USER
PREFERENCES

continues

Listing 32.5. continued

```
// check to see which image size
// and resolution to display, Netscape, image 1
function ns_show1() {
    if (theimagesize == "0") {
         if (theimage == "0")
        document.therock2.document.images[0].src="diopsl.jpg";
        else
         document.therock2.document.images[0].src="diopsh.jpg";
        document.therock2.visibility="inherit";
        document.thetext.top=170;
        }
    else {
        if (theimagesize == "1")
        document.therock1.document.images[0].src="diopll.jpg";
        else
         document.therock1.document.images[0].src="dioplh.jpg";
        document.therock1.visibility="inherit";
        }
    document.thetext.visibility="inherit";
}

// check to see which image size
// and resolution to display, IE, image 1
function ie_show1() {
    if (theimagesize == "0") {
         if (theimage == "0")
        document.images[1].src="diopsl.jpg";
        else
         document.images[1].src="diopsh.jpg";
        document.all.item("therock2").style.visibility="inherit";
        document.all.item("thetext").style.pixelTop=170;
        }
    else {
        if (theimagesize == "1")
        document.images[0].src="diopll.jpg";
        else
         document.images[0].src="dioplh.jpg";
        document.all.item("therock1").style.visibility="inherit";
        }
    document.all.item("thetext").style.visibility="inherit";
}

// check to see which image size
// and resolution to display, Netscape, image 2
function ns_show2() {
    if (theimagesize == "0") {
         if (theimage == "0")
        document.therock4.document.images[0].src="cinnabarsl.jpg";
        else
         document.therock4.document.images[0].src="cinnabarsh.jpg";
        document.therock4.visibility="inherit";
        document.thetext2.top=180;
        }
    else {
        if (theimagesize == "1")
        document.therock3.document.images[0].src="cinnabarll.jpg";
```

```
        else
          document.therock3.document.images[0].src="cinnabarlh.jpg";
          document.therock3.visibility="inherit";
          }
      document.thetext2.visibility="inherit";
    }

// check to see which image size
// and resolution to display, IE, image 2
function ie_show2() {
    if (theimagesize == "0") {
        if (theimage == "0")
          document.images[3].src="cinnabarsl.jpg";
        else
          document.images[3].src="cinnabarsh.jpg";
        document.all.item("therock4").style.visibility="inherit";
        document.all.item("thetext2").style.pixelTop=180;
        }
    else {
        if (theimagesize == "1")
          document.images[2].src="cinnabarll.jpg";
        else
          document.images[2].src="cinnabarlh.jpg";
        document.all.item("therock3").style.visibility="inherit";
        }
    document.all.item("thetext2").style.visibility="inherit";
}

//-->
</SCRIPT>

<SCRIPT language="javascript" src="present.js">
</SCRIPT>

</HEAD>
<BODY onload="setup()">
<DIV id="inset"
style="position:absolute; left:2%; top:2%; width:98%;
height:98%; background-color:ivory">
</DIV>
<LAYER name=layerinset width=90% height=90% top=5% left=5%
    bgColor="ivory">
</layer>
<DIV id=formdiv style="position:absolute; left: 2%;
top: 2%; width:80; height:50">
<form>
<INPUT type=button value="Save Preferences" onClick="open_window()"><p>
<INPUT type=button value="   Switch Images   " onclick="switch_images()">
</FORM>
</DIV>
<DIV id="therock1" style="position:absolute; left: 250;
 top: 60; width: 200; height: 194; visibility:hidden">
<img id=imagelrg width=200 height=194>
</DIV>
<DIV id="therock2" style="position:absolute; left: 250;
top: 60; width: 100; height: 94; visibility:hidden">
<img id=imagesm width=100 height=94>
```

continues

Listing 32.5. continued

```
</DIV>
<DIV id=thetext style="position:absolute; left: 250;
top: 270; width: 300; visibility:hidden">
Dioptase is from the Greek words <em>dia</em>
 meaning "through" and <em>optasia</em>
 meaning "view". The sample pictured was from
the Tsumeb mine, in Nambia, SW Africa.
Dioptase is a Basic copper silicate,
CuSiO<sub>2</sub>(OH)<sub>2</sub>.<br>
Hardness: 5<br>
Cleavage: Perfect in three directions<br>
Specific Gravity: 3.3 to 3.4<p>
</DIV>


<DIV id="therock3" style="position:absolute;
left: 250; top: 60; width: 200; height: 219; visibility:hidden">
<img id=imagelrg width=200 height=219>
</DIV>
<DIV id="therock4" style="position:absolute;
left: 250; top: 60; width: 100; height: 110; visibility:hidden">
<img id=imagesm width=100 height=110>
</DIV>
<DIV id="thetext2" style="position:absolute; left:
250; top: 285; width: 300; visibility:hidden">
The name is from a location in India, supposedly. The sample pictured
is from the Hunan Province, in China. Cinnabar is a Mercury Sulfide, HgS.<br>
Hardness: 2 - 2 1/2<br>
Cleavage: Perfect in three directions<br>
Specific Gravity: 8.0 to 8.2
</DIV>

</BODY>
```

Instead of individual functions for switching the image and text based on the browser, you could also create a new object that contains information such as the image source, size, location, and other information, and create a new instance of the object for each paired text-image elements. These instances can be loaded into an array, and the information accessed and used to make the change, similar to that shown in the following code block:

```
function image_obj(lowsrc, hisrc, texttop, element_name, text_element) {
    this.lowsrc = lowsr;
    this.hisrc = hisrc;
    this.texttop = texttop;
    this.element_name = element_name;
    this.text_element = text_element);
...
objs["0"] = new image_obj("diopsl.jpg", "diopsh.jpg", 170)
...
if (theimagesize == "0") {
    document.all.item(objs["0"].element_name).src = objs["0"].src;
```

COMPANION **Website** Figure 32.5 contains the Web page when the page is showing one of the images, and Figure 32.6 contains the Web page with the second image. Try the file `maindoc2.htm`, setting the image to the first or the second image and then refresh the Web page. The image that was displayed before the page was reloaded is displayed when the page is loaded again.

FIGURE 32.5.

Second version of the main Web page with the first image displayed.

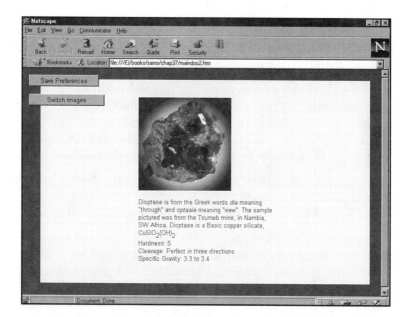

FIGURE 32.6.

The main Web page with the second image displayed.

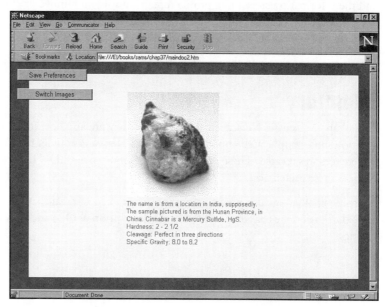

Cookies and OPS

The Open Profiling Standard is a new standard the Internet industry is considering. With OPS, information about the Web page reader is accessible by any company with Web pages accessed by the reader. The profile would only contain information that the reader decides to provide, and provides this information only when in agreement.

Among the types of information the OPS can contain is address and company information. If you have ever had to provide this information when requesting free or beta downloads, you will probably appreciate the advantages of OPS.

If you are a Web browser with special interests, such as kite flying or collecting animation cells, this type of information can also be included in the OPS and accessed by companies. If you collect rare minerals, there are several sites to shop. For you, the OPS could include information such as what type of minerals you collect, or what sizes, and so on—and the Web sites can then use DHTML to fine-tune their page display to fit your interests.

If some of this makes you nervous, with shades of "Big Brother is watching you," remember that the information contained within your own personal profile is totally up to you. Used correctly, OPS benefits both sides of the Web page, the supplier and the reader.

OPS profiles are not a substitute for Netscape cookies. Cookies were created and are used in order to maintain state information about a page, or perhaps to maintain some information about a Web page display, in order to match the Web page reader's needs. Aside from the format used to create the cookie, there is no data standardization with cookies, as there is with OPS. Additionally, OPS does not have any size restrictions, at least that are known at this time, and the information stored in a profile remains until you remove or alter it. Cookies, on the other hand, are transitory, small bits of information with severe size limitations, and by default are destroyed when the browser session ends.

OPS is complementary to the use of Netscape cookies, it is not a replacement technology.

Summary

This chapter discusses Netscape cookies—what they are and how to set and retrieve them. In addition, an example Web application that uses Netscape cookies to store Web page reader's preferences was created. These preferences are then used with DHTML to alter the Web page to meet these preferences.

Netscape cookies are also used to store information to re-create a Web page using Dynamic HTML. Finally, the chapter provides a brief description of OPS and how it relates to Netscape cookies.

VII
PART

IN THIS PART

Emerging and Alternate Web Technologies

ActiveX Controls for the World Wide Web

by Blake Benet Hall

IN THIS CHAPTER

This book's primary focus has been on Internet development languages and the capabilities they provide. Just as HTML, Java, and JavaScript are all popular to Internet developers, ActiveX—a Microsoft technology—is gaining momentum as an integration technology. Although many of today's technical journals enjoy fanning the ActiveX versus Java debate, the basis of the argument is really unfounded. Java is one of many development languages, albeit one with some very attractive advantages over the others. ActiveX is a technology that can be used to augment, enhance, and extend the features of an end-product that is being created using a development language. The end product may be in the form of a Web page or a custom application. The core of ActiveX technology, the ActiveX control, enables developers to add interactive content to both applications and Web pages by incorporating ActiveX controls. Currently, ActiveX's full capabilities are only realized when the server in use is a Windows NT server and the front-end browser supports ActiveX. ActiveX support is inherent within Microsoft's Internet Explorer and supported via a plug-in within the Netscape Navigator environment.

This chapter's main goal is to show you one way to build an ActiveX control. However, the first section is concerned with providing an overview of the ActiveX control and its environment. Afterwards, you'll look at how to create a simple ActiveX control using Visual Basic 5.0, and insert it into a Web page.

ActiveX Control?

What exactly is an ActiveX control? This section provides two answers to that question, the first being more theoretical and the latter more tangible.

The Elegant Description:

Put simply, in programming terms, an ActiveX control is an interactive object that has a defined and exposed interface. In breaking this definition down:

Interactive in that at runtime, a user may interact with the control directly or interact with another control or application that interacts with the control directly. An ActiveX control by itself does nothing—some external event must occur to initiate its functionality. Internally, these events often correlate to a function or method which the control has exposed to the developer. When creating Web pages with ActiveX controls, it is within these functions that a developer inserts the custom code.

The control is an *object that has a defined and exposed interface* in that there is a finite set of functions or methods that a developer has access to in an ActiveX control. The entire set of these functions is known as the object's *exposed interface*.

A developer using an ActiveX control has a clear understanding of the what the control's capabilities are because the control's functionality and interface are defined and documented by the developer who created the control.

The Real-World Description:

ActiveX controls have evolved from what was once known as an OLE or OCX control. The controls exist in files with the extensions .ocx and .dll. Note that an .ocx or .dll file can contain one or more ActiveX controls and that this relationship is not one-to-one (one control per file). As you soon see, an ActiveX control alone—and therefore the file that contains it—may be composed of several other ActiveX controls.

Some ActiveX controls are referred to as lightweight controls, as they are designed to be as small as possible. This allows them to be downloaded quickly and enables several controls to be used together on the same page, or in the same application, without creating a performance burden.

Once downloaded to the local PC, the control automatically registers itself and becomes available to the browser.

When properly licensed, an ActiveX control can be included or used by any application in the MS Windows environment. Licensing issues are discussed in the section "The Security Discussion" later in this chapter.

> **NOTE**
>
> Currently, development is in progress to extend OS support for ActiveX to the UNIX and Macintosh environments.

The Benefits of ActiveX Controls

While the ActiveX control has several advantages, the single most hyped benefit is that of reusability. Because the controls have a defined interface, a defined functionality, and are accessible from a variety of programming languages, they can be used in various development projects.

ActiveX controls can be viewed as the building blocks of an application or as the glue that ties together disparate technologies. If you are creating a Web page to facilitate a Web user entering his or her user name, password, and selecting OK, you could use an ActiveX text control for the user name/password and ActiveX button control for the OK button.

In this scenario, the ActiveX controls are part of the Web page's building blocks. Now say there is a need to access some Java functionality within that page. By incorporating a Java applet into the page and linking it to the ActiveX control via scripting, you can tie the ActiveX control into any Java functionality, and conversely, allow the applet access to some Windows OS-specific features not available to the applet. While this does raise some security issues, this scenario depicts ActiveX as the glue between the applet and any needed OS or ActiveX functionality not supported via the applet.

On the other side of the fence, if you're an ActiveX control developer, you don't relish the idea of your control being available for download to anyone who has access to the Internet. Without some security for the ActiveX control itself, your control could be freely distributed throughout the world and end up being used by hundreds of companies in their development efforts. Thus, the ActiveX security umbrella has to allot for bad users who might try to pirate your control.

Protecting the User

There are two scenarios in which an ActiveX control could wreak havoc. Obviously, the first scenario involves a less-than-reputable developer who purposely creates an unsafe control. The second scenario involves a safe control that can be manipulated by the scripting in the Web page and, unintentionally, exhibit a behavior that is unsafe to the client system.

An Unsafe Control

To protect the user from an unsafe control, a digital signature technology is used in conjunction with ActiveX controls. A *digital signature* contains pertinent information about the control's developer. A developer obtains a digital signature from a third party known as a *certificate authority*, and once obtained, the developer is said to have a *digital certificate*. Prior to a control being downloaded to the user's system, the user is presented with a dialog box (depicting a certificate) containing the information about the control and its developer. This dialog box allows the user to either accept or deny the download.

> **NOTE**
>
> Within the browser options, a user can choose to accept all certificates—but normally that is not done, because most users like to have some level of control over their systems.

In brief, the unique digital signature is created by combining and encrypting a unique section of the control's code and the control developer's personal information. When the control is downloaded for the first time, this signature is decrypted by the browser and a subset of the signature information is stored on the user's system. In any subsequent downloads of the same control, the same process occurs with the additional step of comparing the previously stored information with the newly decrypted information. The user is warned if they do not match; if they do match and a newer version exists, the newer control is downloaded.

Note that it is the certificate authority, which issued the developer's certificate, who gets involved in any legal issues should a security breach occur. More detailed information on obtaining a digital signature can be found on the VeriSign Web site, a popular certificate authority, at http://www.verisign.com.

A Safe Control Manipulated to Be Unsafe

Developers are required to attest to the integrity of their control. Because a control on a Web page relies somewhat on the scripting within the page to perform various duties, the developer must specify that the control is safe both for scripting and initializing.

A control is said to be safe for scripting if—and only if—it does not breach security regardless of how it is scripted into the page.

A control is said to be safe for initialization if—and only if—it does not breach security, regardless of what parameter values are sent to it at initialization time. Initial values can be sent to the control via the HTML OBJECT tag, which is used to embed the control within the page.

By default, browsers do not download a control that is not safe for scripting or initialization. However, forcing the developer to assert these items as safe realistically requires that the control be thoroughly tested by the developer.

As you can see, ActiveX security really relies on the respectability of the developer and the fact that developers honor the trust given them, in exchange for the increased functionality they are given via ActiveX.

Protecting the Developer

As with most commercial software modules, there is a license associated with ActiveX controls. It is via the use of this license that developers can protect their controls. An ActiveX control really has two licenses: one that allows runtime access to the control, and one that allows design-time access to the control.

Design-time access allows other developers to use your control in their products, for their own benefit. Normally, design licenses are obtained directly from the control's developer and include the rights to redistribute the control for runtime usage.

Runtime access to the control designates a user's machine as able to run and operate the control within running applications on that machine. Runtime licensing is the real concern on the Web. This licensing information is normally stored in the registry of the client PC using the control. This procedure works well for packaged software that is purchased outright—when the software is installed, the proper licensing information is stored in the registry of the system. However, when accessing ActiveX controls on the Internet, this licensing information can be kept in a file on the Web server and referenced via the HTML OBJECT tag that embedded the control. When the control is loaded, the license information is retrieved from the remote file, allowing the user to have a temporary runtime license for that control.

Developing a Simple ActiveX Control in Visual Basic

In this section you look at how to create an ActiveX control using Visual Basic 5.0 and insert it into a Web page.

> **NOTE**
>
> Although the example uses VB 5.0, you can download a special version of the VB development environment called the Visual Basic Control Creation Edition (VBCCE) from Microsoft at `http://www.microsoft.com/vbasic/controls/`. This freely downloadable software enables you to create ActiveX controls using VB without need for the Visual Basic development product.

There are three models to choose from when creating ActiveX controls using Visual Basic:

1. *Develop a control from scratch*—When developing a control from scratch, you are responsible for drawing the control.

2. *Enhance an existing control*—You can use a control that is already developed and simply enhance its functionality.

3. *Create a control from existing controls*—You use existing controls to create a new control.

COMPANION Web site This example steps through creating an ActiveX control from a few existing controls. The control you develop is fairly simple—it uses the Internet Transfer Control (Inet), which is included in VB 5.0. The Inet control implements the HTTP and FTP Internet protocols. This example adds some common Windows controls (buttons, textboxes, and the like), and uses functionality provided by the Inet control to create a simple FTP control. The FTP control, which really tends to lean toward an insertable application, can then be placed on a Web page and utilized as a small FTP interface. All of the source code is located in this book's Companion Web Site.

Bear in mind that this control code is not verified for scripting or initialization. It's sample code for the purpose of this chapter and because you have the code now, feel free to hack on it and rebuild it safe-scripted, or anything else of that sort. While the code is safe, the control via scripting is not verified and hasn't been sent initialization parameters. That said, take a look at ActiveX controls in Visual Basic.

Working with ActiveX in VB5

Start VB and select project type ActiveX Control as shown in Figure 33.1.

After selecting the project type, your screen should look something like that depicted in Figure 33.2. As a VB developer, the first thing you notice is that you now have a `UserControl` object where you would normally have a `Form` (when you develop an `.exe` file). The `UserControl` object can be viewed very much as the `Form` is when you are developing standard VB `.exe` files. The `UserControls` are managed in much the same way in that they, too, are stored in plain text files which have a `.ctl` file extension (`Forms` have a `.frm` extension). Just as graphical elements that you store in a `Form` are stored in `.frx` files, graphical elements for a `UserControl` are stored in `.ctx` files.

Now you need to make the Internet Transfer Control available to your project, which is accomplished by simply inserting the Internet Transfer control into your project. Select Project|Components from the menu.

From within the Controls tab, select the Internet Transfer control and the Plugin control as shown in Figure 33.3. The Inet control has a dependency on the Plugin control. You need to insert it into the project as well. Later, when you package this control for distribution, you see that this dependency checking is done for you when the distribution is created. If, at that time, you are missing a dependent control, you only need to re-open your project and insert it. Also, notice that VB Service Pack 2 has been installed—that is why the (SP2) is shown in Figure 33.3. This is available from the Visual Basic area on the Microsoft Web site; it's about a 7.5MB download.

FIGURE 33.1.

Project type selection should be ActiveX Control.

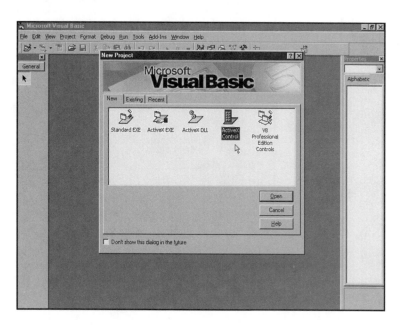

FIGURE 33.2.

An ActiveX project is created with a UserControl *by default.*

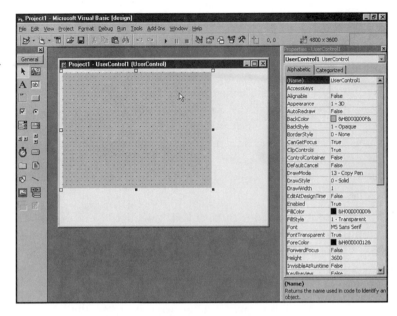

FIGURE 33.2.

An ActiveX project is created with a UserControl *by default.*

FIGURE 33.3.

Select the Inet and plug-in controls via the Components tab.

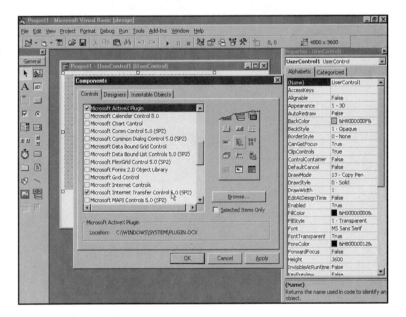

Now, you're ready to insert some controls and tie them in with the Inet control.

Figure 33.4 depicts the end result user interface for the FTP control. On one hand, it makes sense if you were surprised that you went from a blank `UserControl` in Figure 33.3 to a populated `UserControl` in Figure 33.4. However, this entire process is very similar to that of using VB to create an application; thus, you only need to put the Inet control, textboxes, labels, button, and a listbox onto the screen exactly as you would when working with `Forms`. At this point, you can either mock up your own screen or follow along via the code on the Companion Web Site. The notable difference between developing standard `.exes` modules and ActiveX controls is in the distribution and security arena. It should be apparent to you now why Microsoft is providing the special Visual Basic Control Creation edition freely on its Web site (`http://www.microsoft.com/vbasic/controls/`). They have made it very simple for programmers to create basic ActiveX controls.

FIGURE 33.4.

The FTP control with the Inet control and several common controls.

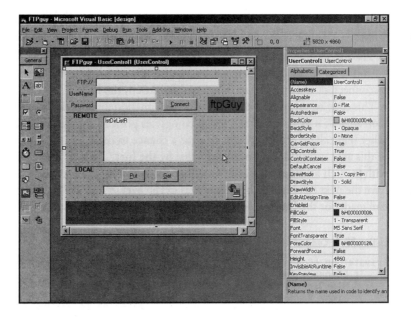

Looking at Figure 33.4, the top controls are used to enter the site, user name, and password. Once those fields are entered, the user clicks the Connect button. Once connected, a directory/file list is retrieved from the remote system and displayed in the listbox. The lower text box is for entering the local file information. The Put and Get buttons enable the user to transfer a file to the remote system and to retrieve a file from the remote system, respectively. Also, once connected, the Connect button toggles its functionality and becomes the Disconnect button. The colored block at the bottom of the screen displays the current status of events and related error messages.

Listing 33.2. continued

```
Dim targetFile As String
Dim i, j As Integer

If Trim(txtLocalFile.Text) = "" Then
    lbStatus.Caption = "Bad local file specification"
    DoEvents
    Exit Sub
End If

j = Len(Trim(txtLocalFile.Text))
For i = j To 1 Step -1
    Select Case Mid(Trim(txtLocalFile.Text), i, 1)
        Case ":"
        Case "/"
        Case "\"
            Exit For
        Case Else
            targetFile = Mid(Trim(txtLocalFile.Text), i, j)
    End Select
Next i

Inet.Execute Inet.URL, "PUT " _
& Trim(txtLocalFile.Text) & " " & targetFile
Do
    DoEvents
Loop While Inet.StillExecuting = True
DoEvents
DoEvents

End Sub
```

In Listing 33.3, Inet_StateChanged() is shortened, as most of the messages are purely informational. You should note three areas: Inet_StateChanged() is basically called (or *raised* in event lingo) whenever any data streams are transferred to or from a host via the Inet control. The states are numbered 1 through 12 and are documented within the help files. Line one denotes a state of icError (State = 11), which is an error; this error message, and for that matter, all of the informational messages that Inet_StateChanged() offers, are printed in the colored status box of the FTP control. Line two denotes a state of icResponseCompleted (State = 12); this is called when a PWD, LS, DIR, or other data-related command is sent to the remote system. Because the volume of data being returned could be quite large, it is received (in line three) by calling the GetChunk method of the Inet control. Note that the data is sent back from the remote system unfiltered, so the carriage-return and linefeeds are used as filename delimiters and then stripped out, allowing the file or directory to be added to the listbox.

Listing 33.3. Monitoring the events.

```
Private Sub Inet_StateChanged(ByVal State As Integer)
    Dim varData As Variant
    Dim rcvData As String
```

```
        Select Case State
            Case icNone        '0
                lbStatus.Caption = ""
            Case icHostResolvingHost       '1
                lbStatus.Caption = "Looking up Host"
                Screen.MousePointer = vbHourglass
  .
  .
  .
1       Case icError
                lbStatus.Caption = "Comm Error : " & Inet.ResponseInfo
                 Screen.MousePointer = vbArrow
            DoEvents
2       Case icResponseCompleted
                'Here if we do an ls or dir...
                'Get a chunk.
                Screen.MousePointer = vbHourglass
                DoEvents
                rcvData = ""
                varData = Inet.GetChunk(1024, icString)
                DoEvents


                Do While Len(varData) > 0
                    rcvData = rcvData & varData
                    ' Get next chunk.
                    varData = Inet.GetChunk(1024, icString)
                    DoEvents
                Loop

                'slam it in the list box stepping over the CR/LF
3               If Len(rcvData) > 0 Then

                    Dim istart, iend, ifound As Integer
                    Dim strsearch As String
                    istart = 1
                    strsearch = Chr(13) 'return

                    lstDirListR.Clear
                    lstDirListR.AddItem ".." ' for CD ..

                    If Asc(Mid(rcvData, 1, 1)) > 13 Then
                        Do
                            ifound = InStr(istart, rcvData, strsearch)
                         lstDirListR.AddItem Mid(rcvData, istart, ifound - istart)
                            istart = ifound + 2  ' skip the linefeed
                            DoEvents
                        Loop While Asc(Mid(rcvData, istart, 1)) > 13
                    End If
End If
Screen.MousePointer = vbArrow
            lbStatus.Caption = "OK"
        End Select

        DoEvents
End Sub
```

In Listing 33.4, The MouseDown() and MouseUp() listbox events are used to facilitate a directory traversal or file selection. Note that the directory names always contain the separator (slash or backslash) characters, and filenames do not. So, if in the MouseDown() event you realize that a filename was clicked, don't issue the CD command (change directory) and do not force the re-retrieval of the directory contents because no traversal occurred. This generic logic might work across different FTP servers if it's beefed up to support the oddball. It's been used against Microsoft's IIS without problem and it should be fine for the majority of FTP software. This is a good time to take notes as an ActiveX developer, because you need to work to resolve compatibility issues and account for problems if you want to mark your control as safe.

Listing 33.4. Obtaining a remote directory list.

```
Private Sub lstDirListR_MouseDown(Button As Integer,
                    Shift As Integer, X As Single, Y As Single)
    If Button <> vbLeftButton Then
        Exit Sub
    End If
    'make sure directory is selected
    If (lstDirListR.SelCount = 0 Or
lstDirListR.ListCount = 0) Then
        Exit Sub
    End If
    If lstDirListR = ".." Then
        If DirLevel = 0 Then
            Exit Sub
        Else
            DirLevel = DirLevel - 1
        End If
    Else
    If (InStr(1,lstDirListR, "/")=0 And
    InStr(1,lstDirListR,"\") = 0) Then
            Exit Sub
        Else
            DirLevel = DirLevel + 1
        End If
    End If
    Inet.Tag = "CD"
    Inet.Execute Inet.URL, "CD " & Trim(lstDirListR)
    Do
        DoEvents
    Loop While Inet.StillExecuting = True
    DoEvents
End Sub

Private Sub lstDirListR_MouseUp(Button As Integer,
                    Shift As Integer, X As Single, Y As Single)

    If Inet.Tag = "CD" And Button = vbLeftButton Then
'we just changed directories
        Inet.Tag = ""
        DoEvents
        Inet.Execute Inet.URL, "DIR "   'do a dir
        Do
```

```
        DoEvents
    Loop While Inet.StillExecuting = True
    DoEvents
End If
```

Testing

Testing is really a pleasure in this environment. You can create your control and then simply include it in a normal Standard EXE project type, put it on a form, and debug it. You can debug the control from within the Form environment. Add that fact to the more powerful developing environment you get with Visual Basic 5.0 and the bugs get weeded out fast.

Once the OCX has been generated, as depicted in Figure 33.5, you can create a Standard EXE project and add your control by selecting Project | Components off the Main Menu. You should be able to select it from the available components just as the Inet control was selected earlier.

FIGURE 33.5.

Generating the control by selecting File\Make .OCX.

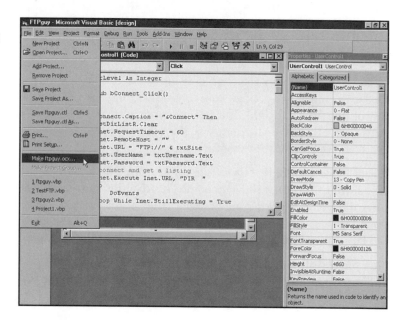

Internet Distribution

Creating the distribution package is the Application Setup Wizard's main job. However, prior to leaving the development environment and running the Setup Wizard, you need to determine whether you require licensing.

Setting up licensing is a two-step process: First you need to select Project | Properties from the Main Menu. Then select the Require License Key option, as shown in Figure 33.6, and save the project.

FIGURE 33.6.

Enabling licensing for your ActiveX control.

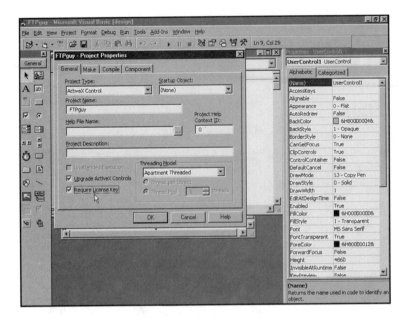

Next, you need to locate and run a program called LPK_TOOL (LPK_TOOL.exe). This tool is used to create a license pack for your control. LPK_TOOL.exe can be found in the \Tools directory of your VB CD-ROM. If that route is not available to you, you need to download the ActiveX SDK from the Microsoft Web site. Once the ActiveX SDK is unpacked and installed, LPK_TOOL.exe is in the \Bin subdirectory.

Figure 33.7 depicts LPK_TOOL. control is included in the license pack file that is generated. If your control does not show up in the list, reconfirm the previous step and make sure you marked the project as requiring licensing. After locating and adding your control into the license pack, choose the button Save & Exit , and provide a name for your license pack. Keep this filename and location handy. You need it when distributing your control on the Internet.

Now you're ready for the last step, which involves running the Application Setup Wizard shown in Figure 33.8. The Application Setup Wizard can be found in the VB 5.0 program group.

Be sure to select the Internet Download Option. Figures 33.8 through 33.11 take you through the wizard's steps.

One advantage to this is that they will be automatically updated when new releases come out. If you don't care for this, select the other option which ends up being local, unless you have your own Web site that you use as a component repository.

In this dialog box you can individually select the safety level associated with each of your controls.

FIGURE 33.7.

Running the Licensing tool to create your license pack.

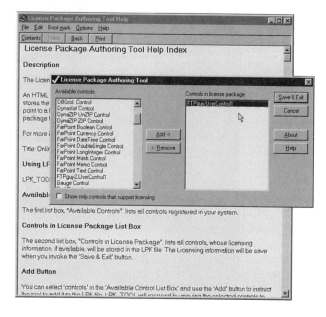

FIGURE 33.8.

Creating the Internet download distribution.

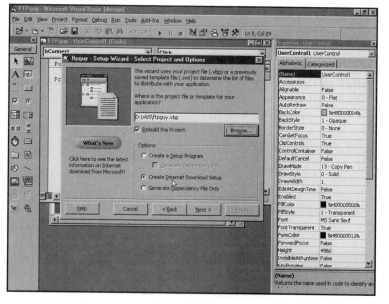

The final two screens prior to the build commencing, are not shown here—one is for adding any ActiveX servers you may rely on, and the final screen before building the distribution displays your complete file dependency.

FIGURE 33.12.
The Internet Explorer,
sporting ftpGuy.

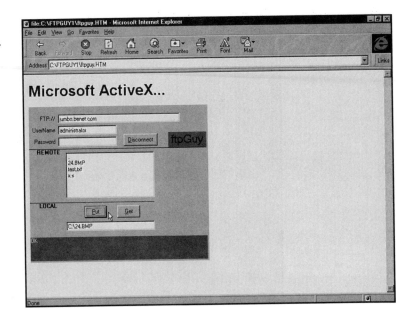

Summary

Trying to cover the basics of ActiveX controls in one chapter is a no-win situation. No matter how much is covered here, there are other areas of ActiveX technology that are on the rise. ActiveX servers are gaining momentum in certain circles. With the current licensing scheme of ActiveX and its integration into the Windows environments, it won't take long for ActiveX to be incorporated into corporate back office systems, which are not even related to the Internet. Software that updates itself can diagnose when some required files are missing and automatically fetch them—all in time.

This is really where the Internet philosophies differ; it's not really one technology versus another and who can achieve market share the quickest. The real key is defining a technology model that both scales and continues to remain cohesive when new pieces are added. The ActiveX model or approach is really quite sound.

You should have some idea after what you just read that: The controls work together to form a single functional application (control), the resultant control is flagged as requiring a license, the license tool generates a license pack, and then everything is pulled together by generating the .ocx file where its dependent modules are also collated and a stand-alone distributable package is created. Once it goes out the door, software in an entirely different arena can take that package and enable it on client systems where another related technology has the capability to automatically update it.

XML

by Simon North

IN THIS CHAPTER

CHAPTER

34

XML, which stands for Extensible Markup Language, is an extremely simple dialect of SGML (Standard Generalized Markup Language). XML has been developed to fill the gap between the power and complexity of SGML at one end of the spectrum, and the inadequacy and simplicity of HTML at the other end of the spectrum.

This chapter covers the following topics:

- The purpose and nature of XML
- XML's syntax and structure rules
- XML document type declarations (DTDs)
- How to decide whether you need a DTD
- XML's linking mechanisms (XLL)
- XML's style language (XS)
- Converting HTML documents into XML documents
- XML's future

After reading this chapter, you should be familiar with the basic concepts of XML and understand the substantial improvements that XML can offer in comparison to HTML. You should be able to write simple XML documents, create basic XML document type declarations (DTDs), and convert existing HTML documents into XML documents. You should also have a basic understanding of XML's style language, XS.

> **NOTE**
>
> Be warned that XML is not yet finished. The specification consists of three parts, and each part has reached a different stage. Part 1, covering the basic language, is now in its third revision but is still only a draft. Part 2, covering linking, is now in its second draft version. Part 3, covering the style language, is a very rough draft that has virtually no formal status at all. Although the specification is already fairly stable, it is still possible for quite radical changes to be made to any part of XML.

What Is XML?

XML is an extremely simple dialect of SGML. In order to understand XML properly, you need to know a little about SGML first.

At its simplest, SGML is a language that provides the tools for defining markup languages. HTML is such a markup language, called an *SGML application*, consisting of a well-defined set of elements (enclosed in tags), attributes (such as `color`), and entities (such as `&copy;`).

Since its initial formalization as an ISO standard in 1986, SGML has consistently faced a problem of its own creation. In trying to be truly "generalized," it had to be powerful. In being powerful it became complex, and in becoming complex it became difficult to learn, time-consuming to implement, and expensive.

The Internet (or more precisely, the World Wide Web) required something simpler, something less demanding of both human and computer resources, and so HTML was born.

HTML has been an excellent markup language, for its purpose, but the years between its development and now have seen that purpose grow and change in ways that no one could have even guessed. HTML is now being put to uses that push the very edge of what is possible and, despite attempts to patch it with proprietary extensions, it is reaching its limits. Modern Web applications require more than the simple addition of a few more tags can offer.

XML is an attempt to find a common ground between SGML and HTML. Rather than being another SGML application, XML is, like SGML, a metalanguage for defining markup languages: *XML applications*. XML provides a means for you to define your own applications, to define your own markup language so that you can encode the information in your Web documents far more precisely than can be done in HTML. Combine XML with the processing power that languages like Java and ActiveX can provide, and you have the means to produce intelligent documents, documents that can be understood by your applications so that the information can be processed in ways that would be absolutely impossible with HTML.

XML is not intended to be a replacement for HTML. XML is meant to be a supplement and an alternative to HTML, when it is needed. XML and HTML can happily coexist, each being used for what it is most suited; HTML for "quick and dirty" applications such as Web pages, and XML for applications that need more intelligent documents and more processing ability.

XML Documents

An XML document need not necessarily look so different from an HTML document (and, as you see later in this chapter, it need not take much effort to convert an HTML document into an XML document). Just like an HTML document, an XML document consists of a mixture of text and markup (tags). Where XML documents do really differ is at the conceptual level, in particular validity and being well-formed.

Validity

Reflecting their closer relation to SGML than HTML, XML documents can be validated to ensure that their structure and content conform to the rules defined for that type of document. As in SGML, these rules are specified in a document called the document type declaration (DTD).

Unlike other markup systems (such as HTML and TeX), the use of a DTD in SGML and XML means that you can actually check, or *validate*, documents. Validation means that you can ensure that all the elements that a document should contain are actually all present, that they are in the right order and, to a limited extent, that they contain the data that they should contain.

The section "The XML Document Type Declaration" gives more information about the DTD; for now it is enough for you to understand that for an XML document to be valid it must have a DTD and its contents must conform to the rules expressed in that DTD. The specific rules for validity are described when the objects they apply to are described.

Well Formed

To save Internet bandwidth, to reduce the amount of processing required (and consequently the speed of interpretation), and to account for unknown, and unpredictable, delivery conditions, it is unreasonable—and even impossible—to insist that a DTD is always available. You may not even want the kind of control that validity would impose (after all, Web browsers do not check HTML documents for validity). To allow for a "looser" delivery of XML documents, a major departure from SGML's formality has been made, and XML introduces a totally new concept of "well formedness."

Well-formed XML documents do not require a DTD (hence XML's slightly incorrect reputation for being DTD-less SGML). Even if a DTD is present, they do not require reference to the DTD in order to be correctly processed. (XML's environment is envisaged as a two-tier layer consisting of an "XML processor" module that reads XML documents on behalf of the application and gives access to their content and structure.) Of course, for an XML document to be correctly processed without reference to the information concerning its structure that would have been contained in its DTD, certain concessions have to be made. Well-formed XML documents have the following requirements:

- Must start with a required markup declaration (more on this later) that says that a DTD is not required:

  ```
  <?XML VERSION="1.0" RMD="NONE" ?>
  ```
- Must contain one or more elements.
- Must have all the elements nested inside each other, and all tags must be balanced (for every start tag there must be an end tag).
- Must have all attribute values enclosed in quotation marks.
- Must have empty element start tags closed with the special /> string, or they must be made nonempty by adding a specific closing tag (for example, <HR></HR>).
- Must not have any markup characters in character data (markup characters must be escaped using the predefined entities).
- All element attributes must be of CDATA type (character data), because there is no way to define them as being otherwise without a DTD.

These well-formedness constraints will make more sense when you come to the objects to which they apply. However, before getting too involved in the fine details of validity and well-formedness, take a look at some of the basic rules that apply for all XML documents.

XML Rules

An XML document has an entity called the *document entity*, which serves as the starting point for the XML processor (and may contain the whole document, like the HTML element that contains a complete HTML document).

Entities must each contain an integral number of elements, comments, processing instructions, and references, possibly together with character data not contained within any element in the entity, or else they must contain nontextual data and no elements.

The logical and physical structures (elements and entities) in an XML document must be synchronous. Tags and elements must each begin and end in the same entity, but they may refer to other entities internally.

Start Tags and End Tags

A start tag marks the beginning of every nonempty XML element. An end tag containing a name that is the same as in the start tag marks the end of every element.

If an element is empty, the start tag may be the whole element and the tag can take a special form: `<name/>`.

Comments

Comments use the same syntax as in HTML:

```
<!-- this is a comment -->
```

However, they must be written using *exactly* this syntax; spaces in the start (`<!--`) and end (`-->`) strings are forbidden. Comments may not be nested.

The string `--` (two hyphens) must not occur in comments.

Comments may appear anywhere except in CDATA sections, in declarations, or in tags.

Declaring XML Documents

The first line of an XML document consists of an XML declaration that specifies the version of XML being used:

```
<?XML VERSION="1.0" ENCODING="UTF-8" RMD="NONE" ?>
```

Note the use of the question mark; this statement is technically a "processing instruction." All ?XML processing instructions are reserved.

The ENCODING declaration identifies the character set in which the document is coded (unlike HTML, which favors ASCII, XML favors Unicode, which allows foreign character sets to be used far more easily than in HTML).

The required markup declaration (RMD) specifies whether or not DTD processing is necessary, and it is here that you can identify your document as being (potentially) valid, or "just well-formed. The possible values of this declaration include:

- NONE—The XML processor can parse the containing document correctly without first reading any part of the DTD.

- INTERNAL—The XML processor must read and process the internal subset of the DTD, if provided.

- ALL (the default)—The XML processor must read and process the declarations in both subsets of the DTD, if they are provided.

The XML Document Type Declaration

The XML document type declaration (DTD) consists of element and attribute declarations that define the allowable element structure of an XML document of a specific type.

The document type declaration must appear before the first start tag in the document:

```
<!DOCTYPE letter SYSTEM "letter.dtd">
```

The DTD is contained in the file `letter.dtd`.

The part of the DTD contained in an external file is called the *external subset* of the DTD. Just as with CSS1 style sheets, where styles can be defined externally in a style sheet or internally in the same document, a DTD may also directly include another, internal, subset:

```
<!DOCTYPE letter [
    <!ELEMENT address (#PCDATA)>

<!-- this part contains the entity, element and attribute -->
<!-- declarations using exactly the same syntax as an external -->
<!-- document type declaration -->

]>
<letter>
<!-- the body of the document comes here -->
</letter>
```

Together, these two subsets make up the document type declaration (DTD), and they must not both be empty.

If both the external and internal subsets are used, the internal subset is read first. Entity and attribute declarations in the internal subset take precedence over those in the external subset.

The name in the DTD must match the name of the root element in XML documents of that type.

The following sections look more closely at the contents of the XML DTD.

Element Declarations

Every element type that appears in a valid XML document must be declared once in the DTD. An element declaration constrains an element's type and its content. For example, the element declaration states that the element BOOK contains a FRONT element followed by a BODY, which is followed by a BACK element:

```
<!ELEMENT BOOK (FRONT, BODY, BACK)>
```

All three elements must be present, and they must appear in this order.

The declarations of the elements that are allowed to be used inside an element are called their *content models.* The contents of an element instance must match the content model declared for that element type.

The language for specifying the content models of elements uses the following syntax:

- ( )   Surrounds a sequence or a set of alternatives.

- ,   Separates the element types in a sequence (read as "followed by;" "A,B" means "A" followed by "B").

- ¦   Separates alternative element types in a list of alternatives ("A|B" means "A OR B").

- ?   Follows an element or group of elements and indicates that it occurs zero times or once ("A,B?" means "A" or "A,B").

- *   Follows an element or group of elements and indicates that it occurs zero or more times ("A,B*" means "A" or "A,B,B…").

- +   Follows an element or group of elements and indicates that it occurs one or more times ("A,B+" means "A,B" or "A,B,B,B…")

The content of an element may be *element content* (it may only contain other elements) or *mixed content* (it may contain character data mixed with elements).

Character data is declared as the #PCDATA, parsed character data, type. The # symbol (SGML's reserved name indicator) distinguishes this element type name from any other element type called PCDATA (which is a perfectly legal name that can be used anywhere). Parsed character data (or simply character data as far as XML is concerned), is character data that is to be parsed (that is, processed) to determine whether each character is markup or simply character data. Any markup characters (tags and entity symbols) appearing in parsed character data will be interpreted. Markup characters that are not meant to be interpreted must be *escaped* (using entity references) or hidden (using CDATA sections).

If an element contains mixed content, the character data part must be declared first, and the content model must use OR (¦) separators, like this:

```
<!ELEMENT address (#PCDATA ¦ street ¦ number )>
```

Empty elements are declared using the keyword EMPTY, but be careful that they really are empty when they appear in the XML document.

An element declared using the keyword ANY may contain child elements of any type and number, mixed with character data.

Attributes

Attributes assign certain properties (size, color, alignment, and so on) to a class of element. Because many properties are usually declared at the same time, attributes are declared in *attribute list declarations.*

Attribute list declarations specify the name, data type, and default value (if any) of each attribute associated with a given element type:

```
<!ELEMENT person (#PCDATA)>
<!ATTLIST person
    forename    CDATA       #REQUIRED
    surname     CDATA       #REQUIRED
    age         NUMBER      #IMPLIED>
```

Attributes themselves may appear only within start tags. For example:

```
<person forename="Fred" surname="FLINTSTONE" age="5">
```

When more than one attribute list declaration is provided for a given element type, all of their contents are merged.

When more than one definition is provided for the same attribute of a given element type, the first declaration counts and later declarations are ignored.

Attribute Remapping

To avoid conflicts with elements whose attributes have the same names (such as when an internal and external DTD subset declare the same attributes), attributes can be declared as equivalent using the XML-ATTRIBUTES attribute.

This attribute must contain pairs of names. In each pair, the first name must be ROLE, HREF, TITLE, SHOW, INLINE, CONTENT-ROLE, CONTENT-TITLE, ACTUATE, BEHAVIOR, or STEPS. The second name is treated as though it was playing the role assigned to the first.

Attribute Types

XML attribute types are of three kinds: a string type, a set of tokenized types, and enumerated types.

A *string* type may take any literal string as a value.

A *tokenized* type has varying lexical and semantic constraints:

- An ID type must be a valid NAME symbol. The name must not appear more than once in an XML document as an ID.

- An IDREF must match the value of an ID attribute of some element in the XML document.

- ENTITY and ENTITIES types must exactly match the name of an external binary general entity declared in the DTD.

- NMTOKEN and NMTOKENS types must consist of a text string consisting of a letter or an underscore followed by one or more letters or digits.

- Notation attribute names must match one of the notation names included in the declaration.

Enumerated type values must match one of the NMTOKEN tokens in the declaration. The same NMTOKEN should not occur more than once in the enumerated attribute types of a single element type.

Attribute Default Values

To avoid having to explicitly declare attributes for every element, you can declare default attribute values in the DTD. If a default value is declared and the attribute is omitted, the attribute is treated as if it were present with its value being the declared default value.

The attribute's declaration provides information on whether its presence is required and, if not, how an XML processor should react if the declared attribute is absent in a document:

- #FIXED—The document is invalid if the attribute has a different value from the default.

- #REQUIRED—The document is invalid if there is a start tag for the element type that does not specify a value for the attribute.

- #IMPLIED—If the attribute is omitted, the XML processor must simply inform the application that no value was specified.

If the attribute is neither #REQUIRED nor #IMPLIED, the value contains the declared default value.

Whitespace Attribute

In HTML documents, multiple blank (white) spaces are reduced to a single whitespace. There are, however, occasions when extra white spaces mean something, and you want to keep them. The XML-SPACE attribute can be used to identify elements in which the whitespace is to be treated as significant by applications. The value of this attribute determines what is to be done with the whitespace in the element:

- DEFAULT—Means that the default whitespace processing is acceptable.
- PRESERVE—Means that all the whitespace should be preserved.

Entities

Entities are similar to the sort of macros that you would expect to find in a word processing package; they are short strings of characters that can be used as abbreviations for large pieces of text (or markup) and are expanded when they are encountered by the XML processor.

Entities may be either binary or text. A text entity contains text data, which is considered to be an integral part of the document. A binary entity contains binary data with an associated notation (notation declarations are explained later).

Only text entities may be referred to using entity references; only the names of binary entities may be given as the value of entity attributes.

If the same entity is declared more than once, the first declaration encountered is binding.

In a well-formed XML document, the name given in an entity reference must exactly match the name given in the declaration of the entity. Entity reference must not contain the name of a binary entity, and binary entities may be referred to only in ENTITY or ENTITIES type attributes.

Parameter Entities

Parameter entity references may be used in a variety of places within the DTD. Parameter entities provide a convenient means of reusing markup code in many places without having to type the code more than once. For example, to declare a parameter entity you would use something like this:

```
<!ENTITY % font (em¦tt¦bold¦strong)>
```

You would refer to it like this:

```
<!ELEMENT body (para, %font;)*>
```

Parameter entity references are always expanded immediately upon being recognized, and the DTD must match the relevant rules of the grammar after they have all been expanded.

In well-formed XML documents, parameter entities must not contain direct or indirect references to themselves.

General Entities

If the definition of an entity is just a value, it is called a *general entity* (or internal entity), and its replacement text is given in the entity declaration. For example:

```
<!ENTITY Shortcut "This is a block of text that I am going to
use very often, but only really want to type once">
```

These entities are for use in the XML document and they are referred to like this:

```
&Shortcut;
```

External Entities

If an entity is not an internal entity, it is an external entity. External entities can be used to include text from another file. For example:

```
<!ENTITY commontext SYSTEM "http://www.there.com/boiler/plate.xml">
```

The keyword SYSTEM identifies a URL, which may be used to retrieve the entity. In addition, an external identifier may include the PUBLIC keyword and a public identifier. The XML processor may try to generate an alternative URL from this, but if it is unable to do so, it must use the URL specified with the SYSTEM keyword.

Each external text entity in an XML document may use a different encoding for its characters. XML provides an encoding declaration processing instruction, which, if it occurs, must appear at the beginning of a system entity, before any other character data or markup. In the document entity, the encoding declaration is part of the XML declaration; in other entities, it is part of an encoding processing instruction.

In order to validate an XML document, an XML processor must include the content of an external text entity. If it is not attempting to validate an XML document, the XML processor does not need to include the content of an external text entity.

External entities are also used to include nontext objects, such as graphics files. Nontext external entities must include a notation (NDATA) declaration, for example:

```
<!ENTITY myface SYSTEM "../images/me.gif" NDATA GIF>
```

Notations identify by name the format of external binary entities, or the application that can handle the format. Notation declarations provide a name for a notation and an external identifier that allows an XML processor or its client application (such as a browser plug-in) to locate a helper application capable of processing data in the notation.

```
<!DOCTYPE BOOK SYSTEM "BOOK.DTD" [
<!-- Figures for this chapter: -->
<!ENTITY chap1.fig1 SYSTEM "0101.PCX" NDATA PCX>
<!ENTITY chap1.fig2 SYSTEM "0132.PCX" NDATA PCK>
]>
```

It's worth noting how much more freedom this gives you over the format than you get in HTML. The format is no longer tied to a specific file type (extension), but depends instead on what you declare it to be.

In a valid XML document, the name of the notation used in an entity declaration must have been declared.

Predefined Entities

As stated earlier, the ampersand character (&) and the left angle bracket (<), which would normally be interpreted as markup, must be escaped using either numeric character references or the strings & and <.

In addition, the right angle bracket (>) may be represented using the string >, the apostrophe or single-quote character (') may be represented as ', and the double-quote character (") may be represented as ".

Well-formed documents need not declare the amp, lt, gt, apos, and quot entities, but valid XML documents must declare them before using them. All XML processors must recognize these entities whether they are declared or not.

Conditional Sections

Parameter entities can also be used in DTDs to turn the sections of markup that they enclose into *conditional sections*. These conditional sections can be used to allow DTDs to be "customized" for individual documents. This is achieved by including the parameter entity declarations in the document's internal DTD subset so that they can be used as "switches":

```
<?XML VERSION "1.0" RMD="ALL"?>
<!DOCTYPE BOOK SYSTEM "strict.dtd" [
<!ENTITY % DRAFT "INCLUDE">
<!ENTITY % FINAL "IGNORE">
<![%DRAFT;[
<!ELEMENT BOOK (AUTHOR_COMMENTS*, FRONT, BODY, BACK)>
[[>
<![%FINAL;[
<!ELEMENT BOOK (FRONT, COPYRIGHT, BODY, BACK, SOFTWARE)>
]]>
]>
<BOOK> ...
```

The preceding code sets the value of the parameter entity DRAFT to "INCLUDE" and the value of FINAL to "IGNORE" in this document. The final version of the document would simply swap the values of these two parameter entities.

CDATA Sections

CDATA sections (character data sections) allow you to enter even large amounts of markup characters without having to escape every single & and < character, and to otherwise "hide" blocks of characters from the XML processor. CDATA sections can occur anywhere that character data might occur. They begin with the sequence <![CDATA[, and end with the sequence]]>, for example:

```
<![CDATA[ <P>This text will not be 'seen' & processed.</P> ]]>
```

In the special case of CDATA sections, *character data* is any string of characters not including the sequence]]>, which terminates the CDATA section.

CDATA sections cannot be nested.

DTD or Not?

I've gone to a lot of effort to explain XML DTDs and what they contain, but all that information begs the simple question "Do you need a DTD?" This is a simple question to ask, but a very hard one to answer. The easy answer is "only if the external subset contains any unspecified attributes that have default values, entity references, or if white space occurs directly within element types that have element content."

The hard answer is, of course, much harder to give and more or less comes down to some considerations rather than some off-the-shelf rules.

Ask yourself what kind of checking you want to do on the documents. If the documents are to be generated by a program, the chances are that you will be able to tune the program to produce the correct XML code, and validity is not a concern.

Consider what you are going to do with the documents after they have been created. If you are going to reuse the content, or process it in any way (such as converting it into HTML), a DTD gives you a formal structure that can be processed externally to derive rules for processing the documents.

Do not let the seeming complexity of a DTD put you off: A DTD only needs to be as complex as you want or need it to be. On the other hand, it can be as simple as you want or need it to be, consisting perhaps of only a few elements. For example, there is a proposed DTD in circulation for Internet FAQs (frequently asked question documents) that only has three or four elements—a Q element for a question, an A element for an answer, and a few others to cover linking to other questions and answers. Hopefully, as XML becomes more widely accepted, there will eventually be a ready supply of off-the-shelf XML DTDs, just as there is for SGML.

XML Linking

Linking is one aspect of XML that I have studiously avoided up to this point. XML provides much more powerful links than either SGML or HTML and deserves to be treated separately in order to do it full justice. Built on the experience acquired from years of research into linking, XML's linking mechanisms (otherwise known as XLL, which stands for XML Link Language) are based on ideas taken from HTML, HyTime (Hypermedia/Time-Based Structuring Language, ISO 10744:1992), and an SGML application used extensively in academia called the Text Encoding Initiative (TEI).

XML links are interoperable with HTML. They use the same HREF attribute and give its value the same general meaning as in HTML.

The value of an HREF is a URL identifying the *resource* that is the target of the link, optionally qualified by # and a *fragment identifier*, or ? and a query. XML links also conform to RFC 1738's conventions governing the characters that can appear within the URL itself.

However, XML's links *extend* HREF links by the following:

- Allowing absolutely any element type to be the source of a link
- Defining additional properties and behaviors for all links
- Introducing the concept of *out-of-line* links
- Defining the precise meaning of the fragment identifier when the target of the link is an XML document

Link Types

XML allows any element type to act as a linking element. This is achieved by specifying the reserved attribute XML-LINK for each element that is to act as a linking element. In addition, the

- ■ REPLACE—On following the link, the target should replace the source where the link started.
- ■ NEW—On following the link, the target should be displayed or processed in a new context (such as a new browser window), without affecting the context of the source where the link started.

HTML link behavior matches that specified by the EMBED attribute for IMG elements and RE-PLACE for A elements.

ACTUATE

The ACTUATE attribute specifies when a link should be followed:

- ■ AUTO—When encountered. The display or processing of the source is not considered complete until this is done.
- ■ USER—Not until there is an explicit external request to do so.

HTML link behavior matches that specified by the AUTO attribute for IMG elements and USER for A elements.

Addressing

XML's HREF attributes are interoperable with HTML. However, XML provides support for more sophisticated addressing within the target resource when it is an XML document. You can use this special addressing from within HTML pages to address parts of XML documents.

When a locator identifies a target that is an XML document, the locator value may contain a URL or a fragment identifier, or both.

A URL, if present, is treated as a standard URL, and identifies the *containing resource* that is the target of the link (the document). If no URL is given, the document in which the link is contained is taken to be the "containing resource."

Any *fragment identifier* is treated as an *extended pointer*. If an extended pointer is provided, the target resource is a *subresource* of the containing resource. A fragment identifier is preceded by a *connector* that identifies how and where the fragment is to be located and processed:

- ■ # A standard HTML-style fragment; the whole of the containing resource is to be delivered to the client, which then has the job of locating the fragment for itself.
- ■ ?XML-PTR= An XML query; the server interprets the fragment identifier (extended pointer) and delivers *only* the requested fragment to the client.
- ■ ¦ An XML-specific connector; either of the two approaches just listed can be used to fetch the requested resource.

Extended Pointers

Starting from the root element (the element named in the DTD), an element that contains other elements is considered to be their parent and they in turn are its children. By expanding these parent-child relationships, it is possible to map out a tree of the element structure of an XML document. (This is not normally possible in HTML, because there is little or nothing to prevent you from using, for example, H1, H2, H3, and H4 elements in any order you like, even though in a structured HTML document you should use them hierarchically.)

Extended pointers operate on the element tree defined by the elements in the XML document. They describe the elements within the document in terms of various properties, such as their type or attribute values, or simply by counting them.

The basic form of an extended pointer is a series of location terms, each of which specifies either an absolute or a relative location.

Absolute Location Terms

In an absolute location, each *location term* works in the context of a location source. By default, the location source for the first location term is the *root element* of the XML document. Each extended pointer can start with one of the following location terms:

- ROOT—The ROOT keyword specifies that the location source is the root element of the source. This is the default behavior.

- HERE—The HERE keyword specifies that the location source for the first location term of the series is the linking element containing the locator rather than the default root element.

- DITTO—The DITTO keyword specifies that the location source for its first location term is the location source specified by the entire first pointer.

- ID—The ID keyword specifies that the location source for the first location term is the element in the source that has an attribute of type ID with a value matching the given name (that is, ID(Name)).

- HTML—The HTML keyword selects the first element whose type is A and which has a NAME attribute whose value is the same as the supplied NAME value (this is the same as the # in an HTML document).

Relative Location Terms

A relative location term consists of a keyword, followed by one or more *steps*. The allowed keywords are the following:

- CHILD—Selects child elements of the location source

- DESCENDANT —Selects elements appearing within the content of the location source (for example, the element tree beginning at this element)

- ANCESTOR —Selects elements in which the location source is found (for example, the element tree beginning at the parent of the current element)

- PRECEDING —Selects elements that appear before the location source

- PSIBLING —Selects sibling elements that precede the location source (for example, the other children of the parent element that come before this element)

34

XML

■ `FOLLOWING` —Selects elements that appear after the location source

■ `FSIBLING` —Selects sibling elements that follow the location source (for example, the other children of the parent element that come after this element)

Selecting Targets

The elements that match a location reference are called *candidates*. Candidates can be selected by their occurrence number, element type, attribute name, and attribute value.

A keyword limits the possible candidates of a location reference to those elements that have the required property in relation to the location source. The keyword is followed by one or more *steps*. Each step defines an *instance*, an optional *element type*, and an optional *attribute type* and *value*.

The *instance* counts the candidates. It can be a positive number (that is, counting forward from the first candidate), a negative number (counting backward from the last candidate), or the special value `ALL` to select all the candidates:

```
(4) - select the fourth candidate location
(-2) - select the second-to-last candidate location
```

The instance can be followed by a comma and an optional, but recommended, *element* type. This can take the following values:

■ `*CDATA`—Selects pseudoelements containing only text

■ `*`—Selects any element type

■ `Name`—Selects elements with the type `Name`

For example:

```
(3,P) - selects the third <P> element
(-1,EXAMPLE) - selects the last <EXAMPLE> element
(2,*CDATA) - selects the second untagged span of text
```

The element type, if specified, can be qualified by an *attribute name* and *value*. The attribute name can take the following values:

■ `*`—Matches any attribute name

■ `Name`—Specifies the attribute type `Name`

The attribute value can take the following values:

■ `*IMPLIED`—Matches attributes for which no value was specified, and no default exists

■ `*`—Matches any value

■ `Name`—Matches the value `Name`

■ `"value"`—Matches the value that is quoted

The following example selects the first child element of the location source that is a <P> element for which the FONT attribute has been left unspecified:

```
CHILD(1,P,FONT,*IMPLIED)
```

Extended Pointer Ranges

A fragment identifier can contain a single extended pointer, or two extended pointers separated by the string .. to define a range, or span of text.

The fragment is assumed to be everything from the start of the first extended pointer's target (the *location source*) to the end of the second one. This allows you to select a range of elements as the target of the link rather than (as in HTML) the whole document.

The following example selects the text that starts at the beginning of the first child element of the location source that is a <P> element, and ends at the end of the last child that is a <P> element:

```
(CHILD(1,P) .. (CHILD(-1,P)
```

Extended Link Groups

An extended link group element is used to store a list of links to other documents that together constitute an interlinked document group.

Each document is identified using the HREF attribute of an extended link document element, which is a child element of the GROUP. The value of the HREF attribute is a locator.

These elements are recognized by the use of the XML-LINK attribute with the value GROUP or DOCUMENT.

The GROUP element contains one or more DOCUMENT elements, each pointing to a resource (or a subresource, using the extended pointer syntax) that forms part of the document group.

For example, if an XML document contained the following code, and GROUP and DOCUMENT had been identified as linking elements, documents bookmarks1.xml and bookmarks2.xml would be processed to look for links that involve this document:

```
<GROUP>
<DOCUMENT HREF="http://www.home.com/bookmarks1.xml"/>
<DOCUMENT HREF="http://www.home.com/bookmarks2.xml"/>
</GROUP>
```

Fixed XML-LINK Attributes

To avoid having to declare the special XML-LINK attribute every time you use an element, you can declare it once, in the DTD, as a fixed value:

```
<!ATTLIST MYLINK
          XML-LINK CDATA #FIXED "SIMPLE">
```

34

XML

XML Style

In principle, CSS1 (Cascading Style Sheets, level 1) style sheets can be used to apply simple formatting to XML documents. XML documents are like HTML documents in that they contain elements with names, IDs, and so on—the same blocks that CSS1 uses to define its formatting rules for HTML documents.

However, CSS1 is specifically designed around HTML, and some of its features rely on HTML-specific coding practice. For example, pseudoclasses, such as `A:link`, `A:visited`, and `A:active`, allow links to look different when they are selected or after they have been followed. Pseudoelements, such as the `:first-line` and `:first-letter` pseudoelements, and normal classes used by CSS1 would also have to be added as attributes to elements in your XML DTDs to allow their values to be used in the CSS1 style sheets for XML documents.

Alongside or possibly instead of CSS1, XML has its own style language called *XS* that is far more powerful than CSS1.

> **NOTE**
>
> XS is still in a very early stage of development; currently, the standard has not developed beyond a discussion document.

XS is based on a profile of DSSSL, called DSSSL-o ("o" for online). DSSSL (Document Style and Semantics Specification Language: ISO/IEC Standard 10179:1996) is a language based on Scheme, a dialect of the LISP programming language. DSSSL supports the transformation, querying, and processing of SGML documents. The transformation aspect of DSSSL is not supported in XS, and the style sheet part has been cut down to the bare essentials.

How XS Works

XS is essentially a data-driven style mechanism. When an XML document is to be formatted (either for printing on paper or display on a screen), one or more XS style sheets will be read. The style sheets to be used can be specified in the XML document itself, or the user can select them.

The processing of the XML document is determined by scanning the XML document's structure and merging it with the *formatting specification* that is derived from the active style sheets. These instructions are then used to create *flow objects*, such as paragraphs and tables, which determine the coding applied to the document. This merging process produces a tree structure of flow objects called the *flow object tree*.

XS supports *construction rules*, that declare, in effect, what to do with an element. More precisely, they state what flow objects are to be created, and what characteristics each flow object is to have. For example, an element construction rule for the P element might specify that a paragraph flow object is to be added to the flow object tree, with the following characteristics:

```
font-size: 12pt
first-line-start-indent: 18pt
quadding: left
```

This will cause the characters in the paragraph to be set in 12 points, with an 18-point indent at the start of the first line, and the paragraph will be left-justified.

XS Processing

Even though it has been reduced to its essentials, XS can still be considered a full programming language that can be used to perform calculations, test for conditions, and so on. XS can be used to build up complex instructions for the processing of individual elements or even characters within an XML document.

Almost any aspect of an XML document's structure can be used to control its processing. Most construction rules operate at the element level, but you can easily refine their behavior by testing for properties of an element, such as its attributes and their values, or its ancestor elements.

Although by default the whole document will be processed, and in its original order, XS gives you access to the full element structure at any point in the document. This means that you can include parts of a document from elsewhere in that document so that, for example, you can create a table of contents from the chapter headings, and place it at the start of the document. It is also easy to suppress parts of the document that you do not want to be seen in this context, thus enabling such features as conditional content, dynamic content, and access-controlled content.

Converting HTML into XML

If your HTML code already conforms to one of the many HTML DTDs that are in public circulation, the code may already be very close to being valid XML. To turn an HTML document into a valid XML document, you have to do four things:

1. Add an XML declaration with a required markup declaration (technically, this is only optional, but you should do it).
2. Acquire a valid XML DTD (or XML version of the DTD you want to use).
3. Add a document type declaration.
4. Ensure that the document is well formed, especially by doing the following:

   - Check that all elements have a start tag and an end tag and that they are nested properly.
   - Check that all attribute values are enclosed in quotes.
   - Convert the empty elements into XML format (for example, `<IMG SRC="file.gif"/>` or `<IMG SRC="file.gif"></IMG>`).

Appendixes

VIII
PART

HTML 4.0 Reference

by Bob Correll

IN THIS APPENDIX

HTML 4.0 is an ambitious attempt to meet the needs of Web developers worldwide, both casual and professional. This appendix provides a quick reference to all the elements and attributes of the language.

> **NOTE**
>
> This appendix is based on the information provided in the *HTML 4.0 Specification W3C Working Draft 8-July-1997,* which can be found at `http://www.w3.org/TR/WD-html40/`.

In order to make the information readily accessible, this appendix organizes HTML elements by their function in the following order:

- Structure
- Text phrases and paragraphs
- Text formatting elements
- Lists
- Links
- Tables
- Frames
- Embedded content
- Style
- Forms
- Scripts

Within each section the elements are listed alphabetically and the following information is presented:

- Usage—A general description of the element
- Start/End Tag—Indicates whether these tags are required, optional, or illegal
- Attributes—Lists the attributes of the element with a short description of their effects
- Empty—Indicates whether the element can be empty
- Notes—Relates any special considerations when using the element and indicates whether the element is new, deprecated, or obsolete

> **NOTE**
>
> Several elements and attributes have been *deprecated,* which means they have been outdated by the current HTML version, and you should avoid using them. The same or similar functionality is provided using new features.

> **NOTE**
>
> HTML 4.0 introduces several new attributes that apply to a significant number of elements. These are referred to as %coreattrs, %i18n, and %events and are explained in the last section of the appendix.

Following this, the common attributes (those with a % in front of them) and intrinsic events are summarized.

Structure

HTML relies upon several elements to provide structure to a document (as opposed to structuring the text within) as well as provide information that is used by the browser or search engines.

<BDO>...</BDO>

Usage	The bidirectional algorithm element is used to selectively turn off the default text direction.
Start/End Tag	Required/Required
Attributes	lang="..."—The language of the document.
	dir="..."—The text direction (ltr, rtl).
Empty	No
Notes	The dir attribute is mandatory.

<BODY>...</BODY>

Usage	Contains the content of the document.
Start/End Tag	Optional/Optional
Attributes	%coreattrs, %i18n, %events
	background="..."—Deprecated. URL for the background image.
	bgcolor="..."—Deprecated. Sets background color.
	text="..."—Deprecated. Text color.
	link="..."—Deprecated. Link color.
	vlink="..."—Deprecated. Visited link color.
	alink="..."—Deprecated. Active link color.
	onload="..."—Intrinsic event triggered when the document loads.
	onunload="..."—Intrinsic event triggered when document unloads.

A

HTML 4.0 REFERENCE

| Empty | No |
| Notes | There can be only one BODY and it must follow the HEAD. The BODY element can be replaced by a FRAMESET element. The presentational attributes are deprecated in favor of setting these values with style sheets. |

Comments <!-- ... -->

Usage	Used to insert notes or scripts that are not displayed by the browser.
Start/End Tag	Required/Required
Attributes	None.
Empty	Yes
Notes	Comments are not restricted to one line and can be any length. The end tag is not required to be on the same line as the start tag.

<DIV>...</DIV>

Usage	The division element is used to add structure to a block of text.
Start/End Tag	Required/Required
Attributes	%coreattrs, %i18n, %events
	align="..."—Deprecated. Controls alignment (left, center, right, justify).
Empty	No
Notes	Cannot be used within a P element. The align attribute is deprecated in favor of controlling alignment through style sheets.

<!DOCTYPE...>

| Usage | Version information appears on the first line of an HTML document and is a Standard Generalized Markup Language (SGML) declaration rather than an element. |

<H1>...</H1> through <H6>...</H6>

Usage	The six headings (H1 is the uppermost, or most important) are used in the BODY to structure information in a hierarchical fashion.
Start/End Tag	Required/Required
Attributes	%coreattrs, %i18n, %events
	align="..."—Deprecated. Controls alignment (left, center, right, justify).

Empty	No
Notes	Visual browsers will display the size of the headings in relation to their importance, with H1 being the largest and H6 the smallest. The `align` attribute is deprecated in favor of controlling alignment through style sheets.

<HEAD>...</HEAD>

Usage	This is the document header, and it contains other elements that provide information to users and search engines.
Start/End Tag	Optional/Optional
Attributes	`%i18n`
	`profile="..."`—URL specifying the location of META data.
Empty	No
Notes	There can be only one HEAD per document. It must follow the opening HTML tag and precede the BODY.

<HR>

Usage	Horizontal rules are used to separate sections of a Web page.
Start/End Tag	Required/Illegal
Attributes	`%coreattrs, %events`
	`align="..."`—Deprecated. Controls alignment (`left`, `center`, `right`, `justify`).
	`noshade="..."`—Displays the rule as a solid color.
	`size="..."`—Deprecated. The size of the rule.
	`width="..."`—Deprecated. The width of the rule.
Empty	Yes

<HTML>...</HTML>

Usage	The HTML element contains the entire document.
Start/End Tag	Optional/Optional
Attributes	`%i18n`
	`version="..."`—URL of the document type definition specifying the HTML version used to create the document.
Empty	No
Notes	The version information is duplicated in the `<!DOCTYPE...>` declaration and therefore is not essential.

`<META>`

Usage	Provides information about the document.
Start/End Tag	Required/Illegal
Attributes	`%i18n`
	`http-equiv="..."`—HTTP response header name.
	`name="..."`—Name of the meta information.
	`content="..."`—Content of the meta information.
	`scheme="..."`—Assigns a scheme to interpret the meta data.
Empty	Yes

`<SPAN>...</SPAN>`

Usage	Organizes the document by defining a span of text.
Start/End Tag	Required/Required
Attributes	`%coreattrs, %i18n, %events`
Empty	No

`<TITLE>...</TITLE>`

Usage	This is the name you give your Web page. The TITLE element is located in the HEAD element and is displayed in the browser window title bar.
Start/End Tag	Required/Required
Attributes	`%i18n`
Empty	No
Notes	Only one title allowed per document.

Text Phrases and Paragraphs

Text phrases (or blocks) can be structured to suit a specific purpose, such as creating a paragraph. This should not be confused with modifying the formatting of the text.

`<ACRONYM>...</ACRONYM>`

Usage	Used to define acronyms.
Start/End Tag	Required/Required
Attributes	`%coreattrs, %i18n, %events`
Empty	No

<ADDRESS>...</ADDRESS>

Usage	Provides a special format for author or contact information.
Start/End Tag	Required/Required
Attributes	%coreattrs, %i18n, %events
Empty	No
Notes	The BR element is commonly used inside the ADDRESS element to break the lines of an address.

<BLOCKQUOTE>...</BLOCKQUOTE>

Usage	Used to display long quotations.
Start/End Tag	Required/Required
Attributes	%coreattrs, %i18n, %events
	cite="..."—The URL of the quoted text.
Empty	No

Usage	Forces a line break.
Start/End Tag	Required/Illegal
Attributes	%coreattrs, %i18n, %events
	clear="..."—Sets the location where the next line begins after a floating object (none, left, right, all).
Empty	Yes

<CITE>...</CITE>

Usage	Cites a reference.
Start/End Tag	Required/Required
Attributes	%coreattrs, %i18n, %events
Empty	No

<CODE>...</CODE>

Usage	Identifies a code fragment for display.
Start/End Tag	Required/Required
Attributes	%coreattrs, %i18n, %events
Empty	No

\<DEL>...\</DEL>

Usage	Shows text as having been deleted from the document since the last change.
Start/End Tag	Required/Required
Attributes	`%coreattrs`, `%i18n`, `%events`
	`cite="..."`—The URL of the source document.
	`datetime="..."`—Indicates the date and time of the change.
Empty	No
Notes	New element in HTML 4.0.

\<DFN>...\</DFN>

Usage	Defines an enclosed term.
Start/End Tag	Required/Required
Attributes	`%coreattrs`, `%i18n`, `%events`
Empty	No

\<EM>...\</EM>

Usage	Emphasized text.
Start/End Tag	Required/Required
Attributes	`%coreattrs`, `%i18n`, `%events`
Empty	No

\<INS>...\</INS>

Usage	Shows text as having been inserted in the document since the last change.
Start/End Tag	Required/Required
Attributes	`%coreattrs`, `%i18n`, `%events`
	`cite="..."`—The URL of the source document.
	`datetime="..."`—Indicates the date and time of the change.
Empty	No
Notes	New element in HTML 4.0.

\<KBD>...\</KBD>

Usage	Indicates text a user would type.
Start/End Tag	Required/Required

Attributes	%coreattrs, %i18n, %events
Empty	No

`<P>...</P>`

Usage	Defines a paragraph.
Start/End Tag	Required/Optional
Attributes	%coreattrs, %i18n, %events
	align="..."—Deprecated. Controls alignment (left, center, right, justify).
Empty	No

`<PRE>...</PRE>`

Usage	Displays preformatted text.
Start/End Tag	Required/Required
Attributes	%coreattrs, %i18n, %events
	width="..."—The width of the formatted text.
Empty	No

`<Q>...</Q>`

Usage	Used to display short quotations that do not require paragraph breaks.
Start/End Tag	Required/Required
Attributes	%coreattrs, %i18n, %events
	cite="..."—The URL of the quoted text.
Empty	No
Notes	New element in HTML 4.0.

`<SAMP>...</SAMP>`

Usage	Identifies sample output.
Start/End Tag	Required/Required
Attributes	%coreattrs, %i18n, %events
Empty	No

`<STRONG>...</STRONG>`

Usage	Stronger emphasis.
Start/End Tag	Required/Required

Attributes	%coreattrs, %i18n, %events
Empty	No

_{...\}

Usage	Creates subscript.
Start/End Tag	Required/Required
Attributes	%coreattrs, %i18n, %events
Empty	No

\^{...\}

Usage	Creates superscript.
Start/End Tag	Required/Required
Attributes	%coreattrs, %i18n, %events
Empty	No

\<VAR>...\</VAR>

Usage	A variable.
Start/End Tag	Required/Required
Attributes	%coreattrs, %i18n, %events
Empty	No

Text Formatting Elements

Text characteristics such as the size, weight, and style can be modified using these elements, but the HTML 4.0 specification encourages you to use style instead.

\<B>...\</B>

Usage	Bold text.
Start/End Tag	Required/Required
Attributes	%coreattrs, %i18n, %events
Empty	No

\<BASEFONT>

Usage	Sets the base font size.
Start/End Tag	Required/Illegal
Attributes	size="..."—The font size (1–7 or relative, that is, +3).
	color="..."—The font color.
	face="..."—The font type.

Empty	Yes
Notes	Deprecated in favor of style sheets.

`<BIG>...</BIG>`

Usage	Large text.
Start/End Tag	Required/Required
Attributes	%coreattrs, %i18n, %events
Empty	No

`<FONT>...</FONT>`

Usage	Changes the font size and color.
Start/End Tag	Required/Required
Attributes	size="..."—The font size (1–7 or relative, that is, +3).
	color="..."—The font color.
	face="..."—The font type.
Empty	No
Notes	Deprecated in favor of style sheets.

`<I>...</I>`

Usage	Italicized text.
Start/End Tag	Required/Required
Attributes	%coreattrs, %i18n, %events
Empty	No

`<S>...</S>`

Usage	Strikethrough text.
Start/End Tag	Required/Required
Attributes	%coreattrs, %i18n, %events
Empty	No
Notes	Deprecated.

`<SMALL>...</SMALL>`

Usage	Small text.
Start/End Tag	Required/Required
Attributes	%coreattrs, %i18n, %events
Empty	No

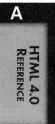

A

HTML 4.0
REFERENCE

<STRIKE>...</STRIKE>

Usage	Strikethrough text.
Start/End Tag	Required/Required
Attributes	%coreattrs, %i18n, %events
Empty	No
Notes	Deprecated.

<TT>...</TT>

Usage	Teletype (or monospaced) text.
Start/End Tag	Required/Required
Attributes	%coreattrs, %i18n, %events
Empty	No

<U>...</U>

Usage	Underlined text.
Start/End Tag	Required/Required
Attributes	%coreattrs, %i18n, %events
Empty	No
Notes	Deprecated.

Lists

You can organize text into a more structured outline by creating lists. Lists can be nested.

<DD>...</DD>

Usage	The definition description used in a DL (definition list) element.
Start/End Tag	Required/Optional
Attributes	%coreattrs, %i18n, %events
Empty	No
Notes	Can contain block-level content, such as the <P> element.

<DIR>...</DIR>

Usage	Creates a multi-column directory list.
Start/End Tag	Required/Required
Attributes	%coreattrs, %i18n, %events
	compact—Deprecated. Compacts the displayed list.

Empty	No
Notes	Must contain at least one list item. This element is deprecated in favor of the UL (unordered list) element.

`<DL>...</DL>`

Usage	Creates a definition list.
Start/End Tag	Required/Required
Attributes	`%coreattrs, %i18n, %events`
	`compact`—Deprecated. Compacts the displayed list.
Empty	No
Notes	Must contain at least one `<DT>` or `<DD>` element in any order.

`<DT>...</DT>`

Usage	The definition term (or label) used within a DL (definition list) element.
Start/End Tag	Required/Optional
Attributes	`%coreattrs, %i18n, %events`
Empty	No
Notes	Must contain text (which can be modified by text markup elements).

`<LI>...</LI>`

Usage	Defines a list item within a list.
Start/End Tag	Required/Optional
Attributes	`%coreattrs, %i18n, %events`
	`type="..."`—Changes the numbering style (`1`, `a`, `A`, `i`, `I`), ordered lists, or bullet style (`disc`, `square`, `circle`) in unordered lists.
	`value="..."`—Sets the numbering to the given integer beginning with the current list item.
Empty	No

`<MENU>...</MENU>`

Usage	Creates a single-column menu list.
Start/End Tag	Required/Required
Attributes	`%coreattrs, %i18n, %events`
	`compact`—Deprecated. Compacts the displayed list.

Empty	No
Notes	Must contain at least one list item. This element is deprecated in favor of the UL (unordered list) element.

`<OL>...</OL>`

Usage	Creates an ordered list.
Start/End Tag	Required/Required
Attributes	%coreattrs, %i18n, %events
	type="..."—Sets the numbering style (1, a, A, i, I).
	compact—Deprecated. Compacts the displayed list.
	start="..."—Sets the starting number to the chosen integer.
Empty	No
Notes	Must contain at least one list item.

`<UL>...</UL>`

Usage	Creates an unordered list.
Start/End Tag	Required/Required
Attributes	%coreattrs, %i18n, %events
	type="..."—Sets the bullet style (disc, square, circle).
	compact—Deprecated. Compacts the displayed list.
Empty	No
Notes	Must contain at least one list item.

Links

Hyperlinking is fundamental to HTML. These elements enable you to link to other documents.

`<A>...</A>`

Usage	Used to define links and anchors.
Start/End Tag	Required/Required
Attributes	%coreattrs, %i18n, %events
	charset="..."—Character encoding of the resource.
	name="..."—Defines an anchor.
	href="..."—The URL of the linked resource.
	target="..."—Determines where the resource will be displayed (user-defined name, _blank, _parent, _self, _top).

rel="..."—Forward link types.

rev="..."—Reverse link types.

accesskey="..."—Assigns a hotkey to this element.

shape="..."—Enables you to define client-side imagemaps using defined shapes (default, rect, circle, poly).

coords="..."—Sets the size of the shape using pixel or percentage lengths.

tabindex="..."—Sets the tabbing order between elements with a defined tabindex.

Empty	No

\<BASE>

Usage	All other URLs in the document are resolved against this location.
Start/End Tag	Required/Illegal
Attributes	href="..."—The URL of the linked resource.
	target="..."—Determines where the resource will be displayed (user-defined name, _blank, _parent, _self, _top).
Empty	Yes
Notes	Located in the document HEAD.

\<LINK>

Usage	Defines the relationship between a link and a resource.
Start/End Tag	Required/Illegal
Attributes	%coreattrs, %i18n, %events
	href="..."—The URL of the resource.
	rel="..."—The forward link types.
	rev="..."—The reverse link types.
	type="..."—The Internet content type.
	media="..."—Defines the destination medium (screen, print, projection, braille, speech, all).
	target="..."—Determines where the resource will be displayed (user-defined name, _blank, _parent, _self, _top).
Empty	Yes
Notes	Located in the document HEAD.

A

HTML 4.0 REFERENCE

Tables

Tables are meant to display data in a tabular format. Before the introduction of HTML 4.0, tables were widely used for page layout purposes, but with the advent of style sheets this is being discouraged by the W3C.

`<CAPTION>...</CAPTION>`

Usage	Displays a table caption.
Start/End Tag	Required/Required
Attributes	%coreattrs, %i18n, %events
	align="..."—Deprecated. Controls alignment (left, center, right, justify).
Empty	No
Notes	Optional.

`<COL>`

Usage	Groups columns within column groups in order to share attribute values.
Start/End Tag	Required/Illegal
Attributes	%coreattrs, %i18n, %events
	span="..."—The number of columns the group contains.
	width="..."—The column width as a percentage, pixel value, or minimum value.
	align="..."—Horizontally aligns the contents of cells (left, center, right, justify, char).
	char="..."—Sets a character on which the column aligns.
	charoff="..."—Offset to the first alignment character on a line.
	valign="..."—Vertically aligns the contents of a cell (top, middle, bottom, baseline).
Empty	Yes

`<COLGROUP>...</COLGROUP>`

Usage	Defines a column group.
Start/End Tag	Required/Optional
Attributes	%coreattrs, %i18n, %events
	span="..."—The number of columns in a group.
	width="..."—The width of the columns.

align="..."—Horizontally aligns the contents of cells (left, center, right, justify, char).

char="..."—Sets a character on which the column aligns.

charoff="..."—Offset to the first alignment character on a line.

valign="..."—Vertically aligns the contents of a cell (top, middle, bottom, baseline).

Empty   No

`<TABLE>...</TABLE>`

Usage   Creates a table.

Start/End Tag Required/Required

Attributes %coreattrs, %i18n, %events

align="..."—Deprecated. Controls alignment (left, center, right, justify).

bgcolor="..."—Deprecated. Sets the background color.

width="..."—Table width.

cols="..."—The number of columns.

border="..."—The width in pixels of a border around the table.

frame="..."—Sets the visible sides of a table (void, above, below, hsides, lhs, rhs, vsides, box, border).

rules="..."—Sets the visible rules within a table (none, groups, rows, cols, all).

cellspacing="..."—Spacing between cells.

cellpadding="..."—Spacing in cells.

Empty   No

`<TBODY>...</TBODY>`

Usage   Defines the table body.

Start/End Tag Optional/Optional

Attributes %coreattrs, %i18n, %events

align="..."—Horizontally aligns the contents of cells (left, center, right, justify, char).

char="..."—Sets a character on which the column aligns.

charoff="..."—Offset to the first alignment character on a line.

valign="..."—Vertically aligns the contents of cells (top, middle, bottom, baseline).

Empty   No

A

HTML 4.0
REFERENCE

`<TD>...</TD>`

Usage	Defines a cell's contents.
Start/End Tag	Required/Optional
Attributes	`%coreattrs`, `%i18n`, `%events`

`axis="..."`—Abbreviated name.

`axes="..."`—axis names listing row and column headers pertaining to the cell.

`nowrap="..."`—Deprecated. Turns off text wrapping in a cell.

`bgcolor="..."`—Deprecated. Sets the background color.

`rowspan="..."`—The number of rows spanned by a cell.

`colspan="..."`—The number of columns spanned by a cell.

`align="..."`—Horizontally aligns the contents of cells (`left`, `center`, `right`, `justify`, `char`).

`char="..."`—Sets a character on which the column aligns.

`charoff="..."`—Offset to the first alignment character on a line.

`valign="..."`—Vertically aligns the contents of cells (`top`, `middle`, `bottom`, `baseline`).

Empty	No

`<TFOOT>...</TFOOT>`

Usage	Defines the table footer.
Start/End Tag	Required/Optional
Attributes	`%coreattrs`, `%i18n`, `%events`

`align="..."`—Horizontally aligns the contents of cells (`left`, `center`, `right`, `justify`, `char`).

`char="..."`—Sets a character on which the column aligns.

`charoff="..."`—Offset to the first alignment character on a line.

`valign="..."`—Vertically aligns the contents of cells (`top`, `middle`, `bottom`, `baseline`).

Empty	No

`<TH>...</TH>`

Usage	Defines the cell contents of the table header.
Start/End Tag	Required/Optional
Attributes	`%coreattrs`, `%i18n`, `%events`

axis="..."—Abbreviated name.

axes="..."—axis names listing row and column headers pertaining to the cell.

nowrap="..."—Deprecated. Turns off text wrapping in a cell.

bgcolor="..."—Deprecated. Sets the background color.

rowspan="..."—The number of rows spanned by a cell.

colspan="..."—The number of columns spanned by a cell.

align="..."—Horizontally aligns the contents of cells (left, center, right, justify, char).

char="..."—Sets a character on which the column aligns.

charoff="..."—Offset to the first alignment character on a line.

valign="..."—Vertically aligns the contents of cells (top, middle, bottom, baseline).

Empty   No

\<THEAD\>...\</THEAD\>

Usage	Defines the table header.
Start/End Tag	Required/Optional
Attributes	%coreattrs, %i18n, %events

align="..."—Horizontally aligns the contents of cells (left, center, right, justify, char).

char="..."—Sets a character on which the column aligns.

charoff="..."—Offset to the first alignment character on a line.

valign="..."—Vertically aligns the contents of cells (top, middle, bottom, baseline).

Empty   No

\<TR\>...\</TR\>

Usage	Defines a row of table cells.
Start/End Tag	Required/Optional
Attributes	%coreattrs, %i18n, %events

align="..."—Horizontally aligns the contents of cells (left, center, right, justify, char).

char="..."—Sets a character on which the column aligns.

charoff="..."—Offset to the first alignment character on a line.

valign="..."—Vertically aligns the contents of cells (top, middle, bottom, baseline).

bgcolor="..."—Deprecated. Sets the background color.

Empty   No

Frames

Frames create new "panels" in the Web browser window that are used to display content from different source documents.

<FRAME>

Usage   Defines a frame.

Start/End Tag   Required/Illegal

Attributes   name="..."—The name of a frame.

src="..."—The source to be displayed in a frame.

frameborder="..."—Toggles the border between frames (0, 1).

marginwidth="..."—Sets the space between the frame border and content.

marginheight="..."—Sets the space between the frame border and content.

noresize—Disables sizing.

scrolling="..."—Determines scrollbar presence (auto, yes, no).

Empty   Yes

<FRAMESET>...</FRAMESET>

Usage   Defines the layout of FRAMES within a window.

Start/End Tag   Required/Required

Attributes   rows="..."—The number of rows.

cols="..."—The number of columns.

onload="..."—The intrinsic event triggered when the document loads.

onunload="..."—The intrinsic event triggered when the document unloads.

Empty   No

Notes   FRAMESET can be nested.

<IFRAME>...</IFRAME>

Usage	Creates an inline frame.
Start/End Tag	Required/Required
Attributes	`name="..."`—The name of the frame.
	`src="..."`—The source to be displayed in a frame.
	`frameborder="..."`—Toggles the border between frames (`0`, `1`).
	`marginwidth="..."`—Sets the space between the frame border and content.
	`marginheight="..."`—Sets the space between the frame border and content.
	`scrolling="..."`—Determines scrollbar presence (`auto`, `yes`, `no`).
	`align="..."`—Deprecated. Controls alignment (`left`, `center`, `right`, `justify`).
	`height="..."`—Height.
	`width="..."`—Width.
Empty	No

<NOFRAMES>...</NOFRAMES>

Usage	Alternative content when frames are not supported.
Start/End Tag	Required/Required
Attributes	None.
Empty	No

Embedded Content

Also called inclusions, embedded content applies to Java applets, imagemaps, and other multimedia or programattical content that is placed in a Web page to provide additional functionality.

<APPLET>...</APPLET>

Usage	Includes a Java applet.
Start/End Tag	Required/Required
Attributes	`codebase="..."`—The URL base for the applet.
	`archive="..."`—Identifies the resources to be preloaded.
	`code="..."`—The applet class file.
	`object="..."`—The serialized applet file.

alt="..."—Displays text while loading.

name="..."—The name of the applet.

width="..."—The height of the displayed applet.

height="..."—The width of the displayed applet.

align="..."—Deprecated. Controls alignment (left, center, right, justify).

hspace="..."—The horizontal space separating the image from other content.

vspace="..."—The vertical space separating the image from other content.

Empty	No
Notes	Applet is deprecated in favor of the OBJECT element.

<AREA>

Usage	The AREA element is used to define links and anchors.
Start/End Tag	Required/Illegal
Attributes	shape="..."—Enables you to define client-side imagemaps using defined shapes (default, rect, circle, poly).

coords="..."—Sets the size of the shape using pixel or percentage lengths.

href="..."—The URL of the linked resource.

target="..."—Determines where the resource will be displayed (user-defined name, _blank, _parent, _self, _top).

nohref="..."—Indicates that the region has no action.

alt="..."—Displays alternative text.

tabindex="..."—Sets the tabbing order between elements with a defined tabindex.

Empty	Yes

<IMG>

Usage	Includes an image in the document.
Start/End Tag	Required/Illegal
Attributes	%coreattrs, %i18n, %events

src="..."—The URL of the image.

alt="..."—Alternative text to display.

align="..."—Deprecated. Controls alignment (left, center, right, justify).

height="..."—The height of the image.

width="..."—The width of the image.

border="..."—Border width.

hspace="..."—The horizontal space separating the image from other content.

vspace="..."—The vertical space separating the image from other content.

usemap="..."—The URL to a client-side imagemap.

ismap—Identifies a server-side imagemap.

Empty   Yes

\<MAP>...\</MAP>

Usage   When used with the AREA element, creates a client-side imagemap.

Start/End Tag   Required/Required

Attributes   %coreattrs

name="..."—The name of the imagemap to be created.

Empty   No

\<OBJECT>...\</OBJECT>

Usage   Includes an object.

Start/End Tag   Required/Required

Attributes   %coreattrs, %i18n, %events

declare—A flag that declares but doesn't create an object.

classid="..."—The URL of the object's location.

codebase="..."—The URL for resolving URLs specified by other attributes.

data="..."—The URL to the object's data.

type="..."—The Internet content type for data.

codetype="..."—The Internet content type for the code.

standby="..."—Show message while loading.

align="..."—Deprecated. Controls alignment (left, center, right, justify).

height="..."—The height of the object.

width="..."—The width of the object.

border="..."—Displays the border around an object.

`hspace="..."`—The space between the sides of the object and other page content.

`vspace="..."`—The space between the top and bottom of the object and other page content.

`usemap="..."`—The URL to an imagemap.

`shapes=`—Enables you to define areas to search for hyperlinks if the object is an image.

`name="..."`—The URL to submit as part of a form.

`tabindex="..."`—Sets the tabbing order between elements with a defined `tabindex`.

Empty   No

\<PARAM\>

Usage	Initializes an object.
Start/End Tag	Required/Illegal
Attributes	`name="..."`—Defines the parameter name.
	`value="..."`—The value of the object parameter.
	`valuetype="..."`—Defines the value type (`data`, `ref`, `object`).
	`type="..."`—The Internet media type.
Empty	Yes

Style

Style sheets (both inline and external) are incorporated into an HTML document through the use of the STYLE element.

\<STYLE\>...\</STYLE\>

Usage	Creates an internal style sheet.
Start/End Tag	Required/Required
Attributes	`%i18n`
	`type="..."`—The Internet content type.
	`media="..."`—Defines the destination medium (`screen`, `print`, `projection`, `braille`, `speech`, `all`).
	`title="..."`—The title of the style.
Empty	No
Notes	Located in the HEAD element.

Forms

Forms create an interface for the user to select options and submit data back to the Web server.

`<BUTTON>...</BUTTON>`

Usage	Creates a button.
Start/End Tag	Required/Required
Attributes	`%coreattrs, %i18n, %events`

`name="..."`—The button name.

`value="..."`—The value of the button.

`type="..."`—The button type (`button`, `submit`, `reset`).

`disabled="..."`—Sets the button state to disabled.

`tabindex="..."`—Sets the tabbing order between elements with a defined `tabindex`.

`onfocus="..."`—The event that occurs when the element receives focus.

`onblur="..."`—The event that occurs when the element loses focus.

Empty	No

`<FIELDSET>...</FIELDSET>`

Usage	Groups related controls.
Start/End Tag	Required/Required
Attributes	`%coreattrs, %i18n, %events`
Empty	No

`<FORM>...</FORM>`

Usage	Creates a form that holds controls for user input.
Start/End Tag	Required/Required
Attributes	`%coreattrs, %i18n, %events`

`action="..."`—The URL for the server action.

`method="..."`—The HTTP method (`get`, `post`). `get` is deprecated.

`enctype="..."`—Specifies the MIME (Internet media type).

`onsubmit="..."`—The intrinsic event that occurs when the form is submitted.

`onreset="..."`—The intrinsic event that occurs when the form is reset.

`target="..."`—Determines where the resource will be displayed (user-defined name, `_blank`, `_parent`, `_self`, `_top`).

`accept-charset="..."`—The list of character encodings.

Empty   No

<INPUT>

Usage   Defines controls used in forms.

Start/End Tag   Required/Illegal

Attributes   `%coreattrs`, `%i18n`, `%events`

`type="..."`—The type of input control (`text`, `password`, `checkbox`, `radio`, `submit`, `reset`, `file`, `hidden`, `image`, `button`).

`name="..."`—The name of the control (required except for `submit` and `reset`).

`value="..."`—The initial value of the control (required for radio buttons and checkboxes).

`checked="..."`—Sets the radio buttons to a checked state.

`disabled="..."`—Disables the control.

`readonly="..."`—For text password types.

`size="..."`—The width of the control in pixels except for text and password controls, which are specified in number of characters.

`maxlength="..."`—The maximum number of characters that can be entered.

`src="..."`—The URL to an image control type.

`alt="..."`—An alternative text description.

`usemap="..."`—The URL to a client-side imagemap.

`align="..."`—Deprecated. Controls alignment (`left`, `center`, `right`, `justify`).

`tabindex="..."`—Sets the tabbing order between elements with a defined `tabindex`.

`onfocus="..."`—The event that occurs when the element receives focus.

`onblur="..."`—The event that occurs when the element loses focus.

onselect="..."—Intrinsic event that occurs when the control is selected.

onchange="..."—Intrinsic event that occurs when the control is changed.

accept="..."—File types allowed for upload.

Empty   Yes

<ISINDEX>

Usage	Prompts the user for unput.
Start/End Tag	Required/Illegal
Attributes	%coreattrs, %i18n
	prompt="..."—Provides a prompt string for the input field.
Empty	Yes
Notes	Deprecated.

<LABEL>...</LABEL>

Usage	Labels a control.
Start/End Tag	Required/Required
Attributes	%coreattrs, %i18n, %events
	for="..."—Associates a label with an identified control.
	disabled="..."—Disables a control.
	accesskey="..."—Assigns a hotkey to this element.
	onfocus="..."—The event that occurs when the element receives focus.
	onblur="..."—The event that occurs when the element loses focus.
Empty	No

<LEGEND>...</LEGEND>

Usage	Assigns a caption to a FIELDSET.
Start/End Tag	Required/Required
Attributes	%coreattrs, %i18n, %events
	align="..."—Deprecated. Controls alignment (left, center, right, justify).
	accesskey="..."—Assigns a hotkey to this element.
Empty	No

A

HTML 4.0
REFERENCE

This appendix provides an overview of the attributes with which you can control the appearance of your HTML documents through style sheets. The World Wide Web Consortium (W3C) set the current standard for style sheets as Cascading Style Sheets 1 (CSS1). W3C's complete recommendation for CSS is located at the W3C Web site at `http://www.w3.org/pub/WWW/TR/REC-CSS1`.

Basic Syntax

All styles within a style sheet definition follow the same basic syntax. You'll notice that there are a lot of opportunities to add other attributes or members of a group:

```
SELECTOR[.class] [,SELECTOR2[.class2]] ...
{ attribute1: value1 [;
  attribute2: value2] [;
  ... ]                  [;
  attributen: valuen] }
```

The SELECTOR is how the style is referenced within the rest of the HTML page. It uses one of the existing HTML tags, such as <CODE> or <P>, along with an optional class to create additional sub-styles. A class is a subset of a selector, allowing the same element to have a variety of styles. For example, you could color-code block quotes to identify sources or speakers.

In addition to the standard HTML tags, you can use two other values for a selector: first-line and first-letter. The first-line value sets the style for the first line of text in a document or several passages within a document, such as a paragraph or block quote. The first-letter value creates drop caps and other special effects on the first letter in a document or passage.

Groups of selectors and their classes are separated by commas. Any member of the group receives the same style as any other member in the group. For example, if you wanted all headings to be displayed in red, you could list H1 through H6 with the attributes to set the color to red. All other tag attributes, such as size, would remain unaffected.

Another option is contextual selectors, which tell the browser what to do with a certain tag when found nested within the parent tag.

```
OUTER_SELECTOR INNER_SELECTOR {attribute:value}
```

This means that when the INNER_SELECTOR is used within the OUTER_SELECTOR, the style is used. Otherwise, other occurrences of INNER_SELECTOR are handled according to browser default.

After making all of the selector and group definitions, use a curly bracket along with a series of attributes and their values. Mate each attribute with its value by using a colon and separate each pair from the next pair by using a semicolon. The values within a definition, such as the name of a typeface or a color value, are not case-sensitive. For example, for font-family, you can have Garamond, garamond, or GARAMOND, and it will all work out the same in the browser.

As with all good syntax, you can place style definitions in three ways within a document: with an embedded style sheet, with a linked style sheet, and with an inline style sheet.

Embedded Style Sheet

The `<STYLE>` tags contain an embedded style sheet. As a matter of structure, the format of an HTML page with an embedded style sheet is as follows:

```
<HTML>
<HEAD>...</HEAD>
<STYLE>...</STYLE>
<BODY>...</BODY>
</HTML>
```

The `<STYLE>` tags contain the list of selectors and styles.

Linked Style Sheet

The linked style sheet is a `.css` file that contains nothing but a set of `<STYLE>` tags and their contents. Identify the style file within an HTML document using the `<LINK>` tag in the head:

```
<HEAD>
<LINK rel=stylesheet href="filename.css" type="text/css">
</HEAD>
```

At runtime, the browser will load the style in the `.css` file and use it to format the document. If the HTML page also includes an embedded style sheet that conflicts with the linked style sheet, the embedded version takes precedence.

Inline Style Sheet

The last option, inline style sheets, uses style sheet syntax, although it's technically not a style sheet implementation. This option uses the style sheet nomenclature to customize single incidents of tags within the document:

```
<TAG style="attribute1:value1; ...">
```

Essentially, this is a way to customize HTML tags on a case-by-case basis. When you use all three forms of syntax, they occur in a cascading form of precedence. The highest priority is inline, followed by embedded, then linked.

Style Attributes

Several classes of attributes are used within the definition for a selector. The following sections cover each of the attributes within a class.

There is a predictable way the rules are applied when faced with conflicts between styles on a page. To determine how an element will appear on the page, follow these rules, in order:

1. First, find all the declarations that apply to the element in question. Style declarations apply if the selector matches the element in question. If no declarations apply, the element's style is inherited from its parent, or, if no parent applies, with any unspecified values handled according to browser defaults.

2. For multiple declarations, any styles marked "!important" carry more weight than unmarked declarations.

3. Next, comes origin priority. The author's style sheets override the reader's style sheets which override the browser's default values. Linked styles are considered of the same origin as the author.

4. Next comes specificity. A more specific selector overrides less specific selectors. For example, if you set BODY as black text on a white background, then set BLOCKQUOTE as red text on a white background, then a block quote within the body will be red, since BLOCKQUOTE is more specific than BODY.

5. Sort by the order in which the styles are specified. If two rules have the same weight, the last definition wins. So, a linked style sheet at the beginning of the document sets the first style. Any discrepancies between the linked style and an embedded style default to the embedded style. If for some reason the embedded style includes two definitions for the same element, such as two sets of properties for BLOCKQUOTE, then the last BLOCKQUOTE wins.

Using these rules, you can accurately predict how your style sheet will be applied when interpreted by a browser.

Fonts

There are no current standards for typefaces and their use on different user machines, so you'll need to choose carefully and include several options to achieve the desired effect for the user.

The font-family Attribute

The font-family attribute lists font families in order of preference, separated by commas. Two types of variables are used: family name and generic family.

```
BODY {font-family: Garamond, Palatino, Serif}
```

A family name is the name of a specific typeface such as Helvetica, Garamond, Palatino, or Optima. Enclose font names with spaces in quotes, such as "Gil Sans". The generic family is one of five choices that classifies the typeface by its style and is recommended as the last option in a font-family list:

■ Serif: Fonts with accents at the tips of the lines (for example, Times)

■ Sans-serif: Fonts without finishing accents (for example, Helvetica)

■ Cursive: Scripts that more closely resemble hand-drawn calligraphy (for example, Zapf Chancery)

- Fancy: Special-use decorative fonts (for example, Comic Book Sans)
- Monospace: Fonts that maintain uniform spacing despite letter width (for example, Courier)

The font-style Attribute

This attribute specifies the type of treatment a font receives and is represented by the values normal, italic, or oblique. The normal value is also referred to as Roman in some typeface references. The oblique value is similar to italic except that it is usually slanted manually by the system rather than by a separate style of the font, such as italic.

```
BODY {font-style: italic}
```

The font-variant Attribute

Similar to font-style, this attribute sets small caps. Its two values are normal and small-caps.

```
BODY {font-variant: small-caps}
```

If there is no true small caps version of the typeface, the system will attempt to scale the capital letters to a smaller size for lowercase letters. As a last resort, the text will appear in all capitals.

The font-weight Attribute

A number of values for this attribute set the darkness or lightness of a typeface. The primary values are normal and bold. You can substitute these values with one from a list of values from 100 to 900. If a typeface includes a "medium" weight, it will correspond to 500. Bold is represented by 700.

```
BODY {font-weight: bold}
```

Two additional values are bolder and lighter, which increase the weight from the current parent weight by one level, such as 200 to 300 for bolder or 700 to 600 for lighter.

The font-size Attribute

Four properties can define the size of a font in a style—absolute size, relative size, length, or percentage.

- Absolute size: This method is represented in several ways. The first is with a value that represents its size relative to other sizes within the family (xx-small, x-small, small, medium, large, x-large, xx-large). You can also use a numerical value, such as 12pt (12 points).

  ```
  BODY {font-size: 18pt}
  ```

- Relative size: This method sets the size relative to the parent style. It can be one of two values, smaller or larger, and it adjusts the size up or down the scale of sizes. If a font doesn't include a mapping to size names, a scaling of 1.5 is recommended between sizes. For example, a 10pt font would be scaled larger to 15pt or smaller to 7pt.

  ```
  P {font-size: smaller}
  ```

- Length: This method is another form of relative size that sets the size by the scale factor of the width of an em, such as 1.5em.

  P {font-size: 2em}

- Percentage: This method is also a relative specification that multiplies the size of the parent font by the percentage value to achieve the new size, such as 150%.

  H3 {font-size: 300%}

The font Attribute

This attribute provides shorthand for setting all of the previous attributes under one umbrella. The order of the attributes should be font-style, font-variant, font-weight, font-size, line-height, font-family. Place no commas between each of the attribute values, except for listed font families:

BODY {font: small-caps bold 14pt garamond, palatino, serif}

Color and Background

These elements set the color values for the text (foreground) and the area behind the text (background). In addition to setting a background color, you can also define a background image. All color values are defined using the same methods as the color attribute.

The color Attribute

This attribute defines the color of the text element and is specified using one of the color keywords (such as red). You can also define the color using a hexadecimal triplet, denoting the mix of red, green, and blue (such as rgb(255,0,0)).

BLOCKQUOTE {color: rgb(0,255,255)}

The background-color Attribute

This attribute sets the background color for a style. You can set this attribute independently of a background color for the document to enable you to highlight text in a different manner.

BLOCKQUOTE {background-color: blue}

The background-image Attribute

This attribute specifies a background image for a style element. Use it in conjunction with background-color to ensure a substitute effect if the image becomes unavailable. If the image is available, it will display on top of the background color.

BLOCKQUOTE {background-image: url(logo.gif)}

The background-repeat Attribute

If the background image should be repeated (tiled), use this attribute to define how. Its values include repeat, repeat-x, and repeat-y. The repeat value indicates that the image should be tiled normally. The `repeat-x` value repeats the image in a single horizontal line, and the `repeat-y` value repeats the image in a vertical line.

```
BLOCKQUOTE {background-image: url(logo.gif);
           background-repeat: repeat-x}
```

The background-attachment Attribute

This attribute, an extended feature of background images not seen in HTML before, sets whether the background image is attached to the foreground text (`scroll`) or anchored to the background (`fixed`). This feature is apparent only when the user scrolls across a selection of text.

```
BLOCKQUOTE {background-image: url(logo.gif);
           background-attachment: repeat-x}
```

The background-position Attribute

When you use a background image through normal HTML, the starting point is always the top left of the screen. With a style sheet, you can specify a starting point anywhere within the box that contains the style content.

You can specify the image's starting position in three ways. The first way is with key word locations. For horizontal placement, your choices are `left`, `center`, or `right`. For vertical placement, your choices are `top`, `center`, or `bottom`. Alternatively, you can represent the position as a percentage of the available area, with `0% 0%` being the top left (default) and `100% 100%` being the bottom right. The last option is to specify an actual measurement in centimeters or inches.

If only one value for the placement is given, it's used as the horizontal position. If both values are given, the first is evaluated as horizontal and the second as vertical.

```
BLOCKQUOTE {background-image: url(logo.gif);
           Background-repeat: repeat-y;
           background-position: right top; }
```

The background Attribute

This shorthand attribute, similar to `font`, enables you to define a set of values for the background in one stop. The order is `background-color`, `background-image`, `background-repeat`, `background-attachment`, `background-position`.

```
P { background: black url(logo.gif) repeat-y fixed right top }
```

Text

This set of style attributes covers the values that can affect the appearance of text, but not by directly changing the typeface. This includes values for spacing, underlining, blinking, and strikethrough. It also supports some of the positioning attributes, including left and right justification and indents.

The word-spacing Attribute

This attribute indicates an addition to the default amount of space between individual words and is specified in *ems*. An *em* is the space occupied by the letter *m* and is the baseline for determining widths within a font. To return the value to its default, use 0em or normal.

```
BODY { word-spacing: 1em }
```

The letter-spacing Attribute

The letter-spacing attribute is similar to word-spacing, except that letter-spacing adds an extra bit of spacing between individual letters. In addition to the default method the browser uses to determine spacing, additional letter spacing is also affected by text alignment.

```
BODY { letter-spacing: 0.2em }
```

The text-decoration Attribute

This attribute is more closely related to its cousins in the font family. It specifies extra text flourishes, such as underline, strike-through, and blinking. The four values are none, underline, overline, line-through, and blink.

```
STR.blink { text-decoration: underline blink }
```

The vertical-align Attribute

This attribute sets the vertical position of the text either to an absolute reference or in relation to the parent element. It supports a range of values and keywords:

- Baseline. Aligns the baseline of the style with the baseline of the parent element.
- Sub. Assigns the style to a subscript relative to the parent element.
- Super. Assigns the style to a superscript relative to the parent element.
- Text-top. Aligns the top of the text with the top of the parent's text.
- Text-bottom. Aligns the bottom of the text with the bottom of the parent's text.
- Middle. Aligns the vertical halfway point of the element with the baseline of the parent plus half of the x-height of the parent (x-height is the height of the lowercase x of the font).
- Top. Aligns the top of the element with the tallest element on the current line.
- Bottom. Aligns the bottom of the element with the lowest element on the current line.
- Percentage. Using a positive or negative percentage value, raises or lowers the element beyond the baseline of the parent:

```
SUB { vertical-align: -10% }
```

The `text-transform` Attribute

This attribute sets the capitalization of the affected text to one of four choices: `capitalize` (first letter of every word), `uppercase` (all letters in capitals), `lowercase` (all letters in lowercase), and `none`.

```
STR.caps { text-transform: uppercase }
```

The `text-align` Attribute

This attribute moves beyond the standard HTML `left-right-center` alignment to provide full justification (`justify` left and right). If a browser doesn't support `justify`, it will typically substitute `left`.

```
BLOCKQUOTE { text-align: justify }
```

The `text-indent` Attribute

The `text-indent` attribute, specified in an absolute value measured in ems or inches, defines the amount of space that is added before the first line.

```
P { text-indent: 5em }
```

The `line-height` Attribute

This attribute sets the distance between adjacent baselines using a length (in ems), multiplication factor, or percentage. Factors are indicated without any units, such as `1.5`. When you use this method, the child inherits the factor, not the resulting value.

```
DIV { line-height: 1.5; font-size: 12pt }
```

In this instance, the line height becomes 18 points and the font size remains at 12 points.

Margins, Padding, and Borders

Each element created in a style sheet is presented in its own "box." All of the styles from the element inside the box are applied, although the box itself can have its own properties that define how it relates to adjoining elements on the page. Length is specified in inches (`in`), centimeters (`cm`), ems (`em`), points (`pt`), or pixels (`px`).

Box properties are divided into three basic categories. Margin properties set the border around the outside of the box, padding properties determine how much space to insert between the border and the content, and border properties define graphical lines around an element.

Additional properties of the box include its width, height, and physical position.

The `margin-top`, `margin-bottom`, `margin-right`, and `margin-left` Attributes

These four attributes set the amount of space between the element and adjoining elements, whether defined by length, percentage of parent text width, or handled automatically.

```
BLOCKQUOTE { margin-top: 4em;
             Margin-bottom: auto }
```

The margin Attribute

The margin attribute provides a shorthand method for setting the four margin values.

When you specify the four values, they are applied, in order, to the top, right, bottom, and left. If you provide only one value, it applies to all sides. If you use two or three values, the missing values are copied from the opposite sides.

```
BLOCKQUOTE {margin: 4em 2em}
```

The padding-top, padding-bottom, padding-right, and padding-left Attributes

These attributes set the distance between the boundaries of the box and the elements inside the box. It can use any of the physical measurements or a percentage of the parent's width.

```
BLOCKQUOTE {padding-top: 110%; padding-bottom: 115%}
```

The padding Attribute

The padding attribute provides a shorthand method for setting the four padding values.

When you specify the four values, they are applied, in order, to the top, right, bottom, and left. If you provide only one value, it applies to all sides. If you use two or three values, the missing values are copied from the opposite sides.

```
BLOCKQUOTE {padding: 10pt 12pt}
```

The border-top, border-bottom, border-right, and border-left Attributes

These four attributes set the style and color of each border around an element. Specify styles with one of the border style keywords: none, dotted, dashed, solid, double, groove, ridge, inset, and outset. For more information on these, see the information on border-style later in this chapter.

Specify colors using a color keyword. For more information, see the border-color later in this chapter.

```
BLOCKQUOTE {border-left: solid red}
```

The border-top-width, border-bottom-width, border-right-width, and border-left-width Attributes

These attributes define a physical border around the box, similar to the border used for HTML tables. In addition to defining a specific width in ems, you can also use the keywords thin, medium, and thick. Using a measurement in ems results in a border whose width changes in relation to the size of the current font.

```
STR {border-right-width: 2pt;
     border-left-width: 2pt }
```

The border-width Attribute

The border-width attribute provides a shorthand method for setting the width of the four borders.

When you specify the four values, they are applied, in order, to the top, right, bottom, and left. If you provide only one value, it applies to all sides. If you use two or three values, the missing values are copied from the opposite sides.

```
BLOCKQUOTE {border-width: medium 0pt 0pt thick}
```

The border-color Attribute

This attribute sets the color of all four borders and uses one color keyword as its value. You cannot set the color of each side independently.

```
BLOCKQUOTE {border-color: yellow}
```

The border-style Attribute

The border's appearance can take on several different settings, represented by none, dotted, dashed, solid, double, groove, ridge, inset, and outset. The last four values are represented in 3D, if the browser supports it. Alternatively, the browser also can present all the variations as a solid line, except none.

Like border-color, the style is applied uniformly to all four sides.

```
BLOCKQUOTE {border-style: groove}
```

The border Attribute

The border attribute provides a shorthand method for setting all the border variables, including width, style, and color. It sets the values for all four sides at the same time, overriding any individual settings that may have been set previously for the same element.

```
BLOCKQUOTE {border: 1.5pt double black}
```

The height Attribute

This attribute sets the overall height of the bounding box that contains either the text or image element. If the content is text, scrollbars are added as needed so that all of the material is still available to the user. If the content is an image, it's scaled to fit inside the area. You can set a physical value or use auto to let the browser allocate space as needed.

```
BLOCKQUOTE {height: 100px}
```

The width Attribute

Similar to height, the width attribute sets the overall width of the bounding box that contains the element. If the content is text, scrollbars are added as needed so that all of the material is still available for the user. If both elements are used with an image and the value of one element is auto, the aspect ratio for the image is maintained.

```
BLOCKQUOTE {width: auto}
```

The float Attribute

This attribute sets a value similar to the align attribute used in HTML. The three possible values are left, right, and none. The none value allows the element to fall where it may, and the other two values force the element to the left or right of the screen with text wrapping around the opposite side.

```
BLOCKQUOTE {float: right}
```

The clear Attribute

This attribute mimics the clear attribute used with the HTML <BR> tag and uses the same keywords as float. If you use it with right or left, elements will move below any floating element on that respective side. If you set it to none, floating elements are allowed on both sides.

```
BLOCKQUOTE {clear: left right}
```

Classification

These attributes control the general behavior of other elements more than actually specifying an appearance. In addition, classification includes the attributes for list items, identified in HTML with the <LI> tag.

The display Attribute

This attribute identifies when and if a style element should be used. Four keywords determine its behavior:

- Inline. A new box is created within the same line as adjoining text items and is formatted according to the size and amount of content within its borders, such as an image (IMG) or text (STR).

- Block. A new box is created relative to the surrounding elements. This is common with elements such as H1 and P.

- List-item. Similar to block, only list item markers, which behave more like inline content, are added.

- None. Turns off the display of the element in any situation, including for children of the element.

```
IMG {display: inline}
BLOCKQUOTE {display: block}
```

The white-space Attribute

The name of this attribute is a bit misleading because it relates to how spaces and line breaks are handled. The choices are normal (in which extra spaces are ignored), pre (as in preformatted HTML text), and nowrap (in which lines are broken only with <BR>).

```
BLOCKQUOTE {white-space: pre}
```

The list-style-type Attribute

This element sets the type of markers used for a list. Your choices are disc, circle, square, decimal, lower-roman, upper-roman, lower-alpha, upper-alpha, and none.

```
LI.outline1 {list-style-type: upper-roman}
LI.outline2 {list-style-type: upper-alpha}
LI.outline3 {list-style-type: decimal}
```

The list-style-image Attribute

In lieu of a text marker for the list item, you can also specify the URL of an image to use. If the image is unavailable, the text marker is used as default.

```
LI.general {list-style-image: url(bullet.jpg)}
```

The list-style-position Attribute

The two values for this attribute, inside and outside, determine the formatting of text following the list-item property. The outside value, the default value, lines up the additional lines of text beyond the first line with the first character in the first line. If you use the inside value, the second and following lines are justified with the list item marker.

```
LI {list-style-position: inside}
```

The list-style Attribute

This attribute is a shorthand element for the list-style-type, list-style-image, and list-style-position attributes.

```
OL {list-style: lower-alpha outside}
UL {list-style: square url(bullet.jpg) inside}
```

I

INDEX

MACMILLAN COMPUTER PUBLISHING USA

A VIACOM COMPANY

Technical ---- Support

If you need assistance with the information
provided by Macmillan Computer Publishing,
please access the information available on our
web site at **http://www.mcp.com/feedback.** Our
most Frequently Asked Questions are answered
there. If you do not find the answers to your
questions on our web site, you may contact
Macmillan User Services at **(317) 581-3833** or
email us at **support@mcp.com**.